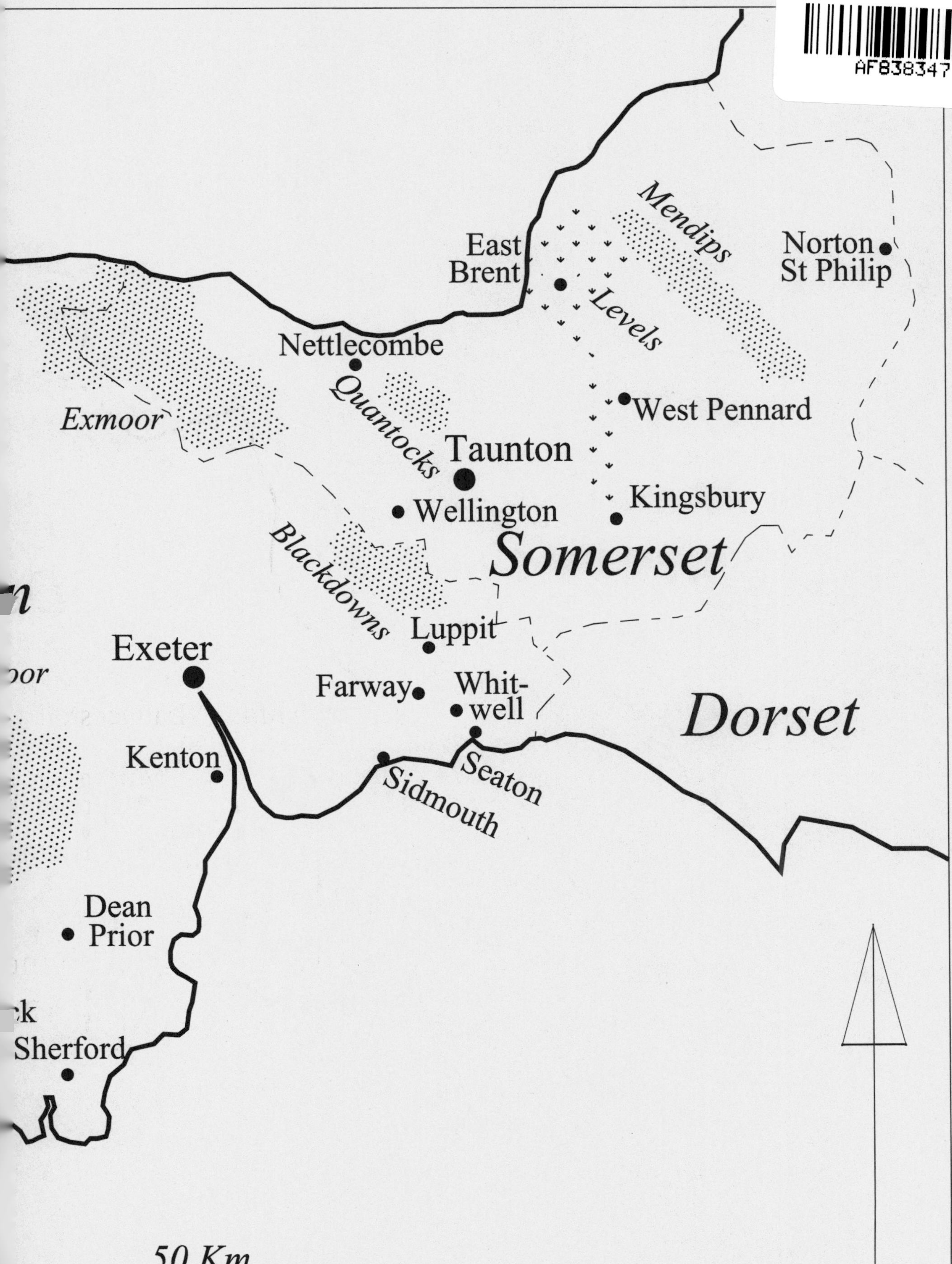
Mendips
East
Brent
Norton
St Philip
Levels
Nettlecombe
Quantocks
West Pennard
Exmoor
Taunton
Wellington
Kingsbury
Somerset
Blackdowns
Luppit
Exeter
Farway
Whit-
well
Dorset
Kenton
Seaton
Sidmouth
Dean
Prior
Sherford
50 Km
50 Miles

West Country Farms

A typical south-western two-storey porch, at Wrey Manor, Lustleigh, Devon, dated 1680. Probate inventories suggest that the rooms over such porches were often used as studies (photo N.W. Alcock)

West Country Farms

House-and-Estate Surveys, 1598–1764

Nat Alcock
and
Cary Carson

Oxbow Books

Published by
Oxbow Books, Oxford, UK

ISBN 978-1-84217-299-5

A CIP record for this book is available from the British Library

This book is available direct from

Oxbow Books, Oxford, UK
(Phone: 01865-241249; Fax: 01865-794449)
oxbowbooks.com

and

The David Brown Book Company
PO Box 511, Oakville, CT 06779, USA
(Phone: 860-945-9329; Fax: 860-945-9468)

End papers: The Region: Location of estates and principal physical features

Cover illustration: Thomas Rowlandson, Camelford, Cornwall, c. 1800 (British Museum, Department of Prints and Drawings). Rowlandson's image gives visual expression to the West Country villages captured in words in the house and estate surveys. (Copyright, The British Museum)

Printed in Great Britain by
Short Run Press, Exeter

In memory of Maurice Barley,
a pioneer in the use of house-and-estate surveys

Contents

List of Illustrations

Plates (between pages 32 and 33)

Figures

Maps

Tables

List of Surveys

Crown Estates

Key letter	*Date*	*Place (and survey reference)*
CN	1606	Carnanton, Cornwall (TNA E315/388, ff.135-171)
L	1606	Launceston, Cornwall (TNA LR2/207, ff.149-208)
NP	1608	Norton St. Philip, Somerset (TNA LR2/202, ff.167-199)
WE	1607	Wellington, Somerset (TNA LR2/255, ff.174-208)
KB	1608	Kingsbury, Somerset (TNA LR2/202, ff.199-253)
EB	1606	East Brent (Burton, Sislington, Singhampton), Somerset (TNA LR2/225, ff.53-107)
WP	1606	West Pennard, Somerset (TNA LR2/202, ff.105-159)

Detailed Surveys

Key letter	*Date*	*Place (and survey reference)*
K	1598	Kenton, Devon (D.R.O. 1508M/London Estate Vals/4)
C	1602	Cornish Manors (Treverbyn Courtenay, Landreyne [in North Hill], Crofthole, Tregamere) (TNA E315/404, ff.65-91)
SH	1606	Sherford, Devon (B.L. Add. Ms. 21605, ff.35-42)
F	1609	Farway, Devon (S.R.O. DD/WO, box 43)
W	1609	Whitwell, Devon (S.R.O. DD/WO, box 43)
SA	1609	Seaton, Devon (S.R.O. DD/WO, box 43)
SB	1682	Seaton, Devon (S.R.O. DD/WO, box 43)
N	1619	Nettlecombe, Somerset (S.R.O. DD/WO, box 43)
TA	1709	Tavistock Abbey — Bedford Estates, Devon (D.R.O. L1258/surveys/whole estate 2)
H	1709	Hurdwick — Bedford Estates, Devon (D.R.O. L1258/surveys/whole estate 2)
O	1709	Oreston — Bedford Estates, Devon (D.R.O. L1258/surveys/whole estate 2)
P	1709	Plymstock — Bedford Estates, Devon (D.R.O. L1258/surveys/whole estate 2)
M	1709	Milton — Bedford Estates, Devon (D.R.O. L1258/surveys/whole estate 2)
SM	1764	Sidmouth and Sidford, Devon (D.R.O. 1334M/M5)

Conventions and Abbreviations

Crown Estate Tables

The information is arranged in the order: domestic buildings; ancillary buildings; farm buildings (barn, stable, cattle housing, hay or straw storage, wain house, other buildings). A consistent column order is retained as far as possible, though irrelevant columns are suppressed in individual tables, and the column headings indicate the particular terms used in each survey. Freeholdings are omitted (apart from the few for which details are provided in the survey).

Symbols used are as follows:

° or *	: building present, size unspecified (* if mentioned in the notes).
= or ≡	: buildings with combined functions (combination and size given in the notes).
Letter	: Subdivided column as explained at the column head (e.g., hay or straw houses coded H or S).
Number	: building of size specified (for units, see captions).

Summary Tables for Farm Buildings

The information is arranged in the order: barn, stable, cattle housing, hay or straw storage, wain house, other buildings; irrelevant columns are suppressed in individual tables. The symbols are as in the Crown Estate tables. Holdings are omitted if they have no farm buildings; details are given in the captions.

Units of Measurement

Units of area	1 acre (0.404 hectare) = 4 rods (sometimes called yard or virgate). 1 rod = 40 perches. In all tables, areas above 10 acres have been rounded to the nearest acre.
Currency units	£1 = 20 shillings(s). 1s = 12 pence (d). The frequent sums of 3s 4d, 6s 8d, 13s 4d, etc., are relics of the use of the mark 13s 4d (2/3 of £1)].

Abbreviations

Ag.Hist.	J. Thirsk, ed., *Agrarian History of England and Wales* (Cambridge). vol. IV (1967); vol. V(i) (1984); vol V(ii) (1985).
B.L.	British Library, London
D.R.O.	Devon Record Office, Exeter
M.L.W.L.	R.E. Latham, ed., *Revised Medieval Latin Wordlist* (London, 1965).
O.E.D.	*Oxford English Dictionary* (Oxford, 1888-1928)
S.R.O.	Somerset Record Office, Taunton
TNA	The National Archives, London

Preface

To John Taylor's tenement there is an enterye, a hawle, a kytchen, a butterye, a mylkehowse, a shopp, five chambers overheade, a stawle, a barne, a maltehowse, a howse for fatt oxen, an olde bakes [*bakehouse*] and a wayne howse ... *[1619 Survey of Nettlecombe, Somerset: entry N35, accompanied by details of John Taylor's 62 acre holding and a note of his lease including his age (38) and that of his wife (45)]*

The discovery of such descriptions as this, repeated for every villager in seventeen diverse West County communities, led the authors to the realisation that they could be used to paint landscapes of individual farming communities caught at one moment in time, pictures that come as close as written records ever can to the archaeological excavation of entire village sites. The existence of such remarkable historical evidence became apparent to the present authors almost by accident.

One of us–Nat Alcock–found and used a solitary survey of this type (called by us house-and-estate surveys) in a study of Bedfordshire buildings, supposing it to be virtually one of a kind. W. G. Hoskins subsequently dispelled this notion by calling our attention to a series of Willoughby estate surveys for Devon and Somerset. His information inspired a deliberate and thorough search for similar West Country records that might illuminate social conditions, economic opportunities, and housing standards in that part of Britain. This search led to the corpus of documents upon which this study is based and also to our joint involvement. The other author–Cary Carson–had been searching for information about the physical environment of seventeenth-century West Countrymen, many thousands of whom were soon to emigrate to North America. These surveys provide such evidence to a remarkable degree.

It soon became clear that we could best exploit their richness collaboratively. In the chapters of Part I we have analysed successively their evidence for the social structure of the communities described, for house type and development, and for farm buildings in the context of their agricultural economy.

It also became apparent to us that these extraordinary documents deserved special treatment. Their evidence for housing standards and for investment in agricultural buildings is illustrated to the fullest extent by the texts of the documents themselves. The distillation from them of generalities and trends can only give a very inadequate impression of their content and, in particular, of the unique place of each tenant, his home and farmstead, within his community. For this reason and because scholars have never before put them to intensive use, we decided that our study must contain more than a general analysis. We have therefore included in Part II calendars or abstracts of our sources, using the original language as far as possible, to present their uniquely informative descriptions of the homes and farmsteads in the score of south-western villages they cover. Each chapter is introduced by a discussion of the individual character of the villages and farms concerned.

We had originally intended that the book should have a third part, contrasting the houses and farms that New World settlers from the West Country left behind them with those they created on the other side of the Atlantic. However, this outgrew its original home and will now appear as a separate publication.

We thank the British Library, the National Archives, the Devon Record Office, and the Somerset County Record Office for permission to publish the texts of the surveys they hold. Requests for a reproduction of images from Trevelyan archives, in Somerset Record Office, have remained unacknowledged. We are also grateful to the late W. G. Hoskins for allowing us to exploit his original discovery of the south-western house-and-estate surveys, and for sharing copies of them with us. Some of the initial research was supported by the National Endowment for the Humanities, and some documents were analysed by Dr. Susan Sutton. Members of the Vernacular Architecture Group, especially Peter Child, Kay Coutin, and John Dallimore, have provided us with much information about standing buildings. Preparation of the volume for publication was ably carried out by Greg Brown of the Digital History Center at the Colonial Williamsburg Foundation in Virginia, and by Val Lamb at Oxbow Books. All these we also thank.

NAT ALCOCK
CARY CARSON

Part I

West Country Communities

A Thanksgiving to God for his House

Lord thou has given me a cell
 Wherein to dwell;
An little house, whose humble Roof
 Is weather-proof
Under the sparres of which I lie
 Both soft, and dry
Low is my porch, as is my Fate,
 Both void of State;
And yet the threshold of my door
 Is worn by th' poor
Who thither come, and freely get
 Good words, or meat;
Likeas my Parlour, so my Hall
 And Kitchin's small;
A little Butterie, and therein
 A little Byn
Which keeps my little loafe of Bread
 Unchipt, unflead;
Some brittle sticks of Thorne or Briar
 Make me a fire
Close by whose living coals I sit
And glow like it.

Robert Herrick, from '*Noble Numbers*', 1647

Glebe Terrier

A Glebe Terrier of the House and Glebe lands belonging to the Vicaridge of Dean Prior given in to the Bishops Registry August [1680] by Will. Pearse, vicar, John Head and John Lavers, Churchwardens.
Imprimis: One dwelling house consisting of one Hall, one parlour, one kitchen, one cellar, one brewhouse, fower chambers, one study, the walls of stone.
Item: Out houses belonging to it are one Barne, one stable....[glebe land totalling seventy acres]
[Devon Record Office, Exeter Diocesan Records, Glebe Terriers, Dean Prior, 1680]
Robert Herrick was from 1629 to 1647 vicar of Dean Prior, a village in South Devon thirteen miles north-east of Plymouth.

Instructions to a Court of Survey

To view all the houses and buildings. . . and present the number of bayes therof and the ruynes and decayes thereof. [see p. 7]

CHAPTER 1

Introduction

Robert Herrick's architectural plan in verse (opposite) was not written for the benefit of future historians nor even for his practical neighbours, the churchwardens, who had the responsibility of reporting the condition of the church's property to the Bishop of Exeter. As historical evidence for a small West Country house, it is tantalising in its concreteness, yet baffling and ultimately defeating in its singularity. So too are those other documents familiar to English historians and often used to write the history of rural communities in the sixteenth and seventeenth centuries. Probate inventories, deeds and leases, terriers, and especially England's extraordinary treasure of surviving early houses and farm buildings, provide a wealth of information. Yet all are biased, generally towards the larger and the wealthier property holders, giving short shrift to those of small means. While each of these familiar sources partly compensates for the others' shortcomings, neither singly or together do they present a complete picture of communities in the English countryside.

In the past social historians and students of vernacular architecture have been content to let a fragmentary record stand for the whole. They saw no alternative to using the incomplete sample of buildings and documents that accident had spared, nor any compelling reason not to. Today we are not so easily satisfied. As social history is increasingly understood to be the history of society in its entirety, it becomes ever more important to find—or to reconstitute—sources of information that reveal communities in complete cross-section.

The house-and-estate surveys presented in this book go a long way toward remedying the deficiencies that historians encounter in other record groups. Surveys generally compile information about tenant householders' rents, conditions of tenure, and sizes of holdings. Some also assemble data on field names, sizes, locations, relative worth, and sometimes their state of cultivation or agriculture use. On estates where tenure was for life, the age of the tenant (and sometimes the ages of members of his family as well) was vital to property valuation. What sets the house-and-estate surveys apart from conventional manorial surveys and other documents that record property-holding and tenure, is the further information they give concerning the fixed assets of the farms, namely the houses, outhouses, and farm buildings. While terriers and inventories sometimes illuminate particular dwellings and farmsteads, these surveys come closer than any other documents to providing information about all village property-holders regardless of their wealth. In house-and-estate surveys, we have a source from which to re-create a picture of the village scene in rural England that includes land, rents, agricultural buildings, domestic service buildings, and dwellings—all associated with named individuals and virtually complete from mere cottagers to the largest leaseholders.

The comprehensiveness of these surveys commends them to a generation of scholars who raise issues about the social history of rural England that require a knowledge of its entire population. Local communities were subject to powerful forces of economic and cultural integration starting in the period covered by the earliest of these West Country surveys, the closing years of Elizabeth's reign and the opening decades of the seventeenth century. Rapid economic growth brought new-found prosperity to landowners and property holders in the middle and upper ranks of society who found themselves in a position to exploit opportunities provided by expanding national markets. By the end of the century the contrasts between the upper and lower ranks of society, or even between the middle and the lower, were not just measured in terms of wealth, status, and power, but were reinforced by marked differences in living standards, education, and cultural outlook.

This transformation proceeded variously in different parts of the country until the end of the eighteenth century. The weight of the evidence from the surveys in Somerset, Devon, and Cornwall span too little of this period to follow the full course of change in south-west England. Instead they provide vivid still-life pictures of communities during these events. Their unsparing record of every villager's land holdings, dwelling and service buildings, and the structures each employed to make his living, enable historians to study two aspects of social differentiation that were experienced directly by the men and women involved. Most acutely felt were the effects of different standards of living. The size and quality of housing contributed most to people's creature comforts in an age when domestic furnishings were still sparse even among the better off. Economic opportunity is another measure that social historians have learned to heed. Often they ask how a person's place in the village hierarchy affected his or her prospects for the future. The surveys studied here throw light on that question by supplying information about the specialised agricultural buildings that equipped farmers to capitalise on the crops they could grow or the stock they could pasture. Opportunity knocked loudest not just for those with the largest holdings. Equally, farmers needed the appropriate animal shelters, storage barns, and work buildings for by-employments that could take advantage of changing market opportunities. Both making money and spending it were activities in which everyone was engaged and by which every community sorted out winners from losers. The house-and-estate surveys give us material to study both.

Our seventeen house-and-estate surveys relating to south-west England (the three counties of Somerset, Devon and Cornwall) fall into two groups.[1] Two Cornish surveys and five for Somerset, all dating from the opening decade of the seventeenth century, are part of a series that recorded Crown estates located throughout England. Ours all follow the same form, even to the point of exhibiting the same handwriting. The descriptions of farmsteads they give are comprehensive, but sparse compared to the remaining surveys. These ten documents, ranging in date from 1598 to 1764, are from six separate record groups and have no intrinsic link apart from the architectural information they contain.

Fortunately, as a whole they provide a wide geographical coverage of the whole region, save only North Devon. Most importantly, they describe all the major micro-economies in the three counties.

Eight of the surveys were made in a period of twenty years between 1598 and 1619, a sufficiently narrow span of time over which to make valid comparisons. The two eighteenth-century surveys give a chronological perspective, showing significant changes both in living standards and in the agricultural economy.

We have organised the book to draw out from the surveys instructive contrasts between regions, between large and small landholders, and between the seventeenth century and the next. This introductory chapter continues with a look at the geography of south-west England, in particular its several agricultural zones, each of which in different ways so conspicuously enriched its farmers by the end of the sixteenth century that prudent landowners were encouraged to survey their property. The chapter concludes by considering the surveys themselves as historical documents, the context of events in which they were made, their content, and the method of their production. We have also included in Part II a representative selection of images of the surveys themselves, to illustrate their individual character.

In chapter 2 we examine the information presented in the surveys about the social structures, economic patterns, and demographic characteristics of the village communities they record. Their portraits of farmhouses and cottages are the subject of chapter 3. The survey descriptions, comprehensive but terse, are enlarged upon by reference to standing buildings and to probate inventories, which both can illustrate and illuminate the surveyors' data.

Chapter 4 gives similar treatment to the farmsteads, concentrating on the different combinations of farm buildings needed to exploit the diverse agrarian economies in the region. Standing farm buildings are not as numerous or as informative as dwellings, but a few specimens do survive, and they repay careful study, especially in combination with inventories, which define the local terms farmers attached to buildings in the farmstead.

Each village, its farms, and its survey is considered in detail in the second part of the book. Its regional setting, its topography, and the history of the estate are described. The survey evidence for the economic and social structure, for the houses, and for the farm buildings is then related to the level of sophistication of living standards and to the development of the agrarian economy.

Each of these sections is followed by an abstract of the survey itself.

South-western England in the Seventeenth Century

The house-and-estate surveys presented here come from one corner of England, the extreme south-western counties of Somerset, Devon, and Cornwall. This is mainly grass-growing country with thin, upland soils best suited for raising cattle and sheep. Down off the moors, the fertile river valleys, coastal plains, fens, and forest pasture land provided farmers in the region with opportunities to diversify both crops and stock.

In all, the region supported five discernibly different agricultural systems, each represented by at least one of the surveyed villages or estates (see Location Map on endpapers).[2]

Norton St. Philip, surveyed by the Crown's appraisers in 1608, is located in the heavily forested, hilly country along Somerset's eastern border with Dorset and Wiltshire. The landscape here was dotted with hamlets and small, scattered family farms, the woodland in between used for grazing dairy cows and some flocks of sheep. Many farmers were also seasonal craftsmen, supplementing an income from cheese and wool with by-employments as weavers, glove and lace makers, and (by the middle of the seventeenth century) stocking knitters. The few nucleated settlements like Norton St. Philip that had some arable land grew small amounts of grain, but never enough to make the region self-sufficient.

To the west, the hills spill down onto the Somerset Levels. This was true fen country, drowned by winter floods that brought wild fowl and eels and left behind enriched soils that every summer grew luxuriant grass for fattening cattle, feeding milk cows, and grazing horses. The pasture commons were so spacious and unstinted that frequently the only land that farmers owned was hay meadow, with some plough-land for barley, beans, oats, and wheat. Kingsbury borders on the fens. Its survey shows that in 1608 it was sharing in the economies of the two regions it straddled, fenland and wood pasture. There is no such ambiguity about West Pennard. Situated five miles due east of Glastonbury, its farmers held large tracts and were clearly fenmen.

Towards the coast, fenland becomes marshland. A justice of the peace for Brent Hundred, one of four rural neighbourhoods surveyed in 1606, described 'the husbandry of these places [as] consisting much in grazing and most proper for it'.[3] Farmers on these fertile coastal marshes bred and fattened stock in large numbers, selling beef to ships' victuallers in Bristol.

Rearing, feeding, and dairying were also important in a few mixed farming areas, which comprised yet another microeconomy in this otherwise predominantly pastoral region. The heavier soils of the Exe Valley and the vales of Taunton Deane and Wellington with their markets along the sea coasts, encouraged stockmen and dairy farmers to diversify into various cultivated crops. Those around Wellington, another of the surveyed Crown estates, combined some grain growing (mainly wheat) with specialisation in fruit and hops. Landholding farmers in Kenton were well placed to sell the grain they raised to merchants coming and going along the River Exe. The village poor of Kenton, numerous as usual where arable land required field hands, had to make do with what they could grow in small cottage gardens or could buy with the little money they made from weaving fine kerseys, Exeter having been for many centuries a centre of that industry.

The ribbons of arable land that issue from Exmouth, Teignmouth, Dartmouth, and Plymouth also hem the south coast of Devon and Cornwall.[4] Coastal agriculture is represented in this study by the surveys of Seaton and Sidmouth, both of which were also fishing villages as were Plymstock and Oreston at the mouth of the Tamar.

It is difficult to be sure how significant field crops were in the economies of these coastal villages, for their arable soils formed a narrow band of fertile land where the uplands folded into river valleys or tipped down to the sea. For example, Sherford, a Devon estate surveyed in 1606, lies less than four miles inland from Start Bay, yet its inhabitants were predominantly herdsmen. Even in Kenton some farmers looked for their livelihood to the higher ground away from the river. For them it was still convenient to retain the ancient custom of stabling their cattle in what are known now as 'long-houses', farmhouses with cow-stalls attached.

These are reminders that throughout the whole region moorland was never more than a few miles away. Fully half the surveys take us up into this grazing country, to Nettlecombe on the north-east slopes of the Brendon Hills, to Farway and Whitwell in the broken country of East Devon, to the Bedford estates along the western fringes of Dartmoor, and into Cornwall, most of which was one great moorland pasture. Looking carefully at the Cornish manors surveyed between 1602 and 1606 and at the Bedford estates appraised in 1709, one finds communities advantageously situated on the edges of the moors with opportunities for various lucrative by-employments, among them carting, pack-horse transport, and some grain growing. Sheep and cattle raising were clearly the dominant activities, but the Hurdwick survey gives evidence of fruit growing in addition to grain production. Like other villages west of Dartmoor it also produced a coarse woolen cloth, which was distributed through Tavistock, an up-and-coming borough whose property attracted the attention of the Bedfords' assiduous estate managers.

Every community in this as any other region experienced a distinctive blend of influences from its geography, geology, land ownership, and even the personalities of its inhabitants. Thus, generalisations about the whole region based on evidence from one or a few villages must always be speculative and uncertain. On the other hand, the surveys presented here—self-selected by their content but random with respect to most of the determinants of the character of a community—cover a wide range of conditions in south-west England. They cannot tell us what proportion of the region's population shared the experiences, say, of the fishermen of Oreston, or the sheep farmers of Launceston, but we believe that this sample is qualitatively representative of the life of the region as a whole.

The Estates

The seventeen estates with which we are concerned were large enough to need careful administration. They were viewed by their surveyors as natural units of ownership, but they are far from uniform, either in size or in nature. Indeed, their varying character as estates reflects the differing agrarian and topographical characteristics of the region. Although each of the south-western counties held landowners with large estates, they also included a substantial body of independent freeholders, owners of their own farms as well as perhaps of some tenanted properties. These freeholders are particularly characteristic of the dispersed settlement found especially in Devon and Cornwall.

Their farms often originated in medieval colonisation of the waste (assarting), with the grant of the property by charter from the lord of the manor. When an estate was built up by acquiring such freeholdings piecemeal, by gift or purchase, the result was what we see in the Launceston survey, the former property of Launceston Priory. It comprised some 130 properties, scattered through half-a-dozen parishes near the town. The other Cornish manors shared, though less markedly, something of the same character, as did the Nettlecombe estate in Somerset. By contrast, estates such as Kenton have nucleated villages with manor and parish more or less coterminous, and with the estate owning almost all the farms and cottages.

Most of the Somerset Crown estates are of this type, although Wellington, the borough itself, where many of the tenants probably lived, is not included in the survey despite being a Crown property. The other Devon estates are intermediate in character, including some scattered farms but with a high proportion of the parish in one ownership.

The Surveys (Figures 23-28)

Like all documents, estate surveys in general and house-and-estate surveys in particular need to be placed in their historical context before they can be properly interpreted. They were produced by estate administrators who included both professionals and amateurs. Indeed, on a small estate the landowner himself might serve as his own steward, bailiff, rent-collector, and surveyor. However, not every steward prepared estate surveys, let alone with the detail found in the house-and-estate surveys. We need, therefore, to examine why and how these surveys were made. Their accuracy depends very much on the manner of their making, while their scope reflects the surveyors' estimation of the estate's assets.

Reasons for surveying estates

The greatest number of house-and-estate surveys date from the late sixteenth and early seventeenth centuries, although some were made as late as the second half of the eighteenth century and a few even into the early nineteenth.[5] Two circumstances explain the keen interest of Tudor and Stuart landowners in this commonplace tool of estate management and especially the decision of some surveyors to include information about dwellings and farm buildings. As rising prices for agricultural products inflated land values in the second half of the sixteenth century, enterprising landlords took steps to keep rents abreast. Private landowners, colleges, corporations, and Crown officers hired professional surveyors and auditors to reappraise estates, compile *valors*, and search out long neglected feudal rights. Many Crown surveys (including seven of the documents used in this study) were compiled in the opening years of James I's reign as part of a scheme to improve the king's revenues when intransigent parliaments refused to provide what he regarded as an adequate income.[6] Private landowners also felt pinched by the pressure of inflation and were no less eager than the king to raise rents on their own estates.[7]

The tendency of prices to outrun income from leases enhanced the value of good farmland for its tenants, who received larger profits than they had been used to. Increasingly, as the sixteenth century progressed, they tended to spend some of that surplus enlarging and improving their dwellings and farm buildings.

The obligation to provide housing had always rested on tenants. In those earlier ages most ordinary buildings were too poorly built to be carried as assets on landlords' books.[8] That changed significantly in the sixteenth century as houses and outbuildings were rebuilt in better quality materials that enhanced their durability, longevity, and inevitably their value. These improvements caught the eye of needy landlords and tempted the likes of Willoughby d'Eresby in Lincolnshire, the Earl of Pembroke in Wiltshire, and the Trevelyans in Somerset to include dwellings and farm buildings for the first time in their calculations of rents and entry fines.[9]

Such improvements were less frequently recorded in later surveys. The reason may be that the quality of housing became more uniform, making differences between individual farmsteads less important. It may also reflect the growing practice of landlords in the late seventeenth and eighteenth centuries to assume responsibility for building and maintaining tenant farms as a way of further extending their control over the management of their estates. Whatever reasons explain the declining use of houses-and-estate surveys in later periods, their popularity around 1600 is both a consequence and a record of a fundamental transformation in English rural life.

Compiling the surveys

Estate surveys seem to have been prepared by two methods, one that might be called 'traditional' and the other 'professional'. The first type was compiled using as informants the villagers themselves, who were summoned by the landlord's steward to a special meeting of the manor court known as a 'court of survey'. What a jury of villagers was asked to do on such occasions is explained in the instructions attached to one of the surveys used in this study, that of East Brent, Somerset, in 1606.[10]

EST BRENT MANER

[Articles for the Jurye for Survye to enquire and presente]

1. Imprimis to enquire and presente the names of all the tenantes, freeholders, copieholders and that hold by lease or leases, or at will, any landes, tenementes & hereditamentes within the said mannor, and all other that hold of the Kinges majestie by lease anye rectories, tithes, landes and tenementes within three myles of the said manor.
2. Item to enquire what incroachmentes by inclosure, buildinge or otherwise hath formerly ben made upon the waste within the said mannor, what the quantitye of the same is and the true yerelye value thereof and the lyke of concealmentes.
3. Item to view all the houses and buildings holden by Lease or copie within the said mannor, and present the nomber of bayes thereof, and the ruynes and decayes thereof, by whom and what charge will replace the same.
4. Item to number the trees upon everye parcell of lease land and copiehold land, and how many loads of tymber, and how many loads of firewood wilbe of each tenante.
5. Item to view the meetes and boundes of the said

> manor, and to present the same and deliver their presentment under their handes unto John Maye esqr. before [St Matthewes *erased*] Michaelmas daye next.

A professional survey might be combined with this traditional court of survey, or it might be conducted separately. Either way, its distinguishing characteristic was the surveyor's precise measurement, on the ground, of all fields in each holding '*per diligentem et exactum visum, perambulacionem et mensurationem*' in the words of the Nettlecombe survey (p. 152). Such pole-and-chain work was relatively easy on the landscape of enclosed fields found in south-west England, although comparison of survey figures with those of later maps shows that the challenge of calculating the exact areas of irregular fields sometimes defeated the surveyor's skills. Exact measurements were much harder to obtain for open field holdings, which often consisted of a patchwork of hundreds of separate strips. In these cases (as at Kenton among the surveys used here) resort was frequently made to the traditional practice of recording nominal sizes.

The reliability of either type of survey is good, it seems, where qualitative information is presented. For mensuration, the professional surveyor provided the more exact figures. His areas were usually computed to the last perch whereas village estimates tended to round off acres to whole numbers. The valuations assigned to parcels of land were probably fairly accurate, as experienced working farmers must have had an excellent sense of current land values in their own neighbourhoods, and the presence of sworn juries is likely to have discouraged deliberate exaggeration or misstatement. There may have been room for greater error where a survey included descriptions of houses and farm buildings. It remains to be seen (in Chapter 3) whether a steward or villagers assembled at a manor court could be expected to produce a full and accurate inventory of the buildings in the village.

The surveyor's concerns.

The instructions given to the jurors of East Brent, as quoted above, enumerate in order of priority those features of his employer's estate that a surveyor was expected to appraise. The conditions governing tenure and the value of land, measured by its fertility, by the buildings located on it, and by its timber resources, were the assets that a landowner had to manage wisely to offset his liabilities.

Rents and fines were his chief sources of income. Consequently, surveyors paid greatest attention to the conditions of tenure appertaining to each holding. These determined its potential profitability to the manorial lord. Of three main forms of tenure, *freeholds* were of least value because such property had been all but transferred out of the lord's control. His only remaining profit came from a small fixed rent, sometimes supplemented by a further small sum–customarily one year's rent–paid when a freeholder died. In the surveys presented here, the freeholds are listed first and generally include only the most cursory details since further information was of no account in calculating the value of the property to the landlord.[11]

Copyholders and *leaseholders* also paid an annual rent, often fixed by custom and insulated against inflation. But when a tenant died or his lease expired, the lord could exact a large entry fine before disposing of the holding again at the same or an increased rent. Thus, the income was substantially larger than just that from rents and could periodically be increased as land values rose. Copyhold tenure was the standard tenure in the medieval period, persisting into the seventeenth century and occasionally later. Each holding was recorded in the manor court roll, the tenant receiving a so-called 'copy of court roll', which he was required to produce on such occasions as a court of survey. Tenancy was for life, and by custom a copyholder's widow could retain it for her lifetime, although not necessarily if she remarried. Succession was usually not inherited.[12] Heirs often sought and obtained the reversion to a holding before the tenant's death by paying an appropriate fine. A holding could also be surrendered to the lord with a new tenant specified, again for a fee.

The normal form of leasehold tenure in South West England was by the three-life lease, which gradually superseded copyhold during the sixteenth and seventeenth centuries. In our surveys, leasehold was becoming significant by 1619 in Nettlecombe, and in Seaton the 1682 resurvey shows that since 1609 virtually every tenancy had been converted at its renewal to a three-life lease. In both the eighteenth-century surveys, this tenure was almost universal. The three lives were those of named people living at the time the lease was granted, and the tenancy lasted either for ninety-nine years or the lifetime of the longest-lived of those named. Usually those were the tenant, his wife, and one child, although unrelated people were occasionally involved, as in some of the Bedford and Sidmouth leases. A tenant could by this arrangement assure the succession to his immediate family. To extend it even further, new lives were often added or a reversion obtained while the original lease was still in effect. Such liens on the future were expensive, and the large entry fines tenants had to pay were often recorded. The surveyors' scrutiny extended too to the annual rent, small as it was, and the 'heriot' that was due on the death of each of the 'lives'. Most landlords with an eye to long-range financial planning instructed their surveyors to record the ages of the surviving lives, useful information for them when it came to forecasting the future value of holdings and useful now for historical demographers.

After the terms of tenure, the surveyor's main concern was with the land itself—the number of fields, their sizes, and the uses to which they were put. Calculations based on value per acre produced estimates of the anticipated annual value of the entire holding. This information shows typically the contrast between the very profitable meadow land, the ordinary pasture or arable, and the marginal moorland fit only for rough grazing.

The few surveys that describe houses and farm buildings are a measure of the lesser importance that most surveyors accorded these assets. Clearly though, some were coming to appreciate that well-constructed buildings enhanced the value of tenant holdings.

The last two provisions in the stewards' instructions to the villagers at East Brent concerned the trees and the manor boundaries. The first represented a capital asset treated sometimes like an emergency fund. Leases were often careful to prohibit tenants from felling timber, although they were usually allowed to collect firewood and hedge-trimmings. The trees belonged to the lord, to be sold off if he should find himself short of ready cash.

In respect to the manor boundaries, the East Brent jurors failed utterly in their duty; the survey contains only a blank sheet headed 'Boundes'. So too the other Crown estates. The survey for Kenton, however, and an early Cornish survey (p. 100) do fulfil the requirement. They show very clearly that recorded metes and bounds were the steward's attempt to define the common lands of the manor. The information was useful for excluding strangers' stock that might otherwise have trespassed undetected. It could also help in collection of mining royalties.

Everywhere surveyors' concerns and procedures were similar. However the surveys they made varied considerably. Not only were they themselves variously skilled, but each region, indeed each village, expressed its own personality in the portrait that surveyors unconsciously created. As modern historians, we have our own reasons to be glad for these vignettes, but once we are satisfied that we understand how and why they were made, our interests turn from the painters to their subject—to the landscape and the figures in it.

[1] House-and-estate surveys are extremely rare, making up less than 1% of all surviving estate surveys. In identifying our corpus (list, p. xiii), we have examined all likely surveys in the National Archives and the Devon Record Office. The only such surveys found in the Somerset County Record Office are those originally identified by W.G. Hoskins; correspondence with the Cornwall and Dorset Record Offices indicated that neither held examples, although later sorting has identified two Somerset surveys in Dorset and one has come to light in a private collection now in the Cornwall Record Office (below).

For England as a whole, two lists have been published of known house-and-estate surveys: N.W. Alcock, 'A Provisional Handlist of Detailed House-by-House Surveys', *Vernacular Architecture*, **1** (1970), 13; N.W. Alcock, 'Further House-and-Estate Surveys', *Vernacular Architecture*, **5** (1974), 27.

At an advanced stage in the preparation of this study four further surveys came to light, too late to be fully assimilated. The first is earlier than any of the previously known examples, dating to 1558, and covers twenty-five holdings in Compton Dundon, Somerset, belonging to the Strangeway estate (Dorset Record Office, D/FSI, Box 16B). It lists the total number of couples on each holding, adding together those in different buildings. The same estate re-examined its property in this village in 1615-16, when the surveyor listed the names of the individual rooms (Dorset Record Office, D/FSI, Box 15). The information in this survey has been summarised in Somerset Vernacular Building Research Group, *Somerset Village: Compton Dundon*, Crewkerne, 2004.

The third newly-discovered survey is a companion survey to that of Norton St. Philip which has strayed from the Public Record Office. It was also taken in 1606 and describes twenty-five buildings on the manor of Hinton Charterhouse, Somerset (Duchy of Cornwall Office, Muniment Room Backshelf 22. DCO Surveys). The fourth, of 1618, relates to the estates of the Arundell family of Lanherne, Cornwall and is reported to include some information on tenant houses (Cornwall Record Office, AR2/1346; H. S. A. Fox and O. J. Padel, eds., *The Cornish Lands of the Arundells of Lanherne, Fourteenth to Sixteenth Centuries*, Devon and Cornwall Record Society NS41, 1998, pp. 1, xcix).

2 The authors wish to thank Joan Thirsk for kindly making available to them the worksheets she used to compile the map of farming regions in England published in *Ag. Hist.*, IV, Fig. 1, 4.

3 TNA SP16/533/3.

4 Although Thirsk's map of farming regions shows this littoral as a continuous belt around the south coast, it was probably interrupted, Dartmoor coming very close to the coast east of Plymouth.

5 Alcock, 'Provisional Hand-list', 13.

6 For a general background to the Crown surveys, see R. Hoyle, 'Vain Projects' in J. Chartres and D. Hey (eds.) *English Rural Society 1500-1800* (Cambridge, 1990), 73-101.

7 *Ag. Hist.*, IV, 268-273; large parts of the 1606-9 Devon surveys of the Willoughby estates are in the hand of John Willoughby himself (see p. 110).

8 Borne out by the general absence of building accounts for tenant houses in estate documents, apart from rare exceptions in the 15th century. See C. C. Dyer, 'English peasant buildings in the later Middle Ages', *Medieval Archaeology*, 30 (1986), 19.

9 For Willoughby d'Eresby's survey see M. W. Barley, *English Farmhouse and Cottage* (London, 1961), 87. The Pembroke surveys are printed in E. Kerridge, *Surveys of the Manors of Philip, First Earl of Pembroke and Montgomery, 1631-2*, Wiltshire Archaeology and Natural History Society Records Branch (Devizes, 1953). John Trevelyan's 1619 survey of Nettlecombe is examined in the present book.

10 TNA LR 2/225, f. 109.

11 Burgage tenure, found only at Crofthole, in the 1602 Cornish survey, was normally similar to freehold tenure.

12 This was the case on most or all southwestern manors, but in some places the copyholders succeeded in establishing that their holdings did pass by inheritance, and also that fines were fixed at the very nominal values of the early sixteenth century. Such copyholds were of no more value to the lord than freeholds. Cf. *Ag. Hist.*, IV, 293, 684-5, and Hoyle, 'Vain Projects'.

CHAPTER 2

The Communities and their Social Structure

The social order in pre-industrial England is at once self-evident and enigmatic. Any reader of seventeenth-century documents encounters the social labels of village society—yeoman, husbandman, and labourer—in addition to the usual occupational terms for artisans—carpenter, tanner, blacksmith, fisherman, and tailor—and among women, of course, spinsters and widows. Social naming gave definition to perceived distinctions in the village hierarchy. That much is obvious. But were the names grounded in economic reality? Did English villages contain three categories of householder with access to successively greater economic resources? The surveys can help answer a question that has long puzzled social historians.[1] In the process they also describe society in the West Country communities whose farming practices and standards of living will be explored in subsequent chapters.

The Size of Landholdings

The surveys uniformly provide two items of economic information for each tenant—the rent he paid and the size of his landholding. Rents might be expected to be the more useful, inasmuch as they presumably reflect the real or potential earning power of the holding and avoid such problems as the quality of the soil or the proportion of meadow to arable. Unfortunately they are notoriously unreliable at this period. Not only was the degree of profit taken by the landlord variable, but the annual rent was a fraction, often a small fraction, of the outgoings from the holding.[2] Substantial sums were often required for entry fines to renew leases. Although the surveys often record these payments, we lack sufficient information about average length of tenure to convert the annual rent into an accurate measure of the financial burden that a landlord could expect his tenant to bear.[3]

Can we use the recorded size of the holding as reliable evidence of the tenant's economic position, or is this also biased by invisible factors? Variations in land type and quality are not significant in comparing two farms within the same community where everyone would need access to arable, pasture and meadow, but the correlation of farm sizes in one survey with those in another may well be affected by differences in the overall quality of land in the two villages. A more important question is whether the surveyed land was actually that farmed by the named tenant. Did he lease or own extra land, or perhaps sublet part of his holding?

Some of the surveys give direct evidence for subletting when they list, for example, a main house and a small house on the same holding. These sublet tenant houses did not share equally in the resources of the holding.[4] They were identical to other landless cottages on the estate, except that they happened to lie within or adjacent to a larger property. Thus they would not alter the effective size of the main holding.

The possession of extra land might arise either from a sub-tenancy, from a tenancy to another landowner, or from a freeholding. The surveys themselves indicate the extent to which both leasehold and freehold land without buildings was available. Holdings that lacked farmsteads were farmed by the tenant or owner of another property.[5] For the surveys studied here, the overall impression is that additional land-holdings hardly distort the survey evidence on holding size, apart from one or two unusual places such as Wellington (see p. 167).

The strongest confirmation that the landholdings in the surveys give a valid measure of economic position comes from the coherence of the patterns they delineate. These are examined in Figure 1 (A-Q) by

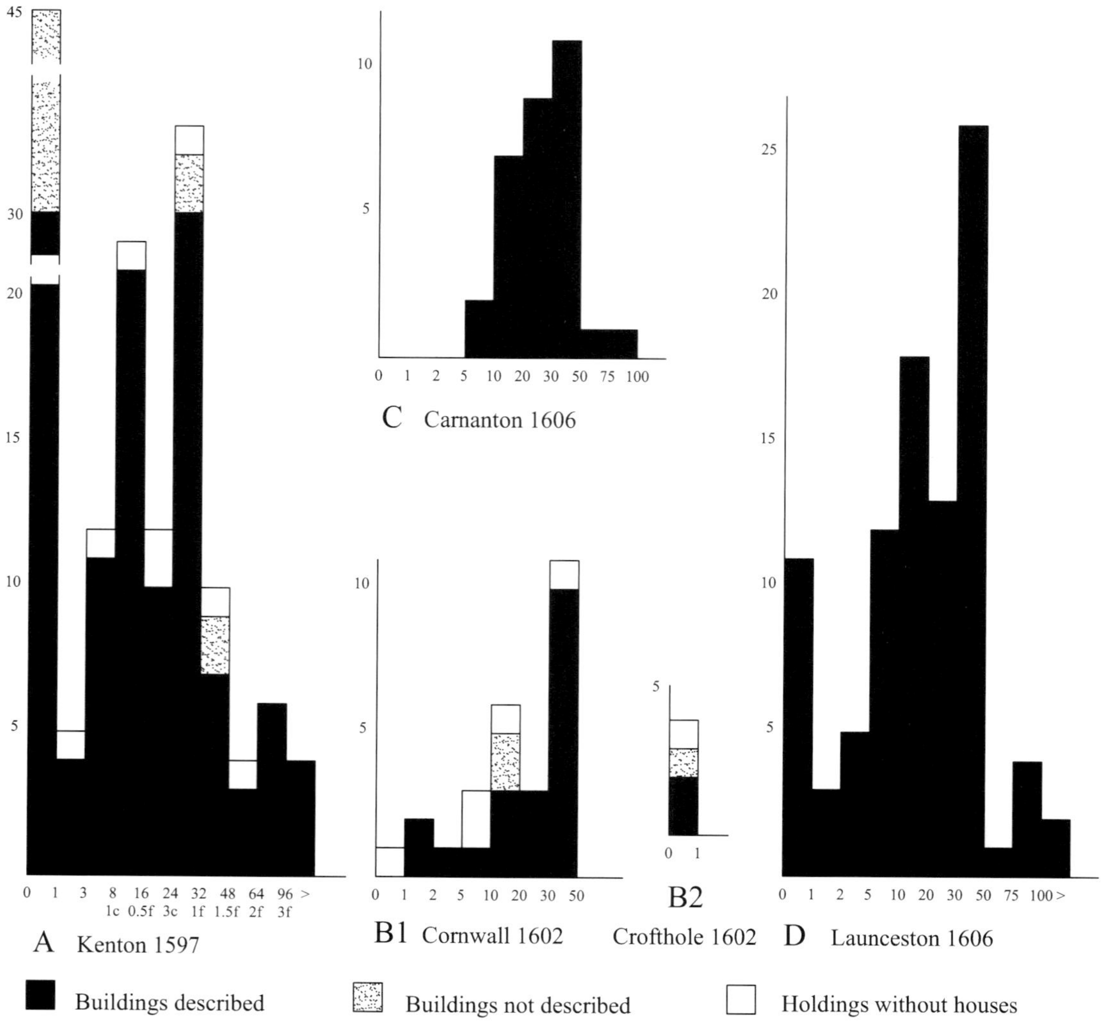

Figure 1a. The size of holdings (A-D). The horizontal axes indicate the ranges of holding size in acres; the vertical axes the numbers of holdings of the corresponding size. The three categories represent (a) holdings with buildings that are described in the survey (b) those with buildings that are not described (usually named as 'house and barn', etc.) (c) holdings without houses. For Kenton, the second row of symbols identify the size in 'claws' and 'furlongs' (see p. 73).

dividing the holdings into groups by size, then plotting for each group the number of tenants with holdings in that category. The resulting profiles characterise the distribution of farms for each community. Thus presented, the surveys provide a new and effective tool for understanding the social make-up of the community and its economic rationale.

None of these diagrams show a random scatter of holding size. Instead, they demonstrate three or four distinctive patterns, which correlate well with what we know about the regional economies. The simplest pattern is a single broad hump, centred at about thirty acres. This is seen at Carnanton, Farway, and West Pennard (Figure 1: C, F, L). It corresponds to an agrarian economy dominated by pastoral farming, the least labour-intensive in the region. The providers of unskilled labour, the smallholders and landless cottagers, were conspicuously absent in these communities.[6]

These smallholders make their first appearance in surveys that conform to a second pattern, showing the same broad concentration in the middle range coupled with a low peak for holdings of an acre or less. We can group together several such estates, where the smallholders make up only an insignificant proportion of the whole community, for example, in the Cornish estates (apart from Carnanton), Sherford, Wellington, East Brent, and Hurdwick (Figure 1: B1, D, E, J, M, N). These manors also lie in areas of pre-

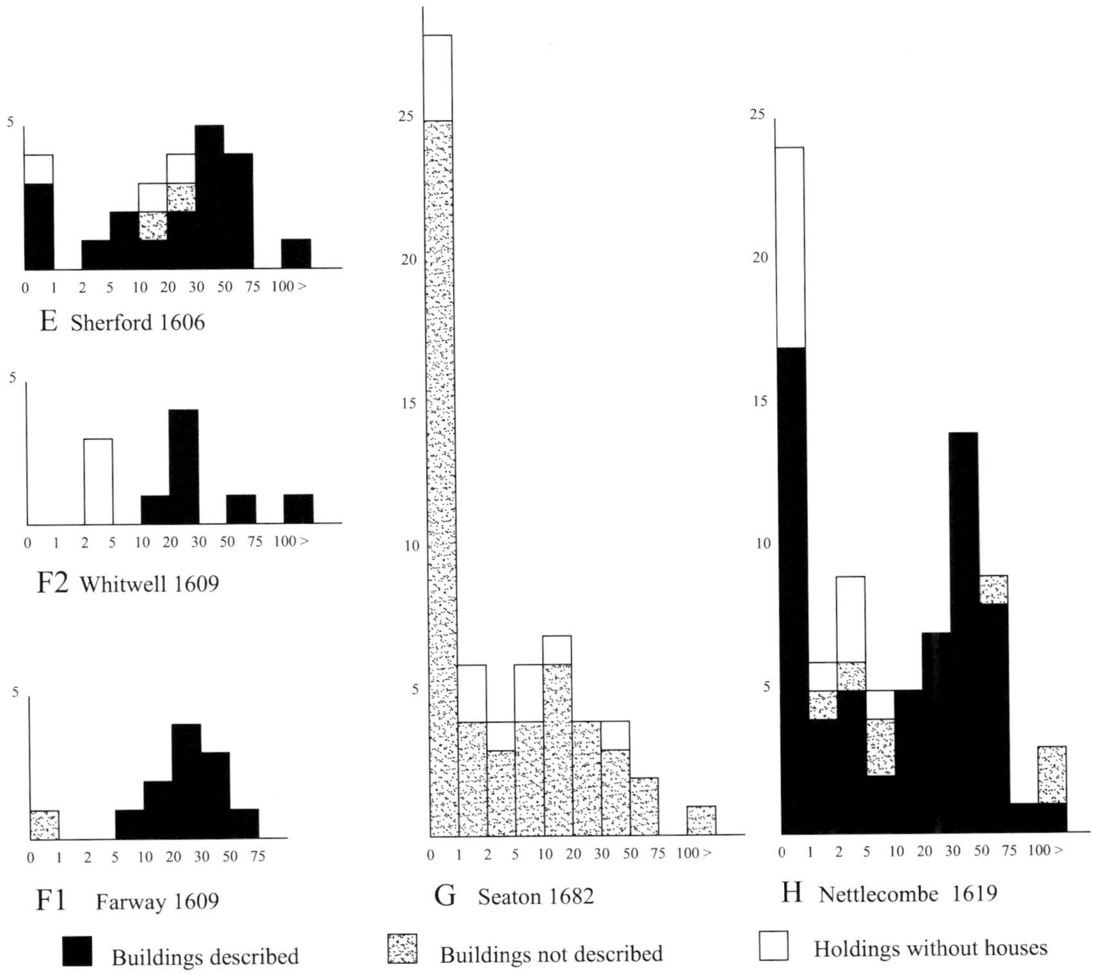

Figure 1b. The size of holdings (E-H)

dominantly pastoral farming, and we can deduce that *their* tenants had diversified only a little into arable farming in this mixed agrarian economy.

A third group of estates show the same overall pattern, but with a much larger proportion of cottagers (up to about a third of all the holdings). Kenton, Nettlecombe, and Kingsbury are the clearest examples (Figure 1: A, H, K), while Seaton and Plymstock (Figure 1: G, P) may also belong to this group. The simple explanation, that these villagers engaged predominantly in arable farming, is surely correct for Kenton with its open field system. Elsewhere alternative livelihoods existed. As well as eking out a living by working for others, householders with little or no access to farming resources may have turned to craft work. Such was probably the case in Nettlecombe, where specialised buildings suggest that butchery and meat processing played a larger role than elsewhere (see pp. 59, 150). Yet another possibility existed at Kingsbury where wide tracts of adjoining fenland could be freely used for summer pasture. Here, even landless cottagers were provided with a good living, as is demonstrated by the remarkable size of some of their houses.[7] Had we the information available, we would expect to see just such a pattern for Wellington borough (as opposed to the manor which was surveyed); probably it was composed of a number of small but prosperous holdings that used the surrounding manor land for their farming (the blank parts of Figure 1: J).

Cottagers with alternative livelihoods dominate the final social pattern. They are most obvious at Oreston (Figure 1: O), a fishing community where agriculture was non-existent and where none of the cottages came

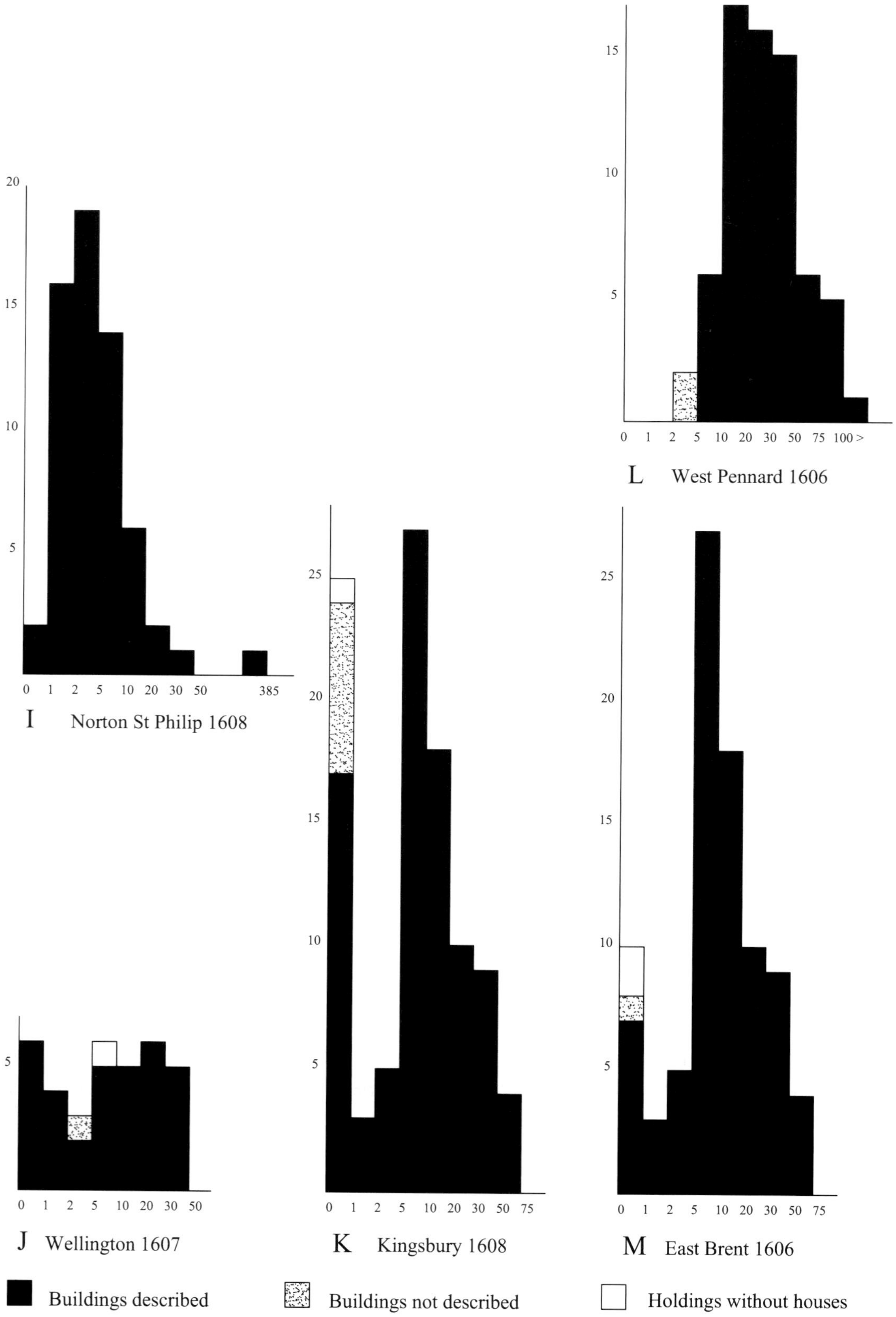

Figure 1c. The size of holdings (I-M)

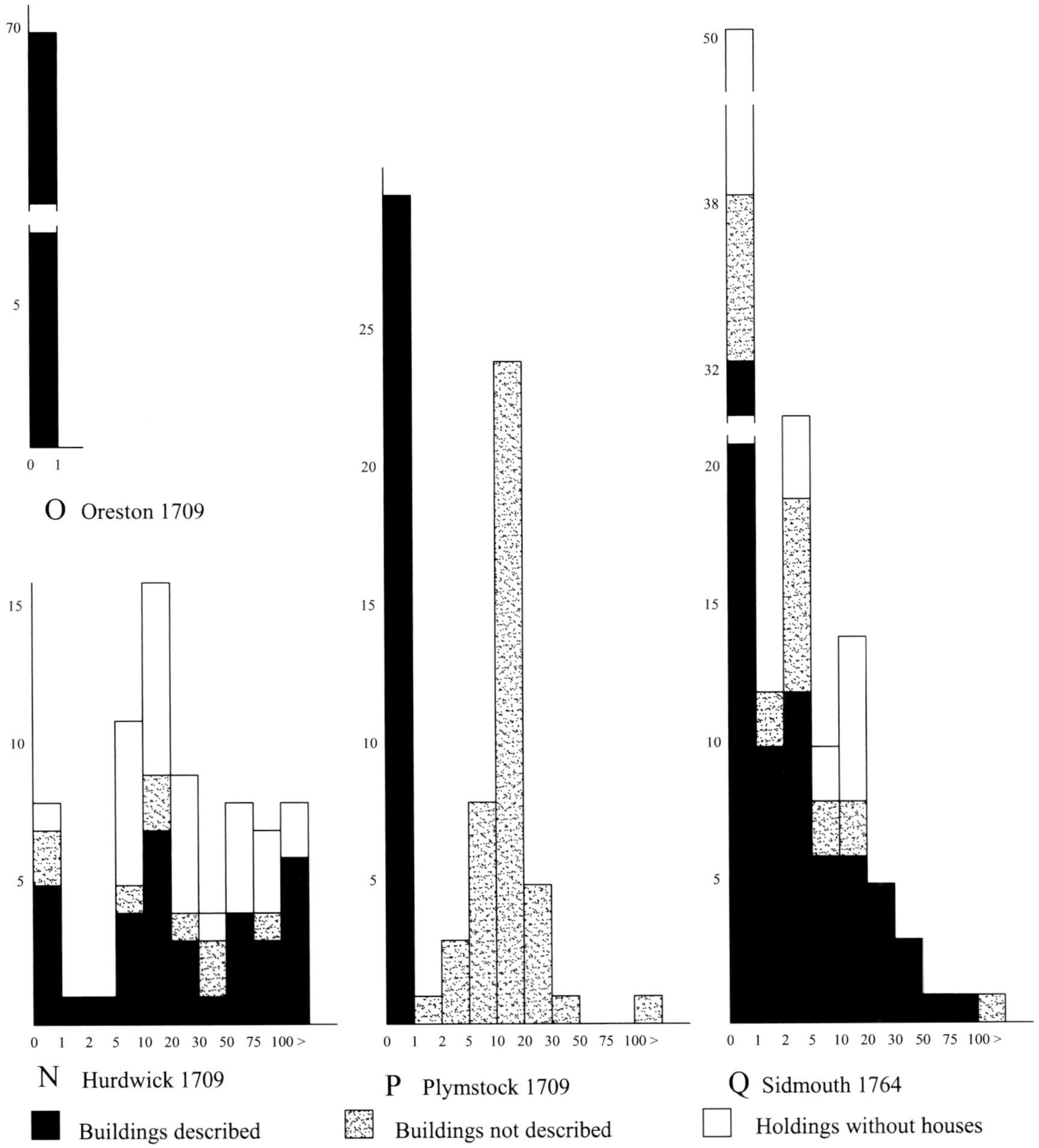

Figure 1d. The size of holdings (N-Q)

with more than a garden plot. Evidence to be discussed later (p. 185) shows that seafaring *per se* was not the mainstay of every household although it underpinned the village as a whole. At Norton St. Philip (Figure 1: I) the local crafts were home-based weaving and stocking-knitting, so that some agriculture could profitably be pursued. As a consequence, most villagers held a few acres of land, and a couple had more than twenty. The bulk of the manor's land (almost 400 acres) was held by one man. Despite his legal position as a tenant of the Crown, he must have played the role of resident squire in the village community.

The other estates are intermediate between the patterns already described. Plymstock (Figure 1: P) closely resembles Kenton, but from its location it seems unlikely to have engaged so heavily in arable farming. It lies just a mile inland from Oreston, perhaps not too far for fishermen to have lived there also. Most likely its villagers were craftsmen, perhaps making goods associated with the fishing trade. Seaton (Figure 1: G) also had a few farms accompanied by a large number of cottages, and here we have firm evidence that their tenants were craftsmen as well as mariners (p. 128). The tenants of Sidmouth (Figure 1: Q) pursued more varied occupations and included many seamen among their numbers. The presence of a greater proportion of prosperous craftsmen may explain its rather different profile, which appears to combine the holding pattern of Norton St. Philip with a group of pastoral farms.

Social structure

A direct correlation between social status and economic position cannot be tested with the surveys themselves because they do not record status or occupation. Indirectly, however, the economic hierarchies that they embody suggest the underlying social stratification of each community. The most characteristic economic pattern does not reveal the traditional tripartite social division into yeomen, husbandmen, and labourer. Rather it shows a marked separation into two groups. At the lower end of the scale came the landless cottagers, those holding 'cottages' in the surveys. In an agricultural community most of these would undoubtedly have been 'labourers' to their neighbours. The other group ranged from the most prosperous to the least prosperous farmers. It is reasonable to suppose that the lesser members of this group would have been called 'husbandmen' and the superior ones 'yeomen', with perhaps a few 'gentlemen' at the upper end.

No firm divisions existed within this group. People probably moved from one category to another in their neighbours' estimations without significant change in their economic circumstances. Indeed, it is not uncommon to find seventeenth-century wills in which the testator describes himself as a 'yeoman', while in the accompanying inventory his more realistic neighbours call him 'husbandman' and *vice versa*. Two of the early surveys, Kenton in 1598 and Launceston in 1606 (Figure 1: A, D), show just such a partial separation between larger and smaller farms. For Kenton, the distinction arises in part because the holdings were described not in statute acres, but in conventional terms of yardlands (there called farthings) (32 acres), half farthings, and so on. However, it may also reflect customs of an earlier period when the social distinction between yeoman and husbandman corresponded to a distinction between the holders of one yardland and those who held only a half.

For two estates, Seaton and Sidmouth, we have been able to supplement the surveys with evidence from series of leases, which usually do include social labels and craft descriptions.[8] Neither community was principally engaged in farming. Both had a strong dependence on seafaring, and Sidmouth in particular had a considerable urban character. People holding cottages, therefore, engaged in a wide range of occupations. They included one or two yeomen and husbandmen, but virtually no labourers. Both estates had a rural hinterland, and the leases also inform us about the social distinctions in those parts of the community.

The most surprising feature in these leases is the relative unimportance of husbandmen, both in numbers and in economic status. At Seaton only two or three are recorded and their largest landholding was no more than four acres, while Sidmouth had a few more, some holding up to seven acres. The leases that refer to husbandmen are concentrated around 1700, suggesting that the term itself was falling out of use in the early eighteenth century. By contrast, yeomen covered the economic hierarchy very broadly. Their holdings ranged from the largest available (about sixty acres) down to those of ten or fifteen acres and even included a few of the landless cottages, possibly sublet to labourers or craftsmen. For similar properties in Sidmouth, we can clearly see the beginnings of a landlord class (p. 210), gentry holding directly from the lord of the manor and subletting to lowlier members of the community. Gentlemen as well as yeomen are also found as tenants of the larger farms (thirty to sixty acres), which a century earlier would have been uniformly occupied by yeomen. The progressive downward movement of social labels is, of course, entirely to be expected, as everyone tended to assume the most prestigious status to which they might aspire. It also corresponds to evidence from elsewhere for the erosion during the seventeenth century of the term 'husbandman'.[9]

In these generalisations, it is important not to lose sight of reality, which is inevitably more varied and less regimented. For instance, four successive leases survive for the sixty-three acre holding, Porch House, Sidford (SM115; pp. 38, 210, 221). In 1651 it was leased to a merchant, who presumably employed a bailiff for the day-to-day running of the farm. He was succeeded by a mariner, one of a number who held farms, again presumably as a part-time occupation.

The mariner's son called himself a gentleman, while the tenant after 1754 was a yeoman.

The surveys give clear descriptions of the economic standing of householders, from the wealthy squire at Norton St. Philip to the poor widow in the cottage at his gate, but they reveal nothing about the household itself. Although the household—that is the 'family', comprising everyone living in the house—changed as children were born, grew up and left home, its composition was always an important factor in determining the size, plan, and use of the house.[10] In the middle of the period covered by the surveys, a yeoman with a mixed or arable farm of 60 acres might be expected to have two or three 'servants in husbandry' living in his house, while his wife might find a maidservant or two useful in the dairy. All these extra people would make the men's and maids' chambers essential parts of his house. However, his was not the only household type, and this pattern seems to have been an innovation of the late sixteenth and early seventeenth century, whether driven by or reflecting the increase in house size.[11] The range of houses in Kenton, the most purely arable of the villages surveyed, suggests that the bulk of the seasonal agricultural labour was provided by day-labourers who lived in their own cottages. These cottagers were concerned that their children move out as soon as they were of an age to be gainfully employed, to ease the crowding in houses with just one or two chambers. A different pattern again might be seen in farming communities specialising in pastoral husbandry. The smaller need for continuous care for farm animals was satisfied by rather fewer servants.

Unfortunately, the evidence to identify and select between these models is sparse indeed because of a lack of census-type listings before the mid-nineteenth century. A partial insight into household sizes in the early seventeenth century in Devon and Cornwall comes from an unusual source.[12] In 1623 and 1630, following harvest failures in the preceding years, parish officers were instructed to report on those households having surplus corn, indicating their size, corn stocks, and arable acreage. The surveys survive for two south Devon hundreds in 1623 and a Cornish one in 1630. The overall household sizes ranged from 40 down to 1, with a mean of 9.6 people. The largest households were clearly those of resident gentry, and it seems unlikely that many of the tenanted farms in the estate surveys approached this size. However, the information is otherwise of little direct use to the present study because of the absence of evidence on farm sizes; the recorded arable acreages probably correlate poorly with the total acreages.[13]

Sherford is one of the parishes covered in 1623, but disappointingly only one of the eight households listed, that of Arthur Wakeham (SH1) can be identified in the 1609 survey.[14] His household of eleven people seems appropriate for the thirteen room house and 72 acre farm (second largest in the Sherford survey). It provides our only specific information on household size in the surveyed villages.

One pre-census household listing has survived for a Devon parish, Wembworthy, in 1780.[15] Wembworthy lies in north Devon about midway between Dartmoor and the north coast. It has a dispersed settlement pattern and probably shared a mixed farming economy with most of the communities covered in the estate surveys, in particular with the east Devon parishes such as Farway. This listing is later than any of the surveys, but the sparse evidence for servants suggests that little change in the employment of living-in servants took place in the eighteenth century, before a major switch to non-resident labour began in the years around 1800.[16] The relatively late date does have one important advantage. The farms named in the listing can immediately be identified in the 1780 Land Tax assessment, followed through year-by-year to 1832, and readily linked to the 1838 Tithe Map from which farm acreages can be directly determined.[17]

Correlation of these acreages with household size (Table 1) shows just the relationship expected from the model of a mixed farming community. The twenty-one households of landless cottagers ranged between two and six people, with three the most common. All were made up of direct family members alone, and the largest units were those with several young children. The nineteen farms in Wembworthy were large, with only one of less than 50 acres; fourteen lay between 50 and 120 acres and four were larger still.[18] All their households were notably larger than for cottagers, generally with five to seven members. The largest farms included the three largest households, with twelve, eleven, and eleven members respectively. Almost all the farms had one maidservant (two on the two largest farms). The households also included one

Table 1: Household and farm size in Wembworthy, 1780

No	Place	Acr.	Family Members	Servants		Total	Notes
				Male	Female		
1	Leigh Wood	600	7	3	2	12	
3	Rashleigh	222	6	3	2	11	1 apprentice
4	Labdon	173	3	2		5	
13	Wembworthy Down	163	6	4	1	11	2 apprentices
16	Kennydown	118	2	4	1	7	2 apprentices
8	Higher Upacott	106	6	1	1	8	1 apprentice
5	Stone	102	3	1	1	5	
7	Upacott	91	7	1		8	1 apprentice
17	Goses	90	5			5	
9	Cumb	83	3	1		4	
12	Yealands	81	3	2	1	6	1 apprentice
11	Biddebear	78	4	1	1	6	1 apprentice
10	Paddons	74	3	1	1	5	
2	Sales	72	7			7	
15	Down	72	6	2		8	
14	Allywill	(50)	5	1	1	7	2 apprentices
18		(50)	5			5	
20	Laurances	25	9			9	2 lodgers
24	Rashleigh Mill	(7)	2			2	
21	[Bowrings?]	(5?)	4			4	
19	Hob	?	5	2		7	2 apprentices
6			5			5	
22			6			6	
23			6			6	aged lodger
25			5			5	
26			6			6	lodger

Notes: The number column gives the order in the listing. Entries 27 to 41 relate to cottagers holding no land and with only family members in their households. Their household sizes were: 2 (twice), 3 (eight times), 4 (twice), 5 (three times). From Devon R.O. 1165Z/Z1.

to four men servants, one or two of whom were identified as apprentices; several of the latter appear to have been members of cottager families.

Thus the households were of three types: small family groups for cottagers with the junior family members in service elsewhere, the intermediate households on middling farms with a couple of servants, and the big households on large farms of up to a dozen people comprising both immediate family members and servants.

Demographic Evidence

The surveys offer two forms of evidence that can be regarded broadly as demographic. The sex distribution of tenants can be established for all the estates (Table 2). Seven of the surveys also include the age of the tenant at the time the survey was taken (Table 3). The Bedford estate and Sidmouth surveys include even more demographic information among the details of the three-life leases, such as the ages of children. To make further use of this evidence would require complex statistical analysis, and it would produce results peripheral to the main purpose of this study. We have therefore examined only the basic demographic information.

The distribution of tenants by sex is remarkably variable (Table 2). Women, for example, occupied between 8% and 52% of the properties. The normal pro-

Table 2: Sex distribution of tenants

Place	Cottages		Farms		Overall		Overall F as
	M	F	M	F	M	F	% of M & F
Kenton (1597)	36	7	77	14	113	21	17
Cornwall (1602)					27	4	13
Carnaton (1606)					25	7	22
Launceston (1606)	16	2	68	6	84	8	9
Sherford (1606)					20	5	20
Farway & Whitwell (1609)					15	3	17
Seaton (1609)					12	13	52
Seaton (1682)	24	8	12	6	36	14	35
Nettlecombe (1619)	20	12	42	16	62	28	35
East Brent (1606)	11	2	65	12	76	14	15
Kingsbury (1608)	18	0	60	7	78	7	8
Norton St. Philip (1608)	19	5	34	4	53	9	16
Wellington (1607)					33	4	11
West Pennard (1606)					52	16	24
Bedford Estates (1709)							
general					80	15	16
Oreston cottages	41	29					41
Plymstock cottages	16	11					40
Sidmouth (1764)	30	15	10	6	40	21	34

Notes: Multiple tenancies are counted as one, as far as possible. The overall figures are the sums of the preceding columns. When the number of cottage holdings is too small to be significant, only the overall figures are given. Cottage holdings are of three acres or less.

Table 3: Ages of tenants when surveyed

	Cottages						Farms					
	Men			Women			Men			Women		
Place	Mean	Number	Range	Mean	Number	Range	Mean	Number	Range	Mean	Number	Range
Kenton	34	32	5–60	40	7	22–60	48	77	24–84	61	14	17–90
Seaton	40	17	20–60	46	2	40–51	54	8	26–82	46	3	40–55
Nettlecombe	49	8	33–83	53	7	36–80	54	25	20–81	57	9	44–72
Bedford general	–	–	–	–	–	–	48	44	20–60	51	9	40–70
Oreston	50	21	28–70	47	15	28–60	–	–	–	–	–	–
Plymstock	44	6	35–50	48	5	22–60	–	–	–	–	–	–
Sidmouth	44	9	27–66	49	9	27–70	39	7	22–66	59	2	58–60

Note: The round numbers recorded for ages in the Kenton survey show that these figures are approximate. Cottage holdings are of three acres or less.

portion for female tenants in most of these rural communities seems to be 15-25%, although Launceston and Kingsbury were significantly below the average, for reasons that are unclear. The situation among the Kingsbury smallholders, with eighteen male tenants and no women whatsoever, is particularly surprising.

Most of the village with the largest proportions of women share a common characteristic. They were cottage communities, particularly those with maritime connections such as Oreston. Presumably a high mortality among fishermen and mariners was responsible. At Oreston, evidence for the size of the cottages (see p. 185) suggests strongly that these fishing widows were supporting themselves by running lodging houses and that the number of seafarers in the community was considerably larger than the number of independent households suggests.

The proportion of women tenants at Seaton in 1609 was larger than anywhere else. Although the total numbers involved are not very great, the disequilibrium between men and women seems too extreme to be merely a statistical fluctuation. Some recent disaster might account for it, but a study of the survey suggests otherwise. Some of the entries are entirely normal, such as Elizabeth Starre, who held SA12 during her widowhood 'according to custom'. The descriptions of other tenants are less standard, for example, Katrina Chapman, described as 'now wife of Richard French' (SA24). A few read very strangely indeed. SA28 was held by two copies of court roll granted for the lives (not separately distinguished) of

> *Agnes Tyler now the wife of William Taylor, the same William Taylor, and John Taylor, his son and John Taylor, the son of a certain John Taylor, senior* [perhaps the brother of William Taylor].

The customs of the manor of Seaton must have been very unusual in their treatment of women, although whether both widows and spinsters were concerned is not clear. Usually a widow's rights disappeared on marriage or remarriage. She would, for example, lose her right of 'free bench' (retention of the property during widowhood). Sometimes her rights were taken over by her new husband, who held 'in right of his wife'. In Seaton, however, the women seem to have retained their legal existence on marriage and to have continued to hold property.

The limited evidence for tenants' ages is summarised in Table 3, subdivided by sex and by size of holding. The average age and the range of ages at the moment the survey was taken has been calculated for each section of the community. With considerable effort, most of these surveys could also yield the length of each tenure and the age of entry to the holding. A margin of error would still remain for widows, whose tenure was usually based on a grant to their husbands, as well as for tenants by three-life leases who either were not the original grantee or who held by leases in reversion, that is starting at the expiration of some earlier lease.

Otherwise the impressions of the relative maturity of the different groups is much as might be expected. Throughout the surveys women tenants were some years older than the men, reflecting the predominance of widows who had outlived their husbands. The principal exception was Oreston, where the evidence of tenant age reinforces that of the high proportion of women tenants in demonstrating the important role of women in that community.[19] The widows holding larger farms in Kenton must have been a remarkable group of matriarchs, including two ninety-year olds and one octogenarian (although the figures are clearly not precise). Strikingly, they also included the youngest woman tenant, a lass of seventeen, although this is nothing compared to the extraordinary grant of a copyhold in the same village to a boy of five. Both examples imply that the succession of tenants in Kenton was much more dependent on custom than on either capability for farming or (presumably) the ability to put down a lump sum as an entry fine.

On each estate, the tenants of cottages were younger than the tenants of farms, and at Kenton and Seaton the difference exceeded ten years, because all the very old tenants held farms rather than cottages. The age evidence is not consistent with the notion that a young man might start out as a cottager and in due course take over the tenancy of a proper farm. It seems rather that once he obtained a holding, he was likely to continue there until his death. Further support for the presence of distinct communities of farm and cottage tenants comes from an examination of tenants' names at Kenton. Of the 43 distinct cottagers' surnames, only six are found among the 75 farm tenants names. For only one pair, John Ewinge, aged 50, and John Ewinge the younger, aged 30 (K103 and K117) is a father/son relationship likely. Certainly the system of three-life leases, with the frequent granting of reversions, led to farms being occupied by one family for generations. The variation in age from place to place was considerable, and the differences must have had a significant effect on the social character of the villages. However, from the evidence considered here we cannot do more than draw attention to the contrast between the average age of farmers in Sidmouth (42) compared to those in Seaton (54) or of cottagers in Nettlecombe (49) as against Kenton twenty years earlier (34). With considerable further study, additional evidence from parish registers or other sources might explain whether the differences arose from accidents of disease or health (such as the local incidence of plague) or whether they reflect such social factors as age at marriage, family size, and spacing between children.

Viewed as a whole, the surveys illuminate a wide range of social arrangements from the Kenton matriarchs and the Oreston fisherwomen to the Sidmouth landlords and the Norton St. Philip squire. Overall they show how the same ingredients—landless labourers, smaller and greater farmers, and occasional gentlemen—combined in different ways under the influence of different economic conditions to produce communities with extremely varied social structures.

[1] *Ag. Hist.*, IV, 303, 396-7.

[2] The low profits of the Crown estates in the early 1600s was one of the main reasons for the compiling their surveys.

[3] Several of the surveys provide valuations of the land, which should be more useful; however, they are not consistently available.

[4] The descriptions often indicate which part of the property was sublet, and the secondary houses are invariably associated with little or no land.

[5] This evidence gives, of course, a general view of the land available both to outsiders and to local people. It does not tell us how much extra land was held by tenants of the estate. Freehold property can also be studied from wills, although these survive sparsely in south-west England.

[6] In principle, labor could be provided by an adjoining community. A similar profile can be seen for a hamlet in Warwickshire, which undoubtedly concentrated on arable farming. The nearby main village contained the labourers' cottages. However, the dispersed settlement of the West Country villages makes such an explanation unlikely. See N. W. Alcock, *Stoneleigh Villagers, 1597-1650* (Coventry: University of Warwick Open Studies, 1975), 4.

[7] Including, for example, a seven-bay house on a three acre holding (p. xx).

[8] See Part II, pp. 127 and 209.

[9] *Ag. Hist.*, IV, 734-5.

[10] In this period, the 'family' included everyone living in the house; A. Kussmaul, *Servants in Husbandry in Early Modern England* (Cambridge, 1981), 5; P. Laslett, *The World We Have Lost* (London, 1971), Ch. 1, note 10.

[11] Kussmaul, *Servants,* 117.

[12] Todd Gray, ed., *Harvest Failure in Cornwall and Devon: The book of orders and the corn surveys of 1623 and 1630* (Redruth: Institute of Cornish Studies, 1992). Some 640 households are described in all, but these are estimated to include only a third of the total population, occupying possibly a quarter of the houses. Publication of a full study of household size at this period in the south-west is promised.

[13] For example, the total absence of 'oat' (i.e. spring corn) tillage in many Cornish parishes.

[14] The list also includes two members of the Reynell family, whose farms might perhaps be those of one or another Randall in 1609. The overall poor correlation seems worse than might have been expected after only 14 years, and it is likely that several of the 1623 householders were not tenants of the Willoughby estate.

[15] Devon R. O. 1165Z/Z1.

[16] Kussmaul, *Servants*, 120.

[17] Devon R. O.

[18] There seems to have been only one smallholding (5 acres) among the forty-one households listed; it comprised four family members.

[19] The anomaly for women holding larger tenancies in Seaton is based on too few people to be significant.

CHAPTER 3

The Houses

The house-and-estate surveys provide evidence available from no other source to study both the whole house and all the houses. They avoid the problems common to standing buildings and probate inventories alike. They have not had parts demolished, nor have their rooms been passed over by a perfunctory inventory-taker. Most important, they avoid the bias towards larger houses typical both of surviving buildings and of the houses of people sufficiently wealthy to require the compilation of an inventory. Further, the surveys show the vital relationship between a house and the amount of land associated with it, information that can rarely be obtained from other sources.

Ultimately the surveys invite generalisations about life styles and standards of living, some aspects of which are seen more clearly than others. The evidence is particularly good for the size of houses and its correlation with the occupant's economic position in his or her village. Consideration of social status raises still other questions about the diversity of living conditions within a region and whether some economies allowed higher living standards than others. The surveys undoubtedly demonstrate variations in the size of houses more fully than do standing buildings. Surviving structures as a sample are skewed by the disappearance of small houses and separate service buildings. Ironically, further distortions in the physical evidence are a consequence of the very survival in south-western England of many fifteenth- and sixteenth-century buildings. In their original forms they were simpler in plan and more uniform in size than they had become one and two centuries later when they were recorded in the surveys. Architectural studies tend to emphasise the original appearance of such structures and pay less attention to subsequent modernisations, in part due to the difficulty of disentangling complex alterations. The evidence of the surveys effectively corrects this foreshortened historical prospective.

After the size of the house, the arrangement of rooms deserves to be considered. Here the surveys are less revealing. Although they provide occasional information on the organisation of interior space, a comprehensible picture emerges only when the surveys are compared to standing buildings, revealing both the expected similarities and some instructive differences.

The names of rooms give the best clue to their changing uses, with the passage of time, from one place to another, and among tenants of differing economic status. Service rooms and ancillary buildings identify the varying facilities available to householders, ranging from a cottager's single living room, to the kitchen, dairy, bakehouse, brewhouse, and pound house that accommodated each activity separately on a big farm. The surveyors' choice of names was immediately intelligible to his contemporaries, but they must be translated for modern ears. For this, the probate inventories are the best guide, itemising the contents of each room and thus suggesting their functions.

This chapter is first concerned with the additional evidence needed to interpret the surveys, that provided by standing buildings, to address the question of room arrangements, and by inventories to tell us how rooms were used. Then follows an overview of the survey evidence for house size, house plan, and the pattern of everyday activities implied by the names and functions of the rooms, bringing together the result of the individual studies presented in Part II.

House Construction and Plan

A few house-and-estate surveys from other parts of the country record materials and methods of construction, but none of those from the south-west give this information. The omission is not surprising in view of the uniformity of existing buildings throughout the region. Walls are almost invariably solid.[1] Over much of the peninsula, stone is the principal building mate-

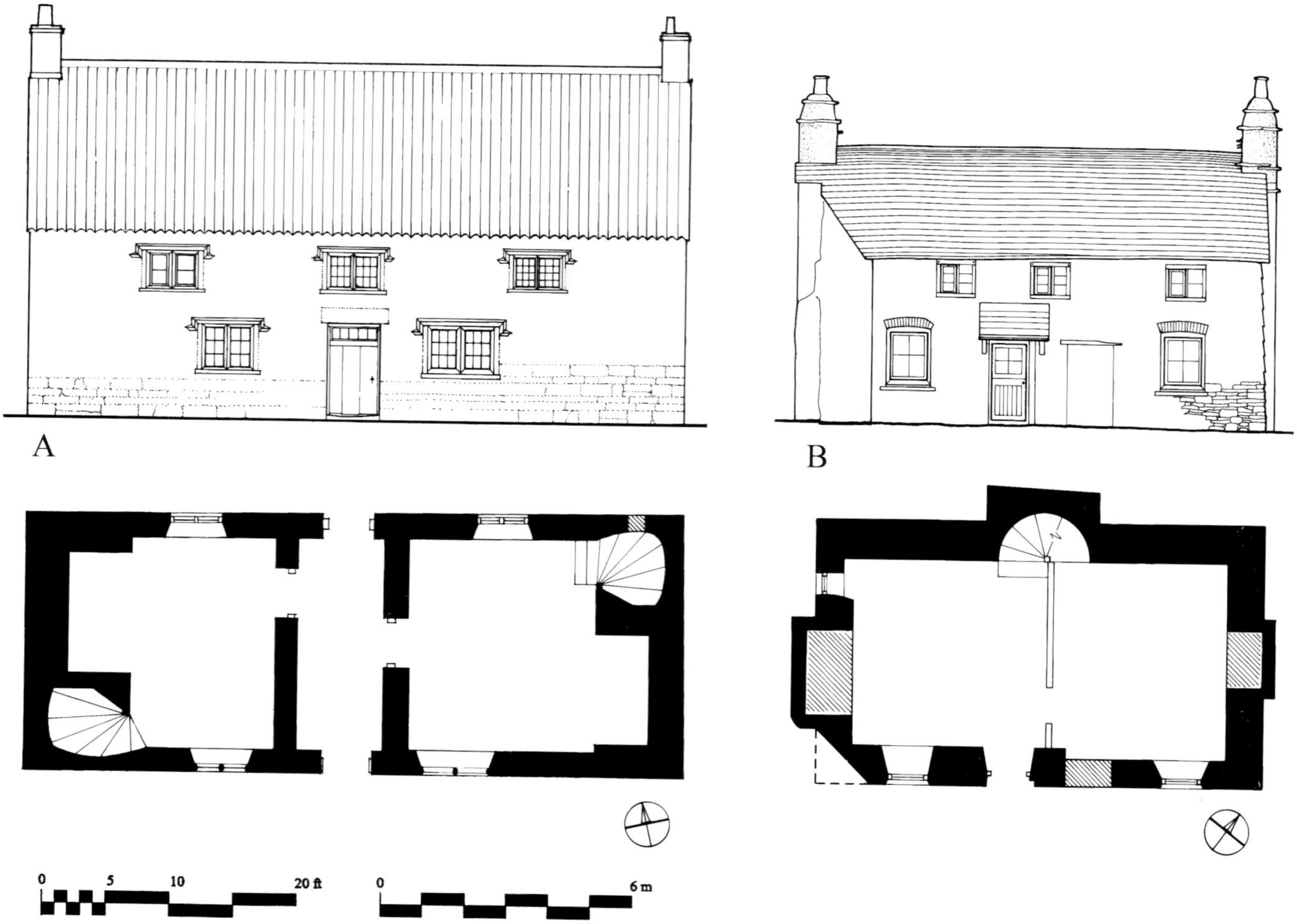

Figure 2. Two room houses: A: Burt's Cottage, Knole, Somerset, B: Staple Cottage, Dartington, Devon

rial, ranging from the Somerset limestone and lias, through the Dartmoor granite, to the irregular slate stone characteristic of South Devon and most of Cornwall. By contrast, in East Devon and South Somerset walls are of 'cob', mud laid wet to a thickness of about 2 ft. 6 in. (0.75m.). Despite the lowly connotations of this material, it is found in houses of yeoman status downwards, from the medieval period to the eighteenth and nineteenth centuries. The roof is usually of thatch, although in Cornwall by the seventeenth century, various forms of slate were beginning to be preferred. Interior walls in Somerset and East Devon are generally of timber, either filled with wattle and daub or (particularly on the ground floor) of 'stud-and-panel' construction.[2] Further west, especially in Cornwall, solid internal walls are commonplace, while sophisticated timberwork is almost unknown.

The surveys occasionally use names such as 'chamber within the hall' that suggest room arrangements, but they do not describe house plans as a whole. It might be possible to remedy this deficiency directly by identifying such of the surveyed houses as still stand—and it is likely that a number exist though they have not been sought for systematically.[3] Fortunately, such a search is hardly necessary since the many standing buildings that have been studied conform to sufficiently few regional plan-types for us to infer the character of those surveyed.[4] Both existing houses and those described demonstrate that housing standards in the southwest, with the exception of Cornwall, were among the highest in the country. They stand in contrast to the meagre one-or two-room houses that were still the norm in some parts of seventeenth-century England.[5]

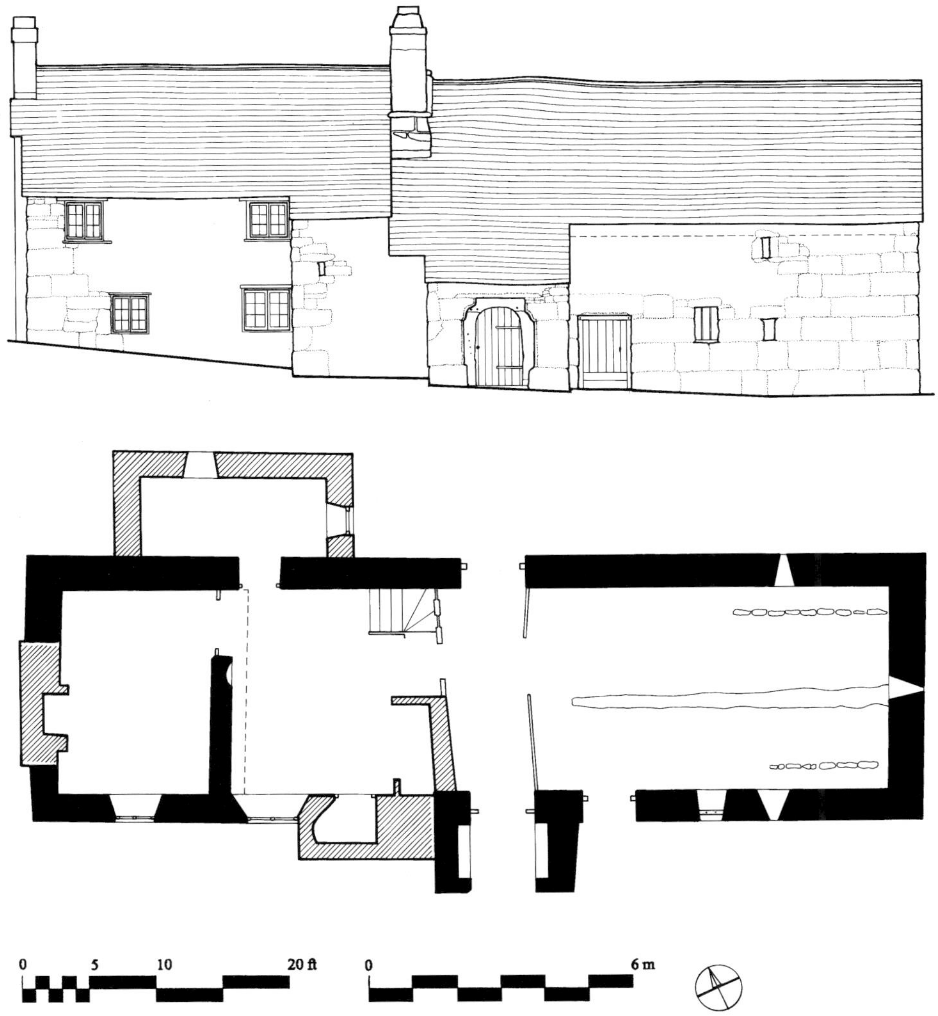

Figure 3. A long-house: Sanders, Lettaford, Devon (cf. Plates IIa-b)

The typical south-western house is rectangular with a single range of rooms. The plans can most easily be classified by the number of main rooms on the ground floor, which correspond to the 'bays' of the surveys. Sometimes supplementary additional domestic rooms are accommodated either in wings or combined with farm buildings, but these were usually additions to the original structure. Cross-passages are almost universal in all but the smallest houses built before the mid-seventeenth century.

A major distinction can be made between small houses, those with two main rooms, and larger ones.[6] About half of the small houses have cross-passages, as with Burt's Cottage, Knole, Somerset (Figure 2A). Staple Cottage, Dartington, Devon (Figure 2B) illustrates the alternative type, entered directly into the one main heated room. This hall now has a service room beside it and three chambers over. The house reached its present form in the seventeenth century, but when built in the early sixteenth century, its open hall was accompanied only by a ground floor chamber (the later service room).

The great majority of larger houses share a single basic layout, a *three-room-and-cross-passage* plan. The central room is always the *hall*. The most important variable is the use of the room across the passage. In one type, this is a *shippon* (the West Country dialect word for a byre or cattle stall) resulting in the so-called *long-house* plan. With the domestic accommodation limited to only two main rooms, long-houses

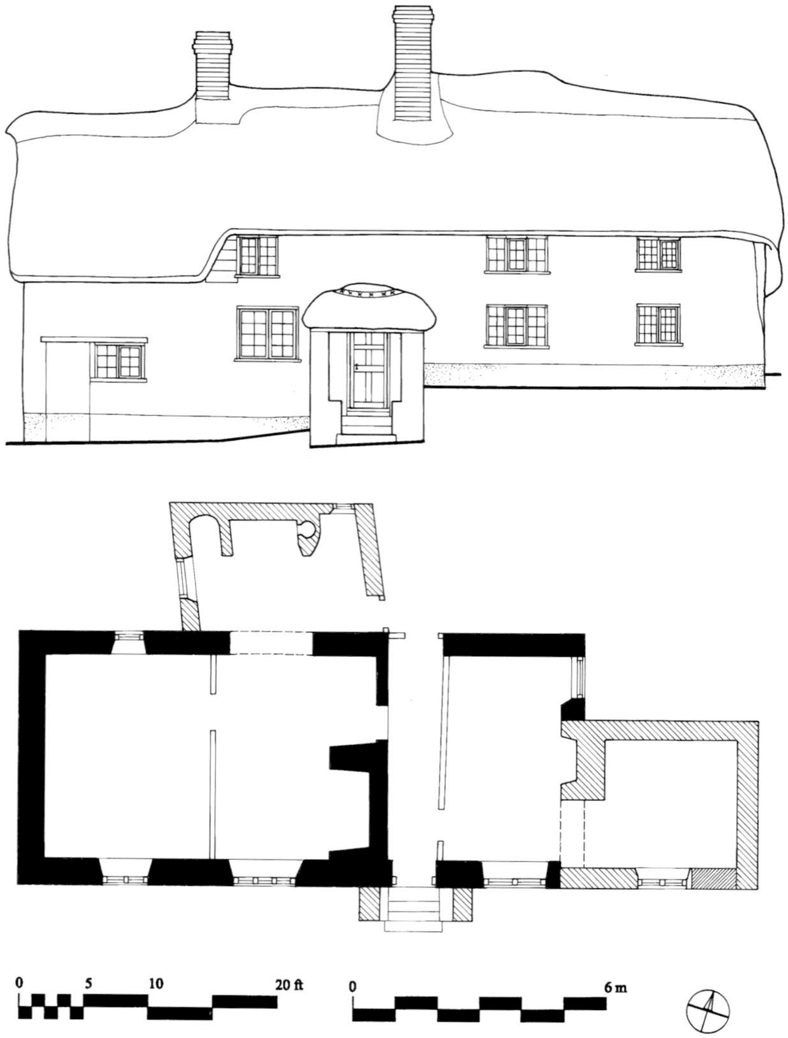

Figure 4. A three-room house with the hall only heated: Kites, Stockland, Devon

were very much the homes of small farmers. They can be associated with a specific agricultural economy, moorland mixed farming on a small scale, with few enough cattle for them to be housed in the shippon.[7] They are of great historical significance, as they have been shown by excavation to have been a very common form of medieval peasant house.[8] However, only in localised areas of the south-west did long-houses continue in use sufficiently late in the post-medieval period to have survived to the present day. They are ubiquitous on Dartmoor and its southern and western fringes.[9] The evidence of the surveys significantly extends their coverage in the early seventeenth century, indicating the former presence of long-houses in both Somerset and east Cornwall, with a few examples also recorded from one of the east Devon villages. Figure 3 shows a characteristic long-house, originally of the early or mid-sixteenth century. The inner room (the typical 'room within the hall') may have been a buttery or dairy, but it is at least as likely that both it and the original chamber above were for sleeping. Two further chambers were added, one in the later sixteenth century over the passage ('in the chamber over the entry') and the other in the seventeenth century when the hall was ceiled. At this stage, the inner room may well have become a buttery. The lean-to room on the north was added in the seventeenth century, almost certainly as a dairy, a typical addition to long-houses.

In the more typical three-room plan house, which

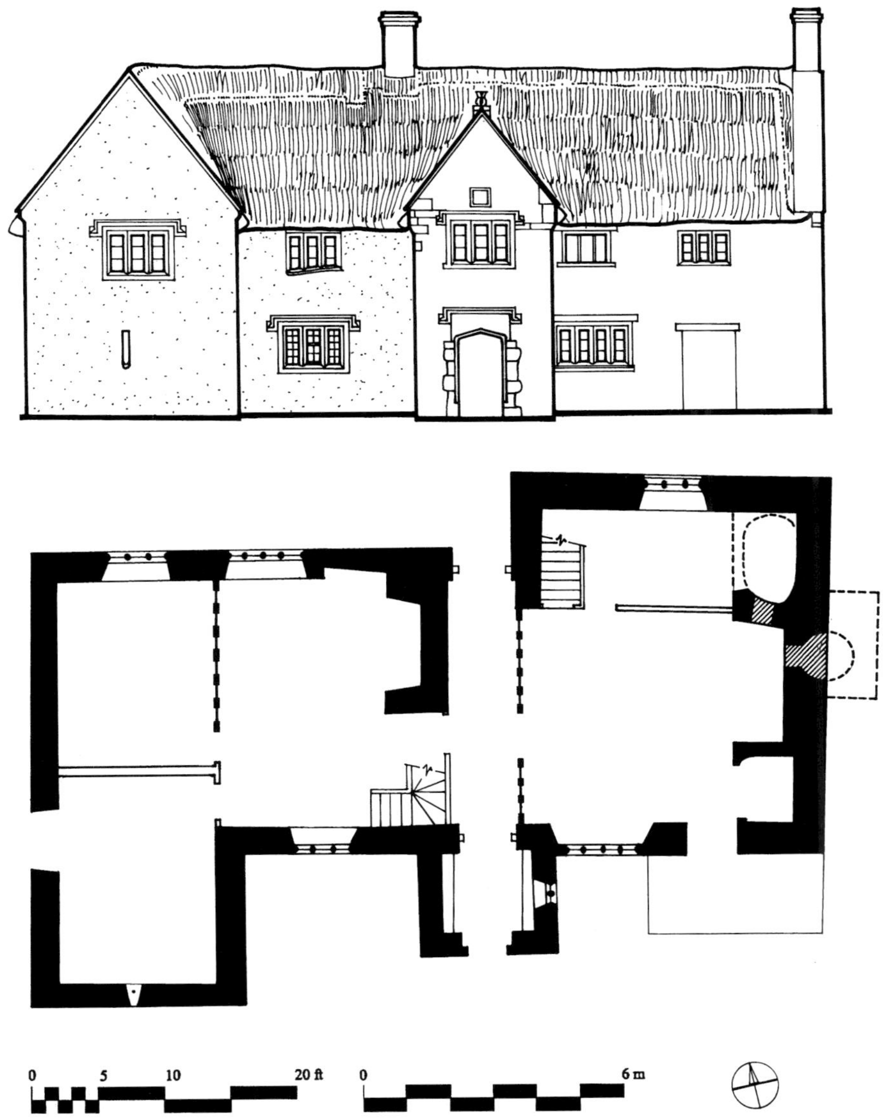

Figure 5. A developed three-room plan: Brome Farm, Isle Abbotts, Somerset (cf. Plate IIIa)

often had stud-and-panel partitions (Plate Ib), the third room was either a kitchen or a service room. Figure 4 shows the simplest form, with only the hall heated at first. The inner room and the original room over it were almost certainly chambers, while the room across the passage was a buttery. As improvements, upper rooms were constructed over the buttery, passage and hall, and a kitchen or bakehouse was added in the rear wing.

The fully developed three-room plan is seen in Figure 5. The inner room is a heated parlour, and across the passage is a kitchen with a service room behind it. A two-story porch is a frequent feature, as here (cf. Frontispiece). In still larger houses, the plan is greatly elaborated, making it almost impossible to identify the use of all the rooms from the plan alone. However, the example in Figure 6 also began as a three-room house (see also Figure 11).

More imposing even than such elaborated farms are those that use a courtyard layout. One house described in the surveys clearly had this plan (NP61, p. 167). A handful of courtyard houses survive, such as Roscarrack, St. Endellion, Cornwall, and Littlehempston Rectory, Devon, but the clearest and most remarkable representation is the glebe terrier of c. 1600, High Bickington Rectory (Figure 7).[10] In link-

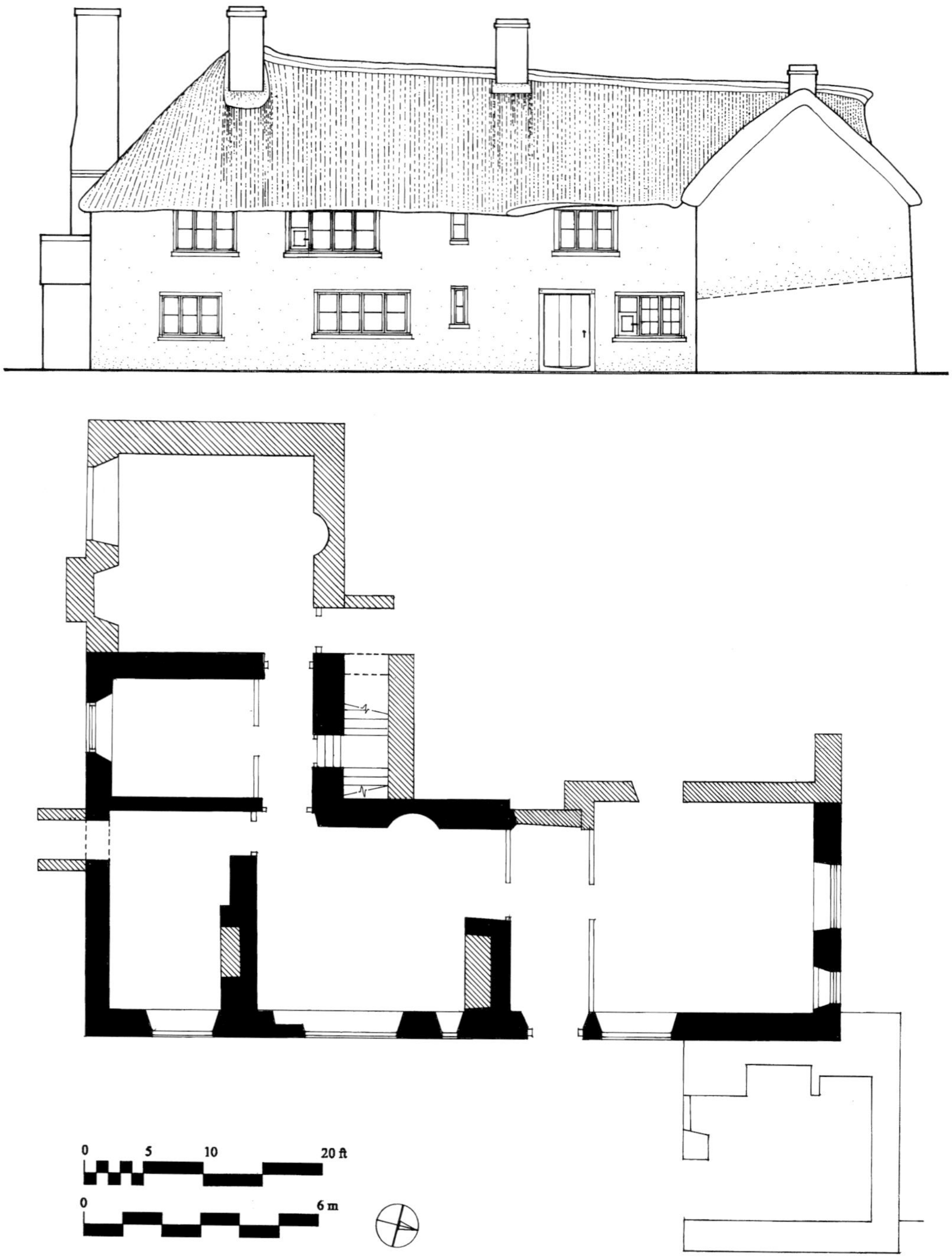

Figure 6. An elaborated plan, based on a three-unit house: Great Cliston, Sampford Courtenay, Devon

ing the names of rooms and buildings to their layout, this drawing provides a key to the organisation of a large West-Country farm, that illuminates the survey descriptions.

At High Bickington, the main court was entered from the south (left on the plan) through a wall with minor buildings against it, probably constructed as lean-tos—poultry house, milk house and dross house. The main range, open hall, entry, and parlour (with two chambers above) lay on the right hand with a

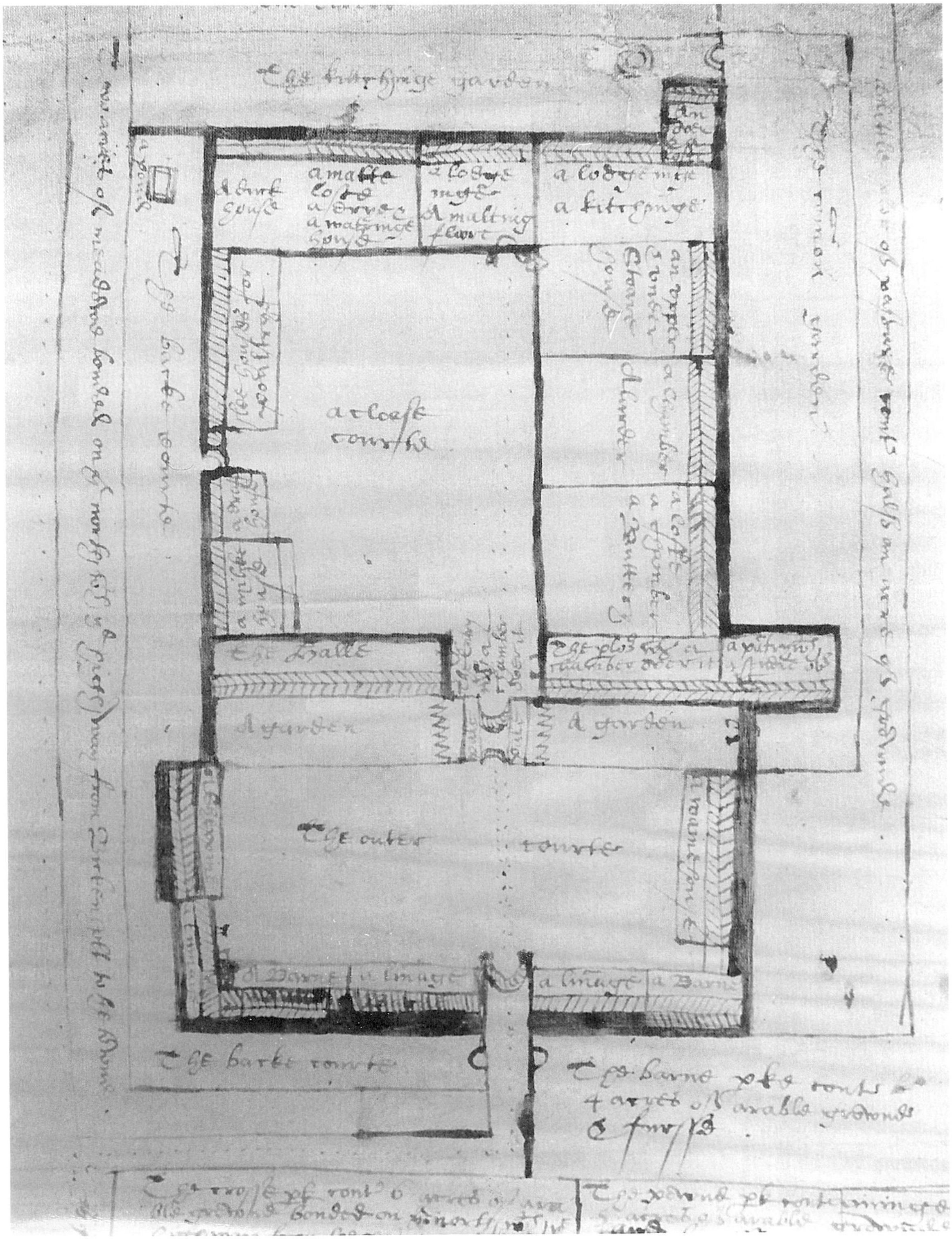

Figure 7. Schematic plan of a courtyard house: High Bickington, Devon, c. 1600

Beyond the house itself, the rector drew out the fields of his glebe schematically, labelling them with their names and acreages. North is apparently to the right (Central part of a glebe terrier, Devon Record Office; Exeter Diocesan Records, Glebe terriers, High Bickington; reproduced with permission of the Diocese of Exeter).

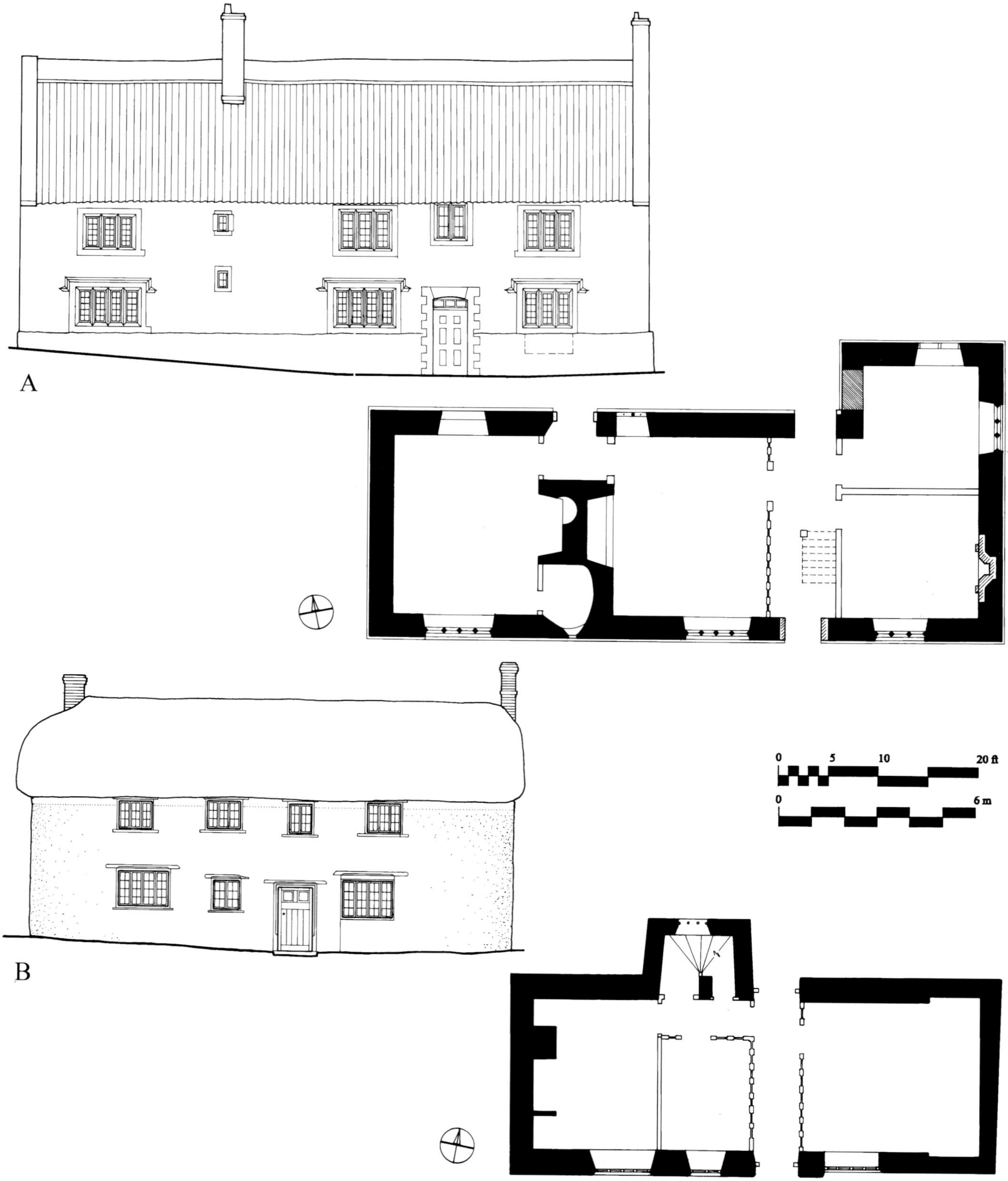

Figure 8a. Innovative house plans (A-B)
A: Wick Farm, Curry Rivel, Somerset, of 1661 (cf. Plate IVb), B: Southtown, Sampford Courtenay, Devon

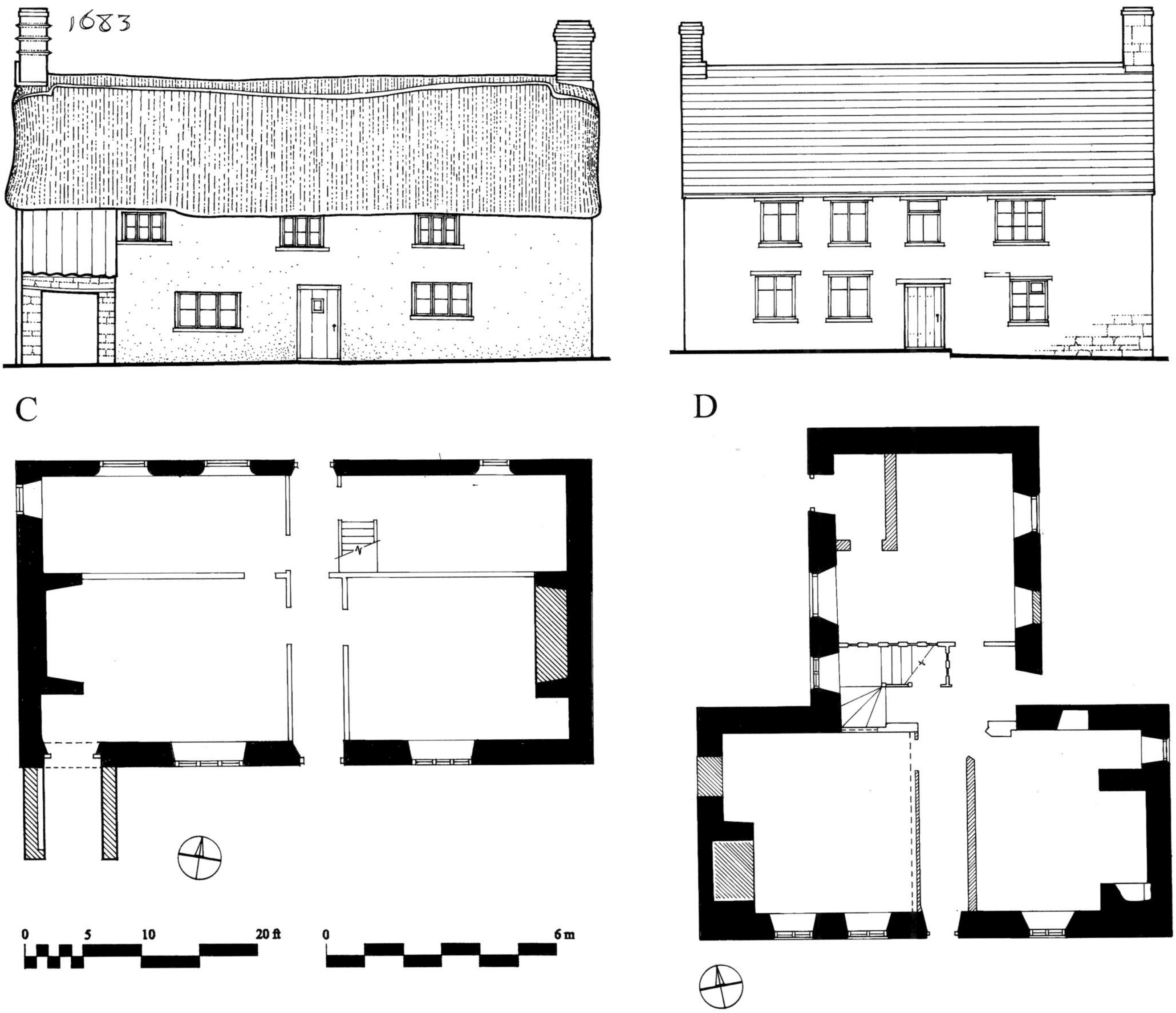

Figure 8b. Innovative house plans (C-D)

C: Moxhayes, Membury, Devon, of 1683 (cf. Plates Va-b), D: Hale Farm, Cucklington, Somerset

pantry and the rector's study in a projection. The service rooms extended round the other sides of the court, with chambers over them, becoming steadily more work-a-day moving away from the parlour, down to the malting loft, kiln, 'watering house' (also for brewing), and the duck house in the southwest corner next to the poultry house. Through the entry past the gardens, an arch (or perhaps a high gate) in a fence led to the outer court with all the farm buildings: the wain house, two barns, three linheys (see pp. 47, 50-1), and a shippon, all built up against the perimeter wall.

Before about 1600, departures from the three-room-and-passage arrangement were very rare, but many houses built after that date experimented with novel plans (Figure 8). The 'lobby entry' plan (Figure 8A), is important, because its parallels can be recognised in the standard seventeenth-century house plan in East Anglia, and its rare appearances in the Southwest can be attributed to influences from eastern England.[11] The key feature is the presence of a door leading onto a chimney stack, generally with two back-to-back fireplaces serving hall and parlour. Lobby-entry houses usually contain a third room at one end, either a heated kitchen or a service room. The example

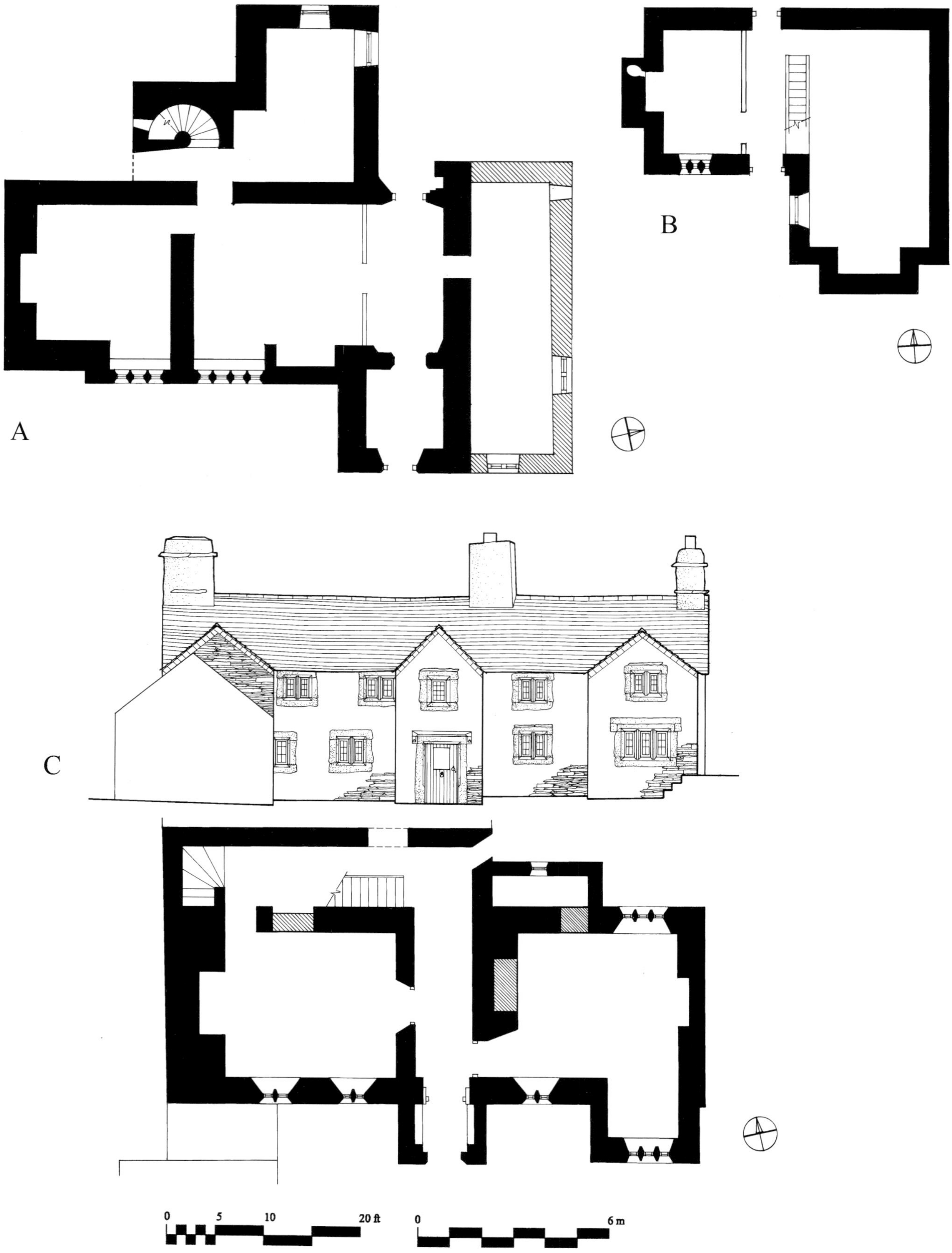

Figure 9. Cornish house plans.
A: Welltown, Forrabury (cf. Plate VIa), B: Trewhiddle, St Austell, C: Redevallen, Trevalga, of 1642 (cf. Plate VIb)

Plate Ia. Townsend, Stockland, Devon. The earliest identified medieval house of three-room plan in Devon (tree-ring dated to c. 1260) (photo: N.W. Alcock).

Plate Ib. Owls Castle, Stockland, Devon. A typical stud-and panel screen, dividing the hall from the inner room in a medieval Devon house (photo: N.W. Alcock).

Plate IIa. Sanders, Lettaford, Devon. A classic Devon longhouse: general view (photo: N.W. Alcock).

Plate IIb. Sanders, Lettaford, Devon. A classic Devon longhouse: interior of the shippon (photo: N.W. Alcock).

Plate IIIa. Brome Farm, Isle Abbotts, Somerset. A house with a developed three-room plan. (photo: Cary Carson).

Plate IIIb. Porch House, Sidford, Devon (see p. 38). Water-colour of 1855 (P.O. Hutchinson, History of Sidmouth (manuscript), City Library, Exeter; reproduced with permission).

Plate IVa. Ellishayes, Combe Raleigh, Devon. A large early seventeenth century East Devon farmhouse (photo: N.W. Alcock).

Plate IVb. Wick Farm, Curry Rivel, Somerset. A farmhouse of innovative plan, dated 1661. (photo: Cary Carson).

Plate Va. Moxhayes, Membury, Devon. An innovative small house dated 1683: general view (photo: N.W. Alcock).

Plate Vb. Moxhayes, Membury, Devon. Painted decoration in the best chamber (photo: N.W. Alcock).

Plate VIa. Welltown, Forrabury, Cornwall. A substantial farmhouse of around 1600 (photo: N.W. Alcock).

Plate VIb. Redevallen, Trevalga, Cornwall. A Cornish gentry house dated to 1642 (photo: N.W. Alcock).

Plate VIIa. Poltimore, Farway, Devon. A fifteenth-century house with a remarkably complete early farmstead (photo: Cary Carson).

Plate VIIb. Great Moor, Sowton, Devon. Large seventeenth or eighteenth century barn of cob (now demolished) (photo: N.W. Alcock).

Plate VIIIa. Woolstone, Sandford, Devon, a typical small seventeenth or eighteenth century West Country barn (photo: N.W. Alcock).

Plate VIIIb. Lower House, Payhembury. A complete yard of linheys, characteristic Devon buildings for sheltering cattle and storing hay (photo: N.W. Alcock).

illustrated, Wick Farm, Curry Rivel, Somerset, is unusual in retaining an old-fashioned cross-passage accompanying the novel lobby entry. A second innovative form, unusual outside the south-west, is the house with a central unheated service room (Figure 8B).[12] In yet another variant, a two-roomed house with gable chimneys was developed to provide extra service accommodation by including either rear lean-tos (Figure 8C) or a rear wing (Figure 8D). Both these houses also reflect the growing concern for personal privacy through the provision of a lobby at the head of the stairs with the bedchambers leading off it.

In Devon and Somerset innovative plans are inevitably in a minority, because many serviceable houses survive from the sixteenth century and earlier. However, Cornwall retains fewer early houses and therefore provides a considerable range of alternatives to the three-room-and-passage plan. It is also apparent that two-room plans are more frequent than further east. Figure 9 shows a selection of Cornish plans, including an example with an entrance at the end of one long side, a substantial house using a two-room plan, and one where an L-shape was chosen by the builder rather than imposed by the site.

For a full picture of the accommodation provided, upper floors need to be considered as well as ground plans. Here, the evidence of the detailed surveys is particularly important, because they span just that period when complete upper floors were becoming universal. Standing buildings suggest that in East Devon, inner rooms were the earliest to be floored, starting in the late fifteenth and early sixteenth centuries. Floors were inserted over the rest of the house during the course of the next century and a half. Houses newly built from the early seventeenth century onwards almost always had complete upper floors. The evidence from Somerset is similar, but as with other trends, improvement took hold more slowly in south Devon and Cornwall. The accuracy of the dates for inserted floors assigned from architectural evidence is not good enough to delineate this development more precisely.

The Rooms of the House (Table 4)

The original use of most rooms in existing buildings is a matter of guesswork. The surveys name each room but the significance of these names is not immediately obvious, because their functions do not generally correspond to modern usage. Fortunately, the lists of furnishings and equipment in probate inventories[13] define the functions of the rooms named. The use of the main rooms is clear-cut. Not so the storerooms and service rooms; whatever their names, they usually accommodated several activities.

Some names present special problems. In ordinary use, the 'cellar' contained drink in barrels, and from the evidence of existing buildings would almost always be at ground level, not underground. However, in fishing villages, 'cellar' typically meant a *fish cellar* (also above ground) for storing fish, salt, nets, and so forth (cf. Inv. 100). 'Shop' occurs more frequently in the surveys than in the inventories, probably because the latter generally correspond to a higher social level. Although goods might occasionally have been sold from shops, the word principally meant *workshop*. For example, in a carpenter's house the shop contained 'his workeing tooles and other lumber' (Inv. 242).

The most difficult distinction to draw is that between a 'parlour' and a ground floor 'chamber'. In early houses the ground floor chamber was simply a sleeping room (Invs. 1 and 25, of 1531 and 1592), perhaps also containing a chest for storage. It seems that a parlour was very similar, still apparently unheated in the early seventeenth century when the word came into use at the local level (Invs. 39 and 55, of 1605 and 1623).[14] In other houses the parlours were clearly the best living rooms, very well furnished and usually with fireplaces. Sometimes such parlours contained no beds (Invs. 61, 94, 97), but in others the best bed was still to be found there (Invs. 65, 105, 130). Clearly, a gradual change was occurring. As the habit of sleeping upstairs grew more widespread, the term parlour took on in these small houses the 'best living room' connotation that it had long had in great houses. Therefore it is not easy to be sure what was meant by 'parlour' in the surveys, but it seems reasonable that, when the surveyor recorded a mixture of 'chambers' and 'parlours', he saw a significant difference between them. We may perhaps suggest that the presence of a fireplace was considered characteristic of a parlour, though the inventories do not strongly support this.

One part of the house that is occasionally mentioned in the inventories (Invs. 34, 105), but is in-

Table 4: Domestic room names and uses

Room Name	Use
Living rooms	
Hall	Main living and eating room; often the only heated room, when it would also function as the kitchen.
Kitchen	Food preparation and cooking; sometimes also food storage.
Parlour	[See text]
Chamber	Ground or upper floor; sleeping room, also used for storage, sometimes specialized (apple, cheese, wool chamber).
Study	As the modern meaning, a room for writing or reading; also for keeping documents of importance
Service rooms	
Buttery; Larder(house); Pantry	Storage of food and utensils. 'Larder' was particularly for food storage, and was standard in the early 17th century, while 'pantry' was used in the 18th century.
Dairy(house); Milkhouse; Dey house	Making and storing butter and cheese; also storing utensils.
Drink house; Cellar	Storage of drink, e.g. barrels of beer. [See text]
Cider house; Poundhouse	Making and storing cider; the 'pound house' refers particularly to the apple crusher.
Bakehouse (Bakes); Brewhouse; Malthouse; Kilnhouse; Dry(house)	Nominally for baking bread, brewing beer and malting barley for beer in the 'kiln' (drying oven); however, the inventories suggest that these uses were often interchanged or combined.
Wringhouse	Cheese-making, specifically the room holding the cheese-press (wring).
Wood house	Storing firewood.
Miscellaneous	
Entry	Passage, occasionally with miscellaneous furniture.
Porch room	The upstairs room in a two-storey porch, often the study.
Shop	[See text]
Cockloft	Storage loft in the roofspace.

cluded silently in the surveys, is the 'roof', presumably over an open hall or kitchen where sides of beef and bacon were hung until this became impractical with the introduction of upper floors over these rooms. In taller houses, the space in the roof above the ceiling was occasionally used for storage, taking the name cockloft.

The Evidence of the Surveys

The size of houses

Although not every survey lists the rooms of the houses in detail, they all give the size in one form or another. This must have been the single most important piece of information for the surveyors. For us, it is the key to the general picture of housing in the community and its correlation with status.[15]

Most of the surveys record house size specifically for each holding. This information was part of the instructions for the surveyor's jury at East Brent (p. 7), which required him to give the number of bays in each house. The use of the term 'bay' in the Southwest is at first sight unexpected, for the word is derived from timber-framed construction in which the rectangular house is divided into structural units by timber-framed transverse walls. Each of these structural units constitutes a bay, each is exactly or nearly the same size, and each normally contains one ground floor room, longitudinal divisions being rare. The lengths and widths of bays are fairly consistent, and so they give a useful, though rough guide to the size of the house.[16] For barns the usage was slightly different because they rarely had internal partitions; nevertheless, the bay structure was still apparent in the main wall-posts and tie-beams, and the bays could still be counted. The word had been in common use since the medieval period in court rolls, deeds (occasionally), glebe terriers, and other documents.

For houses with solid walls, including those built of stone, rubble, and cob (as throughout the South-west), the use of 'bay' was less accurate because there was no requirement for structural transverse walls at regular intervals and so the rooms could potentially be of very different sizes. However, marked variation in room size was not customary, and the surveyors still employed 'bays' to mean the number of main ground-floor rooms.[17] In reverse, when the rooms are named, we can approximate the house size in bays by counting the number of ground-floor rooms (excluding the 'entry', which would not have been counted as a bay).

In the Crown surveys, whose main text is in Latin, the term 'bay' itself is rare. Instead, they use a Latin equivalent, 'spacia'.[18] The correspondence is shown in the Norton St. Philip survey where 'bay' and 'spacia' are used interchangeably, while one Launceston entry starts in the usual form: *Jana Bligh clamat tenere unam messuagium* [claims to hold one messuage]... *viz. domum mansionalis* [house] *4 spacias, coquina* [kitchen] *2 spacias, cum le bakehouse 2 spacias, horreum* [barn] *5 spacias cum le oxestall et le leanye*.[19] It then continues in English: 'Memorandum that the said Jane claimeth to hold parcell of the lands above mencioned with the barne and oxestall containing 5 bayes...'.

The Kenton survey describes its buildings by their 'couples'. At first, this sounds like a count of the number of roof trusses, but in fact it appears to have been used equivalently to the size in bays. This identification is suggested because the smallest buildings are of *one* couple, which must therefore represent a room-sized unit.[20] The term is also used at Farway and Seaton, in addition to a description of the rooms in each house.

Occasionally, house-and-estate surveys give dimensions for buildings. The only systematic use in the present group is at Sherford. The lengths of some lean-tos are given in feet, but for the main buildings 'poole of timber', eight feet in length, are used.[21] This coarse unit and the absence of widths makes the figures rather uninformative, but they do suggest that most rooms were about sixteen feet long.

The evidence for size from all the surveys can therefore be presented as the number of bays or its equivalent in ground-floor rooms (Table 5). As far as possible, all domestic rooms have been counted, including shops and kitchens, even though the latter might occasionally have been detached. The ancillary buildings—malthouses, brewhouses and bakehouses—have been omitted.[22] The table is divided into cottage holdings (those with very little land),[23] smaller farms and larger farms. The division between the farms is not kept at a single acreage, but is chosen to correspond approximately to the peak of each distribution of holding size; thus the two groups broadly represent the more and the less prosperous farmers.

The most obvious similarity everywhere is the presence of true cottages on the smallest holdings—a recognisable group of small houses, typically with two bays, less often with three. We know from other evidence that many were the homes of labourers, the lowest social class in the farming community, who had to support themselves by working for others, because their holdings were too small to be self-sufficient. Small holdings were also occupied by craftsmen whose extra earnings could provide better and larger houses.[24] As illustration, the craft earnings at Norton St. Philip that produced the community's remarkable economic structure (pp. 15, 167) were accompanied by unusually large 'cottages'.[25] Both the seaside villages, Sidmouth and Seaton, also had larger than average houses in this group, but for different causes. In the Seaton houses the extra rooms were chambers, apparently to accommodate large households, but at Sidmouth a number of bigger houses were of good quality, clearly not supported by either farming or fishing. Instead, they were inns, or the homes of tradesmen and craftsmen, and also of rentiers, a new class in the society of the town.

By contrast, Oreston was purely a fishing hamlet, full of small cottages including an unusual number of one-bay houses. They must have been a consequence of the very constricted site (Map 12). It is significant that just such dense settlements are found for other fishing villages, both in England and the New World.[26] The only other concentration of one-room houses was at Kenton, where again the site was constricted, this time by the open fields. The small Kenton houses, as well as the subsidiary houses on a number of the holdings there, were certainly for the farm labourers.

The one-bay cottage fell below the normal standards for accommodation in the seventeenth and eigh-

Table 5: Numbers of domestic ground-floor rooms

Place	Type	Cottage Holdings 1	2	3	4	5+
Kenton (1598)	C	10	33	16	1	1
Cornwall (1602)	D	1	3	2		1
Launceston (1606)	B	1	7	5	2	5
Sherford (1606)	D	2				
Farway & Whitwell (1609)	D	1				
Seaton (1609)	D		4	10		1
Nettlecombe (1619)	D	2	12	6	2	1
Norton St. Philip (1608)	B	2	2	5	5	2
Wellington (1607)	B		7	2	1	
Kingsbury (1608)	B		8	8	5	
East Brent (1606)	B	1	6	2	2	1
Oreston (1709)	D	15	28	17	7	2
Plymstock (1709)	D	4	16	9		
Bedford (Hurdwick & Milton) (1709)	D	1	4	1		
Sidmouth (1764)	D	5	15	15	13	1
Totals		45	145	98	38	15

Place	Type	Small Farms 1	2	3	4	5	6+	Split Ac	Large Farms 1	2	3	4	5	6+
Kenton (1598)	C		5	17	8	7	5	30		4	16	8	5	8
Cornwall (1602)	D		3	2	1			30		2	4	2		
Launceston & Carnanton (1606)	B		10	14	8	4	5	20	1	3	15	15	7	16
Sherford (1606)	D	1	3	4				40		1	3	1	1	1
Farway & Whitwell (1609)	D		3	7	2			40			2		3	
Seaton (1609)	D		3	7	6	2		20		1		2	5	
Nettlecombe (1619)	D		2	8	5	2		30		2	8	7	5	1
Norton St. Philip (1608)	B			6	10	8	9	10		1			1	6
Wellington (1607)	B		2	6				10		2	8	3	1	1
Kingsbury (1608)	B		3	14	5	6	3	10		1	1	6	10	18
East Brent (1606)	B	1	6	19	7	4	2	30			3	16	3	7
West Pennard (1606)	B		4	20	11	2	2	30			5	7	4	11
Bedford (Hurdwick & Milton) (1709)	D		3	4	2			30		1	5	6	2	
Sidmouth (1764)	D	(1)	6	8	2	1		10		1	6	6		
Totals		3	53	137	62	36	26		1	19	76	79	47	69

Notes: In the Type column, B = bays, C = couples (bays), D = descriptions of rooms. Identified kitchens and shops are included whether detached or not, but malthouses and brewhouses are omitted. Cottage holdings: three acres or less, except for Norton St. Philip (two acres or less). The Split column gives the dividing acreage between small and large farms.

teenth centuries, even for farm labourers and fishermen. The survey descriptions, however, reveal a mitigating feature of one-bay buildings. All had an upstairs chamber, although the same was not true of the two-room cottages. Bearing in mind that by the nineteenth century, the one-up and one-down cottage had become the norm in the south-west,[27] it seems possible that the cottage with one living and one sleeping room provided the minimum accommodation for a family over the whole period, its arrangement gradually changing between the sixteenth and the nineteenth century from horizontal to vertical. Such medieval documents as have been studied corroborate this view, showing that one-bay cottages were rare.[28]

Analysing house size in relation to farm size reveals intriguing distinctions. The most notable impression among the smaller farms is one of uniformity, with twice as many houses of three bays as of any other size. The larger farms did include a number of substantial houses with six or more ground-floor rooms (20%), which were rare on the smaller holdings. They also included as many with four rooms as with three rooms. Houses of three to four rooms in plan fulfilled both the physical needs and cultural expectations of almost everyone in these rural communities. Houses had not yet become differential expressions of economic standing and social aspirations.[29]

Geographically, differences are more marked. The 1602 Cornish survey shows a concentration of two-bay houses, not surprising where the farming economy was poor, despite possible contributions from tin-mining. The effect on building traditions persisted through the seventeenth century.[30] Similar two-bay houses occur at Launceston, but a considerable number of the larger farms there carried bigger houses. These can be attributed to architectural as much as economic choices, because they reflect the numerous detached kitchens at Launceston, each of which contained two or three bays instead of the single room/bay of a kitchen located inside the house.

The strongest contrast to the poverty of the Cornish small farms comes from the prosperous farmsteads at Norton St. Philip. There a diversified economy supported large houses even on holdings of less than ten acres. The largest building there, with twenty-three bays, was the George, an inn of national standing. The marshland villages of Somerset, particularly Kingsbury, enjoyed similar prosperity, to judge by their houses.[31] Leaseholders experienced more varied living conditions at Wellington and Nettlecombe with an even distribution of moderate-sized buildings, resembling those on the East Devon estates which shared similar economies and building traditions.

With all the seventeenth-century surveys falling within twenty-one years of each other, chronological development can hardly be expected. In contrast, the two eighteenth-century surveys appear to show that the passage of a century brought about a significant contraction in house size. However, this is to ignore changes in the upper floors, where the survey picture is clear. In the early seventeenth century, houses were incompletely floored; by the eighteenth complete upper rooms were almost universal.[32] Again, the seventeenth-century surveys reveal regional contrasts. The Cornish houses had few rooms on upper floors, corresponding to their general poverty. In East Devon, full upper floors were more common, though it is noteworthy that of three new-built houses in Farway and Whitwell, one was not yet fully floored (F16). At Sherford, virtually all the houses had full upper floors, which is surprising as its houses otherwise give a rather backward impression. All in all, the documents catch the transition in progress, but cannot fully separate its stages. It is therefore easy to understand why the eighteenth-century houses appear comparatively small. By then every house had a full complement of both upstairs and downstairs rooms for living space. By contrast, the large houses of the Launceston survey may be partly explained by the rarity of upper floors; the space in the house that the kitchen would later occupy was still taken up by ground-floor chambers.

Plan types

Comparisons between existing buildings and the survey descriptions must be inferred. For the two-room plans, the only problem is whether there was a passage, the matter being resolved only at Nettlecombe where the 'entry' was systematically recorded. The standard plan was a 'hall and chamber', and of some fifteen examples in Nettlecombe only one had an entry. The same plan was usual on the Cornish manors and at Seaton, but at Sherford and in one Farway house the hall was paired with a service room—a buttery, a kitchen, or a dairy. This was made possible in the Sherford houses by their chambers already being on the upper floor.

Among the larger houses, the layout is clear for one group, the long-houses, in which one end was a byre. None of the surveys covers Dartmoor itself, where long-houses were ubiquitous, and remained so until the twentieth century. In Sherford, the survey shows them on six or seven of the twelve farms. Some had the classic plan with just hall and inner room, described in two cases as a shop and a parlour. The others were larger, with a kitchen as well as a hall and another room. In the area south of Dartmoor itself, of which Sherford is typical, the long-house must have passed out of use not long after the survey was taken, because in standing buildings of the seventeenth century the evidence of conversion from long-houses is very rare. A few long-houses were also noted in Kenton and Launceston (seven and four respectively representing about five percent of the holdings). The descriptions of the latter are particularly clear '*domum mansionalis cum bovite sub uno tecto*' (house and shippon under one roof). The Launceston examples are not unexpected. On the fringes of Bodmin Moor, not far to the west, archaeologists have located a number of 'platform' houses and house sites; excavations have shown some to be thirteenth- to fifteenth-century long-houses.[33] Notwithstanding this archaeological evidence, existing houses in the area show no specific long-house features. No long-houses are noted in Hurdwick (situated very near Dartmoor) despite the fact that long-houses can still be found in several adjoining parishes. This discrepancy points to the same pattern as at Sherford, that the long-house was obsolete by 1600 and rapidly passed out of use thereafter. The Kenton examples may be similarly explained, but their presence at all in a predominantly arable village is surprising. In the Somerset surveys, long-houses are only certainly recorded at East Brent in an area where husbandry was pastoral, but not combined with mixed farming in the moorland fashion. Detailed fieldwork has not yet been carried out in this area.

Equally significant is the absence of long-houses from certain other localities. None at all are mentioned in the East Devon and West Somerset (Nettlecombe and Wellington) surveys. It has been suggested that the standard three-room-and-cross-passage plans in this area are derived from long-houses.[34] However, structural evidence is lacking, and the surveys show the absence of even a residual long-house tradition by the early seventeenth century.

The other three-unit plans leave a mixed impression. The chamber (or rarely another room) 'within the hall' occurs fairly frequently. This room was entered from the hall, and thus was beyond or 'within' it when viewed from the entrance. The room on the other side of the passage was usually a kitchen or milkhouse, although three houses had just a hall and two chambers (C36, C42, F12). Less common was the alternative arrangement with hall, kitchen and milkhouse, but neither chamber nor parlour.

Where more than three rooms are named, there is little chance of identifying the plan precisely. In some houses, one room of the basic plan may have been subdivided to provide both buttery and milkhouse in one bay. In W11, these rooms are said to be 'between the hall and the chamber', suggesting that it had the novel plan with central service rooms. Viewed more generally, the larger houses had halls combined with all possible permutations of chambers, parlours, kitchens, milkhouses, butteries, and occasionally other rooms as well. These descriptions correspond to standing houses having a core (often a medieval three-unit house) expanded by extensions, wings, or lean-tos. One identified house, Porch Cottage, Sidmouth (SM115), is characteristic, with fifteen or sixteen rooms when surveyed in 1764 (Plate IIIb; Figures 10-11; see also p. 210). These houses show how many ways rich but conservative farmers could find to adapt a traditional plan.[35]

A vignette of their standard of life comes from two documents, subsidiary to the Seaton survey, that list the 'landlord's fixtures' in two of the largest farms (p. 120). These fixtures included panelling between the hall and parlour, with a bench fixed to it, a feature of which traces remain to the present day in many Devon farms. Various doors were specially noted (some with locks) as also were shelves, racks and an iron bar in the chimney. One of the houses had three built-in tables and one bedstead. In the other, the windows of the major ground-floor rooms and of one chamber were glazed; the other rooms had only shutters.

The surveys demonstrate that the mixed farming lands of Devon and Somerset provided the wherewithal for a comfortable life and that local building traditions were sufficiently advanced to support it.

Room use

Building traditions in the West Country show signifi-

Figure 10. Porch House Sidford (SM115). Photograph of 1894.
The position of the surviving date-stone at the base of the nearest chimney stack can just be seen. It carries the initials N I E for Nicholas and Elizabeth Isaac and the date 1574.
(Copyright Sidmouth Museum)

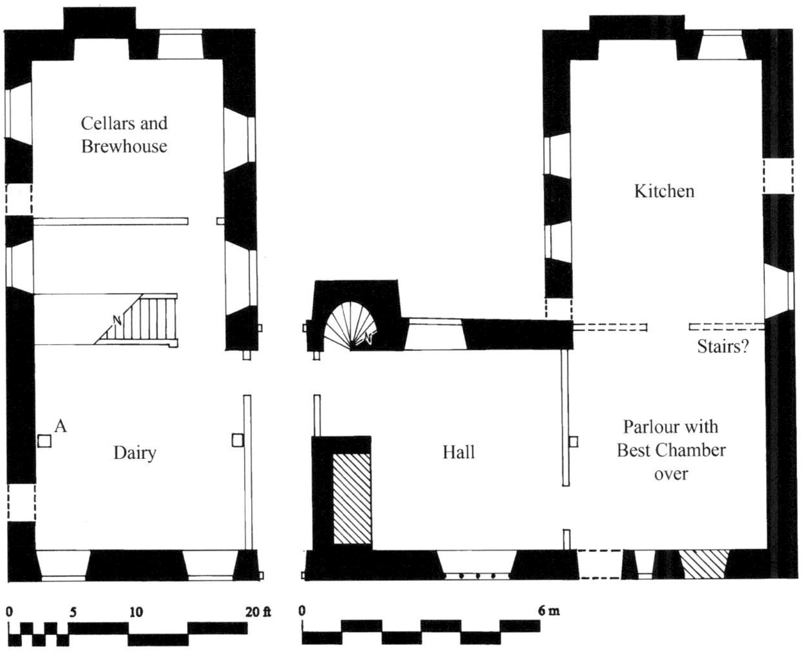

Figure 11. Porch Cottages, Sidford (the former Porch House, SM115) (cf. Plate IIIb)

Ground floor plan, with some 19th-century features omitted. The room names are suggested from a comparison of the 1764 survey and the plan. At A, the beam is supported by an octagonal stone post, which may well be derived from the 'Porch'. We thank J. Marr and R.E. Wilson for the survey, and the owners and occupiers of the five cottages for permission to examine them.

cant changes during the period covered by the surveys, improvements that led to greater comfort and a more modern lifestyle. During the seventeenth and eighteenth centuries houses were enlarged, but not by adding ground-floor rooms. Instead, much of the extra space came from inserted upper floors. This development decidedly affected the use of rooms. In the early surveys, ground-floor chambers were frequent while parlours were rare (one in Cornwall in 1602, one in Sherford, two in Farway and Whitwell, five in Seaton). At Nettlecombe in 1619, parlours were commoner, while ground-floor chambers were disappearing (for example, in the 20-104 acre group seventeen parlours and twelve chambers). Simultaneously, as the inventories show, parlours were becoming living and not sleeping rooms. By 1709 and 1764, the change was complete. Indeed, as far as chambers were concerned, the word was used exclusively for upstairs rooms. It could be argued that the change was purely semantic, that the 'under rooms' were still being used as sleeping chambers. Inventories still list beds in ground floor rooms on occasion, but the exclusive use of the term 'chamber' for an upstairs room shows that people who slept downstairs knew they were old-fashioned, and the pressure for them or their children to rearrange the house was overwhelming.

Significantly, the eighteenth-century surveys describe the cottages more simply, usually giving just the numbers of under rooms and over rooms (or chambers). The practice must be explained by the removal of chambers to the upper floor, leaving the ground floor rooms in these small houses less clearly differentiated in function and consequently less easily identifiable.

In superior houses two further changes took place among the domestic rooms. The first is the appearance of closets accompanying chambers, both at Hurdwick (H25) and Sidmouth (SM74, 89). The second follows the increasing importance of the parlour. The favour it was coming to enjoy led some householders to want two parlours and others a house with parlour and kitchen but no hall, rather than hall and parlour, or hall and kitchen.

Service rooms and subsidiary buildings

Changes also affected the service rooms, and particularly the ancillary buildings. It has been generally considered that the detached kitchen was the primary service building associated with a medieval or sixteenth-century house, although the evidence for this is mostly drawn from houses of manorial or higher status.[36] One writer has claimed that detached kitchens were standard in Devon at a lesser social level.[37] The suggestion is based on a few references in glebe terriers and on the identification of one or two particular buildings as kitchens. Much more extensive fieldwork by the present authors and others shows that these buildings are extremely rare, and hardly any other undisputed examples of detached kitchens have been found. The surveys provide a valuable corrective. In Kenton, some of the kitchens were detached (four out of twelve), while Launceston and Carnanton between them had fifteen (with an unknown number integral). In the other Devon surveys they were rare, as also at Nettlecombe and on the Somerset Crown estates.[38] The sole exception was Norton St. Philip, with nine detached kitchens.

The surveys, however, show that the situation was more complex, because other heated ancillary buildings—malthouses, brewhouses and bakehouses—were considerably more numerous than detached kitchens. They occurred frequently in the East Devon and Somerset houses and contributed twenty-eight examples at Launceston and Carnanton. In contrast, detached kitchens were non-existent by the eighteenth century at Hurdwick and Sidmouth and other heated ancillary buildings were rare.

A clear sequence of development can be recognised in the more substantial farmhouses, although the initial stages of the transformation are not fully documented. Heated service buildings were usually added in the course of the sixteenth century. They were as often called kitchens as malthouses or bakehouses, although their functions overlapped. By the beginning of the seventeenth century, improvements were well under way in the houses themselves. The insertion of some upper floors produced more space and meant that the kitchens could be incorporated into the houses. The detached kitchens were no doubt converted into malthouses and bakehouses.[39] Later in the seventeenth century and into the eighteenth century, the need for separate bakehouses diminished. Stone, cloam, and brick ovens, which are very often found inserted into hall and kitchen chimneys, replaced bakehouses.[40] Wring houses are another specialised space that came into use in the seventeenth century. They held the cheese wring (press) that had earlier been kept in the kitchen or milkhouse.[41] Malthouses and brewhouses probably disappeared when cider became the preferred everyday drink (as indicated by the presence of a number of poundhouses at Sidmouth). Flooring over the whole of the house freed still more space in the main range, and more of the service functions were transferred to it. This process was not completed by the time the eighteenth-century surveys were compiled, and many of the houses they record still had some ancillary buildings.

Sidmouth showed peculiarities in its unusual number of cellars and the appearance of woodhouses (the only other example being at Nettlecombe). Some of the cellars may have been for fish, but the others had probably taken over the storage function of the brewhouses. What the woodhouses meant for the pattern of domestic life in eighteenth-century Sidmouth is unknown, although possibly they held fuel for smoking fish.

The ancillary buildings show a strong correlation with farm size. Thus, at Nettlecombe, apart from a couple of bakehouses on farms of fourteen and seventeen acres, the malthouses, brewhouses, bakehouses and wringhouses were numerous only on farms of thirty acres upwards. These represented the upper end of the scale of domestic (rather than agricultural) economy, which started at the two or three rooms of labourers' cottages. With the exception of butter, cheese, and eggs, the produce of the service buildings was not intended for market.[42] The difficulty of transporting such things as barrels of cider forced isolated farmers to make their own. The service buildings on large farms produced foodstuffs for home consumption by the entire household, the family, the children, and particularly the hired hands and house servants (who slept in the men's and maids' chambers mentioned in inventories).[43] As an extreme example, a farm of forty-eight acres at Nettlecombe (N34), in addition to its hall, parlour, kitchen and eight upper rooms, included a storehouse, two butteries, a butter house, a milkhouse, a brewhouse, a malting house, and a bakehouse.

The comparison between the graphic detail of this description and the unidentifiable rooms in the plan of Great Cliston (Figure 6) demonstrates one of the particular strengths of the surveys in understanding the physical setting and the economy of these farming households. Such insights into the individual houses in each of these villages permeate the texts that are given in fuller form in Part II.

[1] Timber-framing was often used in urban buildings, which are outside the scope of this study. It is also noteworthy that the upper parts of storied porches in Devon were often of timber, no doubt to reduce the weight on the porch posts (Frontispiece).

[2] Nine to eleven inch vertical studs set into head and sill beams, grooved along their sides to take the twelve to eighteen inch wide panels (Plate Ib).

[3] This applies particularly to the areas of dispersed settlement in East Devon and Somerset, where many early houses survive, cf. Figure 5 in N. W. Alcock, 'Vernacular Architecture: Historical Evidence and Historical Problems', in I. M. Quimby, ed., *Material Culture and the Study of American Life* (Winterthur, 1978).

[4] For Cornwall see V. M. and F. J. Chesher, *The Cornishman's House* (Truro, 1968). For Devon, this section is based on work by N. W. Alcock (partly published), and for Somerset on that by C. Carson and E. H. D. Williams (mostly unpublished).

[5] M. W. Barley, *The English Farmhouse and Cottage* (London, 1961); R. W. Brunskill, *Vernacular Architecture of the Lake Counties* (London, 1974).

[6] Houses with one-room plans are extremely rare among surviving buildings.

[7] N. W. Alcock, 'Devon Farmhouses II', *Trans. Devonshire Assoc.*, 101 (1969), 83.

[8] J. G. Hurst and M. W. Beresford, *Deserted Medieval Villages* (London, 1971), 107.

[9] They have also been claimed in Dorset, on rather insubstantial evidence; see R. Machin, *The Houses of Yetminster* (Bristol: University of Bristol, 1979). Recent work also suggests their occasional presence around Exmoor.

[10] We thank Veronica Chesher for drawing this document to our attention. Although the terrier is undated, and only the rector's name (John) is legible, this is sufficient to identify him as John Johnes, rector 1593-1619; the terrier probably belongs to the earliest surviving series of c. 1600.

[11] Royal Commission on Historical Monuments, *West Cambridgeshire* (London, 1968), xlix.

[12] The unheated central room is commonest in Dorset, and is discussed in detail by Machin, *Yetminster*. The type was frequently used from the 1620s onwards, and the earliest example found was of 1592. By the later seventeenth and the eighteenth centuries this plan became more widely distributed, moving north-eastwards across England; M. W. Barley, 'Rural Housing in England' in *Ag. Hist.* V(ii), 659.

[13] The great majority of Devon inventories were destroyed in 1942. Most of the survivors have been published: M. Cash, *Devon Inventories of the Sixteenth and Seventeenth Centuries*, Devon and Cornwall Record Soc. NS11 (Torquay, 1966). Numerical references are to the inventories as listed there. The texts of a further group of 250 inventories for the parish of Uffculme, Devon, a peculiar of Salisbury diocese, are given in Peter Wyatt, ed., *The Uffculme Wills and Inventories*, Devon and Cornwall Record Soc. NS40 (Torquay, 1997). Comparatively few of these

inventories include room names. Cornish and Somerset inventories also survive from the seventeenth century, but no analyses have been published.

[14] Both were clearly yeoman inventories, although this is only stated for Inv. 55.

[15] Most of the surveys include a few holdings for which the surveyor has failed to record house details. These are indicated by shaded squares on Figure 1. Their distribution indicates that these omissions do not introduce any significant bias.

[16] In existing buildings, bays usually range from 10 to 12 ft. in length, by 14 to 18 ft. in width.

[17] The roof structure was divided into true bays, but roof framing members normally were concealed. Three Norton St. Philip entries (NP27,42,52) use 'felda' or 'filda', which apparently had the same meaning as bay. The word has also been recorded from Wiltshire (G. E. Dartnell & E. H. Goddard, *Glossary of Wiltshire Words* (London: English Dialect Soc., 1893)). One other entry (NP26) gives a full description, of the type found in the detailed surveys, 'a shop, a hall, a chamber, two other chambers, a stable, in all five bays'.

[18] The more usual Latin term was 'baia'. 'Spacias/spaciam' is almost invariably abbreviated in the texts to 'spac'.

[19] TNA LR2/207, f. 198; L93 in Table 13.

[20] A single bay building has either one truss at each end, or solid gables, giving either two or zero trusses. The earliest identified south-western survey, that of 1558 (see p. 9) also counts couples, but here the presence of a single figure for the total number of couples on each holding suggests that the surveyor's concern was for the value of the timbers themselves, rather than of the buildings. In the context of an increasing interest in manorial resources, it would seem to be a straightforward development to go from this primitive procedure to specifying the size of each building.

[21] The length of a poole is given in SH1; see also p. 109. The term is presumably an example of 'pole' as a unit of length (O.E.D.); this was normally 16-18 ft. long; O.E.D. cites one example of a 9 ft. unit. 'Poole' were also used occasionally in the Farway survey.

[22] The inaccuracy caused by one of these being in the main range should be insignificant, because the descriptions with names show that this combination was rare. Similarly, axial divisions, which would also cause errors, are uncommon in standing buildings.

[23] Contemporary documents normally group such small holdings under the heading of 'cottages'.

[24] Their presence has been noted in other areas, for example, in one Warwickshire village where the labourers and the craftsmen were living on the smallest holdings. The craftsmen were very much more likely to leave inventories, and they also had more substantial houses. See N. W. Alcock, *Stoneleigh Villagers* (Coventry: University of Warwick Open Studies, 1975).

[25] Kingsbury shows the same pattern to a lesser extent, apparently for the same reason.

[26] H. C. Forman, *Early Nantucket and its Whale Houses* (New York, 1966).

[27] These have been observed both as new-built houses, often attached to each other in blocks, and as subdivisions of earlier houses and cottages.

[28] E.g., R. K. Field, 'Worcestershire Peasant Buildings', *Medieval Archaeol.*, 9 (1965), 112.

[29] Sir Cyril Fox and Lord Raglan in their pioneer work *Monmouthshire Houses* (Cardiff, 1951-54), Vol. II, 109-110, noticed that some small houses were very highly decorated, leading to a similar deduction, that extra money, beyond that needed for a normal-size house, was spent on decoration rather than on a larger house.

[30] Cf. Chesher, *Cornishman's House*.

[31] In contrast to Launceston, very few detached kitchens are found, and so the number of bays reflects the size of the main house only.

[32] Evidence for flooring is less complete than that for bay sizes, because upper floors were not recorded at Kenton or on the Crown estates.

[33] D. Dudley and E. M. Minter, 'The Medieval Village at Garrow Tor', *Medieval Archaeol.*, 6 (1963), 272-294. This article includes a partial gazetteer.

[34] Barley, *English Farmhouse*, 110.

[35] Barley, *English Farmhouse*, 111.

[36] M.E. Wood, *The English Medieval House* (London, 1965).

[37] Barley, *English Farmhouse*, 102, 222.

[38] The Hurdwick survey lists few kitchens of any sort.

[39] David Martin has noted the disappearance of detached kitchens in Sussex around 1600 and suggested a connection with their incorporation into the houses. However, he attributes this to the use of brick for good chimneys, rather than the extra space created by upper floors, see D. Martin, *Historic buildings in East Sussex*, I (No. 2), 18-20 (Rape of Hastings Architectural Survey, 1977).

[40] Cloam, a very coarse pottery, was often used for ovens, which were dome-shaped, 12 to 18 inches in diameter (rather smaller than those built of stone or brick). All these ovens opened onto the hearth, were pre-heated with brushwood or embers, and then left to bake the bread slowly.

[41] Five examples of wring houses are listed for the period after 1660 in the Uffculme inventories, compared to only one in the previous half-century; Wyatt, *Uffculme Wills*; Peter Wyatt and Robin Stanes, *Uffculme, a Peculiar Parish*, Uffculme, 1997, 79. Cider-making also required a press, called a cider wring; this was apparently kept in the pound-house or the barn, rather than in a special building (see Uffculme inventories nos. 72 and L6).

[42] Beer, sold in the village alehouse and made by its keeper, is another exception although no alehouse can be recognised among the survey descriptions.

[43] Cf. Charles Vancouver, *General View of The Agriculture of the County of Devon*, (London, 1808), 359ff.

CHAPTER 4

The Farmsteads

While dwellings are a source of information about social organisation, family life, and standards of living, the buildings of the farmstead shed light on the agricultural economy. Pastoral farming demands different structures from the barns and granaries needed for large-scale arable farming. The broad picture has long been clear, distinguishing region from region. Much less is known about variations at the local level. Were all village farmers occupied in the same way? How did a cottager's livelihood differ from that of his yeoman neighbour? At the microscopic level, the buildings of the farmstead offer a source of information that can distinguish between one farmer's good fortune and another's hard struggle.

Surviving buildings themselves tell us little. Almost everywhere the physical record has been defaced by the relentless destruction and replacement of farm buildings. As crops, economies, and farming practices change, farmers have always modified or razed buildings no longer needed for the jobs they were built to perform. Consequently, groups of early farm buildings are very rare, and even these few are almost always later than the dwellings they accompany. The impossibility of knowing which structures may be missing from a surviving group of period buildings further complicates the historian's task.

The surveys come to the rescue. They are a source of information that can compensate for the loss of the buildings themselves. Their record of every structure in use at the time each survey was made, however abbreviated the format, opens two new dimensions on the study of regional agricultural history. The wide geographical distribution of the surveys through several farming regions enables historians to estimate the differing importance of farm buildings among the capital assets that farmers needed to engage in different agricultural economies. Second, the comprehensiveness of the surveys within each estate reveals, in the enumeration of farm buildings, the different degrees to which villagers needed and used special-purpose agricultural buildings to exploit the local economy. They make clear how, in different regions, wealth was shared among a broader or narrower class of men. Such matters figured greatly in the choice that many people faced in the seventeenth century, whether to emigrate, to the nearest town, to Ireland or the American colonies, or to stay at home competing for whatever economic opportunities the neighbourhood afforded. These are familiar issues for social and economic historians, whose conclusions from other evidence can be tested and refined in the light of the surveys.

To study local and regional agricultural economies using the surveys we must first determine which basic operations each farmstead engaged in. When one farm is compared with others in the same village and in other villages in the same region, we can reconstruct with a fair degree of confidence the mixture of agricultural activities that contributed to a locality's livelihood. Farm buildings represented much of the capital equipment with which each farmer exploited the economic potential latent in his land and in the markets that lay within his reach. Beyond the ubiquitous barn found in all but the poorest farmyards, specialised structures for housing animals and storing or processing the harvest enabled better-equipped farmers to engage in a greater variety of income-producing activities than their poorer neighbours. Well-to-do farmers would certainly have reinvested some of their earnings in land, labour, livestock, and additional capital improvements. But, as we have already seen in the chapter on the houses, profits from farming in the sixteenth and seventeenth centuries went increasingly to support higher standards of living. The house-and-estate surveys illustrate this essential connection between the means of production and one of its principal ends. In so doing, they offer scholars a rare opportunity to investigate the 'great rebuilding' in the most intimate of all possible contexts, the rural community, comparing one farmstead with its neighbour down the lane.

To understand how agricultural buildings of different kinds contributed to the everyday work of the farmstead, this chapter begins by examining the function of each recorded type of farm building, supplementing internal evidence from the surveys themselves with information from probate inventories. Then comes a general discussion of characteristic farmstead groups in each of the major agricultural sub-regions in the area. The chapter concludes by looking closely at two sample estates to see whether their economic potential was being differently exploited by large landholders, who could command the use of specialised farm buildings, in comparison to the more slender resources of their less prosperous neighbours.

The Buildings of the Farmstead

The farm buildings inventoried in the surveys cannot be analysed as straightforwardly as the houses. Rarely described in more than size, their names only indicate their primary function—storing crops, sheltering stock or implements, performing farming tasks, or (on some farmsteads) engaging in by-employments related more or less closely to the agriculture of the region. It is only possible to guess at the secondary functions they may have served, especially on the smaller farmsteads—cattle in the barn, for instance, hay over the cowshed, hens in the hog house.

The names themselves are found in great variety, and the meaning of the terms (Table 6) needs careful consideration. The probate inventories offer little help; only one in ten give the names of farm buildings. Nor do the rare early standing structures fill the silences left by the records. Apart from barns, farm buildings dating from before 1700 are too rare to establish recognisable patterns. Their original function is now often a matter of guesswork, and secondary uses are even more obscure. Sometimes though, a combination of all the evidence throws a little light on the meaning of the buildings' names and the purposes for which they were built.

Barns for corn and grass storage

The barn was the largest and best-built structure in the farmstead. Consequently, many early barns have survived the farming improvements of the eighteenth and nineteenth centuries as well as mechanisation in the twentieth. Two examples illustrate the type (Figures 12-13; see also Figure 21 and Plates VIIb, VIIIa). The first is probably of the sixteenth century and contains a very unusual feature, an integral shippon, discussed in the next section. The other dates from the early eighteenth century. Each has the height and unobstructed interior space ideal for storing crops in bulk. Neither is particularly long; most surviving examples have three to five bays.[1] The big opposed doors are also typical, allowing a loaded wagon to be driven into the central bay for unloading. However, the use of such doors had developed gradually, in line with the replacement of packhorses by wagons. Barns of the sixteenth and early seventeenth centuries often have one or both doorways too small or low or awkwardly placed in relation to ground level to admit carts (Figure 12A). Later, barn doors usually allowed room for a cart with a high load to be driven right through the wagon-way (Plate VIIb), and sometimes had porches on one or both sides for extra shelter.

The prime use of the barn was the storage of crops in sheaf. Threshing was done on the floor—often boarded or flagged for the purpose—between the doors, which, when open, provided a draught for winnowing. Hand-flail threshing was a labour-intensive and back-breaking task, but one that could wait for the slow winter months. The threshed corn needed more protection from vermin than the barn could supply, and it was always stored above ground. A very few southwestern farms had free-standing granaries or garners set on staddle-stones, and these may have been an eighteenth-century innovation (Figures 15 and 19).[2] Elsewhere, the grain was kept in an upper room. This might be over an outbuilding (e.g. the malthouse at Leigh Barton in 1709; p. 206), but often was in the house itself, in the 'corn chamber' listed in some inventories. In the surveys, chambers in houses are hardly ever described in detail, and as a result their use for grain-storage is certainly under-represented.

Few farm descriptions mention separate storage for hay, and we deduce that it was generally housed in the barns. The Devon probate inventories confirm the practice. They also show that barns had other uses as well. Ladders and other tools often ended up there, as did thatching reed, spars for roof repairs, furze and broom for cattle bedding, and packhorse gear.[3] Crops were also not always stored where expected.

When a yeoman of Sidbury died in January 1621,

Table 6: Farm building names and uses

Corn and grass storage	Barn [*horreum*] Haybarn or hayhouse Hayloft Strawhouse Granary (Recorded in inventories as part of the house: corn chamber, cheese chamber, apple chamber)
Housing for stock	Cowhouse or cowstall Shippon [*shepina*] Stall Oxstall or oxhouse [*bovite*] Calfhouse Linhey Stable [*stabulum*] Sheephouse or sheeppen Fold Asshouse [*asinum*] Hogscote, hogsty, or pighouse Henhouse or poultry house Dovehouse
Implement shelters and other storage	Wainhouse Cart house Store [*staur*] (Pumphouse, woodhouse, coalhouse are associated with the farmhouse rather than the farmstead)
Working buildings	Poundhouse (ciderhouse in inventories) Yoking house (Malthouse, ovenhouse, wringhouse are associated with domestic rather than agricultural work)
Buildings for by-employment or crafts	Tanhouse or barkhouse Soaphouse Dyehouse Rackhouse Shelfhouse 'Palace' or fish-cellar (Workhouse, workshop, and shop are associated with the farmhouse)

Italic names in square brackets are the equivalents used in the Latin surveys, though these are accompanied by some English terms, e.g. 'le waynehouse'.

he left a 'mow' (a yard for ricks which probably stood on staddle stones) with wheat and barley, while his barn was filled with hay and straw.[4] Barns were to the farmstead what the hall was to its house—the catch-all for whatever objects or activities lacked accommodation in special-purpose structures.

Separate hay-barns were sometimes useful on larger farms. The surveys show that they were generally smaller than corn-barns. Thus, on farms where two barns survive, we can probably recognise the hay-barn in the smaller. In standing buildings, the second barn shows no particular features to distinguish it, apart from generally being later.[5]

The absence of a hay-barn need not mean that hay

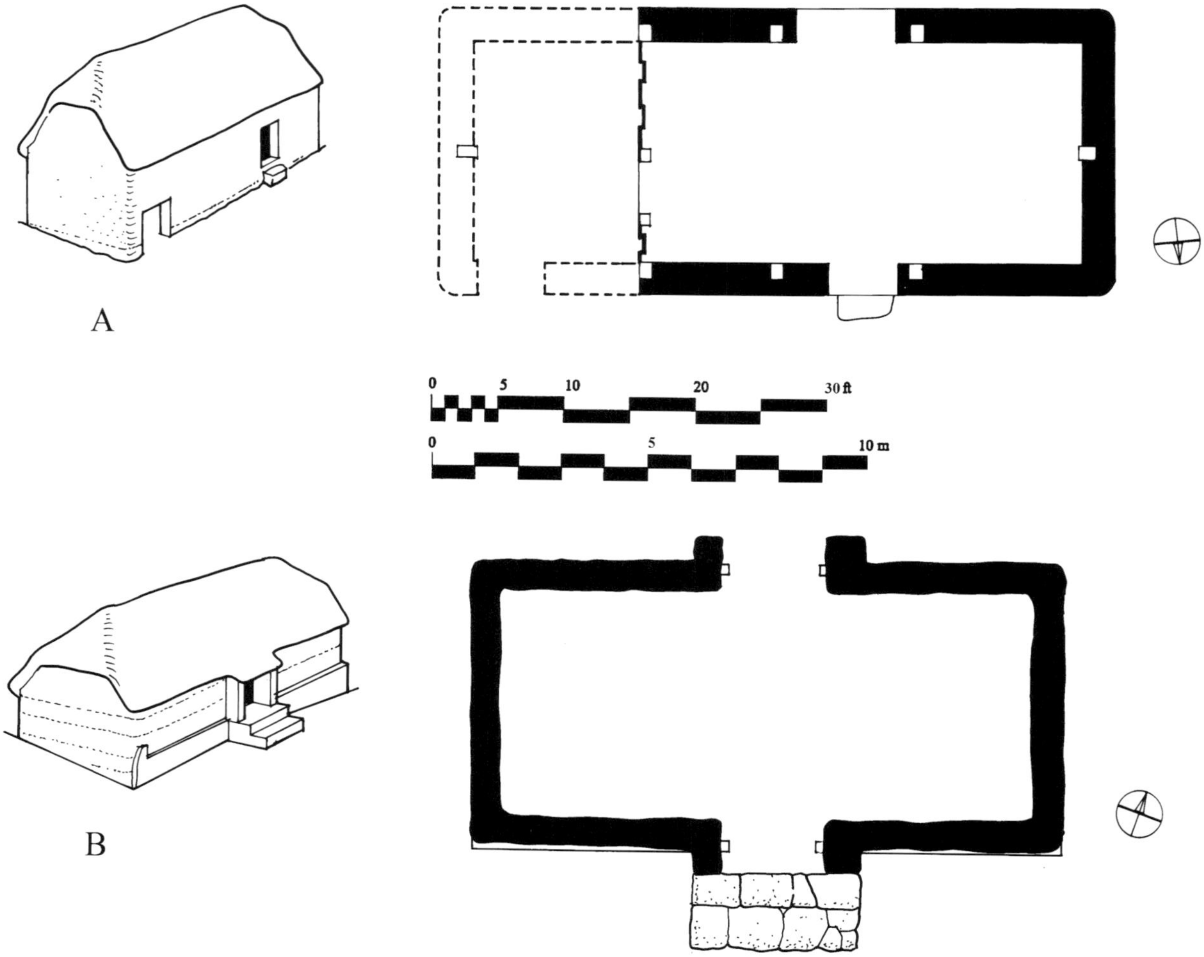

Figure 12. A: Higher Farm, Stockland, Devon, a sixteenth century barn combined with an ox-stall or shippon (in the demolished eastern bay). B: Woolstone, Sandford, Devon, a typical small seventeenth or eighteenth century West Country barn (cf. Plate VIIIa).

Figure 13. Higher Lettaford, North Bovey, Devon. Barn and linhey in the farmyard (photo N.W. Alcock).

was not given special treatment although it does suggest that hay needed less storage room. Besides taking up part of the barn, hay was also kept in lofts over the stable or shippon where it was later to be used. This convenient location is recorded in 1609 in Farway and in later surveys as well. From surviving structures, we know too that it was kept in the lofts of linheys. The recording of hay-lofts in the surveys is certainly incomplete, as neither the Kenton nor Crown surveys say anything about upper floors in farm buildings.

Occasionally the straw also required separate storage. It was used primarily as animal bedding, although it might do double duty as fodder or for thatching. We have no evidence to suggest that straw-houses had a very different appearance from hay-barns, though they may have been smaller still. In the same way, the occasional hay-houses listed in the surveys were probably much the same as the hay-barns.

Housing for stock.

The variety of animal housing and the many names for it are an indication of the importance of pastoral husbandry in the region. Distinguishing the various meanings can be difficult. Structures for housing cattle were the most important and were called by four or five separate names plus a couple of Latin equivalents. Two of these are straightforward, *cowhouse* and *oxstall* (or sometimes *cowstall* and *oxhouse*). These were used respectively for milking cattle and for stalling draught oxen, or occasionally for fattening stock.

Of the general terms, *shippon* is essentially equivalent to cowhouse. The one or two references to 'shippon for fat oxen' indicate that this arrangement was unusual, requiring special explanation. *Stall* is a more complex term. Its principal meaning was oxhouse. In the Somerset Crown surveys, stall and *bovite* (from *bos*, an ox) are used as alternatives. In contrast, in Farway, Seaton, and Nettlecombe, stall and shippon alternate and clearly have identical meanings. By the eighteenth century, stall had vanished from the regional dialect, leaving shippon and oxhouse as the standard Devon terms. However, by then some Devon farmers had only the buildings they called linheys (described below).

The inventories show the complexities behind the formal terms. Stalls and shippons contained hay, presumably in lofts, but also boards and timber and no doubt other sundries put under cover out of the weather. One farm had its oxstall, but also great and little stalls for *kine* (cows).[6] All contained planks for the stalling.

Identifying surviving shippons and especially oxhouses is much more difficult than finding barns, because relatively few survive. Some early shippons exist as part of long-houses (see Figure 3 and Plates IIa-b), organised as rectangular spaces with a central drain, the cattle tethered in two rows, their heads to its side walls. A unique example of a shippon or perhaps an oxstall combined with a barn is seen in Figure 12A. Here, the cattle were apparently tethered across the barn and fed through the partition. Perhaps we can infer that early free-standing shippons would have been long buildings with a single entrance and either narrow, with a single row of cattle, or wider, with two rows tethered facing each wall, both with a hayloft over. Surviving early examples are of the narrow form, either with a series of doors set at intervals, corresponding to the spacing of two or three cows (Figure 16A), or open-sided (Figure 15C). This type was particularly common in Somerset where it continued into the nineteenth century and beyond. Early oxhouses have simply not been identified, which is hardly surprising if their only distinguishing feature was the wooden stalling that would be removed if the oxhouse was converted to another use.

From the late seventeenth century, cattle farmers in Devon and Somerset came to favour a distinctive new type of building, the *linhey*, often set away from the main farmstead.[7] It combined shelter for beef cattle in an open-sided shed with a hayloft above, again open on one side (Figures 16B, 17B, Plate VIIIb). Characteristically, the roof was carried on two-storey timber posts, but cylinders of rubble masonry and even standing stones (orthostats) were also used. Understanding the development of the linhey as a farm building type is complicated by a parallel development of the meaning of the name. In the sixteenth century (persisting later in Cornwall), linhey had its primary meaning of 'lean-to' referring for example to a lean-to room along the side of a house. It then came to be used for a lean-to free-standing shed. It had one side open, as in the *lynne over the plumpe* [pump], used for storing tools and wood.[8] Such makeshift sheds must have recommended themselves for cattle shelter, especially for the less pampered bullocks and fattening stock, if not for the milking cattle and oxen.

Figure 14. Manor Farm, Charlton Mackrell, Somerset. Large stable with loft (above) and open-fronted cowhouse (below) (cf. Figure 15) (photos John Dallimore).

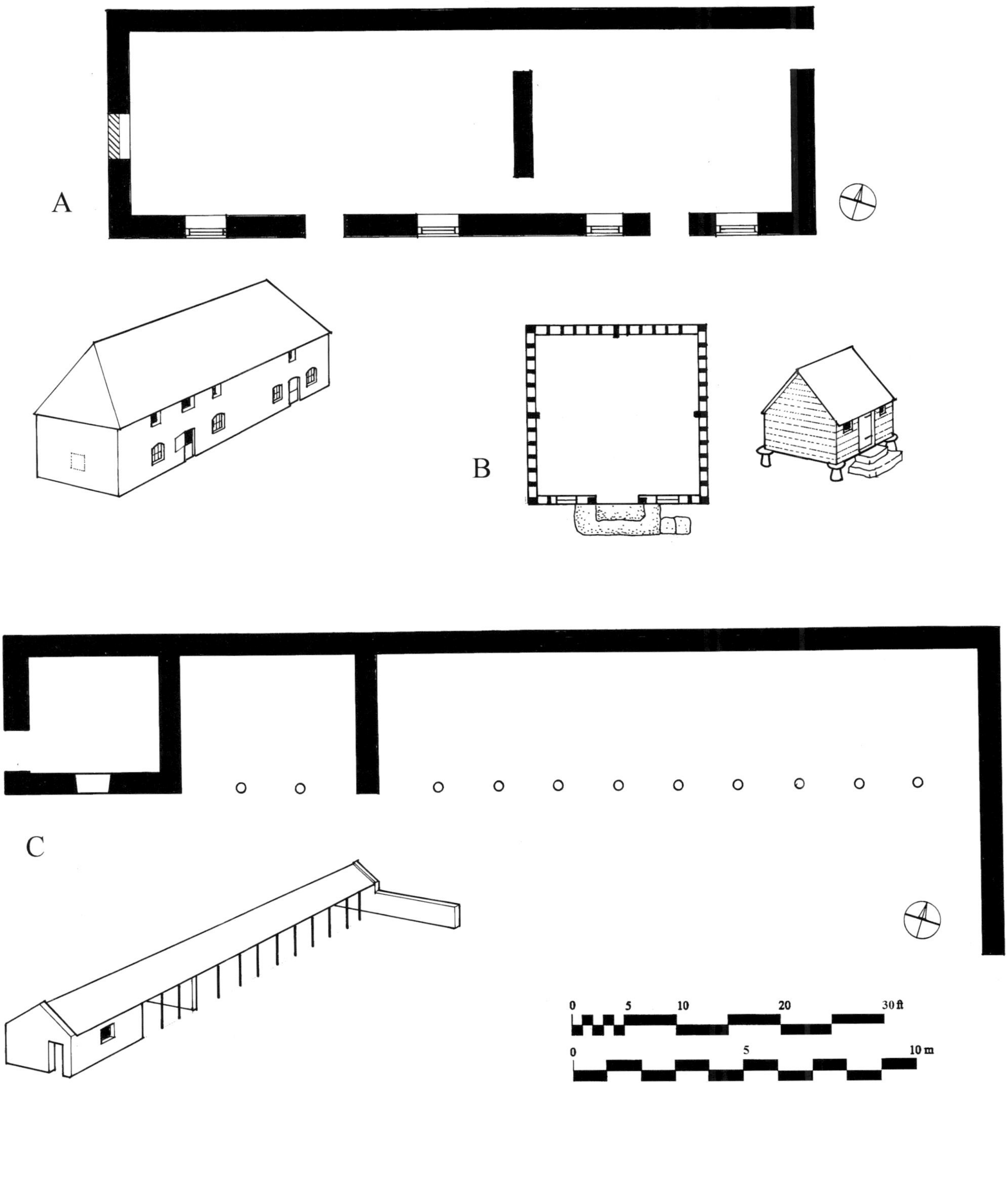

Figure 15. Farm buildings at Manor Farm, Charlton Mackrell, Somerset (cf. Figure 14): A: stable with loft, B: granary (cf. Figure 19), C: cowshed (based on survey by John Dallimore).

Figure 16. Eighteen century farm buildings. A: Higher Southtown, West Pennard, Somerset. Cowhouse (above) (cf. Figure 17A) (photo John Dallimore), B: Upton Hellions, Devon. Linhey (below) (photo N.W. Alcock).

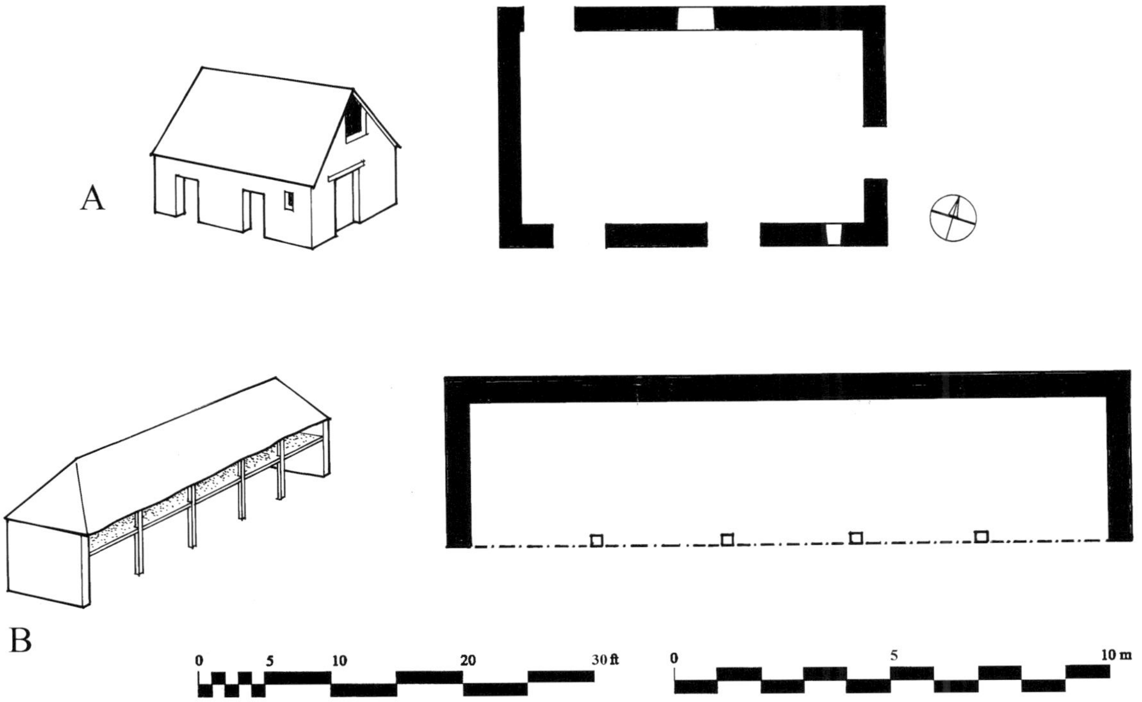

Figure 17. Eighteenth century farm buildings. A: Higher Southtown, West Pennard, Somerset. Cowhouse (cf. Figure 16A) (based on survey by John Dallimore), B: Linhey at Hellions Barton, Upton Hellions, Devon.

The important development of adding a hayloft apparently took place in the course of the seventeenth century.[9] The lofts were no doubt modelled on those already used over shippons and stables.

Our knowledge of *stables* is much more limited. By the late eighteenth century the stable was often a well-designed building, different from the shippon in having windows and only one door (Figure 15A). By then it housed the most valuable animals on the farm, the draught and riding horses. Earlier stables have disappeared or gone unrecognised. We must suspect first, that as housing for pack ponies, they would have been less substantial and, second, that they would have differed little from shippons, apart from the stock they housed. As we have seen, both often had haylofts over. The inventories show that stables were also used for all the paraphernalia associated with saddle and packhorses—saddles, bridles, dung pots for moving manure, panniers, and 'crookes' to fasten them to the horses' flanks. Stables at Kingsbury, Somerset, are described as 'le cut' or 'cutting'. This term is not recorded elsewhere, but probably refers to a small stable cut off from a barn.

Sheephouses or *sheep pens* pose even knottier problems. From our general information about farming practice in the region and from a dearth of existing buildings, we would deduce that houses for sheep were not provided in the south-west. On the other hand, the Cornish surveys show their presence explicitly in the early seventeenth century. Their form can only be guessed, but their description by numbers of bays indicates that they were roofed, although they may have been lower and narrower than buildings for other stock. The *folds* occasionally mentioned elsewhere were probably the more usual open sheep-pens, used at lambing time and for close inspection of stock.

The remaining stock buildings need little comment. *Pig-houses* may have been somewhat different from

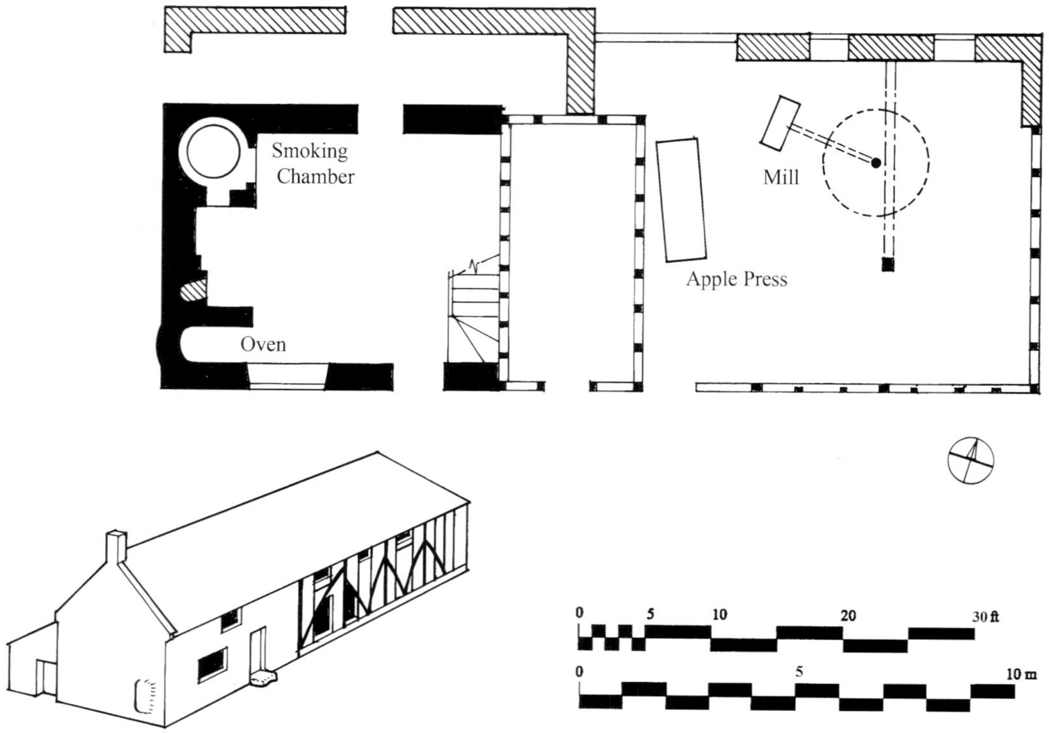

Figure 18. Hilliards, Curry Rivel, Somerset. Poundhouse, converted from a shippon in 1744 (dated roof timber), with a bakehouse and smoking chamber added earlier (based on survey by John Dallimore).

Figure 19. Osmore, Membury, Devon. Granary on staddle stones (cf. Figure 15B) (photo N.W. Alcock).

Figure 20. North Bovey, Devon. Granite ash-house (photo N.W. Alcock).

sties or *hogscotes,* because Devon had a tradition of housing pigs in sections of larger buildings rather than in separate sties.[10]

Implement shelter and other storage

Of the shelter buildings, *wainhouse* and *carthouses* were probably similar, single story buildings with one side or end open so that carts or wagons could be wheeled in (Figure 21B). Most of the *stores* recorded were incorporated in barns and must have been small subdivided sections or perhaps lean-to's like the 'end-sheds' at Farway. The inventories do not mention stores, but they may well have been present, containing some of the miscellaneous tools and lumber listed in the barns. The various working buildings probably had very few distinguishing features, and indeed probably changed function from time to time in response to changing needs. The *pound house* illustrates this specifically. It contained the equipment for crushing apples for cider making. Initially the mechanism consisted of a large round stone trough with a stone wheel rolling around in it over the apples. The 'apple-mill', which spread slowly after its invention in 1664, achieved the same result more compactly, the apples being crushed between two toothed rollers. The pound house would also contain the apple press, which extracted the juice from the crushed apples.[11] Inventories also use the term ciderhouse, where cider barrels were stored, together with the cider-making equipment.[12] None of the cider-making gear placed great demands on the building that contained it, and indeed at the end of the eighteenth century William Marshall described the pound house as 'a mean shed or hovel, without peculiarity of form'.[13] No doubt this would apply equally to many of the other minor buildings of the farmstead. Our example of a pound-house (Figure 18) illustrates just this aspect. It was converted from a seventeenth-eighteenth century building of very rough construction, which had perhaps been a shippon. The building was too small for the cider-mill, and so a lean-to addition was provided. Before this, the original building had already been extended for a bakehouse, with smoking chambers.

One storage building of which we have examples, but which finds no mention in either the surveys or the inventories, is the ash-house (Figure 20). It was used for collecting the wood ash from the farmhouse hearth, valuable as fertiliser, but of little monetary significance.

The only other working buildings listed in the surveys with a specifically agricultural function were the *yoking houses* at Leigh Barton (pp. 188, 206). From their names these were clearly used for harnessing oxen, but neither we nor any of a number of agricultural experts we have consulted can suggest what features might have been found in a building with this specialised function. The *fish-cellars* ('palaces' in dialect) stand rather outside the range of agricultural buildings, because they were found in the fishing communities and were located on the quayside or the beach (p. 33).

Illustrating entire historic farmsteads from standing buildings is even more difficult than delineating individual building types. However, a very few fairly complete farmsteads have survived, as a record of the many that have vanished. Figure 21A shows the overall layout of a large farm, illustrating the irregular layout and agglomeration of buildings of various dates that is typical of the region. In contrast Figure 21B illustrates a farmstead with just one block of buildings incorporating a barn and a motley collection of service functions.

By-employments

Buildings for minor farm industries were clearly distinguishable to the surveyors by their use, probably because they had some specialised fittings. Externally most must have resembled other minor buildings on the farmstead. The tanner needed a store for his bark, the *barkhouse* which may also have contained his 'mill' for crushing the bark, while he would use his *tanhouse* for working on the leather, especially scraping it.[14] The specialised buildings of the soap-maker and the dyer would contain vats for boiling fat or cloth. The *rack-houses* and one *shelf-house* were presumably similar, but their particular function is obscure. The fittings of all these buildings have one thing in common—that they could easily be removed, leaving a simple building identical to many others on the farmsteads in the region.

Farmsteads and the Regional Economies

Farmers in each locality used the agricultural buildings they inherited or built new to take best advantage of the economic opportunities that their neighbourhood afforded. Their choices were guided by the traditions of their forefathers and the examples of their neighbours. Consequently, the farmsteads on

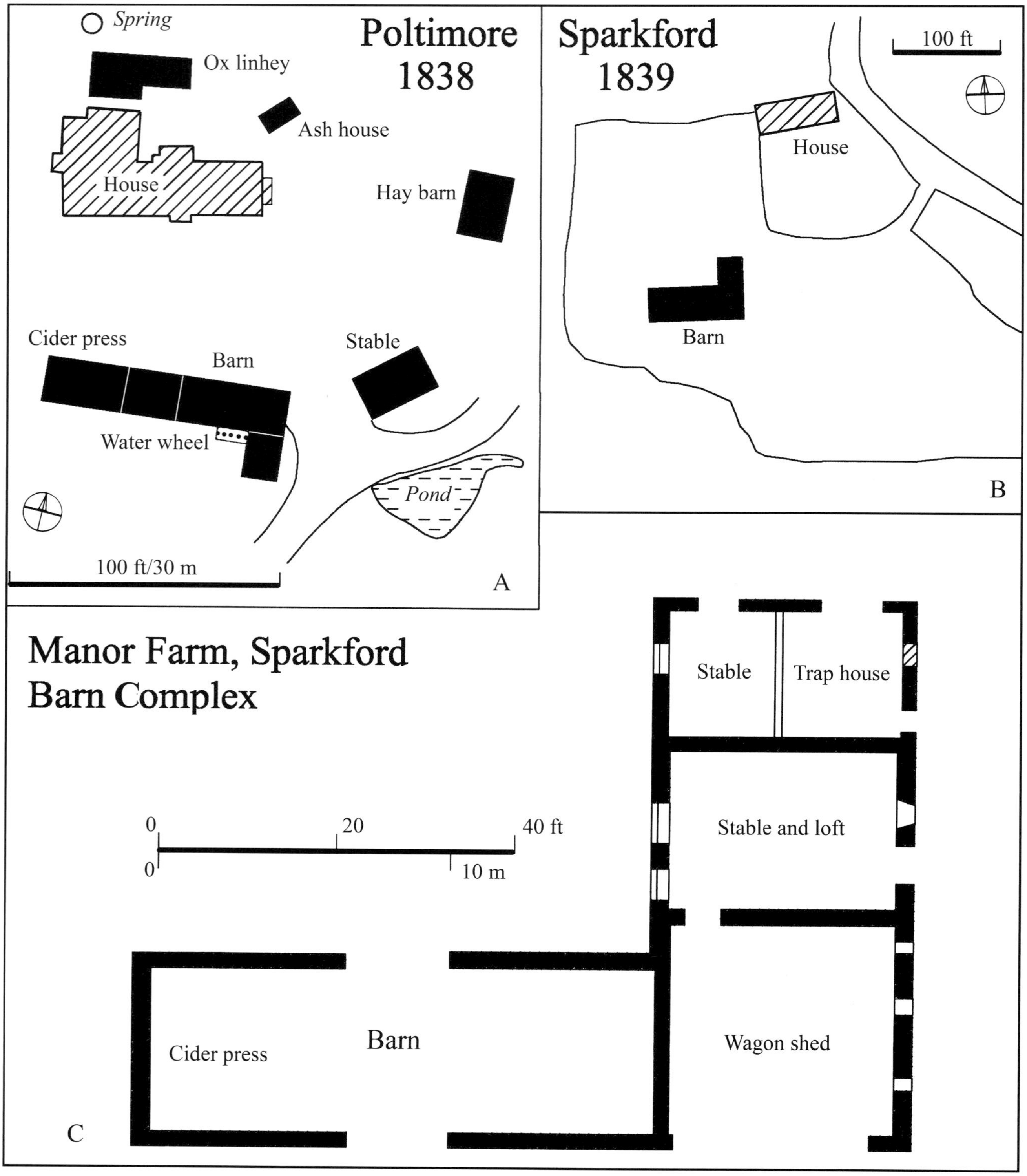

Figure 21. Farmstead layouts

A: Poltimore, Farway Devon, A farmstead including a large range of buildings of many different dates as shown on the Tithe Map of 1838 (surveyed by Desmond Williams), B: Manor Farm, Sparkford, Somerset, a small farmstead with just a barn and adjoining wagon shed as shown on the Tithe Map of 1839, C: The barn complex at Manor Farm, Sparkford (surveyed by John Dallimore)

one estate, no less than the farmhouses, showed similarities that marked them out from farmsteads in other regions where different mixes of crops, stock, and by-employments required somewhat different combinations of farm buildings.

The characteristic pattern of farmsteads on each of the surveyed estates are revealed by arranging the farms in order of increasing size (tabulated in Part II) and then plotting the proportion of farms containing each type of agricultural building (Figure 22: A-Q). So presented, farmsteads with similar combinations of buildings are found to cluster into groups according to farm size. We learn from the Cornish surveys (Figure 22: B), for example, that barns and oxhouses were common on farms larger than thirteen acres, but only farmers holding more than forty acres were likely to have a stable as well. The identification of such configurations demonstrates two points about these villages. First, they show the truth of the logical deduction that the amount of land that a farmer held was roughly equivalent to his real worth in relation to his neighbours. Indeed, the correlation between the size of holdings and their level of capital improvement is our principal assurance that landholding is a tolerably accurate measure of an individual's economic standing in the community. Second, the clustering of buildings of similar function implies a connection between wealth (or 'worth') and economic opportunity. Land was a fixed asset valued at the appropriate fraction of what a farmer paid to purchase a freehold or acquire a lease. Improvements to the farmstead in the form of fences, farm buildings, and equipment were needed to make a living from the land—a modest living for smallholders 'of little working capital' or a better one for those who had enough land and could afford the capital to realise its full potential.[15]

Seemingly minor variations among agricultural buildings in the surveyed estates show how finely tuned these West Country farmsteads were to local economic opportunities. The farm buildings are the historian's key to understanding these variations. Broadly speaking, the whole of Somerset, Devon, and Cornwall was pasture country, but a closer look reveals that farmers almost everywhere were actually engaged in mixed agriculture. The very close examination that these surveys alone make possible shows that the region supported the five distinct farming economies that have been described in Chapter 1. The listings of farm buildings give an unintended record of West Country farmers' varying strategies for making livings from the land.

Arable farming. Our ability to say anything at all about farmsteads in those few places where cereal production predominated depends on an accident of agricultural history. When surveyed in 1597 Kenton (Figure 22: A) still retained its medieval open field system. Farmers large and small employed numerous labourers to cultivate communal strips of land using ploughs drawn by oxen. Virtually every landholder stored the harvest in a two- or three-bay barn and half to two-thirds kept the plough oxen in a stall. These two structures were an arable farmer's minimum requirements unless he provided his own transportation to market, in which case he might want a wainhouse to shelter the carts. The larger farmers at Launceston, for instance (Figure 22: C), carried their cereal crops to the town market in wains.

The farmsteads on one other estate bear some resemblance to Kenton's because there too grain growing was unusually important. The main Cornish manor surveyed in 1602, Treverbyn Courtenay (Figure 22: B), lay on a flat, fertile coastal plain, and, while it was not farmed communally, its barns and oxhouses on farmsteads of all sizes and its largish number of labourers suggest parallels with Kenton and strengthen the picture of the typical arable farmstead. But only so far. The estate also contained substantial amounts of rough common grazing land, and it is obvious from the sheep houses on some farmsteads that farmers up and down the social scale at Treverbyn Courtenay pastured flocks on these moors. Horses—and the stables to house them—were another sign that some of these Cornishmen had access to sidelines not open to the Exe River cultivators. Some of the stables adjoined cottages in the town of St. Austell and may indicate that a few fortunate labourers sometimes supplemented their meagre incomes by hiring out a packhorse or two.

Such auxiliary enterprises notwithstanding, the surveys of Kenton and Treverbyn Courtenay identify the basic farm buildings needed to engage in the cultivation of crops—a grain barn for the unthreshed harvest and stalls with hay and straw lofts overhead for the plough teams. Structures serving these two or three functions appear on farmsteads wherever fields were tilled and grain grown, no matter how secondarily.

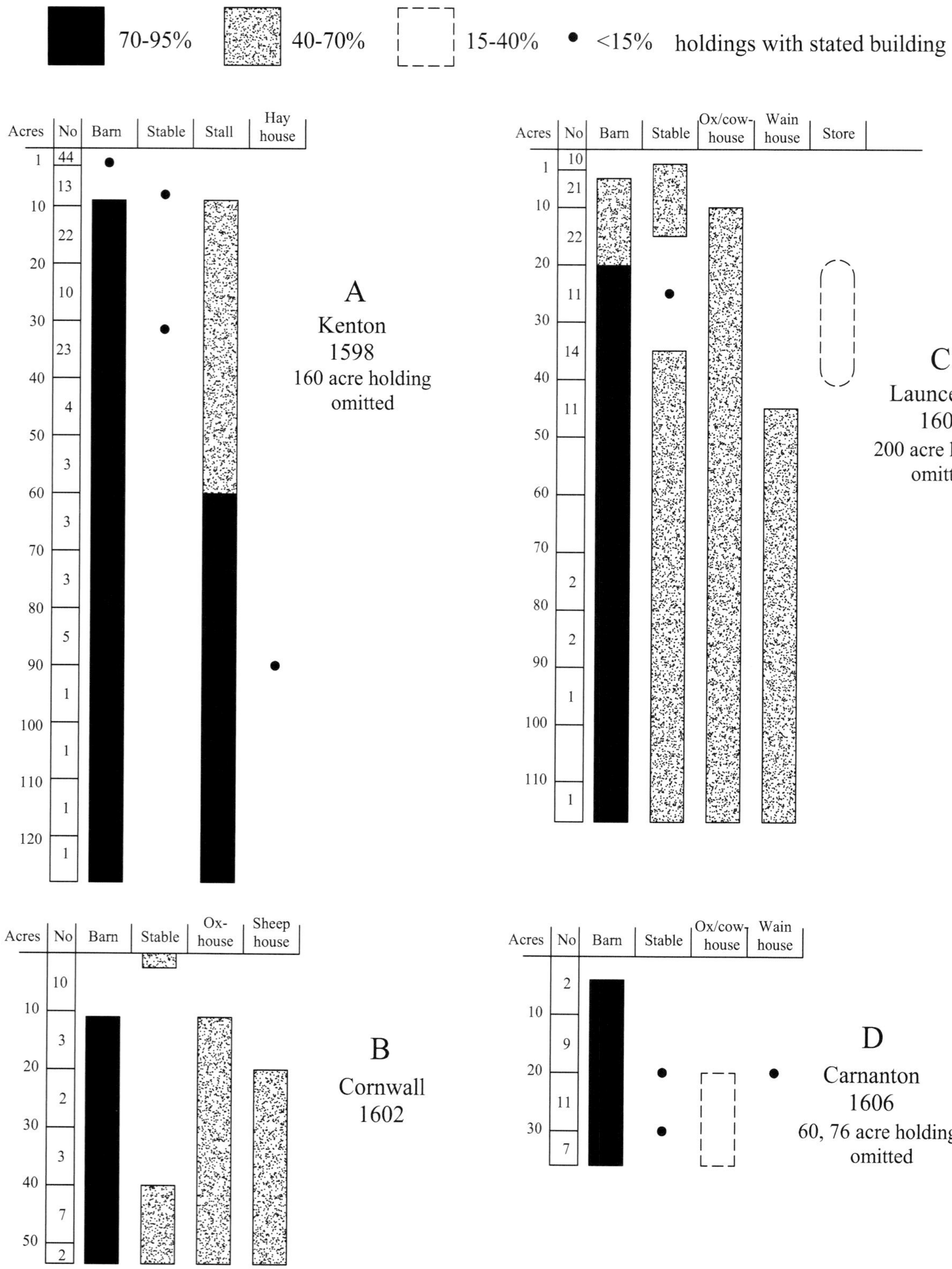

Figure 22a. Farm building patterns (A—D)

The different shadings correspond to the proportion of holdings with buildings of each type. The patterns should be viewed as impressionistic, rather than precise, because judgment of the limits for the zones plotted is necessarily subjective. Square- or round-ended blocks indicate sharp or gradual cut-offs.

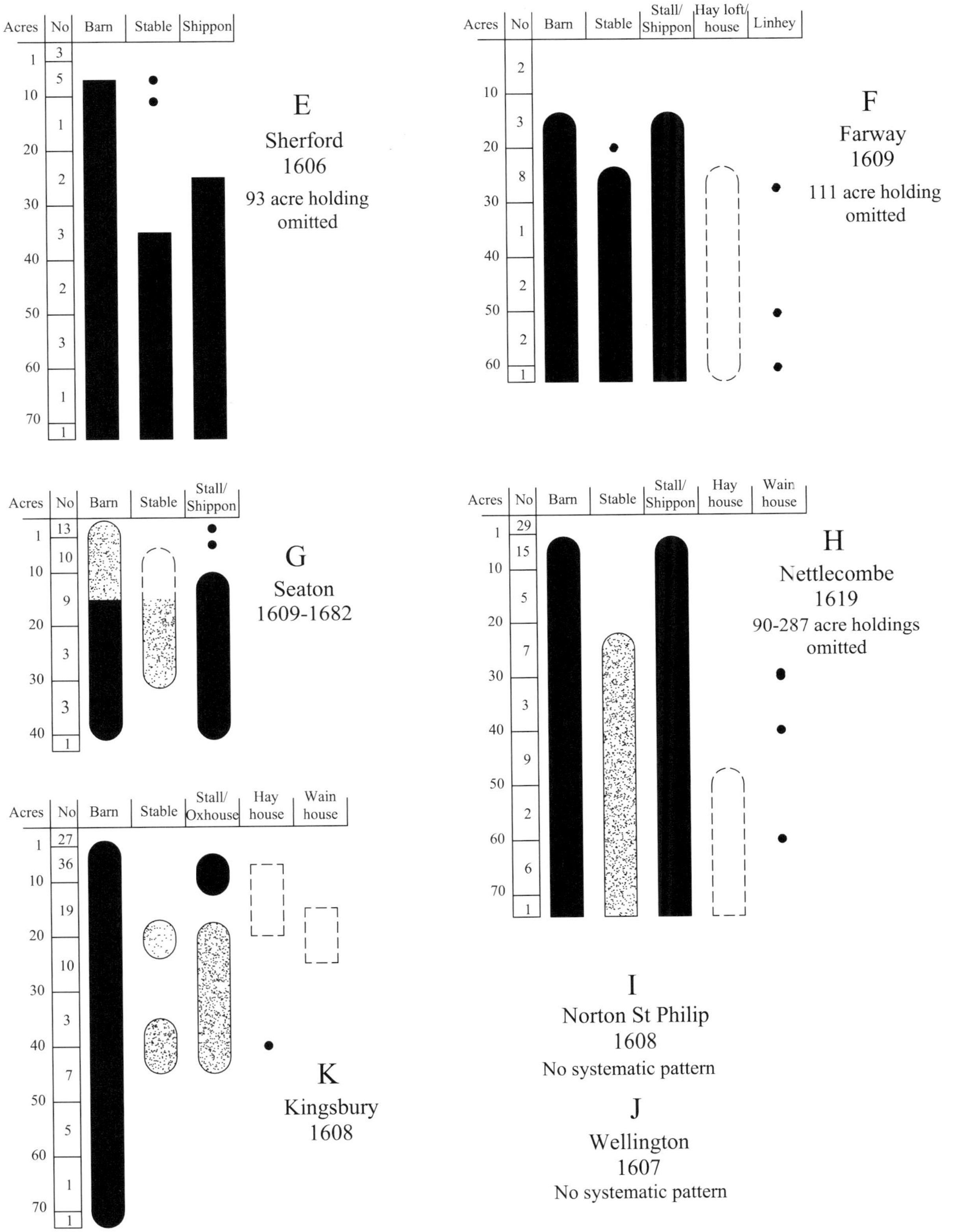

Figure 22b. Farm building patterns (E—K). For identification of shadings see Figure 22a.

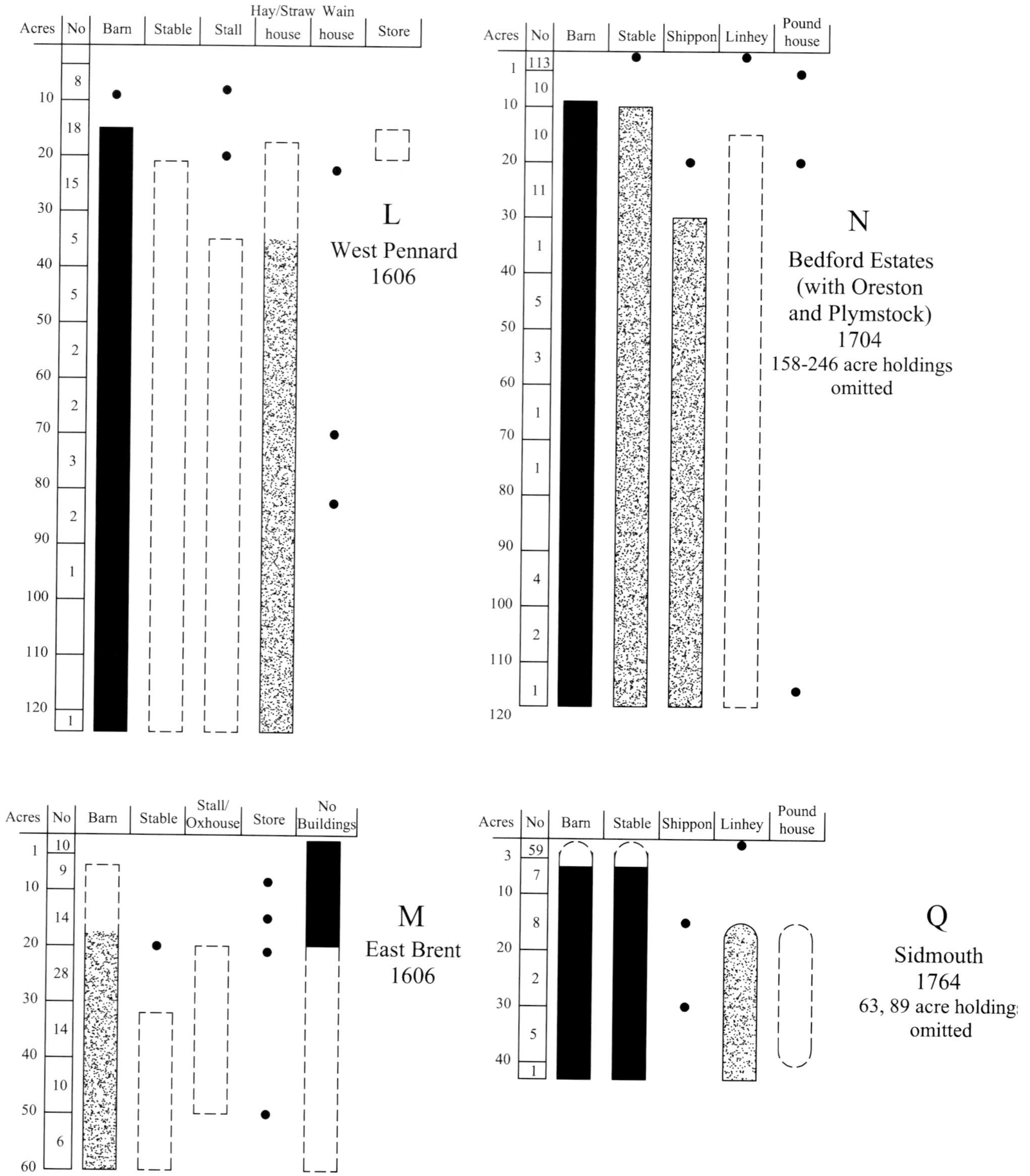

Figure 22c. Farm building patterns (L—Q). For identification of shadings see Figure 22a.

Moorland pasture

Grazing sheep, pasturing dairy cattle, and fattening steers produced a different farmscape. The only absolutely essential building for pastoral farming was a barn. Sometimes that alone was enough. Almost the simplest of all West Country farmsteads belonged to the graziers of Carnanton (Figure 22: D) who ran sheep on the high moors. They had little use for structures other than open folds (usually too insubstantial to attract a surveyor's notice) and barns to store hay and fodder for the flocks.

Dairymen by contrast found it prudent to provide substantial shelter for valuable milking cows. Stalls and shippons were almost as common as barns on farmsteads at Sherford, Farway, Seaton, and Nettlecombe (Figure 22: E-H). Good housing for animals and dry storage for fodder and bedding would have sufficed, had not these Devon herdsmen also dabbled in tillage and done a little stock-raising ('ranching') for the meat market as well. Stables on the larger farms (everywhere but Seaton) may indicate the presence of riding horses or pack ponies; more likely they housed plough horses, which in local practice were harnessed in tandem with oxen. The oxen themselves were tethered in stalls or shippons, while the dairy herd had sometimes been moved into cowhouses. A few farmers at Nettlecombe and Sherford provided separate housing for 'fatte oxen', which they were probably raising for a commercial meat market. At Seaton, too, stockmen built barns and shippons like their inland neighbours at Farway and Whitwell, but in the coastal fishing village small to middling leaseholders, not the larger farmers, needed stables. The difference may be accounted for by the fact that farming was a seasonal activity for those Seaton men who were primarily fishermen and artisans. Only the tenants of the largest pastures may have chosen not to diversify into by-employments requiring horses and stables.

The essential moorland farmstead rarely required more than a barn for winter feed and general storage of small arable crops and agricultural equipment. When sheep were not grazing on the moor, they could huddle in open folds, although sometimes they were provided with roofed shelter. Dairy farmers needed stalls and shippons to house their herds. All other buildings were optional, depending on whatever sidelines graziers found profitable.

Fen and marshland grazing

At lower, more temperate altitudes, pastoral farmers could engage in high volume, fast turnover, stock raising. Sometimes they required no buildings at all, not even barns. Their nearness to the stockyards at Bristol enabled small landholders living at East Brent (Figure 14: M) to drive their grass-fed steers to city markets before the winter rains flooded the pastures. They could manage with no permanent shelters whatsoever. However, even ranchers could use a barn, if only to store supplies of hay and bedding straw that came in handy in early spring before the grass was ready for grazing. Several stockmen at West Pennard (Figure 22: L) owned not a single stall or stable, yet fattened cattle in such numbers that they needed hayhouses or strawhouses as well as barns to store fodder. They probably sold most of their summer animals to butchers and victuallers at the end of the season, but any herds that were over-wintered on the open fenland pastures can have had no more than makeshift shelters to protect them during the coldest spells. Kingsbury's largest leaseholders appear also to have sold their animals on the autumn meat market, thereby eliminating all need for shelter buildings (Figure 22: K). In place of lean-to haylofts and strawhouses, they built large, six- and seven-bay barns, generally the only farm buildings they had.

The fenland farms that most resembled farmsteads elsewhere in the larger region belonged to dairymen and those who combined cow-keeping with small-scale arable farming. The surveyors of West Pennard and East Brent recorded stalls, stables, and oxhouses on approximately every third farmstead they listed. Such buildings were somewhat more frequent at Kingsbury, as could be expected on the fen borders. Permanent shelters made sense for saddle-horses, plough teams, and, most important, dairy cattle. Three or four long-houses, still in use in East Brent and West Pennard, preserved all that was left of an ancient cow-keeping tradition, by now rapidly giving way to specialised market farming.

No region better illustrates how different agricultural enterprises among near neighbours—ranching for some, dairying and cheese-making for others, and perhaps not a little arable farming for more fenmen than we can identify from the surveys—led to practical investment decisions that were visible in every farmyard in central Somerset. As elsewhere, barns were the fen and marshland grazier's usual first choice of buildings for fodder and grain storage, although here, unlike elsewhere, a stable, a stall, or a store-room occasionally took its place—or sometimes no building at all. The next most common structure was generally one to shelter over-wintered animals, an oxhouse, cowhouse, stall, or stable. These buildings served farmers' and stockmen's chief employments. But the watery world of the Somerset Levels also supported a profusion of supplementary activities augmenting the regional economy, from withy-collecting and basket-making to eel-fishing and cheese-making. Often workhouses, shelf-houses, storerooms, and lean-tos were added to barns and animal shelters, buildings as miscellaneous as the by-employments they sheltered.

Wood-pasture

The forested hills along Somerset's eastern border with Wiltshire and Dorset were home to a swarm of small leaseholders who eked out poor livings as part-time farmers and seasonal craftsmen and regularly exported surplus sons and daughters to North America through the port of Bristol. Settled in hamlets or on isolated farms in forest clearings, these woodland farmers seldom required even a barn. Their few dairy cows and small flocks of sheep foraged freely most of the summer. Lean-tos and makeshift shelters must have provided such protection for animals and for such stores of hay and straw as were needed during winter, if housing and storage buildings were lacking. Stables were nowhere commonplace, but they outnumbered barns. They were probably intended primarily for packhorses, used to transport woollen cloth, leather gloves, lacework, and cheeses produced by cottage artisans throughout the region. Theirs were home industries, their shops sometimes combined under the same roof with their dwellings. Occasionally a traveller through these hills would come upon homesteads with a separate tanhouse, wool-house, or workshop.

Probably more small-scale arable farming took place than can be discerned in the surveys. Only a few large landholders at Norton St. Philip, the one recorded estate in this part of Somerset, grew cultivated crops on a scale that required barns for small grains and storage fodder. Besides their large barns, these farmsteads in nucleated villages resembled those in other mixed farming regions where saddle and pack horses were kept in stables and cattle and oxen in stalls.

Later eighteenth-century pastoral farms

Even as early as the first decade of the seventeenth century, surveys of the estates closest to Bristol show that demand from that growing metropolis and overseas shipping centre was already offering inducements to enterprising countrymen who were willing to give up traditional farming practices in favour of specialised, high-volume, commercial production of meat, horses, and dairy products. A hundred years later such new opportunities caused farmsteads to be rebuilt throughout the whole region. Surveys of the Bedford estates in south Devon recorded fewer stables and shippons in 1709 than there had been a century earlier. They were fast being replaced by the animal shelter— the linhey—that became the characteristic south-western farm building in the eighteenth-century as dairymen increasingly turned to stock fattening. In a parallel development, more farmers were building field barns located some distance from the main farmstead, but convenient to the herds of cattle that ate the fodder stored there. Some quite large operators had learned that there were high profits to be earned in a low-overhead seasonal market for cattle that required no barns or stalls at all. The Bedford estate surveys also record a scattering of pound houses, suggesting that technical improvements in cider production equipped some enterprising Devon farmers to supply yet another demand for commercial agricultural products (Figure 22: N).

These changes were complete by the time Sidmouth was surveyed in 1764 (Figure 22: Q). Pound houses were numerous on the larger farms. The linhey had completely ousted the shippon, just as cattle fattening dominated the stockman's economy. Probably peculiar to Sidmouth itself was the fact that stables had become the most numerous farm buildings of all, partly because they had always been common on the smallest holdings in such seaside communities. It may also be true that horses had become the principal pack animals for transporting fish, garden produce, and craft-work for the inhabitants of a village that was growing into a real town.

All in all, West Country farmers engaged in forms of husbandry that required relatively few agricultural buildings and generally small ones at that. It is no surprise that today the surviving farmsteads of the region do not rival the splendid tithe barns and granaries of Essex, Sussex, or even nearby Bradford-upon-Avon, Wiltshire. Indeed, there is a paucity of historic farm buildings throughout Somerset, Devon, and Cornwall—and we know now that there always was. Even barns, common as they were in most parts of the Southwest, gave place to stables on some of the forest farms along the borderlands and not infrequently to stalls, storerooms, or occasionally, in the fens and marshes, to no buildings whatsoever. Only among arable farmers and moorland graziers were barns almost a necessity, for the one to store his unthreshed harvest and for the other his winter fodder. Otherwise most medium to larger farmsteads had barns, but they were not used consistently for the same purposes. As a general utility building, a West Country barn might hold crops, fodder, bedding straw, tools, workrooms for by-employments, and stalls for animals. It all depended on the neighbourhood and on a given farmer's mix of agricultural activities.

Besides barns, the other characteristic buildings were those used to house animals—stalls, stables, ox- and cowhouses (and later linheys). The surveys suggest that they were usually small, one or two bays. Many must have been inexpensively constructed, the best of cob or rubble and the less good of wattle and daub fixed to scrappy timber frames such as can still be seen here and there in central Somerset (Figure 18). As already noted, the few stalls or cowhouses listed in the Norton St. Phillip survey, together with the absence of folds in the surveys of the manors that occupy upland pasture lands known to have supported flocks of sheep, lend some weight to speculation that flimsy timber building traditions probably included forms of ephemeral, impermanent, maybe even earthfast construction suitable for seasonal animal shelters. Likewise, the lean-tos and workhouses in the fenland parishes suggest a widespread knowledge of jerry-building among farmers who skimped on farm buildings to invest their working capital in land and livestock and spend their earnings on dwellings and household furnishings.

Economic Opportunities Among Neighbours

Historians can discover important variations in farming systems from one region to another by close analysis of historical records such as these estate surveys. Three hundred years ago country people formed their own impressions of regional differences intuitively, from far-away farmers whom they met only infrequently at fairs and markets, from itinerant hired hands, from hearsay. John Aubrey, a Wiltshireman, was only repeating common lore when he described the forest dwellers on the borders of Somerset as 'slow and dull' and 'heavy of spirit'. He saw a familiar connection between economy and character: farmer-craftsmen from that 'dirty clayey country ... only milk cows and make cheese', he explained. No wonder 'they feed chiefly on milk meats, which cool their brains too much and hurts their inventions'.[16]

Villagers made similar personal judgements about their near neighbours. Every community had its haves and have-nots, its go-getters, its slackards, its innovators, and its 'olde stickes' (called such by the steward of Nettlecombe). It was common knowledge that so-and-so tilled the best bottom lands on the manor, or that one lucky man had inherited a barn and stable new-built by his father, or that another only leased enough acres to graze four cows. Such assessments provided the context in which everyone sized up his or her own position and future prospects. These intensely parochial considerations weighed in the balance when many men and women in the seventeenth-century had to choose either to remain at home and compete for the opportunities offered there or pull up stakes and seek their fortune elsewhere. Such local perceptions, such bodies of common knowledge, are usually beyond historians' powers to recover. At best the sources sometimes tell us whether a particular locality or industry experienced good times or bad. Individuals living there or engaged in those occupations are presumed to have assessed their opportunities accordingly.

House-and-estate surveys give historians a tool capable of greater magnification. With it we can examine particular villages and see how circumstances offered the inhabitants of one a variety of livings different from those available to other villagers in the same farming region. Just as it is a misleading oversimplification to characterise the West Country economy as purely pastoral, important evidence is overlooked if one assumes that its mixed agricultural activities were everywhere more or less the same. Men and women did migrate to other counties, towns, and colonies to escape poor harvests and depressed markets that affected whole regions, but just as often they responded to strictly local circumstances. When historians' sources of information permit particularly close examination of rural England, we are surprised to discover that the range of conditions and variety of choices were greater than we otherwise imagined. The surveys provide one of those rare close-up pictures of country life 300 years ago. Carefully studied, their village scenes begin to approximate the view a resident of one of these West Country estates had of his or her community.

The lens that brings this prospective into focus is the same set of tables used to study the characteristic farmsteads of each region, the ordered lists of leaseholders arranged seriatim by size of holding, from the smallest to the largest, on which farm buildings of similar function are observed to occur in clusters (Figure 22). The name given to each farm building implies a specific farming activity; a farmstead's buildings together indicate the sum of activities by which the leaseholder made his living; the number of acres he leased established his rank among his neighbours; and the fact that he and his immediate peers owned similar farm buildings and therefore must have farmed in similar ways becomes a rough and ready guide to the variety of agricultural pursuits open to men and women of different means in the same village. To put it in economists' terms, the tabulated surveys constitute a roster of village producers, grouped according to the resources—land and capital improvements—that each employed to make the best living he or she could afford.

Analysis of all twenty-two surveys would produce twenty-two sets of unique results. Inasmuch as our purpose in this introduction to the documents is to show other historians how the surveys may be used to measure the keen responsiveness of West Country farmers to market opportunities, a case study of two manors will serve as demonstration. We have chosen Kingsbury and West Pennard (Figure 22: K, L; Tables 26, 27) as our examples, because both lay within a two- or three-day walk from Bristol. Historians can doubtless invent many other uses for the detailed tables. Those for Kingsbury and West Pennard help to test the hypothesis that local circumstances in seventeenth-century England pushed some villagers to seek opportunities elsewhere and encouraged others to stay at home.

The farms at Kingsbury had much in common with those in West Pennard, fifteen miles away across the Somerset Levels. As we have seen, both manors were extensively engaged in fen pasture agriculture, West Pennard completely and Kingsbury in part. Kingsbury lay alongside Muchelney-Thorney Moor, but its southern boundary touched the Ham Hills and the edges of the wood pasture region. The social profiles of both manors were similar in that most farmers came from the middle ranks of village society (Figure 1: K, L). Those from West Pennard usually held ten to fifty acres; at Kingsbury the middle group included more smallholders of five to twenty acres.

Middling farmers in both communities were overwhelmingly stockmen. Smart cattlemen at West Pennard put relatively little money into buildings and more into larger leaseholds of pasture on the verdant Queen's Sedgemoor. Agatha Nashe (WP21) was typical of the villagers who held from ten to twenty-five acres. She lived in a three-bay house with adjoining orchard and garden and probably filled her two-bay barn with spring fodder and bedding straw for the cattle she grazed on sixteen acres of grasslands. Like all but five leaseholders in this group she had no stall or cowhouse to shelter her steers. Nor did she need one, for she undoubtedly sold the entire herd to drovers every autumn. Her cows were her principal profit every year, but like others in her circumstances she may have cut peat or woven baskets to make ends meet. That the storeroom incorporated in her barn was reserved for some necessary by-employment is indicated by the fact that most storerooms in the village adjoined barns belonging to the lesser leaseholders. Those with larger pastures than Agatha Nashe's were not so likely to bother with by-employments, at least not those that required storerooms. Just a few additional acres gave men like John Cooke (WP32) an advantage that he and others like him pursued by fattening greater numbers of cattle and building separate hayhouses to store supplies of feed consumed by the spring yearlings.

Arable farmers and perhaps dairymen and stock breeders were found among the wealthier middling farmers in West Pennard who held at least twenty acres and usually more than thirty. Their farmsteads came with a barn, a stable or stall (never both), and a structure (usually free-standing) for storing hay or straw. These tenants of approximately twenty to thirty-five acres practised a form of husbandry that required year-round shelter for cattle or horses, and sometimes separate buildings for surplus stores of hay and straw. It is tempting to identify this group of men and women as West Pennard's dairy farmers. If so, two of them at least probably stored cheeses in their shelfhouses, which, though fairly rare, cluster at this end of the list.

There were ranchers in this group too, stockmen with barns, but no buildings for housing animals. These men built no supplementary hayhouses, unlike their neighbours who leased somewhat larger holdings. Nor did they try to squeeze storerooms into their two- and three-bay barns in the manner of Agatha Nashe and her like. Perhaps careful tabulation reveals here an economy of scale. Some ranchers needed only a barn. The smallest operators found room in that building for by-employments as well. Slightly larger cattlemen built hayhouses (maybe quite cheaply) rather than enlarge their modest barns. Middle-sized ranchers had just that much more wealth to build barns that met all their needs for storage of hay and straw. Only those who occupied parcels larger than thirty-seven acres consistently needed largish barns and also separate hay or straw houses.

Typical of pastoral villages throughout the South-west, West Pennard had few cottagers at the bottom of society and still fewer large farmers at the top. Only twelve villagers leased fifty acres or more. With two exceptions, the largest landholders in West Pennard chose not to concentrate exclusively on fattening cattle. For men like John Rawlyns (WP58) the main opportunity lay in a combination of economic activities that took full advantage of their considerable assets. Rawlyns and two other large landholders sublet smaller parcels to poorer tenants. Rawlyns himself presumably lived in the large, seven-bay house on his fifty-nine acre leasehold. His farmstead contained a four-bay combination barn and stall, a straw house, and a cowhouse. The latter suggests that dairying was part of his business. The stall and barn combination, plus the separate straw house, may be evidence of either arable farming or over-wintered stock rearing. Some of Rawlyns's peers had stables rather than stalls, because either they ploughed with horses or ran horse farms. The presence of a few wainhouses on these larger holdings may be taken as further indication that the cultivation of marketable crops was only feasible for the most prosperous farmers on the manor. Yet even the good livings they made required a relatively modest investment in buildings. Only David Warren, the biggest landholder of all (WP68), owned the full complement of farm buildings common to arable farming regions, including, besides a barn containing oxstalls, a combination stable and cowhouse, and a dovecote above the kitchen. Fen pasture agriculture offered the most prosperous landholders in West Pennard attractive opportunities to speculate profitably in animals with a smaller investment in buildings than elsewhere.

The fens were excellent 'poor man's country' as well. Remarkably, no landless labourers lived in West Pennard. The smallest holdings were two to four acres, and only fifteen farmers on the manor leased fourteen acres or less. More than half of them were content with only their house. While some of the remainder may occasionally have worked for their neighbours as hired hands, six owned their own barns, two kept stables, four had stalls for cows, and here and there these smallholders had a work house, store room, or hay house. In other words, the dozen or so poorest villagers had access to the same opportunities that other men turned to good advantage. The grass was just as green in their smaller pastures, the only difference being that it fed fewer cows and horses. Their store rooms and work houses show that they were no strangers to the by-employments that might supply extra income and lift them into the ranks of the middling farmers.

The Kingsbury poor were remarkable in ways quite different from the smallholders of West Pennard. First of all, some on this estate shared in two pastoral economies, fen and forest. Fifteen were true cottagers in the sense that they leased less than a single acre; indeed, the surveyor described six of them as dwelling in 'cottages'. More to the point, in contrast to the smallholders of West Pennard, the twenty poorest inhabitants of Kingsbury owned between them no more than a single barn, one store house, a lean-to, and, if a miller's specialised buildings are added to the sum, a stable and a granary. The presence of so many cottagers and small leaseholders gives the social profile of Kingsbury (Figure 1: K) a superficial resemblance to other manors where arable farming employed significant numbers of rural labourers. Kingsbury too had farmers who raised grain in addition to other activities. Were these nearly landless men their hired hands?

Perhaps the cottage dwellers were. But the others lived in houses much too large to belong to mere labourers. The curious fact that many of Kingsbury's poor leased dwellings three and four bays long—one of seven bays was the sixth largest house in the parish!—clearly indicates that some of these smallholders engaged in lucrative activities that required no farm buildings. Some may have run summer cattle on the common marshes, buying yearlings late enough in the spring to avoid any need for hay, bedding straw, or a storage barn and selling all the fattened animals before the onset of winter. There is another possibility. John Luccocke (KB17) is identified in the survey as a tailor, a clue to the likelihood that others in his circumstances may have followed craftsmen's trades in the tradition of the wood-pasture region. Whatever the explanation, the 'poor' smallholders of Kingsbury appear not to have been impoverished.

The group of middling farmers, which bulks large in the social profile of Kingsbury, starts abruptly with a group of five small-scale cattlemen reminiscent of the small-holding ranchers of West Pennard. Most owned only a barn, presumably for the storage of spring fodder for cattle that were run on the Sedgemoors at the northern edge of the manor. Thomas Lye (KB24) and Robert Seagar (KB26) were also involved in side-lines of some sort that required separate storerooms, again reminiscent of the catch-all activities of typical smallholders in other fen-pasture villages. These five ranchers on leaseholds of only four and five acres strengthen the impression that graziers enjoyed the use of common pasturage on this manor.

Some others in the village owned only barns with no housing for animals, but they were uncharacteristic of the middling farmers generally. Leaseholders of six to thirteen acres engaged in husbandry that required stalling for cattle, probably dairy cows (for no one in Kingsbury owned a cowhouse). Usually the stall was combined under one roof with the barn. Conceivably they were ox stalls, and these were arable farmers. George Louche (KB48) and John Stokey (KB51) kept oxen in separate oxhouses, but otherwise had no stalls. On the other hand, the presence of only two wainhouses among this group of middling farmers (except a very large five-bay cart shed owned by the miller) suggests that the cultivation of arable crops was a modest undertaking for leaseholders of five to thirteen acres. The hay and straw houses on a few farmsteads of eight to nineteen acres may indicate that a middling farmer's best strategy was to enlarge his herd before he tried to put more acres to the plough.

To succeed at arable farming in Kingsbury a farmer had to lease at least fourteen acres—and acquire a team of horses, which were kept in a stable. Richard Prigg (KB58) was such a man. His farmstead, occupying seventeen acres, consisted of a five-bay dwelling, a similar size barn and stall, a small stable, a separate building for hay or straw, and a wainhouse. Such stables and cart sheds or wainhouses identify these leaseholders of fourteen to almost fifty acres as Kingsbury's successful cultivators. The only discernible difference among them appears to be their scale of operations. The larger ones grew more crops, which required bigger barns to store the harvest. They consistently built structures five and six bays long; their smaller leaseholding neighbours owned barns of only three and four bays.

Forty-plus acres was as large as an arable farm needed to be. Only two leaseholders held more, John Lavor (KB66) fifty-two acres and John Mallet (KB6) sixty-two. Significantly both were ranchers, their only farm buildings large barns. These were the cattle kings whose equal were to be found in other parishes in the fen pasture region.

The cases of Kingsbury and West Pennard show how easily new subjects of historical inquiry open up when historians can increase the magnifying power of their sources. Seen as one piece on a map of farming regions throughout the whole of England, the Southwest fits broadly into a highland economy of pastoral agriculture with pockets of mixed farming here and there. Closer inspection reveals significant differences from one sub-region to another—differences in the animals raised, the products they were raised for, the pastures on which they grazed, and the markets where they were sold. Documents that record sub-regional differences can answer questions that otherwise remain unanswered—and sometimes even unasked—by historians who paint only with broad brushes.

The house-and-estate surveys fit an even stronger lens to the historian's microscope. They may bring into focus only twenty-two estates in all of three counties, but within those communities they allow us to peer inside almost every leaseholder's farmhouse, to tally the buildings on every farmstead, and to record the range of agricultural activities in each of these localities. The surveys reveal what remains invisible in other documents. The sharpness of their picture invites historians to think up questions for the new information to answer.

The previous chapters have addressed historical problems from the surveys' corpus of information about dwellings, the social order, and finally farm buildings and the agriculture economy. By no means have we exhausted all the possibilities. Part II presents the documents themselves in transcripts and tables, so that other students of the region may use them for their own purposes. We believe they have application to an even wider world. Indeed the surveys initially came to the attention of one of us who was searching county record offices for documents that contained information about the everyday experiences of the thousands of young men and women from West Country villages who emigrated to North America and the Caribbean colonies in the seventeenth century. To ask how well or ill their rural English upbringing prepared them for the new lives they made overseas implies a comparison and requires an objective measure of the experience they left behind. The house-and-estate surveys reveal a larger part of this experience than has previously been available to historians.

[1] Larger barns do survive on big farms and estate home farms, but they are relatively much rarer in the south-west than in other parts of the country.

[2] None of the recorded examples seem to be earlier than the eighteenth century but their rarity makes for uncertainty. Uncharacteristically for the south-west, they were timber-framed structures. Their stone staddles were also used under hay or corn ricks, and are recorded much earlier (e.g. Inv. 54 of 1623 in M. Cash, *Devon Inventories of the Sixteenth and Seventeenth Centuries*, Devon and Cornwall Record Soc. NS11 (Torquay, 1966); numerical references are to the inventories as listed there.).

[3] Invs. 44, 55, 136, 196.

[4] Inv. 49. These 'mows' might stand in a special yard or 'mowhay', as in one or two of the Bedford estate farms in 1709. *Ag. Hist.* V(ii), 673.

[5] For example, Poltimore, Farway (Figure 21A, Plate VIIa). The identification here is confirmed by the presence of the water-powered nineteenth-century threshing machine in the larger barn.

[6] Inv. 54.

[7] N. W. Alcock, 'Devonshire Linheys: A Vernacular Tradition', *Trans. Devonshire Assoc.*, 95 (1963), 117; *Ag. Hist.* V, ii, 673.

[8] Inv. 55 (1623).

[9] The earliest surviving examples seem to be late in the century, though they cannot be closely dated.

[10] J. E. C. Peters, *Discovering Traditional Farm Buildings* (Princes Risborough, 1981), 73.

[11] As noted in Chapter 3, it was the cheese-press, rather than the cider press, that had its own 'wring-house', although one Seaton description (SA13) apparently equates the wring house and the pound house.

[12] Invs. 54, 227.

[13] William Marshall, *The Rural Economy of the West of England* (London, 1799), Vol. I, 224.

[14] N. W. Alcock and Nancy Cox, *Living and Working in Seventeenth Century England* (London, 2000), CD-ROM of Randle Holme, *Academy of Armory* (Chester, 1688), Book III, chapter 8, no. 119.

[15] The result was the same, whether this capital was applied to acquire a holding which already had a suitable stock of buildings, or to erect new housing. It was, of course, the value of the farm buildings which prompted the estate surveyor's interest in them.

[16] John Aubrey, 'Natural History of Wiltshire', Bodleian Library, Oxford, Ms. Aubr 1.f2. Quoted in Anthony Powell, *John Aubrey and His Friends* (London, 1948), 38-39.

Part II

The Villages and the Farms

CHAPTER 5

Introduction

The broader view of the South-Western peninsula, as we see it in the house-and-estate surveys, has been presented in Part I. In the sections of Part II we explore the villages one by one, considering the evidence of the surveys for the farmhouses and cottages, the farm buildings, and the agricultural economy. To set the scene, each part starts with a discussion of the topography of the village, its economic structure, and the ownership and history of the estate; this gives the context for the taking of the surveys, and sheds light on any peculiarities they may show. In order to suggest the character of the village, and the influence of settlement patterns on its social structure, each section is illustrated with a map.[1] These show as many as possible of the village and farm names of the surveys, as well as the parish and estate boundaries, and any other important features. Each part ends with a calendared text or an abstract of the corresponding survey.[2] The precise wordings of the descriptions in the more detailed surveys seem to convey, almost by innuendo, more about the nature of the farms than any ordered tabulation can retain. Each survey is introduced by a brief description of the individual features of its manuscript and text.

Editing Methods

The detailed surveys (other than those for the Crown Estates) are presented as calendars, with one typical entry (usually the first) given verbatim. Because of the differing information in each survey, the arrangement varies, but generally the words of the original are retained as far as possible, especially for the building descriptions. Marginal headings and sums are brought into the text, at the start or end of the relevant item, and marginal notes are usually given as footnotes. Punctuation and capitalisation have been modernised throughout; small scribal corrections and erasures are not noted, if they are clearly no more than slips of the pen. Latin is translated, and in headings and verbatim items is given in italics. Square brackets are used for explanatory notes and comments (both in italics), and to mark uncertain or illegible words; parentheses are used for additions to the text not in the original hand, and for a few other items, including the ages of 'lives'. Abbreviations are expanded when this is possible without doubt.

Most of the surveys contain lists of fields arranged in columns, with other columns including area, value per acre and total value. These have been rearranged into continuous text. When the surveyor gives detailed areas in acres, rods (4 rods = one acre) and perches (40 perches = one rod), these are put in the form A1-2-15 for one acre, two rods, fifteen perches, but when the number of acres only is given, this is retained as 1 ac., etc. Similarly, monetary values in pounds, shillings (20s = one pound) and pence (12d = one shilling) were used either for the rate per acre of a field, or its total value per annum; these have been recorded as R 0-6-0, for a rate of 6s per acre. V 2-15-6 for a total value of £2 15s. 6d. a year. Reference numbers have been added for each holding; original numbers in some of the surveys do not usually correspond precisely to these, and have been omitted.

All dates given by regnal year have been converted to modern calendar form; dates between 1 January and 25 March where the year is given explicitly in the text are shown as 1652[/3], etc.

The Crown Estates

The Crown estate surveys present rather different problems. Their treatment of land-holdings is not consistent, and often only the total acreage is given. A typical house description reads:

> *Domum mansionalis iiij spacias, horreum et stabulum iij spacias, gardinum, pomarium et curtilagium continentem per estimacionem ij acris*

The regular form and relative sparsity of the information makes a tabular presentation suitable. The holdings have been rearranged in order of ascending size, but the sequence number of each entry in the original text is given, so that reference back is possible. Then follow the number of bays in the main house (*domum mansionalis*), in other domestic buildings, and in farm buildings. Information about the landholding is condensed to just the total acreage, while details about rents, fines, trees, estimates of value, etc., have been omitted. Tenure was by copyhold, almost without exception.

[1] For most of these, it has been possible to find an eighteenth or early nineteenth-century original as a base, which has both made the location of farms easier, and avoided confusion from recent changes.

[2] Each entry has been given a key letter and number. The key letters are included in the list of surveys on p. xiii.

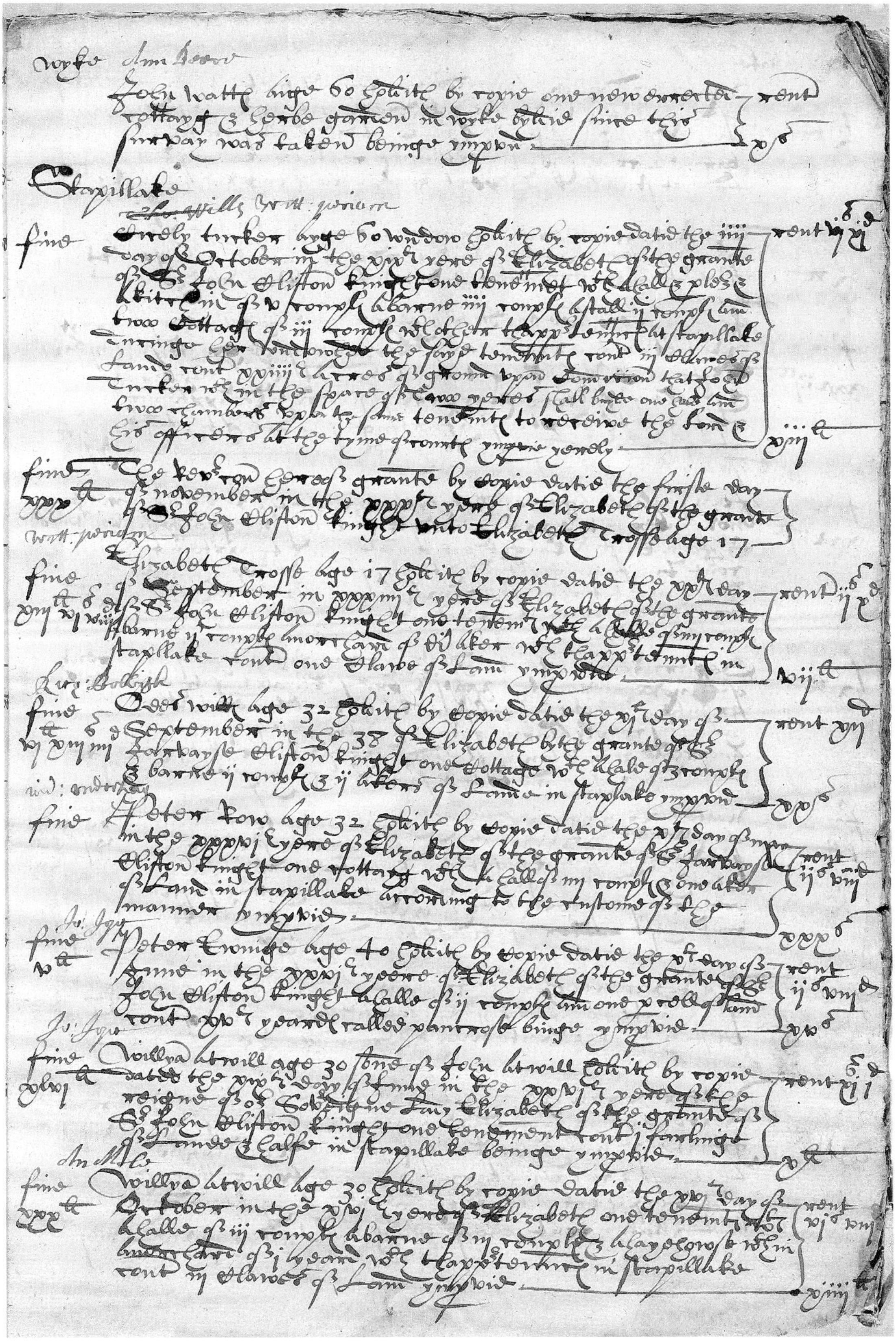

Figure 23. A page from the survey of Kenton, Devon, 1598 (K14-21) (D.R.O. 1508M/London Estate Vals/4, f.3, reproduced by kind permission of the Earl of Devon)

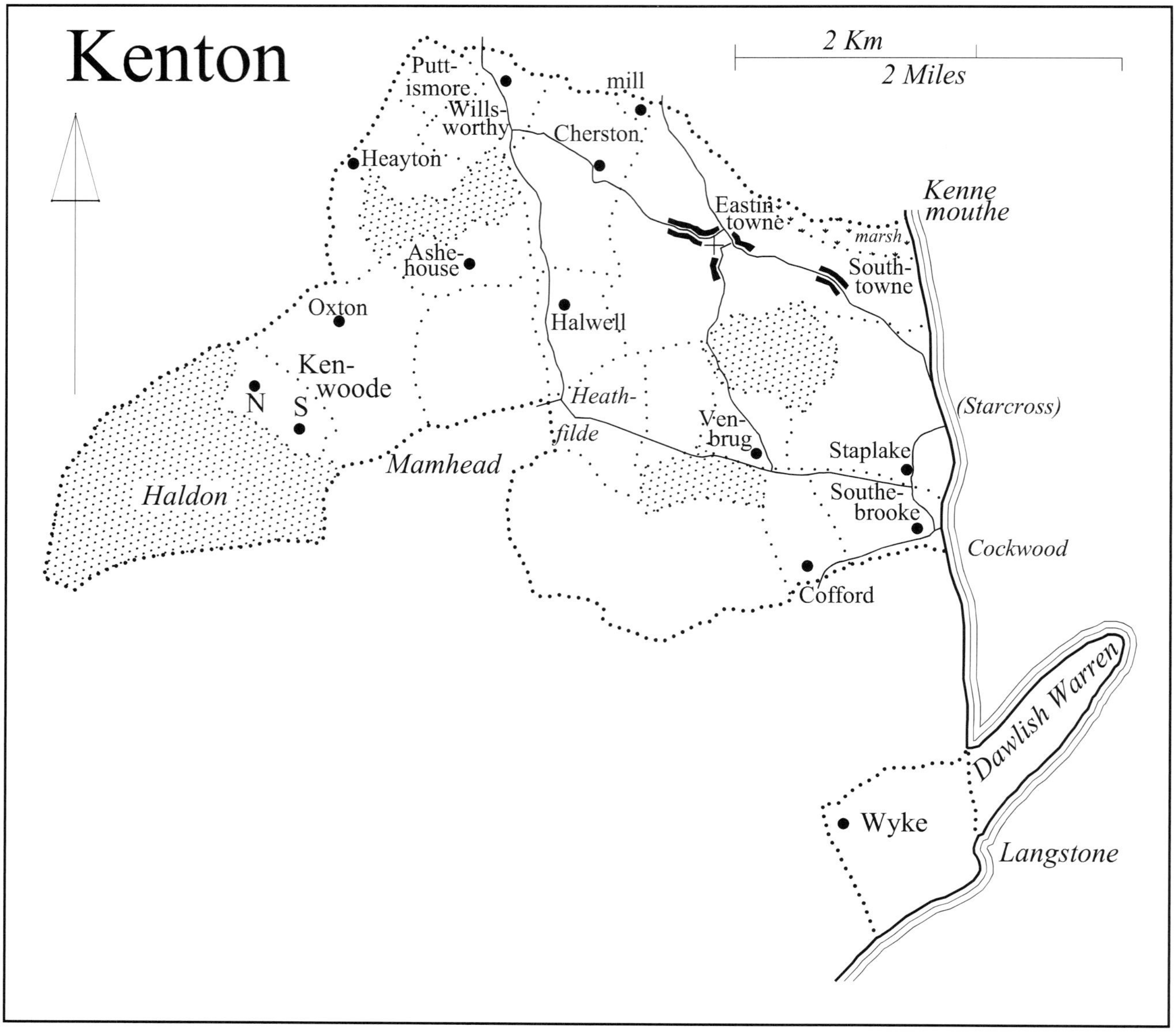

Map 1. Kenton Parish, Devon

This shows the portions of the manor and the centres of the hamlets named in the survey. Solid tone is used on this and the other maps to indicate the extent of nucleated settlements. Commons are stippled (parts being occasionally ploughed). In 1725, the strip-shaped fields were concentrated around the hamlets. Wyke was a detached part of Kenton Parish; Cutridge has not been located. Based on D.R.O. 1508M/Maps/Powderham 1 and on H.S.A. Fox, 'Outfield Cultivation in Devon and Cornwall: a Re-interpretation', in Husbandry and Marketing in the South-West, 1500-1800, *ed. M. Havinden, Exeter, 1973.*

CHAPTER 6

Kenton

Kenton (K): 1598 *Map 1*
Kenton lies on the Devon coast, on undulating land between the Haldon Hills and the Exe estuary. It is an area of good soil that was used largely for arable farming.[1] The survey has a number of distinctive features. Most obvious is the measurement of land in units of clawes and farthings (or farlings), as well as acres and yards (= perches) for small plots; a clawe was eight acres (K15), one quarter of a farthing, which had its normal Devon value of thirty-two acres. No fields were named, and the areas of holdings were recorded as round numbers or simple fractions of farthings. The reason for this is that Kenton retained strip fields until the seventeenth century, a great rarity in Devon where enclosure had normally taken place in the medieval period.[2] With each holding divided into numerous scattered strips, it was difficult to discover its exact area, and the figures in the survey were the traditional, or customary, estimates; a clawe known to be exceptionally large (twelve acres) was noted in K105. Although the true areas may have varied around the nominal values, the general pattern of holding sizes can be taken to be correct.[3]

As normally with open-field communities, the settlements were nucleated. Kenton itself was the main village, divided into Eastintowne and Southetown. The parish contained two smaller settlements, Staplake and Cofford, and several other hamlets. A considerable area of unimproved common pasture lay in the marshes (cf. after K134), while one piece of rough land, Heathfield, had recently been leased (K135-8). Kenton village lies about a mile from the Exe estuary, and the survey gives little evidence that its people had any interest in the Exe or the sea, apart from familiarity with the 'Humber barrel' (p. 78). However, work by H. Fox shows that this impression is misleading, indicating that the 1597 surveyor was more concerned with the agricultural than the maritime assets of the manor.[4] A somewhat earlier survey (1578) lists no less than 50 'cellars' at Starcross, on the bank of the Exe at the mouth of the Staplake Brook;[5] these are ignored in the present survey (apart from the cellar listed under K66). These cellars were mainly held by the village tenants with smaller holdings (up to 20 acres). Fox's study identifies the settlement as a classic example of a developing fishing village which, in the later sixteenth century was at an intermediate stage. Fishing was being carried on as a part-time occupation by the smaller farmers and they had put up permanent buildings for tackle and net storage. The following century was to see the final stage in the development of the settlement, conversion of the cellars to cottages and the separation of the fisher-folk and the farmers.[6]

Apart from the six free-holders (K1-6), tenure was almost entirely copyhold.[7] One unique entry (K15) shows a tenant made responsible for building a hall and two chambers on the holding, to be used by the lord and his officers when holding the manor courts (and presumably by the tenant at other times.) This holding presumably had a convenient location for this purpose, but the description shows no distinctive features. Another cottage (K120) was called 'The Lord's Doghouse', perhaps having been converted from the kennels.

The Houses
A total of 115 entries in the Kenton survey give details of houses, and although the descriptions are rudimentary, they give useful information, which can be treated quantitatively. The main item is the number of 'couples' in each building, and as discussed above (p. 35), this is equivalent to the number of 'bays' or main rooms. As well as couples, the simplest descriptions include only a 'hall', implying at face value one-roomed houses. This is clearly incorrect, because buildings described only as 'halls' typically have three couples (thirty-four examples), but range from one couple (K48, 52, 99, 125) to five (K12, 109); it is implausible that all these had one room only. Secondly, 'chambers' are only mentioned twice in the survey,

Table 7: Kenton: Dimensions of houses (couples)

House type	Acres	Couples								
		1	2	3	4	5	6	7	8	20
Cottages[a]	0–3	4	15	11	1	1				
Kitchens (of cottages)				1						
Second Cottages (single)		1[b]	5	2[b]						
(two cottages together)				2	4	1				
Second Houses (single)		1	2	1						
(two)			1[c]	1						
Houses of middle-sized holdings	4–31		5	17	8	7	5			
Kitchens				1		2	1			
Houses of larger holdings	32–160		4	16	8	5	5	1	1	1
Kitchens				1	2	3	1	1		

[a] *Excluding K145 (one cottage and two other houses), K141 (two little houses) and sixteen cottages of unstated size*

[b] *A three couple cottage and also a three couple cottage and a one couple cottage together (K109)*

[c] *Two little houses and a kitchen (K113)*

Notes: Kitchen bays are included with their houses. In the Table 5 summary, couples are equated to bays; second cottages and houses are included with the cottages.

both times because they were to be built by the tenant (K15, 64). It seems clear that the single mention in the first description (K7) of a 'hall and other rooms' should cover the other houses. Similarly, upper floors are not listed, but were surely present.

The most striking feature of the Kenton survey is the group of forty-eight small-holdings (up to three acres), whose houses are almost all described as 'cottages', in contrast to the 'house' or 'housing' of the larger buildings. About fifteen are not further described; the other houses had mainly two and three couples (fifteen and eleven examples), but included the four houses of one couple and one each with four and five couples (Table 7). For extra rooms, they had just one kitchen (K75), one shop (K116), and one 'little house' (K33). By comparison with the other surveys, the two and three couple cottages must have had a hall and one or two chambers, or one chamber with a buttery or dairy. Those of one couple most probably also had a chamber as well as a hall, but *over* rather than beside the hall.[8] An even more unusual group of small houses were the cottages that formed part of fifteen of the larger holdings (Table 7). Half of these were apparently semi-detached, named as two cottages in one block, with three (K15, 94), four (K70, 118, 151) or five couples (K65). These suggest that the nucleated Kenton villages, surrounded by open fields, had little space for new houses except on existing house plots. The large group of almost landless tenants was almost certainly a consequence of the arable economy of the village, providing employment for many labourers.

The period of the survey seems also to have been a time of rapid increase in this group; as shown both by the secondary cottages just mentioned and by the five 'newly erected' cottages, built between the taking of the survey and the writing of the fair copy (K14, 38-40, 81). Eight of the larger holdings had secondary buildings described as 'houses' rather than cottages (Table 7). These were not just service buildings for the farms, but were again separate dwellings; it would not otherwise have been necessary to describe one (K29) as being two houses. They must have been extremely cramped. K113 had 'two little houses and a kitchen' in its two couples.

The main buildings on the larger holdings (eight acres and over) were 'houses' rather than cottages. They ranged from two couples upwards, but show no correlation of house size with holding size (see Table 7. Overall, there were nine houses of two couples, thirty-three of three couples, sixteen of four, twelve of five, ten of six and one of seven couples. The village also included one house of eight couples (K57), a 'fair farmhouse' of twenty couples (K56), and a 'very convenient gentleman house with all other necessary housing' (K152).

For some houses, rooms other than the hall are named. Commonest were kitchens (twelve examples), but they were rivalled by the bakehouses (ten examples), concentrated on the largest holdings.[9] However, there was a significant distinction: eight of the bakehouses, but only four of the kitchens, were detached. The seven malt-houses and one brew-house were all separate. Only one house had more than one of these buildings (K96 with kitchen and brew-house), and so in practice their uses must have overlapped. One cellar is also recorded (K66), probably for fishing gear, while two houses had shops, i.e. workshops (K73 and 140, a smith's shop).

Six of the houses had parlours named as part of the main houses, in three cases combined with kitchens, and in one with a shop (K73). These were all smaller farms (sixteen to twenty-four acres), suggesting that other parlours may have been overlooked. The problem of how the parlours were distinguished from chambers is unsolved (cf. p. 33); it would be neatly explained by assuming that parlours were heated, and so were singled out with the kitchens. Unfortunately, there is nothing in the survey to confirm this suggestion, while the slight evidence of the inventories suggests that most parlours were still unheated at this date.

The Farm Buildings (Table 8)

Arable farming along the river Exe required stalls to house the oxen used as draught animals in the old-fashioned arable economy, and barns to store the harvest of unthreshed grain. Both were common in Kenton. Barns were found on seventy-nine holdings, virtually all those larger than three or four acres. Most were two and three bays long and none more than four, except when combined with other buildings. Nearly half were so combined, either with the stall, the dwelling, or occasionally a malthouse, stable, or hayhouse. Forty-six were free-standing.

Stalls were the next most common farm building, with thirty-eight recorded examples. They occurred intermittently on the smaller farms, but on almost all the holdings of sixty-four acres and upwards. They were modest buildings. Only for the six that were free-standing do we know the exact size, either one or two bays, but the rest must also have been small. Most were joined to barns; eleven were combined with the farmer's dwelling. Four of those (K23, 63, 93, 102) also included the barn and may only represent a convenient arrangement of house and adjoining farm buildings. Of the rest, four had only 'hall and stall' (K8, 9, 141, 150), one also a parlour (K45), another a kitchen (K26), and still another a bakehouse (K13). These seem too numerous to be accounted for by chance and probably represent a residual longhouse tradition. If the oxen ate hay, it may have been stored in unrecorded lofts over outbuildings, for only a few of the largest landholders owned hayhouses. On the other hand, meadows being at a premium in the Exe Valley, the ox teams may have fed on straw and cereal crops kept in the barns.

Pack horses were so rare in the flat country around Kenton that only three farmers needed stables. The absence of shippons similarly suggest a scarcity of herds, but deceptively perhaps, for stock may have been pastured year-round on the upland commons. It is surprising that not even the largest farmers built wainhouses, common in other arable regions. The explanation might be that corn merchants rode out from Exeter to make purchases farm by farm, and sent their own wagons later to transport the crop to market.

1 Cf. p. 5. It is described in H. S. A. Fox, 'Outfield Cultivation in Devon and Cornwall', in M. A. Havinden, ed, *Husbandry and Marketing in the Southwest, 1500-1800* (Exeter, 1973).

2 No formal enclosure took place, but strips were being exchanged actively in the sixteenth and seventeenth centuries, and they were then enclosed informally, leading to a confusion of small closes.

3 Another interesting feature of the survey is the boundary perambulation with which it starts; this follows a tradition extending back to the bounds of Anglo-Saxon charters.

4 Harold Fox, *The Evolution of the Fishing Village: Landscape and Society along the South Devon Coast, 1086-1550* (Leicester, 2001), esp. 115-122.

5 The name (Stercrosse in 1578) signifies a cross set up by the stair leading down to the beach landing place; this reference precedes by more than a century the first mention of the village identified in J. E. B. Gover, A. Mawer, and F. N. Stenton, *The Place-Names of Devon* (Cambridge, 1931-2), vol. II, 500.

6 See also p. 185.

7 Eight holdings carried notes 'beware of socage' (e.g., K62), presumably because this gave the tenant special rights. Socage is normally equivalent to freehold, but here probably implied copyhold tenure with right of inheritance rather than with the succession of tenants being at the lord's choice.

8 Compare the one-bay houses in the other surveys (p. xx).

9 In three cases (K140, 141, 146) called 'barkehouse', which could indicate a tanner's storehouse. This seems less likely than a scribal idiosyncracy.

Table 8: Kenton: Dimensions of farm buildings (couples)

Ms. Number	Acres	Barn	Stable	Stall	Hay House	Notes
K17	2	2				
K101	2½					
K116	3					
K19	3¾					
K16	8	2				
K22	8	2				
K49	8					
K62	8	=				hall + barn(5)
K66	8	=				hall + barn(3)
K67	8	=	=			barn + stable(2)
K86	8	=		=		barn + stall(3)
K102	8	=		=		hall + barn + stall(5)
K104	8	2				
K105	12	=		=		barn + stall(3)
K23	13	=		=		hall + barn + stall(6)
K26	16	=		=		hall + kitchen + stall(6); barn + cottage(3)
K31	16	3		=		malt-house + stall(3)
K32	16					
K47	16	2				
K54	16	2				
K60	16					
K68	16	2				
K69	16	=				hall + barn(4)
K71	16	=		2		hall + barn(4)
K72	16	2		2		
K73	16	2				
K87	16	=		=		barn + stall(2)
K95	16	=		=		barn + stall(3)
K97	16	1				
K98	16	=		=		barn + stall(3)
K103	16	2		1		
K114	16	=		=		barn + stall(3)
K115	16	2				
K118	16	2				
K121	16	=				hall + parlour + kitchen + barn(6)
K12	24	3				
K15	24	4		2		
K21	24	3			•	
K25	24	=		=		barn + stall + malthouse(3)
K35	24	4				
K53	24					
K61	24	3				
K63	24	=		=		hall + barn + stall(6)
K70	24	=		=		barn + stall(3)
K93	24	=		=		hall + barn + stall(6)

Table 8 *continued*

Ms. Number	Acres	Barn	Stable	Stall	Hay House	Notes
K111	31	2				
K7	32	=	=			barn + stable(5)
K9	32	2		=		hall + stall(4)
K10	32	=				hall + barn(4)
K27	32	3				
K29	32	3				
K43	32	2				
K44	32	=		=		barn + stall(3)
K45	32	2		=		hall + parlour + stall(5)
K46	32	2		1		
K50	32	=				hall + barn + malthouse(6)
K59	32	2		=		stall + other house(2)
K64	32	3	2			
K65	32	3				
K80	32	3				
K90	32	2				
K94	32	=		=		barn + stall(3)
K96	32	=		=		barn + stall(3)
K106	32	2				
K126	32	3				
K142	32	=		=		barn + stall(3)
K145	32	3				
K24	38	2				
K84	40	3				
K13	48	3		=		hall + barkehouse + stall(5)
K34	48	2				
K85	48	2		1		
K119	48					
K147	48	= =		=		two barns + stall(5)
K57	50					
K88	64	=		=		barn + stall(3)
K146	64	2		=		stall + barkehouse(4)
K151	64	3				
K144	72	=		=		barn + stall(4)
K150	72	4		=		hall + stall(5)
K8	80	4		=		hall + stall(5)
K148	88	3		=	=	stall + hayhouse(3)
K56	96					
K143	96	=		=	=	barn + stall + hayhouse(6)
K141	104	4		=		hall + stall(6)
K11	128	=		=		barn + stall(4)
K140	160	3=			=	barn + hayhouse(6); barkehouse(3)

Note: No farm buildings are listed for the 44 cottages with less than 1 acre.

Survey of Kenton: 1598 (Figure 23, p. 71)

(Devon Record Office, 1508M/London — Estate Vals./4; Courtenay muniments)

This paper volume is unpaginated but contains sixteen sheets; these are sewn together and were originally a gathering, but the right hand halves of each bifolium have been cut away. With them, the final one or two sheets of the text may have been lost, because the survey does not have a note on commons after its final section. Most of f.1 is torn away; if it carried an original title, this is missing, and this sheet has only a few later jottings of small disbursements; f.2r. now carries an eighteenth-century title, *Survey of the Manor of Kenton: 40th Q Eliz.* Apart from the initial damage and a few tattered edges, the manuscript is in good condition and easily legible. The court of survey was taken in September, 1598, but entries were clearly being added to and altered for some time afterwards, before this copy was written (cf. K14, 41).

K7 and 8 give the full form of the entries; in the calendared items the tenant's age is put in parentheses. Only K135-8 were held by lease, the remainder being copyhold, including the reversion; the words *by copy* are therefore omitted. The last entry of each description is the most uncertain. It reads *ymproved* or *being ymproved*, referring to a sum in the margin. This is taken to be the value per annum (most probably the potential value) and is given as V£10, etc.

All entries give the name of the grantor; these have been omitted, but can be found from Table 9.

Table 9: Names of grantors of Kenton copyholds

Name	Earliest Use	Latest Use
Richard Pollard, the King's Surveyor	9 Aug. 1542	(only K72)
Ralph, Earl of Westmoreland (d. 24 April 1549)	10 June 1545 (K9)	13 Aug. 1548 (K66, 146, 147)
Katheryn, Dowager Countess of Westmoreland (d. 14 May 1555)	30 Sept. 1553 (only K71)	
Henry, Earl of Westmoreland (d. 10 Feb. 1564)	15 Sept. 1547 (K93) (in error)	14 April 1556 (K144)
William Clifton, Esquire	4 April 1557 (K140)	20 June 1562 (K148)
Sir John Clifton	9 Oct. 1564 (K57)	13 May 1593 (K117)
Sir Jarvise Clifton	2 Oct. 1593 (K30, 51, 118)	Lord when the survey was taken

TEXT

The view and particular survey and terrear of Sir Jervaise Clifton, knight, of all the almanner messuages, landes, tenementes, cottages, milles, culver hous[es], and all other edifices and buildinges with all other meadowes, pastures and landes errable with feedinges, severally devided, togeather with all and almaner of woodes, underwoodes, hedgerowes, moores, marices, furses, heathes, comones, fishinges, watter courses, rentes and services, with all and almanner of liberties, royalties, comodities, emolumentes and profittes belongin and appertayninge to this manner of Kenton within the County of Devon, renovaty [*sic*], renewid and made by the othes [*oaths*] of all the tennantes there, and by Robarte Wadham, gentleman, surveyer of the manner aforesayd, taken the 20th day of September [*1598*].[1]

The perambulacion, precincte or envyronynge of this whole manner with the severall bounds and meares aboute the same, vewed and taken by Robarte Waddam, gentleman, surveyor their, accompanyed with the 12 men and other the customary tennantes of the same manner, that is to saye, Hugh Crosse, John Clogge, Thomas Geffer, John Edmonde, Robarte Spicer, Robart Hinde, John Farringdon, Henry Lucombe, Steven Lowe, Roger Phelpe, John Atwill, Willyam Atwill, Robarte Samson, John Pascew, John Thorne, John Healwill, Rychard Froste, Emanuell Lutton, Willyam Clarke, John Ewens, John Babbishe, John Lyell, [John] Gyles, Rychard Sealey and others, beinge all sw[orne] the 20th day of September [*1598*].

[1] Given as a regnal year.

Beginynge at Wyke bondes, at the watter of Shutterton Bridge adioyninge to the grounde of Peter Pyne in Dawlish, and from thence to the commone which [is] betweene John Thorne and John Clogge, which is an 160 akers, which lyeth full to the mayne seay, and so farder by Haldon bounes, begyninge from Mamhead Penne, where the forches stode, and so southe by the heapes of stones til yea come to the farther heape of stones upon the h[ill], and from thence stright west by a ditch untill ye come to the easte ende of Haldon Parke, to the farder side of [?the] watter wher standeth a holly tree, and from [? the said] tree northeweste to the highway which leadith to Garlandes Crosse, and from Garlandes Crosse a little farder to Perrymans thorne, and from thence eastwards to Haldon yeat, which leadeth to Heayton. The commone[2] of this and Haldon Parke belongeth to these three tenements, and enter commoners [*inter-commons*] with other lordes lands.

And so be Eastintowne and Westingtowne boundes, begyninge from Mabynes marshe to the water which cometh from Powderham milles, which dothe parte the landes of Sir Willyam Courtney from the mannor of Kenton, untill yee come to Kennemouthe Poynt, and so fourth by the watter untill yee come to Cockewoode Lake, and from thence upe to Cofford at Mr. Lutton' Bridge adioyninge to his grounde. The first common[3] from Mabbynes marshe to the brooke at Efforde belongeth to Eastingtowne, and from thence to Kenmouthe poynte the common[4] belongith to the tennantes of Southeintowne; the reste of the commone[5] from Kenmouthe to Budlake belongith to the tennantes of Staplake, and from Budlake all the commones[6] untill ye come to Studdelcome belongithe to the tennantes of Southebroucke, and from Southbrake [*sic*] untill ye come to Mr. Lutton' Bridge at Cofford belongith to the tennantes of Cofford.[7] And from the Poynte at Kennemouth right over Cuppie until yee come to the Rocke at Lymston, and from the Rocke of Limston dowewardes all Wonley, and from thence to Sheely and Littel Wonley, adioyninge to Sir Thomas Dennes Lande, and so forthe as farre as a man may see a Humber barrell, and so alonge Tingmouth bondes, beginyng from Tolewales wher the Lorde here to fore kepte aconnte to the Lady Brayes lande, and so to the Watter of Tanne, and thence Southest and by easte to Doggehill, and from Doggehill Southe-east and by east into the seay as farre as a man may see an Humber barrell, and so to the Passage Poynte, and the halfe deale of the channell to Tolewalles, by which lande the Lord of this manner hath of every shipene that douthe unlade salte their, twoo busselles, and of every small barke one bushell, and of every stranger that anckerith their 4d.

The Free Tennants

K1. Willyam Courteney, knight, holdithe freely certen landes and tennementes in Sheverston, alias Cherston, in the parishe and manner of Kenton, by the eight parte of a knight fee, and rent at the feaste of St. Mychell, and suite of courte twise by the yeere, rent 40s.

K2. Willyam Courteney, knight holdith a wattercourse unto the milles of Powdram, and payeth for the same yerely more rent 18d.

K3. Thomas Fulford, esquyer, holdith freely certen landes and tenements in Mutleigh and Melhuysh within the parish of Tetborne Mary, and within the mannor of Kenton, by the eight parte of a knightes fee, suit of courte twise in the yeere, and yerely rent of 10s.

K4. Willyam Clifton esquyer holdith certen landes and tenementes called Oxoton, within the manner of Kenton, by the eight parte of a knight fee, suite of courte twise by the yeere, and the yerely rent of 40s.

K5. Emanyell Lutton, gentleman, holdith certen landes within this maner by the ight parte of a knightes fee, sute of courte twise by the yeere, and the yeerely rent of 3s 4d.

K6. Willyam Harwood holdith freely certen landes within Willsworthy, within this manner of Kenton, by the eight parte of a knightes fee, suite of courte twise by the yeere, and the yerely rente of [*blank*].

The Customary Tennantes: Wyke

K7. Hugh Crosse, age 80, holdith by copie granted by William Clifton, esquire, datid the 30th day of May in the first yeere of Elizabeth [*1559*], one tenement with a hall with other roomes of 4 couples, a barne and a stable of 5 couples, and one farthinge of land with thappertanances in Wyke, except the woodes and underwoodes and Kenton Woode, ymproved [*value*] £10. Rent 10s 9½d.

Heriot 2s.[8] Fine £20. (1668 Mrs Hardon)[9]

K8.[10] John Clogge, age 65, holdithe by copye the 20th daye of September in the 33rd yere of Elizabeth [*1591*] of the grante of Sir John Clifton, knight, one tenement with a hall and stall of 3 couples, a barne of 4 couples, an orchard of one yerd with thappertenances, cont' one farthinge, and one farthing and one halfe of waste lande, beinge ymprovide [*value*] £13 6s 8d Rent 13s 6½d. Heriot 2s 6d. Fine £50. (Geo. Carpenter)

K9. Joane Pyne (90) holds during her widowhood, date 10 June 1545, one tenement with a hall and stalle, 4 couples, a barne of 2 couples, orchard of ½ yeard, 1 farthing of land,

2 There are marginal notes in this section (notes 2-7). The first is: *This common conteinyth 400 akers*, followed by the names of the three tenants: *Videlicett of Rychard Towill, Joane Kenwood, Jasper Towill.*

3 *Eastowne commones.*

4 *Southetowne commones.*

5 *Staplake commones.*

6 *Southebroucke commones.*

7 *Cofford commones.*

8 These sums and the *ymproved* value are in the right margin; the fine is in the left margin.

9 In the left margin; see p. 78.

10 This is a standard entry.

V £8, rent 9s 6½d, heriot 2s 6d, fine £6 13s 4d. (Widow Lamshed)

Reversion to Rychard Dunstable, alias Baker (36), date 3 Oct. 1596, fine £42.

K10. Robarte Spicer (42) holds, date 3 Nov. 1592, one tenement with a hall and barne 4 couples, a bakehouse of 1 couple, an orchard of 1 yerd, one farling of land, V £9, rent 9s 6½d, heriot 2s 6d, fine £34. (Tho. Coming)

K11. John Thorne (70) holds, date 1 April 1585, one tenement with a hall 3 couples, a stall and a barne with 4 couples, orchard of 1 yerd, and 4 farlings of land in Wyke and Pitt, V £30, rent 36s ½d, fine £23 6s 8d. (Grace Thorne) Reversion to Nycholas Thorne (40), his son, date 5 April 1585, fine £60.

K12. John Farringdon (67) holds, date 18 Feb. 1577, one tenement with a hale of 5 couples, a barne of 3 couples, a maltehouse of 2 couples, orchard of a yeard, 3 clawes of land, V £7, rent 7s 2d, fine 40s. (William Willcox)

K13. John Drew (36) holds, date 14 May 1593, one tenement with a halle and stalle and bakehowse of 5 couples, a barne of 3 couples, orchard of ½ acre, and a maultehowse of 3 couples, 1½ farling of land in Wyke, V £10, rent 11x 8d, fine £30.[11] (William Meadway)

K14.[12] John Watts (60) holds one new errected cottayg and herbe garden in Wyke, byldid since this survay was taken, V 10s rent [*blank*]. (Ann Beere)

Stapillake

K15. Cicely Tucker (60), widow, holds, date 4 Oct. 1577, one tenement with a hall and parler and a kitchin of 5 couples, a barne of 4 couples, a stall 2 couples, and twoo cottages of 3 couples with other thappertenances at Stapillake, during her widowhood; the said tenementes contain 3 clawes of land, 24 acres; consideration that John Tucker, within two years, shall buyld one hall and twoo chambers upon the same tenementes, to receive the lord and his officers at the tyme of courtes, V £13, rent 6s 11d, fine [*blank*]. (William Periam[13]) Reversion to Elizabeth Trosse (17), date 1 Nov. 1588, fine £30.

K16. Elizabeth Trosse (17), date 20 Sept. 1592, one tenement with a halle of 4 couples, a barne 2 couples, an orchard of ½ acre, in Stapllake, one clawe of land, V £7, rent 2s 10d, fine £13 6s. (William Periam)

K17. [?Odec'] Willes (32) holds, date 11 Sept. 1596, one cottage with a hale of 3 couples, a barne 2 couples and 2 acres of land in Staplake, V 20s, rent 12d, fine £6 13s 4d. (Richard Dolbish)

K18. Peter Row (32) holds, date 10 May 1594, one cottayg with a hall of 4 couples and 1 acre of land in Stapillake, according to the custome of the manner, V 30s, rent 2s 8d, fine [*blank*]. (Widow Underhay)

K19. Peter Ewinge (40) holds, date 10 June 1584, a halle of 2 couples and on percell of land containing 15 yeards called Pancrofte, V 15s, rent 2s 8d, fine £5. (Jo. Jope)

K20. Willyam Atwill (30), son of John Atwill, holds, date 19 June 1584, one tenement containing 1½ farlinge in Stapillake, V £10, rent 11s 1d, fine £46. (Jo. Jope)

K21. Willyam Atwill (30) holds, date 16 Oct, 1574, one tenement with a halle of 3 couples, a barne of 3 couples, and a hayhouse within an orchard of 1 yeard, 3 clawes of land in Stapillake, V £13, rent 6s 8d, fine £30. (An Mole)

K22. Margery Trulowe (90) holds, date 7 May 1565, one tenement with a hall of 3 couples, a barne 2 couples, 1 claw of land at Stapillake, except Kenton woodes, V £6, rent 2s 6½d, fine £10. (Rob Mole)

Reversion to Willyam Atwill (30), date 10 Oct. 1575, fine £10.

K23. John Pascew (60) holds, date 1 Nov. 1588, one tenement with a halle, barne and stalle of 6 couples, orchard of 1 yerd, third part of a farling and third part of one clawe of land, V £6, rent 3s 9d, fine £28. (Eman'[14] Hellwill)

K24. John Healwill (50) holds, date 5 Nov. 1588, one tenement, one farling and two partes [*two-thirds*] of one clawe of land, a halle, kittchin of 3 couples, barne of 2 couples, orchard of 1 yerd, V £9, rent 7s 8½d, fine £28. [Widow Hellwill)

K25. Geffery Rewe (40) holds, date 4 Nov. 1590, one tenement with a halle of 3 couples, a barne and stalle and maltehouse of 3 couples, an orchard and 3 clawes of land, except one cottaig and halfe and aker [*sic*] of land to the same, V £11, rent 5s, fine £10. (An Saymons)

K26. Walter Drew (65) holds, date 3 Nov. 1582, one tenement with a hale, kitchin and stall of sixe couples, a barne and cottag of 3 couples, orcharde of 3 yerdes, in Stapillake, ½ farling of land, V £14, rent 7s 5d, fine £50. (Widow ?Awnnan)[15]

Reversion to Willyam Drew (35), date [*blank*], fine £50.

K27. Walter Drew holds, date 4 Sept, 1561, one tenement with a hale of 3 couples, a barne 3 couples, two cottayges of 4 couples, orchard of 1 yerd, in Stapllake, 1 farlinge of land, V £14, rent 8s 10d, fine £25. (Thomas Walls)

K28. John Fowckes (46)[16] holds, date 13 Sept. 1594, one cottaige twoo couples, with one yerd of land to the same cottayg, V 20s, rent 2s 8d, fine £4.

K29. John Lacomb (26) holds, date 28 April 1596, one tenement with a halle of 3 couples, a barne 3 couples, with twoo other howses of 3 couples, all in decay, one farlinge of lande in Staplacke, V £6, rent 8s 8d, fine £120. (John ?Bond)

[11] There is an almost illegible original note, perhaps *terre [?do] mine*.

[12] In original hand.

[13] *Thomas Wills*, erased.

[14] *Widow*, erased.

[15] *Robert Cragg*, erased.

[16] An original note: *Andrew Venard, tenent of this cottage, ut alter pagin'* [i.e. K37].

K30. Rychard Cooke (40) holds, date 2 Oct. 1593, one cottage with a hall with 3 couples, and ½ acre of land to the annixd, in Staplake, V 15s, rent 2s, fine £6. (Chris Towly)

K31. John Lackington (56) holds, date 2 Sept. 1574, one tenement with a hall and parler of 5 couples, a barne 3 couples, a maulte howse and stall 3 couples, orchard of 1 yerd, ½ farling of land in Staplake, except Kenton woodes, V £16, rent 12s 1½d, fine £50. (Thomas Mery)

K32. Anthoney Blackestone (50) holds, date 30 March 1579, one tenement with a hall, kitchin, parler 4 couples, orchard of 1 yerd, ½ farling of land, V £16, rent 7s 6d, fine £40. (David Croppe[17])

K33. John Shapley junior (40) holds, date 4 Oct. 1591, one cottayge with 2 couples, a littell howse, an orchard of 1 yerd, with halfe a rode of land to the same in Staplake, V 10s, rent 2s 8d, fine £6. (Richard Lux)

K34. Baldwin Allynge (60) holds, date 11 Dec. 1576, one tenement with a hall of 3 couples, barne 2 couples, a kitchin 2 couples, all in decay, 1½ farling of land, V £8, rent 11s 2½d, fine £93 6s 8d. (Geo. Alling)

K35. Baldwin Allynge (60) holds, date 4 Oct. 1591, one tenement with a hall of 4 couples, a barne of 4 couples, a garden of 1 yerd, 3 clawes of land, V £10, rent 6s 9½d, fine £50. (Thomas Wills)

K36. Nycholas Crammer (30) holds, date 3 Oct. 1595, one cottage having 2 couples and one acre of land to the same belonging, V 20s, rent 16d, fine £4. (Thomas Moale)

K37.[18] Andrew Venard (50) holds, date 11 Oct, 1598, one cottage with one yeard of ground, late in the tenure of John Foukes, V 12s, rent 2s 8d, fine [*blank*]. (William Wotton)

K38. Agnes Morrish (35) holds one new errected cottaig since this survaye, and one acre of land to it now belongin, V 30s, rent 2s 8d, fine [*blank*].

K39. Nicholas Sealy (16) holds by copy one new erected cottayge since this survay and one rode of land to it now belongin, V 15s, rent 2s 8d, fine [*blank*].

K40. Anthoney Lange (30) holds by copie one new errected cottaige and herbe garden granted since this survay, V 20s, rent 4s. (William Bolster)

Stapillake Comones: Memorandum that all the comones from Kenmouth Poynte to Budlake belongith to the tennants of Stapillake, as before in the perambulation is mencioned and declared.

Cofford

K41. Cicely Tucker (60) holds, date 28 April, 1589, one cottaige with a hall of 3 couples, garden and orchard of 1 yeard and ½ acre of land in Cofford, V 16s, rent 2s 8d, fine [*blank*].[19]

K42. Roger Phelpe (43) holds, date 11 Dec.[20] 1583, one cottage with a hall of 2 couples, orchard and garden of ½ yeard, and one close of land in Cofford, V 20s, rent 2s 8d, fine [*blank*]. (William Cassely)

K43. Rychard Froste (40) holds, date 3 Nov. 1591, one tenenent with a hall of 2 couples, a barne 2 couples, and a cottage of 2 couples, orchard and garden of ½ acre, one farling of land in Cofford, V £8, rent 8s 4½d, fine £60. (Widow Bussell)

K44. Rychard Froste (40) holds, date 3 Nov. 1591, one tenement with a hall and kitchen with 4 coupls, a barn and stall 3 couples, to litell howses with a kitchin of 2 coples, one cottayge of 2 coples, orchard and garden of 1 yerd, 1 farling of land in Cofford, V £8, rent 8s 4½d, fine £60 and one barrel of red wine.[21] (Widow Bussell)

K45. Rychard Sealey (27) holds, date 20 July 1573, one tenement with a halle, parler and stall of 5 couples, a barne with 2 couples, 1 farling of land in Cofford, except Kenton woode, V £8, rent 8s 4½d, fine £49. (Stephen Low)

K46. Rychard Cheese (24) holds, date 11 May 1594, one tenement with a hall of 4 couples, a barne of 2 couples, a stall 1 coupl, orchard and garden of 1 yerd, 1 farling of land in Cofford, V £8, rent 8s 4 1.2d, fine [*blank*]. (Thomas Underhay)

K47. John Burgen (28) holds, date 6 Nov.[22] 1593, one tenement with a hall of 3 couples, a barne 2 couples in decay, orchard and garden of 1 yeard, ½ farling of land, V £5, rent 4s, fine £31. (Elizabeth Drew)

K48. Christoper Philpe (35) holds, date 4 Oct. 1591, one cottaige with a hall of 1 couple, orchard and garden and one rode of lande in Cofford, V 20[s], rent 2s, fine 53s 4d. ([*blank*] Phillpe)

K49. John Fowckes (?46) holds, date 11 May 1594, one tenement, 1 clawe of land in Cofford, howsinge of 5 couples, orchard and garden one yeard, V 53s 4d, rent 3s 2d, fine £16. (?Alce Card)

K50. Geffery Rewe (39) holds, date 10 May 1596, one tenement with a hall, a barne and maltehowse of sixe couples in decay, one howse of to couples, orchard and garden of 2 yeard, 1 farling of land in Cofford, V £8, rent 8s 4½d, fine £40. (An Saymons)

K51. John Langmead (30) holds, date 2 Oct. 1593, one cottag with a hall of 3 couples in decay, and 1 yerd of land, orchard and garden of ½ yerd in Cofford, V 13s 4d, rent 2s 8d, fine £5. (Ja. Hollman)

K52. Margery Perry (22), spinster, holds, date 10 May 1596, one cottaige with a hall of 1 couple and tenne yeards of land, orchard and garden, to herself and to her next marryer, in Cofford, V 12s, rent 2s 8d, fine 40s. (George Browne)

---

[17] *Widow Wanard*, erased.

[18] Cf. K28.

[19] This whole entry is erased, and there is an original note: *Note that Thomas Faremouth hath this cott'* [i.e. K55].

[20] *April*, erased.

[21] *Ultra unum dolum vini rubri*.

[22] *May*, erased.

K53. Phillipe Thorne (36) holds, date 11 May 1594, one tenement, 3 clawes of land in Cofford, a howse of 4 couples, orchard and garden of ½ acre, V £5, rent 6s 4½d, fine £25. (Robert Pulling)

K54. Willyam Clarke (30) holds by copy made to Anne Yeard and to her next marryer, date 4 Nov. 1591, one tenement with a hall of 3 couples, a barne of 2 couples, orchard and garden of ½ yeard, ½ farling of land in Cofford, V £5, rent 4s 4d, fine £26 13s 4d. (John Northamme)

K55. Thomas Fayremouth (34) holds, date 11 Oct. 1598, one cottage, late in the tenure of Cicely Tucker widdow, lying in Cofford, V 20s, rent 2s 8d, fine £3.[23] (Stephen Shurton)

Cofford Commones: Memorandum that all the commones from Southbroucke untill ye come to Mr. Lutton' Bridge belongith to the tennantes of Cofford, as in the perambulation of this manner before is declared.

Cutridge

K56. Thomas Jeffery (47) holds, date 9 Sept. 1574, one tenement, 3 farlinges of land, with a fairr farmehowse of 20 couples, orchard and garden 1 acre, V £30, rent 6s 8d, fine £160.

Reversion to Thomas Jeffery (12), son of the said Thomas date 11 Oct. 1596, fine £70.

K57. John Edmonde (84) holds, date 9 Oct. 1564, one tenement, [?50] acres of ground, one howse of 8 couples, orchard and garden ½ acre, V £12, rent 3s 11d, fine £13 6s 8d.

Reversion to Willyam Jeffery (7), son of Thomas Jeffery, date 11 Oct. 1596, fine £60.

K58. The Lady Margarett Denyes holdith 30 acres of land during her widdohood, payinge yerely rent 12d, V £5.

Eastintowne

K59. Robarte Hine (40) holds, date 4 Nov. 1590, one tenement with a hall 3 couples, barne 2 couples, stall and another howse 2 couples, a cottaig of 2 couples, orchard and garden ½ acre, 1 farling of land, V £12, rent 8s 7½d, fine £30. (William Lux)

K60. Thomas Hutchins (64) holds, date 11 Sept. 1564, one tenement with a dwelling howse of 5 couples, kitchin 2 couples and a maultehowse of 2 couples, orchard and garden a yerd, ½ farling of land in Eastintowne, V £7, rent 3s 8½d, fine £18. (Widow Clarke)

K61. Willyam Rorcke (66) holds, date 14 Sept. 1594, one tenement with a hall 3 couples, a barne 3 couples, orchard and garden of 1 yerd, 3 clawes of land in Eastintown, V £9, rent 8s 2d, fine £32. (Widow Downe)

K62. Robarte Wenarde (50) holds, date 3 Nov. 1592, one tenement with a hall and barne of 5 couples, orchard and garden of 1 yerd, 1 clawe of land and one percell of lande in Eastintown, V £6, rent 2s 11d, fine £6.[24] (Jo. Vennard)

[23] A note refers back to the earlier entry (K41).

[24] Note: *Beware of sockige*.

K63. John Wise (34) holds, date 1 Oct. 1584, one tenement with a hale, barne and stall of 6 couples, orchard and garden ½ acre, 3 clawes of land, V £10, rent 8s 2¾d, fine £40. (Jo. Hooper)

K64. Nycholas Lucombe (48) holds, date 3 Nov. 1592, one tenement with a hall 3 couples, a kitchin 2 couples, a barne 3 couples, a stable 2 couples, one garden and orchard 1 yeard, 1 farlinge of land in Eastintowne. The said Nycholas by covenante at his cost and charge, shall prepare in the sayd tenement two chambers and stable rome for six horses with strawe and litter, during his owne lyfe and his widowes estate, and 3 beddes, V £10, rent 10s 6¼d, fine £76. (Thomas Jope)

K65. Joane Hollyes (60), widow, holds, date 23 Nov. 1558, one tenement with a hall 4 couples, a barne 3 couples, 2 cottaygs of 5 couples, a maulte howse of 2 couples, orchard and garden ½ acre, 1 farling of land, V £10, rent 8s 7½d, fine £34. (Thomas Russell)

Reversion to John Cowse, deceased, and the fine not all payed, fine £35, payd 17s 10s.[25]

Reversion re-granted to Rychard Hollies (20), date 22 Oct. 1598, fine £54.

K66. Margery Borro (50), widow, holds, date 13 Aug. 1548, one tenement with a halle and barne of 3 couples, orchard and garden 1 yeard, one seller, 1 clawe of land in Eastintowne, £4, rent 2s 6d, fine 53s 4d. (William Drayson)

Reversion to William Towill (33), date 30 Mar. 1579, fine £13 6s 8d.

K67. Richard Bricknall (50) holds, date 7 Oct. 1583, one tenement with a hall of 2 couples, a barne and stable of 2 couples, orchard and garden 1 yerd, 1 clawe of land in Eastintowne, V £5, rent 2s 6d, fine £10. (La. Bricknall)

K68. Robarte Searle (62) holds, date 18 April 1569, one tenement with a hall of 4 couples, a barne 2 couples, orchard and garden ½ acre, ½ farling of land in Eastintowne, V £7, rent 4s 5½d, fine £32. (Widow Ewing)

Reversion to John Dier, date [*blank*], fine [*blank*].

K69. Rychard Wise (66) holds, date 11 May 1594, one tenement with a hall, and barne of 4 couples, orchard and garden 1 yerd, ½ farling of land in Eastintowne, V £7, rent 6s ¼d, fine £52. (Henry ?Dar)

K70. Joane Downe (54), widow, sokewoman, holds during her life, one tenement with a hall of 3 couples, a barne and stall of 3 couples, two cottayges of 4 couples, orchard and gardin 1 acre, 3 clawes of land in Eastintowne. The issue of the sayd Joane Downe is not to have it for that shee marryed to a stranger that was no sockeman. V £8, rent 8s 1¾d, Sockage. (Widow Cunett)

K71. Cicely Bremellcombe (50), widow, holds, date 30 Sept. 1553, one tenement with a hall and barne 4 couples, a stall 2 couples, orchard and garden 1 yerd, ½ farling of land in Eastintowne, V £7, rent 4s 5½d, fine £4. (George Wills)

[25] Perhaps in error for £17 10s.

Reversion to Stevon Frier, fine £30.

K72. Agnes Mathew (68) holds, date 9 Aug 1542, one tenement having a hall of 3 couples, a barne 2 couples, a stall 2 couples, orchard and garden 1 yeard, ½ farlinge of land in Eastintowne, V £7, rent 10s 1¼d, fine £6 13s 4d. (... Wills)

K73. Robarte Parker (30) holds, date 5 July 1585, one tenement with a hall and parler and shope of 4 couples, a barne 2 couples, one other howse 1 couple, orchard and garden ½ acre, ½ farling of land, 1 acre of land in Cowton, V £8, rent 6s 10½d, fine £35.[26] (William Parker)

K74. John Lome (28) holds, date 28 April 1596, one tenement with a hall of 2 couples, orchard and garden ½ yeard, one close of lande called Browneshay ½ acre, in Eastintowne, V 20s, rent 4s, fine £5. (Robert Weston)

K75. Robarte Payne (60) holds, date 13 Sept. 1594, one cottayg with a hall and kitchin of 3 couples, with a garden and orchard in Eastintowne, V 20s, rent 5d, fine £20. (Widow Stone)

K76. Thomas Russell (26) holds, date 1 Nov. 1588, one howse with a hall of 2 couples, orchard and garden ½ yeard in Eastintowne, called the stable, and 4 yeards of land annexid to the foresayd howse, V 30s, rent 2s, fine 20s. (Thomas Russell)[27]

K77. Willyam Raffe (30) holds, date 14 April 1597, one cottaige with a hall of 2 couples, garden and orchard 1 yeard, ½ acre of land in Eastintowne, V 30s, rent 4s, fine £3. (William Craner)

K78. John Colwill (56) holds, date 33 [*sic*] Sept. 1596, one tenement and 1 farlinge of land, 32 acres, in Eastintowne, with 5 couples, V £10, rent 8s 6¼d, fine £30. (Edward Dolling)

K79. Alice Westebrooke (60) holds, date 3 Mar. 1591, one cottayg of 2 couples, orchard and garden ½ yeard, and a parcell of land 4 rodes, at Eastintowne, East end, V 10s, rent 3s 4d. (George King)

K80. Margery Easton (60), widow and sokewoman, holds during her life, one tenement with a hall of 3 couples, a cottayg of 3 couples, and a barne with 3 couples, a littell cottayge of 1 couple, orchard and garden 3 yerds, 1 farling of land in Eastingtowne, V £10, rent 8s 9¼d, socage. (Thomas Thore)

K81. George Shutlock holds one cottayg and hearbe garden, latly erected, V 20s, rent 12d. (?Liz Bayly)

K82. Robarte Giles holds one cottayge and littell orchard and herbe garden, lately surrendered out of the tenement now John Lowes.[28] V 40s, rent 4s, fine £32. (William Bastard)

[26] Note: *Beware of sockaige*.

[27] *George Wills*, erased.

[28] Presumably K74 (John Lome).

K83. Willyam Teage holds certayne grounde, 5 acres or theirabout, lying at Wowerlande, lately surrendered out of the tenement of Humfery Towill, and a new rent 4s, V 30s, fine £6. (William Balsler)

Eastintowne Comones: Memorandum that the firste comones from Malbyns Marshe to the broucke at Efford belongith to the tennantes of Eastintown, as before in the Perambulacion of this mannor is expressed.

Venbrug[29]

K84. Henry Lucombe (50) holds, date 25 May 1573, one tenement with a dwellinge howse with 2 couples, barne 3 couples, kitchin 3 couples, garden and orchard ½ acre, 1 farling and 1 claw of land in Cofford, V £10, rent 11s, fine £64. (William Pulling)

K85. Steven Lowe (40) holds, date 2 Oct. 1590, one tenement with a dwelling howse of 3 couples, barne 2 couples, stall 1 couple, orchard and garden, 1½ ferlinge of land, V £9, rent 13s 2d, fine £64. (Thomas Underhay)

K86. Christian Hillyng (60), widow, holds during her widowhood only, date 24 Mar. 1574, one tenement with a dwelling howse 2 couples, barne and stalle 3 couples, garden and orchard 1 yeard, 1 clawe of land, V £5, rent 2s 8d, fine £12. (William Pulling)

K87. John Bobbishe (50) holds, date 4 Oct[30] 1574, one tenement with a dwelling howse of 2 couples, barne and stall 3 couples, a bakehowse 1 couple, ½ farling of land, V £7, rent 2s 8d, fine £30. (Richard Wills)[31]

K88. Robarte Clement (30) holds, date 4 Nov. 1594, one tenement with a dwelling howse of 2 couples, barne and stalle of 3 couples, bachowse 1 couple, orchard and garden ½ acre, 2 farling of land in Hallwill, V £10, rent 16s 9d, fine £20.[32] (John Clement)

K89. John Callow (46) holds, date 4 Nov. 1586, one cottaige with an orchard and garden and 2 acres of land in Kenton Woode, V 30s, rent 4s, fine 53s 4d.[33] (John Gentle)

K90. Thomas Streete (60) holds, date 4 Sept. 1585, one tenement with a dwelling howse with 2 couples, a barne of 2 couples, garden and orchard 1 yeard, ½ farling of land in Venbridge, V £5, rent 4s, fine nil. (Jane Whitman)

K91. Francies Allynge (36) holds, date 3 Nov. 1592, one tenement, 1½ farlinge in Southebeere, V £9, rent 13s 8d, fine £64. (John Whitcom)

Reversion of Christian Hillynge tenement[34] to John Shont (22), date 11 Oct. 1596, fine £20. This tenement hath 1 clawe of land in Venbridge.

[29] Also Venbridge in the headings of later pages.

[30] *November*, erased.

[31] ... *Pulling*, erased.

[32] Note: *Beware of sockaige*.

[33] Note: *Beware of sockaige*.

[34] I.e. K86.

Southebrooke

K92. Jerman Tege (50) holds, date 1 Nov. 1595, one cottage with a halle of 3 couples, orchard and garden ½ yeard, 3 yeards of land, V 20s, rent 3s 4d, fine £8. (?Rich. Henson)

Reversion supposed to be granted to Nycholas Wills (8), date 4 Nov. 1596, fine £4.

K93. Marryon Samson (60), widow, holds, date 1 Sept. 1547, one tenement with a hall, barne and stall of 6 couples, orchard and garden, 3 clawes of land, 24 acres, V £6, rent 6s 6d, fine £9. (Widow[35] Wills)

Reversion to Robarte Sampson (30), date 4 Nov. 1596, fine £30.

K94. Robarte Sealey (40) holds, date 21 July 1572, one tenement with a halle with 3 couples, a barne and stall 3 couples, two cottayges of 3 couples, orchard and garden well fruited, 1 farlinge of land in Southebrouck, V £10, rent 8s 7½d, fine £30. (Robert Crappe)

K95. Willyam Skorche (66) holds, date 22 April 1561, one tenement with a hall of 3 couples, a barne and stall of 3 couples, with an other howse of 3 couples, orchard and garden 1 yerd, ½ farling of land in Southebroucke, V £6, rent 4s 5¼d, fine £17. (Jo. Bobbysh)[36]

K96. John Rewe (27) holds, date 3 Nov. 1587, one tenement with a hall and kitchin of 4 couples, a barne and stall 3 couples, a brewehowse of 4 couples, orchard and garden 1 yeard, 1 farling of land, V £10, rent 8s 7d, fine £16.[37] (Jo. Rowe)

K97. The same John Rewe holds, date 4 Oct. 1590, one tenement with a hale of 3 couples, a barne 1 couple, all in decay, orchard and garden ½ yeard, ½ farling of land in Southebroucke, V £6, rent 4s 5d, fine £30. (Jo. R[?ewe])

K98. Willyam Drew (35) holds, date 2 Oct. 1590, one tenement with a hall of 3 couples, a barne and stall 3 couples, orchard and garden ½ acre, ½ farling of land in Southebrooke, V £6, rent 4s 5¼d, fine £45. (Thomas Wills)

K99. Thomas Willes (35) holds, date 4 Nov. 1586, one cottaig with a hall of 1 coupl, orchard and garden ½ yerd, V 13s 4d, rent 16d, fine 40s. (Thomas Helley)

K100. Robarte Sampson (50) holds, date 18 June[38] 1583, one tenement with 3 couples, orchard and garden ½ acre, one parcell of land ½ acre, V 20s, rent 3s 4d, fine 40s. (Ja. ?Pigte)

Southebrooke Commones: Memorandum that from Budlake, all the the comons untill yee come to Studdlecome belongyith to the tennantes of Southebrooke, as it is in the perambulacion of this manner before expresste.

[35] *Nicholas*, erased. Either the grantor, or the date of grant of this tenement must be wrong, (see p. 78).

[36] *Widow Wills*, erased.

[37] Note: *Beware of sockaige*.

[38] *January*, erased.

Southetowne[39]

K101. Moryce Danyell (60) holds, date 8 Aug. 1580, one cottaige with a hall 3 couples, orchard and garden 1 yeard, 1 acre of land in Bonhay, one other acre and 1 yeard of land, V £3, rent 3s 4d, fine 40s. (Jam. Clarke)

K102. John Mediate (50) holds, date 5 April 1585, one tenement with a halle, barne and stall of 5 couples, orchard and garden, 1 clawe of land, V £3 6s 8d, rent 2s, fine £26 13s 4d.

K103. John Ewinge (50) holds, date 8 Oct. 1586, one tenement with a hall of 3 couples, a barn 2 couples, a stall 1 couple, orchard and garden 1 yeard, ½ farlinge of land in Southeintowne, V £8, rent 4s 7½d, fine £30.

K104. John Gyles (50) holds, date 15 Mar. 1559, one tenement with a hall of 3 couples, a barne of 2 couples, orchard and garden 1 yeard, 1 clawe of land, V £5, rent 2s 8d, fine £11. (Jo. Crooke)

K105. Robarte Langford (50) holds, date 30 Mar. 1579, one tenement with a halle of 3 couples, a barne and stall 3 couples, garden and orchard, 1 clawe of land in Southetowne; their is 12 akers of grownd to this clawe. V £8, rent 3s 5d, fine £38. (Widow Lucombe)

K106. Robarte Burden (30) holds, date 1 Nov. 1588, one tenement with a hale of 3 couples, a barne of 2 couples, orchard and garden ½ yeard, 1 farlinge of lande in Efford, V £9, rent 10s 7½d, fine £26 13s 4d. (Jo. Barfette)

K107. Christopher Marshall (50) holds, date 1 Oct. 1591, one cottayg with a hall of 2 couples, orchard and garden 1 yeard, in Southetowne, ½ acre of land lying in Littell Bonehaye, V 30s, rent 3s 4d, fine £4. (Jo. Qucke)

K108. The same Christopher holds, date 11 May 1594, one cottayge with a hall of 2 couples, orchard and garden ½ yerd, 1 acre of land, V 30s, rent 4s, fine £8. (Widow Meale)

K109. Rychard Whittocke (50) holds, date 11 April 1591, one cottaige with a hall of 5 couples, orchard and garden ½ yeard, 1 acre of land, V 30s, rent 2s, fine £13 6s 8d. (Jo. Roade)

K110. Nycholas Ball (5) holds, date 10 May 1597, one cottaige with a hall of 2 couples, orchard and garden ½ yerd, 3 yards of land in the bacsid of the cottaig, V 30s, rent 3s 4d, fine £13 6s 8d. (Ed. ?Man)

K111. George Bawden (30) holds, date [*blank*], one tenement with a hale of 3 couples, a barne of 2 couples, orchard and garden of ½ acre, 1 farlinge of land containing 30 acres, and one peece of lande at Powderham Bridge 1 acre, V £9, rent 8s 8½d, fine [*blank*].[40] (Jo. Barsett)

K112. Elizabeth Cade (55) holds during her widdowhood, date 9 Sept. 1574, a cottaig with hall of 3 couples, orchard and garden of 1 yerd, 1 acre of land, V 40s, rent 3s 4d, fine £6 13s 4d. (Symon Quick)

[39] Also Southeintowne in the headings of later pages.

[40] Note: *dest' copia* [copy destroyed]. The grantor, Sir John Clifton, indicates a date between 1564 and 1593.

K113. Nycholas Rode (60) holds, date [*blank*], one cottaige, orchard and garden, ½ acre of land, V 6s 8d, rent 16d, fine [*blank*].[41] (Jo. Roade)

K114. Willyam Easton (30) holds, date 2 Oct. 1593, one tenement with a hall of 3 couples, a barne and stalle 3 couples, a cottaige 2 couples, orchard and garden 1 yeard, ½ farlinge of lande, V £8, rent 4s 5½d, fine £40. (Jo. Headon)

K115. Peter Seley (60) holds, date 4 Nov. 1577, one tenement with a halle with 3 couples, a barne 2 couples, orchard and garden 1 yerd, ½ farlinge of land, V £8, rent 4s 5½d, fine £5. (Nico. Wills)

K116. John Mole (30) holds, date 11 May 1594, one tenement, being a cottaig, with a halle and a shope of 3 couples, orchard and garden and 3 acres of land in Southeingtowe [*sic*], V £3, rent 3s 4d, fine £18. (Widow Doble)

K117. John Ewinge the younger (30) holds, date 14 May 1593, one cottaige with a hale of 2 couples, orchard and garden and ½ acre of land, V 20s, rent 2s 8d, fine 40s. (Jo. Morish)

K118. Thomas Willes (35) holds, date 2 Oct. 1593, one tenement with a hall of 2 couples, barne 2 couples, and two cottaiges of 4 couples, orchard and garden 1 yerde, ½ farlinge of lande in Southeingtowne, V £6, rent 4s 5½d, fine £48 10s. (Jo. Band)[42]

K119. John Babb (55) holds, date 11 Oct. 1578, one tenement of 6 couples, 1½ farlinge of land in Southeingtowne and certen other parcells of lande to the same tenement belonging, V £20, rent 14s, fine £150.[43] (Widow Lickey)

K120. Thomas Avery (26) holds, date 6 Nov. 1593, one cottaige with a halle of 2 couples in Southeingtowne, called the Lordes doghowse, V 26s 8d, rent 8d, fine £4.

K121. Alice Mower (50), widow, holds, date 10 Oct. 1575, one tenement with a hall, parler, kitchin; and barne of 6 couples, a cottage with 2 couples, orchard and garden 1 yeard, ½ farlinge of land called the Westerhalfe Farling, V £8, rent 4s 5½d, fine £17. (Jo. Jope)

K122. Nycholas Lucombe (50) holds, date 11 Oct. 1598, one tenement with a convenyent howse, orchard and garden [1] yerd, 1 farlinge of ground in Efford, late held by George Couck, V £12, rent 8s 7½d, fine £160. (Will. Towill)

K123. Jeffery Shapley (20) holds, date 14 May 1593, one cottaige with a halle of 2 couples, orchard and garden, ½ acre of land in Southeintowne, V 20s, rent 2s 8d, fine 40s. (Edward Allen)

K124. Rychard Luxe (30) holds, date 21 April 1591, one parcell of lande 12 yerde, lying in the lower parte of a close called Bonehaye, V 10s, rent 2s, fine 40s.

K125. Robarte Simones (30) holds, date 4 Nov. 1594, one cottaige with a hall of 1 cople, orcharde and garden ½ yerd, 6 perches of land, V 6s 8d, rent 2s, fine 20s. (William Davis)

K126. Thomas Addies (50) holds, date 1 Oct. 1580, one tenement with a hall of 3 couples, a barne 3 couples, orchard and garden of 1 yerd, one farlinge of lande in Southetowne, V £9, rent 9s, fine £35. (Dimond, widow)

K127. Alice Dalkinge (60), widow, holds, date 26 Jan. 1587, one cottage with a hale of 3 couples, orchard and garden ½ yerd in Southetowne, 1 acre of lande in Bownehaye, V 30s, rent 4s, fine £3 6s 8d. (Widow Warren)

K128. Roger Langeford holds one cottayge, 1 acre of land, V 30s, rent 4s. (Roger Langford)

K129. Thamsin Babb, widow, holds one cottayge and 2 acres of land, orchard and garden ½ acre, V £3, rent 4s. (?Al. Shorte)

K130. John Cocke holds one cottayge and 20 yeardes of land, V 20s, rent 4s. (Thomas Skinner)

K131. George Mole holds one cottaig and hearbe garden, V 20s, rent 2s. (Thomas ?Gibs)

K132. Stevon Elliote holds one cottage, 1 acre of land and herbe garden, V 20s, rent 4sp. (Jeffery Elliotte)

K133. Marke Creede holds one cottaige, 1 acre of lande and garden, V 30s, rent 4s.

K134. John Larance holds one cottag and herbe garden, V 20s, rent 4s.

The tennantes of Southeintowne doo paye for their marshe yeerly, rent 18d. Which common the Lorde may inclose at his pleasure, V £5. This marshe is 80 akers belongin to Southintowne.

Southtowne Commones: Memorandum that the comones from Efford Brooke to Keynmouthe Poynte belongith to the tennants of Southeintowne, as in the perambulacion of this manner before is sett downe.

Heathfilde

K135. Emanyell Lutton (30) holds by indenture dated 10 Sept. 1574, for his life, halfe of the Heathe filde, with licke condition to thothe[44] leses, V £10, rent 6s 8d, fine £50.

K136. Rychard Marting (30) holds by indenture, dated 30 June 1584, the fifth part of cer[tain] ground called Kenton Heath Filde, by estimacion 20 acres of lande, to himselfe and to such a wooman as he should take to wife, fine £41.[45]

K137. Larance Hopper (35) holds by indenture dated 10 Sept. 1574, the fifthe parte of the sayd Heathfilde called Kenton Heathefilde, for his life, with sute of courte and with condition for non-payment of the rent a re-entery, V £4, rent 2s 8d, fine £20.

K138. John Hopper (50) and Rychard Hopper (40) hold by indenture dated 16 Oct. 1583, a tenth parte of the said lande

[41] As for K111, the copy had been destroyed; again the date was 1564-93.

[42] *Nico Wills*, erased.

[43] Note: *Beware of sockaige*.

[44] Probably for the other.

[45] Value and rent absent. Original note: *Memorandum this parcell was afterward demised ut infra* [as below]. See K 138a.

aforesayd, for their lives, sute of courte and condition for non-payment, V 40s, rent 16d, fine £12.

K138a. George Broucke (22) and Willmot Doble (23) hold by copy, date 11 Oct. 1598, the reversion of a tenement in Heathefilde, 1½ farlinge of land, in the tenure of Elizabeth Trencher,[46] V £4, rent 2s 8d, fine £20.

Northe Quarter

K139. John Skyner (50) holds, date 11 Oct. 1595, one close of pasture, V 30s, rent 2s, fine £3 6s 8d. (Jo. Towill)

K140. Joane Jope (45), widow, wife of John Jope the elder, holds during her widowhood, date 4 April 1557, one tenement with a dwellinge howse, a smithe shope of 6 couples, a hay howse and a barne of 6 couples, and other barne 3 couples, and a barkehowse[47] 3 couples, orcharde and garden ½ acre, and another howse by the walter,[48] in Liston, 5 farthinnges of land, V £24, rent 29s 7d, fine £10.[49] (Jo. Jope)

Reversion to John Jope the younger (19), date 5 Nov. 1592, fine £90.

K141. Simon Kenwood (27) holds, date 6 Nov. 1593, one tenement with a hale and stalle of 6 couples, a backhowse 2 couples, a barne 4 couples, orchard and garden 1 yerd, to littell howses, 3 farlings and 1 clawe of land, V £24, rent 28s, fine 200. (Jo. Symons Charles Skiner)[50]

K142. Peter Sely (60) holds, date 16 Sept. 1582, one tenement with a dwelling howse and bakehowse of 4 couples, barne and stalle of 3 couples, orchard and garden 1 yeard, 1 farling of land in Liston, V £10, rent 8s 4½d, fine £20. (William Periam)

K143. Thomas Hutchin (64) holds, date 11 May 1594, one tenement with a dwelling house of 5 couples, kitchin 2 couples, maltehowse 2 coupls, barne hayhowse and stalle 6 couples, orchard and garden ½ acre, in Liston, 3 farlinges of land, covenant to finde the lordes officers' horses' meat at all courtes, V £20, rent 25s 3d, fine £120. (Widow Downs)

K144. Roger May (70) holds, date 14 April 1556, one tenement with a hale of 4 couples, kitchin 2 couples, barne and stale of 4 couples, orchard and garden ½ acre, 2 farlings and 1 clawe of land and 1 acre of meadow, 16 yeards of wode, V £13 6s 8d, rent 22s, fine £10. (Widow Moale)

K145. Willyam Smalridge (30) holds, date 14 May 1593,[51] one tenement with a dwellinge howse of 3 couples, one cote and to other howses, a barne of 3 couples, orchard and garden 1 yerd, 1 farlinge of land and certen other lands in Wilsworthy, V £10, rent 12s 4½d, fine £40. (William Jope)

K146. Richard Towill (80) holds, date 13 Aug. 1548, one tenement with a dwellinge howse of 5 couples, stall and barkehowse of 4 couples, barne 2 couples and to outhowses, orchard and garden ½ acre, 2 farlinges of land in Haldon, one pece of lande called Toddismore, V £20, rent 18s 5d, fine £9 3s 4d.[52] (William Towill)

Reversion to Emanyell Towill (28), his son, date 4 Oct. 1591,[53] of the said two farlings of land at Haldon, aliase North Kenwood.

K147. Rychard Hopper (80) holds, date 13 Aug. 1548, one tenement with a dwelling howse of 3 couples, to barnes and a stall of 5 couples, a maltehowse of 2 couples, orchard and garden ½ acre, 1½ farling of land in Liston, V £12, rent 17s 2½d, fine £8 10s. (Thomas Harris)

Reversion to Rychard Hopper the younger (40), date 3 Oct. 1596, fine £60.

K148. George Casley (60) holds, date 20 June 1562, one tenement with a dwelling howse of 3 couples, a hayhouse and a stale of 3 couples, barne 3 couples, bakehowse 2 couples, orchard and garden 3 yeards, 2 farlings 3 clawes of land in Heyton and Wilsworthy, V £14, rent 24s 8d, fine £60. (Jo. Cassly)

K149. Emanyell Towill (30) holds, date 4 Nov. 1596, one tenement, 2 farlings of land at Hayton, V £10, rent 16s 9d, fine £26 13s 4d. (William Towill)

K150. John Britnall (70) holds, date 26 Oct. 1572, one tenement with a dwelling howse and stalle of five couples, barne 4 couples, bakehowse 2 couples, orchard and garden 3 yardes, 2 farlings of land and 1 clawe of wast lande in Puttismore and Hayton, V £20, rent 24s, fine £20.

Reversion to Othy Brictnall (30), his sonne, date 10 May 1596, fine £75.

K151. Joane Kenwoode (80), supposed a sockewooman, holds a dwelinge howse and 2 farlings of land, which house hath a hall of 3 couples, to cottages with 4 couples, a barne of 2 couples, all forfytid, V £20, rent 19s 11d.

K152. John Atwill (64) holds, date 4 April 1558, one tenement with a very convenyent gentleman house with all other necessaryes, housinge and orchard and garden 3 acres of ground, five farlings of land, called Ashehowse, V £60, rent 40s, fine £16. (Will. Atwill)

Reversion to Willyam Atwill (30), sonne of the said John Atwill, date 10 Oct. 1584, fine £26 13s 4d.

K153. The same John Atwill holds also, date 26 July 1569, one tenement at Myll, 1 farlinge of lande and two griste milles, except Kenton Woode, V £60, rent £4 18s 3d, fine £100. (Richard Atwill)

Reversion to John Atwill (40), the younger, date 10 Oct. 1584, for his life according to the coustom, fine £40.

[46] See K136. It seems likely that Elizabeth Trencher had been Rychard Marting's wife.

[47] Backehouse is possible, but less likely.

[48] For *water*?

[49] Note: *Beware of sockaige*.

[50] Two names are given. The second is perhaps the tenant of the two little houses.

[51] The grantor is given as Sir Jervaise Clifton, presumably in error.

[52] Note: *Beware of sockaige*.

[53] Again, the grantor is Sir Jervaise Clifton, presumably in error.

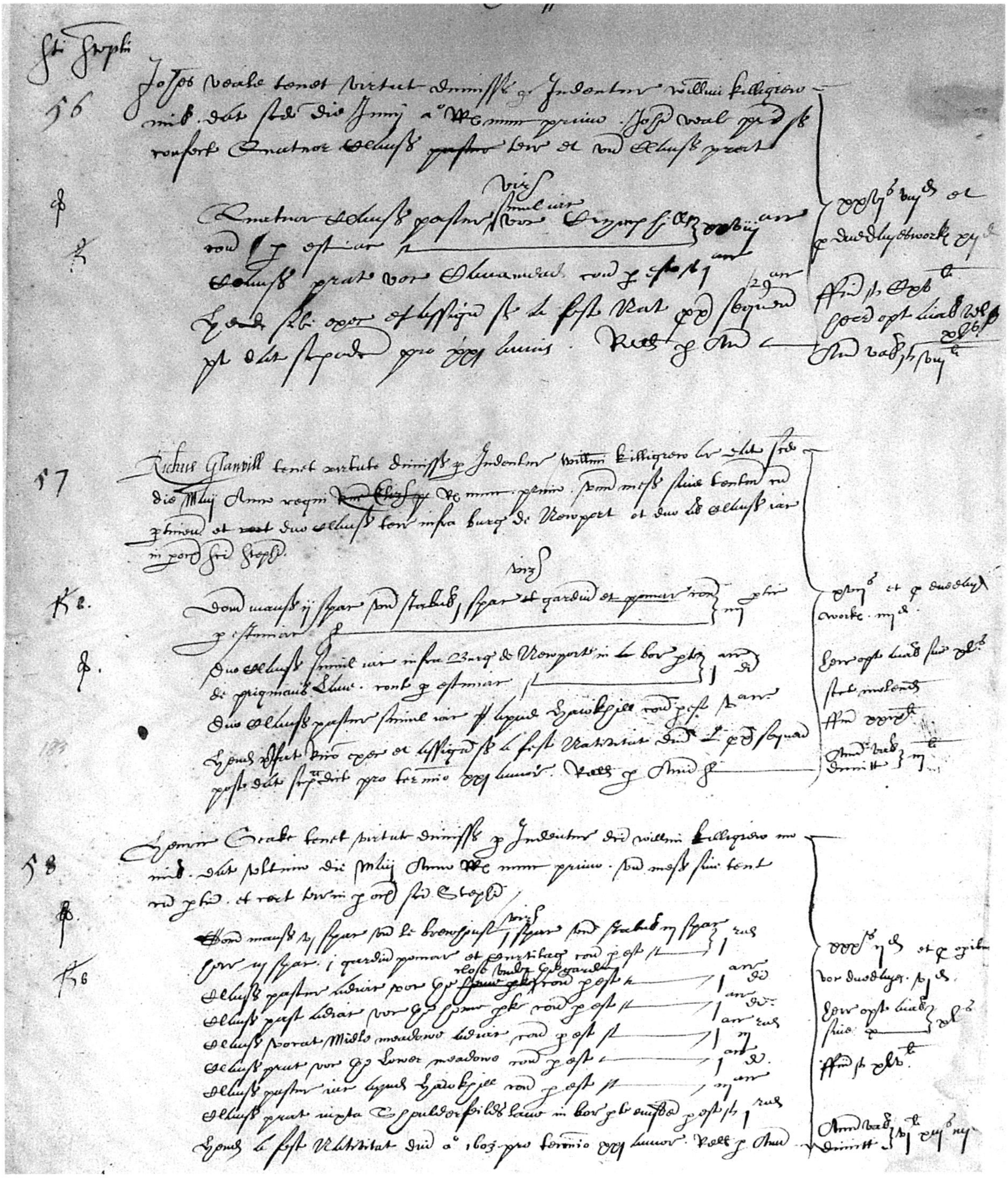

Figure 24. Part of the Crown survey of Launceston, Cornwall , 1606 (TNA LR2/207, f. 5)

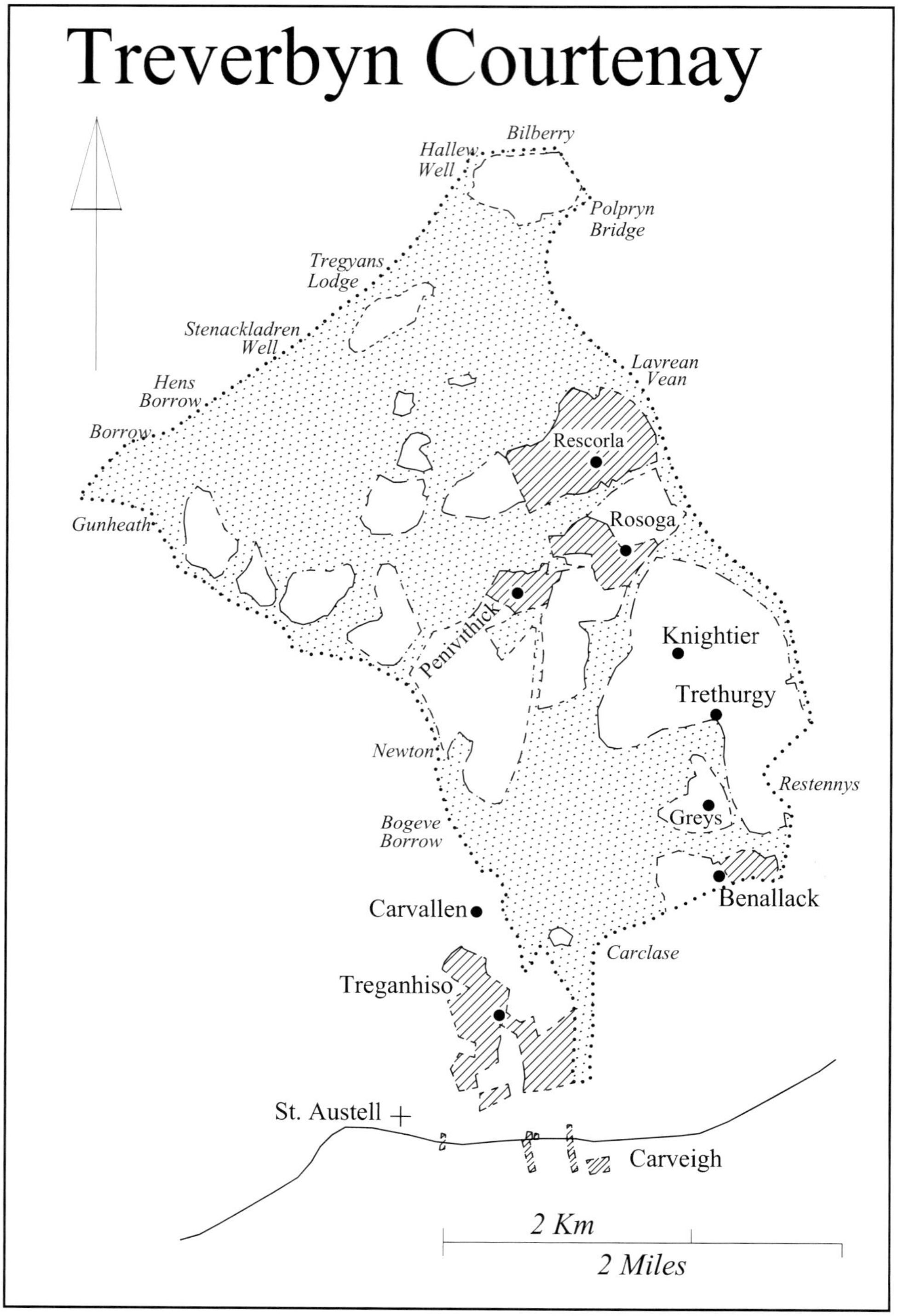

Map 2. Treverbyn Courtenay Manor, Cornwall

The main boundary surrounds the commons (stippled) of the manors of Treverbyn Courtenay and Treverbyn Trevanion (Cornwall R.O. A.D. 455); this corresponds very closely to the survey description (p. 100). Land owned by the Duchy of Cornwall in 1831 is shaded (Survey Volume S.b.2, Duchy Office, Buckingham Palace Gate, London); small tenements in St. Austell, and three fields at Menagiveners (?C23) cannot be located. Other enclosed land is left blank. Duchy holdings at Carvallen (C21) and Greys (C25) had been sold in 1799.

CHAPTER 7

Cornish Manors

1602 Survey (C) *Map 2*

This survey brings together descriptions of widely scattered lands in South and East Cornwall. Nominally it covers the five manors of Treverbyn Courtenay (or Courtnay), Landreyne, Northill, Crofthole (or Crafthole) and Tregamere. By the standards of midland England, only the first, with a manor court, would merit the name of manor. Before 1538, they belonged to the Courtenay family and were forfeited when Henry Courtenay, Marquess of Exeter, was attainted; they were assigned to the Duchy of Cornwall by Henry VIII. At the end of Elizabeth's reign, the Crown was illegally selling Duchy manors, including this group which was bought in 1601 jointly by Lord Stanhope, Michael Stanhope and John Molesworth.[1] The surveys were prepared by the new owners. After 1603, the sales were rescinded, and the manors eventually recovered, but not in time to be included in the 1606 Crown Surveys.[2]

The manor of Treverbyn Courtenay, despite its formal structure, was topographically extraordinary (Map 5). The original manor of Treverbyn was divided in the fifteenth century between the Courtenay and Trevanion families,[3] and it is clear that this was a physical division, apart from common rights and a mill (C33). The overall layout is shown in a nineteenth century map of the common land.[4] Treverbyn occupied the north-east part of the enormous parish of St. Austell, and the whole manor was a vast common, with islands of enclosed lands. Only a small part of these belonged outright to Treverbyn Courtenay, the rest consisting of the fourteen freeholdings of the manor and the land of Treverbyn Trevanion. However, some of the Duchy holdings lay outside the apparent manor boundary, in St. Austell town (C16-18, C32),[5] Carveigh (C15) and Treganhiso (C19-20). These had presumably been purchased at some date and were considered part of the manor for convenience.[6] Tenure in Treverbyn was apparently by copyhold (stated for C15), with a few leaseholders (e.g. C29), but the large number of freeholdings is notable.

Both Landreyne and Northill were in North Hill parish (Map 6), which included several other manors;[7] both were no more than groups of farms, although Landreyne did have five freeholdings.[8] In contrast, Crofthole in Sheviock parish had 17 separate holdings, but was correctly not a manor but a borough.[9] Most of the holdings were free burgages, but four had customary tenants, having presumably fallen into hand at some period and been granted out on less favourable terms. Tregamere, in St. Columb Major, was again a very small estate.

The 1602 survey gives much more detail about the farmsteads than does the Kenton one; apart from the commons, it shows fully enclosed fields,[10] grouped around the farmyard ('courtlidge' or 'town-place'), the garden and orchard, 'mowhay' (rick-yard) and occasionally 'hemphay' (small plot for growing hemp or flax). Although the farms were fairly large (cf. p. 12), this was partly because they included rough or moor ground: 'Noddon, being a rocky peece of land inclosed' (C37). In compensation, it was 'very likely for tynne', and tin-working could clearly supplement farming income, as well as bringing in a toll of £10 per year to Treverbyn Courtenay from the 48 mines on Treverbyn Common. The enormous commons must have made pastoral farming far more important than arable husbandry, though no doubt enough grain was grown on the enclosed fields for the farmers' own use.

The Houses

The Cornish 1602 survey gives details for only twenty-one houses, but they are sufficient to establish a clear pattern. The descriptions are explicit, apart from one uncertainty. Only four mention upper rooms, raising the suspicion that some have been omitted. This is probably justified for houses such as C19, with only a hall and service rooms mentioned; however, the sev-

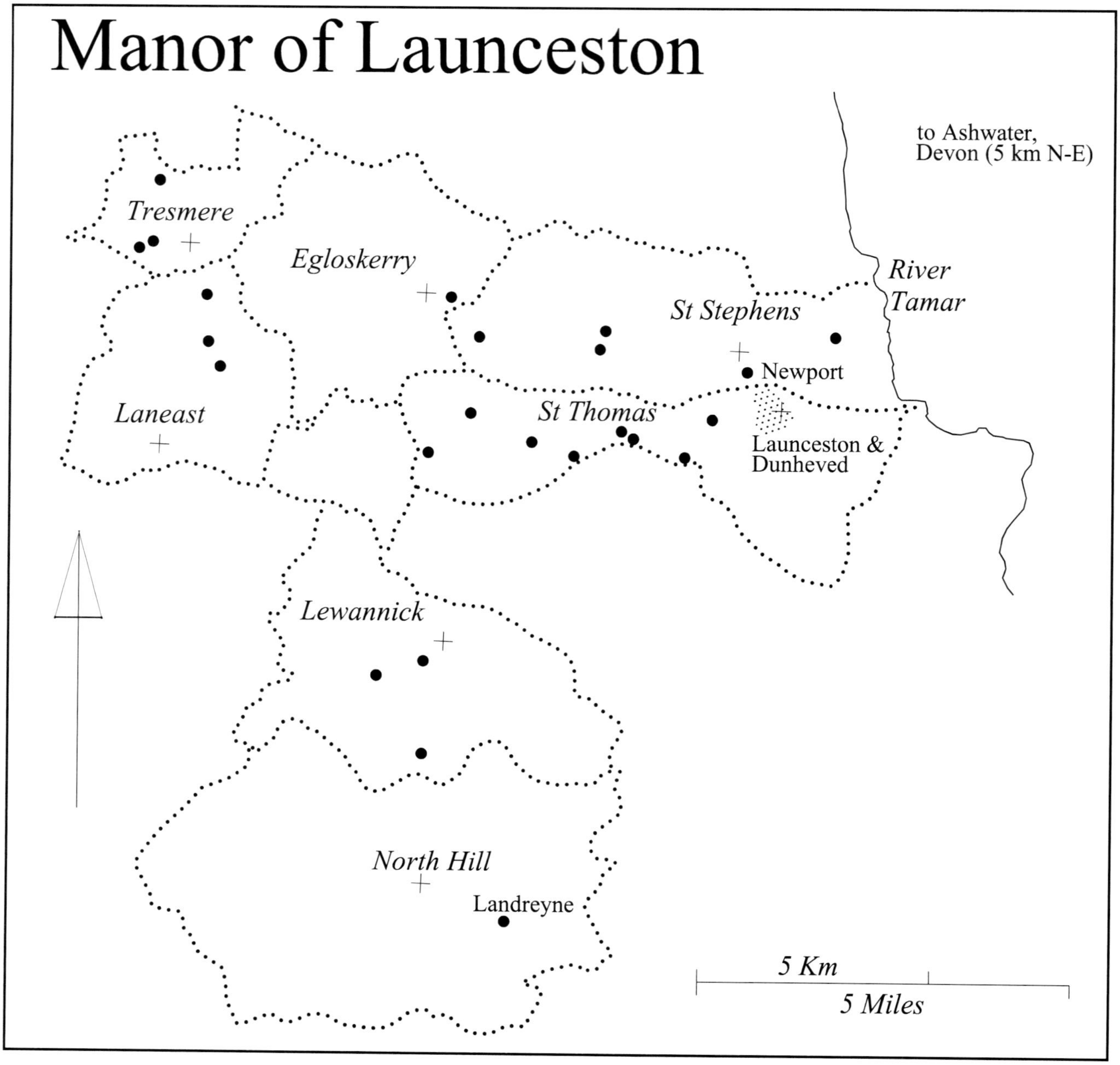

Map 3. Manor of Launceston, Cornwall

Located named holdings are marked (about 75% of the total). The remainder are almost all known to lie within the parishes shown. Landreyne and North Hill (part of the Treverbyn estate) are also shown. Parish boundaries are dotted.

eral smaller houses with chambers on the ground floor seem likely to have just had ground floor rooms.[11] This view is reinforced by the generally mean impression that the houses give.

The holdings fall into two distinct groups. The four in St. Austell town and the three in Crofthole borough, with no more than an acre or two each, clearly differ from the farms, most commonly of 30-50 acres. In the first group, two houses were of two-room plan; hall and chamber (C18), and chamber and cellar (C44).[12] The latter was perhaps not a normal house, because the tenant also held another burgage (C58). Two others were little bigger: halls with a chamber at the upper end (i.e. an inner room), together with a kitchen (C16), or a cellar (C17). There is no reason to think that these had upper rooms. Two did have their halls chambered over, with either a shop and cellar (both with rooms above, C32), or with a smith's shop.[13] The final town house was described as a 'fair house', and indeed had six ground floor rooms: hall, two chambers, buttery, cellar and kitchen (C46).

Small houses might be expected to be associated with small-holdings, but the modest scale of Cornish houses as a whole is brought out by the farmhouses, which were hardly more spacious. Four had only a hall and chamber (C26, 39, 40, 62); others added a second chamber (C36, 42), a kitchen (C25, 61), a chamber and buttery (C37),[14] or a kitchen and dairy (C15). Three rather larger houses followed the same pattern: hall,[15] buttery, kitchen and milkhouse. The chambers over that were specified for C20, were presumably also present in C19 and C28. C35 had the unique combination of hall, parlour and chapel (certainly with upper chambers). It was perhaps the original manor house of Landreyne.[16]

The distinction between the two groups becomes clear in their ancillary buildings. The village houses together had only three stables (C17, 32, 46). The farms had eight bakehouses and one dry-house (malthouse). The dairy of one house (C37), accompanied by a cellar (chambered over) and a bakehouse, seems to have been in an outbuilding, as it is mentioned after the barn and ox-house. The pattern of these ancillary buildings resembles that at Launceston and Carnanton (below), although there the kitchens were detached, which seems not to be the case for the houses described in 1602 (see p. 40).

1606 Crown Estates *Map 3 (Fig. 24, p. 87)*

The two long Crown surveys for Cornwall[17] give detail similar to that of the Kenton survey, the number of bays (spaces) in each unit of building (summarised in Tables 12 and 13, pp. 95-99). They cover two manors, both originally the property of Launceston Priory, annexed after the Dissolution to the Duchy of Cornwall. The compact group of farms making up Carnanton lay in or immediately adjoining to St. Mawgan in Pydar, on the North Cornwall coast (Location Map), quite near Tregamere (p. 89); included twenty-four houses. The so-called manor of Launceston (Map 3), with about 130 properties, did not include full rights over either of the ancient twin boroughs of Launceston and Dunheved, but consisted mostly of rural holdings, covering most of the parish of St. Thomas, and also scattered through half-a-dozen adjoining parishes with one outlier in Devon. It included some urban properties, in the suburb of Newport north of the town (twelve holdings), in Boughty, apparently a southern suburb (8), and a few in Launceston (1) and Dunheved (2) themselves. The manor had presumably been built up by piecemeal purchase, and was administered as a unit for convenience. Only ninety-two of the properties had houses, and the tenants of most of the rest seem to have lived in Launceston to judge by the proximity of the land to the town. Despite their rather different make-up, the pattern of farm sizes was similar in the two areas, with a peak at about thirty acres (Figure 1C-D, p. 12). However, the suburban houses gave the Launceston estate another peak at 0-2 acres; it is likely that the tenants of some of these also held land from other owners.

The Houses (Table 10)

It is probably because of their access to other resources that the smaller Launceston holdings were not simply cottages. One house had a single bay, seven had two bays and five had three, but four, five, six, and eight and eleven bays were also represented. Two also had kitchens (one and three bays), the latter accompanied by a three-bay stable, a pound-house and lean-to; this holding must have included land not part of the Crown estate.

The houses of the larger holdings (5 acres upwards) showed few distinctions, either between Launceston and Carnanton, or with holding size. Three-bay houses were commonest (39), with a substantial minority of two (13) and four bays (24), and a few ranging up to 10 bays. One holding of 44 acres had only a one-bay house (12 ft. square), but this cannot possibly have been the main house of the holding; like the two largest Carnanton holdings (60 and 76 acres), which had no houses, the tenant must have had a separate main farm, from which the rest of the land was run. This small house was presumably lived in by a farm labourer. Other evidence can be seen for sub-tenants on the smaller Launceston holdings; three holdings had three separate houses each, and another four or five had two houses. This again is probably a result of their suburban situation.

The ancillary buildings in these surveys are particularly significant, because the descriptions indicate that they were almost certainly separate buildings.[18] The Carnanton houses included only two kitchens, one

Table 10: Launceston and Carnanton: Dimensions of houses (bays)

Place	Acres		Number of bays in house									
			1	2	3	4	5	6	7	8	9	10+
Launceston	0–3½	All houses	1	7	5	2	2	3		1		1
		Houses with kitchens						1		1		
	5–20	All houses		8	11	6	1	2		2		1
		Houses with kitchens								2		
	21–40	All houses			8	9	1	1	2	1		
		Houses with kitchens				1	1		1	1		
	>40	All houses	1	2	3	3	1	2	2	2		1
		Houses with kitchens				1	1	1	1	1		
Carnanton	5–20	All houses		2	3	2	3					
		Houses with kitchens					1					
	21–40	All houses		1	4	3	5	2	2		1	
		Houses with kitchens						1	1			

Note: Kitchens, chambers, cubiculi *and milkhouses are included in the number of bays.*

associated with a milkhouse and bakehouse, one other bakehouse, and a malthouse. However, at Launceston, ancillary buildings were remarkably numerous. They included no less than twenty-six bakehouses,[19] and thirteen kitchens, whose uses probably overlapped as only one house had both. Less common were the backhouses (2), brewhouses, and malthouses (two of each individually and one house with both). The most interesting are the buildings that would be expected to form part of the main houses; two milkhouses, one buttery, two called 'cubiculum'[20] and one parlour and 'le chamber'. The last, at least, can hardly have been fully detached, and was perhaps in a wing. The same may have been true of some of the other rooms, but not many of the kitchens, simply from their number, in view of the linear house-plans that fieldwork shows to be normal.

A number of buildings are recorded whose purposes are rather ill-defined: 'lean-to's' and 'other houses' (which may not have been separate dwellings). Most of the former were certainly for farm use (e.g. L21: *stall or lean-to*), but L7, which lay in Launceston itself, had a *small house called a lean-to* that may well have been domestic.

Six of the Launceston houses combined farmhouse and farm buildings, with one store, one stable and four oxstalls or houses (*bovite*). Their descriptions show particularly clearly that these were of longhouse type, for example 'house and oxhouse under one roof' (*domus mansionalis et bovite sub uno tecto*) (L70).

The Farm Buildings *Tables 11, 12, 13*

The 1602 survey and the surveys of Carnanton and Launceston all give similar evidence of a mixed agricultural economy based primarily on cattle and sheep rearing, but including some arable farming.

Barns were present almost everywhere apart from a few of the holdings with less than fifteen acres. They ranged in size from two and three bays on the smallest holdings to buildings four, five, and six bays long on farms of twenty-five acres or more. Most barns were self-contained, but a few were coupled with stables, stalls, shippons, linheys, and (on three Launceston farms) storehouses.

The pastoral farmers in Carnanton and on the Cornish manors seem to have specialised in sheep, the flocks finding shelter from the region's wet and windy weather inside 'sheephouses' or under so-called 'shepe pens' (a term not to be confused with the word 'shippon'). These 'houses' and 'pens' must have been roofed, because their sizes are described in bays, but they may have been low and narrow. One of the Carnanton holdings had sixty acres of land with just a three-bay sheep house (though as it lacked a dwelling, it must have been held in combination with some other property). The larger Carnanton holdings that lacked any farm buildings at all may also have been used for sheep, but have had relatively sheltered positions on the estate, whose coastal location makes it exposed to westerly winds. Launceston had only three sheep pens; its pasture was used more for grazing

Table 11: Cornwall, 1602: Occurrence of farm buildings

Ref. Number	Acres	Barn	Stable	Ox House	Sheep House	Wain House	Other buildings; Notes
C45	¼	•		*			no house; * cowhouse
C44	½						
C17	1		•				
C47	1						smith's shop
C16	1¼						
C18	1¼						
C24	1¼						
C46	1½		•				other little houses
C32	2¾		•				
C39	9						
C40	11						
C61	14	•		•			
C62	16	•					
C30	18	•			•	•	lenny
C15	22	•		•		•	
C42	24						
C21	38						
C19	40	•	•	•	•		lenny house and other small houses
C20	40	•	•		•		
C31	45						
C26	45	•			•		
C36	45	•	•	•	•		
C28	47			•	•		
C35	50	•	•				
C25	51	•		•	•		
C37	52	•	•	•	•	•	

Note: Holdings with no described buildings or without buildings are omitted.

steers, occasionally sheltered in the linheys, and dairy cows, tethered, fed and milked in structures variously termed 'cowhouse' or 'shepina' (shippon). Fodder may have been stored in lofts, for separate hayhouses were rare.

Numerous oxhouses on farmsteads larger than ten to twenty acres indicate that pasture farming was widely mixed with grain growing. Some larger landholders preferred plough horses and so built stables rather than oxstalls. A few had both, including five of the eight most substantial farmers in the Launceston district. Pack and cart horses must account for some stables, but horses were also used to plough in tandem with ox teams, a practice whose antiquity was noted 200 years later by William Marshall, who wrote that 'oxen have ever been the plow team of the district, sometimes with horses before them, but more generally alone'.[21] Both customs seem to be reflected in the buildings recorded in 1606. The increased amount of housing for draught animals on the larger holdings matches the larger barns needed to store the more abundant crops harvested by farmers who tilled more land than their neighbours. These men also had the greatest need for wagons, and indeed wainhouses appear in all three surveys on farms of about twenty acres upwards and become common on Launceston farmsteads larger than forty-one acres.

On the smallest holdings, stables were not uncommon, generally as the sole outbuilding associated with the property. Many were located in the urban centres of Launceston and St. Austell, a feature recurring in other towns for which survey evidence exists. Holding L62 included a structure containing a stable, a backhouse, and an *asinum*. This can only mean 'ass-house', but just how donkeys figured in the farm's economy is difficult to imagine, as neither asses or their shelter find any mention in contemporary farming literature outside the pages of Holy Writ.

[1] Cf. note 23 on p. 105.

[2] From evidence in the Duchy of Cornwall Office, notably Particulars and Warrants, and a list of purchasers (D.b.2). We are most grateful to the staff there for elucidating this confusing situation. A further survey was taken in 1650 but it shows very little correlation with that described here (and does not give details of houses); presumably the poor administrative control of the estate had not prevented further alienation and reorganisation. See N. J. G. Pounds, ed., *Parliamentary Survey of the Duchy of Cornwall*, Devon and Cornwall Record Soc., NS25, 27 (Torquay, 1982, 1984).

[3] Later recognised as the two manors of Treverbyn Courtenay and Trevanion. Anon. *Complete Parochial History of Cornwall* (Truro 1867-72), Vol. I.

[4] Cornwall R.O. AD.455 (undated, but apparently early to mid-nineteenth century). The manor was surveyed and mapped by the Duchy in 1831 (Duchy Office, S.b.2., Volume of Surveys and Maps), and the overall pattern is also shown on a set of the first edition 1 inch Ordnance Survey maps (1813) with contemporary annotations (Duchy Office). In the 1831 survey, a few holdings are noted as having been sold in the 1790s, but apart from these, the holdings and many of the fields are immediately identifiable with those described in 1602.

[5] The town apparently lacked borough status, and only received a market grant in 1661, *op. cit.* in note 3.

[6] Cf. the Launceston estate, p. 91.

[7] *Op. cit.* in note 3, IV, 5-11.

[8] Not included in the 1602 survey, but mentioned earlier in the same volume.

[9] M. W. Beresford and H. P. R. Finberg, *English Medieval Boroughs: A Handlist* (Newton Abbot, 1971).

[10] Although the 1606 Crown survey does mention open fields at Tregurrion in Carnanton.

[11] Such one story houses are mentioned in glebe terriers, e.g. at Forrabury in 1679. R. Potts, *Cornish Glebe Terriers*, Devon and Cornwall Record Soc. NS19 (Torquay, 1974).

[12] 'Seller' can be taken to mean cellar, not solar, as the latter term had fallen out of use by about 1600 and in any case would be used as an alternative to, rather than in conjunction with 'chamber'.

[13] With another 'little dwelling house' at one end (C47).

[14] This also had domestic out-buildings, noted below.

[15] The 'fair house' of C20 seems simply to imply the hall, like the 'fair hall' of C19.

[16] Only one other Cornish parlour is noted, in a Launceston house.

[17] A couple of other surveys from the 1606 series survive for Cornish property, but they cover only freeholdings and give no building details. For a typical entry from a Crown survey, see p. 70.

[18] They have, for example, the form *domus mansionalis iij spacias, coquina ij spacias.*

[19] The bakehouse shared between L35 and L38 must obviously have been detached.

[20] Apparently meaning 'bed-chamber', (MLWL) but the difference between this, the normal *camera*, and *le chamber*, used in L75, is not clear.

[21] William Marshall, *The Rural Economy of the West of England* (London, 1799), I, 116.

Table 12: Carnanton, 1606: Dimensions of surveyed buildings (bays)

Ref. Number	Ms. Number	Acres	House	Kitchen	Ancilliary Buildings: Other Domestic Buildings	Ancilliary Buildings: Bake House	Ancilliary Buildings: Malt House	Farm Buildings: Barn	Farm Buildings: Stable	Farm Buildings: Ox House	Farm Buildings: *Bovite*	Farm Buildings: Cow House	Farm Buildings: Wain House	Farm Buildings: Store	Farm Buildings: Other Farm Buildings	Places; Notes
CN1	19	6	2													Tregurryon
CN2	6	7	3					2								Trevaryan
CN3	29	10	3													Trevaryan
CN4	9	12	4					*								Trevaryan;* barn decayed
CN5	4	12	4					2								Trevaryan
CN6	12	14	2					3								Tregurryon
CN7	30	14	2													Tregurryon
CN8	18	18	3	2				2								Tregurryon
CN9	11	19	5					5								Carneton
CN10	5	20	3					1								Trenowe
CN11	32	20					4									Carnanton; malthouse only
CN12	28	21	9					3	=	3			=			Trenowe; stable + wainhouse(4)
CN13	17	22	5			3		4					•		2 shepepens	Trevaryan
CN14	26	22	3					2							outhouse(1)	Trenowe
CN15	10	23	2					4								Trenowe
CN16	3	25	2	2	milkhouse(2)	1		3								Carlogas
CN17	16	25	5					*			3					Tregurryon; * half of barn(2)
CN18	24	26	7					3								Tregurryon
CN19	7	30	4		2nd house(2)											Tregurryon
CN20	8	30	6					3?		=					shop(=)	Tregurryon; shop + oxhouse(4)
CN21	15	30	4					1				*				Tregurryon; * one le shippon
CN22	25	30	4	2				=		=					sheep-house(4)	barn + stall(4)
CN23	13	31	5				2	3	2							Tregurryon
CN24	20	34	3					3								Trewyne; both CN24 and CN25 held by local gentry
CN25	21	34	3													
CN26	14	35	4					3			3					Tregurryon
CN27	22	35	•					•								Trewyne
CN28	27	35	5					4								Trewince
CN29	2	36	5					2						2	hayhouse(2)	St. Columb Minor
CN30	23	60													sheephouse(3)	Penbuthen; sheephouse only
CN31	31	76								•						Carnanton; oxhouse only

Table 13: Launceston 1606: Dimensions of surveyed buildings (bays)

Ref. Number	Ms. Number	Acres	House	Kitchen	Ancilliary Buildings: Other domestic rooms and housing	Ancilliary Buildings: Bake house	Ancilliary Buildings: Malt house (M) Brew house (B)	Farm Buildings: Barn	Farm Buildings: Stable	Farm Buildings: Ox-house (H) Stall (S) *Bovite* (B)	Farm Buildings: Cow house (C) *Shepina* (S)	Farm Buildings: Wain House	Farm Buildings: Store	Farm Buildings: Other buildings	Places; Notes
L1	120	0	5	=					=					pound-house(3) leanto	Boughtey; stable + kitchen(3)
L2	121	0	3												Boughtey
L3	122	0	3		*										* court hall of Newport
L4	125	0	2*		2 houses(2, 2)*										Borough (Boughtey) * 3 tenements in all (Boughtey)
L5	71	¼	4												St. Stephen
L6	113	¼	5	1											Newport
L7	64	¼	3											small house called lean-to	Beast St., Launceston
L8	112	¼	3												Newport
L9	74	½	5												St. Stephen
L10	79	½	2												St. Stephen
L11	87	½	2		2nd house(4)			2							St. Stephen, 2nd house adjoins [?the barn] (Ms.defective)
L12	70	1	2												St. Stephen
L13	85	1	3						2						Newport + St. Stephen
L14	110	1	2												Newport
L15	72	2	6												St. Stephen
L16	38	2½	11						2						St. Stephen
L17	80	3	1												Dunheved
L18	82	3	3		backhouse(3)				2						St. Stephen
L19	67	3½	5						3						Bridge, Launceston
L20	57	5	4					3							St. Stephen
L21	68	5	3					2	2	S*					St. Stephen; * house called le stall or lean-to
L22	118	5	3					4							Boughtey; St. Thomas
L23	59	6	2						1						St. Stephen
L24	86	6	3						2						Newport + St. Stephen
L25	92	6	3	2+3*	2 other blds(3)										Newport; * kitchen + other kitchen

Table 13 *continued*

Ref. Number	Ms. Number	Acres	House	Kitchen	Ancilliary Buildings: Other domestic rooms and housing	Bake house	Malt house (M) Brew house (B)	Farm Buildings: Barn	Stable	Ox-house (H) Stall (S) *Bovite* (B)	Cow house (C) *Shepina* (S)	Wain House	Store	Other buildings	Places; Notes
L26	115	6	6		other bld(3)										Boughtey, St. Thomas
L27	54-5	6½	-					3							Landreyne
L28	84	8	3	2	other house(3)	2		3	2						St. Stephen + St. Thomas
L29	53	8½	3			1		3						le lean-to	Lewannick
L30	40	9¼	3												Newport
L31	60	9¼	6				1B	3	3						St. Stephen
L32	31	10	4												Higher Trebursye
L33	18	10	3					2		3B					Bodgall
L34	111-2	12	4						3					shop(3)	Newport
L35	117	12	=			2*			=						Kemyhall[?]; house + stable(3); * bake-house(2) jointly with L38
L36	15	12	2			3		4		3B					Bodgall
L37	46	13	2												Kemyhall[?]
L38	48	13	2			2*					2S				Kemyhall[?]; * see L35
L39	41-2	14	4					3							St. Thomas
L40	45	14	=						=						Kemyhall[?] house + stable(4)
L41	103	14	4					2							Lanall, Lewannick
L42	117	14	2*		2 houses(2,2) *										* 3 tenements(2,2,2) in Baseheghey(?), St Thomas
L43	19	15	3			2		3		3B					Laneast
L44	75-8	16	4		2nd house(2)				o					leane*	St. Stephen; * two mills
L45	123	16	4	4	higher house(2)			4	6					shop(2)	Newport
L46	30	17	*							*					* house now bovite, 20ft long by 13ft broad
L47	83	17	=		3 other houses (6,2,2)	=									St. Stephens + Dunheved; house + bakehouse(10)
L48	90	17	3					=					=		Trebursey, St. Thomas
L49	51	18	2												Lewannick
L50	91	20	3												Newport
L51	104	20						=					=		Carnoden; barn + store(3)
L52	107	20						3							Trelake, St. Stephen
L53	127	20	3					3		3S					St. Neot

Table 13 *continued*

Ref. Number	Ms. Number	Acres	House	Kitchen	Ancilliary Buildings			Farm Buildings							Places; Notes
					Other domestic rooms and housing	Bake house	Malt house (M) Brew house (B)	Barn	Stable	Ox-house (H) Stall (S) *Bovite* (B)	Cow house (C) *Shepina* (S)	Wain House	Store	Other buildings	
L54	105	21	3					3		2S					Kynnyshall
L55	52	23	3					2	1		1S				Kinihall, Lewannick
L56	14	23	3		*cubiculum*(2)		2M	3*		2B					North Tregere; * new-built barn
L57	61	24	3	3	milkhouse(?2)										St. Stephen; [?way]nehouse [Ms. defective]
L58	21	24	6			1		3			3C+2S	4			Causpenheale
L59	22	24	=			2		3		=B		2		lean-to adj. bakehouse	Causpenheale; house + *bovite* adj(7)
L60	23	24	6					3		3B					Causpenheale
L61	99	26	3			=		=+			=S		=+	le lean	Tregadillick; barn + store(4), bakehouse + *shepa'*(2)
L62	43	27	4		backhouse(=)				=					ass-house (*asinum*)(=)	St. Stephen; stable + backhouse + *asinum*(6)
L63	16	30	4			2		=						shepepen(=)	Laneast; barn + shepepen adj(4)
L64	32	30	=	2				4		=H					Ashill, St. Stephen; house + oxhouse(4)
L65	63	31	4					4							Dutston, Launceston
L66	100	31	=	2				=+		=S	=+S			le leyntooe	Tregadillick; house + le stall(4); barn + *shepa'*(4)
L67	106	31	3			2				3S					Trebursey, St. Thomas
L68	88	32	3			1		=					=		St. Stephen; barn + store(5)
L69	36	32	=					2+4					=		Kernisk(?), St. Stephen; house + store(3); 2 barns
L70	20	33	=			2		3		=B		3		shepepen(2)	Lutcot; house + *bovite* under one roof(6)
L71	108	33	3			2		3			2C				Colehaye
L72	119	34	3			1		3	1						North Trebursey
L73	17	35	3		*cubiculum*(1)	2				3B					Kessell
L74	116	35	7				2M 3B	5	==					strawhouse(3)	Landreyne, St. Thomas; two stables(4)
L75	126	35	3		le parlor(2); le chamber(2)				2	5S					Tresmannion(?)

Table 13 *continued*

Ref. Number	Ms. Number	Acres	House	Kitchen	Ancilliary Buildings: Other domestic rooms and housing	Ancilliary Buildings: Bake house	Ancilliary Buildings: Malt house (M) Brew house (B)	Farm Buildings: Barn	Farm Buildings: Stable	Farm Buildings: Ox-house (H) Stall (S) *Bovite* (B)	Farm Buildings: Cow house (C) *Shepina* (S)	Farm Buildings: Wain House	Farm Buildings: Store	Farm Buildings: Other buildings	Places; Notes
L76	24	38	4			2		4		2B					Kessell
L77	8	40	4	3				5		2B					Doddyston, St. Thomas
L78	39	40	3					4							Lower Truscott, St. Stephen
L79	56	40	7						4						St. Stephen
L80	98	41	2	3	other bld(2)			o	o					maltmill + wheatmill(3)	Athall, Tresmere, Laneast
L81	13	41	4			3		5	2	3B		3			North Tregere
L82	26	43	•						4						Wollacott; house decayed
L83	34	44	8		backhouse(1)			2							Nether Truscott, St. Stephen
L84	25	44	1												Wollacott; house 12 ft. square
L85	89	45	2			2		6	4						High Hall, Laneast
L86	12	46	5	3				5	1			2			North Tregere
L87	10	47	3			3	2M	4		3B					Trevallet
L88	11	49	3	4				4	2			3		hayhouse(2) outhouse(2)	North Tregere
L89	7	50	3		milkhouse(1)	2		4	1	2B					Trevallet, St. Thomas
L90	3	73	3			2		2	1	3B	=C	=			Tresmere; cowhouse + wainhouse(5)
L91	97	80	2							2H					Trewant, Lewannick
L92	37	83	3					5	2			3			Trevallet, St. Thomas
L93	101-2	89	4	2		2		=	2	=S				leany(=)	Carmolor, St. Thomas; barn + oxestall + leany(5)
L94	6	92	6		2nd house	3	3B	4	2	4B					Thorne, [Egloskerry?]
L95	5	117	2		buttery(2)		2B	3	1	3B	2C	3			Egloskerry
L96	133	c.200	=	=				=	=					other blds(=) mill(2)	Newhouse grange; house + kitchen(10); barn + stable + other blds(6)

Notes: The column for 'Other housing' includes 'houses' (domus), *buildings* (edific') *and tenements* (tenem'). *On the few occasions where a tenant holds two consecutive properties, the acreages are combined. Holdings with no buildings are omitted, as follows (acreages in brackets) Ms. 4(46), 9(24), 27–9 (10,10,11), 33(6), 35(1), 44(9), 49–50(1¼, 1½), 58(29), 62(3), 65-6(4, 3), 69(2), 73(4), 81(1), 93–6(32, —, 26, 3), 114(2), 128–30(22, —, —). Ms. 129 was at Ashwater, Devon.*

Survey of Cornish Manors: 1602
(Public Rec. Off.: E315/404; Augmentation Office Miscellaneous Books)

This book contains several unrelated paper volumes of surveys, bound up together. The volume examined here, which occupies ff. 65-91, deals with a group of Cornish manors. It starts (ff. 1-11, original foliation) with a survey of them all (datable after 1598 from internal evidence); after two blank folios, comes the survey transcribed here (ff. 14-22v). It is followed by a further survey of Landreyne, and an index (f. 25v).

The survey poses no problems of legibility, and few of interpretation. It is worth noting that occasionally sums are recorded in the left margin, in addition to the rent; these are probably actual or suggested entry fines, and are here labelled [*fine*].

The first survey contains (f.5) a description of the commons of Treverbyn Courtenay, which is of interest both in comparison to the Kenton survey, and for its evidence of the importance of tin mining. It reads:

The commons of the mannor are bounded as followes. viz. from Carwallen to Bogeve burrow; from thence [*omitted hereafter*] to Newton Bridge; to the corner of Gunheath; to a borrow on the west of Crowse Gellyn; to Hennsborrowe; to Stenackladren well; to a rock between Owen and Treverbyn Courtney; to Tregyans Lodge; to a thorne in Gwethen Bryny; to a well betweene Melynnys and Hallew; by Polpryn to Bilbery; and so to Polpryn Bridge; to three stones; and so to another stone by Lawallon; to the ponyon [*gable*] of a house of Lavrean Vean; to a Lodge; and so to Junnys; and so to a stone at Restennys Lane End; and to the end of Carracles; to a crosse; and so to Carwallen.

All this common is full of Tynnworkes and very likely for tynne. The names of the tynnworkes:

[*column one*] Polpryn; Great Beame; Mewan Beame; Gwethen Barra; Corgell Downe; the old Corgell Downe; Halewyn and Haloybett; Newe Worke; Dolphyns Worke; [?Noxe] Lane Gwenvos; Crebelleskes; Will. Gumnos Work; Brasse; Kerrowe; Hie Shilfe; Legoes Worke; Lewastes Beame upon Hill; Cricktoll and Good Fortune; Penweness; the Brasse; [*column two*] Quarter Worke; Verkaren; Crickelase; Garra; Little Cricktell; Litle Godd Fortune; Litle Spare; 2 workes in Davies Moore; Penhoe; Greywill; Screda; Penivitheck Moore; Single Rose; Gelaffer; Nynestones; Bolassack; Whethon; Corlogals Borowe; White Myne; Hallase Moore; Treverbyn Moore; [*column three*] Our Lady Beame; Knighter in Othe; Rescorla Moore; the Stenyestenyck; [?Menhie] Parkes.

TEXT

[f.14r] *A Survey of the Manor of Treverbyn Courtney in the County of Cornwall, taken 29 March* [1602]
Manor of Treverbyn Courteney: Free Tenants there

C1. *Hugo Trevanyon, knight, and the heirs of Pollerde hold one tenement called Kayrnamanyn containing 60 ac. of land and they pay thence per year 2s 7d.*

C2. *Nicholas Boyer for one tenement called Trevenoth in Treverbyn containing one ferling* [farlingum] *of land 13d.*

C3. *John Rescorla for one tenement in Hallas containing one ferling of land pays per year 4s.*

C4. *William Lower esquire, for one cottage with garden and croft in the town [*villa*] of St. Austell pays per year 19d.*

C5. *Edward Tripcony for one tenement called Carvere with three closes of land pays per year 2s 6d.*

C6. *Edward Penwarne, esquire, for one tenement called Knightier containing 30 ac. of land, per year 2s 3d.*

C7. *John Trehauke [? Trehanke] for one tenement called Russells containing 3 ac. of land per year 4s.*

C8. *Christopher Woolcocke for one tenement called Ewynheth containing 30 ac. of land, 2s 8d.*

C9. *Richard Lavrean for one tenement in Knightier containing 30 ac. of land, 2s 6d.*

C10. *Richard Trethowell for one tenement in Trethirgye pays per year 19½d.*

C11. *John Stoddon and John Carlyan for one other tenement in Threthirgie pay per year 19½d.*

C12. *Thomas Bere for one tenement called Odgabere pays per year 5s 8d.*

C13. *Thomas Davye for one tenement in Knyghtior pays per year 19½d.*

C14. *Martin Tristeane for one tenement called Penhiere containing 9 ac. of land pays 4s 2d.*

Total of the free tenements: 37s 10½d

Manor of Treverbyn Courteney: Customary Tenants there

C15. Carveigh alias Carvergh. John Reynold by copies of court roll bearinge date the fyveth daie of September in the seventh yere of the raigne of Quene Elizabeth that now is

[*1565*], holdeth in Carveighe alias Carvergh one messuage contayning a hall, a chamber at the upper end thereof, a kytchin, a deyhouse, a barne, an oxe house, a wayne house, a courtlidge, a bee garden, a mowhaye, a garden, an orcharde, worthe by the yeare 30s; two closes of land called West Parkes contayneng 3½ ac., worth by the yere 40s;[1] Parke Bawden, 1¼ ac., 16s 8d; a moore under the same. ½ ac., 5s; St. Austell Parke, 40 [?*perches*],[2] 6s; the close behind the garden, 60 [*p*..], 4s; the Castell Close 2½ ac., 25s; a close called Polpit, 3 ac., 30s; close by the lane, ½ ac., 6s 8d; the Down Close, 3½ ac., 16s; the Myddle Close, 3½ ac., 17s 6d; the Whomer Close, 3 ac., 20s; a stitch of land called Polcatch, ¼ ac. 2s 6d.

Annual rent 15s 3d [*Fine*] £88 *Annual value* £10 19s 3d.[3]

C16. St. Austell Towne. Maude Light, a widow, during her widowhood holdeth there one messuage contayning a hall, a chamber at the upper end thereof, a kytchyn, a curtlage, a backside, a garden, worth by the yere 20s; a medowe, 1 ac., 13s 4d, in the hedges therof ashes and elmes to value of 10s; a litle medowe before the dore, ¼ ac., 5s.

[*Rent*] 7s[*Annual value*] 43s 4d.

Reversion [*blank*]

C17. St. Austell Towne, Henry Nicollas and Elizabeth his daughter holde there one messuage contayning a hall, a chamber at the upper end therof, a seller, a stable, a backside, a garden, worth by the yere 20s; one close of land and a litle garden in the same, 13s 4d; Castell Parke, lac., 10s.

[*Rent*] 6s 8d [*Annual value*] 43s 4d.

C18. St. Austell Towne. Henry Buffitt holdeth there one messuage containing a hall, a chamber, a backside, a garden, per annum 13s 4d; the meadow under the vicarage, 70 [?*p*.], 6s 8d; a little garden by the same, 2s 6d; Quarry Park, ½ ac., 6s 8d; Rock Park, ½ ac., 6s 8d; Longe Parke, ¼ ac., and 20 [p.], 5s; a garden by the litle lane, 2s.

[*Rent*] 6s [*Annual value*] 42s 10d.

C19. Treganhiso. Gregory Rowse holdeth there a messuage and tenement containing a faire hall, a buttry, a kitchin, a milkehowse, a bakehouse, a barne, a stable, an oxen howse, a sheepe howse, a lenny house and other smale houses, a backside and a towneplace, per annum 33s 4d; a litle garden before the house, 20 [?*p*..],[4] 2a; an orchard, ¾ ac., 13s 4d; the litle medow, ½ ac. 6s 8d; a close called [?Caroures],[5] ½ ac., 5s; the close above the house, 2½ ac., 25s; close under the Church Waie, 5 ac., 50s; Polkear, 5½ ac., 44s; Great Close, 6½ ac., £3 lls 6d; Crosse Parke, 3½ ac., 35s; two Downe Closes, 20 ac., 30s; Gwallen, 13 ac., 26s.

[*Rent*] 15s 3d [*Fine*] £90 [*Annual value*] £17 1s 10d.

C20. Treganhiso. John Trelevan holdeth there a faire house, a kytchen, a buttry, a mylkehouse and certen chambers over them, a barne, a stable, a sheep house, a bakehouse, a mowhaye and thre gardens contayning 56 perches, per annum 40s; 2 litle orchardes, 5s; one close called the Bovetowne, 3 ac., 36s; a backside, 6 p. 12d; East Park, 3½ ac., 35s; Litle Park, ¾ ac., 8s; the close next the Churchtowne, 5 ac., 40s; the Undertowne, 2 ac., 26s 8d; Furse Parke, 3 ac., 20s; the Farther Close, 2½ ac., 16s 8d; the Myddle Close, 4 ac., 16s; the Homer Downe Close, 6 ac., 20s; the Farther Downe Close, 10 ac., 25s.

[*Rent*] 10s 2d [*Fine*] £80 *Annual value*] £14 14s 4d.

C21. Carwall alias Carwallen. Nicholas Sawle holdeth there in the right of Jane Sawle, widow, a messuage and one close of land in the south parts of the same, 8 ac., 32s, and three other closes of very course downe land, 30 ac., 45s.

[*Rent*] 6s 4d [*Fine*] £30 [*Annual value*] £3 2s 8d.

C22. Benalleck. John Menheire holdeth there a tenement, Rovelles, contayning a close called the Furse Parke, 2 ac., 5s; one other close by the same, 1½ ac., 10s; a Broome Close, 9 ac., 36s; a litle peece of land by the old walls, ½ ac., 2s; a plott of furse land and a more therby near adioyning, 4 ac., 4s.

[*Rent*] 5s 2d [*Fine*] £26 [*Annual value*] £3 2s 8d.

C23. Menagwynsdy. Margery Tonkin holdeth there a litle meadow, 1 ac., 8s; two other closes, 9 ac., 45s; *Inquire by whose concession because she did not show a charter.*

[*Rent*] 4s 3d [*Fine*] £20 [*Annual value*] 53s.

C24. Trethirgie. Agnes Penwitheck, widow, holdeth there a quarter of one acre of land, worthe by the yere 2s.

[*Rent*] 4d.

C25. Greyth. John Josep holdeth there a messuage and tenement containing a hall, a chamber, a kitchen, an oxen house, a barne, a sheepe house, a towne place, per annum 25s; 2 closes called Barne Parkes, 6 ac., 36s; a medow behind the barne, 1 ac., 6s 8d; Stone Parke, 2¾ ac., 11s; Furse Parke, 10 ac., 25s; Laye Close, 4 ac., 20s; 2 litle meadowes behind the house, lac., 6s 8d; the Hall Parke, 2½ ac., 12s 6d; Cross Parke, 5 ac., 15s; a close called Boscawen, 11 ac., 55s; Greythlond, 8 ac., 40s; *Inquire if it is included in the copy or not*;[6] a severall common belonging to the same, 20s, and a moore ful of old tynnepites, 5s.

[*Rent*] 12s 4d [*Fine*] £90 [*Annual value*] £13 12s 4d.

---

[1] The name or description of each close is followed by its area and annual value. The words *containing* and *annual value* are omitted hereafter.

[2] The areas of several closes include a number (here 60), followed by a space. The clearest example (C40) reads 1 acre and half and 10, while C39 has 3 quarters and 20. This is interpreted as perches but it is puzzling that these are named explicitly in a few other entries.

[3] The annual rent and value are in the left and right margins respectively, although they are only labelled for this holding.

[4] Here the space contains a single letter, perhaps c.

[5] Smudged and uncertain, with a superscript letter, perhaps c.

[6] *Quere* in the margin.

C26. Rescorla. John Penhale holdeth there one messuage and tenement contayning a hall, a chamber at thend therof, a barne, a shepehouse, a backsyde and a mowhaye, a litle plot of ground called a meadowe, 20 p., per annum 13s 4d; Parke above the lane, lac., 5s; Litle Parke, ¾ ac., 5s; New Parke 3½ ac., 23s 4d; the Bovetowne, 1½ ac., 6s; Gwele Meors, 4½ ac., 22s 6d; Gwele Nowa, 3¼ ac., 8s 8d; Furse Parke, 9 ac., 18s; Newe Parke, 5 ac., 8s 8d; parke before the dore, 1¼ ac., 12s 6d; French Furze, 9 ac., 27s; the Carne [?Carue], lac., 3s 4d; the close before Reseyghan, 3½ ac., 17s 6d; the close before Tremoughe, 1¼ ac., 5s.

[*Rent*] 12s 8d [*Fine*] £50 [*Annual value*] £8 15s 4d.

C27. Rescorla. Thomas Roseveor holdeth there a tenement containing an olde peare of walls, a garden, a close called the Old Field, 1¼ ac., 6s 8d; the Bove Towne, 2 ac., 8s; the Long Close, 3¼ ac., 20s; the fourth parte of a Furse Close next Kerrowe, 3¼ ac., 6s 6d; the commons and furse belonging to this tenement, 20s.

[*Rent*] 3s 3d [*Annual value*] £3 1s 2d.

C28. Rescorla. Thomas Roseveor, *in the right of his sometime wife* Guinivore, holdeth there a messuage and tenement wheron there is a hall, a buttry, a mylk howse, a kytchin, an oxen howse, a shepe house, a dry house, certen old walls, a mowhaye, worth by the yere 20s; a litle close called the Will Parke, 1¼ ac., 8s 4d; Newe Parke, 2¼ ac., 9s; a litle stich above the hosue and a hempe haye, ¼ ac., 18d; Gwell Meor, 3 ac., 20s; Higher Croft, 2 ac., 8s; Gwell Nowth, 4½ ac., 18s; Furse Parke next Kerrowe, 10 ac., 20s; the close before Resigham, 4 ac., 32s; the Croft, 2 ac., 13s 4d; Great Parke, 3¼ ac., 26s; the moore under the towne, 11 ac., 16s 6d; a close called the Haye and a litle plot at the upper end therof, 1 ac., 50 [*?p.*]; 12s 6d; the Wortfolde, 2 ac., 10s; certen commons and furse in the same, 20s.

[*Rent*] 9s 9d [*Fine*] £80 [*Annual value*] £9 15s 2d.

Ther is belonging unto this village of Rescorla a certen severall common bordering uppon the west and south west parte therof called White Myne Downes alias Hengengever and Blacke Poole, contayning one hundred acres and more and are worth by the yeare, [*blank*] whereof there belongeth unto the Mannor of Treverbyn Courtney seven partes and the eight parte therof to John Rescorla and so of the whole village accordinglye.

C29. Higher Rosoga. John Killiowe, esquier, holdeth there by lettres patentes from Her Majestie which he showed not, a house, a garden, a plott of land about the same, worth by the yere 6s 8d; 4 closes next Hallas Blackpoole, 20 ac., £3; the Bovetown, 3 ac., 9s; a litle close next the same, 2 ac., 8s; 2 closes above the lane and a litle moore therin, 5 ac., 15s; 2 Furse Closes against Rescorla, 4 ac., 16s; a litle close under the watering, 1½ ac., 7s 6d; 3 other closes under the water that runneth to the house, 13 ac., £4. The third parte of all this tenement belongeth unto Mr. Trevanyon. And hath a common in a moore on both sides the land, viz. the east and west parts, worth by the yere, 10s.

[*Rent*] 5s 3d [*Fine*] £26 13s [*Annual value*] £6 19s 1d[7]

C30. Rosoga. John Vyvian holdeth there a faire house, a kytchin, a barne a wayne house, a sheephouse, a lenny, three litle gardens, a mowhaie, per annum 20s; 2 closes under the towne, 3½ ac., 21s; the Croft, 1½ ac., 7s 6d; a litle medow, 60 [*?p.*], 4s 6d; Parke Enhall, 3½ ac., 35s; Parke Ensouth, 5½ ac., £3 6s; Gwele Hunse, 1¼ ac., 8s 4d; Newe Parke, 1¼ ac., 8s 6s; Gwele Hunse 1¼ ac., 8s 4d; Newe Parke, 1¼ ac., 8s 4d; parke by the lane, lac., 5s; Longestone, 60 [*?p.*], 5s.

[*Rent*] 6s 3d [*Annual value*] £9 8d.

C31. Penivithecke. John Phelip holdeth there a house, a litle garden, worth 5s; a litle meadowe, ½ ac., 5s; the Lower Parke, 5 ac., 16s 8d; parke before the dore, 7 ac., 23s 4d; parke behind the house, 3 ac., 7s 6d; the Litle Downe Parke, 3 ac., 6s; the Great Downe Parke, 10 ac., 15s; Penivithecke Ball, 15 ac., 15s; Longstone Parke, lac., 18d.

[*Rent*] 6s [*Annual value*] £4

Ther is uppon the southwest parte of this tenement a severall common of 7 ac., wherin are divers old tynnworkes, worthe by the yere [*blank*].

C32. St. Austell Towne. John Carlyan holdeth there, *Inquire by what right*, two[8] tenementes contayning a hall,a chamber over the same, a shop, a sellar and chambers over, a stable, a backside or curtlage, worth by the yere 20s; a litle close called the Kill Parke, 30 p., 3s; a close uppon the Playeng Place, ¼ ac., 3 s 4d; the garden under the towne, 10 p., 2s; a close called Parcell of Carvergh Fieldes, 1½ ac., 24s; a litle orchard, 10 p., 2s 6d; Quarry Parke, ½ ac., 6s 8d; High Crosse, ¼ ac., 4s; one other close called Wrennageddell, 6s 8d.

[*Rent*] 8s 6d [*Annual value*] £3 12s 2d.

There are growing uppon this tenement certen elmes to the value of 20s. *Inquire*: Theis tenementes were surrendred in court but no copie therof grannted by the steward, and therefore *in the lord's mercy*.[9]

There is also a common there called Hensborrow Common contayning about foure hundred acres, wherof Mr Trevanyon doth clayme the one halfe, and an other common called Caroles which was lately leased by her Majestie as it is supposed for certen yeres, which should seme to be belonging wholy to the Quenes Manner of Treverbyn Courtney, which doth contayne 200 ac. or nere therabouts, in which ther is a very good tynworke, called by that name. Ther are also in all these commons tynneworkes, the toll tynne wherof is worth most commonly £20 by the yere, of which toll tynne Trevanyon hath alwayes the half. All the severall land and commons within the Mannor are likely for tynne, and the toll tynne is devided equally, aswell in the severall as com-

[7] Replacing £10 8s 2d.

[8] *Messu[age]* erased.

[9] *Quere* in margin, also £4 3s 10d at the foot of the page.

mon, betwene the Quene and Mr Trevanyon, and the farm tynne of the severall land to the lord of the same wholye.

C33 Treverbyn Myll. There is also the halfe of a griest myll in the tenure of Richard Kendall, gentleman, at the rent of 7s per annum, grannted by lettres patentes from her Majestie about 32nd of her raigne [1589-90] unto one Richard Sawle for certen eyres yet enduring, which was not shewedd, and is worth by ther yere £3.

[*Rent*] 7s [*Fine*] £30 [*Annual value*] £3

C34 The knocking mylle. Ther is also a knocking mylle for tinne which is supposed to be grannted unto the said Sawle by the same demyse, the rent therof 3s 10d, and is now converted to a tucking myll, worth by the yere 20s.

[*Rent*] 3s 10d [*Annual value*] 20s.

Total of the convencyonary rents £7 11s 2d.

To be improved £120 1s 1d besides the tynne and profittes of the commons and all perquysites of court which may be very well worth £20.[10]

[f.19r] *Manor of Landreyne*

C35. Landrene. Nicholas Willes holdeth there a messuage and tenement contayning a hall, a parlor, a chappell, a barne, a stabell, a mowhaie and a litle garden behind the chappell, and one other litle garden, ½ ac., worth by the yere 20s;[11] the moyty of the towne plac, lac., 6s 8d; a bakehouse decayed, nil; a close called Easte The Towne, 13 ac., £7 16s; a moore adioyning to the same, 2½ ac., 12s 6d; Easter Medow, 2 ac., 20s; Wester Meadowe, 5 ac., 25s; Borowe Parke, 4½ ac., 52s; Cholwell, 3 ac., 36s; Middell Parke, 3 ac., 36s; Highe Land, 5 ac., 55s; Kytchcroftes, 10 ac., £5.

[*Rent*] 14s 1d [*Annual value*] £25 19s 3d.

There are certen tres, viz. oakes, aishes and witchalse[12] growing uppon this tenement and in the moytie of the towne plac, worthe to be sold 40s.

C36. Landreyne. Gran Harvy, widowe, holdeth there a messuage and tenement contayning a hall, a chamber at the upper end therof, a chamber below the same, an oxenhouse, a shepe house, a barne, a stable, a garden, a mowhay, an orcharde, per annum 30s; a close called Bovitowne, 6 ac., £4; Easter Towne, 3 ac., 30s; a Moore Medow, 3½ ac., 23s 4d; the Wester More Medowe, 5 ac., 25s; Burrowe Parke, 3¾ ac., 45s; Churche Parke, 7 ac., £4 4s; two closes called the Newe Parkes, 7 ac., £3; Kichecroftes, 10 ac., £5.

[*Rent*] 13s 7d [*Annual value*] £24 14s 4d.

There are certen tres, viz. oakes, aishes and witchalse growing uppon this tnement and in the moyty of the town place, worth 20s.

Quere [?antea] de Kitchcroftes quia [. . .]

Inquire: The land called Kitchcroftes is thought to be parcell of the Mannor of Northill and not of Landreyne, and the said Harvy and Willes do paye their rent in this sort, viz. to the feodary of the Duchye 7s 7d and for their rent of Landrene 5s 9d and for the rent of Kitchcroftes 9d.

C37. West Berry; Yeo. William Master holdeth there a messuage and tenement conteyning a hall, two chambers at the upper end therof, a buttry, a chamber over the same, a bakehowse, an oxenhouse, a barne, a stable, a mylkehouse, a waynehouse, a shepe house, a seller and chamber over the same, a curtlage, a backside, a garden 3 orchardes, per annum 46s 8d; a medow, 1 ac., 13s 4d; Bridg Parke, 3 ac., 30s; Underhill, 1¾ ac., 11s 8d; the Hill, lac., 5s; Wood Parke, 1¾ ac., 6s 3d; Calvern Parke, 1¾ ac., 7s 6d; Bovehay, 3 ac., 15s; Grene Parke, 1½ ac., 5s; Will Park, 1 ac., 3s 4d; the close next Noddon, 1 ac., 2s; Noddon, being a rocky peece of land inclosed, about 35 ac., 35s.

[*Rent*] 10s [*Annual value*] £9 10s 3d.

There is uppon this tenement a wood contayning 14 ac., leased unto Thomas Vincent, gentleman, by lettres patentes from her Majestie as he reporteth, the coppies young springes therof much distroyed with beastes, wherin Mr Vincent hath tenn yeres to expire of his terme, as himself reporteth. The soyle rocky and very unapt for wood.

There groweth uppon this tenement (and Landreyne)[13] tymber trees in the hedges and closes therof, worth to be solde sixtene poundes or theraboutes.[14] This also and the close called Noddon are very likely for tynne and may be worth by the yere [*blank*].

C38. Pallismyll. The said William Mayster holdeth also the greist mills of the mannor and a litle garden therunto belonging.

[*Rent*] 18d [*Annual value*] £6 13s 4d.

C39. Westmolla. Richard Wering holdeth there a messuage and tenement containing a hall, a chamber, a bakehouse, an orchard, a garden, a mowhaye, worth by the yere 13s 4d; three litle closes called Hollandes, 3 ac., 30s; 2 litle closes called High Landes, 22s; one close called East Parke, 1 ac., 12s; the Bovetowe [*sic*] lac. 50 [?*p.*] 16s; Washpoole Medowe, ¾ ac., 10s; Westparke, 1 ac., 6s 8d; Crosparke, ¾ ac., 20 [?*p.*] 6s 8d; a moore medowe under the same, ¾ ac., 8s; a common in a marrish peeic of land lyeng in the west parte of this tenement, 3s

[*Rent*] 2s 6d[*Annual value*] £6 7s 8d.

There are growing uppon this tenement 6 smale oakes, foure smale elmes and two litle ashes, worth 3s 4d.

C40 West Molla. Robert Finge holdeth there a messuage and tenement containing a hall, a chamber, a bake house decayed, a litle garden, a mowhaye, per annum 13s 4d; 2 closes called the High Landes, 2 1/1 ac., 26s 6d; a little

---

10 £120 5s 1d *bisides* at the foot of the page.

11 30s erased.

12 Perhaps elms, rather than hazels.

13 Interlined.

14 One line heavily crossed out.

close at the lower end therof, ¾ ac., 10s; Underway, ¾ ac., 10s; Undertowne, 1 ac. 50 [?*p*.], 16s, 8d; the Bovetowne, 1½ ac., 10 [?*p*.], 20s; Highe Crosparke, 1¾ ac., 11s 8d; Nether Crospark, 1¼ ac., 10s; a moore medow under the same ¾ ac., 10s; a common in the west parte therof, 3s 4d.

[*Rent*] 2s 6d [*Annual value*] £6 9s 2d.

C41. Blowing mill and a house. Henry Spore, esquier, holdeth there the blowing myll and house lyeng nere Colsabridge alias Bery Yeo Bridge, and is worth by the yere 13s 4d.

[*Rent*] 10d.

(Nicholas Willis holdeth there one tenenment, parcell of the Barton, *by letters patent as it is said*, for certen yeres, per annum [*blank*].)[15]

Total of the annual rent of the Manor of Landreyne by appraisal[16] £80 2s 5d.

[f.20v] *Manor of Northill*

C42. Northill alias Northpill. William Blighe holdeth there a hall, 2 chambers, a bakehouse decayed, a backside, a faire orchard, ½ ac., per annum 20s; a litle medow, ½ ac., 5s; Buttes Parke, 2½ ac., 25s; Globall, ½ ac., 20 [?*p*.], 7s 8d;[17] Rack Parke, lac. 30 [?*p*.], 12s 6d; Waye Parke, 2½ ac., 16s 8d; 3 Northe Parkes, 5¼ ac., 26s 3d; Crosse Land, 1¼ ac., 5s; 3 closes called Longe Landes, 7 ac., £4 4s; Hall Parke, 1½ ac., 13s 6d; Old Parke, 1½ ac., 13s 6d.

[*Rent*] 11s [*Annual value*] £10 16s 1d.

C43. Newham. Henry Spore, esquier, holdeth there one close next Treswell, 8 ac., 36s; a litle more under the same, ½ ac., 2s; the Middle Close, 15 ac., £3 15s; the close next the lane, 6 ac., 20s; the Long East Close, 6 ac., 30s; 3 ac., of marrish groundes in the same, 9s.

[*Rent*] 5s [*Annual value*] £8 12s.

[f.21r] *Manor of Crofthole*

C44. Bryanthaies. Ferdinando Spiller holdeth there a messuage, a seller, a chamber, and a litle garden, worth by the yere 20s; ½ ac. land, 10s.

[*rent*] 9d [*Annual value*] 30s.

C45. Sone. Walter Sone holdeth there a stable, a barne, a cow house, a litle garden, 10p, 23s 4d; ¼ ac., medowe land, 6s 8d.

[*Rent*] 9d [*Annual value*] 30s.

C46. Gills Hayes and Weshehayes. Tristram Harrye holdeth there 2 burgages or tenementes called Gillwalles alias Gillhaies and Welshes[18] alias Welsehayes, wheron ther is a faire house containing a hall, a chamber at the upper end therof, a buttrey, a seller and chamber at thend therof, a kytchin, a stable and other litle houses, a backside, a garden, an orchard, 30 p., all worth by the yere 40s; one medowe and a litle orchard in the same ½ ac., 13s 4d; one other medowe, 50 p., 7s.

[*Rent*] 18d [*Annual value*] £3 4d.

The medow which he holdeth there called Willhayes contayning ½ ac., at the rent of 18d, is parcell of the land above mencyoned.

C47. High Howse. John Nannber holdeth a messuag and tenement called Highe House wherin ther is a hall, a chamber over the same, a litle dwelling house at thend of the hall, a smythes shop, two litle gardens, 10 p., all worth by the year 40s; a meadow, 1 ac., 26s 8d.

[*Rent*] 9s 4d [*Annual value*] £3 6s 8d.

All these tenementes are there called burgages and other tenementes which any free tenantes have within the same are called free burgages, and every one, as well free as convencyonarie, have a like quantity of land belonging unto them, viz. a quarter of an acre to each of them, as I was enformed, and it is very likely to be true, for every full burgage payeth 9d per annum as the convencyonary doth.

Total of convencionary rents 13s 10d.

[f.21v] *Crofthole*

In the whole village are [*blank*] fre burgages.

C48. Thomas Smyth, esquyer, holdeth there fyve free burgages an a half, and payeth yerely 4s 1½d.

C49. John Skynner[19] holdeth there fower free burgages and payeth by the yere 3s.

C50. Thomas Sone one free burgage, 9d.

C51. William Brooken and others one free burgage, 9d.

C52. John Creiffell one free burgage, 9d.

C53. John Smyth of Shevyocke 2 free burgages, 18d.

C54. John Moreshead one free burgage, 9d.

C55. John Fostreate one free burgage, 9d.

C56. Jeffery Michell one free burgage, 9d.

C57. Walter Cample[20] and others one free burgage, 9d.

C58. Ferdinando Spiller one free burgage, 9d.

C59. John Dwayne one free burgage, 9d.

C60. John Skynner holdeth there one house and payeth by the yere 12d.

Total of free burgages [*blank*]

The whole rent of the manner yerely payd unto Her Majestie is [*blank*] wherof the Reve yerely payeth out of his owne purse 4½ d, which is not known who ought to paye the same.

[15] This item has been added in another hand, perhaps that of the following survey.

[16] *Appriamen* for *Appretiamentum*.

[17] 9s erased.

[18] *Walls* erased. The name in the heading is clearly *Weshehays*, not *Welshehaies*.

[19] *Quere* in margin.

[20] *Quere* in margin.

[f.22r] *Manor of Tregameer*

C61. Tregamere. James Hawke holdeth there a messuage and tenement wheron there is a hall, a chamber, a kitchyn, a barne, an oxenhouse, a mowhay, a garden, all worth 12s; the close called Cross Parke, 4 ac., 24s; three closes called West Parkes, 8 ac., 32s; the meadow unmder the house, 2 ac., 16s.

[*Rent*] 10s 10d [*Annual value*] £4 4s.

There are growing in the hedges of this tenement 8 smale elmes worth 3s 4d.

C62. Tregamere. John Calwaye holdeth there a hall, a bakehouse, a chamber over the hall, a barne, a mowhaye, all worth 12s; a close called Crossparke, 4 ac., 26s 8d; the narrow close next the water, 2½ ac., 20s; a moore under the same, lac., 2s; the close above the hill, 3 ac., 15s; the Litle Hill, 1¼ ac., 4s; the Great Hill, 3 ac., 9s; the moore under the same, 1 ac., 2s 6d.

[*Rent*] 10s 10d [*Annual value*] £4 11s 2d.

C63. The same John Calway holdeth there a tuckinge myll, worth by the yere 13s 4d.

[*Rent*] 2s 4d [*Annual value*] 13s 4d.

There are growinge uppon Calwayes tenement 12 smale oakes worthe 6s 8d.

C64. The Griest Myll. Thomas Vyvyan, gentleman, holdeth there the moytie of a greist myll and the weare and leate belonging to the same, worth by the yere 40s.

[*Rent*] 3s 4d.

C65. Trevethick. Thomas Arundell, esquier, holdeth there a messuage and tenement wheron ther is a very faire houyse, a garden and an orchard, a common in the towne plac, worth by the yere 40s; the meadow under the garden, 2 ac., 21s; 2 moores, 6 ac., 26s 8d; a close by the same, 2 ac., 13s 4d; the North Park, 10 ac., 50s;[21] 2 closes under the lane and a moor under the same, 5 ac., 16s 8d; the Common Close, 3 ac., 12s.

[*Annual value*] £8 9s[22]

C66. Tremayne. John Vyvian holdeth there the moytie of a tenement called Tremayne contayning 50 ac. of arrable and pasture, worth by the yere £12 10s; and 10 ac., of marrishe land, 20s; and the moytie of a medowe contayning 2 ac., 8s.

[*Annual value*] £13 18s.

There is also a hedweare which William Gilbert holdeth at will and the myll decayed, the rent therof by the yere 6d, *and worth nothing more*.[23]

---

[21] 8 ac., 40s erased.

[22] No rent is given for C65 and C66.

[23] The page continues with the next survey, in a different hand, entitled *Landreyne by Mr. Moleswort hes Booke of Survey.*

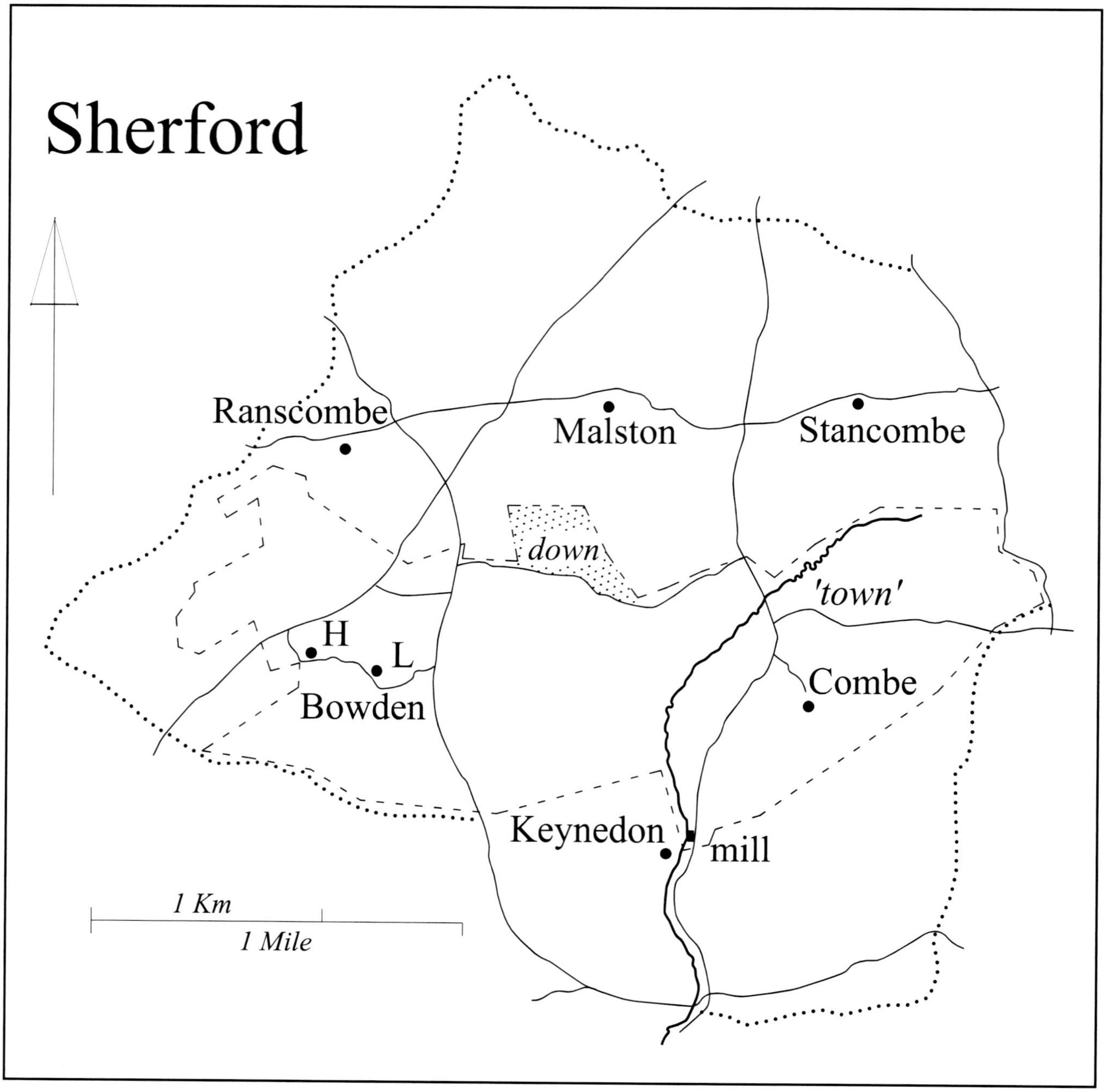

Map 4. Sherford parish, Devon

The 1659 survey shows that SH6, 7, 9, 21, 22 were in Bowden, while SH31 can be tentatively identified with Ranscombe (though this was later in separate ownership). Holdings SH14, 23, 24, 27 were certainly in Sherford Town, the settlement around the church (probably with most of the remainder). SH5 was Combe (see British Lib. Add. Mss. 21608, p. 146). The dashed line shows the boundary of the manor in 1786 (from a map owned by Mr. R. Cuming, and studied with his kind permission). Keynedon, Malston and Stancombe were independent manors in Sherford parish, in separate ownership. H=Higher, L=Lower.

CHAPTER 8

Sherford

Sherford (SH): 1609 *Map 4*

The group of surveys considered in chapters 8-10, for Sherford (1606), Farway, Whitwell and Seaton (1609), cover most of the estates of John Willoughby of Payhembury, Devon.[1] Sherford was well separated from the bulk of his property, which was in East Devon; it lies in the extreme south of Devon, in the area known as the South Hams. It has moderately good soil, overlying the South-Hams slate, which is used in all the existing buildings (coming from small local quarries). The sea is too far away for it to provide direct employment, although a local charity provided for the support of orphans of seamen.

The Sherford survey is the last of a long series. The extra detail it gives, compared to the earlier ones, must have been found particularly useful, encouraging John Willoughby (who wrote it himself) to survey the rest of his estate in 1609. The properties were resurveyed in 1682, but for the Sherford this second survey gives little further information about buildings.[2] Another partial survey, taken in 1659, was added to until 1680.[3] This can be fairly well correlated with that of 1682, but the relationship with the 1606 description is complex. It is clear that there had been substantial rearrangement of holdings, leading to consolidation of farms into larger units. Not all these changes can be followed precisely but, for example, both SH3 and SH22 were split up; the land of SH3 was leased by the owner of the adjoining manor, Stancombe, while about twenty acres of SH22 were combined with SH20 (giving a total of sixty-five), and the remaining forty were leased to Nicholas Sumter. He also held both SH1 and SH32, with other smaller holdings—a total of at least 200 acres.

Unexpectedly, Sherford seems to have been in a state of economic and demographic decline, in contrast to the other estates examined here and to the general trends of the late sixteenth and seventeenth centuries. This decline is seen in the decayed or destroyed cottages in 1606 (SH4, 8, 29), as well as in those falling into ruin during the seventeenth century. Some new cottages did appear by 1682, while the 'Church-house' (SH24) was converted into two cottages in 1608.[4] This economic stagnation may well be an example of the general depression found by Fox[5] in south as opposed to east Devon and attributed by him to the lack of a cloth industry.

A close study has been made of the Sherford documents, in conjunction with fieldwork, in the hope of identifying a number of the houses on the ground.[6] This has been unsuccessful, but not because of the gaps between the surviving surveys. In the two main concentrations, Bowdon and the 'Town' around the church, no buildings retain any substantial portions of seventeenth-century work.

The Sherford survey includes no free-holdings, although there were some large independent properties within the parish. Although it is not directly stated in the survey, tenure was by lease; the court books[7] contain no copyhold grants in the seventeenth century. SH31 and 32, for which 2,000 year leases are mentioned, had probably been mortgaged by John Willoughby.

The Houses

The twenty house descriptions for Sherford give room names, with one extra feature: the number of 'poole of timber'. At first sight, this could be the 'couples' of the Kenton survey, but the note in SH1, 'being 8 foote in every poole', is not consistent with this. Also, minor rooms are given a measurement in feet (e.g. SH14), and the only satisfactory interpretation is that the 'pooles' give the length of the buildings. Most of the houses had about two poole for each room in the plan, reasonable enough, allowing for the roughness of the measurements; 16 ft. is rather larger than the normal internal length of rooms, but is not too far from common external dimensions.[8]

The most remarkable aspect of the Sherford survey is the number of long-houses recorded from a part of Devon where they are now unknown. SH5 is a characteristic example, with a hall, kitchen, buttery and shippon, and three rooms over, of 8 poole (64 ft.). It also had a separate dairy, and a new malthouse with a room over adjoined the barn that was the only other building for the thirty-one acre farm. Seven of the twelve substantial farms had shippons as part of the farmhouse. Although their plans were varied, this large group shows a tradition different from those found elsewhere in Devon, and clearly stemming from the long-house. Three of these houses (SH7, 9, 14) had the shippon accompanied by two domestic rooms (hall with shop, inner room and parlour respectively), and may have had the classic long-house plan, a cross-passage with shippon to one side, hall and inner room to the other. SH14 also included a buttery and dairy whose length is given in feet, suggesting they were in a lean-to (cf. SH2); this is a characteristic addition to the long-house plan, presumably because the space on the other side of the passage is taken up by the shippon (cf. Figure 3). Three others were larger, with hall and two rooms: kitchen and buttery (SH5, 22); kitchen and inner room (SH21). These may represent long-houses with an extra room added, but may otherwise have followed the old tradition in having the shippon in the main range, but perhaps not in the traditional position. Extra rooms, perhaps in added wings like the malthouse of SH5, were common among these long-houses—bakehouses (SH7, 9, 14), a buttery (SH14), dairies[9] (SH9, 14, 21, 22), and one parlour (SH21). SH3 should probably be included with the long-houses, though it was unusual, having a hall, with a separate buttery, shop, malthouse and shippon. This probably indicates an L-shaped building (if not one more complicated) which is reflected in its subdivision in 1659. The hall made up one unit, with an entry (passage) along the back (i.e. away from the street) and a derelict second section contained the remainder.

The farms of the other substantial holdings lacked integral shippons. SH2 and 32 were particularly large; the first had eight rooms in plan, and the other contained a hall, parlour, kitchen, dairy, larder and porch, with six chambers over (perhaps including one over the porch), and also with a bakehouse and chamber over.[10] SH6, 20 and 31 were rather smaller, and in more than one range. None had a parlour, and only SH20 a kitchen; SH31, like SH3 and 7, included a 'shop', suggesting that they were craftsmens houses.

Most of the houses of the smaller holdings were of two bays, hall and buttery (SH27, 30), or hall and kitchen (SH23). Two had a hall alone (SHI5, 26), though the first of these also had a malthouse, and the other a 12 ft. linhey[11] which may have been domestic and not agricultural. The 1605 description of the latter, 'one house and ladder room', gives a vivid impression of the type of upper room to be expected in these houses.

Two houses had three rooms, (SH2, 13); one was not further described, but the other contained hall, inner room and kitchen. There was also the Church-house (SH24), which was clearly an unusual building, 64 ft. long, with only two rooms on each floor, and was, as noted, later divided into two cottages.

In one major respect, the Sherford houses differ from those so far described. Hardly any had ground floor chambers,[12] and instead, the sleeping rooms had clearly been moved upstairs. Most of the houses were fully two-storied, although a few followed the older style, with only one or two bays ceiled (SH9, 13, 27; SH21).[13] A significant number of the secondary buildings also had chambers over them. A natural result of this improvement was that ground floor rooms could take on more varied uses, as parlours, butteries or kitchens, although cooking was still more often done in the hall (ten houses), than in the kitchen (eight houses).

The Farm Buildings (Table 14)

As elsewhere, cottages and small holdings were accompanied by few farm buildings. Nine properties with less than twelve acres had between them only two barns (SH8, 15), two linheys (SH13, 26), and two stables (SH2, 23), one combined with a 'working house', the pair 'being builded as lynneys'. The larger farmers all owned barns, some two. The other characteristic agricultural building was the shippon. Those still incorporated in long-houses have been mentioned above. Others were freestanding (SH 3-4, 6, 31, 32) or attached to a barn (SH20). The survey seems to have caught this village in the midst of that familiar transformation in which the cattle were being relegated to separate outbuildings leaving the farmhouse entirely free for domestic uses.

Other changes were afoot in Sherford. Shippons were losing their traditional association with dairy

Table 14: Sherford: Dimensions of farm buildings (poole(p))

Ref. Number	Acres	Barn	Stable	Shippon	Linney	Other buildings and notes
SH26	0				*	* perhaps domestic
SH27	0					
SH30	0					
SH4	3					
SH13	3				•	
SH2	7	3p	*			* stable + working house as linneys
SH8	7					
SH15	7	3p				
SH23	12		1p			
SH21	25	6p		=		house + shippon(10p)
SH6	28	6p		3p		
SH3-4	31	5p		4p		
SH7-8	33	5p		=	•	house + shippon(6p)
SH14	35	4p	2p	=		house + shippon(6p)
SH20	45	= =	=	=		barn + stable(3p); barn + shippon(8p)
SH9	46	= =	=	=		house + shippon + barn(12p); barn + stable(5p)
SH5	56	•		=		house + shippon(8p)
SH22	58	6p	*	=	*	house + shippon(20p); *linney or stable(2p)
SH31	60	6p	2p	*		*cowhouse(2p)
SH1	72	* *	*			*two barns + one stable(12p)
SH32	93	* *	*	*+3p		*two barns + stable + shippon + dovehouse(22p); second shippon for fat oxen(3p) (also held 90 ac. more (SH12, 18)

Notes: mill and parish house omitted. A 'poole' (8 ft) appear to be roughly equivalent to a bay.

cattle and becoming shelters for oxen, by implication in SH31, which had both a shippon and a cowhouse, and explicitly in SH32, where there were two shippons, one of 3 poole (24 ft.) 'for fatte oxen'. Furthermore, seven of the eight largest farms (except SHl) had stabling for horses in addition to shippons. They may have been riding or pack horses, or, if draught animals, they may have been harnessed in tandem with the ox teams that were still used for ploughing in the nineteenth century. In any case, agricultural practices were apparently changing, arable farming and the use of horses becoming more prevalent. This seems to have led first to the conversion of shippons for oxen and then gradually to the appearance of more stables.

The largest farm (SH32) also boasted a dovehouse, an unusual building to find on a lesser holding than a manor house. It was combined with two barns and a stable. That there were no wainhouses in Sherford, even on this holding, is no surprise, considering that south Devon lacked both level ground and good roads.

[1] They are now in the Trevelyan estate archives, because his granddaughter, Mary Willoughby, married Sir George Trevelyan in 1656. Her father died in 1681, leaving her as his heiress, and this was obviously the cause of the new surveys being taken.

[2] The relationship between the surveys is considered under Seaton (p. 127); the notes to the Sherford text include a few details from 1682.

[3] S.R.O. DD/WO, Box 44; a considerable number of miscellaneous notes are in B.L. Add. Mss. 21608, and leases survive among the B.L. Add. Charters.

4 B.L. Add. Mss. 21608, f. 77.

5 H. S. A. Fox, 'The Chronology of Enclosure and Economic Development in Medieval Devon', *Economic Hist. Rev.*, 2 ser. 28 (1975), 181-202.

6 By K. Coutin. We are most grateful to her for allowing us to use her findings.

7 B.L. Add. Mss. 21606.

8 With three holdings, John Willoughby optimistically attempted to add pooles and perches (SH27, 27, 30). He perhaps had the equivalence of 'rod, pole and perch' in mind (although the Sherford 'poole' is much shorter than the standard 16½ ft. rod), and he apparently further confused the linear and areal measures with the same names.

9 For SH21, this was 20 ft. long, attached to the north side of the hall, a typical position for a lean-to dairy. The buttery and dairy of SH14 may have been similar.

10 A buttery had been added to this on the land of an adjoining holding (SH25), but it is not certain that this was always used as part of the house.

11 A lean-to building (cf. SH2) no doubt similar to the dairy of SH21.

12 Only the 'inner' or 'other' rooms of SH9, 19, 20 and 21 were possible chambers.

13 SH3 had no upper rooms named in 1606, but it also had no ground floor sleeping rooms, and the 1659 descriptions include two upper chambers.

Survey of Sherford: 1606 (Figure 25)

(British Library. Add. Mss 21605. Trevelyan muniments)

This volume contains a long series of surveys for Sherford, starting in 1543. These were originally on separate paper sheets, bound up in the 19th century (probably by the British Museum after they were presented by the Trevelyan family). Ff. 35-42 (modern foliation) contain the 1606 survey, the last one covering Sherford. It is in good condition, apart from a few tattered edges. The editing is slight, as there is little redundant information. The use of units poses some problems. The areas of fields are given as acres and rods (usually), but also as acres and yeards (e.g. SH32); these have both been converted to the form A 1-2-0, etc. However, *yeards* is also used (e.g. SH3) for the areas of the courtyard, with figures like *20 yeards*, which are far too large to be rods; here apparently yeards must be perches (which are also used in SH3). For *pooles*, see p. 107.

The hand is characteristic, well-formed and slightly ornate, and from many signed documents in Add. Mss. 21608, can be seen to be that of John Willoughby, the land-owner himself.

Unusually, the 1606 survey does not give information on rent and type of tenure. It has therefore been compared with the immediately preceding survey, of 1605 (f. 30ff), and rents have been added from this. The footnotes also give some more information from this survey, from one of 1659 (Somerset Rec. Off. DD/WO Box 44), and one of 1682 (see p. 127).

TEXT

[*f. 35v*] 1606. Sherford. Survey booke made by the enformacion of the tenantes themselves

[*f. 36v*] Sherforde Survey Anno 1606;

12 August 1606

A particular noate of every tenement, howse or howses, cottage and severall parcell of lande, and meadow, and pasture, and by what names they are called, and of what vallew, as it was then vallewed by the tenantes them selves, viz.

SH1. Mr. Arthur Wakeham, his tenement. Inprimis one dwelling howse (being in all 8 under roomes and 5 over roomes) conteyninge 7 polle of timber (being 8 foote in every poole),[1] too barnes one stable conteyninge 12 poole of timber, V-0-0,[2] one courtalaige, one herbgarden, A 1-0-0, V 2-0-0.[3]

Courthayes, A 4-0-0, R 1-0-0, V 4-0-0; Warde meadowe and the grove (½), A 6-2-0, R 1-6-8, V 8-0-0; one close called Renthayes, A 0-2-0, V 0-6-8-; too New Parkes, A 4-

1 The two bracketed phrases are interlined, in the original hand.

2 Interlined above *stable*

3 £3 bracketed against all the preceding items.

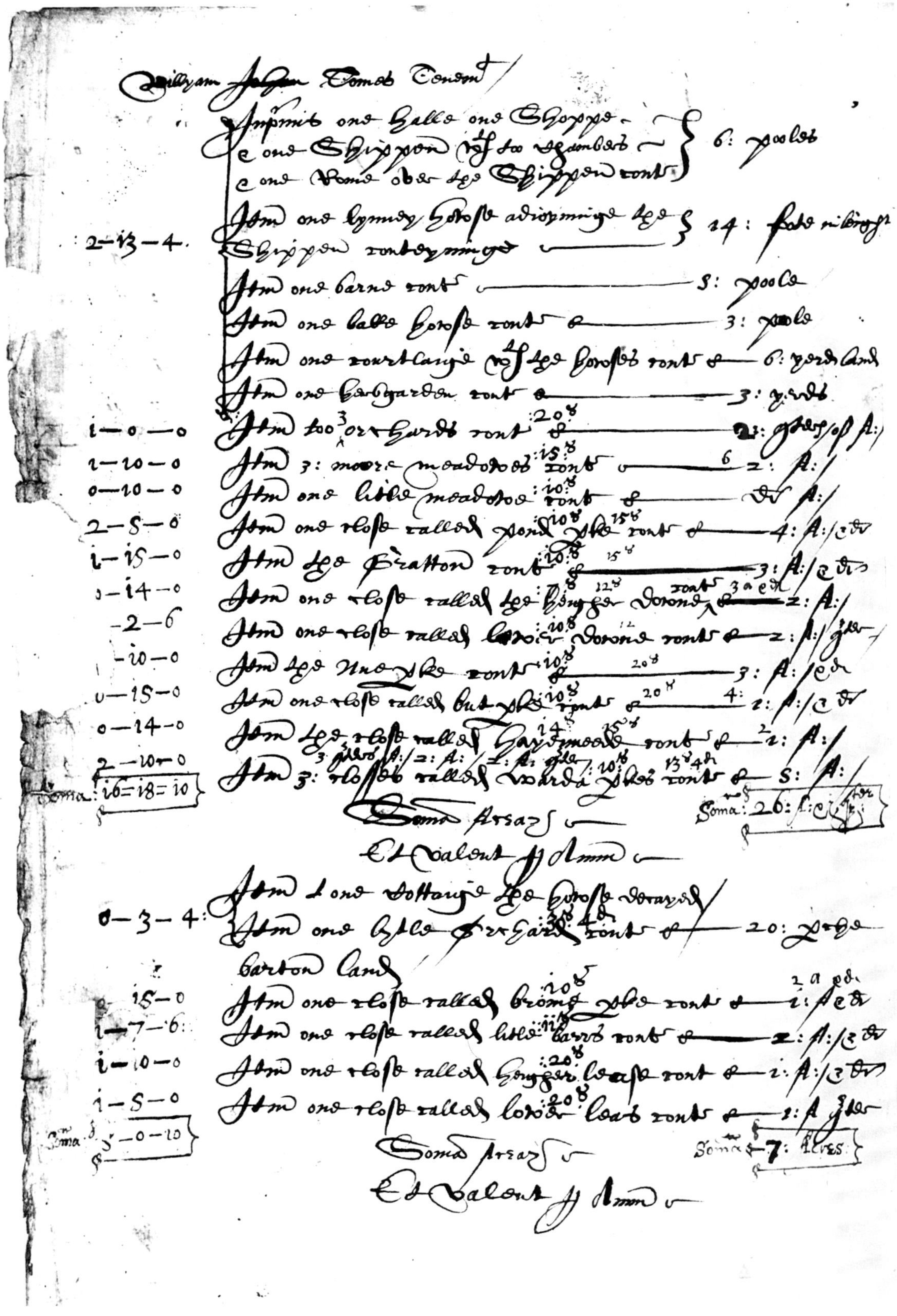

Figure 25. A page of the survey of Sherford, Devon, 1606, in John Willoughby's hand (SH7) (B.L. Add. Ms. 21605, f. 37v, reproduced with permission)

0-0, R 0-14-0, V 2-16-0; Baylshayes, A 4-0-0, R 0-15-0, V 3-0-0; Wilparke, A 4-2-0; R 0-16-0, V 3-12-0: Broadparke, A 0-6-0, R 0-10-0, V 3-0-0; 3 Middle Downes (6½, 6, 2½)[4], A 15-0-0, R 0-11-0, V 7-15-0; Furshill, A 6-0-0. R 0-7-0, V 2-2-0; Raweridge, A 9-0-0, R 0-6-0, V 2-14-0; too Blockewills (5,5), A 11-0-0, R 0-13-4, V 6-13-4; Court meadowe, A 1-1-0, R 1-13-4, V 1-13-4;[5] the 2 Balles, in tillage, A 8-0-0, R 0-15-0; 2 other closes, 8 or 9 ac., R 0-1-15.

Sum A 72-0-0, V 48-12-8 [Rent £2 6s 10d].

SH2. George Feare his tenement, one cottage viz. Inprimis his dwellinge howse beinge 3 under romes and three upper romes, 4 poole, one barne 3 poole, one stable and one workinge howse, beinge builded as lynneys, 34 foote in length; one courtlaige, too herbgardens (1 yerd) and one orchard (½ ac.,), A 0-3-0, V [*Total*] 3-6-8.

Too closses called Milparkes (2½, 1½), A 4-0-, R 1-10-0, V 3-0-0; 3 Newparkes (3 yards [*each*]), A 2-2-0, R 0-13-4, V 1-10-0.

Sum A 7-2-0, V 7-16-8 [*Rent 15s 3d*].

SH3.[6] Robert Horseman his tenement; Inprimis one halle howse, 2 poole, one buttery (1 poole), one shoppe (3 poole), one malt howse (3 p.), and one shippen adioyninge (3 poole), 10 poole, one barne 5 poole; one courtlage, 20 yeards,[7] V 2-0-0; One herbgarden and too orchards, A 1-0-0, R 0-15-0, V 0-15-0.

1 meadowe (*called* East meadow),[8] A 1-2-0; R 1-0-0, V 1-10-0; the Perycke Parke, A 3-0-0, R 0-18-0, V [2-1]4-0; one close called Ester Parke, A 6-0-0, R 0-10-0, V [3]-0-0; Middle Parke, A 4-0-0, R 0-10-0, V [2]-0-0; the Gratton, A 4-1-0,[9] R 0-13-4, V [2]-16-8; the Hill, A 3-0-0, R 0-10-0, V [1-1]-0; Raweridge, A 4-2-0, R 0-6-8, V 1-[10]-0.

Sum A 28-0-0, V [15]-15-8 [*Rent, with* SH4 *18s 10½d*].

[4] This and the component acreages are interlined.

[5] The next two items are inserted in the original hand. They are apparently omitted from the sums.

[6] In 1659, this was split into three holdings. The bulk of the land was leased separately, while Richard Horseman held part of the house: *one haule with the chamber over, the entry lyinge on the bacside of the hall, the lower orchard, the west side of the court, and the wast ground adioyninge againste the howse.* By 1682, this had become: *one hall and chamber over the same, one milkhouse, one entry, one piggs-roofe behind the same, and one garden lying in the bacside.* Ann Edwards, widow, had the third part in 1659: *all those severall decaied walls, roomes and garden, being part of a tenimente once Richard Horsmans, and allsoe the chamber over the entry, the decayed walls sometymes beinge a malthouse and shippinge, and the orchard on the east side of the house.*

[7] See p. 110 for *yeard.*

[8] Interlined.

[9] Given as *4 acres 40 perches.*

SH4. Robert Horseman. One cottaige, the howse decayed, one orchard, A 0-2-0, V 0-10-0.

One meadowe caled Westermeade, A 1-0-0, R 1-0-0, V 1-0-0; one close lyenge between Comeslake and Canesparke, A 1-2-0, R 0-10-0, V 1-0-0.

Sum A 3-0-0, V 2-10-0.

SH5. Walter Gittisham his tenement: Inprimis one halle, one kitchen, one buttrey and one shippen with three over romes 8 poole, one new malt howse and one rome over the same with a barne adioyninge 8 poole, 1 dery howse 2 poole; one courtalaige, A 0-1-0; too herbe gardens, 6 yeards, V [*total*] 2-13-4.

Too orchards, A 1-0-0, R 0-13-4, V 0-13-4; 1 meadowe, A 1-2-0. R 1-5-0, V 1-17-6; too closses called Fordhayes (3, 2½), A 5-2-0, R 0-13-4, V 3-13-4; the Heigher Bottom, A 5-0-0, R 0-10-0, V 2-10-0; the Lower Bottom, A 4-2-0, R 0-11-0, V 2-9-6; the Pericke Parke, A 1-2-0, R 0-10-0, V 0-15-0; Thester Quarrye Parke A 5-0-0, R 0-10-0, V 2-10-0; the Wester and Middle Quarrye Parkes, A 7-0-0, R 0-10-0, V 3-10-0; one close called the Heigher Hill, A 4-0-0, R-10-0, V 2-0-0; one close called the Lower Hill, A 3-0-0, R 0-10-0, V 1-10-0; Shindell Quarye Parke, A 6-0-0, R 0-10-0, V 3-0-0; Pond Parke, A 4-2-0, R 0-13-4, V 3-0-0; one close called Mowe Parke, A 1-2-0, R 0-13-4, V 1-0-0; Wester Hill Parke, A 4-0-0, R 0-10-0, V 2-0-0; Puskyn Parke, A 2-0-0. R 0-10-0, V 1-0-0.

Sum A 56-2-0, V 34-2-0 [*Rent 30s 3d*].

SH6. Thomas Marche the youngers tenement: Inprimis one halle howse, one buttrey with too chambers over the same 5 poole, on syder howse adioyninge the buttrey 2 poole, 1 bakehowse with a litle rome over parte theirof 4 poole, one shippen 3 poole, one barne 6 poole; one courtalaige containing with these howses 20 yeards; one herbgarden 4 yeards; V [*total*] 2-13-4.

2 Orchards, A 0-2-0, R 1-0-0, V 1-0-0; 1 meadowe, A 1-0-0, R 1-0-0, V 1-0-0; one close called Puskin Parke, A [4-0-0], R 0-14-0, V 2-16-0; the Perycke Parke, A 1-1-0, R 0-14-0, V 0-17-6; one close called the Ball, A 4-0-0, R 0-7-0, V 1-8-0; 1 close called Blacke Will, A 1-2-0, R 0-7-0, V 0-10-6; one close called the Lane and Lane Parke, A 1-2-0, R 0-7-0, V 0-10-6; three closses called Tapisyeat, A 6-0-0, R 0-9-0, V 2-14-0; three closses called Rawerudges, A 4-2-0, R 0-13-4, V 1-7-0; Butfurlonge, A 4-0-0, R 0-13-4, V 2-13-4.

Sum A 28-2-0, V 17-10-2 [*Rent 15s 10½d*].

SH7. Willyam[10] Tomes tenement: Inprimis one halle, one shoppe and one shippen, with too chambers and one rome over the shippen 6 pooles, one lynney howse adioyninge the shippen 14 foote in length, one barne 5 poole, one bake howse 3 poole; one courtlaige with the howses 6 yerdland; one herbgarden 3 yerds; V 2-13-4.

[10] *Jolyon* erased.

Too (3)[11] orchards, A 0-2-0, R 1-0-0, V 1-0-0; 3 Moore meadowes, A 2-0-0, R 0-15-0, V 1-10-0; one litle meadowe, A 0-2-0, R 0-10-0, V 0-10-0; one close called Pond Parke, A 4-2-0, R 0-10-0 (0-15-0)[12] V 2-8-0; the Gratton, A 3-2-0, R 0-10-0 (0-15-0), V 1-15-0; one close called the Heigher Downe, A 2-0-0 (3-2-0), R 0-8-0 (0-12-0), V 0-14-0; one close called Lower Downe, A 2-1-0, R 0-10-0 (0-12-0), V [1]-2-6; the Nue Parke, A 3-0-0 (3-2-0), R 0-10-0 (1-0-0), V [1]-10-0; one close called But Parke, A 1-2-0 (4-0-0), R 0-10-0 (1-0-0), V 0-15-0; the close caleld Haymeede, A 1-0-0 (2-0-0), R 0-14-0 (0-15-0), V 0-14-0; 3 closses called Wardaparkes (¾, 2, 2¼), A 5-0-0, R 0-10-0 (0-13-4), V 2-10-0.

Sum A 26-1-0, V 16-18-10 (*Rent 28s 5½d*).

SH8.[13] Item one cottaige, the howse decayed; one lytle orchard 20 perches, V 0-3-4.

Barton land: one close called Brome Parke, A 1-2-0 (2-2-0), R 0-10-0, V 0-15-0; one close called Litle Barrs, A 2-2-0, R 0-11-0, V 1-7-6; one close called Heigher Lease, A 1-2-0, R 1-0-0, V 1-10-0; one close called Lower Leas, A 1-1-0, R 1-0-0, V 1-5-0.

Sum A 7-0-0, V 5-0-10.

SH9. Nicholl Sumpters tenement: Inprimis one halle, one inner rome with a chamber over, one shippen, one barne, one dery howse and one bakehowse 12 poole, one other barne and stable 5 poole; one courtlaige with these howses 20 yeards; one herbgarden 2 yeards; V 2-6-8.

One orchard, A 0-2-0, R 0-13-4, V 0-13-4; one meadowe, A 1-2-0, R 0-13-4, V 1-0-0; the Moorehayes, A 1-1-0, R 0-15-0, V 0-18-9; one close called Bakehowse Parke, A 1-2-0, R 0-10-0, V 0-15-0; the litle Parke, A 1-0-0, R 0-10-0, V 0-10-0; 2 closses called the Downe, A 5-0-0, R 0-9-0. V 2-5-0; the Basterd Parke, A 5-0-0; R 0-6-8, V 1-13-4; the Heigher Heele, A 5-0-0, R 0-6-8, V 1-13-4; the Middle Heele, A 5-0-0, R 0-6-8, V 1-13-4; the too Lower Heeles, A 4-0-0, R 0-7-0, V 1-8-0; the Mery Pittes, A 1-0-0, R 0-7-0, V 0-7-0; the Litle Heele, A 1-0-0, R 0-7-0, V 0-7-0; the Crosse Parke, A 4-0-0, R 0-10-0, V 2-0-0; the [?Newe] Parke, A 3-0-0, R 0-10-0, V 1-10-0; the Lamb Parke, A 2-0-0, R 0-6-8, V 0-13-4; the Mere Parke, A 5-0-0, R 0-11-0, V 2-15-0.

Sum A 46-3-0, V 22-19-1 [*Rent 29s 9d*].

SH10. Grace Randall: One close called Cowparke, A 11-0-0, R 1-6-8, V 14-13-4; one meadowe called Cowparke Meade, A 2-0-0, R 1-6-8 (1-10-0), V 2-13-4.

Sum A 13-0-0, V 17-6-8 [*Rent 26s 8d*].

SH11. Mr. Richard Halls: Inprimis one grist mill and treble myll called Lakes Mill 3 poole; one mille poole 20 perches; V 10-0-0. One orchard, 5 yeards, R 0-5-0 V 0-5-0.
Total V 10-5-0 [*Rent 11s*]

SH12. Willyam Randall: Inprimis too closses called Well Parkes, A 9-2-0, R 0-1-6, V 6-17-9; too closses called Cames Parkes, A 12-0-0, R 0-11-0, V 6-12-0.

Sum A 21-2-0, V 13-9-9 [*Rent 29s 4d*].

SH13. Nicholas Stone his cottaige: Inprimis one halle, one kitchin, one inner rome, one chamber over the halle 5 poole, one lynney 10 foote; one courtlaige with the howse 8 perche; V 1-0-0.

One herbe garden, A 0-0-4, R 0-8-0, V 0-8-0; one orchard and a meadowe, A 0-3-0, R 0-13-4, V 0-13-4; one close called Pericke Parke, A 2-0-0, R 0-14-0, V 1-[8]-0.

Sum A 3-0-0, V 3-6-8 [*Rent 6s 8d*].

SH14. John Taylor his tenement: Inprimis one halle, one parlour and one shippen, with too chambers over the same 6 poole, one barne 4 poole, one stable 2 poole, one bakehowse 3 poole, one buttrey, one dery howse 20 foote, V [2-13]-4. Too courtlaiges and howse rome 16 perches; one herbe garden 4 perches, V [*both*], 0-5-0;

3 orchards, A 0-3-20, R 1-2-0, V 1-2-0; one close called Longe Parke, A 1-2-0, R 0-13-4, V 0-16-8; one close called Lower Parke, A 2-2-0, R 0-11-0, V 1-7-6; one close called Whippaparke, A 2-2-0, R 0-11-0, V 1-7-6; 2 Middle Parkes, A 5-0-0, R 0-10-0, V 2-10-0; 2 Quarrye Parkes, A 4-0-0, R 0-8-0, V 1-12-0; 3 Downes, A 10-0-0, R 0-7-0, V 3-10-0; one meade called Wood Mead, A 2-1-0, R 0-13-4, V 1-9-2; Barton land: One close called Fursparke, A 5-0-0, R 0-10-0, V 2-10-0; one meade called Warde Meade, A 2-2-0, R 1-10-0, V 3-15-0.

Sum A 35-2-0, V 22-18-2 [*Rent 30s*].

SH15. Richarde Smith his cottaige: Inprimis one halle, one chamber over the hall 2 poole, one malt howse 1 poole, one barne 3 poole, V 1-0-0.

One herbgarden. A 0-0-4, R 0-4-0, V 0-4-0; one orchard, A 0-1-0, R 0-10-0, V 0-10-0; one close called Lower close, A 2-2-0, R 0-13-4, V 1-13-4; Middle close and one other litle close adioyninge, A 2-2-0, R 0-14-0, V 1-8-0; the too Heigher closses, A 2-2-0, R 0-14-0, V 1-15-0.

Sum A 7-2-0, V 6-10-4 [*Rent 12s*].

SH16. Mr. Richard Halls: Inprimis one wood called the Lords Wood, A 24-0-0, R 0-8-0, V 6-0-0; one meade called the Mill Meade, A 2-1-0, R 1-7-0, V 3-0-0.

Sum A 26-1-0, V 9-0-9 [*Rent 10s*].

SH17. Willyam Halls holdeth one close called Luscomb, A 30-0-0, R 0-9-0, V 13-10-0. [*Rent 26s 8d*]

SH18.[14] Willyam Randalls downes: Inprimis one close called Lower Wilparke, A 2-0-0 (4-0-0), R 0-10-0 (0-16-0), V 1-0-

---

[11] Interlined.

[12] All the following rates and a few of the areas have been changed, apparently in the original hand; these revisions are given in parentheses. The original figures seem to have been used for calculating the values.

[13] Probably held by the previous tenant, who had *four barton closes called Twichhills* in 1605.

[14] As for SH7 many of the figures have been altered. See also SH32.

0; Rowdon Hill, A 5-2-0 (6-0-0), R 0-6-8 (0-16-0), V 1-16-8; one close called Gratton, A 10-0-0, R 0-6-8, V 3-6-8; Stone Parke, A 6-0-0, R 0-7-0, V 2-2-0; Wheaton Arrishe, A 8-0-0, R 0-7-0, V 2-16-0; Tounge close, A 3-2-0, R 0-6-8, V 1-13-4; Warde Yeate, A 6-0-0, R 0-6-8 (1-0-0), V 2-0-0; Beat Hill, A 8-0-0, R 0-6-8, V 2-13-4; Bottom Parke, A 10-0-0, R 0-7-0, V 3-10-0; Furse Hill, A 10-0-0, R 0-6-8, V 3-6-8.

Sum A 69-0-0, V 23-14-8.

Willyam Randalls Lamparke, A 12-0-0, R 0-18-0 (1-0-0), V 9-0-0.

SH19. Roger Costerd in the right of his wiff: Inprimis 3 meadowes called Court Meads, A 6-0-0, R 1-0-0, V 6-0-0; too closes called by the name of Court Meads (2½, 2½), A 5-0-0, R 0-10-0, V 2-10-0.

Sum A 11-0-0, V 8-10-0 [*Rent 20s*].

SH20. Thomas Marches tenement: Inprimis one halle, one kitchin and one other rome, with fower chambers over them 7 poole, the milkehowse and buttrey, and one chamber over the buttrey 3 poole, one barne, one stable 3 poole, one other barne and shippen 8 poole, one bake howse 3 poole; the courtlaige with the howses 27 perches; V 3-3-4.

One herbgarden, A 0-0-8, R 0-10-0, V 0-10-0; one orchard and one wast plott of ground, A 1-0-0, R 1-0-0, V 1-0-0; the Furshill, A 9-0-0, R 0-7-0, V 3-3-0; the Fowle Will, A 5-2-0, R 0-10-0, V 2-15-0; the Broad Parke, A 5-2-0, R 0-10-0, V 2-15-0; the Reapinge Parke, A 4-0-0, R 0-10-0, V 2-0-0; the Will Parke, A 2-0-0, R 0-13-4, V 1-6-8; the Coate Parke, A 3-0-0, R 1-0-0, V 3-0-0; Redwoodes Parke, A 4-2-0, R 0-14-0, V 1-15-0; Three Shillinges Parke, A 2-2-0, R 0-14-0, V 1-15-0; the Cross Parke, A 3-0-0, R 0-6-8, V 1-0-0; the West Meade, A 2-0-0, R 1-0-0, V 2-0-0; one wood, A 3-0-0, R 0-5-0, V 0-15-0.

Sum A 45-2-0, V 28-6-0 [*Rent 33s 4d*].

SH21. Marye Brownes tenement, clere £12: Inprimis one halle, one kitchin[15] and the rome within the halle, with one chamber over the kitchin, and one shippen 10 poole, one parlour with a chamber over 2 poole, one litle derye howse adioyninge the north side of the hall 20 foote, one barne 6 poole; one courtlaige with the howse rome 20 perches; V 1-3-4.

One herb garden, A 0-0-2, R 0-2-0, V 0-2-0; one pece of ground, A 0-2-0, R 0-2-0, V 0-2-0; one close called Furze[16] Parke, A 1-2-0, R 0-13-4, V 1-0-0; one close called Lower Parke, A 2-0-0, R 0-13-0, V 1-6-0; Middle Parke, A 2-0-0, R 0-13-0, V 1-6-0; the Litle Downe, A 2-0-0, R 0-13-0, V 1-6-0; the South Downe, A 3-2-0, R 0-13-0, V 2-5-6; 3 closses of land called Middle Parkes, A 8-2-0, R 0-9-0, V 3-16-6; Quarrye Parke, A 5-0-0, R 0-9-0, V 2-5-0.

Sum A 25-0-0, V 14-2-4 [*Rent 14s 10½d*].

[15] *One parlour* erased.

[16] ?*Whipstone* erased.

SH22.[17] Willyam Gyles tenement: Inprimis one halle and one chamber over, one kytchin with a chamber over, and one buttry with a chamber over, and one shippen with a lofte over 20 poole, one lynney for a stable 2 poole, one dery howse 2 poole, one barne 6 poole, one lynney adioyninge the barne, 20 foote; one courtlaige with the howse rome 26 perches; V 1-3-0.

One herb garden, A 0-0-6, R 0-5-0, V 0-5-0; one orchard, A 0-2-0, R 0-8-0, V 0-8-0; one meadowe, A 1-0-0, R 1-0-0, V 1-0-0; Shuttaparke, A 1-2-0, R 0-14-0, V 1-1-0; Lower Shuttaparke, A 1-2-0, R 0-14-0, V 1-1-0; the Gratton, A 6-2-0, R 0-13-0, V 4-4-6; the litle parke below the waye, A 2-0-0, R 0-13-0, V 1-6-0; the Crosse Parke, A 5-2-0, R 0-13-0, V 3-11-6; the litle parke above the waye, A 2-0-0, R 0-14-0, V 1-8-0; Downe Parke, A 5-0-0, R 0-12-0, V 3-0-0; Heigher Downe, A 3-0-0, R 0-6-8, V 1-0-0; the Wester Downe, A 5-0-0, R 0-6-8, V 1-13-4; the Middle Downe, A 3-0-0, R 0-6-8, V 1-0-0; the Lower Downe, A 3-0-0, R 0-6-8, V 1-0-0; Thester Downe, A 4-0-0, R 0-6-8, V 1-6-8; the Heigher Heele, A 4-0-0, R 0-6-8, V 1-6-8; Thester Heele, A 3-0-0, R 0-6-8, V 1-0-0; the Norther Heele, A 4-2-0, R 0-6-8, V 1-10-0; the litle parke below the Heele, A 2-0-0, R 0-8-0, V 0-16-0; 2 plottes of ground adioyninge the close called the Heele, A 0-0-30, R 0-5-0, V 0-5-0.

Sum A 58-0-0, V 29-5-8 [*Rent 29s 9d*].

SH23. Andrewe Lakes tenement in Sherford Towne: Inprimis one halle, one kitchin, with too chambers over 4 poole, one stable thirunto adioyninge, with a chamber over 1 poole; one herb garden 3 perche; one orchard 20 perche; V 1-10-0.

Too meadowes called Church Meads, A 5-0-0, R 1-8-0, V 7-0-0; one close called Comeslake, A 7-0-0, R 0-11-0, V 3-17-0.

Sum A 12-1-0, V 12-7-0 [*Rent 6s 8d*].

SH24. Item one howse called the Parissoners howse; First too under roomes with too chambers over 8 poole, V 1-0-0.

SH25. Grace Randall:[18] Item one buttrey adioyninge to the hall and parlour 20 foote in breadth, 16 foote in length, V 4-0-0. [*Rent 12d*]

SH26.[19] Richard Horsmans cottaige: Inprimis one halle with a chamber over 3 poole, one lynney 10 foote lenght; one

[17] By 1616, this had been divided. One part was described in 1618 (Add. Mss. 21608, f. 148) as: *a hall, a dairy, a lyttle buttery, with chambers over, a shypen with a lofte over and a stable, the moyety of one barn*. The remainder was described in 1682 as: *a tenement and two farthings of land, viz: the kitchen with a chamber over, the moyety of the barne as now divided*.

[18] In 1605, this piece of land 20ft. by 16ft. was where *William Randall hath now builded his house called a buttrey*, which had been part of John Gyler's tenement. The remainder of the house is apparently SH32, but it is odd that in 1606 it had a different tenant.

[19] In 1605, this was *one house and ladder rome*.

courtlaige with the howse 4 perche; one herb garden 3 perche; one pound adioyninge the said courtlaige 20 foot lenght.

Sum A 12 perches V 0-18-0 [*Rent 8d*].

SH27. Ibote Deringe, widow, her cottaige: Inprimis one halle, one buttrye, with a chamber over 3 poole; one herb garden 1½ perches; one pece of land before her dore 2 perches.

Sum A 6½ perches, V 0-18-0 [*Rent 16d*].

SH28. Mr. Richard Hals, George Reynolls and Willyam Randall: Item one pece of land called Pericke, A 1-0-0, V 0-6-8. [*Rent 2s*]

SH29. Anne Horsman and Marye Teylors cottaige: Inprimis one parcell of wast ground called Puskin, A 0-2-0, V 0-4-0. [*Rent 16d*]

SH30.[20] [?Kathrin] Lawyres cottaige: Inprimis one halle, one buttrie and one chamber over 3 poole; one courtlaige and garden 8 yeard.

Sum A 11 perches [*sic.*], V 1-0-0.[21]

SH31.[22] Andrew Lakes tenement, in lease for 2000 yeares: Inprimis one halle with a chamber over 3 poole, one buttrye with a chamber over 2 poole, one bakehowse, one sider howse with 3 chambers over 5 poole, one milke howse 13 foote lenght, one larder howse 11 foote lenght, one shippen 2 poole, one barne 6 poole, one stable 2 poole, one howse called the shop with a chamber over 2 poole, one howse called the cowe howse 2 poole; too courtlaiges 10 perches.

Too orchards, A 1-2-0; one herbe garden A 0-0-10; one beanehaye, A 0-0-10; one peece of land called the Greene, A 0-2-0; one meadowe, A 1-2-0; one meadowe, A 0-0-31; one other meadowe, A 0-0-20; one peece of land called the Mowehaye, A 0-2-0; Shopp Parke, A 1-2-0; Cowe Parke, A 3-0-0; the Will Parke, A 3-1-0; one close called Smaleaparke, A 4-0-0; Crosse Parke, A 2-0-0; Ball Parke, A 2-3-0; Broade Parke, A 3-2-0; Litle Parke, A 1-2-0; Heigher Hill, A 3-2-0; the Lower Hill, A 0-3-0; the Hill Parke, A 1-2-0; the Quarrye Parke, A 3-2-0; the Grove Parke, A 3-2-0; the Grove A 0-1-0; the 3 Corner Parke, A 0-3-0; one close called the Pasture, A 12-0-0

Sum A [52-1-0], V 30-0-0.

Andrew Lake holdeth too closses of land called Camesparkes, A 8-0-0, R 0-10-0, V 4-0-0.

SH32.[23] William Randalls Tenement, in lease for 2000 yeres: Item 1 hall, 1 parler, 1 kitchen, 1 dayry, 1 larder, 1 portche, with 6 chambers over, containing by estimacion 10 poole, 1 bakehowse with a chamber over, 2 barnes, 1 stable, 1 shippen, 1 dovehowse 22 poole, 1 shippen for fatte oxen 3 poole.

4 Cloases called the Heeles, A (by estimacion) 30-0-0; the Moorehay, A 2-0-0; the Greene Parke, A 1-0-5; the Poole Parke, A 3-0-0; Under Ashe, A 4-0-0; Longe Meadowes 2, A 2-2-0; Lyttle Parke, A 2-2-0;[24] Redford Lake Parke, A 4-0-0; Chapple Parke, A 6-0-0; Lower Myddle Parke, A 6-0-0; Horseparke and Beanehay, A 2-2-0; Ashehay Parke, A 2-2-0; Lange Parke, A 8-0-0; Hyer Myddle Parke, A 5-0-0; Rowdon Hyll, A 7-0-0; North Ball, A 5-0-0; 3 herb gardens, A 0-0-40; 2 orchards, A 2-0-0; 3 courtleyges, A 0-0-40.

Sum A [93-0-0], V 60-0-0.

[20] In 1605, this was *a piece of void ground next the water course called Sherford Lake or Prest Lake, with a dwelling house now built*, with bounds, E: *land of the lord of Sherford manor, called Ford Hayes*; N: *lands of Sir Richard Champernowne, knight, now held by William March*; W and S: *highway from Church of Sherford to Stancomb Crosse.*

[21] There is a note at the foot of the page (the end of the survey, apart from the two holdings leased for 2000 years) *Valent toto per annum 400* [£].

[22] The remaining holdings have only total values. This one, with a rent in 1605 of one peppercorn, was presumably mortgaged.

[23] This and SH18 are absent in 1605, perhaps because they were mortgaged (but cf. SH31). The 1605 entry for SH25 shows that the house of SH32 must then have existed.

[24] Given as *2 ac. 2 yerd.*

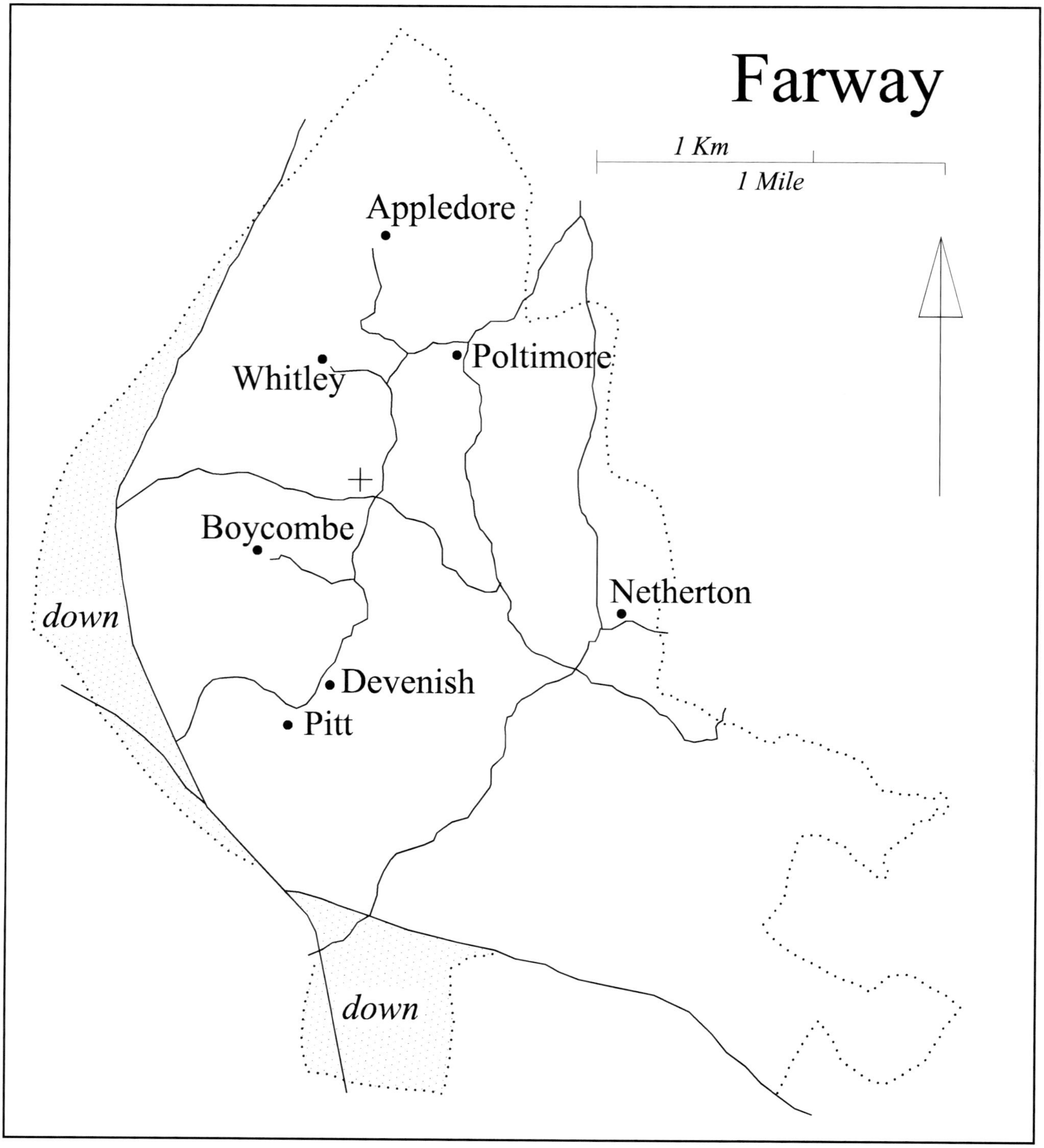

Map 5. Farway parish, Devon

Netherton Hall was the seat of the Prideaux family, owners of Sidmouth (p. 209).

CHAPTER 9

Farway and Whitwell

Farway and Whitwell (F,W): 1609 *Maps 5, 6*
Farway and Whitwell are considered together, partly because the Whitwell survey is short, but mainly because of their similarity.[1] They lie about a mile and a half apart in East Devon, in hilly country where most of the farms are isolated. Farway was the largest though not the only estate in the parish of that name. Whitwell was a small property in the south-eastern part of Colyton parish (immediately north of Seaton parish). Both were re-surveyed in 1682, and almost all the properties can be identified with those in 1609 from internal evidence.[2] The 1682 surveys contain a few house descriptions which are mostly repeated from 1609, but one Farway farm (F2) had been bought, and the description of one Whitwell farm (W10) was probably omitted from the existing copy of the 1609 survey (cf. p. 127).

In 1609 a few tenants held large farms by lease, and the remainder held by copy of court roll. By 1682, these had all become tenants by three-life lease. A church house is mentioned in Farway (F15), apparently fulfilling its original function in 1609; in 1682, it was held by one Nicholas Hutchings for a rent of 1d., but whether for his own use or as trustee is not stated.

The Houses

The Farway and Whitwell surveys describe 20 houses in detail, including two covered in 1682 and not in 1609. In six cases the number of 'pooles' is given, and this presumably meant a length of 8 ft., as for Sherford.[3] More commonly, 'couples' is used. The same meaning of *bay* that seems valid for Kenton is generally satisfactory, and is supported by the '8 couples or couple rooms' of W7 in 1682. There are, however, a few oddities, particularly in W2, which apparently had three rooms in plan but was of five couples, and F12, which had a 'house containing one oven and dry [malt-kiln] without any couple'. This may indicate that the surveyor was on occasion recording actual roof trusses; alternatively, it may have been a lean-to structure. The 'entry' [cross-passage] is noted in these surveys, but only when it had a room over it.

Very unusually, in Farway we have evidence for one of the houses associated with the free-holdings. Boycombe (F2) was purchased between 1609 and 1643, when it was divided into three holdings, which by 1682 had been reunited. The descriptions suggest a house of seven ground floor rooms, with further outbuildings around a courtyard. The house still exists, and has been noted in print with a plan.[4] It is of three room and cross-passage plan, with the service end subdivided and so presumably several of the service rooms were in wings that have now disappeared. The main block of the house, of mid-sixteenth-century date, is of very high quality, finely finished with large and high rooms. The house thus reveals both the strength and weakness of the surveys, in giving complete house descriptions, but leaving date, plan and quality to the imagination.

One of the other free-holdings, Poltimore (Fl), with no survey details, has also been examined and a description published.[5] It is also of larger than average size, though not particularly imposing. In the seventeenth century, it probably contained seven rooms in plan, though two of these were small and partitioned out of others; this plan was the result of several stages of development from a medieval core.

The copyhold tenements of Farway and Whitwell shared one important feature. They were of considerable size, most commonly between twenty and thirty acres, but extending up to more than 100, and with only two having less than ten acres. Of these two, one (F14) had two rooms on each floor, but the other (F5) from its length (only 16 ft.) may have been of one-room plan.

The cottages that were a substantial group at Kenton, and significant in Cornwall and at Sherford, were almost non-existent; the Farway houses were those of farmers, ranging from the modest to the sub-

Table 15: Farway and Whitwell: Dimensions of farm buildings (couples)

Ref. Number	Acres	Barn	Stable	Stall	Shippon	Hay House	Linhey	Notes
F5	1/4							
F14	7							
W6	15	=			=			barn + shippon(3)
F4	18	•						
F10	19	=	=	=		2		barn + stable + stalls(3)
F9	22	2		1			*	* 2 end sheds
F11	22	=			=		*	barn + shippon(3); * 2 end sheds
W11	22	•			•			
F12	24	=		=				barn + stall(4)
W2	25							
W4	26	=			=			barn + shippon(3)
W8	27	2		4			••	
F16	27	=	=			*		barn + stable(4) with hayloft(*) over stable
F13	34	=	3		=	*		barn + shippon(3) with haylofts(*) over them and stable
F8	43	3	=					stable + bake house(3)
F6	50	=			=		=	barn + shippon + lynnage(4)
W10	60	=	=		3p	*	•	barn + stable (5 poole); hayloft(*) over shippon
F7	61	4	•	2				stable adjoining barn
W7	111	=		= =				no house; barn + two stalls(8)

Notes: Most dimensions were recorded in couples, apart from W10 where pooles were used. F15 (the church-house) is omitted.

stantial. The smallest of these farmhouses were of two-room plan; two had hall and dairy (F4) and hall and inner chamber (F14), both with two chambers over. The description of the third (F9) 'one halle, one other halle and 3 chambers over' is very odd, with no obvious interpretation. It is interesting that F4 was newly-built, presumably the appropriate size for an eighteen acre holding.

The commonest plan appears to have been that with three ground floor rooms, although some houses may have had extra rooms in their main structure. The standard type had a hall, inner chamber and kitchen (F10, 13, 16).[6] The last was a 'good howse, new-built', although, surprisingly, it had only one upper chamber, unlike the others which were fully floored. Two houses had a milkhouse instead of a kitchen (F8 fully chambered over, W4 entirely open to the roof, both also with bakehouses), and one had a parlour and no ground floor chamber (W2). F12 had two ground floor chambers, and its only service room was the separate oven and drye.[7] W10 and F7 may have had basically three-room plans, but if so, several of the rooms were subdivided—buttery and dairy together in W10, milkhouses both beside the chamber and in the kitchen in F7 (unique in having these two milkhouses). In W10 the lower end was enlarged, including a cyder room as well as a 'low room'; this was for lodging, i.e., it was a ground floor sleeping room. It also had no less than five upstairs chambers. W11 had three upper rooms, and so presumably a three unit plan with buttery and dairy in one section. Interestingly, the description also suggests that these were in the centre, and taken with its being 'new-built', it may well be an example of the innovative seventeenth-century plan with central service rooms. It also had a separate malthouse and bakehouse.

The four largest houses were not those of the largest farms. One (W6) had a ground floor weaving house (a unique feature) in what was basically a two-room plan (hall and milkhouse); it also included a bakehouse in the main range. F6, F11, and W8 seem to have had five and four room plans respectively, each with at least one ground floor chamber and a milkhouse; only the last had a kitchen.

The overall pattern is not dissimilar to that at Sherford, although the process of improvement seems not to have gone quite so far. Several houses were not yet completely chambered over, many had ground floor chambers, and correspondingly lacked kitchens. Parlours were also rare (only in F6, W2). However, any long-houses that had existed on the estate had been remodelled, in contrast to Sherford.

The Farm Buildings (Table 15)

The farmsteads were remarkably uniform on the two estates. Each holding usually had a barn and a shippon (or a stall, the terms apparently being synonymous descriptions of shelters for milking cows, for they never occur together), and these were often combined into a single range. The larger farms had slightly bigger barns and shippons, and they contained most of the stables, haylofts, and side-set linheys; the latter must have been more commodious than the pairs of lean-to 'end sheds' that served for miscellaneous storage or perhaps for stabling beef cattle on two smaller farms (F9,11). Otherwise the survey is ample witness to the fact that pastoral farming required less variety of building and escaped the extremes of wealth and poverty that were typical in arable regions.

[1] The survey of one further part of the estate survives and is included: Anthonyhaies (W11, p. 125). This was another isolated East Devon farm, in Luppitt, about six miles north of Farway. It was presumably sold before 1682, when it is not mentioned.

[2] Further documentation survives in the Trevelyan archives in the Somerset Record Office and in the British Library, but has not been studied in detail.

[3] Four of these are in that part of the survey in John Willoughby's hand (as in the Sherford survey), with the spelling 'poole'. The fifth (F4) uses the spelling 'pole'.

[4] W.G. Hoskins, *Local History in England* (London, 1959), 125. Cf. also John Cherry, 'Post-medieval Britain in 1976', *Post-Medieval Archaeol.* 11 (1977), 96-7.

[5] E. H. D. Williams, 'Poltimore Farmhouse, Farway', *Trans. Devonshire Assoc.*, 106 (1974), 215-229.

[6] F10 also had a shop and bakehouse, F13 a malthouse.

[7] The description 'chamber before the entry' can perhaps be understood in terms of a house with its lower (third) room towards the road.

Survey of Farway and Whitwell: 1609 (Fig. 26)

(Somerset Rec. Off. DD/WO Box 43. Trevelyan muniments)

The 1609 survey of Farway, Whitwell and Seaton occupies a complete bound volume, written in two hands. The principal hand (1) is very unusual, regular but spiky, very old-fashioned and not easily legible, and for the most part using Latin. The other hand (2) seems to be that of John Willoughby himself, as in the 1606 Sherford survey, and uses English almost exclusively. For the translation of Latin room names, the equivalences of Table 16 (p. 128) are used. The lists of fields usually give the name and area, and a superscript figure which is apparently the value per acre (given here as R 0-6-8, etc.); the total values have generally not been inserted although space is left for them.

The 1682 survey volume contains surveys of Farway, Whitwell, Seaton and Sherford; that for Seaton (ff.18-42) is transcribed completely (in Chapter 10, with that for 1609), but for the others only a few entries are included, mainly in footnotes, as the remainder add little to the 1609 descriptions. Each survey is followed by a summary rental, apparently compiled independently, as they show several variations from the surveys. For Seaton a considerable number of leases also survive. Their information together with that of some other documents is collected in a separate section of Chapter 10, arranged to correspond to the 1682 holdings.

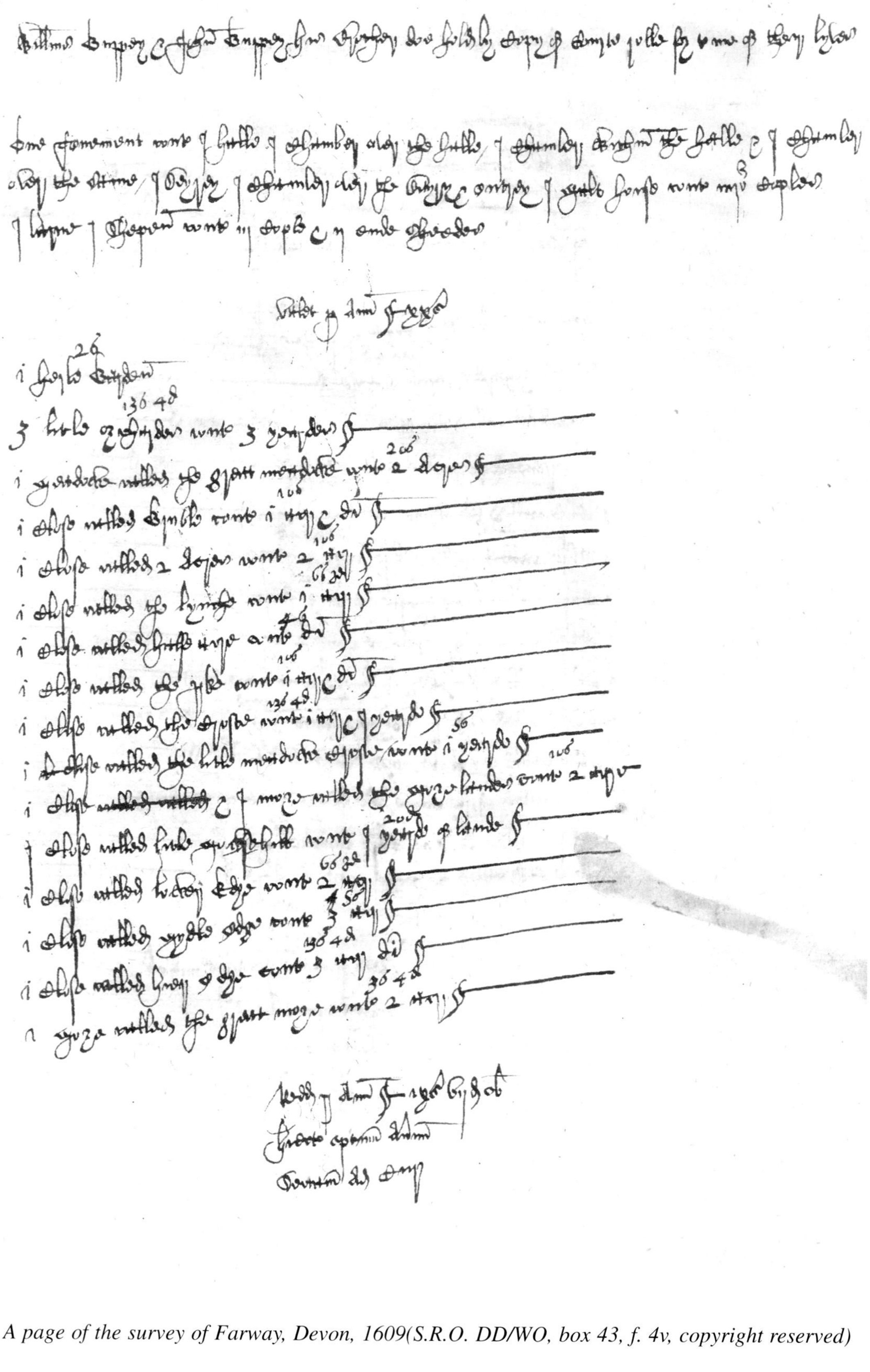

Figure 26. A page of the survey of Farway, Devon, 1609(S.R.O. DD/WO, box 43, f. 4v, copyright reserved)

TEXT

[f.1][1] Farway

A particular survey of the mannor of Farway taken the third day of July 1609,[2] att a courte there holden the same day uppon the oathes of John Clappe, Thomas Coxe, John Floode junior and William Guppye, tenauntes of the same mannor, viz.

[John Floode senior and John Floode junior hold: Inprimis one dwelling howse con']'[3]

F1. *John Arrundell of Treryse in the county of Cornwall esquire and William Tuckefylde hold freely by knight service viz. 4 several holdings with appertenances called Poltymore (160)*[4] *and Whiteley (50) containing by estimacion 210*[5] *acres land, meadow and pasture, and common pasture in severalty, and they make suit of court and render for it per year 12d.*

F2.[6] *William Hoskyns, gentleman, holds freely to him and his heirs by [ ]*[7] *two holdings with their appertenances, of which one called Boycombe (60)*[8] *and another called Abriel Knolle and two other holdings called Apledore (40) and Berysballe (20), containing in all by estimacion 120 acres of land, meadow and pasture, and renders for it per year 13s 6d.*

F3. *Rectory of Farway: [?Archibald] Scadlen, clerk, rector of the parish church of Farewaye holds the rectory of Farewaye, to which pertains one close of land called* the Great Borage *containing by estimacion 4 ac.; another close of land called* the Little Borage *containing 2 ac.;*[9] Parson Wode 3 v.; Shole lac.; Stoneham 1 ac.; Langland 3 ac.; meadow called Wynsam 2 ac.; meadow beside the aforesaid Rectory house 1½ ac.; Mansehyll lac. lv.; Ayshe Grove ½ ac.; lying beside Lansmore and the land of William Hoskyns; 3 ac. land lying beside Landschire in Northyll and the land of the said William Hoskyns; meadow called Kytsmeadowe 3 v.; orchard and curtilage lac; which all and singular from the free gift and disposition of John Willoughby esquire, lord of the manor. Value per annum £80.

Various Lands by Indenture

F4. John Thomas, assignee of William Duke [?miller], as it is supposed claims to hold 1 holding newly erected containing 4 poles, 1 hall, 1 dayrey, 2 chambers over, 1 barn, ¼ ac.; [*value*] 13s 4d.

Hier Est Fyeld 4 ac. R 1-0-0; Lower East fyld 3 ac. R 0-13-4; 1 meadow 3 ac. R 1-0-0; (1 wood called Lisley Wode 8 ac.)[10]; the Lords Woode 8 ac. R 0-13-4.

Herryotte 20s; sute of courte; rent per annum 15s.

F5. Richard Lotte, Elizabeth his wyfe and William Lotte hold by indenture dated 14 April 1590: Inprimis one dwelling howse 2 pooles in length. V 0-8-0; 1 herb garden and 1 orchard 1 yerd, V 0-6-0.

Rent 5s; herryotte nil; sute of courte.

Coppyes

F6. John Floode senior, John Floode junior and Nicholas Floode hold: Inprimis 1 dwelling howse, 1 hall, 1 parlour, 1 mylkehowse, 1 buttery with 1 under chamber and [?5] roomes over the same, 4 cowple in length, 1 bakehouse or maulthowse 2 poole, 1 barne and 1 shyppen and 1 lynnage 4 cowple; value [*blank*]. 2 Herb gardens; 1 orchard 2 ac. R 1-0-0; Pytte Parke 4 ac. R 0-15-0; Myddle Parke 4 ac. R 0-10-0; Hollow close 3 ac. R 0-10-0; the Greate meadow 3½ ac. R 1-5-0; Bramble close 3 ac. R 0-8-0; Lower Chyldyshe 3 ac. R 0-8-0; Coxewoode meadow ½ ac. R 0-10-0; Coxewoode Moore ½ ac. R 0-3-4; Hyer Chyldyshe 5 ac. R 0-10-0; Churchyll Knappe 4½ ac. R 0-13-4; Pownd close meadow 1½ ac. R 0-16-0; all these parcelles before wrytten were some tyme Barton land.

Lands belonging to the tenement called Blackedytche: Blackedytche Moore 6 ac. R 0-6-8; Blackedytche close 2 ac. R 0-6-8; June [?Inne] Downe 6 ac. R 0-4-0; Lyttle Gulles Downe lac. R 0-4-0; halfe an acre of downe lying by Sandford in Haydons Gulles Downe ½ ac. R 0-2-6.

Rent 45s 3½d;[11] heryottes 1; sute of courte.

F7.[12] John Haydon thelder, tennant yn possession, and John Haydon the yonger and Raph Haydon, tennants yn revercion, doo holde for terme of their lyves: One dwellinge house called Wylmoresleigh, 1 halle and 2 romes within the halle,

[1] Hand 2 in English.

[2] Followed by the regnal year.

[3] Erased. The following entries are in hand 1, in Latin.

[4] The individual areas are interlined.

[5] *160* erased.

[6] In 1682, Boycombe was no longer a freeholding and was described (see p. 117).

[7] A long blank.

[8] *40* erased.

[9] Common form is omitted hereafter.

[10] Erased. Hand 2 continues, in English.

[11] *42s.* erased.

[12] Hand 1, but in English. In the 1682 survey Willmore Lea is described as: *All that dwelling house contayning an entry, one hall, one milkehouse and one roome within the hall, one chamber over the milkehouse and low roome, one chamber over the hall, two chambers over the entry, one kitchen, one dayry house, 2 chambers over the kitchen and dayry, one barne, stable and curtilage.*

wherof one ys a mylkehouse, one chamber over the same, 1 chamber over the halle, 2 chambers over the entrey, 1 kychen, 1 mylkehouse yn the kychen, 2 chambers over the kychen, containing yn the whole 4 coples, 1 barne 4 coples, 1 stable aduyninge to the barne, 1 stalle 2 cople; V 40s.

One herbe garden, R 0-6-8; 2 orchardes 2 ac. R-2-0-0; 1 meadowe 2 ac. R 1-4-0; Grene close 4 ac.[13] R 0-13-4; Slade Downe 7 ac. R 0-5-0; Gulleyes Downe 10 ac. R 0-5-0; 1 plot of grounde ½ ac. R 0-5-9; Lower Beryes Crofte close 2 ac. R 0-13-4; Hier Beryes Crofte close 3 ac. R 0-10-0; 1 more to the same adioyning lac. R 0-3-4; 1 meadowe called Cadewell Meade 8 ac. R 1-0-0; 3 closes of berton lande called Furlandes 21 ac. 1 yerd, R 0-12-0.

Rent 50s ld; heriot 2 best beasts: suit to the court.

F8. Thomas Coxe and William Stephens do hold by copy of courte rolle for terme of their lyves: 2 tenements whereof thonn ys called Denche[14] and thother Pytt, 1 halle, 1 chamber within the halle, 1 mylkehouse, 1 chamber over the mylkehouse, 1 chamber over the halle and 1 chamber over the chamber within the halle 3 coples, 1 barne 3 cloples [*sic*], 1 bakehouse, 1 stable 2 coples; V 20s.

3 Herbe gardens ½ v. R 0-3-4; 1 orchard 3 yeards, R 0-10-0; 1 meadow lienge next the barton land lac. R 0-13-4; 1 meadowe called Lange Meade lac. 1 yd. R 0-13-4; 1 meadowe called Hollocke Meade lac. R 0-10-0; Longe Parke lac. R 0-10-0; Thiscel close 3 ac. R 0-13-4; Grene close 3 ac. R 0-13-4; Awne close 1 lac. R 0-10-0; Holme close 2 ac. R 0-13-4; Three Acres 3 ac. R 0-10-0; Ruffe close 3½ ac. R 0-13-4; 1 close therto adioyninge lac. R 0-6-8; 1 close lienge by the Wode lac. R 0-10-0; 1 close lienge also by the Wode 3 yd. R 0-6-8; 1 close lienge by Langeland Yeate 2 ac. R 0-10-0; 1 other close lienage by Langeland Yeate ½ ac. R 0-5-0; Pyt Parke 2 ac. R 0-13-4; Lower Downe close 2 ac. [*rate absent*]; Mydle Downe close 2 ac. R 0-3-4; 1 other close lienge above the Mydle Down close 2 ac. R 0-13-4; 2 other closes called the Hier Downe Closes 2 ac. R 0-13-4; 1 close of barton lande called Braston Wode ½ ac. R 0-5-0; 1 close of barton lande lienge yn the south parte of Leselygh Wode 3 ac. R 0-13-4; 2 mores called Denche More and the More beneath the house 4 ac. R 0-5-0.

Rent 20s; heriot 2 best beasts; suit of court.

F9. John Cadleigh holdeth for term of his life accordinge to the custome of the mannor there: One tenement, 1 halle, one other halle and 3 chambers over the same 4 coples, 1 barne 2 coples, 1 stalle 1 cople, and 2 end shydes; V 20s.

1 Herbe garden, 16th parte of an acre, R 0-2-0; 3 orchardes lac. R 0-13-4; 1 meadowe lienge before the Axe 1 ac. R 1-0-0; 1 meadowe called Halfeacre ½ ac. R 0-5-0; 1 meadowe called Gynnemeade 3 yd. R 0-6-8; Knolles 4 ac. R 0-3-4; Lynch Acre lac. R 0-5-0; the Crofte lac. lyd. R 0-13-4; 1 other close called the Crofte ½ ac. R 0-6-8; Slade Parke 4 ac. R 0-13-4; Blackelande 1½ ac. R 0-10-0; Litle Aryshe lac. R 0-6-8; Acre-hayes 2½ ac. R 0-8-0; 1 close called the more behynde the house 2½ ac. R 0-5-0.

Rent 7s 10½d; heriot best beast; suit to the court.

F10.[15] John Clappe and William Clappe his sonne doe hold by copy of courte rolle for terme of their lyves: One tenement, 1 halle, one chamber within the same, 1 chamber over the halle, 1 chamber over the chamber within the halle, one kychen and one chamber over the kychen, 1 shoppe 3 coples, 1 barne, the stable and stalle 3 coples, and one house called the hayehouse 2 coples, and the bakehouse 2 coples; V 20s.

1 herbe garden 2 p.; 2 orchardes lac. R 0-13-4; 1 meadowe called the Great Meade 2 ac. R 0-12-0; 1 other meadowe called Litle meadowe lyd. R 0-4-0; the Crofte 2 ac. R 0-13-4; Hylle close 2 ac. R 0-13-4; Lang Crafte 3 ac. R 0-10-0; Ayshendune 2½ ac. R 0-8-0; Heigher Wilmore 1½ ac. R 0-10-0; Lower Wilmore 3 yd. R 0-6-8; Butlake More ½ ac. R 0-3-4; Crofte above the Waye 3 yd. R 0-8-0; Downe close 2 ac. R 0-5-0; the More lac. R 0-5-0.

Rent 8s 4½d; heriot best beast; suit of court.

F11. William Guppey and John Guppey his brother doe hold by copy of courte rolle for terme of their lives: One tenement, 1 halle, 1 chamber over the halle, 1 chamber within the halle and 1 chamber over the same, 1 deyrey, 1 chamber over the dayrey and entry, 1 malt house 4 coples, 1 barne, 1 shepen 3 coples, and 2 end sheedes; V 20s.

1 Herbe garden, R 0-2-0; 3 litle orchardes 3yds. R 0-13-4; 1 meadowe called the Grett meadowe 2 ac. R 1-0-0; Gruble 1½ ac. R 0-10-0; Two Acres 2 ac. R 0-10-0; the Lynche lac. R 0-6-8; Halfe Acre ½ ac. R 0-4-0; the Parke 1½ ac. R 0-10-0; the Crofte lac. lyd. R 0-13-4; the Litle Meadowe Crofte lyd. R 0-5-0; 1 close and 1 more called the More Landes 2 ac. R 0-10-0; Litle Mowsehill lyd. R 0-1-8; Lower Edge 2 ac. R 0-6-8; Mydle Edge 3 ac. R 0-5-0; Hier Edge 3½ ac. R 0-13-4; 1 More called the Gratt More 2 ac. R 0-3-4.

Rent 9s 7½d; heriot best beast; suit to the court.

F12. John Saunder doth hold for terme of his life acordinge to the custome of the manor: 1 tenement called Newlande, 1 halle, 1 chamber within the same, 1 chamber befor the entry, 1 chamber over the same 3 coples, 1 barne, 1 stalle 4 coples, and 1 house containing 1 oven and 1 drye withoute any cople; 1 garden and 2 litle orchards ½ ac.; V 20s.

1 meadowe called the Yonder meadowe lac. R 0-10-0; 1 meadowe called the Lower meadowe 3 yd. R 0-9-0; 1 meadowe called the Heigher meadowe ½ ac. R 0-6-0; 1 parcell of meadowe yn common with John Calley 3 yd. R 0-6-0; Combeland 3 ac. R 0-10-0; Langcrofte 3 ac. R 0-3-0;

[13] Apart from those called 'plot' and 'meadow', the closes listed in hand 1 are described as 'one close called ...'.

[14] Devenish in 1682.

[15] In the 1682 survey: *one hall, one chamber or roome within the same, one chamber over the hall, one chamber over the chamber or roome within the hall, one kitchen and chamber over the same, one shop, one barne, one stall, one house called the hayhouse, one house called the bakehouse.*

Three Corner close lac. R 0-6-8; 1 close lienge behind the bakehouse ½ ac. R 0-3-4; 2 closes called the Bynchehills 1½ ac. R 0-10-0; Drye Lease 2½ ac. R 0-7-0; Barne close lac. lyd. R 0-13-4; the Yonder More 3 ac. R 0-7-0; the Mydle More lac. lyd. R 0-7-0; the Heigher More 3 yd. R 0-3-4; the Lower More 2½ ac. R 0-3-4; the More next the house 3 yd. R 0-4-0.

Rent 7s 3½d; heriot best beast; suit to the court.

F13.[16] Robert Mason alias Lake holdeth for terme of his lyfe according to the custome of the mannor: One tenement called [*blank*], 1 hall, 1 chamber within the hall, 1 kytchen with 4 chambers over 5 poole, and 1 maulte howse with ovens and drye, and 1 chamber over, 1 other roome adioyninge to the same maultehowse, 1 stable with a hay lofte over 3 cowple, one barne and shippen with a hay lofte over 3 cowple; V 20s.

3 orchards and 1 herb garden lac. R 20s; 1 meadow called Langemeadow lying above the howse 1½ ac. R 1-0-0; Pownde alias Lange Meade lac. lyd. R 1-6-8; Rounde meadow 3 yd. R 0-12-0; Parke over Waye 5 ac. R 0-10-0; Barneparke 2½ ac. R 0-10-0; Furze Parke 6 ac. R 0-6-8; Myddleparke 3½ ac. R 0-6-8; Bentche Hyll 4 ac. R 0-7-0; Greene Parke 4 ac. R 0-8-0; New Barton 1 ac. R 0-10-0; the moore above the howse lac. R 0-6-8; 1 close above the garden 1½ ac. R 0-13-4; 1 groave called Aller Beare ½ ac. R 0-5-0.

Rent 8s 9½d; heryotte best beast; suit of court.

F14.[17] Alyce the wyfe of John Weaver, Josyas Boyle and Rychard Weaver hold for terme of theire lyves by indenture: One tenement, 1 hall with an inner chamber, with 2 upper chambers; V 13s 4d. [*Rent, etc. absent*]

One herb garden, R 0-0-12; certaine growneds called Newland Pytte 7 ac. R 0-13-4.

F15. The paryshoners of Farway clayme to holde the Church howse, 3 poole of timber, worthe per annum 13s 4d.

F16.[18] Elizabeth the wyfe of Rychard Bucknoll, John and Grace Bucknoll doe holde for terme of theire 3 lyves by indenture dated 20 June 1609: One tenement and dwelling howse (20s), 1 hall, the foarthe chamber, the kytchen and 1 chamber over 5 cowple, 1 barne, 1 stable with a hay loafte over 4 cowple; V 26s 8d.

The orchard and garden ½ ac. R 1-10-0, V 1-3-4; 1 close called Possession ½ ac. R 0-6-8, V 0-6-8; Meane meadow 3 yd. R 0-10-0, V 0-10-0; Langelande meadow lac. R 0-15-0, V 0-15-0; the Moore 3 ac. R 0-6-8, V 1-0-0; the Hygher Downe cloase 2 ac. R 0-7-0, V 0-14-0; 1 parcell of meadow by the same close lyd. R 0-7-0, V 0-7-0; the Downe cloase 2 ac. lyd. R 0-8-0, V 0-18-0; the Pyne close 5 ac. R 0-7-0, V 1-15-0; the Greate close 4 ac. R 0-13-4, V 2-13-4: the Lyttle close 2 ac. R 0-12-0, V 1-4-0; the Bye close 3 ac. R 0-13-4, V 2-0-0; 1 meadow called the Ragge lac. R 0-15-0, V 0-15-0; 1 close below the howse 2 ac. R 0-15-0, V 1-10-0.

Comon for 60 sheepe by custome, and also for catell and horses in sommer tyme uppon the lordes common, worthe yerely to this tenement at the leaste 30s. A good howse new builte. Woode great store. Water: running thorough moste of the grownde. Marle: plentyfull and very good. Good tymber but lyttle.

Sum per year £18 8s; rent 20s; herryotte best beaste or [*blank*]; Suyte of courte.

Boycombe (**F2**) in 1682

This had been split up into four holdings, of which the first three had been re-united. A calendar of the survey follows.

1. Nicholas Pomery holds by indenture, date 26 Aug. 1673: All that parte of the mansion house of the Barton of Boycombe: An entry, hall, parlour, buttery and milkehouse and two chambers over the same hall and parlour, and one chamber over the buttery and milkehouse, a brewhouse and one chamber over the same, and the barn and stall on the north side of the said house, both which barne and stall were built about 30 yeares before, and the stable on the south side of the said barne, and one other stall on the north side of the said brewhouse, and the little court called Dungecourt therto adioyninge, the close court betweene the said mansion house and brewhouse, and the fore curtilage, the herbe garden on the south and southwest side of the mansion house.

One close called the close before the doore and the orchards therto adioyninge, lately made and severed out of and from the same 3 ac.; 3 closes of meadow and one other orchard lately but one close and called Boycombe meadow 10 ac.; two other closes of land or pasture called the Higher Clees and Lower Clees 12 ac.; two other closes of meadow called Cley Meade and Pound Meade 2 ac.; one other close of land called Stilande 7 ac.; 4 other closes of land or pasture and one other orchard formerly one close called Boycombe Wood 9 ac.; the Greate Knolle 10 ac.; the Little Knolle 3 ac.; 3 other closes lately one close called Knolle Moore 4 ac.; 3 closes lately inclosed out of Knolle Hill: Lynch, Stoneborow and Newmoore 9ac; common of pasture upon Farway Downe.

Rent £2 14s; heriot best beast or £4; lives: said Nicholas Pomery (aged 65), John Pomery (32) his son, Thomasine Gold (30), daughter of Nicholas Gould of Woodbury; yearly value £36.

2.[19] Nicholas Pomery holds by indenture, date 10 Mar. 1648: the kitchen and entry [*of Boycombe*], the milkehouse and larder on the southwest side of the said kitchen, and the 3 chambers over the same entry, kitchen, milkhouse and larder, with the south east side of the curtilage called the Back court as the same is allready severed with postes and rayles.

[16] Hand 2. This can be identified as Sallicombe in 1682.

[17] In the 1682 survey: *A hall, an inner chamber, two upper chambers, one shippinge.*

[18] In the 1682 survey: *One entry, one hall, one kitchen, one milkehouse and 4 chambers over the same, one barne, one stall and hayloft over the stall.*

[19] Described in the summary rental as 'Adams tenement', perhaps in confusion with the next part.

One close called Bickenhayes 14 ac.; 3 other closes called the Moores 3 ac.; common of pasture for 20 sheep at all times upon the commons and waste called Knoll Hill and Farway Downe.

Rent 8s; heriot 40s; lives: Nicholas Pomery (dead), John Pomery (32) his son: Dorothy Pomery (dead), his daughter.

3. Nicholas Pomery holds by indenture, date 17 Aug. 1660; All that dwelling house and barne which was late before a barne only, and the lynnage and curtilage on both sides of the same house and barne, and the herbe garden and orchard lying on the south side of the said barne, and two other little orchardes, the one lying on the south side, the other on the north side of the said herbe garden.

One close of meadow lac.; the Little meadow lac.; 3 closes of land sometyme but one close called Barly Arrish 10 ac.; Barne close 2 ac. (late before in the possession of one John Adams); common of pasture uppon Knolle Hill and Farway Downe.

Rent 14s; heriot £3 6s 8d; lives: [*as last]*.

4. Peter Haydon, executor of John Haydon, his father, holds by indenture, date 11 Dec 1624: Whattley 5 ac.; Hole Crofte 4 ac.; common of pasture for 8 sheep upon Farway Downe.

Rent 5s 6d; heriot 10s; lives: Edmund and John Haydon (dead), said Peter (74).

[f.15][20] Whytewell

Court of survey of John Willoughby, gentleman, lord of the said manor, of all and singular the messuages, Lands, holdings, lands [*sic*] and other whatsoever hereditaments of the said manor, held the 5th day of July [1609]. [*Jurors*] Edmund Lowde; Edward Clarke; William Teape; John Butter; John Howper; John Markhyll: sworn.

W1. John Clerke, Agnes his wife and Elizabeth Clerke now wife of Ron' Bylle hold by copy of court roll of the aforesaid manor for term of their lives successively according to the customs of the manor: A certain parcel of barton land lying beside the Water of Axe, containing by estimacion 3 ac.; value per annum 46s 8d; rent 6s; heriot nil; suit of court.

W2. John Howper and [?Pascal] Howper, his brother hold[21]: One holding called Horryford, 1 hall, 1 chamber, over the same hall, one parlour and one chamber over the same, 1 kitchen and 1 chamber over the same 5 couples; 1 garden and 1 orchard lac.; V 40s.

3½ ac. Meadow in Colyford Meade called Hope, R 0-14-0; 1 meadow called Litle Meade lac. R 0-14-0; a close lying in Tayle Lane lac. lv. R 1-5-0; a close lying in Salterne Lane 5 v. R 0-10-0; 4 closes called the Lower Groundes 9 ac. R 0-10-0; Horryford More 5 ac. R 0-10-0; the Hier Grounde 50 ac. R 0-3-4.

Rent 8s 5d; heriot best beast; suit of court.

[20] This is all in hand 1, in Latin, except for the values in W3 and W7.

[21] The words from *by copy* to *customs of the manor* (as in W1) are omitted hereafter (absent for W6, 8, 9).

W3. John Markehill and Agnes Markehill lately wife of William Dyrrey hold: One meadow called Bynche close 3 ac. V 40s.

Rent 3s; heriot nil; suite of court.

W4. John Butter holds: One holding called Boltshayne, 1 hall, 1 chamber within the same hall, 1 house called a mylkehouse 3 couples, also 1 barn and 1 shippen 3 couples; 1 garden and 3 orchards lac.; V 40s.[22]

One parcel of meadow lying in Southeover in Coliford Meade lac. R 1-6-8, V 1-6-8; one other parcel of meadow in Southeover 3 v. R 1-0-0, V 1-0-0; Various[23] parcels of meadow in Northeover in Colyford Meade, lying there in five separate places lac. 1 v. R 1-5-0, V 1-5-0; Shylfes 2 ac. (3 v.)[24] R 1-0-0, V 2-0-0; Foure Acres 2 ac. (3 v.)[25] V 2-0-0; 2 closes called Buckeslades 3 ac. R 0-10-0, V 1-10-0; Underhill lac.[26] V 0-16-0; Whitemare ½ ac.[27] V 0-10-0; Barnehaye 1½ ac. R 1-0-0, V 1-10-0; the Hier Langeland 1½ ac. R 0-13-4, V 1-0-0; Lower Langelande 2 ac. R 1-0-0, V 2-0-0; Yonder Langelande lac. lyd. R 0-13-4, V 0-16-8; West close lac. lyd. R 1-0-0, V 1-5-0; 2 closes called the Crackelandes 4 ac. R 0-12-0, V 2-14-0; Ryecrofte 1½ ac. R 0-12-0, V 0-18-0; comon of pasture per annum for 60 or 80 sheepe. V 4-10-0.

Rent 7s; heriot best beast; suit of court.[28]

W5. John Butter holds: One holding with appertenances called Bakehouse containing 2 couples; V 13s 4d.

Rent 5d; heriot nil; suit of court.

W6.[29] Alice Markehill, widow, lately wife of Thomas Markehill, deceased, and John Markehill, son of the said Thomas, hold, Alice during her widowhood according to custom and John for his life according to the customs of the aforesaid manor: One holding called Boltshayne, 1 hall, 1 chamber over the same hall, 1 house called a mylkehouse, 1 chamber over the same, 1 chamber over the entry of the same holding, one house called the bakehouse, 1 house called the weavingehouse, and 1 chamber over the same 4 couples, also 1 barn and 1 shippon adjoining 3 couples; 1 garden and 2 orchards lac. land; V 40s.

[22] A value of £4 is added in hand 2, as are the values of the closes.

[23] *One* erased.

[24] Erased.

[25] Erased.

[26] *3 v.* erased.

[27] *1 v.* erased.

[28] A total value of £28-10-0 is given, in hand 2.

[29] In the 1682 survey: *A hall and one chamber over the same, one dayry house and chamber over the same, one chamber over the entry, one house called the bakehouse, one house called the weavinghouse, and one chamber over the same, one barne, one shipping*. The same description is used in a single sheet of survey notes (undated but early 17th century) in British Library, Add. Mss. 22173, f.44.

The Crofte 3 v. R 0-13-4; Pecketishaye lac. R 0-13-4; Litle Showle ½ ac. R 0-8-0; North Showle 3 v. R 0-12-0; Downe close 3 ac. R 0-13-4; White Mare lac. R 0-16-0; Underhyll 3 v. R 0-10-0; White Crosse lying beside Nunford 3 ac. R 0-13-4; Litle Cleyes ½ ac. R 0-10-0; ½ ac. meadow in Colesmyl Meade R 0-13-4; 3 v. meadow lying in Southeover in the meadow of Colyton, R 0-15-0; 1½ v. meadow in Northeover in the said meadow, R 0-8-0.

Rent 4s½d; heriot best beast; suit of court.

W7.[30] Edmund Lowde and Richard Lowde his brother hold: One barn and 2 lez stalles containing in all 8 coples; V 20s.

Hier Hampstede (1½ ac.);[31] Lower Hampstede (10 ac.); Litle Hampstede (5 ac.); Longe More (3 ac.); Gratons (16 ac.); White Wilmore (9 ac.);[32] the Lynch (3 ac.); Lower Whitewell Ley (4 ac.); Mydle Whitewell Ley (6 ac.); Hier Whitewell Ley (9 ac.); Downe close (8 ac.); Lynche beside the Downe (3 ac.); the Greate Water Leate (7 ac.); the Litle Water Leate (3 ac.); the Yonder Brodelandes (5 ac.); the Heither Brodelandes (5 ac.); meadow called the Persons Meade (lac. 3r.); Broome close (3 ac.); Lordes Ley; meadow called Litle Meade (1½ ac.); Great Meade (4 ac.); half of one close called Rugcrofte; 4 ac. meadow in Colyford Meade (3 ac. 1r.).

Rent £3 1s 10d.[33]

W8. Edmund Lowde holds in possession, and Robert Lowde, John Lowde and Hugh Lowde hold in reversion by two separate copies for term of their lives successively, according to the customs of the said manor: One holding called Rode, 1 hall, 1 chamber over the same, one chamber within the same hall, 1 chamber over the same, 1 house called the Forthe House, and 1 house called the mylkehouse, and 2 chambers over them 3 coples, also 1 barn with 2 lez lyneys 2 coples, 1 kitchen, 1 chamber over the same, which kitchen contains 2 coples, 1 lez stalle 4 coples; 1 garden and 1 orchard lac.; V 40s.[34] The More 1 ½ ac. R 0-16-0, V 1-4-0; similarly the More lac. R 0-16-0, V 0-16-0; Brome Close 3 yd. R 0-13-4, V 0-13-0; Kinges Crofte lac. ½yd. R 0-13-4, V 0-16-8; Wheat Crofte 4 ac. R 0-13-4, V 2-13-4; Underhyll 5 ac. R 0-13-4, V 2-11-8; Cleyes 4 ac. R 0-13-4, V 2-13-4; similarly Cleyes 4 ac. R 0-13-4, V 2-13-4; Strynges 3 v. R 0-10-0, V 0-10-0; Morrens Meade 1½ ac. R 0-13-4, V 0-16-0; similarly

Morrens Meade, beside Abbots Marshe 5 v. R 1-0-0, V 1-13-4; 3 v. meadow lying in Southeover in Colyford meadow, R 1-0-0, V 0-15-0; common per annum, V 4-0-0.

Rent 6s 8½d; heriot best beast; suit of court.

W9. Francis Carsewill, gentleman, and Robert Carsewill his son, hold by two separate copies, Francis in possession and Robert in reversion, for term of their lives successively, according to the customs of the said manor: One close of demesne land called Due Hope, one orchard and one meadow called Due Hope Meade 3 ac. V 3-0-0.

Rent 3s 4d; heriot nil; suit of court.

Whitwell in 1682 and Luppitt

Four Whitwell holdings are described in 1682, but not in 1609; one of these includes a house description (here called W10).[35] *One further undated description comes from a loose sheet in the hand of John Willoughby, bound up in British Library Add. Mss. 22173 (f.42); it is here called W11, even though it does not lie in Whitwell.*

W10. Benedict Hake holds by indenture, date 10 Mar. 1659[/60]: one dwelling house, a hall and chamber over, one buttery (within the hall), one dayry, and chamber over the buttery and dayry, one entry, one low roome without the entry (being a lodging), one sider house, 3 chambers over the same entry, low roome and sider house (5 poole), one bakehouse and chamber (roome) over, one barne, one lynnage or (and) stable (5 poole), one sheppen (with a hayloft over, 3 poole), one curtilage, one herbe garden.

3 Orchardes 2 ac.; 3½ ac. of meadow in 3 severall places nere together in Northover within Colliford meadow; 1 ac. meadow lying in Colesmill meadow; Underhill 2½ ac.; Badburrow 2½ ac.; Hill close 3½ ac.; 5 other closes called Whitemares 15 ac.; Horne close 1½ ac.; Great Downe close 3 ac.; Little Downe close 1½ ac.; Lords Lea 4 ac.; 20 ac. common or wast called Bolshams common, to be allotted out by John Willoughby, in lieu of all common whatsoever belonging to the said premises.

Rent 9s; heriot best beast or £3 10s; suit of court; lives: said Benedict Hake (52), Mary Butter (46), John Butter (dead).

W11. Luppytt: one tenement called Anthonyhayes: one dwelling house, one hall, one buttery and dayerye, one entry, one grownde chamber and 3 chambers over, 5 poole in length, new buylte and well tymbred. One bakehouse, one maultehouse, one shypen and one barne something decayed. One herb garden, one lardge courte and 3 orchardes containing an acre, 1 shere and 1 yerd [*i.e. 1 rod, 1 perch*] V £2 6s 8d. Longeparke 3 ac; R 0-13-4, V 2-0-0; the parke without the waye 3½ ac. R 0-13-4 V 2-6-8; Lyttle close 2 ac. R 0-13-4, V 1-6-8; Lower Meadowe 2 ac. R 1-0-0, V 2-0-0; Hyer Meadowe 2 ac. R 1-0-0, V 2-0-0; Lyttle Groave 2 ac. R 0-8-0, V 0-16-0; Greate Groave 4½ ac. R 0-10-0, V 2-5-0; The moyetye of 4 ac. of comon which may be enclosed, being alreddy bounded out R 0-6-8, V 0-13-4; Comon of pasture uppon Hartridge Hille, not stynted, V 0-13-4.

Total V 16-7-8

Woode and water greate stoare, and worthe to be soalde at this present besydes ye tymber in all £18.

[30] In the 1682 survey: *houses, closes...late parcell of Whitewell farme, one barne and 2 stalles containing 8 couples or 8 couple roomes.*

[31] The 1609 survey gives no areas, and these have been supplied from that of 1682.

[32] *Whitwell More* in 1682.

[33] A marginal note reads *35 ac. land, 4 ac. meadow*, but this is much less than the actual area.

[34] A value of £4 added in hand 2, as are the field values.

[35] This is also described in a sheet of survey notes of about 1640 (British Library, Add. Mss. 22173, f.74) which contains some further information, given here in brackets

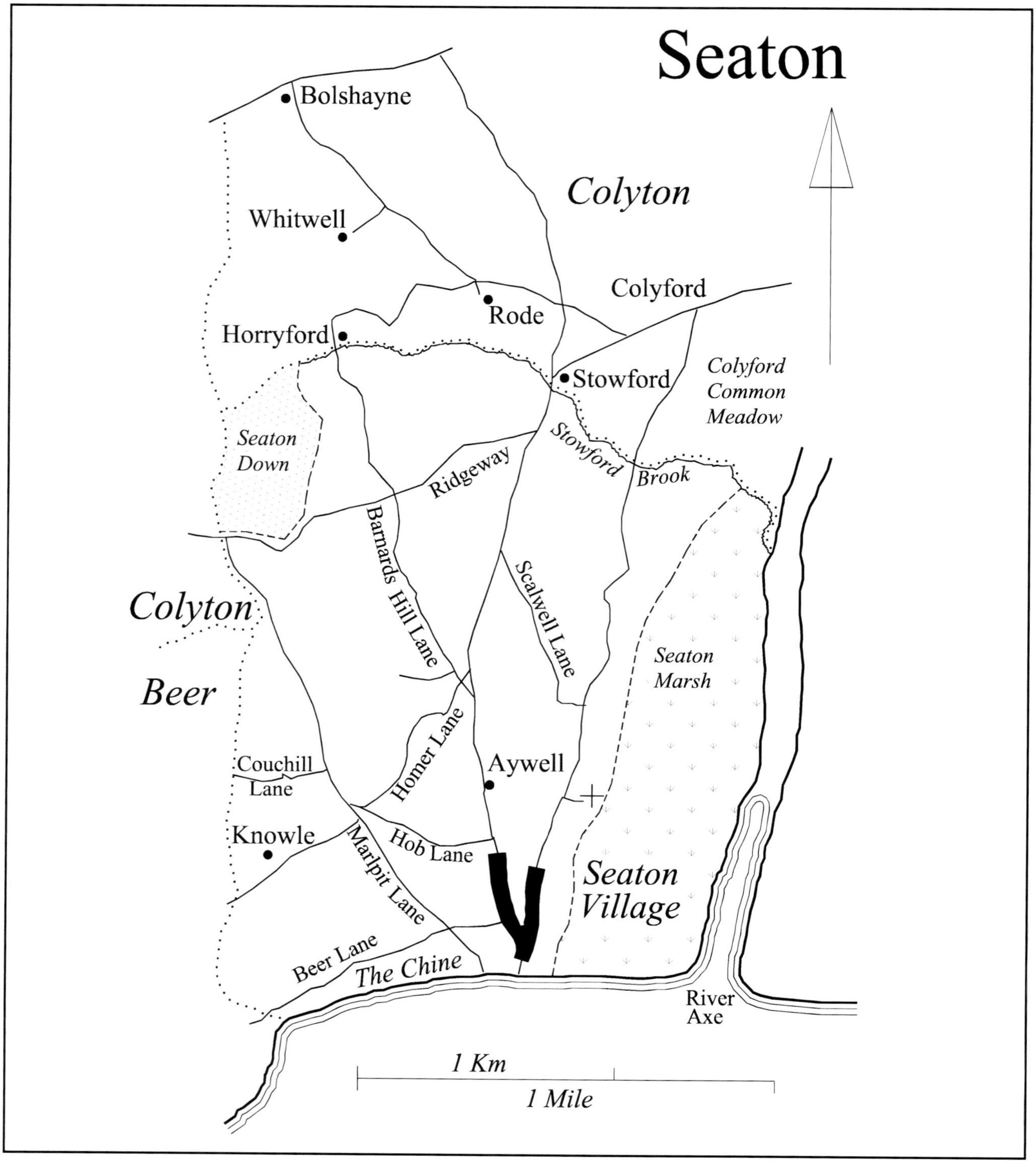

Map 6. Seaton and Whitwell, Devon

Boundaries are dotted. The parish of Seaton also contained the large manor of Beer in its western part, and therefore the western boundary of Seaton manor is approximate; it is drawn to follow the crest of the high hill to the west of the village. The possible western boundary of the Whitwell properties follows a prominent hedge-line. The names of the lanes in Seaton are mostly taken from the first 6" scale Ordnance Survey map (circa 1885). The solid tone gives a suggestion of the extent of the 17th-century fishing village.

CHAPTER 10

Seaton

Seaton: 1609 to 1682 (SA; SB) *Map 6*

Seaton is somewhat similar to Kenton—in good farming land, with most of the houses in a large village. Seaton, however lies on the sea, rather than being a mile away, with a large beach that could be used for landing. Fishing and seafaring were major occupations[1] and have clearly affected the pattern of housing. Like Kenton, much of the land had been in open fields. By the seventeenth century, the common field system was virtually extinct,[2] but most of the properties still consisted of widely scattered small fields with the same names recurring from holding to holding. These names may well have been those of the open fields or their furlongs, and many of them are perpetuated in the names of the network of lanes in the parish (see map 8).

The Seaton surveys present more problems of interpretation than those so far examined, particularly in the relationship between the 1609 and 1682 surveys. Many of the sixty-two holdings mentioned in 1682 cannot be immediately identified among the thirty-two earlier ones. Fortunately, several rentals survive, as well as 140 leases (and counterparts) dating from 1605 to 1691. The latter both add extra detail to the 1682 descriptions, and provide continuity.[3] The most important fact revealed by the leases is that the 1682 document is not an independent survey at all, but gives detailed abstracts of the leases, which were produced at a special court.[4] Its information (apart from the tenants' ages) therefore does not refer to 1682, but at the latest to the date of the lease. Several series of leases reveal that the primary source was the 1609 survey, and that details were copied from lease to lease. This survey covers thirty-two holdings (with twenty-six house descriptions), but a 1608 rental includes fifty-four items, so clearly the survey is incomplete. A specific example is SB11, absent in 1609, though its first lease is of 12 October 1607. This lacks house details, but the next one (1657) contains them. Twelve other holdings absent in 1609 have house descriptions, either in the 1682 survey or in surviving leases. The explanation must be that the 1609 exemplar is an incomplete fair copy, and that the lease descriptions were copied from the original survey.[5] The leases of one or two houses built after 1609 also contain descriptions, presumably following the pattern of the others (e.g. SB22, 25); however, by the later seventeenth century, descriptions were being omitted from the leases on renewal.

Apart from the specifically dated examples, it is therefore necessary to treat the whole body of evidence as relating to the early seventeenth century, and the hope that changes in houses through the century could be charted from the two surveys, is largely unfulfilled. However, the rentals and leases do give an indication of the fluidity of Seaton land-holdings.

The 1609 survey poses additional problems in its very difficult hand (see p. 119-20), and in the use of Latin for room names.[6] The terms used are given in Table 16, with their apparent meanings. Fortunately, many can be identified directly from the descriptions in the later survey; also the scribe sometimes fell back on English: *1 coquinam, 1 le Deyhouse* (SA5).

As at Farway, copyhold tenure was replaced by three-life leases during the seventeenth century. The evidence is incomplete, but it seems that only a few leaseholds existed before 1609, but that thereafter virtually all the holdings were leased. This was also the beginning of a period of rapid change. The fifty-four holdings in c. 1608 had risen by 1616 to no less than sixty-nine. This was the result both of subdivision (e.g. of SA18, 19), and of new building on waste land (e.g. SB64). However the 1682 survey lists only sixty-two holdings; some houses had fallen down (SB50), or been washed into the sea (SB64). As well as subdivision, it is clear that subletting was common in Seaton. As in Kenton, this practice is indicated by several holdings including more than one house (SA1, 5), while the description of SB27 suggests multiple occupancy of one house. Several groups of holdings

Table 16: Latin terms in the 1609 Seaton survey

Latin Term	English equivalent
Antrium	Entry
Aula	Hall
Camera	Chamber
Conolave (SA8)	'Anglice a parlour' (SA8); not in M.L.W.L.
Coquina	Kitchen
Domum brac'	Brewhouse (SB42 = SA2)
Horreum	Barn
Promptuarium (SA5, 8, 12)	Dairy (SB39 = SA8), but from internal evidence in SA12 it means Buttery, and in SA5 it is not a dairy. Buttery is the most likely meaning for all these. M.L.W.L. gives Storehouse.
Shepina	Shippon
Shopa (SA1, 25, 28, 29)	Shop
Spatium (SAl, 4, 19)	Translated as room in SB33 = SA4; used as equivalent to 'bay' in the Crown surveys
Stabulum	Stable
Triclium (SA2, 26, W2)	Parlour (SB55 = SA2l: SB5 = SA26). M.L.W.L. gives 'tricleia' = Bower.

M.L.W.L. = R. E. Latham (ed.), *Revised Medieval Latin Word List*, London, 1965

were also held by the same person (e.g. SA1, 2). The families of Dare, Manston, and Starre were much involved and for the last-named, this was only part of much more widespread interests. Although the Starre family probably lived in Seaton or Beer in the sixteenth century, by the seventeenth they were Exeter merchants. Barnard Starre was an upholsterer, and his son John and nephew (?) Edmond were both grocers: all three apparently held SB58, in succession to an earlier Edmond Starre (died circa 1608). They also bought land in at least one other parish much nearer Exeter, where Edmond Starre (II) lived in the later seventeenth century.[7]

The descriptions for some properties (e.g. SA27: 'one holding and three cottages'), which clearly have only one house, are unconnected with subletting, but probably reflect a situation similar to that found at Bishop's Clyst.[8] There, a populous village with some forty small tenements, dwindled in the fifteenth century to only twelve, whose tenants were regularly listed as 'A. holds four cottages', etc.

The Houses

The numerous building leases and new houses recorded (SB10, 22, 23, 25, 38, 40, 43, 51, 63, 64a, 64b) relate particularly to the smallest holdings, those with less than two acres. These were the homes of Seaton's working people: mariners (numerous), fishermen (SB19, 37), shipwrights (64b), carpenters (27), coopers (17), blacksmiths (18), bakers (36) and tailors (23, 64). From the surveys already examined, we would expect these to be cottages, mostly of two-room plan. In fact, ten of the fifteen described were larger than this, perhaps an indication that the sailors and craftsmen were less poor than the farm labourers who held small-holdings in inland villages. It is noticeable that the houses had fewer service rooms and more chambers than farmhouses of similar size. The implied differences in life style must have involved more people living in each house. The three-room plan houses had hall, inner chamber, and kitchen (SA1, 7, 20, SA30's second house, SA36 and SA25 with a shop), hall and two chambers (SA11, 24), or hall, chamber and 'room or small house' (SB19, SA31); most had two chambers over, though none were fully floored. SA27 is unusual, having hall, kitchen and brewhouse, the absence of a chamber being perhaps understandable as the tenant was a widow. In 1609, it was a seven acre holding, but by 1655 (SB21), it had been leased without its land and was described as 'three low rooms'; clearly they had ceased to have special functions. The largest of these houses was SB27, a complex building with six ground floor rooms. It may have been a farm which had come down in the world, and the description 'dwelling houses' suggests that it was in multiple occupation.[9]

Four houses had a hall and chamber plan (SA17 second house, SA22, SB22, 37), and one had 'two

Table 17: Large farms at Seaton

SA12	
Hall and chamber over	One other small chamber
Buttery and chamber over	Cyderhouse and chamber over
Chamber over entry	Malthouse
Dairyhouse and chamber over	Stable
Larderhouse	Wellhouse
Kitchen and chamber over	Barn
Brewhouse and chamber over	Shippen
Study	
SA21 (SB55)	
Rooms	*Lease Schedule (1641)*
Hall Parlour	In the Hall and Parlour; the waynscote or seeling [*panelling*]; two table bords
Chamber over Hall	In the Hall chamber: one bedstead
Chamber over Parlour	
Kitchen	In the Kitchen: one table borde and side borde
Chamber over Kitchen	
Buttery and Milkhouse, and one Chamber over	[absent in 1609, 'chambers' in 1661] In the Buttery: three shelves; in the Milkhouse: one shelve
Brewhouse and Chamber over	In the Brewhouse: one Gibb [*barrel stand*] and one borde; in the Store Chamber: one cheese rack
Stable	One rack and manger
Shepon or Stall	In the Stall; one long ladder
Barn	[1657: adjoining Robert Trickey's house]
Barn	[1609: absent. 1657: newly erected]
Salthouse	[1609 only]
SB29	
Rooms	*Lease Schedule (1649)*
Hall	The glasse of the Hall window and window leafes [*shutters*]
Parlour	The seeling between the Hall and Parlour with the Bench affixed thereunto. One of the Parlour dores with a locke, the other Parlour dore of seeling. The Iron Barr in the Hall chimney. The glasse of the Parlour window and the window leafes and the bench fastened to the speare [*partition*].
[Entry]	The shelfe behind the Portall The door at the foote of the staires The back and fore dores of the entrie, the Halldoore, the Buttrie doore
[Chamber over Entry]	The glasse of the Chamber window over the entrie, and the doore with a lock and key to the same
Chamber over Hall	The window leaves of the Chamber over the Hall
Chamber over Parlour	The window leaves of the Chamber over the Parlour
Buttery and Chamber over	
Dayrie or Milkhouse on south side of Buttery	
Kitchen	
[Outhouses]	Two doores of two outhouses; without them the back doore
[Bakehouse]	Fower doores to the Bakehouse and [*blank*], with lockes and keyes unto two of them
Stable	The great dore at the end of the wall of the dwelling house.
Little low room commonly called the stall	One mow staddle with six postes [*supports for a hay stack*]

low rooms' (SB8); this had two chambers over, while SA17 and SB37 each had one. Neither of the others were chambered over, and interestingly, neither was old. SA22 was new-built in 1609, and SB22 had been a cellar (presumably a ground-floor storeroom) that by 1657 had been converted to a house. The pair of cottages that formed part of SA7 may well have been smaller still, their total of two couples suggesting that each was of one-room plan. Of the three cottages combined in SA1, one probably consisted of hall and chamber on the ground floor only; one presumably had an extra room, and another an extra shop and a chamber over. It is important to recall, before leaving the cottages, that most of the descriptions probably date from 1609 and so may not be typical of the houses that appeared later.

The farmhouses can be grouped according to their holding size into those with less than ten, less than thirty and more than thirty acres. The ten houses in the first group were quite varied. They included one with only a hall and a room within it (SB44), but with three chambers over, and three houses of three-room plan: hall with kitchen and buttery (SA14), kitchen and brewhouse (SA27, cf. above), or chamber and shop (SA28). The others were more complex, hall and kitchen with various combinations of buttery (SA29, SB14), dairy (SA23, 39), chamber (SA4, 23, SB14), brewhouse (SA2), malthouse (SB14), 'rooms' (SA2, 4, SB14) possibly for storage rather than sleeping;[10] only SA29 was fully floored, the rest each having two upstairs chambers.

As with the earlier surveys, the larger farms (sixteen in all) did not necessarily have larger houses, although they did include the two or three finest houses in Seaton. Indeed, SA18 and SB11, with sixteen and twenty-two acres, had houses with only a hall and inner chamber, with one chamber over. The farms with less than thirty acres also included two with hall, inner chamber and one other room—kitchen in SA7, milkhouse in SA30;[11] this farm, however, included a second house with hall, inner chamber and kitchen. The majority of the larger farms[12] had houses very similar to those on the smaller farms, with no two exactly alike, but rearranging the same components of hall, kitchen (absent from SB2, 3, unlike any in the last group), buttery (absent from SA13, 32), dairy (absent from SA8, 19, 26), ground floor chambers (in SA5, 13, SB2), 'room' or 'little house' (SA19), brewhouse, malthouse and bakehouse. Five houses had parlours, indicating their somewhat higher status, and the proportion of rooms floored over was rather higher than for the smaller farms.

It is worth looking at the three largest houses in more detail, as they represent a style of living significantly better than the typical standards of the early seventeenth century (compared in Table 17). The leases for two of them show a very unusual feature: schedules of fittings that the tenant had to preserve. These are particularly welcome as throwing a little light into the interiors of the farms, which are otherwise invisible.

All three houses had full upper floors. While SA12 possessed a multitude of service rooms, its living accommodation was less developed, although it did include a study. SA21 illustrates some typical furnishings. It also had the only salthouse, probably used for salting meat. SB29 shows the increased comfort that could be found by 1649, with glazed windows in the hall, parlour and one chamber (perhaps over a porch).[13] The room names in the schedule and those in the description, show discrepancies that are disturbing at first sight; these are, however, understandable if the description dates from 1609 and was not updated, while the schedule was compiled after improvements between then and 1649.

The Farm Buildings (Table 18)

Seaton residents who made a living from the land were chiefly pastoral farmers like their inland neighbours at Whitwell and Farway, although this coastal village may also have provided some limited opportunities for arable farming and commercial fruit-growing. Virtually every farmer had a barn and most kept cattle in a shippon or stall (used interchangeably in SA21). Several stables, on the larger farms particularly, indicate the presence of horses, probably for ploughing rather than transport in so far as no stables are associated with any artisan's property. Changes in arable farming practices are hinted at too, in the conversion of a barn and shippon in SA30 in 1609 into a barn and hayhouse by 1682. SA13, the largest farm, had a pound house for crushing cider apples, and SB2 a henhouse.

A group of five very small holdings (SB27, 37, 44, SA2, 14) invite speculation, for in each case the farm buildings hardly seem necessary for the minuscule piece of property (one to five acres). Yet, each one had a barn, and three had another structure be-

Table 18: Seaton 1604–82: Occurrence of farm buildings

Ref. Number	Acres	Barn	Stable	Shippon	Stall	Linhey	Other Buildings	Notes
SA17	0	•						
SB8	0							
SB19	0	6						
SB21	0							
SB22	0							
SA11	1/4							
SA31	1/4							
SB25	1/4							
SA20	1/2					•		linhey perhaps domestic
SA24	1/2							
SA22	1							
SA25	1							
SB37	1	•						
SB27	1 3/4	•			•			
SA23	3 1/4							
SA1	3 1/2							
SA2	3 3/4	=		=				barn + shippon + brewhouse(3)
SA29	4 1/2							
SA14	4 3/4	=	=					barn + stable(4)
SB44	5	•						
SB14	6							
SA28	7							
SA27	8							
SA4	9	•		•				
SB29	14		•		•			
SB5	15				•			
SB3	15	•		•				house adjoins shippon
SA30	16	=		=				barn + shippon(3); in 1660: barn and hayhouse
SA26	16	=	=					barn + stable (3)
SA18	16	4						
SA7	18	=		=				barn + shippon (5)
SA19	19	4	=	=				stable + shippon(2)
SA12	20	=	2	=				barn + shippon(6)
SA21	22	2	=	=				stable + shippon(2); second barn by 1657, and shippon described as 'shippon or stall'
SB11	22	•						
SA5	30	•	•	••				
SA8-10	31	=	=	=				barn + shippon + stable(3)
SB2	33	•		•			hen-house	
SA32	36	•			•	•		
SA13	45	4					pound-house	

Note: The information from both surveys and leases is combined, eliminating duplicates. The occasional dimensions are in couples.

sides, a combination shippon and brewhouse, a stall or a stable. The dwellings of all but one were described as 'cottages', but were the tenants farmers? Yes and no. SB44 was held in 1682 by 'husbandman' Edward Manston, but the resident of SB27 may have been a carpenter like his father, and SB37 had been recently the home of a fisherman. Perhaps what we see here is evidence of seasonal or part-time farming by fishermen and artisans who put out a few steers or cows on the common pasture or kept horses for hire. Usually by-employments were sidelines to farming, but in a varied economy, such as that of Seaton, cattle raising and dairy farming may have been the secondary employments.

1 Demonstrated by the occupations given in the seventeenth-century series of leases.

2 The only record of land apparently still in open field is in the 1660 lease of SB13. The grant involved the surrender of two parcels of open field land, no doubt for consolidation. Common field meadow was still present at Seaton (e.g. SA26), and in part at least, this was in Colyford meadow, shared with the Whitwell properties.

3 Because of the major differences between the surveys, both are calendared, with details of the leases.

4 Originals or counterparts survive for two-thirds of the holdings, including some where the surveys noted 'this lease I could not see'.

5 Few house descriptions are likely to be completely lost, because a number of the entries in the 1608 rental but not the 1609 survey clearly relate to fields not houses.

6 This is almost universal for Seaton and Whitwell but for Farway only occurs in F4; John Willoughby himself never used Latin.

7 N. W. Alcock, 'Fields and Farms in East Devon Parish', *Trans Devonshire Assoc.*, 107 (1975), 109.

8 N. W. Alcock, 'An East Devon Manor in the Later Middle Ages, Part II', *Trans Devonshire Assoc.*, 105 (1973), 141.

9 SB51 was probably also of three-room plan, as its measurements, 40 ft. by 16 ft. are large for two rooms.

10 This confused the surveyors and stewards. SA2's 'lower room' (1609) became an 'under chamber' in 1656; SA4's 'chamber within the hall' became a 'low room' (1655).

11 By 1659, the milkhouse had become a buttery, and it also had a woodhouse, something otherwise unrecorded in Seaton.

12 These are SA5, 8, 10, 13, 32, SB2 greater than thirty acres, and SA7, 12, 18, 19, 21, 26, 30, SB3, 5, 11, 29, less. SB5 is possibly equivalent to SA26, but their house descriptions are not similar, and they are discussed separately.

13 SA32 also had one first floor chamber particularly noted as glazed.

Surveys of Seaton: 1609 and 1682; Leases

The survey texts are described in Chapter 9 (p. 119). Some 140 distinct leases also survive, including both surrendered leases and counterparts (not distinguished here). They are in Somerset Rec. Off. DD/WO boxes 29-30 (and a few in 31), bundled chronologically; although unlisted, they can be identified from the dates given. Rentals of c.1608, c.1618, 1616 and 1668 and a survey or list of leases of 1660, with additions to 1672 also exist (boxes 43-44).

TEXT

[f.7][1] *Seaton* [1609]

Court of survey of John Willoughby, esquire, lord of the said manor, of all and singular the messuages, lands, tenements, meadows, pasture, rents, woods, underwoods, and other hereditaments whatsoever of the said John, of the said manor wherever, together with their appurtenances, held 4 July 1609.

John Manston; John Baker; William Twychen; William Dare; Robert Wodeland; Edward Clerke; Geoffrey Forde; William Redwode.

SA1.[2] *William Twychen and John his son hold 1 cottage*[3] *containing 3 halls, 3 chambers, and 1 room, 1 shop and 1*

1 This survey is all in hand 1 in Latin, except where noted.

2 Marginal note in hand 2: *They are all in togetheere.*

3 Interlined *tria 46s 8d* (presumably the value). This indicates that three cottages, not one was intended.

chamber over, containing 7 couples; 3 gardens ½ ac. Value per annum [blank].

1 close of land called Beare Lane containing 3 v. 13s 4d; 1 other close called Beare Waye containing 1 ac. 1 v. 13s 4d; 1 close called Marle Pytt containing 1 ac. 16s.

Rent per annum 3s 2d; relief, half rent; value per annum [blank].[4]

SA2 (See SB60).[5] The same William and Richard Twychen, his son, hold 1 cottage (20s), 1 hall, 1 kitchen, 1 lower chamber, 2 chambers above 4 couples, 1 barn, 1 shippon, 1 brewhouse 3 couples; 1 garden and 1 curtilage 1 v.

Flete close 1 ac. R 0-12-0; Heathefyld 1 ac. 1 v. R 0-13-4; Yonder Heathfyld 1 ac. R 0-13-4; meadow called Combehill Lane alias Withelake 3 v. R 0-15-0.

Rent 4s 2d; farleu half rent.

SA3. The same William Twychen, John senior, and Richard son of the said William hold: 1 close of land called Lower Salterne Way 2 ac. R 1-0-0.

Rent 8d; farleu 5s.

SA4 (see SB33). Geoffrey Forde and Joan Forde, now wife of Richard Clerke, hold by copy of court roll for term of their lives successively: one holding (20s), 1 hall, 1 chamber within the hall, 1 other chamber over the same, 1 kitchen, 2 other rooms with 1 le lofte over 3 couples, also 1 barn, 1 shippon, 1 curtilage and 1 garden ½ ac.

Close of meadow called Comon Lane Meade 1 v. R 0-4-0; close of meadow called Wilclose 3 v. R 1-0-0; close of land called Great Wellclose 2 ac. R 1-0-0; close of land called Aywell 1½ ac. R 1-0-0; Newe Close 1 ac. 1 v. R 0-12-0; Bussell 1½ ac. R 0-12-0; Bearewaye 1 ac. R 0-7-6.

Rent 3s 2d; heriot best beast.

SA5 (see SB60). John Manston senior, John Manston junior, and Michael Manston, son of John Manston senior, hold by copy of court roll for term of their lives successively: one holding (40s) with 2 tofts, 1 hall, 1 chamber within the same hall, 1 chamber over the hall, 1 small chamber adjoining, 1 kitchen, 1 buttery, 1 le deyhouse, 2 chambers over the kitchen, 1 chamber over le deyhouse 6 couples, also 1 barn, 1 stable, 2 shippens, 2 gardens, 1 orchard 3 v., 1 meadow called Mylmede ½ ac. R 0-6-8; ½ ac. meadow in Colyford Meade, R 0-6-8; meadow at Lydeyeate 3 v. R 0-10-0; Burnardshyll 6 ac. R 1-13-4; Brodeclose 3 ac. R 0-6-8; Marlepytt 3 ac. R 0-6-8; Bossell 1½ ac. R 0-6-8; Lower Bossell 3 v. R 0-5-0; Hoblane 1½ ac. R 0-10-0; close at the end of a lane called Hoblane ½ ac. R 0-3-4; Bearewaye 3 v. R 0-8-0; close lying in Cawsey Lane 1½ ac. R 0-8-0; close lying uppon the Channe 3 v. R 0-5-0; close lying at ?Ropers doore[6] 3 v. R 0-10-0; Beare Lane 3 v. R 0-10-0; Scalwell 2 ac. R 0-10-0; Heathefyeld 1½ ac. R 0-10-0; Fyeldes 1½ ac. R 0-8-0; close lying behynde the barne 1½ ac. R 0-10-0; Marlepytt ½ v. R 0-1-0.

Rent 12s 1½d; heriot best beast.

SA6 (see SB42). John Manston senior, John Manston junior and Marie Manston, son and daughter of John Manston senior, hold:[7] A close called Newe close, divided into three, 8 ac. R 0-6-8; More Acre 5 ac. R 0-10-0; Shortland 1 ac. R 0-10-0; a small parcel of land lying in Holmermeade, R 0-1-0. Rent 3s 4d; heriot by custom 30s.

SA7 (see SB46). William Redwode, Richard Redwode and John Redwode hold: One holding (26s 8d), 1 hall, 1 chamber within the hall, 1 kitchen, 3 chambers over these, 1 barn, 1 shippon 5 couples; 1 garden, 1 orchard 1 v.; 2 cottages beside Beere Lane: 2 couples.

Marlepytt 4 ac. R 0-9-0; Salterne Waye 1½ ac. R 0-3-0; Bossell ½ ac. R 0-5-0; Newcombe 1 v. R 0-4-0; Rudgewaye 1 ac. R 0-9-0; Honydiche 2 ac. 1 v. R 0-9-0; Litle Fyld ½ ac. R 0-5-0; Great Fyeldes 1 ac. 1 v. R 0-9-0; Newe close 3 v. R 0-8-0; Aywell 1 ac. 1 v. R 0-10-0; Stoneborowe alias Fearneborowe 1 ac. 1 v. R 0-10-0; Townesende 1 ac. 1 v. R 0-10-0; Mylclose 3 v. R 0-8-0; Whiteclose 3 v. R 0-8-0; 2 parcels of land called Bowhayes and Barnehayes ½ ac. R 0-5-0; Neithehayes 3 v. R 0-7-0; 1 parcel of land lying in Holmermeade ½ v. R 0-4-0.

Rent 5s 3d; heriot best beast.

SA8 (see SB39). Nicholas Manston, Elizabeth and Katerina, daughters of the said Nicholas, hold: One holding (30s), 1 hall, 1 *conolave, anglice* a parlour within the same, 2 chambers over them, 1 kitchen, 1 buttery and 1 chamber over 4 couples, 1 barn, 1 shippon and 1 stable 3 couples; 1 garden and 1 orchard and curtilage ½ac; value 30s.

Cawsey 3 v. R 0-6-8, V 0-6-8; Knolles 3 ac. R 0-6-0, V 0-18-0; Treeymlands 5 ac. R 0-7-0, V 1-15-0; Homer Meade 1½ ac. R 0-10-0, V 0-15-0; Bawmeshott 3 ac. R 0-8-0, V 1-4-0; Barnarde Hille 2 ac. R 0-6-8, V 0-13-4; Peartlakes 2 ac. R 0-8-0, V 0-16-0; 1 ac. meadow in Colyford Meade, R 0-10-0, V 0-10-0; Worcester ½ ac. V 0-4-0.

Rent 8s 1d; heriot best beast; value,[8] £8 8s.

SA9 (see SB39). The said Nicholas Manston, Dorothea Manston and Katherina Manston, his daughters, hold: 2 closes called Newe close 8 ac. R 0-8-0, V 3-4-0; Lange Acre 2 ac. R 0-10-0, V 1-0-0.

Rent 4s 2d; heriot best beast.

SA10 (see SB39). Nicholas Manston, Elizabeth and Katerina, his daughters, hold: three closes of demesne land called [*blank*] 2 ac.

Rent 22d; heriot [*blank*].

[4] The words *valet per annum* are given at the end of each entry, and after each house description, but with no figures.

[5] These references to the 1682 survey indicate the holdings that may correspond; the identifications are examined below. Common form is omitted hereafter; including the phrases *a close called* in front of each field name.

[6] *Downe* erased.

[7] The phrase *by copy .... according to custom*, as in SA5, occurs regularly (apart from SA14), and is omitted hereafter.

[8] The total values are in hand 2.

SA11. John Hoper alias Dyer, John his son, and Maria, daughter of the said John Howper senior, hold: One cottage, 1 hall, 1 chamber within the same hall, 1 other chamber, 1 chamber over the same chamber, one other chamber over the entry, and 1 loft; 1 garden and 1 orchard 1 v.; V 30s.

Rent 12d; Farleu 6d.

SA12 (see SB58). Elizabeth Starre, widow, late wife of Edmond Sterre, deceased, holds during her widowhood according to custom, and also John Sterre and Jane Sterre, son and daughter of the said Edward and Jane [*sic*], hold: one holding (£4), 1 hall, 1 buttery, 1 le deyryhouse, 1 le larderhouse, 1 kitchen, 1 brewhouse, 1 chamber over the hall, 1 other chamber over the buttrey, 1 chamber over the entry, 1 other chamber over the deyrey, 1 other chamber over the kitchen, 1 le studye, 1 other small chamber, 1 chamber over the brewhouse 7 couples, 1 house called a syder house and one chamber over it, 1 house called a malthouse, 1 stable 2 couples, 1 house called a welhouse; also 1 barn and 1 shippon 6 couples; 1 curtilage, 1 garden and 2 orchards 1½ ac.

2 closes called Couchehill Crosse 4 ac. R 0-3-0;[9] Witheylake 2 ac. R 0-10-0; Barnarde Hille 3 ac. R 0-8-0; Seaven Acres alias Seaven Okes 4 ac. R 0-6-8; Stoford Broke 2 ac. R 0-10-0; Fleete Hylle 2 ac. R 0-10-0; meadow called Common Lane 3 v. R 0-10-0; Barnehaye 1 ac. R 0-10-0; the Litle meadowe 1 v. R 0-5-0.

Rent 10s 6d; heriot best beast.

SA13 (see SB58). Elizabeth Starre, widow, late wife of Edmond Starre, deceased, holds during her widowhood, and John Sterre and Agnes Sterr, children of the said Elizabeth, hold: One holding (53s 4d) called Aywell House, 1 hall, one le parlour within the same hall, 1 chamber within the said hall, one kitchen, 1 le deyhouse, 1 chamber over the hall, 1 chamber over le parlor, 1 chamber over the chamber within the hall, 1 chamber over le deyhouse 5 couples, 1 barn[10] 4 couples, 1 le poundhouse 3 couples; 1 garden and 1 orchard 1 ac. 1 v.

One meadow called Courtemeade 1 ac. R 0-13-4; a close of land called the close above the Waye 1 ac. R 0-10-0; Marle Pytt 4 ac. R 0-10-0; Surley 10 ac. R 0-6-8; Ayshe Grove 5 ac. R 0-8-0; Bossell 7 ac. R 0-6-8; Newe close 1½ ac. R 0-10-0; Wode 1½ ac. R 0-8-0; Bromelea 3 v. R 0-6-8; meadow called Langemeade 3 v. R 0-9-0; meadow called Holmermeade ½ ac. R 0-6-0; More Acre 2½ ac. R 0-8-0; Lower Lydeyeat 1 ac. R 0-9-0; Higher Lydeyeat 2½ ac. R 0-8-0; Castell 3 v. R 0-10-0; Brodeclose 3 ac. R 0-10-0; meadow called Aywell meadow 3 v. R 0-16-0; meadow called Common Lane Meade ½ v. R 0-2-0. (Litle Courte Hill 2 v.)[11]

Rent 26s 9d; heriot best beast; suit of court.

SA14 (see SB62). John Sterre senior of Beare, gentleman, holds for term of his life according to custom: one dwelling house[12] containing two cottages, 1 hall, 1 chamber over the same hall, entry and 1 chamber over, le buttrey and chamber over, and 1 kitchen 3 couples, also 1 barn, stable 4 couples; 1 curtilage and garden 1½ ac.; 1 virgate [?*rod*] of land.

1 close of land lying to the west of the holding 1½ ac.; one close of land lying to the east of the barn 1½ ac.

Rent 3s 4d; farleu 20d; suit of court.

SA15 (see SB43). Thomas Weston and Francis Weston hold: one decayed fulling mill.

One close of demesne land called Abbey Hyl 12 ac. R 0-10-0; one meadow called Hier Abbey Hyll Meade 1½ ac. R 1-6-0; one other meadow called Lower Abbey Hyl Meade 1 ac. R 1-0-0; one meadow lying beside Blackepole 3 ac. R 1-0-0.

Rent 22s 4d; heriot best beast; suit of court.

SA16 (see SB24). Robert Roberts holds: one piece of land called Vyncage, 40 ft. broad and 80 ft. long, on which there is now erected a dwelling house; V13s 4d.

Rent 8d; farleu 4d; suit of court.

SA17. Agnes, wife of John Whyker, John Whyker and Robert Whyker, sons of the said John and Agnes, hold by indenture: 2 cottages containing 2 dwelling houses; 1 hall, 1 chamber over the same hall, 1 chamber within the same hall, one chamber over the same chamber, 1 kitchen to the north of the entry; 1 other cottage, 1 hall, 1 chamber within the same hall, 1 chamber over the same chamber, which [*both*] cottages contain 5 couples; 1 small room to place [?beer]; one curtilage, 1 garden, 1 barn to the east; 1 garden and 1 orchard lying to the west [*?of the street*] containing the same house; all of which is worth per year, let, 53s 4d.

Rent 2s; heriot [*blank*];[13] suit of court.

SA18 (see SB49 and 58). Agnes, wife of John Pyne, John Clerke senior, and John, his son, hold: one holding called Abbots and 1 cottage, 1 hall, 1 chamber within the same hall, one chamber over the entry of the holding, one barn adjoining 4 couples; 1 garden, 1 orchard; V 40s.

2 closes called Longacre 2½ ac. R 0-13-4; Marlepytt 3 ac. R 0-6-8; Honydyche 1 ac. 3 v. R 0-10-0;[14] Hoblane 3 v. R 0-7-6; Fyeldes 2 ac. R 0-6-8; Castell 1 ac. 1 v. R 0-10-0; Scalwell 1½ ac. R 0-10-0; meadow called Budmeade 3 ac. R 1-6-8; meadow called Comon Lane 3 v. R 0-7-6.[15]

Rent 5s 8d; heriot best beast; suit of court.

SA19 (see SB31). Agnes, wife of John Pyne, John Clerke,

[9] SA12 and 13 have a column of figures in the margin in a later hand, possibly a set of values per acre, though they bear little relationship to the original ones. These are omitted.

[10] Followed by *1 le wringehouse* erased, probably corresponding to the *poundhouse* mentioned next.

[11] Added in the hand of the marginal figures.

[12] *Domus mansionalem.*

[13] Over an erasure *Farleu 12d.*

[14] From Honydyche to Budmeade are marked *Solde to R. Starre.*

[15] Marked *Jo. Starre* (part of SB58).

senior, and John, his son, hold: one holding called Hanysheplace, 1 hall, 1 le buttrey within the hall, 1 room outside the entry, 3 chambers over the same 3 couples, 1 kitchen, 1 barn 4 couples, 1 stable and 1 shippon 2 couples; 1 garden, 1 orchard 1½ ac.; V 40s.

Brodeclose 5½ ac. R 0-13-4; Withey Lake 2½ ac. R 0-13-4; Ridgewaye 3 v. R 0-7-6;[16] Moreacre 3 ac. R 0-6-8; Peartlake 2 ac. R 0-10-0; Fleetehyll 2 ac. R 0-10-0; Worster 3 ac. R 0-6-8.

Rent 8s 6d; heriot best beast; suit of court.

SA20 (see SB36). Elena Calley, widow, John Abbot and Maria Abbot, now wife of Peter Dare, hold: one cottage, 1 hall, one chamber over the same hall, 1 chamber within the same hall, 1 kitchen and one chamber over the same kitchen, and le lyney, in all 3 couples; 1 garden and orchard ½ ac.; V 33s 4d.

Rent 12d; Farleu 6d; suit of court.

SA21 (see SB55). Elizabeth Waldron, now wife of Edward Waldron, gentleman, holds: one holding and 3 cottages; 1 hall, 1 chamber over, 1 parlour and 1 chamber over, 1 kitchen and 1 chamber over, 1 house called a bruehouse and 1 chamber over, 1 le buttrey and 1 le deyhouse 6 couples, 1 stable and shippon 3 couples, 1 house called a salthouse 2 couples, 1 barn 2 couples; 2 gardens and 1 orchard ½ ac.; V 40s.

1 v. land beside the barn, R 0-2-0; meadow called Saunders Meade 1 ac. R 0-13-4; Channe 5 v. R 0-16-8; Worceter 5 v. R 0-12-6; Hoblane 5 v. R 0-12-6; Knolle 2 ac. R 0-6-8; Crymeland 2 ac. R 0-6-8; Ayshegrove 2 ac. R 0-6-8; Fyeldes 1 ac. R 0-6-8; Wilclose 1 v. R 0-1-0.

Rent 5s 9d; heriot best beast; suit of court.

SA22. Robert Wodeland senior, Robert Wodeland junior and John Wodeland, sons of the said Robert senior, hold: one messuage lately newly erected, 1 hall, 1 chamber within the same hall 2 couples; 1 garden adjoining 1 v. land, and similarly 3 v. land called Channe on Le Clyffe.[17]

Rent 16d; Farleu 8d; suit of court.

SA23 (see SB32). Elizabeth, now wife of Edward Walrond, gentlemen, and Robert Moxon hold: two cottages, 1 hall, 1 chamber within the same hall, 1 le deyrey house, 1 chamber over, 1 kitchen, 1 chamber over 4 couples; 1 garden ¼ ac.; value, let, 20s.

Crosse close 1 ac. R 0-10-0; Whymplehaye ½ ac. R 0-8-0; Shortland 3 v. R 0-7-6; Aywell 3 v. R 0-7-6; (Lyttlewell close 1 v., belongeth to the greate house only).[18]

Rent 4s ½d; Farleu 2s; suit of court.

SA24. Katrina Chapman, now wife of Richard Frenche, the said Richard Frenche and Richard, his son, hold by two separate copies etc.: One cottage, 1 hall, 1 chamber within the same, 1 chamber to the north of the entry of the cottage; 1 garden and ½ ac. adjoining. V 20s.

Rent 19d; farleu 9½d; suit of court.

SA25 (see SB30). (Christina Babe, widow, holds during her widowhood)[19] Bernard Babe and Alice Babe, children of the said Christina, hold: one cottage, 1 hall, 1 chamber within the same hall, 1 shop and 1 chamber over, 1 kitchen and 1 chamber over 3 couples; 1 garden and 1 orchard and 1 parcel of land 1 ac.; V 26s 8d.

Rent 22d; farleu 11d; suit of court.

SA26 (see SB5). Elena, now wife of Walter Babbe, and the said Walter Babbe, Simon Babbe and Walter Babbe, sons of the said Walter Babbe, hold by two separate copies, etc.: one holding and 4 cottages, 1 hall, 1 chamber over the same, 1 parlour and 1 chamber over, 1 kitchen and 1 le buttrey and 1 chamber over, 1 le seller and 1 chamber over 5 couples, 1 barn, 1 stable 3 couples; 2 gardens 1 v.; V 26s 8d.

Neithehayes 1 ac. R 0-13-4; Crosse close 2 ac. R 0-13-4; 2 closes called Channes 1½ ac. R 0-13-4; Worceter 3 v. R 0-10-0; Rudgewaye 5 v. R 0-13-4; Fyeldes 1 ac. R 0-6-8; Scalwell 2 ac. R 0-10-0; Mylclose 2 ac. R 0-10-0; 1 ac. meadow in Colyford meadow R 0-13-4; Barnardshyll 1½ ac. R 0-6-8.

Rent 6s 8d; heriot best beast; suit of court.

SA27 (see SB21, 55). Alice Palle, widow, holds during her widowhood, and Robert Moxon, her brother, hold: one holding,[20] 1 hall, 1 kitchen, 1 house called a bruehouse 3 couples; 1 garden and 1 orchard 1 v.; V 26s 8d. Bowehayne 3 v. R 0-13-4; Bossell 4 ac. R 0-10-0; Aywell 3 v. R 0-10-0; Hoblane ½ ac. R 0-6-8; meadow called Shortland Meade 1 ac. R 0-13-4; Holmerlane ½ v. R 0-1-0.

Rent 3s 2½d; heriot best beast; suit of court.

SA28 (see SB4). Agnes Tyler, now wife of William Taylor, the same William and John Taylor, his son, and John Taylor, son of a certain John Taylor senior, hold by two separate copies, etc.: One holding and 1 cottage, 1 hall, 1 chamber within the same, 1 chamber over the same chamber, 1 shop, 1 chamber over the same 3 couples; 1 garden ½ v. V 16s. Combehil Lane 2 ac. R 0-8-0; Holmerlande Meade ½ ac. R 0-6-0; Lydeyeates 3 v. R 0-10-0; Wilclose ½ ac. R 0-6-0; Castell 3 v. R 0-6-0; Fleetehill 1½ ac. R 0-13-4; Wode 1 ac. R 0-6-0; Common Lane 1 v. R 0-2-6.

Rent 3s; heriot best beast; suit of court.

SA29 (see SB56). Maria Phylippes alias Batt, and Thomas Phylippes alias Batt, hold: one holding, 1 hall, 1 chamber over the same, 1 le buttrey and chamber over, 1 kitchen and chamber over, 1 ley deyhouse and chamber over, 1 house adjoining containing 1 hall and 1 shop 6 couples; 1 curtilage and garden 1 ac.; V 40s.

Hier Hoblane ½ ac. R 0-5-0; Lower Hoblane 3 v. R 0-10-0; White Crosse ½ ac. R 0-6-8; Fleete close 1 ac. R 0-10-0; Mylmeade 3 v. R 0-10-0.

---

16 From Ridegwaye to Fleetehyll are marked *Ro. Starre*.

17 Interlined *Surrendered into the lord's hand*, apparently referring to Channe.

18 Added in hand 2.

19 Erased.

20 *And 1 cottage* erased.

Rent 4s 11d; heriot best beast; suit of court.

SA30 (see SB12). Margaret Furneaux, widow, holds during her widowhood, and Richard Furneaux, her son, and Maud Furneaux, now wife of Nicholas Andrewe, hold: one holding, 1 hall, 1 chamber within the same, and another chamber over the same, 1 house called a mylkehouse and 1 chamber over 4 couples, also 1 barn, 1 shippon 3 couples; 1 house beside Hornes Lane, 1 hall, 1 chamber within, 1 kitchen, and 1 garden and orchard ½ ac. also 1 garden and orchard belonging to the first holding ½ ac. V 40s. Langacre 2 ac. R 0-13-4; Holmermeade 1½ ac. R 0-10-0; Rudgeway 2 ac. R 0-6-8; Salterne Way 1 ac. R 0-8-0; the Hier Holmer 1½ ac. R 0-10-0; the Lower Holmer 3½ ac. R 0-8-0; Bawmeshot 4 ac. R 0-10-0.

Rent 6s; heriot best beast; suit of court.

SA31 (see SB17). Matilda Beste, widow, holds during her widowhood, and Edward Beste and Jane Beste, now wife of William Colloppe, hold: one cottage, 1 hall, 1 chamber within the same hall, 1 chamber over the same and 1 small house adjoining 2 couples; 1 garden and 1 orchard 1 v.; V 20s. Rent 16d; farleu 8d; suit of court.

SA32 (see SB1).[21] John Starre of Horryford holds[22] 2 tenements contayning one dwelling howse, one hawle, 1 entrye, 1 kytchen and 1 lyttle howse adioyninge to the kytchen, 1 dayry howse and 3 chambers over, with 1 chamber glazed with 3 lockes and keyes to the severall doores, 1 barne, 1 stawle and 1 lynney and 1 courte, 1 herb garden, 1 orchard ¾ ac.; worth by the year £2 16s 0d.

One crofte 1 ac. R 1-0-0, V 1-0-0; Hyer Grownde 4 ac. R 0-16-0, V 3-4-0; the Lyttle Hyer Grownde 2 ac. R 0-13-4; Hyer Horryford Yeate 3½ ac. R 0-14-0, V 2-9-0; Hyer Bottome cloase 3 ac. R 0-16-0; V 2-8-0; Lower Bottome cloase 3 ac. R 0-16-0, V 2-8-0; Hayne Leaze close 3 ac. R 0-13-4, V 2-0-0; Longe cloase 2 ac. R 0-15-0, V 1-10-0; Maunders cloase, with a coppes of ½ ac. to the hed thereof 3½ ac. R 0-15-0, V 2-12-6; Mead End cloase 2 ac. R 0-13-4, V 1-6-8; Heckstarres cloase 3 ac. R 0-15-0, V 2-5-0; the Woode cloase 1 ac. R 0-15-0, V 0-15-0; 1 meadow at Stowforde Brooke 1 ac. R 1-10-0, V 1-10-0; 1 meadow at Comon Lane called Pynes Meadow, lying in common with Mrs. Elizabeth Starre, widow, equally to be devyded betweene them, the whole meadow contains in all 1½ ac. R 0-13-4, V 0-13-4; 1 other parcell of meadow bownded out with the said Mrs. Starre, lying by Comon Lane, containing neere ½ ac., R 0-7-0, V 0-8-0; 1 parcell of meadow lying neere the Read Downes, changed every yeare with William Newtons tenement, containing each parte ¾ ac. R 0-13-4, V 0-13-4; further, common in Seaton Downe and Seaton Marshe, V 5-0-0.

Total Value 32-19-4.

SA33. Seaton: At the court there held, 8 April 1600, there came to the said court, William Redwoode, Richard Redwoode, his brother, and John Redwoode, son of the said William, and took by the grant of Richard Willoughby, gentleman the reversion of one close of land called Crosse Close, parcel of one messuage called le Churchehowse, which messuage John Starre al. Steares there now holds for his life. To have and hold the said reversion, and the said close, from the death of the said John Starre, or otherwise if the said reversion shall take place, to the said William Redwood, Richard and John Redwoode, for their lives, rent 2s 6d per year, and 5s in the name of a heriot or farleuia. And they gave the lord for fine 20s.

The 12th of November 1592: William Redwoode saylor, had a sonne baptised named John.

Seaton 1682

[f.18] A survay of the Mannor of Seaton, taken by Robert Leigh att a Court Leett and Court Baron there helde the 26th day of Aprill 1682.

SB1. Edward Drake [of Southleigh, gentleman][23] holdes by indenture of the grante of John Willoughby, esquire, dated 28 Feb. 1658: all that messuage and dwellinge house contayning an entry, one hall, one kitchen, one little house adioyning to the kitchen, one dayry house and 3 chambers over, one barne, one stall, curtilage, garden and orchard containing halfe an acre; and all those closes and parcells of land, meadow and pasture to the same belonging (viz.): one close called the Crofte containing one acre; one close called the Higher Ground containing 4 acres;[24] the Little Higher Ground 2 ac.; the Higher Horriford 3½ ac.; the Higher Bottome close 3 ac.; the Lower Bottome close 2 ac.; Hayneleaze 3 ac.; Longclose 2 ac.; Maunders close 3 ac. with a coppice wood ½ ac. thereto adioyninge; Meaden close 2 ac.; Heckstarrs 3 ac.; Woodclose 1 ac.; one close of meadow lying att Stoford Brooke 1 ac.; one parcell of meadow ¾ ac. lying undevided with Elizabeth Starrs meadow groundes in one close called Pynes Meade att Comon Lane; one other parcell of meadow ½ ac. bounded out from other of the groundes of the said Elizabeth Starr nere Comon Lane aforesayd, and one other parcell of meadow nere Readinges ¾ ac. lying in common with the meadow groundes of the same contentes belonging to the tenement sometymes in the possession of one William Newton, to be enjoyed by course and turnes as antiently. All which premisses are parcell of the Mannor of Seaton and are scituate lying and being in the parishes of Seaton and Colliton or one of them, for 99 years if the said Edward Drake (aged 63 yeares), Ann his wife since deceased, and Edward his sonn (aged 33 yeares), or either of them soe long live, rent 11s 4d payable quarterly, herriott best beast or £4 in leiue therof att the lordes election, and suite of court. Yearely value [*blank*].

Lease. In a lease of 1 Feb. 1655/6 the property is described as late of [*blank*] Starr, widow. Identical with SA32.

[21] This is in hand 2, in English, as is the following transcript of a copy of court roll.

[22] No statement about his tenure.

[23] Information in [ ] is added from the leases and additional information from them is included at the end of each entry.

[24] *One close called* is omitted hereafter.

SB2.[25] Edward Clarke [yeoman] holds, date 9 Oct. 1646, lives: Edward Clarke, his son (deceased), Hannah Clarke, his daughter (deceased), Richard Clarke (52), his son, rent 19s 8d and 2 fatt capons at Christmas or 3s in lieu, heriot £6: One dwelling house, a hall, one ground chamber, one buttery, one dayry, and one under chamber therto belonging, with 3 chambers over, one barne, one sheppen, one henhouse, one bakehouse, one curtilage, 2 herb gardens 1 yd.

2 Orchards 1 ac.; one close by the sea side called the Cliffe 2 ac. 1 yd.; the Higher Beereway 1 ac.; Beane Arrish 1 ac. 1yd; Wosseter 1½ ac.; one meadow called Holmer Meade ½ ac.; Ridgway 3 yd.; Withylake Grove 2½ ac.; Bossell 3 ac.; Burnards Hill 7 ac.; Feilds 1½ ac.; Mooreacre 3 yd.; Townesend 5 ac.; Stofordebrooke 3 yd.; Fleethill 1½ ac.; the Lower Beereway 1 ac. 1 yd.; one meadow lying behind the house 1 ac.; one little plott of ground call Grubb Orchard.

Reversion to Edward Clarke [yeoman], date 20 May 1673, lives Edward (19) and John Clarke (15), sons of Richard Clarke and grandchildren of the said Edward, rent 22s 8d,[26] heriot £6.

Leases: Both lease and reversion exist; the former is endorsed *4 tenements*, and states that the house was lately occupied by Katherine Whicker.

SB3. Edward Clarke [yeoman] holds, date 1 Aug. 1659, lives: said Edward Clarke (82), Elizabeth his daughter (deceased), Mary (43), his daughter, rent 10s 4d, heriott best beast or £3 13s 4d:[27] One dwelling house, a hall, a buttery, a dayry, a malthouse with 3 chambers, one barne, one sheppen with a house adioyninge, one bakehouse, one wellhouse with a chamber adioyning, one herbe garden, one orchard 3/8 ac. One backside 1½ ac.; Higher Backside 1 ac.; Bossehill 2½ ac.; Mooreacre 4 ac.; Spittle close 2½ ac.; Shortland ¾ ac.; Fleetclose ¾ ac.; Beereway ½ ac.; one parcell of meadowe in the end of the said close called Shortland ½ ac.

Reversion to Edward Clarke [yeoman], date 20 May 1673, life: Mary Bussell (17), his grand-daughter, same rent etc.

Leases: Both lease and reversion exist, the latter endorsed *his* [Edward Clarke's] *home tenement*. Two other leases, both of 2 June 1614, are to Elizabeth Clarke, widow; one is apparently a revised version, with the italicised words added: *Shippen with a house adjoining, bakehouse, a well house with a chamber adjoining*. The previous tenant was Edward Clarke.

[25] The remaining entries are calendared by the omission of common form. All were held by indenture for 99 years, or the stated lives, and these (with the ages in brackets), the rent and heriot, are collected at the head of each entry. All tenants owed suit of court, and this is also omitted.

[26] This sum, apparently including the money in lieu of capons, is given in the rental.

[27] In all cases when the heriot is the best beast or goods, with a money alternative, this is at the lord's election.

SB4. Edward Clarke holds, date 24 June 1664, lives: Hannah Clarke, deceased, Deborah Clarke (38), his daughter, Edward Clarke (19), sone of Richard Clarke, rent 2s, heriot 6s 8d: All that cottage, dwellinge house and one garden lying in Seaton.[28] Couchill 1½ ac.; Cassell ¾ ac.; Wellclose ½ ac.; Comon Lane ½ ac.; Fleethill 1½ ac.; one parcell of meadow called Hokmermeade ½ ac.

Leases: There are no originals, but the 1660 survey gives the previous lease, of 14 October 1659, to Dionis Taylor, widow, rent 2s 4d; SB9 was split off in 1668. This is SA28.

SB5. Elizabeth Pyke, widow, executrix of Elizabeth Babb, holds, date 8 Feb. 1659[/60], lives: Elizabeth Babb, deceased, Elizabeth Babb (42), her daughter now called Elizabeth Pyk, rent 6s 5d, heriot £4: one dwelling house, a hall, a parlor, a shopp, one chamber over and one stall, one curtilage and garden.

One close behind the house called Neitherhayes 1 ac.; the Feilds 1 ac. 1 yd.; Stowell 2½ ac.; Fleethill 2 ac.; Burnards Hill 1½ ac.; Rudgway 1 ac. 1 yd.; Marlepitt 3yd,; 2 closes called Crosse closes 2 ac.; Chan 3 yd.; Dunghill 3yd,; one acre of meade in Culliford meadow.

Leases: No originals. This is possibly SA26, with one or two different fields, but the very different house description suggest that the two are not the same.

SB6. John Head [mariner] holds, date 20 Jan 1672, lives: said John Head (43), Jane (43), his wife, William Smith (20), son of Nicholas Smith of Sidbury, rent 3s 4d, heriot 6s 8d: Dwellinge house with an herbe garden lying in the Back Streete in Seaton.

Leases: The original lease notes that this was lately in possession of Amy Manston. In 1660, it seems to be one part of a holding described as (a) *one cottage, a garden, orchard and backside* with (b) *a dwelling house in the backstreete*, which had been leased on 20 Mar. 1634/5 to Robert Trickey. The first part may be SB50.

SB7. Richard Clarke, assignee of William Dare, holds, date 18 Nov. 1657, lives: Elizabeth Dare, deceased, Jane Dare (45), Hannah Dare (40), rent 9s 10d, heriot 25s: One close of land called Crosse 1 ac.; half of all that tenement late in the posession of Allen Marke [Markell] and Thomas Sheires, both deceased, and then of the said William Dare, and of Robert Starre and of William Martyn.

Leases: See SB45.

SB8. John Bacon, assignee of Edward Clarke [yeoman], holds, date 15 Oct. 1658, lives: Mary (43) and Deborah Clarke (38), daughters of Edward Clarke, rent 1s, heriot 1s: Dwelling house called Beere Lane, an entry, 2 low roomes and 2 chambers over the same, one garden and orchard.

Leases: The original exists, granting the reversion of the tenement then held by John Redwood to Edward Clarke.

[28] Noted: *Indorsed on the back of the lease, that Edward Clarke, 24 April 1668, did surrender into Mr. Willoughby's hands the within mentioned dwelling house and garden;* see SB9.

SB9. Richard Forde [mariner] holds, date 1 Oct. 1668, lives: Jane (46), his wife, Thomas (16), his son, Elizabeth (20), his daughter, rent 2s, heriot 4s: A dwelling house and garden.

Leases: The original notes that the property had lately been in the possession of Dionisia Taylor, widow, and that it had been surrendered by Edward Clarke; this is the cottage that formed part of SB4.

SB10. Richard Forde [seaman], holds, date 22 Jan. 1658[/9], lives: said Richard Forde (47), Jane Dare (46), Johan Ford (36), his sister, rent 2s, heriot 5s: A cottage or dwelling house, orchard and garden ½ ac.

Leases: The 1660 abstract of the lease gives Robert Edwards as the previous tenant. From this, it was the cottage and garden, leased on 10 Nov. 1658 to Robert Edwards, butcher, rent 2s. It is first mentioned in a lease of 5 June 1610, to Robert Wodeland alias Mills, fisherman: *a parcel 100 ft. long by 60 ft. broad, for the buyldinge and new erectinge of a convenient mansion and dwellinge house; between William Taylour (S), Johan Babb (W), land in the possession of Allane Markehill (N), and High Street (E);* lately belonging to Abbots Place, held by John and Agnes Pyne (cf. SB49).

SB11. Nicholas Manston, executor to Nicholas Manston his father [yeoman], holds, date 1 July 1657, lives: Nicholas Manston the father, deceased, Joshua Manston (40), his son, said Nicholas Manston (46), rent 9s 2d, heriot 3s 8d, suit of court and mill: Messuage, one hall and one chamber within the hall, one chamber over the hall, one barne, one cottage, one garden; all houses, gardens, orchards belonging to the said messuage and cottage.

Three closes of land called Knolles 8 ac.; Durley 1 ac.; Worseter 3 ac.; one close of meadow or pasture called Hoblane 1 ac. 1 rod; one close of meadow called Heathens Meadow 1 ac.; Aywell 3 ac.; Liddeards 1 ac.; Scalwill 3 ac.; Wood 3 rods.

Leases: The original lease divides the rent into 7s 10d and 1s 4d, the latter probably for the cottage and garden. It had all previously been held by Richard Manston. A lease to John Manston, dated 12 Oct. 1607, covered a tenement and cottage, with the same fields as in 1657, rent 7s 10d.

SB12. Edward Manston junior, executor of Christian Furnace [widow], holds, date 26 Jan 1659[/60], lives: John Weekes, deceased, said Edward Manston (26), rent 6s, heriot best beast or £3: Dwelling house called Furnaces House with severall roomes, curtilage, garden and orchard; one other messuage, 3 low roomes, with an orchard and garden.

Langacre 2 ac.; Bonneshutt 4 ac.; 3 closes called Holmers 4 ac.; Ridgway 1½ ac.; Salterneway ¾ ac.; one meadow called Holmermeade 1½ ac.

Reversion to Edward Manston, [the younger, yeoman] date 3 Jan 1677, lives: Prudence Starr (26), daughter of Elizabeth Starr, Hannah Manston (14), daughter of Josua Manston.

Leases: Both lease and reversion exist. The first describes Furnace's house as: *a hall, a chamber within and a chamber over the same, a buttery, a woodhouse, a hayhouse, a barn*; the whole was then held by Christian Furnace. This is SA30.

SB13. Edward Manston [?senior], assignee of Robert Starr [gentleman], holds, date 13 Nov. 1660, lives: John Starr, deceased, Elizabeth (34) and Prudence Starr (26), rent 1s, heriot 3s 4d: Lands heretofore parcell of a tenement called Abbots Place: Whitecrosse ½ ac.; 2 parcells of land lying by Landskeire in a close called Ridgeway 1 ac. 1yd; Honnyditch 1 ac. 3 yd.

Leases: The original lease was granted in consideration of the surrender of (a) two parcels of land by the landscore on the north side of a close called Ridgeway, (b) two parcels on the south side of Ridgeway, part of land held in leases to Robert Starr the elder and the younger. Whitecrosse (called Little Whitecrosse) was in John Willoughby's possession. For Abbots Place, see SB49. See also SB59.

SB14. Edward Manston junior, assignee of John Weekes [shipwright], holds, date 30 Dec. 1656, lives: John Weekes, deceased, Mary (60), his wife, the said Edward Manston, rent 11s, heriot best beast or £4: Dwelling house containing severall roomes, one orchard, one herb garden adioyninge to the said dwelling house. Withylake 2½ ac.; Easter Worseter 1 ac.; the Burrough 1 ac. 1 yd.; Chan 1 yd.; Dungeon 3 yd.

Leases: The original lease describes the house: *a hall, a chamber within the hall, a buttry, and three chambers over, a kitchen and a room within the kitchen, an entry, a malthouse*; the house and first two fields had been held by Michael Manstone, the last three fields by John Baker.

SB15. Richard Strode and Robert Younge, esquires, as trustees for Mrs. Jane Willoughby, widow, and Madam Margarett Trevelyan, hold, date 4 Oct. 1677, for their lives, the profits to Mrs. Willoughby and after her death to Margarett Trevelyan, rent £1 6s 8d, heriot £4; Close of meadow called Parke Meadow 6 ac.; two closes called the Two Magen Roaddes 12 ac.; Taylors Grove 1 ac.; 2 closes called Parsons closes and Mill Greene; Mill Plott 4 ac.;[29] one meadow called Coksham Marsh 8 ac.; 8 ac. of land, meadow and pasture in Cokesham Marsh.

Leases: These fields were probably part of the demesne. In 1660, Parke Meadow and Colcomb Marsh were let on short Leases:

SB16.[30] Richard Martyn holds, life: now only Richard Martyn (52), rent 3s 4d, heriot 6s 8d: One dwelling house and garden plott, heretofore in posession of John Mills.

Reversion to Richard Martyn [husbandman], date 13 Sept. 1680, lives: John (24) and William Martyn (12), his sons.

Leases: The reversion exists, and from the 1660 survey, the original lease was to John Martyn the elder, husbandman, date 2 Oct. 1649.

SB17. Christopher Manley [mariner] holds, date 20 Dec. 1675, lives: Florence (66), his wife, William (31) and Ed-

[29] Including the previous two.

ward (22), his sons, rent 1s 4d, heriot 10s: Cottage and one little orchard therto adioyning.

Leases: The lease exists, as does one to William Turner of Shildon (Sheldon, near Teignmouth), cooper, dated 8 Jan. 1622, of this cottage and an orchard called Aleywill [Ailewill in an endorsement], previously held by Edward Best and William and Jane Collopp. This is SA31.

SB18. Thomas Head [blacksmith] holds, date 3 April 1675, lives: said Thomas (38), Gertrude (38), his wife, Mary (10), his daughter, rent 3s 4d, heriot 6s 8d: A cottage and garden.

Leases: The original lease notes that the cottage was previously occupied by John Head; he held it in 1660 by a lease dated 20 April 1659, when it was surrendered by Clemans Head, widow. It was therefore the house and garden known as Pytchers, leased to Philip and Clempse Hedde, blacksmith, on 12 Jan. 1617, rent 3s 4d; it has been surrendered by John Starr (see SB47).

SB19. Peter Wootton [mariner] holds, date 30 Aug. 1680, lives: said Peter (28), Joyce (28), his wife, Precilla Pitcher (21), daughter of John Pitcher of Seaton, mariner, rent 3s 4d, heriot 6s 8d: Dwelling house with a garden plott adioyning.

Leases: From the original lease, the cottage was sometime in the possession of John Martyn and then of Joyce Martyn his daughter. In the 1660 survey, despite the change in description and rent, this can only be Chimney Place, held by John Martyn on his life and those of his daughters Grace and Joyce. The lease to John Martyn, fisherman, on 1 Jan. 1647, rent 4s, was of: *a house called Chymney Place, a hall, an under chamber with a chamber over it, an entry, a roome without the entry, a chamber over, and a barn adjoining, 6 coople in length, a garden*. It was between [*blank*] Ford, widow (N) and Mary Myllles (S) and it had been held by John Starre, deceased (see SB47).

SB20.[31] Peter Wootton holds, lives [*as SB19*], rent 3s, heriot 6s: Two closes lying in Seaton 2 ac.; late in posession of one [*blank*] Cheesman, in right of his wife.

Leases: These closes formed part of SB56.

SB21.[32] Presilla Wootton holds, life: now only her life, rent 3s 4d, heriot 6s 8d: Cottage or dwelling house called Sweett Sopp, 3 low roomes, and only the Backside therto adioyning. Reversion to Peter Wotton [sailor], date 30 May 1680, lives: said Peter (28), Joyce (28), his wife.

Leases: Both lease and reversion exist. Before 1655, it was held with other land by Robert Moxam (see SB55). This was probably part of SA27.

SB22. Amy Hooper, executrix of John Cawley, holds, date 20 Dec. 1665, life: now only her life, rent 1s, heriot [*blank*] All that celler now converted into a dwelling house, sometyme in posession of Richard Mallacke.

Reversion to Amy Hooper, date 31 Oct. 1671, lives: John Hooper (30), her son, Amy Hooper (36), her daughter.

Leases: The reversion exists, as does an earlier lease to Richard Mallack the elder, of Axmouth, gentleman, dated 1 July 1657, of a house: *the Seller, containing a hall and chamber over*, then in the possession of John Cawley, rent 6d.

SB23. John Bevis holds, date 5 Dec. 1664, lives: said John (45), Johan (45), his wife, rent 8s, heriot 13s 4d: One cottage and plott of ground called Aywell, in length east and west 120ft., and in breadth at the east end 15ft. with the hedges of the same, and att the west end about 24ft. with the hedges.

Reversion to John Bevis [mariner], date 30 May 1680, life: John (12), his son.[33]

Leases: The reversion survives, describing the cottage as a little house. There are also two leases: 20 April 1614, to John Pylcher, tailor, of a house lately built, and 20 Jan. 1634, to Michael Beavis, husbandman.

SB24. Ralph Lee [sea mariner], assignee of Elianor Robertes, alias James, holds, date 5 Dec. 1664, lives: said Elianor, deceased, said Ralph (52), Alice (46), his wife, Sarah (26), his daughter, rent 8d, heriot 1s 4d: Dwelling house and garden plott, in which the said Elianor dwelled.

Leases: The 1660 survey describes this as: *one little house and garden adjoyninge to the Marshe*; this must be Robert Robertes by the Marshe in the 1608 rental, rent 8d, i.e. SA16.

SB25. William Lee [mariner] holds, date 16 Nov. 1657, lives: said William (50), Johan, his wife, deceased, rent 8s: One cottage contayning 2 couple roomes, lately built by Emanuell Lee, father of the said William, one plott of ground 1 yd., formerly belonging to the Church House.

Leases: The lease also states that the cottage adjoins the house of Richard Mallack, gentleman, and that the church house had become a barn. The holding was lately in the posession of Richard Redwood.

SB26. Joseph Mico [of Branscombe, miller] holds, date 4 June 1678, lives: Elizabeth Starr (60), said Joseph (35), Alice (35), his wife, rent 5s[34] heriot 10s: All those water greist milles and mill houses, together with the plott of ground, garden plott and one close of land called Fleethill [1½ ac.].

Leases: The lease notes the previous tenant as Robert Starr. See SB59.

SB27. Robert Trickey, executor of Robert Trickey [carpenter], his father, holds, date 1 July 1657, lives: Robert Trickey (40), the son, Johan Trickey, deceased, Jane Trickey (30), daughter of Robert Trickey, the father, rent 3s 5d, heriot 6s 10d: All those cottages and dwelling houses, a hall and chamber over the same, a little roome within the hall, a kitchen, a little roome on the south side of the entry and

---

[30] Noted: *This lease I could not see.*

[31] Noted: *Grant indorsed on the backe of the last mentioned indenture.* From this lease, the date was 8 Sept. 1680, and the earlier tenant is given (correctly) as Cheesway.

[32] Noted: *This lease I have not seen.*

[33] Noted: *Extinguished by death.*

[34] As in the lease, but given as 10s in the rental.

chamber over the same, one new built roome adioyning to the said roome within the hall, a seller without the backdore, a barne and stall, and the backside and the gardens 3 yd. Marlepitt ½ ac.; Rudgway ½ ac.

Leases: In the lease, the seller is 'without the backdoore of the dwelling houses', suggesting multiple occupancy. The previous tenant was Christian Dare.

SB28.[35] Jane Trickey, widow, holds, life: now her own life only, rent 10s 4d, heriot 53s 4d: Dwelling house with the backside and garden adioyning; Broadclose 6 ac.

Reversion to Robert Trickey [mariner], date 5 Oct. [1669],[36] lives: said Robert (40), Sarah (38), his wife.

Leases: The reversion notes that this had been held by John Nicholas (or Nicholls), and then Robert Trickey, father of the grantee. Broadclose was leased to Nicholas Darre, mariner, on 10 June 1620, rent 6s (endorsement noting that in 1667, it was held by Jane Trickinge, widow); it had been part of John Clarke's tenement (i.e. SA19). See SB31.

SB29.[37] Johan Gibbs, widow, holds, life: now her life only, rent 13s 6d, heriot best beast or £7 6s 8d: A tenement with 14 acres of land, meadow and pasture.

Reversion to Phillip Weekes and Johan his wife, lately Johan Gibbs,[38] date 19 Aug. 1678, lives: said Phillip (26), said Johan (34).

Leases: The reversion and the original lease survive, the latter to Philip Weekes, of Axmouth, dated 1 October 1649. This describes the house: *a hall and chamber over, a parlour and chamber over, a buttrie and chamber over, a dayrie or milkhouse on the south side of the buttery, a kitchen, a stable, a little low room comonly called the stall.* It also includes a schedule of: *the goodes, implementes of household and other things remayning in and about the house* (given in Table 17). The fields are: The Backside, Bomshoote, Woode, Holmer, Heathfield, Fleethill, Withelake, and Burnards Hill. Earlier, a reversion was granted to Elizabeth Clarke, to succeed Amy Clarke, dated 2 June 1614, rent 5s 10d. This gives essentially the same details, although the phrase *comonly called the stall* is omitted, while Burnards Hill is the subject of a separate reversion to the same tenant, dated 15 July 1614, rent 4s.

SB30. John Roberts alias James [sailor] holds, date 20 April 1668, lives: said John (60), Susan, his wife, deceased, John (24), his son, rent 1s 10d, heriot best goodes or 20s: One cottage, a hall, one chamber or low roome within the same hall, one shopp and chamber over the same, one kitchen and chamber over the same, one garden, one orchard and parcell of land 1 ac.

Leases: The original does not survive, but an earlier lease does, again to John Robertes, dated 1 Feb. 1652. The previous tenant was Sibill Babb. This is clearly SA25.

SB31. Nicholas Stockham [mariner] holds, date 27 June 1659, lives: said Nicholas (44), Joyce (58), commencing on the death of Christian Dare (since deceased), rent 7s, heriot 40s: One dwelling house, with the chambers and roomes therto belonging, one orchard lyinge on the west side of the house 2 ac.

Reversion to Nicholas Stockham, date 27 April 1667, life: Joyce (25), his daughter.

Leases: Both lease and reversion exist. The first is itself a reversion, to Nicholas and Christian Dare; it states that the holding was part of Haymish Place (also Haynes, Haynish or Hamish Place). The previous lease was to Nicholas Dare, mariner, date 16 March 1625, rent 6s. Hany Place was surrendered by John Clarke on 9 June 1620 *[copy of court roll DD/WO box 29]*. The name and tenant identify this as the house and orchard of SA19. See also SB28 and 56.

SB32. Margarett Turle, widow, administratrix of Henry Turle [seaman], her late husband, holds, date 5 Dec. 1664, lives: said Henry, deceased, said Margaret (55), his wife, Margarett, her daughter, deceased, rent 5s 2½d, heriot 10s: Dwelling house called Crosse House, a hall and chamber over the same, a low roome within the hall, a kitchen and chamber over the same, a dayry and chamber over the same, a little garden plott on the east side of the said dwelling house.

Crosse close 1 ac.; Whimplehay ½ ac. Shortland 3 yd.; Aywell 3 yd.; Well close 1 yd.

Leases: The lease qualifies the low roome as: *a chamber or low roome*, and also describes the dairy as *a low roome*. The preceding lease was to William Dare, yeoman, dated 1 Sept. 1654, rent 4s 2½d, with Robert Moxam as the earlier tenant. This is clearly SA23.

SB33. Stephen Witcombe [or Whitcombe, yeoman] holds, date 20 April 1655, lives: said Stephen (70), Elizabeth (38) and Agnes (35), his daughters, rent 3s 6d and a cock or hen at Easter, heriot best beast or £4: Dwelling house; one close of meadow called Comon Lane Meade 1 yd.; Willclose 3yd,; Great Willclose 2ac,; Aywell 1½ ac.; Newclose 1 ac. 1 yd.; Bossell 1½ ac.; Beereway 1 ac.

Leases: The lease describes the house: *a hall, a low room within the hall, a chamber over* [the low room], *a kitchen, two other low rooms, a loft over, a barne and a shippen.* It was previously held by Johan Clarke by copy, and is clearly SA4.

SB34.[39] Stephen Witcombe holds, date 9 June 1676, lives [*as SB33*], rent 6d, heriot 1s: A parcell of land called Vincage [?Vintage] 3 yd.

Leases: This close was probably detached from SB47.

[35] Noted: *This lease I have not seen.*

[36] The survey gives 31 Charles II (1679), but the original reversion shows this to be correctly 1669.

[37] Noted: *This lease I have not seen.*

[38] Marginal note in another hand: *Roger Turner of Yarcombe*, and his name is given in the rental.

[39] Noted: *Endorsed on the back of the sayd mencyoned indenture* [SB33].

SB35. Phillip Hooper [husbandman] holds, date 6 June 1672, lives: said Phillip (30), Anstice Ford (33), his intended wife, Elizabeth Head (16), daughter of Thomas Head, rent 2s, heriot 4s: Dwelling house and garden plott called Hemphay, adioyning to Marsh Lane.

Leases: The lease survives, as does an earlier one to the same tenant, dated 2 October 1649. It was then held by Philip Hooper's aunt, Mary Hooper.

SB36. Thomas Clapp and Christian his wife, administratrix of William Robertes alias James, hold, date 2 Nov. 1664, lives: said William Robertes, deceased, said Christian (45), Christian (24), her daughter, rent 1s and a capon at Christmas, heriot 10s: Dwelling house or cottage, a hall and chamber over the same, one low chamber within the sayd hall, one kitchen and chamber over the same, one lynage, one herbe garden and orchard ½ ac.

Leases: This was leased on 6 Jan. 1655/6 to Joseph Pope of Beer, baker, rent 1s: *a house or cottage, a hall and chamber over, a low chamber within the hall, a kitchen and chamber over, a lynage, a herb garden*. It was in the tenure of Stephen Whitcombe, previously of Ellen Cawley, then of John Abbott. From this description and rent, it is SA20.

SB37. Elianor Paull, widow, executrix of Nicholas Dare [fisherman], holds, date 30 May 1644, lives: Mary Babb, deceased, said Elianor (51), William Trickey (47), rent 3s 2d, heriot 5s: Dwelling house, one hall, one under chamber and chamber over, one barne on the south side of the entry, one curtilage, one garden and one backside 1 ac.

Leases: The lease gives previous tenants: Margaret Oliver, widow, then John Parker.

SB38. Edward Parsons [husbandman] holds, date 10 Oct. 1659, lives: said Edward (55), Mary (28) and Precilla (25), his daughters, rent 6s 8d, heriot 13s 4d: Cottage and garden.

Leases: The lease is endorsed: *house and garden in Trickshire* (cf. SB57); the previous tenant was Jane, succeeding John Hooper, husbandman. His lease, 20 Mar. 1633, states that the plot was held by Robert Endicott and had been forfeited for non-payment of rent, and for letting the house be ruined. John was to rebuild the house to the same size. A parcel was added to the holding, six foot of ground on the lord's waste, between Roger Whicker's house (?SB2 or 64), and Andrea Grey's house (SB57). Robert Endicott had probably succeeded William Endercote, joiner, in his lease of a house and garden, dated 17 Jan. 1616, rent 3s 4d, then in the tenure of Constans Lee, widow.

SB39. John French holds, date 24 June 1670, lives: said John (70), Samuell French, his son, deceased, Sarah French (23), his daughter, rent 19s 1d, heriot two best beasts or £6 13s 4d and for the cottage 10s: One dwelling house, one hall, one parlour within the same, 2 chambers over the same, one kitchen, one dayry, and two chambers over the same 4 couples, one barne, one sheppen, one stable, one garden, one orchard and one curtilage ½ ac.

Hemplott 3 r.; Knolles 3 ac.; Creamelandes 5 ac.; Holmermeade 1½ ac.; Bawmshott 3 ac.; Burnards Hill 2 ac.; Peartlakes 2 ac.; one acre of meadow lying in Collyford Meade; one yard of ground called Worseter; 2 closes of land called Newcloses 8 ac.; Longacre 2 ac.; 2 other closes and one orchard of the same demeasne lands of the said manor, lying nere the churchyard and vicaridge house of Seaton 2 ac. Cottage or dwelling house, curtilage, orchard and garden. Wood 1 ac.; Beaneway 3 r.; Aywell 1 r.

Leases: The original does not exist, but four earlier leases do, three to George Weekes, yeoman. The first (30 Sept. 1630) is of the cottage and three closes, Wood, Beaneway and Aywell, lately held by Joane Babb, rent 1s; this was also leased to Richard Mallacke of Axmouth, gentleman, on 9 May 1635. The others (both dated 10 April 1631, rents 8s 1d and 6s) cover the house and main fields, and New closes, Longacre and the demesne, respectively. Both were surrendered by Nicholas Manston, and can be recognised as SA8 (main property), SA9 (New Closes and Longacre) and SA10 (demesne).

SB40. John Wicker and Christian his wife, executrix of Nicholas Dare [yeoman], hold, date 1 Jan 1647, lives: Johan Trickey, deceased, said Christian (42), Jane Trickey (40), daughter of Robert Trickey [ship carpenter], rent 2s, heriot 6s 8d: Orchard or parcell of pasture ground called Horneslane Orchard 1 ac.

Leases: In the lease, the tenants agree to erect a house, and in 1660 it is described as having a new erected house, but by 1682 it had presumably fallen down.

SB41. John Spinster, assignee of Katharine Spinster, holds, date 31 Mar. 1667, lives: John Spinster junior (30), said Johan (40), Hannah Spinster, deceased, rent 3s 4d, heriot 6s 8d: Dwelling house and garden in the towne and manor of Seaton.

Leases: In 1660, this was: *one cottage in Tricksheare*, held by Agnes Manstone, which had been held by [Thomas] Chase. Earlier, it was leased to Nicholas Manstone, on 17 Jan. 1616.

SB42.[40] Sarah Clapp holds, life: now her life only, premises as below.

Reversion to Nicholas Paull, date 8 July 1680, lives: Sarah (30), now wife of the said Nicholas, John Paull (7), his son, rent 9s 2d,[41] heriot £3: Tenement called Wilslades Tenement, one dwelling house, garden plott, closes of land called the Yonder Heathfeildes, Salterneway and Couchey Lane 4½ ac. Also, tenement called Furnaces Tenement, 4 closes or parcells of land or pasture called Newcloses 8 ac.; Shortlandes 1 ac.; one meadow called Mooreacre Meadow 5 ac.; one plott of meadow lying in Holmermeade ½ ac.

Leases: The 1680 reversion does not survive, but three earlier leases do. These are considered under SB60.

SB43. John Butter [of Branscombe, yeoman] holds, date 5 Oct. 1646, lives: said John (51), Ann (50), his wife, John

[40] Noted: *This lease I have not seen.*

[41] In the rental, given as 5s 2d which, from the leases, is that of the first holding only.

Hooke, deceased, rent £1 2s 4d, heriot 33s 4d: Close of land or pasture called Abby Hill 12 ac.; close of meadow called Higher Abby Hill Meade 1½ ac.; one close of meadow called Lower Abby Hill meadow 1 ac.; one peece or parcell of meadow at Blackpoole 3 ac.

Leases: The lease includes an agreement that if John Butter builds a house, John Willoughby will allow him some timber. This is SA15.

SB44. Edward Manston the elder [husbandman] holds, date 28 Dec. 1652, lives: said Edward (50), Nicholas Manston (46), Joshua Manston (40), rent 3s 4d, heriot best beast or £4: Cottage, an entry, a hall and one low roome within the hall, and three chambers over the same, and a barne, garden and backside 1 yd.

Higher Hoblane 1 ac.; Mooreacre 2½ ac.; Lower Hoblane ½ ac.; Scallwell 1 ac.

Leases: The lease notes that the barn adjoins the entry, and that the previous tenant was Mary Howper, widow. It is endorsed *next below Franckes*.

SB45. Edward Manston the elder holds, date 11 Jan 1658 [/9], lives: said Edward (50), Agnes (48), his wife, Edward (28), his son, rent 2s 6d, heriot 6s 8d: His moyety of one tenement with his part of two gardens 1 rod.

Leases: This and SB7 are two halves of a property that was bought by John Willoughby in 1657 [deeds in DD/WO box 31]. In 1601, half belonged to John Arundell of Trerice, Cornwall (cf. Farway: F1), and half to Allen Markell, also occupier of Arundell's half. The second part passed (12 Dec. 1631) to Allen Markell's daughter Elizabeth, who married William Dare, tenant to Arundell (lease 18 Dec. 1654). This lease was renewed by John Willoughby after he had bought Arundell's half (deed 6 April 1657, lease 18 Nov. 1657, as in SB7). Elizabeth Dare resigned her half to John Willoughby in 1657, and this was then leased to Edward Manston (11 Jan. 1658/9, as in SB45); presumably the house and fields had been physically divided. This lease also included the whole of two fields, the Channe and Little Lane, an adjoining garden and a plot before the hall door. Similarly, SB7 included Crosse Close, which had previously been held by John Redwood (as in SA33).

SB46. Edward Manston [yeoman] and Joshua Manston [his brother], hold, date 29 Sept. 1668. lives: Edward Manston junior (25), son of the said Edward, Mary (19) and Rachell Manston (16), daughters of the said Joshua Manston, rent 5s 3d, heriot best beast or £4: Two tenements or dewlling houses, backside, orchards, garden and curtilage 1 ac.

Bowhay 1 yd.; Marlepitt 4 ac.; Salterneway 1½ ac.; Long Bossell ½ ac.; Higher Bossell ½ ac.; Rudgeway 1 ac.; Newclose 3 yd.; Great Feilds 1 ac. 1 yd.; Little Feilds ½ ac.; Aywell 1½ ac.; Townesend 1 ac. 1 yd.; Fearneburrow 1½ ac.; Little Stock 1 yd.; two other closes called Stoford Brooke and Honyditch 3½ ac.; one parcell of meadow called Whitecross Meadow 1 ac.

Leases: The lease survives, as does an earlier one (18 Nov. 1657) to the then tenant, John Redwood, yeoman. This is clearly SA7, though the field names do not match precisely.

SB47. Joshua Manston, assignee of Nicholas Manston his father [yeoman], holds, date 29 June 1663, lives: said Joshua (40), Edward Manston the younger (26), Mary (40), now wife of the said Joshua, rent £1, heriot £6: Messuage, orchard and garden in Seaton.

Foxenhole 9 ac.; Burnards Hill 4 ac.; Rye Parkes 5 ac.; Stoford Brooke 4 ac.; Hemphay, with the plott behind the barne 1½ ac.; Longmeade 5 ac.

Leases: The first record of this holding is in a lease of 16 Nov. 1605 to John Starr (the son), rent 28s 8d, of Barones Place, 'wherein John Starre the father now dwelleth', Hemphay (1 ac.), a barn and ½ ac. plot, with a messuage called Chimley Place with a curtilage, and a messuage called Pytchers with fields: Maylandes at Reade, Vencage, Burnards Hill, Seaside, a piece at Foxenholes, Withelakes, Fyeldes, a (second) piece at Foxenholes, one acre in More Acre, Rie Parke, an orchard and common for 22 sheep. Of this, Pytchers was surrendered in 1617 (see SB18) and Chymney Place in 1647 (see SB19), while Barones Place was let on a five year lease on 5 Oct. 1653 to John Cheesway, with fields: Hemphay, the backside behind the barn, North and South Mayton at Rode, Stoford Brooke, Langmeades, Feildes, Burnards Hill, Foxenholes, Withilake Grove, Seaside, Vincage and common for 40 sheep on the Marsh. The lease was renewed for a further five years, but in 1663, the property was leased for lives. Of the fields missing from this lease, (North and South Maytown, Seaside and Vincage), SB20 probably covers the first and SB34 the last.

SB48. Hannah Dare, assignee of William Dare, her father, holds, date 25 Mar. 1662, lives: Said Hannah (40), Richard Clarke (52), son of Edward Clarke, Edward Clarke (19), sone of Richard Clarke, rent 10s, heriot 2s 6d: A parcell of ground in the south end of Seaton Downe 7 ac.

Leases: No originals. This was probably a recent enclosure. See SB52.

SB49. Hannah Dare, assignee of William Dare [yeoman], her father, holds, date 5 Dec. 1664, lives: said William, deceased, said Hannah (40), Elizabeth Clarke (18), daughter of Richard Clarke, rent 8s, heriot 50s: Dwelling house, garden and orchard called Abbotts place; close adioyning to the sayd dwelling house 1 ac.; Longacre 2 ac.; Wester Worseter 1½ ac.

Leases: The lease survives, as do earlier leases: 5 June 1610, for the house and orchard (lately John and Agnes Pyne), to Nicholas and William Dare and William Whitaker, all fishermen, rent 3s 4d; 10 Dec. 1622, for the two closes (surrendered by John Clarke), to Robert Dare, mariner, rent 4s. Abbots Place is SA18. See also SB13, 34, and 58.

SB50. Richard Clarke holds, date 29 Sept. 1674, lives: said Richard (50), Richard (12), his son, Jane (15), his daughter, rent 5s, heriot 6s: Messuage, decayed cottage and plott of ground lying in Aywell Green ½ ac. Liberty is given Richard Clarke on the backside of his lease to suffer the dwelling house to fall downe.

Leases: The previous occupant was Mary Newton. See also SB6.

SB51. Anstice Hooper, executrix of John Hooper [sailor], her father, holds, date 16 April 1652, lives: said John, deceased, Joyce Hooper (52) and Margaret Hooper (52), his sisters, rent 4s, heriot best goodes or 10s: Dwelling house lately built by Richard Wheeker on a close of land called Beere Lane, together with the garden adioyning, and the said close called Beere Lane 1 ac.

Leases: The lease survives, as does one of 1 Dec. 1642, to Richard Wheker, husbandman, requiring him to build a house 40 ft. long by 16ft. broad, within one year.

SB52. Edmond Waldron, esquire.[42]

Leases: The rental gives 6s under Edmond Walrond's name, and the 1660 survey identifies the property as the rest of Seaton Downe (cf. SB48).

SB53. A large parcell of Marsh Land, called Seaton Marsh, about 300 acres, is now in hand.

Leases: DD/WO box 35 contains accounts for the enclosing of Seaton Marsh in 1660. The rental also includes 1s, paid by Mr. Starr for drivinge over the Marshe (perhaps for wildfowl).

SB54.[43] Richard Clarke holds, date 15 May 1691, lives: Jane (60), wife of Richard Clarke, Richard Clarke (20), William Clarke (17), rent 1s 4d, heriot nil, fine £14: One acre of meadow, late parcell of Starrs Tenement att Pale.

Leases: The original lease describes this as Badpoole Meadow. For Pale, see SB59.

SB55. Nathaniell Mallacke, gentleman holds, date 30 Dec. 1661, life: Nathaniel Mallack (48), rent 9s 10d, heriot £5: Hall, parlor and 2 chambers over, 1 kitchen and chamber over, 1 bouttery and milkhouse and the chambers over, one brewhouse and chamber over, one shepon or stall, one stable, one barne newly erected, one other barne by Trickys house, one garden and orchard.

The Chan 1½ ac.; Worester 1¼ ac.; Hoblane 1¼ ac.; Knolle 3 ac.; Asshegrove 2 ac.; Crimlands 2 ac.; the Fields 1 ac.; Saunders Mead 1¼ ac.; together with Sweetsopps closes, hereafter described: Bosthill 4 ac.; Aywell 3 yd.; one close to the east of Hoblane 1 ac.; one close in Homerlane 1 yd.

Note: This lease hath a schedule annexed of severall goods, to the house belonging, to returne with the premises.[44]

Leases: The lease was to John Mallack, of Axmouth, gentleman, while the previous one was to Richard Mallack the elder, also gentleman of Axmouth, dated 1 July 1657. In this, the barn adjoins Robert Trickey's house. Sweetsopp had apparently just been split up, its house (SB21) having been leased in 1655. The main holding can be identified with SA21, and Sweetsopp is SA27.

SB56. [Blank apart from two notes.] *Quere: for the demeasne house and other house and tenement wherein Richard Clarke liveth. Memo: Allen Newton gave £65 for the three lives in Manstons lease.*

Leases: This entry was apparently intended to cover the demesne, but it was never filled in. The capital messuage (presumably the demesne) was 'leased' on 25 Mar. 1648, to John Willoughby the younger, together with a messuage previously occupied by Andrew Holwell (but then by John Willoughby), and another at Townsend, previously held by John Starr (cf. SB62). Andrew Hollowell (*sic*) had held by a seven year lease (DD/WO box 31, 21 May 1632, rent £30 15s 4d): fields Marlepitt, Mooreacres, Feylds, Castle, Scalwell, Partelakes, Fleetehill, Ridgeway, Ayewell, Lees Doore, Channe, Beere Lane, Beere Way, Marlepitt Meade, Broadeclose, Scallwell, Hoblane, Aywell; the house of Andrew Hollowell, a garden and fields Higher Hob Lane, Lower Hob Lane, White Crosse, Fleete Close, Mill Meade. It is possible that in 1682, Richard Clarke occupied this.

The second part of this holding is clearly SA29, while the remainder though it cannot be fully identified, may be the lands of SA1, 18 and 19, all of which had been subdivided after 1609. Five closes - Feylds to Fleetehill - are referred to in a bond of 5 Sept. 1613, reserving occupancy to Alice Paule of Beere, during the lives of John Clarke, father and son (presumably the leaseholders).

SB57. Agnes Lee, spinster, holds, date 30 May 1641, life: now her life only, rent 3s 4d, heriot 6s 8d, originally granted to Nicholas Dare [yeoman] for a surrender and £4: One dwelling house and garden in Seaton, heretofore in possession of Thomas Martyn.

Leases: The lease is endorsed *house in Tricksheere*; Thomas Martyn was tenant before 7 Jan. 1616, when the holding was leased to Audrey Gray, widow.

SB58. Elizabeth Starr of Exeter, widow, holds Hill Liveing, lives: Edmund Starr, John Starr and,[45] rent £1 19s 3d.[46]

Leases: This is recognisable from the rent as the two messuages called Aywell and Hill, leased to Elizabeth and Edmond Starr, grocer of Exeter, on 10 Dec. 1657, and again to John Starr, grocer of Exeter, on 10 Sept. 1675. It consisted of a messuage with fields: Marlepitt, Durley, Ayshgrove, Bossell, Newclose, Burnards Hill, Moreacre, Higher Lydyeates, Lower Lydyeates, Broad Close, Castle, Aywell Meadow, Bea Meadow, Long Meadow, Homer Meadow; with a tenement called Hill and fields: Barnhayes, Fleethill, Stoford Brooke, Seven Okes, Burnards Hill, South Hill Crosse, Wythylakes, Little Meadow, Common Lane. Common Lane had only just been added to this holding, having been leased on 5 June 1610 to John Starre, rent 1s; it was then a meadow at Common Lane, lately belonging to Abbots Place (cf. SB49) [Total about 64 ac.].

[42] Noted: *His lease I have not seen, nor severall other leases of this mannor have not ben shewen to me.*

[43] The remaining entries are in different hands, some clearly added later. SB54 is not in the rental.

[44] This schedule is abstracted in Table 17.

[45] Note for the surveyor, to check the lease for the third name.

[46] Under John Starr in the rental. Noted: *See lease.*

The first messuage is SA13, the second SA12.

SB59.[47] Agnes [Dare] holds Pale Tenement and Edward Manstons ground called [*blank*].

Leases: This is only described in the lease to Agnes Dare of 18 May 1691: a house (*Pale tenement* in the endorsement), another dwelling house, Shindle Hall and garden (1 ac.), Seaclose (1½ ac.), Cross Close (1½ ac.), Couchwill Close (3½ ac.), two closes Rudgewayes (1½ ac.), Crimlandes (1½ ac.), two Bossells (10 ac.), Hoblane (1 ac.), Honyditch (2½ ac.), Fursey Slade (5 ac.), Feeldes (3 ac.), Parkelake Meadow (4 ac.), White Cross (5 ac.), Scallwell (4 ac.), Fursley (4 ac.), Heathfield (1 ac.), Parkelake (3 ac.), Ten Acre (10 ac.), Tenn Acre Ragg (1 rod), Mill Parke (5 ac.), ground in the salt Marsh, Rideings (3 ac.), ground in the first common meadow, Culliford Meadow (¾ ac.), all lately held by Elizabeth Starr; also Honyditch (1½ ac.), Whitecross (½ ac.), Rudgeway (1 ac.), all lately Edward Manston (i.e. SB13). Fleetmills, ½ rod of land and one close, Fleetmill (1½ ac.) were excepted, being in the tenure of Joseph Mico (i.e. SB26) [total 75 ac.]. The rent was £2 14s 6d for the main section and 1s for the fields of Edward Manston.

In 1608-10, this was in the tenure of John Starr at Pale (probably not the same as the tenant of SB47, and certainly not as that of SA32); in 1639, it was leased to Robert Starre the younger, and probably fell into hand on the death of his widow Elizabeth, in about 1678, and so was not included in the 1682 survey. SB26 and 54 were separated from it when it was in hand.

SB60. Nicholas Tanner of Dartmouth holds, life: Susanna Clap (26), rent [13s 1d]:[48] Heathins Tenement in Tricksheir, previously leased to Robert Clap, one messuage and 28 acres of land in Trickshear.

Leases: The lease does not survive, but this property can be identified as part of a holding leased on 30 March 1667 to Robert Clapp, merchant of Dartmouth. The holding was in three parts: Willades (Wislades or Wilslades) tenement, rent 5s 10d, Furnaces tenement, rent 3s 4d, and Heathins, rent 12s 1½d, lately Elizabeth Manston's. The first two comprise SB42, and have separate earlier leases: 11 October 1656, to John Wislade, husbandman, rent 4s 10d (lately [widow] Tutchin); 28 April 1659, to Elizabeth Manston, widow, rent 3s 4d (lately Margaret Furnex, widow). Wislade's lease describes the house as: *a cottage with a hall, kitchen, under chamber and two chambers over, 4 couples, a barn, shipping and brewhouse, 3 couples*. These two parts are recognizable as SA2 and SA6.

Heathins is not described in the 1667 lease, but is clearly SB60. It can be followed through the earlier rentals from its name, and identified as SA5.

SB61. William Lee holds, date 29 Dec. 1677, lives: John Edwards (45), Richard Smith senior (40), Richard Smith junior (15), rent 2s 5d, heriot 5s: One dwelling house, one shopp, courtledge, herbe garden and one close called the Backside ½ ac.; Ropers close ½ ac.

Leases: This is probably in the rental under John Edwards, paying 2s 3d; the 1660 survey abstracts a previous lease, of 1 October 1652, to John May. In it, Roper's Close is described as Roper's Doore otherwise Greene Heade (cf. SA5), and it notes the earlier tenant as Spes Ford, widow.

SB62. Joshua Storrick junior, Marie, his wife, and William Dare, hold, life: The said Mary (35), rent 3s 4d, heriot:[49] Messuage, orchard and garden 2 ac., called Townes End.

Leases: The original does not survive, but this seems to be the house, barn and two closes lately held by John Starre of Beere, leased to Robert Dare the younger on 24 March 1658/9, for which the 1660 survey shows that Mary Dare was the last life. In 1648, this was probably in hand, the 'messuage at Townsend previously occupied by John Starre' (see SB56). Previously, it had been leased to Robert Dare, mariner, both on 4 January 1626, and on 10 July 1639, when it was described as a house, barn and three acres of land, lately held by John Starre of Beere. This is SA14.

Further Holdings

Leases for four properties have no identifiable counterparts in the 1682 survey. They are numbered following on from SB62.

SB63. Lease, 10 October 1616, to Robert Welshead, sailor, rent 2s 8d. He has erected a new house on a *void plott near the sea coast*. This is granted to him, with a plot 45 feet in length, 12 feet in breadth. The lease is endorsed: *May 1660, Mary Cawley of Beere in possession, let to Nicholas Hooper*.

SB64(a) and (b). Lease, 2 October 1612, to Edward Manley, tailor, rent 3s 4d. A house to be erected on Seaside Plott, near Seaside, part of the tenement lately held by Walter and Elen Babbe. This was then divided:

(a). Lease, 10 June 1620, to the same, rent 3s 4d. Surrender of the original holding, with a new lease for *the house in the west part of the said* [original] *house and garden, about 48 feet broad by 60 feet long*. Lease, 10 April 1626, to Roger Whitaker, husbandman, rent 3s 4d, *a house and garden, 40 feet by 60 feet*. In 1660, *since carried into the sea*.

(b). Lease, 10 June 1620, to William Trickay, shipwright, rent 2s 8d, following Edward Manley's surrender, of a house to be built on part of Seaside Plot, adjoining the garden of Edward Manley, with ½ ac. of land. In 1660, *since carried into the sea*.

SB65. Lease, 1 October 1623, to Ciprian Phillips, husbandman, rent 3s 4d. *A cottage, garden and plot, as it is agreed to be enclosed*, late part of the tenement of John Clarke (cf. SB31).

SB66. This is a short-term lease, 28 April 1618, to Philip Steyning of Chedley, Somerset, for three years, rent 5s, of a messuage, the Church House, in Seaton (cf. SA33 and SB25).

---

[47] Absent from the rental.

[48] From the rental, where it is paid by Susanna Clap, daughter of Robert Clap.

[49] Noted: *See lease*. In the rental, this is under Mary Dare, who was presumably the wife of Joshua Storrick.

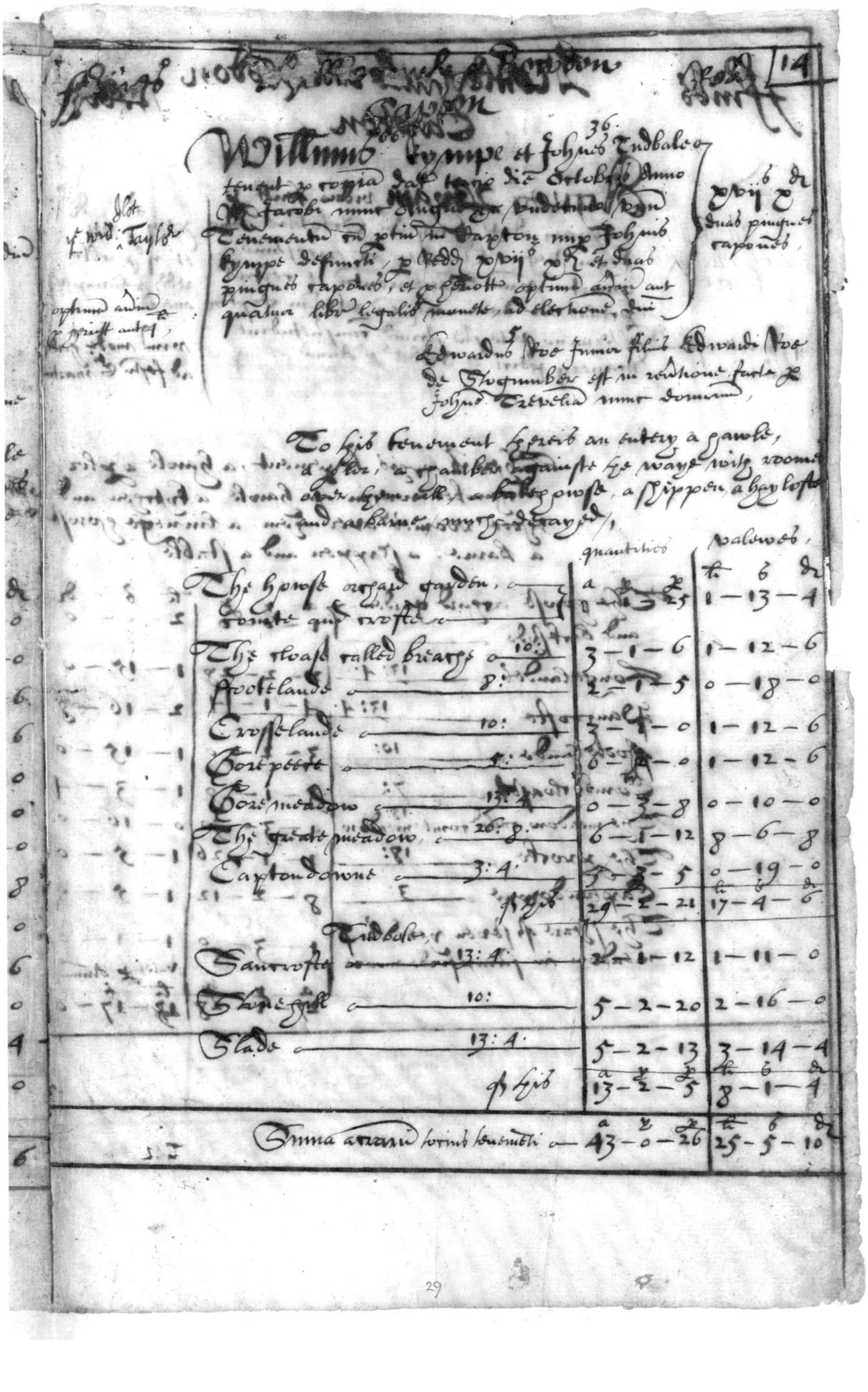

Figure 27. A page of the survey of Nettlecombe, Somerset, 1619 (N38) (S.R.O. DD/WO, box 43, f. 14, copyright reserved)

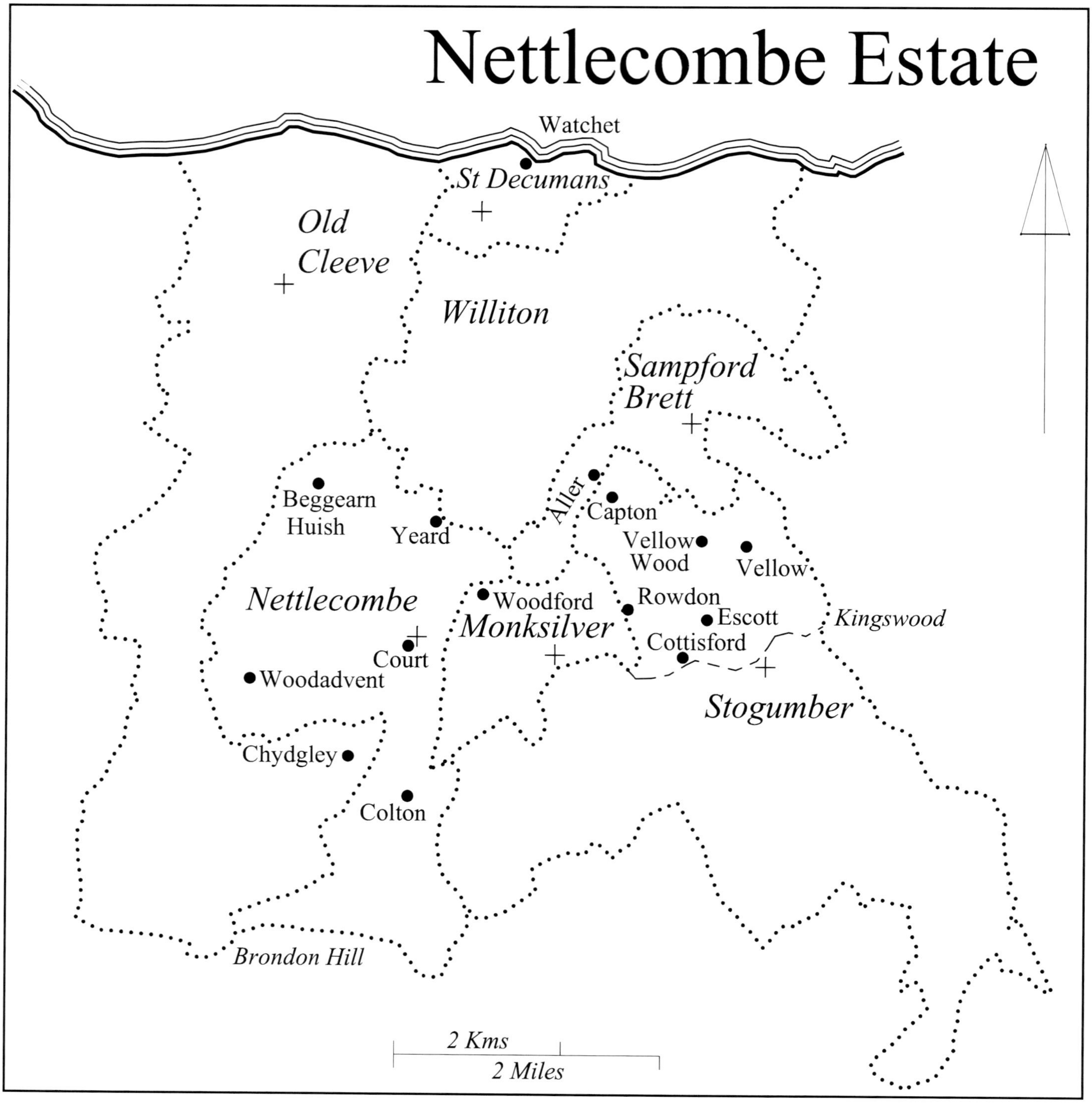

Map 7. The Nettlecombe Estate, Somerset

Based on maps of 1796 S.R.O. DD/WO. Parish boundaries are dotted, and the boundary of the estate in Stogumber is dashed. The location of Churlwood is uncertain, but it may be represented by Kingswood.

CHAPTER 11

Nettlecombe

Nettlecombe (N): 1619 *Map 7*

The Nettlecombe survey is the only one for Somerset that gives full details of houses, but fortunately it is particularly informative, covering sixty-five houses including a few unusually large ones. It deals with the Somerset estates of the Trevelyan family, and it is a remarkable coincidence that their estate archives should also contain the major group of Devon surveys (for the Willoughby estates), as the two families were not connected in the early seventeenth century. The lands are located in a series of hamlets, making up most of the parish of Nettlecombe and part of Stogumber, with a few houses in Monksilver parish (Woodford hamlet), Old Cleeve (Chydgley) and in the town of Watchet in St. Decuman's parish. About 700 acres of common land lay on the Brendon hills.[1] The soil, a red loam, was considered extremely fertile and useful for arable farming.[2] The cloth industry has left clear traces in the rackhouses (N19, 32, 42, 109), and the dye house (N72), and of soap making in the 'sope-houses' (N27, 40).

Apart from the few freeholdings, tenure was predominantly copyhold, but a substantial minority of tenants had leases. A number of the holdings in Escott and Capton had rents levied in barley, while many tenants paid capons (chickens). Five still owed day work, though this amounted to no more than one or two days at harvest time.

The Houses

The most important holding described was the demesne itself (N6) of 293 acres, but apart from the tantalising mention of the 'tennis court', Nettlecombe Court (built by John Trevelyan in 1599) is not described. One other holding (N109) was almost as big,

Buttery within Hall	Higher Hall	Entry	Lower Hall	Entry	Kitchen
					Milkhouse

N109: suggested layout

with 287 acres and a house to match, including two halls and two entries.[3] It may have had the layout shown, with a straight main block and a wing.

The second hall was perhaps used by the servants; if so, this is an unusually early example.[4] (N65 also had two halls, but here the second may have corresponded to a kitchen which it lacked.) The main block had five upper rooms with one over the kitchen. The bakehouse, rackhouse and wringhouse were probably separate.

Two houses were even larger, one (N7) being the home of Francis Trevelyan, brother of the owner of the estate. This had about ninety acres, but the other holding (N34) was not outstanding, with forty-eight acres. Each had entry, hall, parlour, two butteries and milkhouse. N7 had a 'little spence'[5] within the parlour, a brewhouse with a room beside it and a malt chamber above, and four chambers including one over the entry. Unexpectedly it had no kitchen; N34 did have one, together with a remarkable range of service buildings. As well as its butteries and milkhouse, it had a *store-house*, a *butter-house*, brewhouse, malting-house, shopp, bakehowse, *toolehouse*,[6] and 'nine other outhouses' as well as eight upper rooms. Those italicised are recorded in no other Nettlecombe houses.

Most of the houses of the other large farms (considering the twenty-seven with 20 to 104 acres; Table 19)[7] were substantial buildings. However, they were not homogeneous, and show little correlation between size of farm and size of house. The most important distinction seems to be between some smaller and apparently old-fashioned houses, and those that were more modern. Another difference, between those without and those with an 'entry', corresponds to some extent to the house size, but it is probably more significant as reflecting a mixture of building traditions, some derived from eastern England, some from the cross-passage plans of Devon.

The smallest house was N32, no more than a hall and a chamber within it;[8] N33 had two rooms 'within

Table 19: Houses on Nettlecombe farms

Main House	+ Entry	+ Chamber(s)	+ Both	+ Neither
Hall + no functional rooms		32, 33	31	
Hall + one functional room				
P			38	
K		56, 58		
M			28	
Hall + two functional rooms				
PK	36	39		63
PB	65*		42	
KM		43		
BM	35			
Hall + three functional rooms				
PKB	19			27*,66*
PKM				44
PBM	24	108	57	
KBM	55*			67
Hall + four functional rooms				
PKBM	11*,37*,52			
Summary	P	K	B	M
	17 houses	15 houses	13 houses	14 houses

* *N27 and N66 each had a 'little spence'; N55 had a 'little house', probably a store room, and N65 apparently had two halls. N11 also had a study and N37 a stool-house.*
Notes: Farms with 20 to 104 acres are included. P = parlour; K = kitchen; B = buttery; M = milkhouse. N7, 34, 54, 64, 107 are omitted.

the hall' and N56 hall, chamber and kitchen. N31, 28 and 38 had entries, but were no larger, having hall and little inner chamber, hall, little inner chamber and milkhouse, and hall, chamber and parlour respectively. The last had only one upper chamber, over the hall, but the others seem to have been fully floored. These houses probably had simple two or three room plans, either with or without passages. Some also had bakehouses (N31, 32, 33, 38), and there was one rackhouse (N32) and a wringhouse and coalhouse (N56).[9]

The standard rooms found in the larger houses of this group are illustrated by N11, N37 and N52, each with entry, hall, parlour, kitchen, buttery and dairy/milkhouse.[10] The houses showed almost every possible combination of these rooms, with or without an entry and with or without ground floor chambers. It is particularly interesting in relation to the transition from the medieval to the post-medieval forms, that five houses with ground floor chambers had parlours and six did not. Most of the houses had full upper floors, at least over their main ranges, although sometimes the kitchen, buttery or milkhouse seem to have been separate (in a wing or detached) and lacked upper floors (e.g. N11, 37). An interesting distinction is made between 'rooms over' or 'chambers over' over, which were probably equivalent, and the less common 'lofts over' which must imply smaller and less useful spaces. N11 had chambers over the house and a loft over the dairy, while N65 had a bakehouse and a half-loft, presumably covering half of the building.

The most common outbuilding was a bakehouse (fifteen examples), with a number of 'shops' (presumably workshops). The rackhouses (N19, 32, 42 twice), malthouses (N35, 67) and wringhouses (N56, 57, 58) were less common, while one farm had a soap-house (N27), and one a 'plumpe-house' (a dialect form of pump-house; N66). N58 also included a second small house, with a hall and inner chamber, and one loft.

The Nettlecombe survey gives unique evidence that some of these service buildings were detached. In N19, the fields included the Bakes Close, which contained the bakehouse, while N31 had a Bakehouse

Close, and N26 a 'bakes' probably joined to the shippon. In N11, the Home Close and the kitchen in it are listed after three other fields, though the kitchen is also included among the rooms of the house.

In the group of smaller holdings with three to seventeen acres,[11] three of the houses were similar to the larger farms. N23 had an entry, hall, parlour and buttery, while N69 had also a chamber and shop, and N40 a milkhouse (both with bakehouses, though no entries). The tenant of the last may have been principally concerned with soap making, as he had two soap houses as well. Of nine other houses in this group, only two had entries (N20, 45) and all were considerably smaller. Two had hall, kitchen and buttery, with lofts over (N70, 71). N73 was almost identical with hall, kitchen and drink-house, with a chamber over the hall and a 'bad' loft over the kitchen—another (N20) had hall and milkhouse (also a shop and entry) with three chambers over. N45 had just hall and chamber, and N60 had these and also a shop and was called a 'cottage'; it had lofts over, while N45 had one room over the entry and one over the chamber. This must indicate a two room plan with a central passage, and the upper floor may well have partly overlapped the hall. Two houses (N19, 89) were only described as having three and two under rooms, with no first floors mentioned.

Of the twenty-two small-holdings[12] with less than two acres (mostly with only a garden), six were in the town of Watchet, but otherwise they were concentrated in Churlewood, which may well have grown up as a hamlet of cottages. The houses were particularly uniform in design. Eleven had the same basic accommodation of hall and ground floor chamber, although they differed in their lofts. Six had lofts over all (N59, 74, 77, 80, 84, 86), two had a loft only over the hall (N81, 83)[13] and three had no lofts at all (N41, 61, 75). Three of these cottages also had a shop (N75, 77, 84); N59 had a 'little hanging house' (probably a lean-to) and N83 had a wood-house. N95 had a buttery and two shops as well as its hall and chamber (all with lofts). N82 and 79 were slightly different, each with a hall and loft, the first also with buttery and shop, the second with two other unspecified rooms.

The smartest of all these cottages was clearly N88, which had been newly built in Churlewood. It had a hall open to the roof and an inner chamber with loft, and also a shop and a 'pretty under-chamber' at one end.

The houses in Watchet were described just by their number of rooms. Two had one under and one over room (N91, 94); two had two under and one over room (N90, 93) and were probably similar to the 'hall and chamber' houses. N92 had six little rooms, presumably all on the ground floor, and N87 had three under and three over rooms, but was divided into two dwellings. The smallest unit was N15 with two chambers cut off from one end of the Church-house. The Church-house itself was still used for its original purpose by the Nettlecombe churchwardens. It was apparently not very large, with three under rooms and lofts over.

This entire group of cottages contained just one outbuilding, the stable of N84.

The Farm Buildings (Table 20)

When the cottages without barns of Watchet and Churlewood are excluded, Nettlecombe resembles the Devon villages in mixing cattle raising with arable farming, which gave a homogeneous character to its farmsteads. The ever-present barn was almost always accompanied by a separate cattle stall or shippon (the survey uses either description indiscriminately). Haylofts were found on two middle-sized farms (N52, 38) and hayhouses on four larger ones (N34, 55, 43, 62), in one instance (N34) needing to store sufficient winter fodder for stabled horses as well as the cattle filling two shippons; in another case (N55) a hayhouse doubled as a barn. One farmer stacked firewood in a 'woodhouse' under his hayhouse (N43). Linheys were uncommon in the district, and it is hard to tell whether they were used conventionally as shelter for steers, although a 'lynney house [located] against the waye' (N43) and nearer the dwelling and bakehouse than the farm buildings suggests a possible domestic use.

The very frequent 'stalls' and 'shippons' were almost certainly identical, as they are never mentioned together. Another facet of Nettlecombe's pastoral husbandry is revealed by the 'howse for fatt oxen' (N35). No doubt, other shippons were also used for fattening stock. Not all the Nettlecombe farmers were exclusively graziers, and some farmsteads (particularly those with twenty-five acres and upwards) reflect investment in arable farming. Stables are found in increasing numbers, in a few cases on farms without stalls or shippons, and they clearly indicate the use of horses as draught beasts on these larger holdings. Wagons were available on some farms to cart crops to market; five had wainhouses in which to keep them (N57, 42, 35, 63, 109). Rackhouses fitted with drying racks (N19, 32, 42 twice, 109) and wringhouses (N56, 57, 58, 109) give evidence of dyeing and cheese making, while two soap-houses (N27, 40) allude to the slaughtering of cattle, and soap-making on a scale large enough to require specialised outbuildings.[14]

For reasons hard even to guess at, no one in this district chose to live under the same roof with his cows, as was still done by some moorland farmers in East Devon and Cornwall. Nor did they string farm buildings together into long ranges, another common practice elsewhere in the West Country.

[1] Spelled Brondon in the survey.

[2] John Collinson, *History and Antiquities of the County of Somerset* (Bath, 1791), vol. III, 535.

[3] 'Entry' is regularly recorded in this survey.

[4] See Maurice Barley, *Houses and History* (London, 1986), 207, for references to servants' halls in large houses, starting in 1650.

[5] 'Spence', from dispense, i.e., room for serving drink, invariably appears in the surveys as 'little spence'. It probably refers to a small room partitioned off the buttery.

[6] 'Stoolehouse' would be more plausible but the text is clear.

[7] N11, 19, 24, 25, 27, 28, 32, 33, 35-39, 42-44, 52, 55-58, 63, 65-67, 108, excluding N54 where the house described was not the main one, and N64 which was not an independent holding.

[8] N58 also had a subsidiary house, which was the same size as this.

[9] This is the only coalhouse mentioned. If coal did not mean charcoal, it must have come either from the Forest of Dean or from South Wales, by sea to Watchet.

[10] These also had a study (N11), a stool-house (N37) and a shop and brewhouse (N52).

[11] N18, 20, 23, 40, 45, 60, 69-71, 73, 89.

[12] N15, 46, 59, 61, 74, 75, 77, 79-84, 86-88, 90-95. N74 and 75 were the east and west halves of a larger house.

[13] This loft was 'decayed' and presumably more or less useless.

[14] Cf. R. Machin, *The Houses of Yetminster* (Bristol: University of Bristol, 1978), 12.

Table 20: Nettlecombe: Occurrence of farm buildings

Ref. Number	Acres	Barn	Stable	Stall	Shippon	Hay House	Wain House	Wring House	Other buildings and notes
N80	1	•							
N61	2								
N81	2								
N82	2								
N84	2		•						
N89	3								
N60	4	•							
N18	5								
N22	5								
N23	5	•	•		•				
N45	5	•			•				
N12	6								
N73	8	•			•				
N20	9	•		•					
N111	10								
N71	11	•			•				
N70	12	•			•				
N69	14	•	•						
N40	17	•		•					
N58	20	•		•				•	
N44	23	•		•					
N11	24								

Table 20 *continued*

Ref. Number	Acres	Barn	Stable	Stall	Shippon	Hay House	Wain House	Wring House	Other buildings and notes
N110	26	•	•		•				
N39	27	•	•		•				linneage house
N52	28	•	•			*			* haylofts over brewhouse and stable; grist mill
N36	30	••							
N64	30		•						
N33	34	•		•					
N57	34	•	•	••			•	•	
N37	39	•	•		•				
N42	41	•			•		•		
N31	42	•		•					
N32	42	•	•	•					
N38	43	•			•	*			*hayloft (?over shippon)
N19	44	•		•					
N56	44	•			•				
N34	48	•	•		••	•		•	
N55	48				•	•			
N27	50	•		•					
N25	53	•		•					
N65	60	•			•				
N35	62	•		*					*house for fat oxen
N68	62	•	•		•				
N26	63	•			•				
N43	65	•			•	•			woodhouse under hay-house; lynney house
N28	66		•	•					
N66	68	•	•	•					
N62–3	74	*	•			*	•		*N62 included a new barn and the dwelling house had been converted to a hay-house
N7	90	•	•	•					
N24	104	•			•				
N109	287	••	•	•			•	•	

Note: 29 holdings of 1 acre or less, with no farm buildings, are omitted.

Survey of Nettlecombe: 1619 (Fig. 27, p. 145)

(Somerset Rec. Off. DD/WO Box 43. Trevelyan muniments)

This paper volume is bound in a parchment indenture (4 Nov. 1586, relating to the will of Francis Kighley, leatherseller of London). It is in rather poor condition because the ink has rotted the paper, leading to substantial gaps at the head of some pages (but fortunately destroying hardly any significant information). It has an original foliation (1-37), followed by several unnumbered leaves with summary tables, but also has a modern pagination which is used here. The left hand column of each page is headed *Fines*, and when figures are given, they have been transferred to the end of the lease section, labelled [*fine*]. A number of notes have been added in later hands, including the names of some subsequent tenants; the principal hand of these is apparently that of a note to N7, which given the date 1664. The text is in Latin, apart from house descriptions and field names.

TEXT

[p.3] Somerset

Survey of the manors of Nettellcombe, Rowdon and Woodadvent of John Trevelian, esquire, lord of the said manors in the said county, there taken, made and examined by diligent and exact view, perambulation and measurement, as much by Richard Wrentmore, clerk, surveyor of the said John and by order of the same, as by the oaths of John Streete, George Chillcott, Robert Bowden, Richard Ewens, John Thorne, John Hawkins, Simon Bryant and many others of the tenants and homage of the said manors, being there before Richard Pollard, gentleman, capital steward of the said manors, and by him diligently examined, the 20th day of October 1619.

Nettellcombe and Rowdon: Free tenants there

N1. *John Wyndeham, knight, holds freely by military service certain lands and holdings in Chedmarshe by rent, with suit of court, 3s.*

N2. *The same John holds freely by military service certain lands and holdings with their appertenances in Watchett, that were Thomas Ayer's by rent and suite of court 5s [and] 1 lb. cumin.*

N3. *George Lutrell, esquire, holds freely by military service certain lands and holdings in Watchett called Splottes by rent and suit of court, 5s and 1 lb. cumin.*

N4. *John Hewishe holds freely by military service certain lands and holdings in Donyforde by rent and suit of court* [blank]

N5. [Name blank][1] *holds freely by military service 2 ½ ac. called Seland beside Fellow beere by rent and suit of court that were Simon Brit's.*

[p.5] *Nettellcombe and [Rowdon]: Demesne lands*

N6. *John Trevelian, esquire, lord of the aforesaid manors, holds in his own hands the capital messuage, or Le Court Place, with the demesne lands of the same, as follows:* the howses, orchardes, gardens, courts and hopyearde below the tennis courte contayne 4-2-0; the little hoyeard below the churcheyeard 0-1-24; the Conigere 4-3-24; the longe garden with the hopyeard 2-3-26; the Parke meadow 7-0-0; the cloase behinde the barne 2-3-20; the wood called Kynges wood 38-1-0; the wood called Rowdon wood 8-0-15; the cleiss called Westcombes cleiss, whereof the lower furland contayneth 9-3-20, and the upper parte 10-2-20, [*both*] 29-2-0; the cloase called Pilloryes parke 4-3-0; the Courtefeildes about the dead hedge 9-3-22; the Bowlinge Greene and lane below 0-3-8; the peece appoynted to be inclosed 5-0-12; the residew of the cloase 10-1-28;[2] the cloase called Gallis cloase 11-3-24; the hether Lampitts 10-1-16; the yonder Lampitts 9-3-20; the Bromballe 7-0-27; the littell cloase or little Waterleate 1-3-27; the two lower Waterleates devided with the rayles 13-0-10; the yonder upper Waterleate 9-0-13; the hether upper Waterleate 8-1-0; the lower meadow 10-2-0; the higher meadow 11-3-29.

[*Sum*]: The demaynes besydes the parke 223-1-20.

The parke contayneth as in particulers followinge it shall playnely appeare, 70 ac.

[p.6] Nett[ellco]mbe and Rowdon: The Parke

The hether lawne 8-0-0; the myddle lawne 12-2-0; the yonder lawne above the rayles 10-0-0; the parke below the rayles 38-2-0. The whole 70-0-0.

(The ground appointed to make the Parke doth meature all round [?1]8 pannels.)

[1] Note at foot of page: *heirs of Foster, heirs of Preist.*

[2] The preceding four items have total area 26-0-[30].

[p.7] Nettellecombe and Rowdon: [Ye]ard

N7. Francis Trevelian holds by indenture dated the last day of July Anno 30 Elizabeth [1588], from John Trevelian now lord of the said manor, one holding called Yeard for term of his life and rent per annum 19s 10d.

To this messuage or tenement there is a hawle, a parlor with chambers over them, a mylkehowse, and buttery and a little spence within the parlor[3] and three roomes over them, a buttery by the little courte, a brewhouse with a maultchamber over, one under roome within the brewhouse, one chamber over the entrye, one barne, one stawle and a stable.

The howses, orchard, garden and courtilages contayne, A 1-1-30, V 2-0-0;[4] Yeard Hill, R 0-2-8, A 53-0-8, V 7-1-4; Yeard meadow or Myll meadow, R 1-13-0, A 2-3-26, V 4-10-2; the Church meadow, R 1-0-0, A 2-2-0, V 2-10-0; the meadow above the howse, R 1-6-8, A 1-2-4, V 2-0-0; the longe garden and walke, R 1-10-0, A 0-2-16, V 0-15-0; the Waterleates, R [1]-4-0, A 1-3-0, V 2-2-0; the three acre cloase, R 0-12-0, A 3-3-38, V 2-6-8; the Gratton cloase, R 0-6-8, A 4-0-15, V 1-6-8; the Moore, R 0-6-8, A 2-0-4, V 0-13-4; the little cloase, R 0-10-0, A 2-2-18, V 1-5-[0]; the lower Conigere, R 0-12-0, A 1-1-20, V 0-15-0; the higher Conigere, R 0-8-0, A 1-2-0, V 0-12-0; the orchard and hopyeard where the culverhowse is, R 1-0-0, A 0-1-5, V 0-5-0; the Culver cloase, R 0-7-0, A 6-0-33, V 2-2-0; the Rick cloase, R 0-4-0, A 6-1-28, V 1-5-0; the Seven acre close, R 0-4-0, A 5-2-0, V 1-2-0; the close called Graveshеade, R 0-5-0, A 2-1-0, V 0-12-0; the sheare of 5 yeardes of meadow in Samford Moore, A 1-1-0, V 0-15-0.

Sum of acres 101-1-19 V 33-18-[2].

(Jane Towell, widow, sometime wife of Thomas Towell doth now pay me 20s yearely for ye shear in Sandford More, parcell of ye above said tenement, and paid me one yeares rent this present day, being ye 24th of May 1664, due at Lammas last. [and since granted to John Potter])

[p.8][5] Nettelcombe and [Rowdon]: Aller Botler

N8. John Wyndham and Zacharias Wyndham hold by indenture dated 10 Dec. 1621 [*sic for ?1612*], all that farme or messuage called Aller Botler together with that overlande called Vennlandes, 99 years or lives: George Wyndham and Hugh Wyndham sons of Thomas Wyndham esquire, Thomas Francis son of John Francis, rent £4 for the farm, 8s for Venlandes, 6d for suit of court, with suit unto the mill of the said manor, heriot £5.

The howses, bartons, orchardes and gardens, R-1-0-0, A 2-2-0, V 2-10-0; the Lynches with the hopyeard, R 0-8-0, A 4-2-[?0], V 2-0-0; the easter Myddle feilds, R 0-10-0, A 4-2-0, V 2-5-0; the Greate Wydon, R 0-7-0, A 8-2-[3], V 3-0-0; the Little Wydon, R 0-7-0, A 5-3-8, V 2-0-0; the Wester Myddle feilde, R 0-10-0, A 7-1-0, V 3-12-6; the cloase above the house, R 0-10-0, A 10-1-0, V 5-2-6; the Parrocke, R 0-13-4, A 0-2-0, V 0-6-8; the Greate meadow, R 1-6-8, A 4-1-0, V 5-13-4; the Little meadow, R 0-13-4, A 0-2-0, V 0-6-8; the Little Longelande, R 0-10-0, A 7-2-2, V 3-15-8; the Wheate cloase, R 0-10-0, A 8-3-0, V 4-7-6; the Olde cloase, R 0-10-0, A 9-1-[?0], V 4-12-6; Cockhill, R 0-10-0, A 4-0-0, V 2-0-0; the Greate Longlande R 0-8-0, A 9-3-27, V 3-18-0; the Moore, R 0-10-0, A 10-0-0, V 5-0-0; the overlande called Vennlandes, R-0-6-0, A 7-0-0, V 2-2-0; the groundes called [?Haddons], R 0-5-0, A 10-0-0, V 2-10-0; the hill called Aller Hill, R 0-2-6, A 86-0-0, V 10-15-0.

Sum A 208-1-23, V 65-16-8.

N9. Agnes Burges (64)[6] holds during her widowhood one cottage, one orchard and one garden at Yeard, rent 4s.[7] A 0-2-8, V 1-13-4.

The reversion granted to Hugh White by copy dated 10 Oct. 1603 by John Trevelian, in consideration of his good and faithful service.

N10. Thomas Apsley holds one cottage, one orchard and one garden at Woodford by indenture to him, Joan his wife and Michael their son, for their lives, rent 12s and 1 capon at Michaelmas, heriot £1, the reversion not to be granted to any of them. A 2-2-0, V 3-0-0.

N11. John Dyer (40) and Elizabeth Moore (54) hold by copy dated 8 Oct. 1592 one messuage in Nettlecombe, for their lives according to the custom of the manor, rent 10s, heriot best beast, [fine] £20, and all other burdens etc. with common pasture on Brondon hill.

To this there is a hawle, a parlor, a studdie, a buttery, an entery, with three chambers over, a kytchen, a dayrie with a loft over, and a barne and a stable.

The howse, orchard, garden and meadow, A 1-0-0, V 2-6-8; the Higher cloase, R 0-6-4, A 3-1-6, V 1-1-0; the Broad cloase, R 0-6-8, A 5-1-15, V 1-15-0; the Littell cloase, R 0-6-8, A 1-3-30, V 0-12-8; the Home cloase with the hempyeard, kytchen and barne, R 0-10-0, A 3-1-8, V 1-13-4; The Longe cloase or crofte, R 0-8-0, A 4-0-4, V 1-12-0; the Younder cloase, R 0-5-0, A 5-1-24, V 1-6-8.

Sum A 24-1-13, V 10-7-4.

N12. Robert Gore (81) holds by copy dated 4 Sept. 1576, one cottage or holding in Nettellcombe, lately held by George Gore his father, rent 4s 8d, heriot best beast, with common pasture on Brondon hill.

The howse, orchard and crofte, A 1-1-0, V 1-13-4; Broade cloase, R 0-9-0, A 2-0-5, V 0-18-0; Myddle cloase, R 0-10-0, A 1-3-0, V 0-17-6; Quarrye close, R [0-12-0], A [1-0]-0,

[3] The comma after mylkehouse is original, suggesting that both buttery and little spence were within the parlour.

[4] This and succeeding holdings normally give three items after each field name, rate or value per acre, area and total value.

[5] The text from this point is calendared. The main headings on each page are omitted when they repeat that of the previous page.

[6] The numeral (in the original hand) is placed over the name, and is the age of the tenant; as some tenants are described as being dead, these figures were presumably added somewhat after the survey was taken.

[7] Replacing *12d.*

V [0]-12-0, Barne cloase or crofte, R 0-12-0, A 0-3-23, V 0-10-6. Sum A 6-3-28, V 4-11-4

N13. William Graddon (24) and Elizabeth his wife (22) hold one close of land called Crosse cloase by indenture dated 24 May 1619, for their lives, rent 2s and 5 capons at Michalemas, heriot 3s 4d, with suit of court, repossession if the rent 10 days overdue. A 4-1-22, V 2-10-0.

[p.11] Nettlecombe

N14. Francis Clarke (56) holds for his life by copy dated 26 March 1611, one holding in Nettlecombe lately John Bryant's, rent 10s and 3d for common fine, heriot best beast, with common pasture on Brondon hill.

The howses, orchardes, garden, with a parrock and backsyde, A 1-3-20, V 1-[15]-0; the Barne cloase, R 0-8-0, A 1-1-18, V 0-10-0; the Gratton, R 0-8-0, A 1-2-7, V 0-12-0; the Myddle cloase, R 0-6-0, A 1-3-[21], V 0-10-0; the Over cloase, R 0-5-0, A 2-0-37, V 0-12-0; the Quarry cloase, R 0-8-0, A 1-2-22, V 0-12-0; the Waye cloase, R 0-13-4, A 1-0-4, A 1-0-36, V 0-16-4.

Sum A 11-3-1, V 5-7-4.

N15. Thomas Clarke (dead) holds for his life by indenture dated 15 Dec. 1572, one house and one garden adjoining the north end of the Church-house, containing two chambers and a garden, rent 4s and one capon or 12d and one other capon at Michaelmas, suit of court and to the mill, heriot best possession.[8] A 0-0-4.

Reversion granted to Margaret, now wife of Henry Hancock, by indenture dated 7 Sept. 1603, for 99 years or her life, heriot 10s.[9]

N16. The Church-howse havinge three under roomes and a lofte over with a garden thereunto as it is now incloased contayneth 6 perches and is granted unto,[10] [*rent*] 8d.

N17. Agnes Pyne (36), wife of Robert Pyne, holds during her life by indenture dated 31 Oct. 1588 one cottage and garden in Nettelcombe, lately held by Thomas Denber, rent 3s 4d and 2 days in autumn, no heriot. A 0-0-4, V 1-0-0.

Reversion granted to Giles Sweting and his assignees by indenture dated 13 Feb. 1618, for 99 years after the death of Agnes, or lives of Elizabeth, his wife, and Elizabeth, his daughter, with suit of court and to the mill, heriot 3s 4d.

N18. Margaret White (44), widow, holds during her widowhood one holding in Nettlecombe, lately held by John White, her husband, rent 5s 4d, heriot best beast, with common pasture on Brondon hill.

The howse hath three under roomes.

The howse, orchard and garden, A 0-1-0, V 1-0-0; the Nether cloase or meadow, R 1-10-0, A 0-3-20, V 1-6-0; the Hether close, R 0-6-8, A 1-3-12, V 0-12-0; the Yonder cloase, R 0-6-8, A [2-3-0], V 0-18-4.

Sum A 5-2-32, V 3-16-4.

N19. John Thorne (63) holds by copy dated 22 Jan. 1561, one holding and one cottage with a water course to water the meadow of the premises, for life, rent 12s including 6d for water course, 8d for common fine, two heriots best beasts, [*fine*] £40, with common pasture on Brondon Hill.

There is to this messuage an entery, a hawle, parlor, kytchen, and a buttery with fower chambers over, a shopp, a barne, a stawle, a bakehowse and a rackhowse.

The howses, garden and orchard, A 1-0-0, V 3-0-0; Courte cloase, R 0-13-4, A 2-0-7, V 1-7-0; the Bakes cloase, bakehowse and orchard, R 1-4-0, A 2-1-8, V 3-14-0; Chidgeley cloase, R 0-6-8, A 5-0-0, V 1-13-4; Barr cloase, R 0-5-0, A 5-2-2, V 2-17-6; Peaked cloase, R 0-5-0, A 1-3-3, V 0-9-0; the Longe Landes, R 0-6-0, A 6-2-20, V 2-2-0; Brombe cloase, R 0-8-0, A 2-3-0, V 1-2-4; Lower Roade cloase, R 0-8-0, A 3-0-3, V 1-4-0; Higher Roade cloase, R 0-8-0, A 2-0-6, V 0-16-0; the cloase above the Mow cloase (This is now Jo. Farthinge).[11] R 0-8-0, A 6-1-24, V 2-10-0; the Now cloase, R 0-4-0, A 2-0-0, V 0-8-0; the meadowe, R 0-8-0, A 2-0-30, V 0-18-0; the Lagger, R 0-5-4, A 1-3-17, V 0-10-0.

Sum A 44-3-0, V 39-18-10.[12]

N20. Joan (56), wife of Richard Webb, holds for her life by copy dated 13 Oct. 1564, one holding in Nettelcombe with a watercourse and common for 30 sheep on Brondon hill, lately held by Margaret Gilbert, rent 6s 8d and 3d for common fine and 3d for water course, heriot best beast.

It is new granted unto Thomas Webb, Bartholemew Webb and unto Johan Bellamy by copye.[13]

This tenement hath an entry, a hawle, a mylkhowse, a shopp and three chambers over, a barne and a stawle.

The howse, orchard, garden and littell cloase with the well, A [0]-0-26, V 1-10-0; the orchard above the howse, R 0-12-0, A 0-1-12, V 0-4-0; the meadow, R 1-0-0, A 1-0-16, V 1-2-0; the crofte or Over cloase, R 0-15-0, A 1-0-16, V 0-17-6; Bremble cloase, R 0-6-8, A 2-1-0, V 0-15-0; the Furse cloase, R 0-6-8, A 3-0-30, V 1-0-0.

Sum A 9-0-20 [*sic, for 8-2-20*], V 5-8-6.

N21. Maria Edwardes (56) holds by copy dated 3 Oct. 1613, one meadow called Pyttmeade with pasture of the small adjoining wood within the parish of Nettellcombe, for her life according to custom, rent 5s, [fine] £11, heriot Query [*sic*].

The meadow, R 1-6-8, A 1-1-12, V 1-15-4; the pasture of the wood A 1-0-2, V 0-1-8. Sum A 2-1-14, V 1-17-0

Reversion granted to Francis Edwardes and James Edwardes by copy dated 26 April 1617, for their lives.

N22. George Clarke (?36), (Edward (?8) and Elizabeth Clarke (12))[14] hold by copy dated 26 May 1613, one cottage in Nettlecombe, lately held by Luke Clarke, his [*George*]

---

[8] *Optimum Bonum.*

[9] In the rental under her name, with a value of £1.0.0.

[10] Blank, but in the rental under Wardens of Nettlecombe.

[11] An addition in the margin.

[12] Original note *Undervalued.*

[13] In margin. In the rental under Thomas Webb.

[14] Inserted.

father, for their lives, rent 5s, heriot best beast, with common pasture on Brondonhill. The howses, orchard, garden and courte, A 0-1-16, V 1-6-8; the meadow and orcharde, R 1-0-0, A 0-2-1, V 0-10-0; the crofte, R 1-0-0, A 0-2-5, V 0-12-6; the Barlye Earrishe, R 0-10-0, A 1-2-0, V 0-15-4; the Bottome closase, R 0-10-0, A 1-1-25, V 0-14-0; the Hill closase, R 0-6-4, A 1-2-0, V 0-9-6.

Sum A 5-3-27, V 4-7-8.

N23. The same George, (in the right of his wife Elizabeth (56) and Henry Hancock (46))[15] holds by copy dated 18 Sept 1600, one cottage in Nettlecombe, lately held by William Hancocke, with common pasture on Brondon Hill, for life, rent 6s 8d, heriot best beast.

To this messuage there is an entrye, hawle, a parlor, a butterye and three chambers over, a barne, a stable and a shippen.

The howse, orchard, garden and courte, A 0-1-25, V 1-10-0; the Crofte, R 0-13-4, A 0-1-26, V 0-5-6; the Greene cloase, R 0-13-4, A 1-0-0, V 0-13-4; the Oate Earrishe, R 0-10-0, A 1-0-22, V 0-11-6; the Bottome cloase, R 0-10-0, A 1-0-9, V 0-11-0; the Brome cloase, A 1-2-0, V 0-9-0.

Sum A 5-2-2, V 4-0-4.

[p.16] Nettle[Combe and Rowdon]: Woodhowse

N24. Joan Farthinge, widow, holds during her widowhood,[16] two holdings called Woodhowse and the woody pasture called Pookewood with freeth and stakes there for repairing the premises and with common for 100 sheep on Brondon hill, rent 10s and for the woody pasture 6d, two heriots best beasts.

To theise tenementes there is an entrye, a hawle, a parlor, a buttery, a mylkehowse, a kytchen with three chambers over, a bakehowse, a barne and a shippen.

The howses, courtilages, two orchardes with a cloase annexed, A 1-3-8, V 3-0-0; two meadowes above the howse with three groves in them, R 0-18-0, A 5-3-0, V 5-4-0; one other little orchard, R 1-0-0, A 0-1-0, V 0-5-0; the Barne cloase, R 0-4-0, A 1-2-0, V 0-6-0; Broadecombe, R 0-6-0, A 6-3-20, V 2-0-6; Bremell cloase, R 0-6-0, A 4-0-20, V 1-5-0; the little Meade cloase, R 0-10-0, A 1-3-0, V 0-17-6; the Quarry cloase, R 0-6-0, A 4-1-27, V 1-6-8; Moore cloase, R 0-8-0, A 3-1-30, V 1-6-8; Wood cloase or Burchingehedge, R 0-6-0, A 2-1-0, V 0-13-4, Nether Borrowhill, R 0-3-4, A 6-1-12, V 1-0-0; Overborrowhill, R 0-2-6, A 11-3-20, V 1-7-8; Easter Borrowhill, R 0-2-6, A 3-2-30, V 0-9-6; the severall groundes upon the hill, R 0-1-0, A 14-0-0, V 0-14-0; the pasture of Pookewood, R 0-0-10, A 14-0-0, V 0-14-0; the pasture of Pookewood, R 0-0-10, A 36-0-0, V 1-10-0.

Sum A 104-0-27, V 21-5-10.

[p.17] Nettelcombe and Rowdon : Colton

N25. Baldewin Hancocke (52) and Henry Hancocke (49), his brother, hold by copy dated 18 Sept. 1600, one holding called Colton, lately held by Robert Cadworthie, for their lives according to the custom of the manor, rent 10s and 6d for downe rent, heriot best beast, [fine] £60, with common on Brendon hill. There is to this tenement a hawle, a parlor, a butterye and two chambers over, a stawle, a barne and a bakehowse.

The howses, courte and garden, A 0-1-0, V 1-10-0; the meadow, R 1-6-8, A 4-1-0, V 5-13-4; the Trianguler Furse cloase or plot, R 0-3-4, A 2-2-0, V 0-8-4; the grove adioyninge, R 0-6-8, A 1-3-0, V 0-12-0; Myllwaye cloase, R 0-3-0, A 8-1-0, V 1-5-0; the Lower Deane, R 0-5-0, A 5-2-0, V 1-7-6; the Higher Deane, R 0-3-4, A 4-2-0, V 0-15-0; the Higher Brome cloase, R 0-3-4, A 4-0-2, V 0-13-8; the Lower Brome cloase, R 0-4-0, A 2-1-10, V 0-9-0; the cloase called Burrell, R 0-3-4, A 1-1-17, V 0-4-6; the peece called Beacon hill, R 0-1-0, A 10-3-0, V 0-10-9; the peece upon the hill, whereof there is no grannte made, R 0-1-0, A 8-0-0, V 0-8-0.

Sum A 53-2-11, V 13-17-1.

N26. John Hawkins senior (72) (dead),[17] John Hawkins junior (dead) and William Hawkins (dead) hold by copy dated 1 Oct. 1584, one holding at Colton, lately held by John Farmer, with two closes of overland between Pookewood and the road that leads between Colton Crosse and Nettlecombe, for their lives according to custom, rent 11s 8d and 6d for downe rent and 6s 8d for the said two closes, two heriots best beasts, [fine] £90, with common on Brondon hill.

The howse, orchard, two courtes and barne, A 0-1-0, V 1-10-0; the meadow with the shippen, bakes, littell garden and hopyearde, R 1-6-8, A 3-3-0, V 5-0-0; one littell orchard below the meadow, R 1-0-0, A 0-1-0, V 0-5-0; the Little cloase, R 0-8-0, A 1-2-10, V 0-12-0; the cloase called Moore Splatt, R 0-4-0, A 2-3-7, V 0-11-0; the Cleise, R 0-2-6, A 10-2-0, V 1-6-0; the Wheate meadow, R 1-1-0, A 1-0-7, V 1-1-0; Vincen meadow, R 1-0-0, A 2-1-27, V 2-7-8; the Hill cloase, R 0-2-0, A 14-3-0, V 1-10-0; the Lea cloase, R 0-5-0, A 9-3-0, V 2-8-0; the Wood cloase, R 0-4-0, A 9-1-20, V 1-17-6; the Lagger, R 0-4-0, A 7-2-0, V 1-10-0.

Sum A 63-3-31, V 19-18-2.

N27. Joan Kympe (50), widow, holds for her life by indenture dated 26 June 1611, two holdings in Colton, lately held by John Kympe, her dead husband, rent 10s and 12d for downe rent, 12d for common fine, two heriots best beasts, with common on Brondon hill. Remainder to Josia Kympe (33) and assignees for life.

There is to theise tenements a hawle, a parlor, a kytchen, a buttery and a little spence and three chambers over, a barne, a stawle and a sope howse.

The howses, garden and courte, A 0-2-0, V 1-0-0; (Theise parcells are now grannted by deede unto Christian Dyckes and Edmond Dyckes.)[18] Wheat meadow, R 1-6-8, A 1-1-9, V 1-15-0; Ballyeate or Nut-tree, R 0-9-0, A 5-3-0, V 2-12-

[15] Inserted.

[16] Held by John Farthing in the rental.

[17] Possibly added.

[18] Later note, with a bracket down to Bakes Lea.

0; Lower Waterleates, R 1-0-0, A 0-3-0, V 0-15-0; Higher Waterleates, R 1-0-0, A 1-3-10, V 1-16-0; the cloase called Longe [?crosse], R 0-6-8, A 4-1-0, V 1-6-8; Solverleaze, R 0-6-0, A 5-1-0, V 1-11-6; the Bakes Lea, R 0-10-0, A 4-2-24, V 2-6-0; (Richard [?Colard]) the Crosse cloase, R 0-6-8, A 3-1-28, V 1-2-0; (Edward Thorne hath this.)[19] the Over cloase above the howse, R 0-8-0, A 10-1-10, V 4-2-0; the Nether cloase above the howse, R 0-8-0, A 4-2-0, V 1-16-0, the New cloase, R 0-2-0, A 5-0-18, V 0-10-6; the Grove, R 0-6-8, A 1-1-17, V 0-8-0; the Weste meadow, R 1-10-0, A 2-0-0, V 3-0-0.

Sum A 50-0-26, V 24-0-8.

N28. Hugh Locke and Thomas Locke [hold by copy dated] 4th April 1599, two holdings in Colton for their lives, with common pasture on Brondon hill, rent 10s and 12d for downe rent, 1 capon at Michaelmas and one at Easter or 12d for every of them, two heriots best beasts, [fine] £110.

There is to theise tenements an entrye, a hawle, a little chamber within the hawle, one chamber over the hawle, a mylkehowse, a stawly and a stable.

N29. Richard Collard holds by copy dated [?23] Oct. 1612, one cottage, one orchard and one garden in Colton, A 0-0-26, with common pasture for one horse, mare or gelding on Brondon hill, rent 2s 8d, heriot 15s. V 1-10-0.

Reversion granteed to Richard Collard, son of the said Richard by copy dated 26 May 1619, fine £2-4-0.

[p. 21] Nettlecomb and Rowdon: Brondon

N30. Edith Hedford (46), relict and executrix of John Hedford, holds by indenture dated 16 June 1611, that parcell of ground on the hill of Brondon and one howse in the same ground, together with the water and watercourses thereunto appertayninge, and the tyllage of one acre of ground, parcell of the commons of the manor of Nettlecomb, to be had and taken in suche sorte as other the tennantes of the same manor have, for 99 years, lives of her self and John her son, rent 6s 8d and one capon at Michaelmas, heriot 6s 8d, [*fine*] £12, suit of court twice yearly.

This is called the Gore Pece, A 35-2-0, V 5-0-0.

Chydgley

N31. Simon Bryant (66) holds by copy dated 10 Mar. 1584, one holding in Chydgley, lately held by Agnes Sulley, for life according to the custom of the manor, rent 5s and 8d for downe rent, heriot best beast, [*fine*] £60, with common pasture on Brondon hill.

There is to this tenement an entrye, a hawle, a littell chamber within the hawle, two chambers over, a bakehowse, a barne and a stawle.

Reversion granted to the said Simon and his assignees by indenture dated 10 Nov 1618, for 99 years or lives of Joan Honndall, daughter of John Honndall and Simon Chillcott, son of John Chillcott.

[19] Later note, with a bracket to the end.

[p. 22] Nettlecombe and Rowdon: Chydgley Sulleys

The messuage, two orchardes, garden and courte, A 0-3-0, V 1-10-0; the Square meadow, R 1-12-0, A 2-1-0, V 3-12-0; the Hayesed, R [0-8-0], A 3-0-0, V 1-4-0; the Bakehowse cloase, R 0-10-0, A 4-2-8, V 2-6-8; the Higher Half Furlande, R 0-6-8, A 4-1-32, V 1-8-0; the Myddle cloase, R 0-6-8, A 3-1-16, V 1-2-0; the Higher Oateley, R 0-6-0, A 3-2-9, V 1-1-0; Shortelande, R 0-5-0, A 2-3-0, V 0-13-4; Myddle cleis, R 0-5-0, A 3-0-0, V 0-15-0; the Higher Cleis, R 0-4-0, A 2-0-13, V 0-8-0; Higher Lypelande, R 0-10-0, A 1-3-8, V 0-19-0; Lower Sacerley, R 0-5-4, A 2-0-0, V 0-12-0; the grounde above the hedge, R 0-2-0, A 8-0-0, V 0-16-0.

Sum A 42-0-6, V 16-7-0.

N32. The same Simon Bryant (66), Avis Sully and John Gilbert hold by copy dated 19 Oct. 1591, one other holding in Chidsley [*sic*], lately held by Thomas Palmer, for their lives according etc. [*sic*], rent 5s and 8d for downe rent, heriot best beast, [*fine*] £66 132 4d, with common on Brondon hill.

There is to this tenement a hawle, a chamber within the hawle, two chambers over, a bakehowse, a barne, a stawle, a rackhowse and a littell stable.

The howse, orchard, garden and courte, A 0-2-0, V 1-10-0; the Squier meadow, R 1-6-8, A 2-2-0, V 3-6-8; the cloase called Porteweye, R 0-8-0, A 4-2-20, V 1-17-0; the Lower Halfe Furlande, R 0-10-0, A 1-2-0, V 0-15-0; Bromehill or Bromeley, R 0-8-0, A 3-2-13, V 1-8-0; Lower Oatley, R 0-8-0, A 6-0-16, V 2-8-0; the Bovehayes or Bowley, R 0-6-8, A 3-0-0, V 1-0-0; Michell lande, R 0-6-8, A 3-0-34, V 1-1-0; Whittley next the hill, R 0-6-8, A 2-1-30, V 0-17-6; the Halfe Acre cloase, R 0-6-8, A 3-1-20, V 1-1-0; the Lower Lypelande, R 0-10-0, A 1-3-0, V 0-17-6; the Higher Sakerley, R 0-5-0, A 2-2-0, V 0-12-6; the grounde above the hedge, R 0-2-0, A 7-0-0; V 0-14-0.

Sum A 42-0-13, V 17-8-2.

[p.23] Nettlecombe and Rowdon

N33. Simon Slade (55) holds [by copy dated ?20] Aug. 1571, one holding called Slade, for life according to the custom of the manor, rent 6 capons and 10s to the lord of the manor of Baggeren Huishe for all services, heriot best beast; John Slade (36), son of Simon, holds half of the said holding by the surrender of Simon, by copy dated 13 Mar. 1617. Reversion to the said John Slade and Henry Slade (22) for their lives.

The howse, orchard, garden, courtlage and half the crofte, A 2-0-0, V 2-0-0; the moore with a littell hopyeard and the other halfe of the crofte, A 1-2-15, V 1-12-6; the meadowe, R 1-0-0, A 4-3-0, V 4-15-0; the Myddle cloase, R 0-10-0, A 8-0-25, V 4-3-0; the cloase above the howse, R 0-10-0, A 8-2-34, V 4-6-8; the Hill, R 0-5-0, A 5-0-9, V 1-5-4; the cloase called Above[..]he, R 0-8-0, A 4-1-32. V 1-10-0; the cloase called Cameleaze, R 0-10-0, A 4-3-3, V 2-17-6.

Sum A 39-1-38, V 22-10-0.

There is to this tenement a hawle and two lower roomes within the hawle, three chambers over, a barne, a stawle and a bakehowse.

N33a. Jane Stockham holds by indenture [*date blank*], free liberty to fetch potwater over the wood called Kynges woode, rent 16d and one capon at Easter.

[p.24] Nettlecombe and Rowdon: Capton

N34. Robert Bowdon (63) holds by copy dated 10 Oct. 1603, one customary holding in Capton, lately held by George Swyre, rent 20s 4d and ½ measure[20] of barley at Martinmas [*11 Nov.*], heriot best beast.

George Bowdon, (34), son of Robert, is in reversion.[21]

There is to this tenement an entery, a parlor, a hawle, a kytchen, a storehowse, two butteryes, a butterhowse, a mylkehowse, a brewhouse, a maltinghowse, a shopp and 8 other roomes over them, a barne, a stable, two shippins, one hay howse, a bakehowse, a toolehowse with nine other oute howses.

The howses and courtes, A [?0-2-0], V 2-0-0; the garden and orcharde above the howse, A 1-0-0, V 2-0-0; the Higher Honycrofte, R 0-10-0, A 4-[1]-2, V 2-2-8; the Lower Honycrofte, R 0-10-0, A 3-3-0, V 1-17-6; the little meadow and Nurcery, R 1-0-0, A 1-3-16, V 1-16-0; the Greate meadow, R 1-6-8, A 6-2-0, V 8-13-4; the Little Broadcloase, R 0-12-0, A 1-3-0, V 1-1-[0]; Great Broadcloase with the hopyeard, R [0-12-0], A 3-3-20. V 2-6-8; Little Churchhill, R 0-8-0, A 2-0-30, V 0-17-0; Great Churchhill, R 0-10-0, A 5-1-20, V 2-14-0; Churchhill next to Capton, R 0-10-0, A 5-0-0, V 2-10-0; Woodcloase, R 0-10-0, A 4-2-20, V 2-5-0; Capton Downe, R 0-6-0, A 5-0-30, V 1-10-0; the Moore and Allers, R 0-6-0, A 2-3-0, V 0-16-6; the sheare of one yeard of meadow in Sampforde moore, R 0-5-0, A 0-1-0, V 0-3-0.

Sum A 48-3-24, V 35-12-8.

(This is worth £43 per annum besides the houses, garden and orchard. There is now granted to John Potter with this tenement 5 yards of sheare in Sampforde Moore formerly belonging to Yard.)

N35. John Taylor (38) and Katherine Taylor (45), his wife, hold by indenture dated 14 Feb.[22] one holding in Capton and 33 acres of overlande, hawking and hunting reserved, and two closes arable land and pasture, part of Capton Downe, lately inclosed, for 99 years or lives of said John and Katherine, rent 29s 8d and two capons at Michaelmas, heriot best beast, suit of court and to the mill.

Reversion granted by the same deed to Mary Taylor (40), sister of John, for life, with a clause of re-entry if the rent be behinde the space of six monthes and no sufficient distress in or upon the same, or if they or any of them shall doe or procure to be done any voluntary or willfull waste to the value of 40s.

Further reversion to John Taylor, his executors and assignees, for 99 years or the lives of John Taylor (14), eldest son of the said John Taylor, and Robert Taylor (8) his second son; same reservations and re-entry if the rent be behinde by two monthes, or if the sayd John shall assign this estate to any other but unto some one or more of his owne children; covenant to plant two trees of oake, ashe or elme for every tree fallen downe, whether tymber or dokard tree; heriot best beast or £3 at the lord's election.

To John Taylor's tenement there is an enterye, a hawle, a kytchen, a butterye, a mylkehowse, a shopp, five chambers overheade, a stawle, a barne, a mawltehouse, a howse for fatt oxen, an olde bakes and a waynehowse.

The howses, orchardes, gardens and courtes, A 1-3-4, V 3-0-0; the Crofte, R 0-12-0, A 1-3-20, V 1-2-0; Longlandes, R 0-13-4, A 1-3-22, V 1-5-0; Higher Tagewell, R 0-10-0, A 4-0-20, V 2-0-0; Lower Tagewell, R 0-10-0, A 5-0-0, V 2-10-0; Harrwell, R 0-13-4, A 2-1-0, V 1-10-0; Mollon cloase, R 0-13-4, A 4-3-20, V 3-5-0; Somers cloase, R 0-6-8, A 6-2-22, V 2-4-0; Broade Moore, R 0-6-8, A 3-2-0, V 1-3-4; Moorlandes R 0-12-0, A 2-1-6, V 1-7-6; Breach cloase, R 0-8-0, A 3-0-30, V 1-5-0; Breach meadow, R 1-6-0, A 2-2-16, V 3-7-0; Higher Honicrofte, R 0-8-0, A 3-3-6, V 1-10-0; Lower Honycrofte, R 0-8-0, A 4-1-27, V 1-15-0; Capton Downe R 0-5-6, A 4-0-20, V 1-2-0; Higher Wayven, R 0-6-8, A 2-3-36, V 0-18-4; Lower Wayven, R 0-6-8, A 4-0-36, V 1-5-0; the share of three acres and halfe of meadow in Sampforde Moore, A 3-2-0, V 1-15-0.

Sum A 62-3-5, V 32-3-2.

N36. Gilbert Beastlie ([..]) and Joan Beastley (34) hold by indenture dated 13 Feb. 1618, one holding in Capton, lately held by Wiliam Byam, Anne his wife, John Byam, Edward Kellet, Henry Byam, Edward Byam, John Wattes, Christopher Pearse, and James Hurley, rent 12s 8d, heriot best beast or £3 6s 8d at the lord's choice; reserved to the lord one close, parcel of the premises, called Cottiforde cloase, near the place called Cottiforde in Stogumber.

Reversion to Hugh Gore (7), son of Thomas Gore.

To this tenement there is an enterye, a hawle, a parlor, a kychen, with loftes over them, and two barnes.

The howses, orchard, garden and crofte, A 1-0-7, V 2-0-0; Little Henbarow, R 0-12-0, A 0-3-0, V 0-9-0; Longe Henbarow, R 0-12-0, A 0-2-28, V 0-8-0; Lower Crosse cloase with a lane at the lower ende, R 0-13-4, A 3-1-0, V 2-3-4; the Higher Crosse cloase, R 0-13-4, A 4-1-5, V 2-16-8; Broademoore, R 0-8-0, A 7-3-30, V 3-3-4; Moorelande cloase with a fish poole, R 0-10-0, A 3-2-9, V 1-15-0; Capton Downe, R 0-3-4, A 8-2-12, V 1-6-8; the share of a yearde of meadow in Sampforde moore, A 0-1-0, V 0-3-0.

Sum A 30-1-21, V 14-5-0.

N37. Richard Ewens (56) holds by copy dated 12 May 1606, one holding in Capton, lately held by John Ewens, father of Richard, rent 12s and one measure of barley at Michaelmas, heriot best beast.

Reversion to John (dead) and Robert Ewens (20), sons of Richard.

(Robert Dashwood of Vellowwood)

---

20 *Modium*.

21 In margin John Potter (see end of entry).

22 Regnal year of Elizabeth left blank.

To this tenement there is an enterye, a hawle, a parlor, a kytchen, a stoolhowse, with roomes over them, a buttery, a mylkehowse, a barne, a shippen and a stable.

The howses, orchard, garden and courte, A 0-2-0, V 2-0-0; the Crofte, R 0-16-0, A 0-2-32, V 0-11-0; the Pittcloase and orchard, R 0-10-0, A 5-2-16, V 2-15-6; the Hether horsecrofte, R 0-10-0, A 3-1-8, V 1-12-6; the Yonder Horsecrofte, R 0-10-0, A 3-0-6, V 1-10-0; the meadow under the Cleiss, R [1-0-0], A 1-2-15, V 1-11-0; the Cleiss, R 0-6-0, A 3-1-0, V 0-18-0; Combecloase, R 0-10-0, A 2-2-15, V 1-6-8; Longelandes, R 0-13-4, A 2-3-12, V 1-17-0; Sandecrofte, R 1-10-0, A 2-0-12, V 1-0-6; Breache cloase, R 0-13-4, A 2-[1]-15, V 1-11-0; Capton Downe, R 0-3-0, A 11-0-20, V 1-13-4; the sheare of halfe an acre of meadow in Sampforde moore, A 0-2-0, V 0-6-0.

Sum A 39-1-31, V 18-12-6.

N38. William Kympe (66) and John Tudbale (36) hold by copy dated 3 Oct. 1613, one holding in Capton, lately held by John Kympe, deceased, rent 18s 10d and and two fat capons, heriot best beast or £4 at the lord's choice.

Reversion to Edward Roe (5), junior, son of Edward Roe of Stugumber.

(Widow Ilot Taylor)

To this tenement there is an entery, a hawle, a parlor, a chamber against the waye, with roomes over them all, a bakehowse, a shippen, a haylofte, and a barne much decayed.

The howse, orchard, garden, courte and crofte, A 1-1-5, V 1-13-4; the cloase called Breache, R 0-10-0, A 3-1-6, V 1-12-6; Footelande, R 0-8-0, A 2-1-5, V 0-18-0; Crosselande, R 0-10-0, A 3-1-0, V 1-12-6; Gorepeece, R 0-5-0, A 6-2-0, V 1-12-6; Gore meadow, R 0-13-4, A 0-3-8, V 0-10-0; the Greate meadow, R 1-6-8, A 6-1-12, V 8-6-8; Capton Downe, R 0-3-4, A 5-3-5, V 0-19-0.

Sum of this A 29-2-21, V 17-4-6.

Tudbole [*his share*]: Sancrofte, R 0-13-4, A 2-1-12, V 1-11-0; Stone Hill, R 0-10-0, A 5-2-20, V 2-16-0; Slade, R 0-13-4, A 5-2-13, V 3-14-4.

Sum of this A 13-2-5, V 8-1-4.

Sum (total) A 43-0-26, V 25-5-10.

N39. Agnes Byam, widow, holds by copy dated 14 Oct. 1592, a holding and certain parcels of demesne land in Capton, for life according to the custom of the manor, rent 17s 4d and 2s for high rent for Sampforde moore, and one measure of barley at Martinmas, heriot best beast.

(Will Sully of Munksilver)

There is to this tenement a hawle, a parlor, a chamber within the hawle, a kytchen and three roomes over them, a linnege howse, a barne, a shippen and a stable.

The howse, orchard, garden and backsyde, A 1-0-0, V 2-0-0; Longlandes, R 0-13-4, A 2-2-28, V 1-15-0; Pancrofte, R 0-13-4, A 4-1-4, V 2-16-8; Footelande, R 0-10-0, A 3-2-0, V 1-15-0; Combecloase, R 0-7-0, A 3-1-8, V 1-3-4; the meadow called Combe meadow, R 0-18-0, A 1-3-30, V 0-16-0; the Parrocke, R 0-18-0, A 1-1-26, V 1-5-0; Capton Downe, R 0-3-0, A 8-2-12, V 1-5-0; the sheare of seven yeards of meadow in Sampford moore, A 1-3-0, V 1-1-0.

Sum A 27-1-28, V 13-17-0.

(valued in £40 per annum)

N40. Joan Kympe holds for herself and her assignees, being infants: Ursula Kympe (20) and Joan Kympe (17), her daughters, and Baldwin Kympe (4), son of John Kympe, by indenture dated 20 April 1617, one holding and cottage in Capton, lately held by John Byffen, rent 5s 4d and one fat capon at Michaelmas, and ½ measure of barley at Martinmas, heriot best beast or 40s at the lord's choice.

(Ursula Sully)

There is to this tenement a hawle, a parlor, a sope howse, a buttery, a mylkehowse, three chambers over, a barne, a bakes, a stawle and an outer sopehowse.

The howses, orchard, garden and cloase or crofte adioyninge, A 3-3-2, V 4-15-0; Blackelande, R 0-10-0, A 2-2-18, V 1-6-8; Myddle cloase, R 0-12-0, A 1-2-18, V 0-19-0; Headlande, R 0-10-0, A 3-0-24, V 1-11-0; Capton Downe, R 0-3-4, A 3-3-25, V 1-11-0; the meadow called Parke meade, R 0-13-4, A 2-0-0, V 1-6-8; the sheare of one yeard of meadow in Sampforde moore, A 0-1-0, V 0-3-0.

Sum A 17-1-7, V 10-13-4.

N41. Elizabeth Woorth holds the cottage and garden therunto, for life, rent 12d, heriot 3s 4d, A 0-0-6, V 1-0-0.

N42. John Winter (68) holds by copy dated 22 June 1591, one holding in Capton, lately held by John Winter, his father, deceased, rent 14s and 8d for common fine, heriot best beast.

Reversion to Robert (20) and Richard Wynter (18), sons of John.

To this tenement there is an entery, a hawle, a parlor, a milkehowse, a chamber and three roomes overheade, a bakehowse, a shippen, a barne, a waynehowse and rackhowses.

The howses, orchard, garden and courte, A 1-0-4, V 2-0-0; the meadowe, R 0-18-0, A 6-0-4, V 5-8-0; Overshutcloase with a pytt, R 0-12-0, A 2-3-26, V 1-13-4; Lower Shutcloase, R 0-12-0, A 3-2-0, V 2-2-0; Tagewell, R 0-13-4, A 5-0-14, V 3-6-8;

Lower Bromebreache, R 0-13-4, A 2-2-24, V 1-14-0; Higher Bromebreache, R 0-10-0, A 4-0-21, V 2-0-0; Higher Stonehill hath a lymekyll, R 0-13-4, A 3-0-12, V 2-1-0; Lower Stonehill, R 0-13-4, A 3-2-28, V 2-7-0; the cloase called Henborrow, R 0-10-0, A 3-2-24, V 1-16-0; Capton Downe, R 0-6-0, A 5-0-29, V 1-10-0; the sheare of half an acre of meadow in Sampforde Moore, A 0-2-0, V 0-6-0.

Sum A 41-2-26, V 26-4-0.

N43. Robert Bowringe (38) and Barbara (40), his sister, hold by copy dated 17 Oct. 1587, one holding in Capton, lately held by Henry Bowringe, his brother, deceased, for their lives according to the custom of the manor, rent 12s 6d, heriot best beast, [*fine*] £46.

There is to this tenement a hawle, a kytchen, a chamber

within, a mylkehowse, with roomes over them all, a lynney howse agaynst the waye, a bakehowse, a barne, a shopp, a shippen, a hayhowse, and a woodhowse under.

The howses, orchard, garden and courte, A 1-0-0, V 2-0-0; Longelandes, R 0-13-4, A 4-1-4, V 2-16-8; the two Dayehilles, R 0-9-0, A 4-2-12, V 2-0-6; Dayehill meadow, R 0-13-4, A 1-0-4, V 0-13-4; Breache close, R 0-13-4, A 3-2-24, V 2-7-0; the Fower Rowdons, R 0-6-8, A 12-2-6, V 4-4-0; Blacklande, R 0-9-0, A 2-2-20, V 1-3-0; the two Broadecloases, R 0-10-0, A 5-2-26, V 2-16-0; Lower Verneacres, R 0-12-0, A 0-3-0, V 0-9-0; Higher Verneacres, R 0-10-0, A 1-3-24, V 0-18-0; Greate Sancrofte, R 0-10-0, A 3-0-26, V 1-12-0; Littell Sancrofte, R 0-10-0, A 2-0-20, V 1-0-0; the Higher Crofte, R 0-10-0, A 1-2-24, V 0-16-0; the Lower Crofte orchard, R 1-0-0, A 1-2-25, V 1-10-6; (these 3 [*next following*] that are marked out are Robert Dashwoods) Lower Woodcloase, R 0-8-0, A 5-0-0, V 2-0-0; Higher Woodcloase, R 0-6-0, A 3-2-32, V 1-2-0; Parke meadow, R 1-0-0, A 0-2-32, V 0-12-6; Capton Downe, R 0-5-0, A 4-3-14, V 1-3-6; Moorelande meadow, R 0-16-0, A 1-1-6, V 1-0-0; Moorelande cloase, R 0-10-0, A 2-3-22, V 1-8-0; the sheare of halfe an acre of meadow in Sampforde Moore, A 0-2-0, V 0-6-0.

Sum A 65-2-21, V 31-18-0.

N44. Peter Bryant ([..]) holds by copy dated [?20] Oct. 1593 one holding in Capton, lately held by William Bryant, deceased, rent 12s 6d, heriot best beast, common pasture on Chorlewood for six sheep.

Reversion to John (30) and Henry Bryant (36), sons of William.

There is to this tenement a hawle, a parlor, a kytchen, a mylke chamber, with chambers over, a barne, a stawle and a shopp.

The howses, orchard, garden and backsyde, A 0-2-0. V 1-10-0; the Crofte and little orcharde, R 0-13-4, A 1-0-28, V 0-15-0; the Lagger, R 0-13-4, A 0-2-0, V 0-7-0; Greate Headlande, R 0-13-4, A 1-1-20, V 0-18-4; Brome Breache, R 0-13-4, A 1-2-24, V 1-2-0, Sancrofte, R 0-13-4, A 2-2-25, V 1-15-0; Little Headlande, R 0-8-0, A 1-0-12, V 0-8-4; Rowdons, R 0-8-0, A 10-0-24, V 3-0-0; Lower Withenheade, R 0-10-0, A [1-3-0], V 0-17-6; Higher Withenheade, R 0-6-0, A 2-2-18, V 0-17-0.

Sum A 23-3-0, V 11-10-2.

N45. Etheldreda Owen (70) holds during her widowhood by indenture dated [?13] Oct.[23] one holding in Capton, lately held by John Owen, deceased, rent 3s 8d, heriot best beast, with common pasture on Chorlewood for six sheep. (Briants)

There is to this tenement an entery with a chamber over, a hawle, a chamber and one roome overheade, a barne and a shippen.

The howses, two orchardes, garden and courte, A 0-10-0, V 1-3-4; the crofte above the howse, R 0-13-4, A 1-1-4, V 0-16-8; Tagewell, R 0-10-0, A 0-3-2, V 0-8-0; Withenheade, R 0-8-0, A 1-2-0, V 0-12-0; Crosselande, R 0-13-4, A [1-2]-30, V 1-2-6.

Sum A 5-2-2, V 4-2-6.

There is a parrock, some tymes parcell of Crosselande, now remayninge in the lorde's hande without graunte, A 0-0-30, V 0-3-0.

N46. Thomas Bridegood, (54), [?Alice], his wife, and Maria (17), their daughter, hold by indenture dated 7 Aug. 1604, one messuage or inhabited house with garden adjoining, rent 5s, A 0-0-6, V 1-0-0.[24]

There is to this a hawle and a chamber.

N47. William Bragg (dead) holds by indenture dated 10 Sept. 1586, one messuage or inhabited house with garden and adjoining orchard, for 99 years or lives of the said William, Katherine, his wife, and Alice, their daughter, rent 2s 8d, heriot 2s 6d, A 0-1-16, V 1-10-0.

N48. Sir John Sydenham holds Cottifoord [*sic*] meadow, for certen yeares yet to come, rent 40s; the tearme will be ended in September 1631, lease for 50 years dated 30 March 1581, A 10-0-0, V 14-0-0.

N49. Thomas Slocombe (dead), John (dead) and David Slocombe hold jointly Marrish Moore, for their lives, the deed dated 11 April 1578, suit of court twice yearly, rent 13s 4d, heriot 6s 8d, R [?1-6-0], A 5-3-30, V [?8]-5-0.

N50. [Agnes Wipple], widow, holds during her widowhood, [*lands as below*] lately held by Paul Wipple, deceased, rent 18d and one capon at Michaelmas, heriot 6s 8d.

(Robert Wipple is now tennaunt unto these premisses by copy dated [*blank*])

[Overcro]sselande, R 0-13-4, A 1-3-20, V 1-4-6; Headelande, R 0-12-0, A 1-0-0, V 0-12-0; the sheare of half an acre of meadow in Sampforde Moore, A 0-2-0, V 0-6-0.

Sum A 3-1-20, V 2-2-0.

N51. George Conibeere holds by indenture dated 1 July 1619 for himself and his assignees for 99 years or the lives of the said George, Thomas Marshe and Edmonde Marshe, rent 6s 8d and 1 capon at Michaelmas, heriot 10s, with suit to the mill.

(Robert Dashwoode of Vellowwood).

The Poundes, A 7-0-0, V 3-6-8.

[p.38] [Nettlecombe and Rowdon]: Coridon

N52. Thomas [Gore] (33) and Robert Gore (30) hold by copy dated 18 Oct. 1592 one holding in Coridon, for their lives, rent 33s 4d and 3 capons for the mill, heriot best beast.

There is to this tenement [?an entery], a hawle, a parlor, a buttery, a milkehowse, a shopp with roomes over all, a kytchen, a stable, a brewhouse with hayloftes over them, a barne and a griste myll.

The howses, orcharde, garden and courtilage, A 1-3-0, V 3-6-8; the Higher meadow next the howse, R 1-16-0, A 3-2-20, V 6-0-0; the Lower meadow, R 1-16-0, A 2-2-24, V 4-14-0; the Crofte or Parrocke, R 0-16-0, A 1-0-9, V 0-16-0;

[23] Regnal year of James left blank.

[24] Added in margin [*Edward Boone*, erased] *Simon Jacob*.

the Hill, R 0-13-4, A 4-1-22, V 2-18-4; Slade with the lane, R 1-6-8, A 2-0-30, V 2-15-0; the Myddle cloase and [?orchard], R 1-0-0, A 4-0-0, V 4-0-0; the closse called Oate Earrish, R 1-0-0, A 4-0-0, V 4-0-0; Cottiforde cloase, R [1-0-0], A 4-0-0, V 4-0-0.

Sum, besydes the griste myll, A 28-0-5, V 232-10-0.

N53. The same Thomas (33), Hugh Gore (7) and Hellena Gore (4) hold by indenture dated 13 Feb. 1617, one close called Cottiforde cloase, for 99 years or their lives, rent 6s 8d and one capon at All Saints, heriot best beast or £3 3s at the lord's choice, fine £20, R 0-15-0, A 7-1-0, V 5-8-0.

N54. John Knight (33) and Phillepa Lawrence (20) hold in reversion to [..] [?his] father, one holding [and] corn mill in Coridon, with the suit of all the tenants in Vellow, and Coridon to this mill, and the wood called timber[25] for the repair of the same corn mill, also one fulling mill, for their lives, rent 39s 4d and 5s for high rent to John S[...], knight, heriot best beast, fine £140.

The messuage, two orchardes, garden and courtilage, A 1-2-25, V 3-10-0; the Greate meadow, R 1-18-0, A 6-3-0, V 15-8-0; the Little meadow, R 1-16-0, A 1-0-0, V 1-16-0; the Myll closse, R 0-10-0, A 6-0-0, V 3-0-0; Longe cloase, R 0-8-0, A 5-0-20, V 3-2-0; Castel cloase, R 0-4-6, A 2-1-0, V 0-10-0; Newton lane cloase with two acres of coppis woode, R 0-4-0, A 3-0-20, V 0-12-6; Road cloase, R 0-6-8, A 1-0-0, V 0-6-8; Higher Stony closse with a little grove, R 0-6-89, A 2-2-0, V 0-16-8; Lower Stony Cloase, R 0-6-8, A 2-3-0, V 0-18-4; Rix cloase with a great pytt, R 0-6-8, A 4-1-0, V 1-10-0; Hill closse, R 0-8-0, A 2-3-26, V 1-4-0; Wester cloase, R 0-6-8, A 4-3-0, V 1-12-0; Green cloase, R 0-13-8, A 3-0-2, V 2-0-0; one crofte agaynst the orchard, R 0-13-4, A 2-0-0, V 1-6-8; Wood cloase, R 0-6-8, A 1-3-14, V 0-12-0.

Sum (besyde the two mills) A 50-0-27, V 32-4-10.

The littell howse with the orchard and garden betweene two waters, A 0-0-34, V 1-6-8.

This howse hath two under roomes and two over.

[p.40] [Nettlecombe and Rowdon]: Escott

N55. [George Huish] gentleman [?*and another*] hold by copy dated 21 July 1604, two holdings in Escott, lately held by Bridgitte Seller, now wife to the said George Huishe, with common pasture on Chorlewood, rent 22s 2d and 4d downe rent and 2d and two measures of barley at Michaelmas, two heriots best beasts.

(Reversion to John Huishe and William Seller by copy dated 30 Sept. 1620, for fine £100.)

There is to these two tenementes a kytchen, a hawle, a buttery, a dery, a littell howse and an entery; all theise have chamber [*sic*] overhead; a haye howse and a shippen.

The howses, orchard, garden, courte and the Forehead, A 1-0-32, V 2-10-0; the Crofte and Nurserye, R 0-10-0, A 1-0-12, V 0-10-0; the Moore, R 0-8-0, A 1-1-20, V 0-10-0; Heigher Crow crofte with the barne and the Little Moore, R 0-12-0, A 4-3-0, V 2-17-0; the Yonder Crow crofte, R 0-10-0, A 4-2-0, V 2-5-0; Higher Burrowes, R 0-6-0, A 6-0-12, V 1-16-0; the two Higher meadowes, R 1-10-0, A 4-1-12, V 6-6-8; the Lower Burrowes with a littell woode, R 0-9-0, A 7-0-0, V 3-3-0; the Parke meadowe, R 1-6-8, A 3-0-8, V 4-6-8; Wydeyeates, R 0-9-0, A [7-1]-17, V 3-6-0; Longe cloase, R 0-10-0, A 2-0-0, V 1-0-0; Lower Smaleswell, R 0-6-8, A 2-0-31, V 0-14-6; Higher Smaleswell, A 3-3-14, V 1-3-4.

Sum A 48-2-0, V 28-18-2.

N56. [Symon Hawkins] (66) and William Hawkins (33), [?his son] [hold] by copy dated 8 Oct. 1618, a half of a holding and cottage in Escott for their lives, with common pasture on Chorlewode, rent 9s 7d; the said William holds the other half by copy dated 8 Oct. 1618 for his life, rent 9s 7d, two heriots best beasts.

Reversion granted by copy to Christopher Hawkins, son of Christopher Hawkins of Stogumber.

There is to this tenement and cottage a kytchen, a hawle, a chamber within the same, with loftes over them, a shippen, a barne, a wringe howse, a coale howse.

The howses, orchard, garden and courte, A 0-3-20, V 2-6-8; Vellow meadow, R 1-6-8, A 1-0-8, V 1-8-0; the Lower Crofte, R 0-8-0, A 0-3-18, V 0-9-0; the Higher Crofte, R 0-9-0, A 1-0-6, V 0-10-0; Moore meadow, R 1-4-0, A 1-0-32, V 1-8-0; Longe meadow, R 0-16-0, A 2-2-0, V 2-0-0; Rowdon meadow, R 1-0-0, A 1-3-0, V 1-15-0; Litle Cleive, R 0-10-0, A 2-0-34, V 1-2-0; Greate Cleive, R 0-10-0, A 3-3-0, V 1-17-6; Longe closse, R 0-17-0, A 3-2-10, V 3-0-0; Longe Brome, R 0-6-8, A 5-3-4, V 1-18-0; Whitehill, R 0-8-0, A 2-3-10, V 1-2-0; New cloase, R 0-8-0, A 2-0-34, V 0-18-0; Rowdon Hill, R 0-5-0, A 7-3-4, V 2-0-0; Woodlandes, R 0-8-0, A 5-2-0, V 2-4-0; Hayles, R 0-8-0, A 1-1-14, V 0-10-4.

Sum A 44-0-34, V 34-8-6.

N57. John [Streate] (80) [holds] for life by copy dated 16 April [?1589] one holding in Escott, lately held by Joan James, widow, deceased, with common pasture on Chorlewood, rent 11s 8d and 1d and one measure of barley at Martinmas, heriot best beast.

Reversion granted to John (10) and Francis Streate (6), sons of Nicholas Streate by copy dated 31 Mar. 1619.

There is to this tenement an entery, a hawle, a parlor, a buttery, a mylkehowse, and one other litell chamber, with fower loftes over them, a bakehowse with a lofte over, a wringehowse, a barne, two stawles, a stable, a little shopp and a lofte over, and a wayne howse.

The howses, orchard, garden and courte, A 1-1-20, V 2-10-0; the littell meadow in the backsyde, R 1-6-8, A 0-1-16, V 0-10-0; Vellow meadow, this hath a waye under Westlakes howse, R 1-10-0, A 1-2-0, V 2-5-0; the Crofte, R 0-10-0, A 1-1-0, V 0-12-6; Rack cloase, R 0-6-8, A 3-0-20, V 1-0-0; the Wester cloase, R 0-6-8, A 4-3-24, V 1-12-0; Brome cloae, R 0-6-0, A 2-0-20, V 0-13-0; Myddle cloase, R 0-4-6, A 2-3-0, V 0-10-0; Home Sminye, R 0-9-0, A 4-2-8, V 2-0-0; Yonder Smyneye, R 0-9-0, A 4-0-14, V 1-16-0; the dyehowse plot and Footelande meadow, R 1-6-8, A 1-0-0, V 1-6-8; Lower Capton

25 *Lignum vocatum* timber.

Downe, R 0-10-0, A 2-3-20, V 1-8-0; Higher Capton Downe, R 0-10-0, A 1-0-9, V 0-10-6; Lower Snakeshaye, R 0-6-8, A 1-0-30, V 0-8-0; Higher Snakeshaye, R 0-6-8, A 1-1-26, V 0-9-4; Vellow Wood cloase, R 0-6-8, A 1-0-3, V 0-6-8.

Sum A 34-2-10, V 17-17-8.

N58. [Richard Allen] (20) holds for life by [?copy] dated [.] July 1604 half of one holding in Estcott, lately held by William Chapman alias Blackwell, rent 9s and 1 capon at Michaelmas, heriot best beast.

Reversion to William Allen (16).

There is a hawle and two under chambers with loftes over them, a kytchen with a lofte over, and one other dwellinge howse with a lofte over and one chamber within the hawle, a wringe house, a barne and a stawle.

The howse, orchard, garden [and courte], A 1-1-14, V 2-6-8; Greenacre, R 0-18-0, A 1-0-15, V 1-0-0; Longeacre, R 0-13-4, A 1-0-31, V 0-15-10; Snakeshaye, R 0-12-0, A 0-2-10, V 0-7-0; Vellow Woodcloase, R 0-6-0, A 2-0-0, V 0-12-0; the Hether Wayvens, R 0-6-0, A 1-3-0, V 0-10-6; the Myddle Wayvens, R 0-6-0, A 2-1-30, V 0-14-0; the Yonder Wayvens, R 0-6-0, A [2-3-0], V 0-16-6; the Higher Great Wayvens, R 0-6-8, A [7-0-0], V 2-6-8.

Sum A 20-0-20, V 9-9-2.

N59. Joan Hobbs, widow, holds during her widowhood one close of land called the Lagger [?with] a house built on it, lately part of a holding called Cookes, lately held by Thomas Hobbs, her deceased husband, rent 2s, heriot best beast.

Reversion to Henry Hobbs (50), son of the said Thomas.

(Jo. [?Hans] now in posession.)

There is to this a hawle, a chamber, with loftes over, and a little hanging howse.

The howse, orchard, garden and cloase, A 0-3-20, V 1-10-0.

N60. [Joan Cooche] (56) [holds] [?during her widowhood], rent 5s 8d, heriot best beast.

Reversion granted to John and Valentine Darke by copy dated 16 Oct. 1592.

(William [?Darke] and Mary his wife.)

There is to this cottage a hawle, a chamber and a shopp, with loftes over them, and a barne.

The howse, orchard, garden and backsyde, A 0-2-8, V 0-13-6; Vellow Woodcloase, R 0-9-0, A [1-0-0], V 0-9-0; the Over Copcrofte, R 0-8-6, A 1-0-12, V 0-9-0; the Lower Copcrofte, R 0-9-0, A 1-2-0, V 0-13-6.

Sum A 4-0-20, V 3-5-0.

N61. William Dannet (83) (dead) holds during his life a cottage, close called the Crofte, orchard and garden in Estcott, rent 2s 4d, heriot best beast.

Reversion to [?Elena] Bestley (24), wife of John Bestley (30) and John [?the same] by [?copy] dated [?4 May 1618].

(Will. Norman)[26]

There is to this cottage a hawle, a chamber, a lofte over the chamber, a [....] howse to threshe in.

The howse, orchard, garden and backsyde, A 1-3-30, V 3-0-0.

N62. George [Chi]lcott holds [..] according to the custom of the manor, rent 21s 4d and 2d and two measures of barley at Martinmas, heriot best beast, [*fine*] [?£30].

There is to this tenemente a newe barne and the dwellinge howse converted to a haye howse.

The howses, orcharde, garden and court, A 1-2-20, V 2-6-8; the little meadow under Hoare cloase, R 1-10-0, A 0-2-22, V 0-18-6; the Greate meadow, R 1-10-0, A 3-2-4, V 5-5-0; the Great Farthinges, R 0-10-0, A 3-2-20, V 1-16-8; the Myddle Farthinges, R 0-10-0, A 2-0-14, V 1-0-0; the Lower Farthinges, R 0-10-0, A 3-0-0, V 1-10-0; the Hoare cloase with the barne, R 0-10-0, A 2-3-30, V 1-9-0; the Crofte, R 0-10-0, A 1-3-6, V 0-17-6; the Two Acre cloase, R 0-10-0, A 2-0-0, V 1-0-0; Wayes Hill, R 0-8-0, A [2-3]-0, V 1-2-0; the cloase called Slade, R 0-10-0, A 2-1-12, V 1-3-0; Vellow Woodcloase with some woode, R 0-6-0, A 2-2-8, V 0-16-8; the Hither Combehayes, R 0-10-0, A 3-3-30, V 2-0-0; the Yonder Combehayes, R 0-10-0, A 3-3-6, V 1-18-0; the Mares Crofte, R 0-10-0, A 5-2-22, V 2-17-0; the Furse Horse Poole, R 0-6-8, A 4-0-0, V 1-6-8; the Yonder Horse Poole, R 0-9-0, A 2-3-0, V 1-4-0; the Horse Poole next the waye, R 0-10-0, A 4-1-8, V 2-2-0.

Sum A 53-1-2, V 30-12-8.

N63. [George Chilcott] [holds], 12th [.] [1569/70] one holding in Estcott, [?for life] according to the custom of the manor, rent 9s 6d and 1d and one measure of barley at Martinmas, heriot best beast, [*fine*] £17,

(George Chilcotts)

There is to this a hawle, a parlor and a kytchen, with loftes over them, a buttery, a bakes with a lofte over, a stable, a barne and a wayne howse.

The howses, orchard, garden, courtes, allers and mory grounde, A 1-1-0, V 2-10-0; Rownde meadowe, R 1-10-0, A 1-0-[.], V 1-13-4; Vellow meadowe, R 1-10-0, A 1-2-6, V 2-8-8; the Greate cloase, R 0-8-0, A 1-3-0, V 0-17-0; the Little Ham, R 0-8-0, A 1-3-4, V 0-14-0; the Longe Ham, R 0-9-4, A 3-0-34, V 1-10-0; [?Canntehill], R 0-8-0, A 2-0-26, V 0-17-6; Longelande, R 0-10-0, A 2-0-8, V 1-0-0; Dyke cloase, R 0-10-0, A 2-3-8, V 1-7-6; the Waye Acre, R 0-12-0, A 0-3-[?20], V 0-12-6; the Fower Acres, R 0-10-0, A 3-0-0, V 1-10-0.

Sum A 21-3-5, V 15-0-0.

N64. [George Chilcott] [holds one holding] in Estcott, by copy dated 25 Oct. 1568, for his life according to the custom of the manor, lately Cookes, rent 10s 8d and 4d for downe rent and 1d and one measure of barley at Martinmas, heriot best beast, [*fine*] £60, with common on Chorlewood.

There is to this messuage three under roomes, and two over roomes and one stable.

The howses, orchard, garden and courte, A 1-0-6, V 2-0-0; the Great meadow with a grove of three yeardes, A 2-3-8, V 4-4-

[26] Another added note is erased, *I Knowe not who hath this now.*

0; the Little meadow, R 1-16-0, A 0-1-3, V 0-10-0; Keemes Acre, R 0-14-0, A 1-0-3, V 0-14-0; Quarry closae, R 0-6-8, A 3-2-0, V 1-3-4; Longe closae, R 0-10-0, A 3-0-23, V 1-13-4; Lower Bottome closae, R 0-13-6, A 3-1-0, V 2-0-0; Higher Bottome closae, R 0-10-6, A 1-3-20, V 1-0-0; Cookes Hill, R 0-9-0, A 7-2-12, V 3-8-0; the Myddle closae, R 0-12-0, A 3-0-0, V 1-16-0; Cookes Crofte, R 0-12-0, A 1-1-0, V 0-15-4.

Sum A 30-1-2, V 19-4-0.

N65. [Michaell Streate] (66) holds by copy dated 6 April 1609 one holding in Escott, lately held by John Gibbs, deceased, rent 10s and 1 capon at Michaelmas, heriot best beast.

Reversion to John Streate, son of the said Michael.

There is to this tenement an enterye, a hawle, a parler, a mylkehowse and newe hawle, with five loftes over them, a bakehowse with a halfe lofte over, a barne and a shippen.

The howses, orcharde, gardens and courtes, A 2-0-0, V 3-0-0; the Lower Ham, R 0-9-0, A 1-3-0, V 0-15-9; the Higher Ham, R 0-10-0, A 1-1-10, V 0-13-4; the crofte above the barne, R 0-8-0, A 4-0-20, V 1-13-4; the little closae by North Bromecloase, R 0-7-0, A 1-0-14, V 0-7-4; the Brombe closae or Quarry closae, R 0-5-0, A 2-3-0, V 0-13-9; the Higher Lande, R 0-5-0, A 10-2-12, V 2-13-4; the Greate Oate closae, R 0-6-8, A 9-1-0, V 3-2-0; Lambsleaze, R 0-5-4, A 3-2-18, V 1-10-0; Rowden closae, R 0-6-8, A 7-0-0, V 2-6-8; the Furze closae, R 0-6-8, A [7-1]-6, V 2-8-4; the Longe closae, R 0-8-0, A 3-3-20, V 1-10-8; Aishbeere closae, R 0-3-4, A [3]-3-20, V 0-13-4.

Sum A 60-2-0, V 21-8-10.

[p. 49] [Nettlecombe amd Rowdon]: Rowdon

N66.[27] [Samuel Dashwood] (46) and Elizabeth (38) his wife hold by indenture dated 10 Oct. 1606, one tenement called Rowdon and one cloase called Bromballe, reserving Vellow meadow to John Trevelyan, for their lives, reversion to the executors, administrators and assignees of the said Samuell for 99 years or the lives of Robert (14) and John Dashwood (?11), sons of the said Samuell and Elizabeth, rent 36s and 2 capons at All Saints, heriot best beast.

There is to this a hawle, a parlor, a kytchen, a butterye, a mylkehowse, a littell spence within the parlor, a shopp, with chambers over every roome, a barne, a stawle, a stable, a plumpe and plumphouse.

The howses, orchardes, gardens and courtes, A 1-3-26, V 3-10-0; the Moore, R 0-13-4, A 3-2-0, V 2-6-8; the Homelande, R 0-15-0, A 4-2-20, V 3-8-0; the Greate cloase, R 0-8-0, A 18-0-0, V 7-6-0; the Higher Ham, R 0-10-0, A 7-0-25, V 3-10-0; the meadowe, R 1-6-8, A 3-2-15, V 4-15-0; the Lower Ham, R 1-4-0, A 4-2-12, V 5-10-0; the Square cloase, R 0-6-8, A 4-0-23, V 1-7-6; Bromballe, R 0-8-0, A 5-0-20, V 2-0-0; Woode cloase, R 0-6-8, A 3-2-25, V 1-4-2; the Barne cloase, R 0-8-0, A 7-2-0, V 3-0-0; the Little Hill, R 0-10-0, A 4-1-25, V 2-3-10.

Sum A 68-1-31, V 40-1-2.

N67. The same Samuell Dashwood (46) [holds] by copy dated 24 Feb.[28] one meadow called Rowdon meadow, lately held by Marie Tobarne alias Ashwell, lying in the East of a close of the said Samuel called Great cloase, for his life according to the custom of the manor, rent 2s 8d, heriot 10s, A 3-1-0, V 3-5-0.

Reversion granted by copy to Francis Dashwood, son of Samuel.

Vellow Woode

N68. Elizabeth Dashwood (72) and her assignees hold by lease dated 22 Oct. 1612, one messuage called Vellow Wood, one other meadow and a cloase of pasture, sometime held by Nicholas Date, deceased, rent 30s and one capon or 10d, heriot best beast.

Reversion to Francis Dashwood (35) for life, then to Johan Dashwood (30) for life.

There is to this messuage a hawle, a kytchen, a buttery, three chambers over them, a bakehowse and a maulte howse with one chamber over, a milkehowse, a barne, a stable and a shippen.

The howse, orchard, garden and Portelake, A 4-0-33, V 3-2-0; the great meadow called Vellow meadow, R 1-6-8, A 5-2-0, V 7-6-8; the Little meadow, R 0-18-0, A 1-2-10, V 1-6-8; the cloase called Dates Peece, R 0-8-0, A 1-3-20, V 0-15-0; the Home cloase, R 0-6-8, A 3-3-10, V 1-5-0; the South cloase, R 0-4-0, A 3-1-30, V 0-13-6; Flowers Berrye, R 0-4-0, A 4-2-0, V 0-18-0; the Myddle cloase, R 0-6-8, A 5-0-12, V 1-13-4; the Quarry cloase, R 0-5-0, A 5-3-13, V 1-8-0; the cloase called Ruddun Slade, R 0-6-8, A 10-2-30, V 3-10-0; the Barnbe cloase with some wood, R 0-6-8, A 3-3-20, V 1-5-6; the New cloase, R 0-5-0, A 4-0-0, V 1-0-0; the Knap cloase with some wood, R 0-4-0, A 3-0-20, V 0-12-0; the Wood cloase, R 0-2-0, A 4-2-0, V 0-9-0.

Sum A 62-0-18, V 35-4-8.

[p.52] [Nettlecombe and Rowdon]: Vellow

N69. John Gore holds by copy dated 18 Oct. 1592, one messuage in Vellow, for life according to the custom of the manor, rent 13s, heriot best beast, [*fine*] £50.

Reversion granted to George and Francis Gore, sons of the said John, for their lives, by copy dated 9 Oct. 1616, fine £41.

There is to this tenement a parlor, a hawle, a chamber within the hawle, a buttery, with loftes over them, a bakes, a stable, a shopp with a chamber, and a good barne.

The howses, garden and the hill, A 0-3-12, V 3-0-0; the Quarry cloase, R 0-10-0, A 3-3-24, V 1-18-0; the Greene cloase, R 0-10-0, A 1-3-6, V 0-18-0; Oldhayes, R 0-10-0, A 1-2-0, V 0-15-0; the two Broad cloases, R 0-9-0, A 4-1-4, V 1-18-0; the Little cloase, R 0-10-0, A 1-3-20, V 0-18-0.

Sum A 14-0-26, V 9-17-0.

N70. Jo[an Steavens] (52) (dead) and Robert Upcot (18), son of Thomas Upcot, hold by copy dated 6 April 1609, one

[27] This entry is in English, as are N68, 76, 78, 80, 109.

[28] Regnal year of James left blank.

holding in Vellow for their lives according to the custom of the manor, rent 16s and one capon at the Annunciation, heriot best beast, [*fine*] £42.

There is to this tenement a kytchen, a buttery, a hawle, with loftes over them, a barne and a shippen.

The howses, garden, Hayes and Broad hayes, A 0-2-6, V 2-0-0; the little orcharde, A 0-0-38, V 0-7-6; the meadow, R 1-6-8, A 2-2-0, V 3-6-8; the Crofte, R 1-0-0, A 0-2-14, V 0-10-0; the Higher closae, R 0-10-0, A 3-1-12, V 1-13-4; the Lower closae, R 0-18-0, A 3-1-10, V 3-0-0; the Higher Fellande, R 0-10-0, A 1-0-6, V 0-10-0; the Lower Fellande or Cottiford closae, R 0-12-0, A 1-0-20, V 0-13-6.

Sum A 12-2-26, V 12-1-0.

N71. John [Tucker] and Alice Toker hold by copy dated 8 April 1591, one cottage in Vellow, for their lives according to the custom of the manors, rent 8s 8d, heriot best beast.

(Alice Tucker is dead.)

There is to this tenement a kytchen, a hawle and a buttery, with loftes over all, a barne and a shippen.

The house, orchard, garden and courte, A 0-2-10, V 1-13-4; the Crofte, R 0-17-0, A 1-1-20, V 1-3-4; Vellow Beere, R 0-4-6, A 3-0-12, V 0-13-6; the Over Pytlande, R 0-13-4, A 1-2-22, V 1-2-4; the Lower Pytlande, R 0-11-0, A 2-2-5, V 1-7-6; the Bynnhaye, R 0-3-4, A 2-0-5, V 1-6-8.

Sum A 11-0-34, V 7-6-8.

N72. Henry Steavens holds by indenture dated 20 April 1602, one house called a Tannhouse with a garden, A 0-0-18, V 1-10-0, and another house called the Dyehowse and an adjoining piece of land 70ft. long and 33ft. broad, V 0-10-0, rent 4s and 1 capon or 12d at Michaelmas, heriot 4s.

Reversion granted to Christopher Clarke and Robert Upcot for 99 years or their lives for the same rent and heriot.

N73. [Mawde Manninge] (63), now wife of George Burge, and Agnes Manning, now Barne, hold by copy dated 22 Jan. 1562, one holding in Vellow for their lives according to the custom of the manor, rent 15s and for the Hopyeard 8d, heriot best beast, [*fine*] £3.

There is to this tenement a hawle with a chamber over, a drink howse within the hawle, a kytchen with a bad lofte over, a barne and a shippen.

The howses, orchard and garden, A 0-2-0, V 1-10-0; the Hopyeard over the waye, A 0-0-16, V 0-10-0; the Ham, R 1-6-8, A 1-3-0, V 2-6-8; the meadow, R 1-0-0, A 1-1-28, V 1-6-8; the Hether closae, R 0-10-0, A 1-3-30, V 1-0-0; the Yonder closae, R 0-12-0, A 2-2-20, V 1-12-0.

Sum A 8-0-6, V 8-5-4.

N74. [Agnes Barne] (60) and [?Alice] Barne (42), her daughter, hold by copy dated [?12] Mar. 1618, the west part of one cottage in Vellow and the west part of the garden and orchard of the same cottage with common pasture for three sheep on Churlewood common, for their lives, rent 20d and all other burdens, suits and services hitherto due, [*fine*] 30s, A 0-0-25, V 2-0-0.

There is to this parte of the cottage a hawle and a chamber within, with loftes over them.

N75. John Moore (45) and Edward Moore (14), son of William Moore, alias Curtise, hold the east part of the said cottage, garden and orchard, with common pasture for three sheep on the common of Churlewood by copy dated as before, for their lives according to the custom of the manor, rent 20d and all other burdens, suits and services hitherto due, [*fine*] £5, A 0-0-25, V 2-0-0.

(Lawrance Knight hath this now.)

There is to this parte of the cottaige a hawle with a chamber over and one great shopp befoorth the entry.

N76.[29] William Moore alias Courties holds by indenture dated 20 Dec. 1620, one cotage newly builded at Vellow upon the lord's waste for 99 years or the lives of himself, Edward and Johan his children, with suit to the lord's mill, rent 4s and 1 capon or 12d at Michaelmas, heriot 4s, V 0-16-0.

[p.57] [Nettlecombe and] Rowdon; [.] Churlewood

N77. Joan Westlake (80) holds during her life by indenture dated 30 Nov. 1591, one cottage at Churlewood and one acre of land lying to the east and north of the said cottage, lately held by Henry Westlake, husband of the said Joan, rent 4s, heriot best beast, with two days of work at harvest, one to mow and one to make hay.

Reversion after the death of the said Joan to George Westlake for his life, and by another indenture dated 3 Oct. 1617 for 99 years or her life to Agnes now wife of the said George, heriot best beasts or 5s at the lord's choice.

There is to this cottage a hawle, a chamber and a shopp with loftes over them.

The howse and closae above the howse, A 1-0-6, V 1-3-4; the orchard and garden below the howse, A 0-1-30, V 0-18-8.

John Street hath a waye under this howse unto his meadow called Vellow meadow.

Sum A 1-1-36, V 2-2-0.

N78. William Holle (55), Elizabeth his wife (68) (dead) and Robert (16), their son, hold by indenture dated 27 April 1597, one cottage, one orchard and garden and one closae of land and pasture adjoining to the common called Churlewoode, for their lives, the remainder to Robert for his life after William and Elizabeth, rent 2s and 1 capon at Michaelmas or 12d, heriot 6s 8d, [*fine*] £20, suit to the court twice yearly, re-entry if the rent is unpaid for a month or if they refuse their suit or if one of them do not make their dwelling upon the same, A 1-2-26, V 2-10-0.

N79. John Waye (33) holds for life by copy dated 24 June 1618, one cottage in Sweetwell, lately held by John Bestley, rent 4s, heriot best beast.

There is to this cottage a hawle with a lofte over and two other roomes, with a garden and orchard, A 0-0-45, V 2-0-0.

---

[29] Added entry in the main hand of the survey.

N80. Richard Withers (40) and his assignees hold by indenture dated 10 Nov. 1615 for the lives of himself, Grace his wife (40), and Joan (4) his daughter, one cottage called Sweetwell, one garden and orcharde and one acre of land, rent 5s and 1 capon at Michaelmas, heriot 10s, with liberty to sett trees on the banke of the river syde runninge on the west syde of the sayde howse, and uppon warning geven to scoure the mill dyke.

(George Millet)

There is to this a hawle, a chamber, with loftes over them, and a barne.

The howses, orchard and garden, A 0-0-38, V 2-0-0; the close, A 1-0-11, V 0-6-8.

Sum A 1-1-9, V 2-6-8.

N81. Radigan [Goodinough] and her assignees hold by indenture dated 1 Dec. 1618 for her life and the lives of Clement and Katherin (17) her children, one cottage in Churlewood, rent 4s and 1 capon at Michaelmas, no heriot.

There is to this a hawle, a chamber within, with a decayed lofte over the hawle.

The howse, garden and close, A 2-2-14, V 1-13-4.

N82. Thomas Torrington (46) holds by lease dated 13 Aug. 1607 for life, one howse and shopp, one close, A 0-3-0, and one other close, A 1-1-0, [*areas*] by estimation, [*total*] A 1-3-24, V 1-13-4, all sometime part of the common or waste called Churlewood, rent 3s 4d and 1 capon or 12d at Michaelmas, heriot 3s 4d.

Remainer to John Torrington (16), son of William Torrington, brother of the said Thomas, then to John Torrington (16), son of Edward Torrington.

There is to this a buttery, a shopp, a hawle and a lofte over.

N83. Elizabeth [Seller] (50) holds for life by indenture dated 18 Aug. 1606, one cottage lying on the west side of the way leading from Capton to Stogumber, one orcharde, two gardens, and all the trees growinge and standing by the watersyde adjoining near to the meadow of one Nicholas Seller, deceased, all lately held by Geffery Peppen, deceased, rent 3s 8d and one capon or 12d at Michaelmas, heriot 6s 8d, suit of court twice yearly.

Remainder to Elizabeth Seller (18), daughter of the said Nicholas, and to Johan Natcott (18), daughter of John Natcott of Stugumber, husbandman.

There is to this a hawle, a chamber, a wood howse, with a lofte over the hawle.

The howse and garden, orchard and a little plot over the water, A 0-2-8, V 2-0-0.

N84. John Naishen (39) and Dennis (43) his wife hold by indenture dated 30 Oct. 1619, one holding in Churlewood, Stogumber parish, for their lives, rent 4s 6d and 1 fat capon at Easter or 12d, heriot 6s 8d, suit of court.

Remainder to Johan Cheapman (5), daughter of William Cheapman, first husband of the said Dennis.

(Abraham Larcombe now Hyles)

There is to this a hawle, a chamber, a shopp, with loftes over them, and a stable.

The howse, garden, two orchardes with one little cloase, A 1-3-0, V 2-10-0.

N85. Johan Dawe by the name of Johan Torr holds for her life by indenture dated 10 April 1572, all that meadow, mooreland and pasture in common moore next unto Chedmarshe, Stogumber parish, R 0-18-0, A 4-3-10. V 4-6-8, lately held by John Dodridge, rent 6s 8d and one capon at Christmas or 12d, heriot 10s.

Reversion granted by indenture dated 4 Oct. 1601 to Christopher Hawkins and his assignees for 99 years or the lives of the said Christopher and William, his son, rent and heriot the same, except that the capon is due at Easter, [*fine*] £18.

N86. Christian Hodgelande (37) and Johan Leaves (30) hold by indenture dated 25 Oct. 1607, one dwelling howse at Churlewood with an orchard and garden, A 0-0-18, V 1-6-8, for their lives, rent 2s 8d, 1 capon at Michaelmas or 12d, and one day's work at harvest, heriot 8d, [*fine*] £6, suit to the court and to the mill and to inhabit and repair the premises.

There is to this a hawle and chamber, with loftes over.

N87. John Gorwood and his assignees hold by indenture dated 20 Oct. 1614, for the lives of Ellen Gorwood (30) and Walter Gorwood (16), one messuage and garden, A 0-0-32, V 2-10-0, rent 4s and 1 capon at Michaelmas or 12d, one day's work of one able man in the harvest, heriot best beast.

There is to this three roomes under and three above, and is two dwellinges.

N88. Grace Gyll (43) and John (18), her son, hold by indenture dated 2 Aug. 1598 for their lives, one newly erected cottage at Churlewood, rent 4s and 1 capon at Easter or 12d, one day's work at harvest, heriot the best goods, suit to the court twice yearly.

There is to this a hawle without lofte, a chamber within and a lofte over the same, a shopp and a prety under chamber at the sowthe ende.

The howse, garden and orchard, A 0-0-33, V 2-0-0.

N89. John Steavens holds by indenture dated 10 Oct. 1619, for 99 years or the lives of Johan, his wife, George Stephens and Agnes Stephens, their children, a woody grove at Churlewood, rent 2s 8d and 1 capon or 12d at Christmas, heriot 5s.

(Roger Ames hath this now.)

There is to this two under roomes.

The howse, garden and wood, A 2-0-0, V 2-10-0; the cloase before the doore, A 0-3-8, V 0-10-0.

Sum A 2-3-8, V 3-0-0.

There is a common upon the hill of Brondon, Nettlecombe parish, belonging to the lord and certain of his tenants, 700 acres.

There is also one other common called Churlewood, Stogumber parish, belonging to some of the tenants of Estcott and Capton, 38 acres.

[p.65a][30] Tenants in St. Decumans

N90. David Sulley: two roomes under, one roome over, a lyme kill and a lyme house, V 2-10-0.

N91. [*blank*] Palmer of Waycombe: one roome under, one roome over, V 1-10-0.

N92. [*blank*], widow: 6 little roomes, V 2-10-0.

N93. Hugh Sully: 2 roomes under and one over, V 1-5-0.

N94. [*blank*] Palmer: one roome under and one over, V 1-5-0.

[p.65] [Nettlecombe and Row]don: [?Watchet and St. Deaco]mans

N95. Nicholas Sully holds by indenture dated 20 Sept. 1610, one dwelling howse and one peece of land in Watchet in the west side of the bridge there, A 0-0-40, V 3-0-0, rent 2s 8d, and the reversion of [*N96*], rent 16d, the whole for 99 years or the lives of Conant Sullye, David Sullye and Katheren Sullye, his children, heriot 12d, [*fine*]30s, suit of court yearly at Michaelmas.

There is to Sullyes a hawle, a chamber, a shopp, with loftes over them, and a butterye; a little howse adioyninge the bridg, a shopp with a loft.

N96. Isote Wyet holds a dwellinge howse, lyme howse, lyme kyll and garden for her life by indenture dated 2 July 1610, rent 12d.

[p.66] [Nettlecombe and Rowd]on: [Walle]moore

N97. Richard [Slocombe], [Thomas] Slocombe and Andrew Slocombe hold by indenture dated 16 Aug. 1600, theise landes, meadowes and pastures called Wallemore, parish of St. Deacomans, for their lives, rent 8s during the life of Richard, thereafter [?*also*] a capon at Michaelmas, heriot 20s on the death of Thomas or Andrew if they still retain possession, suit of court.

It is bounded with a halter pathway [*bridleway*] leadinge towards Washford on the east syde, and a common meadow and Mr. Lutterell's land on the weste, the lande of Sir John Sydenham the sowthe, and the lande of the sayd Sir John, some tymes Bluntes in fee farme on the northe.

Wallmoore closase, R 0-9-0, A 5-0-0, V 2-5-0; Wallmoore meadow, R 1-0-0, A 2-1-25, V 2-8-4.

Sum A 7-1-25, V 4-13-4.

[p.67] [Nettlecombe and Rowdon]: Smithyeates

(James Hancocke and his assignees holde this.)[31]

N98. John Downe and Elizabeth Downe holde by indenture dated 17 Dec. 1572, theise landes meadowes and pastures called Smithyates, St. Deacomans parish, for 99 years or their lives, starting on the death of James Hancocke, rent 10s, heriot 6s 8d.

It is bounded with the lande of Sir John Wyndham on the easte parte, and the kynges highwaye on the weste, the lande of the sayd Sir John and parte of Mr. Lutterell's on the northe and the lande of the Rectory of St. Deacomans of the sowth parte.

The closase, R 0-12-0, A 5-0-0, V 3-0-0; the meadow, R 1-0-0, A 2-0-0, V 2-0-0.

Sum A 7-0-0, V 5-0-0.

[p.68] [Nettlecombe and Rowdo]n: [Ale]slake

N99. Ellen Byckham[32] holds by indenture dated 2 Feb. 1614, theise parcells called Aselake or Haselake, for 99 years or the lives of William and Aldread Byckham, her sons, rent 6s 8d and 1 fat capon or 12d at Michaelmas at the lord's choice.

It is bounded on the easte and on the weste with the lande of Sir John Wyndham, knight, and on the northe with the land of the sayd Sir John, saving a little parte the lande of Mr. Lutterell, and on the sowthe with the highwaye.

The closase, R 0-7-0, A 4-1-6, V 1-10-0; the meadowe, R 0-13-4, A 3-3-0, V 2-10-0.

Sum A 8-0-6, V 4-0-0.

[p.69] [Rixston] and Woodadvent: Free tenants

N100. John Wyndham, knight, holds freely one holding and 50 acres land, meadow and pasture in Rixston by knight service, rent 12d, suit of court.

N101. George Luttrell, esquire, holds freely by knight service one messuage and 50 acres land, meadow and pasture in Ryxston, rent 12d, suit of court.

N102. William Lacye, gentleman, (lately Erasmus Pyme) holds freely by knight service one holding and 50 acres land, meadow and pasture in Ryxston, rent 12d, suit of court.

N103. [*blank*] Stocker holds freely by knight service three holdings and 60 acres land, meadow and pasture in Illercombe, Dunster parish, rent 2d, suit of court.

N104. [*blank*] Stooke holds freely by knight service one holding and 12 acres land, meadow and pasture in Wollacombe, rent 4d and 1 lb. cumin, suit of court.

N105. George Churchhay (lately Wallgrove) holds freely by knight service two acres meadow and one acre wood in Huishmead and Huishwood, rent 12d, suit of court.

N106. Charles Steininges, gentleman, holds freely by knight service certain lands in Lodehuishe and Togworth, rent 6d, suit of court.

N107. Francis Wyndham, gentleman, holds freely by knight service certain lands in Sandell, rent 6d, suit of court.

N108. George Luttrell, esquire, (lately Hadley) holds freely by knight service one holding and 60 acres land, meadow and pasture in Lodehuishe, rent 12d, suit of court.

[p.71] Woodadvent

N109. Edith How holds for her life by deed indented dated 15 Oct. 1562, four holdings in Woodadvent with the herb-

[30] P. 65a is a smaller sheet of paper, now bound into the survey book. It is in a different hand, and is probably not of precisely the same date; the holdings do not correspond to any of the others listed, unless N90 is the same as N96.

[31] Apparently in the original hand, though the rental gives John Downe.

[32] *Aldered Byckham* in the rental.

age of the wood of Woodadvent (the wood and tymber thereof excepted, rent 26s 8d, heriot four best beasts.

There is to this farme a higher hawle, a buttery within the hawle, the lower hawle, two enteryes, a kytchen, five upper roomes, a mylkehowse, a chamber over the kytchen, a bakehowse, two barnes, a stable, a stawle, a racke howse, a wayne howse and a wringehowse.

(There is paid every yeare to Sir John Strangewayes, knight, 2s 6d, for suite to the Hundred Court of Williton 12d, and to Mr. Fulford for the chiefe rent of Haine Lands 4d.)

The howse, garden, hopyeard and courte, A 1-1-14, V 2-0-0; the Little Pyt Parke, R 0-6-8, A 2-0-24, V 0-14-4; the Great Pyt Parke, R 0-6-8, A 2-3-0, V 0-18-4; Wood meadow, R 1-6-8, A 0-3-26, V 1-2-0; the Lower Hill, R 0-2-6, A 54-3-0, V 6-16-0; Keymey Crofte, R 0-2-0, A 1-1-24, V 0-2-6; the North Hill, R 0-2-6, A 35-3-7, V 4-7-6; the Myddle Hill, R 0-2-6, A 17-0-9, V 2-2-6; New cloase, R 0-6-8, A 13-0-28, V 4-7-0; Yonder Hayne Landes, R 0-5-0, A 21-0-0, V 5-5-0; Hether Haynelande and Longecrofte, R 0-10-0, A 20-1-24, V 10-0-0; Hayne meadow, R 1-10-0, A 2-2-27, V 3-18-0; the meadow and hopyeard above the howse, R 1-0-0, A 1-0-21, V 1-1-0; the two croftes above the howse, Cherry plott and garden, R 0-10-0, A 2-1-22, V 1-3-0; The combe with the wood, R 0-5-0, A 22-1-8, V 5-10-0; But Parke, R 0-6-8, A 5-2-27, V 1-17-0; Little Syson, R 0-6-8, A 5-3-32, V 1-18-0; Great Syson, R 0-5-0, A 10-2-6, V 2-12-6; Venn parke with the grove, R 0-6-8, A 3-3-0, V 1-5-0; Bremble parke, R 0-6-8, A 2-2-29, V 0-17-8; Cradle cloase, R 0-6-8, A 12-2-4, V 4-3-4; Orchard and hopyeard above the howse, R 0-10-0, A 1-3-10, V 0-18-0; the Lower meadow, R 1-6-8, A 2-1-22, V 3-0-0; the Lyftinge, R 0-6-8, A 3-0-4, V 1-0-0; Aishyeate, R 0-13-4, A 1-1-16, V 0-18-0; Starkers Leaze, R 0-6-8, A 4-3-23, V 1-12-0; the Northfeilde, R 0-6-0, A 4-0-30, V 1-4-0; Brombecloase, or Pytlande, R 0-3-4, A 10-3-22, V 1-15-6; the Woode, R 0-1-0, A 10-3-0, V 0-10-0; Quarry cloase and wood, R 0-3-4, A 9-0-0, V 1-10-0.

Sum A 287-3-1, V 74-2-2.

N110. John Woolkott (40) holds by copy dated 22 Nov. 1602, two cottages in Woodadvent lately held by Joan Woolcott, his mother, for his life according to the custom of the manor, rent 7s 4d, heriot two best beasts, [*fine*] £54.

Reversion granted by indenture dated [*blank*] to the said John, his executors and assignees for 99 years or the lives of John and Conand Woollcot, his sons, same rent, heriot two best beasts or £4 at the lord's choice, suit to the lord's mill.

There is to this a hawle, a parlor, a milkehowse, a buttery, a lower chamber, three upper roomes, a barne, a stable and a shippen.

The howses, croftes, orchard, garden and courte, A 1-2-28, V 1-10-0; Butterwell, R 0-5-0, A 3-2-30, V 0-16-8; Hill cloase bettered with lyme, R 0-10-0, A 10-1-29, V 5-3-4;

Crosse cloase, R 0-3-4, A 1-1-0, V 0-4-0; the Cleisse, R 0-3-4, A 2-2-15, V 0-8-6; the Myddle cloase, R 0-4-0, A 2-2-5, V 0-10-0; the Lower cloase, R 0-10-0, A 3-1-0, V 1-12-0; the Weste feilde, R 0-6-8, A 3-2-0, V 1-3-4; Longe Acre cloase, R 0-10-0, A 0-3-30, V 0-9-0; Somerleaze, R 0-6-8, A 3-0-25, V 1-1-0; Earridge cloase, R 0-3-4, A 3-2-26, V 0-12-0.

Sum A 26-2-18, V 13-9-10.

N111. Robert Martyne (68) in the right of Elizabeth (58) his wife, holds by copy dated 20 Oct. 1581 one cottage called Hayne, lately held by Henry Harforde, for life according to the custom of the manor, rent 4s 10d, heriot best beast, [*fine*] £10.

Reversion granted to the said Robert Martine by copy dated 26 Oct. 1587, to hold for life, rent as before and 4d to John Windham, knight for suit of court.

The howse, orchard, garden and the cloase wherein the howse standeth, A 4-0-6, V 2-0-0; the meadow, R 1-10-0, A 2-1-10, V 3-8-4; the Waterleates, R 0-8-0, A 4-0-20, V 1-13-4;

Sum A 10-1-36, V 7-1-8.

[P. 89][33] **N112**. The particulars of the tenement lately in the occupacion of Christopher Knight, deceased.

The messuage, two orchards, garden and courtilage, A 1-2-25, V 4-0-0; The Great meadow, A 6-0-0, V 15-0-0; the Little meadow, A 1-0-0, V 2-0-0; the Mill cloase, A 6-0-0, V 3-10-0; Long close with a grove, A 5-0-20, V 3-6-0; Castle cloase, A 2-1-0, V 1-10-0; Newton Lane close with 2 acres of coppice wood, A 3-0-20, V 1-6-8; Road close, A 1-0-0, V 0-15-0; Higher Stony close with a little grove, A 2-2-0, V 1-10-0; Lower Stony close, A 2-3-0, V 1-10-0; Rix close with a great pitt, A 4-1-0, V 2-10-0; Hill close, A 2-3-26, V [1]-12-6; Wester Close, A 4-3-0, V 3-2-0; one croft against the orchard, A 2-0-0, V 1-15-0; Wood close, A 1-3-[14], V 2-0-0.

Sum A 50-0-27, V 47-19-2.

The ancient yearely rent to be reserved is 39s 4d.

(the old stickes is of opinion yt is worth but £45 10s)

There is a little house with the orchard and garden betweene two waters, which belongs to the mills and amount to 34 perches, worth per annum £2.

[33] Pp. 75-83 contain summary tables: Barley rents for Capton and Escott (75); Capton rents and work days due (76-7); summary of names, areas, values and rents (79-83). These are followed by: a rental for Midsummer 1629 (84-6, in another hand), with some additions to Lady Day 1631; blank (87-8). The final holding (p.89) is in a hand not otherwise used in the survey, on a loose slip of paper.

CHAPTER 12

Somerset Crown Estates

Somerset Crown Estates: 1606-8 (NP, WE, EB, K, WP) *see Location Map*
The surveys of Crown estates in Somerset do not provide the detailed information of the Nettlecombe survey, but they do extend our evidence over the whole county. Geographically, they are well scattered, in areas of markedly different farming economies[1] with, in the case of Norton St. Philip, a view of a community with a social structure quite different from most other West Country villages. All the tenements described in detail were copyhold, apart from eight freeholdings at West Pennard. As explained in Chapter 6, these surveys are presented in tabular form (Tables 23-27, pp. 172-183).

Norton St. Philip (Table 23)
Norton St. Philip lies on the eastern edge of Somerset, and its people combined small-scale farming (particularly dairying) with home-based industry, principally weaving. The economic mixture produced a distinctive pattern of holdings. The normal grouping of farm sizes, clustering about twenty to forty acres, was virtually absent, while the cottage holdings with almost no land were replaced by small-holdings ranging from one to eight acres. The one large farm contained almost as much land as the remaining holdings combined.

Within the smaller holdings (up to eight acres), the pattern of housing (Table 21) was very uneven; even this small range shows some differentiation, with one to three-bay houses concentrated on the smallest holdings. Overall, four bays were commonest, but three and five bays were nearly as frequent, while only two houses each had one or two bays. A significant minority (nine houses) had kitchens, and there was also an outhouse and a backhouse. The eight shops (workshops), the tanhouse, and a wool house reflect the craft economy of the village directly, while the one 'white house' was probably a detached dairy or cheese-storage room. Four abnormally large houses contained nine to twelve bays, and these must have been in multiple occupancy, resembling the holdings with additional two or three-bay cottages on them (NP15, NP19, NP30, NP47, NP48).

The economies of the larger holdings (eleven to thirty-five acres; Table 22) must have come closer to those of normal farms, though it is noticeable that the first four (NP51-54) still lacked any farm buildings. Most had fairly large houses (four to nine bays), though one had only two bays. The magnificent George Inn, which still survives, [2] had the largest domestic accommodation with twenty bays in the main house and three in the kitchen. The building is arranged round a courtyard, now with a nine-bay front range; the side and rear ranges are presumably represented by the remaining fourteen bays in 1606. The George's nineteen acres were no doubt used for pasturing visitors' horses and those available to be hired.

Finally, Geoffrey Flower (NP60) held 393 acres, ten times larger than any one else in the manor. His house can be identified as Norton Grange (now Manor Farm, G.R. ST773559),[3] though only fragments of the seventeenth-century buildings remain.[4] In 1608, its main building was not particularly sizeable, with only eight bays which must have included a kitchen. It also contained a gatehouse and an enormous brewhouse, as well as ranges of farm buildings. It clearly corresponded much more to a manorial demesne or the home farm of a resident squire than to a normal copyhold.

Wellington (Table 24)
The large village of Wellington lies in the west of the county, and like Norton St. Philip, was a centre of the woollen trade. However, at Wellington, the borough itself was separate from its rural surroundings (Wellington manor). Although both fell into Crown hands on the attainder of the Duke of Somerset (1549),

Table 21: Dimensions of Somerset cottages (bays)

Place	Acres	Bays 1	2	3	4	5	6	7	8	9	10	11	12
Norton St. Philip	1–1¾	2	2	5	5	2							
	2–3¾			4	4	4	1	1	1				
	4–8¼			2	6	4	3		1	1		1	
Wellington	0–1¾		7	2	1								
	3–9½			2	6								
Kingsbury	0–2		8	8	5								
	3¼–9½		2	14	5	6	2	1					
East Brent	0–2½	1	6	2	2	1							
	5¾–7¼			1									
West Pennard	4–8½		2	3		1							

Table 22: Dimensions of Somerset farmhouses (bays)

Place	Acres	Bays 1	2	3	4	5	6	7	8	9	10	11	13	14	18	23
Norton St. Philip	11–35		1			1	2	2		1						1
Wellington	12–35		2	8	3	1							1			
Kingsbury	11½–28½			1	4	9	7	3	2							
	30½–64				2	2	1	2	1	1	1	1			1	
East Brent	11–29½	1	6	19	7	4	1	1								
	30½–59½			3	16	3	3	4								
W. Pennard	11–29½		2	17	11	1	2									
	30–121			5	7	4	4	2	1	2	1			1		

the 1607 survey only covers the manor;[5] it therefore describes a rural estate with a typical distribution of holdings, although the farm buildings had unusual features (see below). The houses varied remarkably little in relation to the holding size (Tables 21-22). The smallest holdings (zero to two acres) were dominated by two-bay houses (with one four-bay and two three-bay houses); the remainder ranged from four of two bays to fourteen of three and three of four bays. The only larger houses, one each of five and thirteen bays, were on holdings with respectively fourteen and thirty-one acres. Also, they included virtually no subsidiary buildings, no detached kitchens and only two bakehouses.

Farm Buildings at Norton St. Philip and Wellington

Despite their diverse economies, the agricultural evidence for these two manors can be treated together, because of its sparsity. At Norton St. Philip, so few holdings had any appreciable amount of land that the evidence for agriculture hardly exists. Of the fifty holdings with less than ten acres, eight had barns, whose main use was perhaps for storing fodder. Rather more had stables (thirteen in all), which are more understandable in the context of the need to transport finished goods.

The four larger farms all had barns, but included only one cow stall and a couple of stables. Only Geoffrey Flower's almost manorial tenancy had a full set of buildings, with a large barn of eight bays, a smaller one of five bays, a three-bay stable and a six bay cow stall.

Wellington showed the same lack of farm buildings as Norton St. Philip. Only about half the eight to thirty-five acre holdings even had barns (eleven in all), with in addition no more than a couple of stables, a couple of hayhouses and three stalls. This pattern might imply a concentration on stock fattening, but the large number of holdings without any buildings at all should be remembered. Undoubtedly, these tenants lived in the borough and had their farmsteads there as well, and it may well be that some residents in the manor (whose houses are surveyed) also had additional farm buildings in the borough.

East Brent, Kingsbury, and West Pennard (Tables 25-7)

The three remaining Crown estates in Somerset may have shared to some extent in the county-wide prosperity of the cloth industry. They were, however, particularly well-placed for pastoral farming, and this was their major activity. Each lay adjacent to one of Somerset's marshes, comparable to though smaller than the fens of eastern England.[6] Kingsbury Episcopi was beside Muchelney-Thorney Moor at the confluence of the Parrett and Isle, West Pennard adjoined Queen's Sedgemoor, while East Brent was the wettest, on a hill in the enormous coastal marshes of the River Axe. All these marshes carried vast herds of cattle in summer and yielded good hay as well; in winter, they often stood under water.[7]

The farms on the manors were of similar sizes, though Kingsbury had a group of tenants holding five to ten acres, as well as those with farms of twenty to sixty acres (see Fig. 1K). Several features indicate that the Kingsbury economy had a distinctive character. A majority of the houses on the smallest holdings (zero to two acres) had three and four bays, in contrast to the dominance of two-bay houses at East Brent (Table 22). The houses on the small-holdings at West Pennard and East Brent were also small, with two or three bays each, while at Kingsbury several had five to seven bays. It is clear that economic prosperity at Kingsbury meant that both small-holdings and cottage plots could provide a good enough living to support a substantial house. This prosperity can be attributed to the combination of two factors. Home-based industry was probably important, as at Norton St. Philip. Secondly, extra land was available, partly as parcels to rent (Table 26), and partly as common pasture on the marshes. These extra resources multiplied the productivity and profit of a small village holding.

The prosperity of Kingsbury also influenced the larger holdings, whose houses were significantly larger than at either West Pennard or East Brent (Table 22). All three manors show a general relationship between holding size and house size. Except at Kingsbury, farms of less than thirty acres typically had three bays, with four bays most likely on bigger holdings. However, even small Kingsbury farms most often had five bays, and the larger farms reveal a remarkably even size distribution from three to eighteen bays.

Separate kitchens were uncommon on all three manors (seven in all), but West Pennard included six bakehouses, with two more at Kingsbury. West Pennard also had six *back*houses. None were on the same farms as bakehouses, and they probably functioned as bakehouses or brewhouses, combined with storage of domestic or farm gear.[8] West Pennard also contained five shelf-houses; this term is unrecorded elsewhere, but presumably indicates a building containing shelves. What they stored is not stated, though cheese seems the only obvious candidate. They apparently had a farm rather than domestic context, as one was in the same building as a wainhouse. Storehouses were more common (six, seven and nine on the three manors), and were probably for farm tools, frequently being part of the barn; one only (at East Brent) was in the house. The three outhouses and one cross-house were perhaps in more domestic use, for supplementary storage.

Three houses at East Brent and possibly one at West Pennard included a cow house in the main building. Apart from reinforcing the impression of relatively small houses on these manors, they must represent a residual long-house tradition. One very odd building at Kingsbury included several functions, combining kitchen, oxhouse and dovecote, while what must have been a detached kitchen on the largest holding at West Pennard (WP68) contained a dovehouse.

By comparison with the Nettlecombe survey, we can suggest the rooms most likely to be found in the smaller houses. The two-bay houses are most obvious, and almost certainly contained simply a hall and a chamber, perhaps with one or more lofts; the few one-bay houses must have had a loft-chamber over their living room (cf. N91, 94). Beyond this, Nettlecombe shows the array of possibilities; parlours and kitchens were about equally common in the three to four room plans, and so we might expect hall and chamber with either parlour or kitchen (if the latter was not a detached building). A few houses would presumably have had butteries and milkhouses as well. In the larger houses, the service rooms would no doubt be multiplied, as in N6, 7 and 34 (p. 147).

The Farm Buildings of East Brent, Kingsbury and West Pennard

Because farmers on all three manors were principally engaged in fattening cattle and (in Kingsbury and West

Pennard) maintaining large dairy herds, the principal farm buildings were barns for storing fodder (sometimes overflowing into separate hayhouses) and stalls and stables for wintering stock. On all three estates, barns were frequently combined with animal-housing into a single range of farm buildings, thereby contributing to the compact appearance of these farmsteads. Both stables and stalls were less common than on the Devon estates, indicating a clear differentiation from their mixed economies. The surveys also faithfully record significant differences among the three fenland localities and the microeconomies they represent.

At first glance, Kingsbury exhibits the typically homogeneous characteristics of a pastoral community. Most of its farmsteads, large and small alike, had a barn and a stall; many nothing more. But on closer inspection, distinctions appear that hint at a greater range of opportunities enjoyed by the holders of the larger properties on this manor, as well as at the prosperity enjoyed by smallholders. A close correlation exists between the acreage of land farmed, the number of animals it could support, and the size of buildings needed for their shelter and upkeep. The average size of barns and stalls increased with acreage (from 3.1 bays on farms up to eight acres to 5.3 bays on those above twenty acres). The implications are obvious. The more land a man had use of, the more hay he could cut and the more cows he could over-winter. A concentration of hay and straw houses on farmsteads of eight to twenty acres probably reflects an economy of scale; it cost a small-scale farmer less to build a simple, separate structure than to enlarge his barn. Where a man had more than about twenty acres, he had land enough to diversify into arable agriculture on a scale that not only covered the added cost of building a stable for the plough team and a wainhouse for the farm cart, but also a five, six, or seven-bay barn for his crops and fodder, thus eliminating the need for an extra hayhouse. There is a hint that some of the largest farms chose the alternative either of large-scale grazing, needing only barns, or of summer fattening, when even these could be dispensed with.

Thus, the detailed analysis of the 1608 survey shows Kingsbury to have had a complex agricultural economy with a social order to match. Small farmers were chiefly pastoralists pure and simple. Their wealthier neighbours were graziers too, but supplemented and enhanced their incomes by planting barley, beans, wheat and oats. There can be little doubt that these arable farmers employed the cottagers who otherwise would have been workless had Kingsbury been a strictly pastoral community.

The survey of West Pennard must be read very closely to decipher from its pot-pourri of farm buildings a pattern of agricultural activities. On the face of it and despite its somewhat larger tracts of land, the village looks less prosperous than Kingsbury. Not only were the houses generally smaller, but many farms made do with only a barn. Nor was there any consistency among those with more buildings; barns were coupled with stables, stalls, cowhouses, hay and straw houses, storerooms and shelfhouses in a way that seems to defy reason. But not altogether. Some explanations can be plausibly guessed at and others discerned by carefully scrutinising the survey.

The smallest farms (those of four to fourteen acres) frequently needed only one structure for agricultural purposes—a barn most often, but it could also be a stable, a stall, or a storeroom. Here and on larger properties with barns alone, the scale of operations may have been so reduced (a few milk cows for instance) or so specialised (horse breeding) that a single, multipurpose structure met a farmer's requirements for grain and fodder storage, animal housing, and even work and storage space for by-employments. This suggestion finds some apparent corroboration in a group of slightly larger farms (up to twenty-one acres) where a storeroom, attached to the barn, enlarged the building by a bay or two for general purposes. Indeed, by-employments—cheese-making, fowling and eel fishing, basketry and withy cutting—may have figured importantly in the economy of this manor, thereby explaining the numerous storerooms, shelfhouses, workhouses, sheds and lean-to's. At the same time, such enigmatic buildings contribute to the difficulty we have in deciphering the economy of West Pennard by looking round its farmyards.

One interpretation consistent with the survey information is that stock was fattened on the lush summer pastures but driven to market before the winter floods obliged farmers to provide shelter and feed for the animals. Adequate supplies of hay and bedding straw for the very early spring could be stored in barns, the animals themselves needing no buildings at all.

This possibility is one way to interpret the otherwise curious fact that six hayhouses (WP8, 27, 32, 55, 63) and three strawhouses (WP52, 57, 62) were present on farms with barns, but they had no stalling whatsoever for animals. Ranching, to call it by its modern name, was not a small farmer's shortcut to stock-raising, as might be supposed, for the practice occurred most commonly on holdings larger than twenty acres.

This acreage was also about the smallest that could support dairy cattle and other wintered stock. Cowhouses, stalls, and stables—including one of each incorporated into the three longhouses in the village (WP7 and probably WP24, 59)—appear with some regularity on farmsteads with upwards of eighteen to twenty-two acres. So too the special buildings needed for arable farming—cart sheds and stables, although whether the latter housed draught horses or animals intended for market cannot be decided. Nor is it helpful to observe that stables and stalls were mutually exclusive. All in all, the farmers of West Pennard may have put together better livings than their dearth of farm buildings suggests.

The marshy grasslands surrounding the hamlets of East Brent offered some of the same varied economic opportunities as the sedge moors near West Pennard. Grazing and cow keeping were the mainstays here, supplemented by various by-employments requiring the use of 'stores' usually attached to barns. Some crops may have been cultivated on the larger farms, but the small number of wainhouses (only one [EB40] occurring on a farm with housing for draught animals) suggests that stables accommodated riding horses or breeding stock as often as plough teams. Barns, while the most common building, were not over-large (two to three bays, sometimes four and twice five when combined with a stall or stable). All the more surprising then that no one on the manor owned a hayhouse. The explanation is to be found in the most peculiar feature of the survey—thirteen middle-size to large farms, none of which had any farm buildings at all. These were true ranches where large herds of steers grazed the summer marshlands and then were driven to stockyards in Bristol before the winter flood-waters inundated the pastures. Twelve farmers who owned small barns and nothing else were doubtless ranchers too, but, tending to have somewhat smaller holdings, they may have had to engage in subsistence arable farming and therefore needed barns to store their crops.

Some cattle were over-wintered in the structures variously called (with apparent differentiation) stalls, oxhouses, oxstalls and 'bovite'. Most were attached to barns and three 'bovite' (EB61, 73, 80) were integrated into longhouses. The absence of the term 'cowhouse' suggests that dairy cattle were uncommon in East Brent, larger herds of them at least. A few milk cows could no doubt share a stall with the oxen.

[1] Ag. Hist. IV, 71-80.

[2] E. H. D. Williams, J. and J. Penoyre, 'The George Inn, Norton St Philip', *Archaeol. J.*, 144 (1987), 317-327.

[3] N. L. Flower, 'The Flower Family of Somerset', *Somerset and Dorset Notes & Queries*, 29 (1973), 277-288.

[4] Information from E. H. D. Williams.

[5] The manor was sold by the Crown in 1624-5 (John Collinson, *History of Somerset* (Bath, 1791), II, 481), the borough at some date in the seventeenth century, presumably before 1607.

[6] Ag. Hist. IV, 78.

[7] The West Pennard survey is unique in describing in detail the freeholdings (Ms. nos. 1-8); they show no obvious differences from the other holdings. The East Brent survey is subdivided into Burton, Singhampton, Sislington and East Brent itself. All these are hamlets in the parish of East Brent, with no differences in character between them.

[8] They are clearly distinct from bakehouses in the text. Their use has been established by M. W. Barley from inventory evidence, 'Glossary of names for rooms in houses of the sixteenth and seventeenth centuries', in I. L. Foster and L. Alcock, eds., *Culture and Environment* (London, 1963), 479-501.

Table 23: Norton St. Philip: Dimensions of surveyed buildings (bays)

Ref. Number	Ms. Number	Acres	House	Kitchen	Other domestic rooms/buildings	Shop	Barn	Stable	Other	Notes
NP1	24	0	•							small piece of ground with a house on it (associated with NP25 and 53)
NP2	40a	0	•							former tan-house of NP48
NP3	32	1¼	2							
NP4	17	1⅜	3							
NP5	18	1⅜	3							ruinous
NP6	33	1⅜	=	2		=				house and shop(2)
NP7	35	1⅜	3							
NP8	37	1⅜	1							
NP9	43	1⅜	4							
NP10	50	1⅜	3					1		
NP11	59	1⅜	4							in good repair
NP12	26	1½	5							house 5 'feldas'
NP13	47	1½	3							
NP14	52	1½	5							
NP15	57	1½	4					•		
NP16	54	1⅝	2							
NP17	34	1¾	4		little house					
NP18	36	1¾	1							
NP19	45	2	3	2				1		
NP20	10	2⅜	3	2		•				
NP21	56	2½	3		little house(3)	•	3			
NP22	46	2⅝	4							
NP23	3	2¾	4							in good repair
NP24	48	2¾	3							
NP25	23	3⅛	5							associated with NP1 and 53
NP26	21	3¼	=		chambers(=)*	=		=		* shop, hall, chamber, 2 other chambers, stable, in all 5 bays
NP27	27	3⅜	4							house 4 'fildas'
NP28	38	3⅜	6			•				
NP29	41	3⅜	4		outhouse					
NP30	20	3½	11		2nd house(3)					
NP31	39	3½	5	2						
NP32	51	3⅝	4					2		

Table 23 *continued*

Ref. Number	Ms. Number	Acres	House	Kitchen	Other domestic rooms/buildings	Shop	Barn	Stable	Other	Notes
NP33	53	3¾	3							
NP34	30	4	6				3			barn 3 'feld'
NP35	7	4⅛	4					2		
NP36	42	4¼	4	1						
NP37	49	4¼	3							
NP38	9	5⅛	5				2	*		* two stables of 2 bays [together?]
NP39	11	5½	4	•						well-built and repaired
NP40	12	5½	4			•				
NP41	13	5½	5				3			
NP42	31	5½	10				3			
NP43	25	5¾	4							
NP44	29	5¾	6							
NP45	14	6¼	12					2		ruinous fold, 2 bays
NP46	58	6¼	6	3	little house(3)	4		3		
NP47	15	6½	6					1		
NP48	40	6⅜	4	1	cottage(=)	3	=		tanhouse(3)	barn + cottage(3)
NP49	4	7	3	1	backhouse(2) cottage(2)		2	2		
NP50	62	7	3					2	water-mill	
NP51	61	8	3	1			3	2		
NP52	28	11	7							house 7 'feldas'
NP53	22	16	10							associated with NP25 and NP1
NP54	5	16	2							
NP55	2	17	•							
NP56	16	19	20	3				5		Hospicium called the George
NP57	44	19	4	=	white-house(=)	*	3	2		kitchen + whitehouse [dairy] under one roof(2); * woolhouse(2)
NP58	8	25	6				6			
NP59	55	26	9				•	2	cowstall(4)	
NP60	6	35	7				3			well-built and repaired
NP61	60	385	8		brewhouse(6) gatehouse(4)		8+5*	3	cowstall(6)	* upper and lower barns(8, 5)

Note: Holdings 1 (80ac.) and 19(5 ac.) had no buildings, and are omitted.

Table 24: Wellington: Dimensions of surveyed buildings (bays)

Ref. Number	Ms. Number	Acres	House	Bake-house	Barn	Stable	Stall	Hay House	Other Farm Buildings	Notes
WE1	120	1/8	2							
WE2	115	1/4	4	2						
WE3	6	1/2	2							
WE4	60	1/2	2							
WE5	62	1/2	2							
WE6	65	3/4	3							
WE7	61	1	2							
WE8	88	1	2							
WE9	12	1 1/2	3							
WE10	130	1 3/4	2							
WE11	112	2								a corn mill
WE12	42	3	3							
WE13	23	4 1/2	3							
WE14	133	5	3*							* new built
WE15	104	7	2							
WE16	2	8	3		2					
WE17	10	8 1/4			2					no house
WE18	129	8 1/4	3				*			* stall and other buildings
WE19	83	8 1/2	2							
WE20	15	9 1/2	3*			=	=			* house(3) and adjoining bays(2); stable + stall (4)
WE21	14	12	4		2					
WE22	31	12	4							
WE23	13	14	5		4					
WE24	7	15	3		3					
WE25	71	16	2							
WE26	101	21	3							
WE27	72	21	3							
WE28	69	23	3		2	•				
WE29	9	24	3		3			2		
WE30	4	26	3		=				store (=)	barn + store (3)
WE31	21	26	•							
WE32	8	30	2							
WE33	3	31	3	1	2					
WE34	11	32	4	3	3		=	=		hayhouse + oxstall (4)
WE35	142	33	3							
WE36	89	35	3		3					

Notes: Holdings WE60–62 were held by the same tenant, but as the individual sets of buildings are listed, they have been shown separately. Numerous holdings with no buildings have not been included in the table: (Ms. numbers with acreages in parentheses) 1(7), 16–20 (1, 14, 1, 32, 4), 22(9), 24–30 (8, 22, 5, 4, 13, 9, 1), 32–41 (15, 6, 14, 10, 4, 11 1/4, 1, 14, 6, 31), 70 (78), 73–82 (30, 11, 1½, 3, 1, 3, 8, 4, 1½, 17), 84–87 (12, 1, 15, 2), 90–97 (4, 3, 47, 1, 48, 16, 7, 3), 116–8 (18, 8, 4), 121–128 (7, 9, 10, 5, 20, 10, 10, 32), 131–2 (8, 8), 134–141 (4, 36, 10, 16, 8, 8, 10, 12), 143 (13)

Table 25: East Brent: Dimensions of surveyed buildings (bays)

Ref. Number	Ms. Number	Acres	House	Other Rooms & Domestic Buildings	Barn	Stable	Ox-Stall(S) *Bovite*(B) Stall(St)	Wain House	Store	Notes
EB1	67	0		shop						
EB2	68	0		shop						
EB3	40	0	2							
EB4	96	0	*	outhouse(4)						* cottage (4)
EB5	108	0	5							'The Church House'
EB6	61	1/4	4							
EB7	97	1/4	2							
EB8	98	1/4	2							
EB9	99	1/4	2							
EB10	95	3/4	1							
EB11	55	1	3							
EB12	111	1	4							
EB13	42	1 1/2	2							
EB14	8	2 1/4	3							
EB15	29	2 1/2	2							
EB16	105–7	4	=	shop(=); shop	7					house + shop(2)
EB17	2	5 3/4	•		•				•	
EB18	109	7	•		=		=St			barn + stall; also holds 28 ac. with a stall (1) (Ms.20,104). House 'well and beautifully built'
EB19	28	7 1/4	3							
EB20	81	11	3							
EB21	94	11	3							
EB22	101	12	4		=		=S			barn + oxstall(2)
EB23	86	13	1							
EB24	84	14	5							
EB25	21	15	3		•	•				
EB26	78	16	3							
EB27	93	17	3	outhouse(1)						
EB28	49	18	4							
EB29	10	18	2							
EB30	82	19	3		2					
EB31	80	19	3		2					
EB32	13	19	2		3					
EB33	87	20	3		2					
EB34	100	20	2				1St			
EB35	24	21	2							
EB36	38	21	5		=	=				barn + stable (5)
EB37	76	21	5					2		also holds 21 ac.(Ms.77)
EB38	50	21	3		=		=B			barn + *bovite*(2)
EB39	46	21	3		=		=St			barn + stall (4)
EB40	22	21	7		•	•		•		
EB41	15	22	3		=				=	barn + store (2)
EB42	48	23	4							
EB43	74	23	2	kitchen (1)	2					
EB44	92	23	3		=		=St			barn + stall (3)
EB45	19	23	3							
EB46	60	24	4		=		=B	2		barn + *bovite*(4)

Table 25 *continued*

Ref. Number	Ms. Number	Acres	House	Other Rooms & Domestic Buildings	Barn	Stable	Ox-Stall(S) *Bovite*(B) Stall(St)	Wain House	Store	Notes
EB47	64	24	3(?)		=			=S		barn + oxstall (3)
EB48	27	24	2			2				
EB49	30	24	5							
EB50	37	24	4		2					
EB51	45	24	3							
EB52	88	24	6							
EB53	44	26	•		•		•S			
EB54	90	26	3		2					
EB55	18	26	2							
EB56	66	26	4		=		=S			barn + oxstall (2)
EB57	79	27	3		=	=				barn + stable (5)
EB58	16	27	4		=				=	barn + store (2)
EB59	35	27	3							
EB60	17	29	2		=				=	barn + store (3)
EB61	52	30	=				=B			house + *bovite*(5)
EB62	63	31	7		2					
EB63	23	32	4		2		2S			
EB64	34	32	4		2					
EB65	58	33	4		4					
EB66	56	33	4		=	2	=B			barn + *bovite*(4)
EB67	85	34	7							
EB68	25	34	6		2		3S+2*			* outstall (2)
EB69	39	34	4		=	=				barn + stable (3)
EB70	91	35	3		=	=				barn + stable (2)
EB71	89	36	4		2					
EB72	26	37	4		2					
EB73	51	37	=		=		=B			house + barn + *bovite*(5)
EB74	33	37	4		=	=				barn + stable (2)
EB75	83	38	4							
EB76	59	41	4		=		=B			barn + *bovite*(4)
EB77	41	42	4		•	•	*			* ox house
EB78	1	43	•							
EB79	75	45	5		=	=	2St			
EB80	57	45	=		=		=B	4		house + barn + *bovite*(7)
EB81	36	48	7							
EB82	31	49	6		=	=				barn + stable (4)
EB83	53	49	3		=		=St			barn + stall (4)
EB84	12	50	3		=				=	barn + store (3)
EB85	11	50	4		2				2	
EB86	54	50	4		=		=B			barn + *bovite*
EB87	7	51	4		=		=St			barn + stall (3)
EB88	73	54	4		3					
EB89	9	55	=						=	house + store (5)
EB90	65	57	4		3					
EB91	32	60	6		=	=				barn + stable (4)

Notes: Holdings Ms.1–8 and 44 lay in East Brent itself, Ms.9–43 in Burton, Ms.45–73 in Singhampton, Ms.74–111 in Sislington. Holdings with no buildings are omitted (acreages in parentheses): Ms.3 (5), 4 (30), 5 (30), 6 (8), 14 (4), 20 (26), 43 (10), 47 (27), 62 (10), 69–72 (5, 5, 5, 12), 77 (10), 102–104, (6, 6, 2), 110 (2).

Table 26: Kingsbury, Somerset: Dimensions of surveyed buildings (bays)

Ref. Number	Ms. Number	Acres	House/Cott(C)	Other Rooms & Domestic Buildings	Barn	Stable	Ox House(H) Stall(S)	Straw House(S) Hay House(H)	Wain House	Store House	Other Farm Buildings	Notes
KB1	97	0	C									
KB2	98	0	C									
KB3	99	0	C									
KB4	100	0	C									
KB5	101	0	C									
KB6	8	0	*			•					granary	* millhouse, 2 watermills
KB7	92	0	3									
KB8	93	0	2									
KB9	94	0	2									
KB10	95	0		*								* a shop called le linage house, 16 ft long, 12 ft broad. Perhaps part of KB48
KB11	96	0	2									
KB12	19	1/4	3							1		
KB13	24	1/4	C									
KB14	25	1/4	3									
KB15	56	1/4	2									
KB16	89	1/4	3									
KB15	90	1/4	3									
KB16	91	1/4	2									
KB17	92	1/4	3									
KB18	103	1/4	2									duplicated by Ms. 86a
KB19	26	1/2	2									
KB20	52B	1/2	4		3							
KB21	60	1/2	4									also held 1 1/2 acres (Ms. 30)
KB22	102	1/2	4									
KB23	121	1/2	3									
KB24	50	3/4	2	lean-to(1)								
KB25	128	3/4	4									
KB26	49	1	3									
KB27	44	1 1/4	3									
KB28	124	1 1/4	4	cottage(2)								
KB29	38	2	3									
KB30	57	3 1/4	2									

Table 26 *continued*

Ref. Number	Ms. Number	Acres	House/Cott(C)	Other Rooms & Domestic Buildings	Barn	Stable	Ox House(H) Stall(S)	Straw House(S) Hay House(H)	Wain House	Store House	Other Farm Buildings	Notes
KB31	51	3¾	7									
KB32	83	4¼	3		3							
KB33	13	4½	3		3							also held 6 acres (Ms.109)
KB34	46	5¼	3		=		=S					barn + stall(4)
KB35	17	5½	3		•					•		
KB36	69	5½	3		2*							* barn(2) and le cut
KB37	18	5¾	3		3					•		
KB38	40	5¾	3	+ other bldgs.								
KB39	70	5¾	5		=		=S					barn + stall(6)
KB40	28	6	3									also held 9¾ acres (Ms.105,110)
KB41	37	6	4		3		1S					
KB42	64	6	4	kitchen	•		S		5			millhouse(5)
KB43	87	6	3									
KB44	68	6	3		2		1S		1			
KB45	32	6¼	3		3							also held 12 acres (Ms.137,140)
KB46	75	6¼	5		3							
KB47	77	6¼	3		3		1S					
KB48	78	6¼	=		3		=S					house + stall(4); perhaps included KB9
KB49	3	6½	3									also held 301 acres (Ms.142)
KB50	39	6½	5		=		=S					barn + stall(5)
KB51	84	6½	4		4		1S					barn + stall adjoining; also held 7 acres(Ms.5)
KB52	36	6¾	2		=		=S					barn + stall(2)
KB53	22	7	5		4		S					
KB54	34	7¼	5		3							
KB55	31	7½	4		•		4h					also held 8 acres (Ms.125)
KB56	58	7½	6		2							
KB57	82	7½	4		=		=S					barn + stall(3)
KB58	45	8	3		2		1S		1			
KB59	76	8½	5		3		=S	=H				hayhouse + stall(4); also held 8 acres (Ms.135)
KB60	41	9½	6		=		=S					barn + stall(6)
KB61	20	12	5		•		5S					
KB62	27	12	5		4		3H					
KB63	79	12	4		3							

Table 26 *continued*

Ref. Number	Ms. Number	Acres	House/Cott(C)	Other Rooms & Domestic Buildings	Barn	Stable	Ox House(H) Stall(S)	Straw House(S) Hay House(H)	Wain House	Store House	Other Farm Buildings	Notes
KB64	85	12	4		=		=S					barn + stall(4)
KB65	29	13	5		4		3H	1H				
KB66	57	13	5		4							also held 4½ acres (Ms.126)
KB67	30	13	5		=	=						barn + stable(6)
KB68	16	14	3		3					2		
KB69	88	14	5	kitchen(2)	•			5S	1			also held 22 acres (Ms.72B, 138-9)
KB70	12	15	6		4							
KB71	14	15	6		4							
KB72	65	16	5		3	*			2			stable called a cutting
KB73	80	16	7		5							also held 5½ acres (Ms.131)
KB74	52A	17	5		=	1	=S		1			barn + stall(5); also held 9 acres (Ms.143-4)
KB75	15	19	6		•	•				5		
KB76	48	19	7		=	=					other blds(=)	barn + stable + other bld(4)
KB77	62	19	4		2		2S		1			hayhouse + stall(4)
KB78	73	19	6		4	=		=H				
KB79	66	21	4		•		6+1S		2			
KB80	2	21	•									
KB81	42	21	6	outhouse(3)	=		=S				other blds(=)	Barn + stall + other blds; also held 2½ acres (Ms.112)
KB82	61	21	6		5	2	3S		2			also held 6 acres (Ms.120)
KB83	72	21	5		=		=S					barn + stall adjoining(4)
KB84	63	22	6	bakehouse(1)	7		1*					* oxstall
KB85	43	22	8		3		4S					also held 14 acres (Ms.122-3)
KB86	9-10	25	*								granary	* millhouse, watermill(2)
KB87	81	26	5		*		3S					* two barns(8); also held 4 acres (Ms.130)
KB88	21	29	5	bakhouse(1)	4							also held 8 acres (Ms.119)
KB89	47	31	7		6							
KB90	54	31	4		3		4S*		1		wainhouse*	stall + wainhouse adjoining
KB91	35	37	7	dairyhouse(2)	=	=						barn + stable(6); wellhouse(1)
KB92	55	40	5	crosshouse(2)	5	2		=S	2		wringhouse(=)	strawhouse + wringhouse(5); also held 13 acres (Ms.108)
KB93	23	41	9		5					•		also held 17 acres (Ms.106-7)
KB94	67	44	10		5	1	4S		2			also held 5 acres (Ms.136)

Table 26 *continued*

Ref. Number	Ms. Number	Acres	House/Cott(C)	Other Rooms & Domestic Buildings	Barn	Stable	Ox House(H) Stall(S)	Straw House(S) Hay House(H)	Wain House	Store House	Other Farm Buildings	Notes
KB95	74	45	8		6		5*					stall or oxhouse (5)
KB96	53	46	6		=	3	=S				millhouse(2)	barn + *les stalls* adjoining; also held 11 acres (Ms. 111)
KB97	86	47	5		6		3S					
KB98	7	50	18									
KB99	71	53	4		6							also held 13 acres (Ms.104,111)
KB100	6	62	•									
KB101	1	64+	11									at least 64 acres (Ms. damaged)

Notes: For the cottages (KB 1-5), no holding areas were given, but these were presumably very small. A number of the smaller holdings have their areas expressed in acres and hides, rather than acres, rods and perches ; it has been assumed that a hide is equivalent to a rod. The following holdings consisting only of land are excluded from the table (Ms. numbers, with acreage in parentheses): 4, 5 (5, 7), 10, 11, (1/2, —), 72B (5), 104–120 (11, 3, 9, 7, 13, 6, 7, 2, 3, 5, 11, 4, 8, —, 2, 8, 6), 122–3 (6, 8), 125–7 (8, 5, 2), 129–145 (6, 4, 6, 9, 6, 9, 8, 6, 5, 9, 8, 8, 8, 301, 11, 8, 267).

Table 27: West Pennard: Dimensions of surveyed buildings (bays)

				Ancilliary Buildings			Farm Buildings									
Ref. Number	Ms. Number	Acres	House	Other Rooms & Domestic Buildings	Bakehouse	Backhouse	Barn	Stable	Bovite(B) Stall(ST)	Cowhouse	Straw House(S) Hay House(H)	Wain House	Store	Shelf House	Other Farm Buildings	Notes
WP1	6	4	•				•	•	ST						dovecote, watermill, windmill	
WP2	7	4	•													
WP3	2	5	3				2									held with WP39 and WP58 + 3¾ ac. land (Ms.14)
WP4	101	5	2													
WP5	17	6	3										1			
WP6	55	7½	5													
WP7	4	8	=						=ST							house + stall(3)
WP8	32	8½	2				2				2H					
WP9	78	11	3	workhouse(2) adjoins house				•	B							
WP10	36	11	3		2		2									
WP11	94	12	4													
WP12	62	13	3													
WP13	72	14	3													held with WP66
WP14	23	14	4				1									
WP15	48	14	3				=						=			barn + store(3)
WP16	3	15	3				=		=ST							barn + stall(3)
WP17	59	16	2													
WP18	53	16	3				=	=								barn + stable(3) + 1 ac. land (Ms.21)
WP19	108	16	2				=						=			barn + store(5); held with WP61 + 163 ac. (Ms.106, 109, 110)
WP20	54	17	=	other bldgs(=)												house + other buildings(6)
WP21	20	17	3				=						=			barn + store(2)
WP22	1	17	3											•		
WP23	60	18	4				=						=			barn + store(2); + 3 ac. land (Ms.61)
WP24	76	18	3				2			1	2H					
WP25	79	19	3				2		2B							
WP26	63	20	4			2	2									
WP27	73	20	3				•				H					

Table 27 *continued*

Ref. Number	Ms. Number	Acres	House	Ancilliary Buildings: Other Rooms & Domestic Buildings	Ancilliary Buildings: Bakehouse	Ancilliary Buildings: Backhouse	Farm Buildings: Barn	Farm Buildings: Stable	Farm Buildings: Bovite(B) Stall(ST)	Farm Buildings: Cowhouse	Farm Buildings: Straw House(S) Hay House(H)	Farm Buildings: Wain House	Farm Buildings: Store	Farm Buildings: Shelf House	Farm Buildings: Other Farm Buildings	Notes
WP28	49	21	4	cottage(3) with store(1)		=							=			barn + store(3)
WP29	19	22	4			1	2						2			
WP30	37	22	3				3									
WP31	97	22	3				2	1				••				
WP32	35	23	5		2		2				2H					
WP33	51	23	4				=	=		=						barn + stable + cow stall(4); held with 8 ac. land (Ms.80)
WP34	64	23	4				1									
WP35	12	24	3				2						=		millhouse(=)	store + millhouse(1)
WP36	66	25	3				•			•						
WP37	92	26	3													
WP38	89	27	4			1	3									
WP39	95	27	=				=	=								house + barn + stable(6); held with WP3
WP40	10	29	4				3		1ST		2S					
WP41	50	29	4				3									
WP42	52	30	4				2									
WP43	9	31	4				3	=			2H		=			stable + store(3)
WP44	39	32	3		2		2	1			1H			*		* lean-to shelfhouse
WP45	99	33	3		•		3									
WP46	98	33	6				=	=								barn + stable(4)
WP47	81	33	4				2									
WP48	93	34	5				2		=ST		=H					stall + hayhouse(4)
WP49	47	34	3				3		1ST					•		
WP50	96	35	5				2	•								
WP51	71	38	3			2	=		=ST		2H					barn + stall(3)
WP52	102	38	4				2				2S					+ 6 ac. land (Ms.103)
WP53	68	41	6				3		2ST		2H					+ 7 ac. land (Ms.69)
WP54	56	42	4				=	=			2H	1				barn + stable(4)
WP55	65	42	4			2	3				2H					
WP56	38	48	8				2									
WP57	70	50	4				2				2S				shed	

Table 27 *continued*

Ref. Number	Ms. Number	Acres	House	Ancilliary Buildings: Other Rooms & Domestic Buildings	Bakehouse	Backhouse	Farm Buildings: Barn	Stable	Bovite(B) Stall(ST)	Cowhouse	Straw House(S) Hay House(H)	Wain House	Store	Shelf House	Other Farm Buildings	Notes
WP58	44	59	7				=		=ST	4	2S					barn + stall(4); held with WP3
WP59	67	59	6	other bldg(4)			=	=								barn + stable(2)
WP60	33	69	5				3		2ST					•		
WP61	107	69	3			1	3	2								held with WP19
WP62	40	71	7		2		3				3S	=		• =		wainhouse + second shelfhouse(3); + 21ac. land (Ms.41-2)
WP63	46	75	5				3				3H					
WP64	34	78	14				=		=ST							barn + stall(2)
WP65	58	81	5	other bldg(4)			2									
WP66	45	84	6	kitchen(3) crosshouse(1)			5	1			2S	2+2				held with WP13
WP67	77	98	4	kitchen(2)			3	2			2H					
WP68	91	121	4	kitchen(=)			=+	=*	=+	=*					dovecote(=)	kitchen + dovecote(2); barn + ox-house(=+)(4); stable + cowhouse(=*)(3)

Notes: Three tenants held groups of holdings (3 + 39 + 58; 13 + 66; 19 + 16), but as each had individual buildings, they have been shown separately. Some tenants also held additional land, which has been noted. The following holdings with no buildings have not been included in the table (Ms. numbers, with acreages in parentheses 5 (7), 8 (8), 11 (2), 13–16 (2, 3¾, 3, 6), 18 (2½), 21–22 (1, 11), 24–31 (7, 5, 5, 5, 5, 1, 3½, 8), 43 (6), 57 (6), 74–75 (8, 4), 82–85 (3, 4, 23, 5), 88 (7), 90 (1, 12), 104–6 (12, 2, 43). WP1, 2, 3, 7, 16, 22 were free holdings.

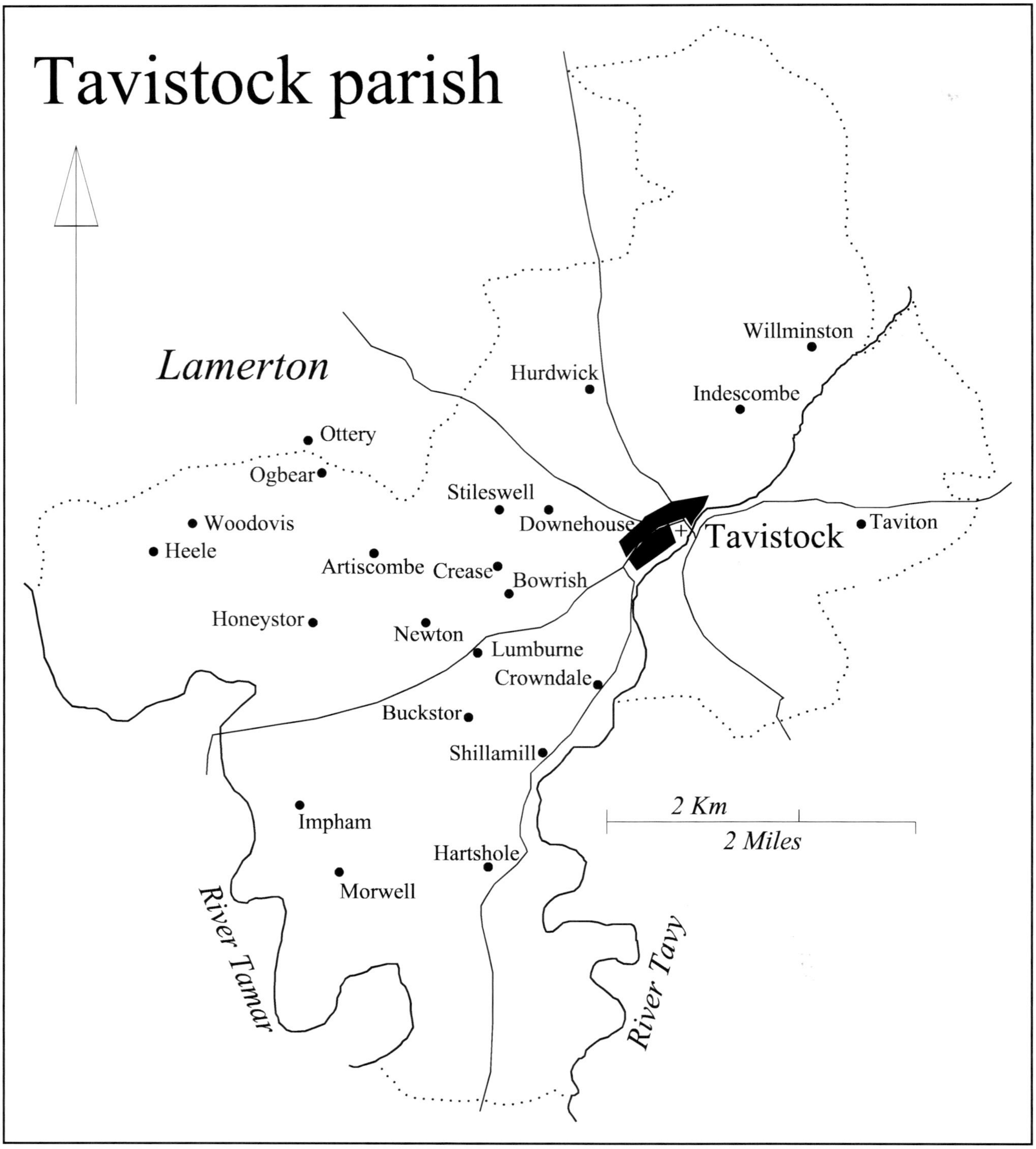

Map 8. Tavistock parish, Devon
Showing the places named in the survey of Hurdwick manor.

CHAPTER 13

Bedford Estates

Bedford Estates (H, M, O, P, TA): 1709
Maps 8-10
The first of the eighteenth-century surveys is the largest of all, with 253 holdings considered here, although not all include houses and not all the houses are described.[1] The Devon lands of the Duke of Bedford, which the survey covers, lay in the south-west of the county, comprising most of what had been the endowments of Tavistock Abbey, including the site of the abbey itself in the town of Tavistock. In 1709 the Duke did not own much property in the town,[2] and the buildings of the abbey (TA1-14) are not analysed here because they are clearly atypical, not only urban but also conversions of monastic buildings. Similarly, the four town houses that were part of the adjacent Hurdwick Manor (H19, 29, 35, 57) are passed over, although it is worth noting that they were very similar to TA1-14. The nearness of the town must also explain why much of Hurdwick consisted of fields only whose tenants did not hold houses on the manor. Hurdwick Barton was the original abbey demesne, and this explains the striking size of its fields. Tenure by this date was entirely by three life leases. Milton (M13-16) shows an unusual survival of one aspect of medieval tenure, with the tenants still owing labour services—one harrowing day, two hay-cutting, two reaping and two carrying days (see p. 206).

The Houses
The Bedford survey described 130 houses, excluding those in Tavistock. Its outstanding feature is that ninety-nine of these were of a character that has hardly appeared in the previous surveys. These were the cottages in the two villages of Oreston and Plymstock, in Plymstock parish. Oreston was a fishing village on the edge of Plymouth Sound, with a harbour and quays; the inhabitants of Plymstock may also have been involved with fishing, but it is a mile from the sea and the cottages were more probably those of farm labourers. Like Starcross in Kenton (p. 75), Oreston grew up from a cluster of huts for foreshore storage, though it seems to have become established earlier as a permanent community and by the date of the survey it retained few cellars.[3] By a fortunate chance, each of the cottages can be precisely located, because when the Bedford estates were resurveyed and mapped for the first time in 1755, a conscientious officer in the Duke's estate office in Tavistock pencilled the plot numbers of the new map on to the old survey (Maps 11-12). However, few if any of the buildings still survive, because they have been swallowed up in the twentieth-century growth of Plymouth.

Plymstock had an ordinary village layout, fairly diffuse and with farms and groups of cottages intermingled. Oreston, tight-packed and made up only of cottages, shows in its different topography its particular function. A corresponding difference appears in the houses. All have simple descriptions—so many ground rooms and so many chambers. Two ground rooms are noted most frequently (28 Oreston, 16 Plymstock) with three rather less common (17 Oreston, 9 Plymstock). However, Plymstock had only four single-room cottages, in contrast to the fifteen at Oreston, perhaps the last houses to be squeezed into the village, and in two cases (O18-19; O64-65) the result of recent division of larger houses. However, seven houses had four ground rooms, one had five (O47) and one even had eight (O45). These were surely not single family houses; they were probably either sublet or used by lodgers.

Only one house had no upper rooms (P4),[4] and most had either the same number of chambers as ground rooms, or squeezed in an extra one upstairs. O10 also had a garret, and O56 probably had cock lofts (over upper floor rooms). Very few houses had other buildings—outhouses at O2, 52 and 56, cellars at O1, 3, 35, 53, 55 and P12, shippons or stables at O36, 56, 58, 60 and P12, and a linhey at O24 (per-

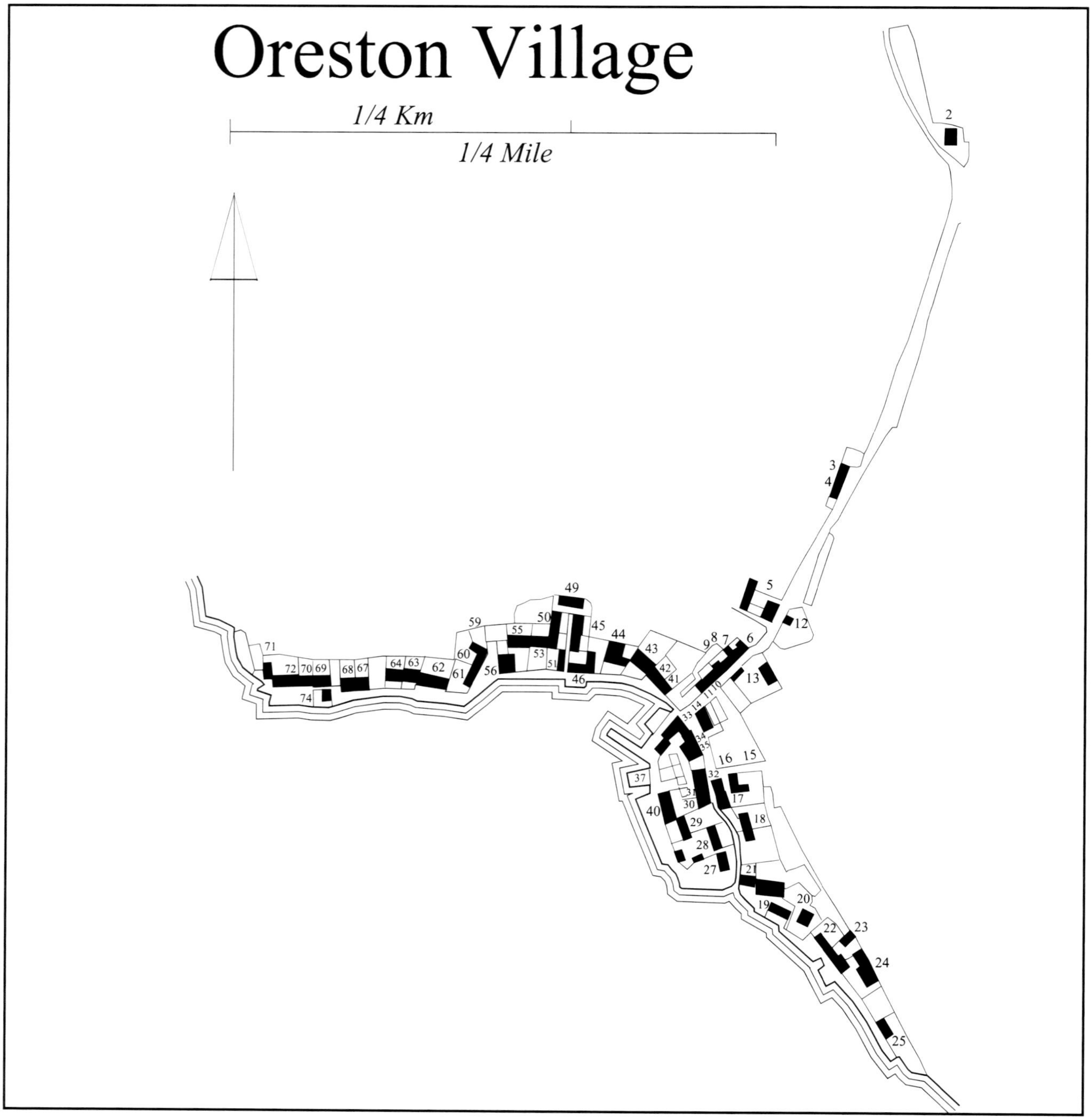

Map 9. Oreston hamlet, Plymstock, Devon

From the map of 1754 (D.R.O. T 1258/M. E24, somewhat simplified). The numbers (from the original) correspond to those added in pencil to the 1709 survey. The main buildings of each holding are shown in black.

haps for domestic use). Plymstock contained one smithy (P22) and one shop (P23). O56 had a 'palace', though this was nothing more unusual than a cellar for bulking and storing pilchards.[5] The two 'permars' of O15 may have been similar, thought the word is unidentified, and the other cellars were probably also fish-cellars.

Oreston boasted the only inn—the King's Arms (O3). It was quite small, with only two under rooms and three chambers, but it did have a brewhouse and two cellars.

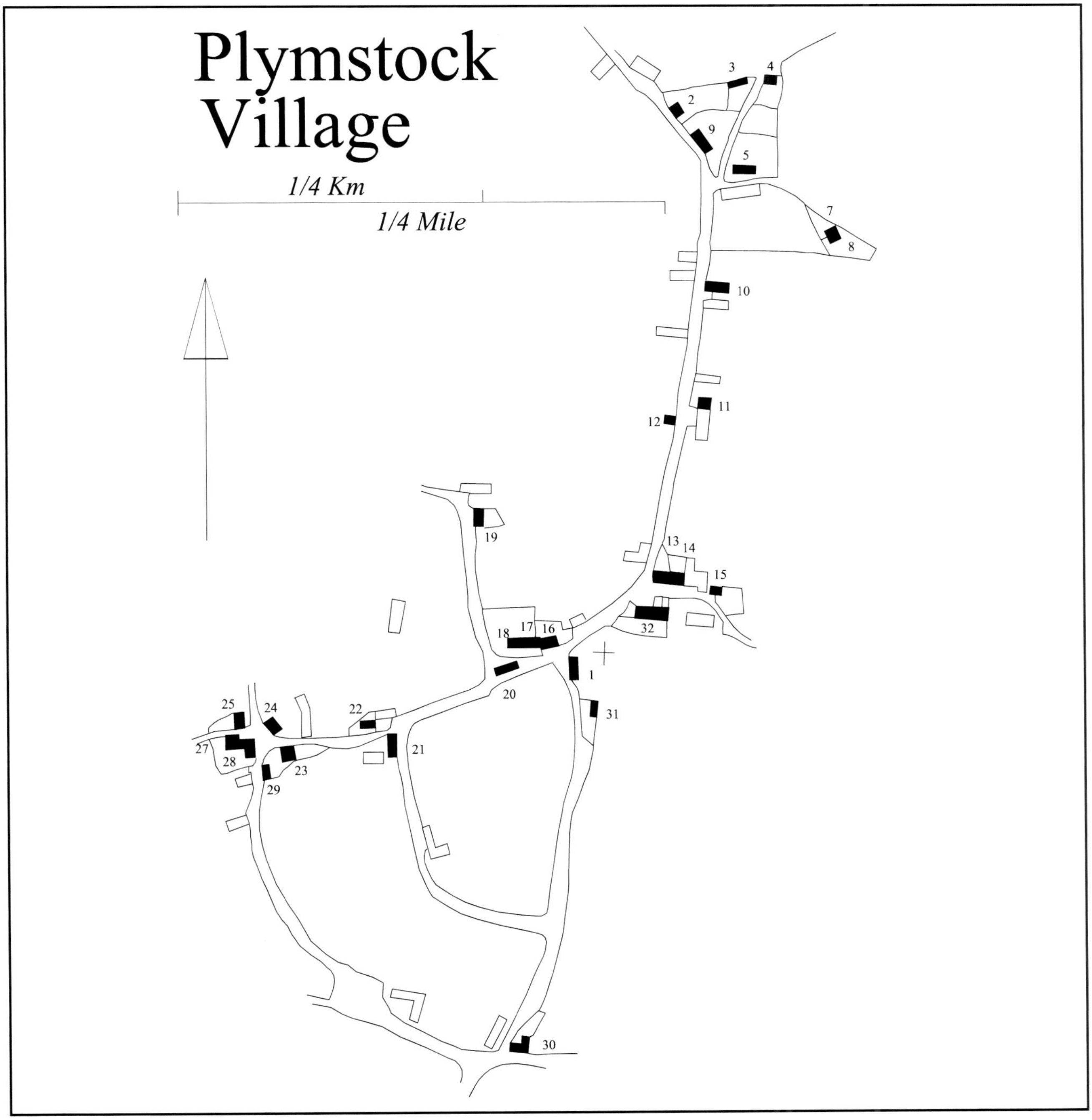

Map 10. Plymstock village

Source as Map 12. The buildings in outline are those of the main farms, which are not described in the 1709 survey.

With the twenty-four houses at Hurdwick, we return to the familiar farmhouse pattern, at a rather higher standard than the earlier Devon examples; this is more likely to reflect the later date than the somewhat larger farm size. Eight houses had four ground floor rooms, eight had three rooms and six had 'two under rooms'. Although the last included the small holdings (H37, 52), two others had more than twenty-five acres, and one was a mill with twenty acres (H34). A solitary 'little house' (H70) had one under room and two chambers. With the three-room houses, the 'hall' appeared as one of the rooms (in all except H37 and 53), usually accompanied by two 'under rooms', but with one parlour (H24) and two shops (H37, 40). For the four room plans, a parlour characteristically accompanied the hall (except for H1, 42); only H1 and H20 had kitchens, while H42 had a shop. H74 was apparently of four rooms, but the description is not quite explicit, 'hall, parlours, milkhouse and drinkhouse'.

These Hurdwick houses were fully chambered over, normally with one chamber for each ground room: H42 and 55 do not mention chambers, but this was probably an accidental omission. Few had domestic ancillary buildings. Two of the three-room plan houses had a bakehouse (H24, 27), and H53 had a 'back-house', just a rear room probably combining several uses. H21, of four rooms, had a separate building containing a milkhouse and a kilnhouse.

Four houses stood on Hurdwick waste (H99-101, 103), probably the result of recent colonisation, as none had any land. They were a mixed group. Two were no more than cottages, with a 'hall and shop', and two 'under rooms', each with chambers over. One was even smaller, with one under room, three chambers and a milkhouse, but was in fact a fulling mill, with the mill room in the same structure. The last was a house of substance—five chambers over a hall, cellar, brewhouse, little parlour and milkhouse. Its presence among the cottages on the waste is not easy to understand.

Two Hurdwick houses, Taviton Barton and Croundwell (H25, 49) have not been mentioned so far. Their farms were substantially larger than any others in the parish (199 and 157 acres), and their houses followed suit. Leigh Barton in Milton (M1, 2) can be grouped with them. It contained two complete farmhouses sharing and dividing the farmyard and its buildings.[6] The two Hurdwick houses show the parlour beginning to dominate the hall: H45 had 'little and great' parlours (cf. H74, above), and H25 lacked a hall but had two parlours instead. Three of the houses had kitchens, three 'a dairy and buttery', and two a cider cellar or house. M2 included a malthouse with granary over—a practical arrangement for keeping the grain dry; it also had a dry-house with a 'pook' [loft?] over. A combined unit at H25 included a malthouse, kiln and brewhouse, with two cellars for storing the resulting liquor. It also had the novel feature of four closets with its eight chambers, as well as more functional corn, apple and wool chambers.

The Farm Buildings (Table 28)

The great majority of the cottage properties in Oreston and Plymstock had no ancillary buildings at all, being the homes of fisherman and labourers. A few cottagers in these seacoast towns and most of the poorest villagers in Tavistock supplemented their wages by keeping a pig, a milk cow or two, and one or more horses, perhaps for hire. Housing this urban menagerie cluttered the tiny house lots with stables or shippons (names probably used interchangeably), hog sties and one carthouse (in Tavistock). They occupied the backsides familiar in many villages, jumbles of pens and huts strung out along side streets and lanes. Significantly, these townspeople had no use for barns.

Genuine farms, starting as small as nine acres, bear an unmistakable resemblance to the Cornish manors surveyed a century earlier. Yet they also show that important changes had ensued. The Duke of Bedford's tenants were still chiefly herdsmen, but more now were likely to shelter cattle in linheys whereas their great-grandfathers had preferred shippons and oxhouses. Those who also engaged in arable farming, still an important secondary element in the economy of the region, relied on horse teams to a greater extent than before. Stables outnumbered oxhousing by the eighteenth century, further contributing to the decline of that ancient fixture of moorland farmsteads, the oxstall. By 1709 farmyards were gradually assuming their modern, crowded appearance, typified in this survey by the large farm at Leigh Barton in Milton Abbot (M1-2). Its courtyards were ringed round with a barn, three oxen houses, two or three shippons with haylofts over, a cowhouse, several pig sties and hog houses, two yoking houses,[7] a pound house, two stables (one with a woodhouse adjoining) and in the Chapel Orchard, well away from the rest, a necessary house. This inventory of specialised farm buildings can be extended in Hurdwick where one large farm (H25) provided separate structures for calves and poultry and another (H54) had the manor's only wainhouse.

Table 28: Bedford Estates 1709: Occurrence of farm buildings

Ms. Number	Acres	No House (X)	Barn	Stable	Shippon	Pound House	Hogs House	Linney	Other Buildings	Notes
O1-71	0									94 of the 99 cottages
P1-30	0									at Oreston and Plymstock
										have no farm buildings
O36	0		••							
O56	0		•						palace	
O58	0			•						
O60	0			•						
P12	0		•							
H99	0									
H101	0						•		fulling mill	
H102	0			•			••	•		
H103	0						•	•		
TA1	0			•			•			in Tavistock
TA2	0						••	•		in Tavistock
TA3	0			•			•		cart-house	in Tavistock
TA4	0									in Tavistock
TA5	0	X		•						in Tavistock
TA6	0							•		linhey house perhaps domestic
TA7	0	X		•						
TA8	0	X		•					loft over stable	
TA12	0							•		linhey house perhaps domestic
TA14	0									
TA9–10	1							••		
H52	1¼									
H70	1¾									
TA13	3	X		•		•				in Tavistock
H29	3									in Tavistock
H37	3¾					•			outhouse	
H17 +H19	7¼									in Tavistock
H20	9	X	•							
H61	9	X	•							
H36	9½		•						2 mills	
H78	10	X	•							
H24	10		•	•			•		3 outhouses	
H34–35	11			•						house in Tavistock
H57	11			•						house in Tavistock
H84	12									
H77	14	X	•							
H15	15	X	•					•		
H16	15	X	•					•		
H46	15		•					•		
H68	16									
H65	18			•	•					
H56	18	X	•							
H40	21		•	•		•				
H38	23		•	•	•				fulling mill	

Table 28 *continued*

Ms. Number	Acres	No House (X)	Barn	Stable	Shippon	Pound House	Hogs House	Linney	Other Buildings	Notes
H30	23	X	•					•		
H58	23	X	•							
H75	24									
H79	25	X	•							
H60	27	X	•							
H55	28		•	•						
H69	29									
H83	29									
H41	30		•	•	•		•	•		
H50	33		•	•			•			
H39	42		•	•	•					
H45	45		•					•		
H42	46		•	•	•			•		
H95	46									
H43	48		•	•	•			•		
H44	53		•	•	•			•		
H81	54									
H74	59		•	•						
H54	66		•	•	•				wain house; 'other house'	
H73	80									
H26 +H31	94	X	••							1 barn on each holding
H85	94									
M2	95		*		*		••••		yoking house, 2 ox-houses	(possibly barn, see survey entry for M1)
H21–3	98		•••	•				•	2 mills	1 barn on each holding
H87–8	102									
H1–4	108		•	•				•		
M1	118		•	•	•	•	••••••		haylofts (over shippon); yoking house	
H49	158		•	•	•	•				
H92	171									
H25	199		•	•	•	•	•••	••	calf-house; poultry house	
H27	246		•		•			•		

Notes: Holdings of land only are omitted, unless held by a tenant with other holdings. Holdings with barns only are included (marked X in column 4), but H7–8, 11, 14, 18, 28, 51, 62, and 94 are excluded. These were all held by David Serjant and/or Henry Vosper, and included four barns, but no dwelling houses.

[1] Six sections of the full survey (ninety-four holdings) are omitted here, as they have no detailed information. At least one other Bedford manor, Werrington, was not included in the survey text.

[2] He bought much more later in the eighteenth century, to obtain political influence in the borough.

[3] Harold Fox, *The Evolution of the Fishing Village: Landscape and Society along the South Devon Coast, 1086-1550* (Leicester, 2001), 149.

[4] The description of O1 is unclear, and it should possibly be included with P4 as having no upper rooms.

[5] J. Wright, *English Dialect Dictionary* (London, 1898-1905). Although fish-cellar is the most likely meaning of 'palace' here, deeds from Dartmouth and Plymouth indicate that it was also used for an enclosure on the foreshore, possibly of reclaimed land enclosed by revetments ('palisades'). H. R. Watkins, *Dartmouth* (Exeter, 1935), vol. I, 71, 74, 150, 161, 162, gives five medieval references (1389-1497); Devon Record Office, Dartmouth Deed, DD6425 is a typical post-medieval example (1745). We thank Chris Henderson of Exeter Archaeology for discussing the use of 'palace' in the south-west and for providing these references.

[6] This is reminiscent of the 'unit system' houses described by J. T. Smith, 'Lancashire and Cheshire Houses; some problems of architectural and social history', *Archaeol. J.*, 127 (1970), 156-181. Unfortunately, no documents have been located explaining the origin of the Leigh Barton complex.

[7] Presumably connected with the yokes of oxen, but the precise function is not clear.

Survey of Bedford Estates: 1709

(Devon Record Office, L1258/Surveys, Whole Estate 2; Bedford Estate muniments)

This survey exists in three versions, a rough copy (*A*: W1258/add.7/3), and two fair copies (*B* and *C*: L1258/Surveys, Whole Estate 1 and 2). *C* is the best and has been used as the basis for this text. The provision of two final copies was normal on the Bedford estate, one being kept in the Devon (Tavistock) estate office, the other in the London office; both *B* and *C* were finally in London, but the latter was probably the Tavistock copy, as it carries pencilled numbers (in the Oreston and Plymstock sections), which key it to the main Tavistock office estate map of 1754 (T1258/M.E24).

The survey contains 13 sections, covering most (but not all) of the Devon estates. Although it was intended that all should contain full details of the houses, and blanks were left for that purpose, they were only completed for six sections. Because of the survey's length, only these sections are calendared. The names given for most holdings in the margin have been incorporated in the text, preceded by [*at*], when it is clear that they are locations, not individual names. The words *by indenture*, and *the premises underwritten for remainder of 99 years* (cf. TA1) are always present and are omitted from the calendar. The dates given are those of the leases, and the bracketed figures after the names of the lives are their ages. Leases without details are omitted from the calendar without comment. In the survey, the lists of fields are in columns: name, rate per acre, area, value, and the last three are abbreviated R, A and V.

TEXT

Anno 1719:General Survey in the County of Devon
[p.l] Hurdwick Mannor: The Abby Scyte

TA1. The Corner House and Stable next the Pound. Value £7 6s 8d.

Eliza Trowt holds by indenture dated the first of June 1691 the premises underwritten for remainder of 99 years if
Walter Troute aged 27 } her sonns, live
John Troute aged 2[*25 in TA3*] }
Rent £l 6s 8d Heriot £l 6s 8d.

A dwelling house viz.: a hall, a parlour, a drinkhouse, 4 chambers over, a stable, a woodhouse, and two little herb gardens and hogshouse, value £7 6s 8d.

TA2. The same Eliza Trowte holds the milkehouse and garden, date l June 1691, rent 5s, heriot 5s, lives, said Eliza (57), Sarah (21), her daughter.

Two under rooms, two chambers over, a herb garden, two hogshouses and court and linny house, V 2-l0-0.

TA3. The same Eliza Trout holds the houses both sides the Higher Gate, date 1 June 1691, rent £1, heriot £1 lives [*as TA1*].

A kitching, a parlour, a shopp, five chambers over, two under roomes and a stable and a carthouse and hoggshouse and two chambers over the East side the gate, V 7-0-0.

TA4. John Edgecomb, mercer, holds the chamber over the Higher Gate, date [*blank*], rent 5s, heriot 5s, lives, said John (34), Anna (26), his wife.

One chamber, V 1-0-0.

TA5. Eliza Penrose holds the stable adjoining to Eliza Trowt's stable, date [*blank*], rent 6s 4d, heriot 6s 4d, lives, Ann Waldron (23), Sarah (15) and Elizabeth (15), daughters of the said Eliza Penrose, V 2-0-0.

TA6. Eliza Foot holds the Mault Kiln house, date 1 June 1691, rent 6s 8d, heriot 6s 8d, lives, Mary Spry (44), wife of William Spry, William (21), their son, John (18), their son.

One lower room and kiln and chamber over, one linney house and chamber over, V 4-0-0.

TA7. Mr. Frank Caunter holds the Dye House, now a stable, date 1 June 1691, rent 13s 4d, heriot 13s 4d, lives John Oake (46), Honor Langford (48), Ann Serjant, daughter of David Serjant junior, V 2-10-0.

TA8. Henry Vosper holds the stable next the Abby Lower Gate, date 1 June 1691, rent 6s 8d, heriot 6s 8d, lives Bevill (25), Amy (27) and Patience Doidge (20), [*all*] children of William Doidge.

A stable and loft over, V 2-0-0.

TA9. Thomas Hornabrooke holds the chamber over the Lower Gate, rent 4s, heriot 4s.

One chamber, V 1-0-0.

TA10. The same Thomas Hornabrooke holds the Hearb Garden, date 1 June 1691 rent £1 6s 8d, heriot £1 6s 8d, lives the said Thomas (46), Patience (40), his wife, Thomas (20), their son.

A hall and parlour, foure chambers over, a linney at the end and court before and little hearb garden, a linney house against the gate, two under rooms, two chambers over, a large herb garden and orchard, A 1-0-0, V 10-0-0.

TA11. John Payne and others hold the Great Hall, date 3 Nov. 1701, rent 4s, heriot 4s, lives Jacob Saundercock (50), Richard Cudlipp (40), gentleman, Walter Shellabear junior (30).

A great hall, now a meeting house and a chapple, V 3-0-0.

TA12. Charity Gendall holds the Dining Roome, date 1 June 1691, rent 10s, heriot 10s, lives said Charity (56), Martha (25), her daughter, Thomas Gendell (22).

A lower roome and loft over, a back court and linney house, V 2-10-0.

TA13. James Bulteel, esquire, holds the Abby Great Orchard, date 1 June 1691, rent £5, Heriot £3, lives said James (26), Azarell Bulteel (56), his mother.

A pound house and pound, a cellar, a stable and two chambers over.

The Great Orchard, pare garden and hearb garden, A 4-0-0, R 3-10-0, V 14-0-0; two meadows, A 3-2-13, R 3-0-0, V 10-10-0.

Sum A 7-2-13, V 27-10-0.

TA14. Arthur Lumley, gentleman, holds in right of his wife the Saxon Scoole, date 1 June 1691, rent £1 13s 4d, heriot £1 13s 4d, lives Thomas Willesford (40), Elizabeth Willesford (35), his wife.

Four under rooms, three chambers over and a large room over all them. A decayed house at each end, and the Dungeon and herb garden, V 5-13-4.

TA15. William Burges holds two Higher Meddows, A 3-2-6, date 1 June 1691, rent £1 13s 4d, heriot £1 13s 4d, lives Eliza (24), Thomassin (22), Mary Burges (20).

TA16. In Hand: the higher Jesops Hay, A 1-2-29, rent £1 13s 4d, heriot £2, V8-15-0.

TA17. Thomas Willesford holds, date 1 June 1691, rent £1 6s 8d, heriot £1 6s 8d, lives said Thomas (40), Elizabeth (35), his wife.

Lower Jessops Hay, A 1-2-35, R 1-10-0, V 3-0-0; Frogg meddow, [A 1-0-33], R 3-0-0, V 3-10-0.

Sum A 2-3-28, V 6-10-0.

TA18. Thomas Willesford holds two Middle Meddows, A 3-1-8, R 2-0-0, V 6-10-0, rent £1 13s 4d, heriot £1 13s 4d, [*lease details as TA17*].

TA19. Thomas Willesford holds two Lower Meddows, rent £1 6s 8d, heriot £1 6s 8d, [*lease details as TA17*]. Outer meadow, A 1-2-12, R 1-10-0, V 2-5-0; Inner meadow, A 1-2-0, R 2-0-0, V 3-0-0.

Sum A 3-0-12, V 5-5-0.

TA20. John Edgecomb holds Dunterfields Meddow, date 1 June 1691, rent £1 6s 8d, heriot £1 6s 8d, lives Martha (45), now wife of William Cole, Sara (20), her daughter, Patience (35), wife of Richard Hawkins.

TA21. George Southall holds Old Wood, date 1 June 1691, rent £1 6s 8d, heriot £1 6s 8d, lives said George (50), Joane (40), his wife, Henry Willcocks (30).

Lower field, A 3-1-5, R 1-0-0, V 3-5-0; Middle field, A 3-1-10, R 1-0-0, V 3-6-0; Higher field, A 3-0-0, R 1-5-0, V 3-15-0.

Sum A 9-2-15, V 10-6-0.

TA22. William Spry holds Common Close (one great field now divided into four fields), A 16-1-0, R 0-18-0, V 14-14-0, date 1 June 1691, rent £2 13s 4d, heriot £2 13s 4d, lives Mary (45), his wife, William (22) and John Spry (18), his sons.

TA23. Walter Shellabear holds, date 1 June 1691, rent £3 6s 8d, heriot £3 6s 8d, lives said Walter (60), his son (30). Dear Parke Hill, A 14-3-4, R 0-17-0, V 12-14-0; meadow under, A 1-2-33, R 2-0-0, V 3-5-0.

Sum A 16-1-37, V-15-19-0.

TA24. Henry Wilcocks holds the Rock Parke, date 1 June 1691, rent £4, heriot £3, lives Bevill Doidge, said Henry (30), Walter Shellabear junior (30).

Grate field and Lane, A 22-1-27, R 1-0-0, V 22-6-0; Hill under, A 2-2-0, R 0-7-0, V 0-16-0; meddow under, A 1-1-0, R 2-10-0, V 3-10-0.

Sum A 26-0-27, V 26-12-0.

TA25. John Payne holds the Rack field and field above, date 1 June 1691, rent £2, heriot £2, lives said John (60), Susanna (65) his wife, Susanna (30), their daughter.

Rack field, A 1-2-0, R 1-10-0, V 2-5-0; field above, A 9-0-33, R 1-0-0, V 9-0-0

Sum A 10-2-23, V 11-5-0.

TA26. Walter Shellabear holds Paynes Ground or three higher fields, date 1 June 1691, rent £1 6s 8d, heriot £1 6s 8d, lives Abell (24), Walter (22) and William Whitechurch (20).

Little field next the gate, A 0-3-0, R 1-5-0, V 1-0-0; field above, next the lane, A 4-1-24, R 0-15-0, V 3-10-0; Inner field, A 4-0-29, R 1-0-0, V 4-0-0.

Sum A 9-1-13, V 8-10-0.

TA27. Walter Shellabear holds Dear Park Downe, etc., date 1 June 1691, rent £3 6s 8d, heriot £3 6s 8d, lives Walter (30), his son, Joan (60), his wife, Nicholas Worth (30). Dear Parke Downe, A 25-0-0, R 0-3-0, V 3-15-0; Easter field under, A 2-0-34, R 0-16-0, V 1-16-0; Midle field, A 3-1-8, R 0-16-0, V 2-16-0; Wester field, R 3-1-2, A 0-16-0, V 2-14-0; Glubs field, R 8-0-10, A 1-0-0, V 8-0-0.

Sum A 41-3-14, V 19-1-0.

TA28. Elizabeth Penrose holds Chaldons Close, date 1 June 1691, rent £2, heriot £2, lives said Elizabeth (55), Sara (21) and Ann (19), her daughters.

The field, A 5-3-24, R 1-0-8, V 8-4-0; the meadow above, A 1-2-0, R 1-16-0, V 2-8-0; the meadow below, A 1-2-12, R 1-16-0, V 2-10-0.

Sum A 8-3-36, V 13-2-0.

TA29. In Hand: Dear Parke Lodge, rent £1, heriot £1. Higher field, A 2-2-0, R 1-16-0, V 4-10-0; Little field, A 0-2-35, R 2-0-0, V 1-0-0; the Hill, A 2-2-32, R 0-13-4, V 1-15-0.

Sum A 5-3-27, V 7-5-0.

[p.18] Hurdwick Barton: Houses and Quillets

H1. Anne Sowton holds, date 10 Dec. 1660, rent 3s 4d, heriot 3s 4d, life Jane Roberts (70).

A hall, a kitching, two under roomes, six chambers, a barne, a stable and a linney.

H2. The same Anne Sowton holds Broome Parks, A 44-1-15, R 0-15-0, V 33-7-6, old V 36-0-0,[1] date 6 Aug. 1675, rent £9 10s, heriot £1, life her own (50).

H3. Anne Sowton holds Great Meddow and Little, A 8-0-0, R 2-0-0, V 16-0-0, old V 17-0-0, date 6 Aug. 1676, rent £5 6s 8d, heriot £1, life her own (50).

H4. The same Anne Sowton holds New Meads, date 9 Aug. 1675, rent £14 10s, heriot £4 or best beast, life her own (50).

Lower field, A 9-0-0, Higher field, A 13-2-9, Grate field, A 26-3-7, Little field, A 3-1-0, meaddow A 3-0-0.

Sum A 55-2-16, old V 55-0-0.[2]

H5. In Hand: North Parkes, A 51-2-23, R 0-14-0, V 36-0-0.

H6. William Oxenham holds the Latches, A 60-0-14, R 0-17-0, V 51-0-0, old V 50-0-0, date 1 Jan 1691[/2], rent £9, heriot best beast or £4, lives John Hillman (60), said William (36).

H7. David Serjant holds Great Briscots, date 3 Nov. 1701, rent £14, heriot £1, lives Walter (50), his son, Althea (50), his [?*Walter*] wife, David (13), his grandson.

Lower field, A 23-3-2, R 0-13-0, V 21-0-0; two Middle fields, A 22-1-36, R 0-17-0, V 19-0-0; Higher field A 25-2-21, R 0-15-0, V 20-10-0; Barne and Watering, A 1-0-20, R 1-10-0, V 1-10-0.

Sum A 72-3-30, V 62-0-0. old V 60-0-0.

H8. David Serjant holds Little Briscots, now devided, A 14-2-15, R 1-4-0, V 17-5-0, old V 12-0-0, [*lease as H7*], rent £4, heriot £1.

H9. John Kinsman holds Bate Parkes, now 3 fields, A 26-2-28, R 0-18-0, V 24-8-0, date 14 Feb. 1698[/9], rent £8 6s 8d, heriot £1, lives Henry Vosper (60), William Doidge (50), John Were (24).

H10. James Tuckett holds East Barton, date 19 Mar. 1704, rent £11 10s, heriot £1, lives said James (50), two sons (20). Field called Forges, A 38-1-4, R 0-13-4, V 25-10-0; the Dinny Colds, A 46-0-0, R 0-14-0. V 32-4-0; meadow, A 2-3-36, R 1-0-0, V 3-0-0.

Sum A 87-1-0, V 60-14-0.

H11. Henry Vosper holds East Barton, date 19 Mar. 1704[/5], rent £11 10s, heriot 10s, lives David Serjant (18), son of David Serjant junior, Honor Serjant (14), his sister, Lydea Serjant (10).

Poole Parke, A 40-0-0, R 0-13-4, V 26-13-4; Barne field or Way Parke, A 36-0-24, R 0-13-4, V 24-0-0.

Sum A 76-0-24, V 50-13-4, old V 65-0-0.

H12. John Anstis holds Longstone, date 23 June 1683, rent £13, heriot £1, life Elizabeth (30), his wife.

Barne field, A 10-2-9; Great field, A 28-0-24; Lower field, A 8-1-30.

Sum A 55-2-14, old V 50-0-0.

---

[1] H2, most of the holdings down to H13, and some later ones have notes of the old value.

[2] No current values are given for H4, H12 and H13.

H13. John Anstis holds Barn Parkes, date 1 Sept 1663, rent £13 6s 8d, heriot £1, life Peter Elford junior (60).

The Quillets, A 11-2-6; Inner field, A 25-3-2; Little field, A 7-0-38; Lower field, A 11-0-8.

Sum A 55-2-14, old V 50-0-0.

H14. David Sergant and Henry Vosper hold Mugglebury, date 3 Nov. 1701, rent £10, heriot £1, lives Joan Wyatt (56), John Roberts (40), David Serjant junior (18).

Higher field, A 27-3-35, R 0-18-0, V 25-4-0; Lower field, A 22-3-21, R 0-16-0, V 18-5-0; meadows, A 6-0-33, R 1-4-0, V 7-5-0.

Sum A 57-0-9, V 50-14-0.

[p.26] Hurdwick Manor, Tavistock Parrish: South East Quarter or Taviton Tything

H15. William Cole holds [*at*] Berkhamsteed Wytham, date 9 Aug. 1675, rent £1 3s 4d, heriot best beast or £1 10s, lives William Doidge (40), Eleanor (36), his wife.

A barn and linney; Higher close, A 3-3-10, R 0-15-0, V 2-13-6; Long meadow, A 1-1-25, R 1-8-0, V 1-18-0; Little meadow, A 1-1-0, R 1-8-0, V 1-15-0; Higher meadow, A 1-1-28, R 1-8-0, V 1-18-0; East Barne field, A 3-2-24, R 0-14-0, V 2-10-0; two fields above way, A 4-0-35, R 0-12-0, V 2-10-0.

Sum A 15-3-2, V 13-4-6.

H16. John Edgecomb holds [*at*] Berkhamsteed Wytham, date 9 Aug. 1675, rent £1 3s 4d, heriot best beast or £1 10s, lives Andrew Doidge (60), Elizabeth (60), his wife, William Doidge (40).

A barn and linney; Barne field, A 2-3-5, R 0-14-0, V 2-10-0; Great meddow, A 3-1-8, R 1-8-0, V 4-7-0; South field, A 2-2-19, R 0-14-0, V 2-7-0; South-west field, A 2-3-20, R 0-14-0, V 2-10-0; Barne parke, A 2-3-8, R 0-15-0, V 2-0-0.

Sum A 15-1-20, V 13-14-0.

H17. John Payne holds Crelake or Vickaridge Ground, A 5-3-10, R 1-6-8, V 7-10-0, old V 7-0-0, rent 13s 4d, heriot 13s 4d, lives William Gill (60), Samuell Gill (56) and Edward Gill (27), his son.

H18. David Serjant holds Crelake or Dyers Field, date 3 Nov. 1701, rent £1 14s, heriot £2, lives said David (70), Walter (50), his son, Lyde (10), son of Walter.

Easter field, A 4-2-23, R 0-18-0, V 4-0-0; Middle field, A 3-2-16, R 0-17-0, V 3-0-0; Wester field, A 3-2-2, R 0-17-0, V 3-0-0; meadow and grove, A 4-0-21, R 1-10-0, V 6-0-0; Barne Parke, A 4-2-30, R 1-8-0, V 6-10-0.

Sum A 20-2-12, V 22-10-0, old V 33-0-0.

H19. John Payne holds Crelake Meddow, A 1-2-0, R 1-13-4, V 2-10-0, and a house in town in West Street, date 3 Nov. 1701, rent £1 2s, heriot £1 2s, lives Dorothy Glanvill (45), Charles Hawke (40), Richard Cudlipp (10), his [*?John*] grandson.

Two under roomes and shopp and 3 chambers over, a bakehouse and chamber over, garden, V 4-0-0. Total V 6-10-0.

H20. John Cudlipp holds St. John's, date 1 Feb. 1689[*/90*], rent 17s 4d, heriot 10s, lives said John (22), Richard (17), his brother.

A Barne and Barne field, A 1-2-32, R 1-15-0, V 3-10-0; Long field, A 3-1-8, R 1-4-0, V 3-18-0; Hill, A 2-2-39, R 1-0-0,. V 2-15-0; meaddow, A 1-1-21, R 2-10-0, V 3-5-0.

Sum A 9-0-20, V 13-8-0.

H21. Julius Glanvill, esquire, holds Forland, date 17 Nov. 1706, rent £4, heriot £2, lives said Juilus (65), John Glanvill (30), his son.

A barn; three Lower fields, A 15-2-37, R 0-14-0, V 10-10-0; field above, A 4-1-3, R 0-15-0, V 3-10-0; Rock field, A 8-2-15, R 0-10-0, V 4-5-0; field above next the Downe, A 6-0-32, R 0-6-8, V 2-2-0; field below it, A 3-3-5, R 0-10-0, V 1-15-0; Hill, A 7-0-3, R 0-5-0, V 1-15-0; field next the barne; Tree field, A 7-3-0, R 0-8-0, V 3-0-0, meaddow, A 5-0-27, R 1-0-0, V 5-0-0; field above meaddow, A 5-2-32, R 0-12-0, V 3-10-0; field above that, A 4-0-20, R 0-8-0, V 2-0-0.

Sum A 67-1-14, [*V 37-17-0*].

H22. The same Julius holds Taviton Keagle Wood and Mills [*same lease as H21*].

Hall, parlour, kitching and under roome, foure chambers over, a stable, barn, linney and killn house and house adjoining to the barne, a milkehouse and chamber over, two mills, V 6-0-0.

Meaddow by the house, A 1-2-19, R 2-0-0, V 3-0-0; Little field beyond the wood, A 0-3-24, R 1-2-0, V 1-0-0; Splatt and orchard, A 0-1-15, R 1-1-0, V 0-5-0.

Sum A 2-3-18, V 10-5-0.

H23. The same Julius holds Taviton alias Grafftons tenement [*same lease as H21*].

Way Parke, A 6-1-9, R 0-15-0, V 4-14-0; field above that, A 5-3-32, R 0-15-0, V 4-10-0; field above that and barne, A 2-1-32, R 1-8-0, V 3-0-0; field above the wood, A 6-0-25, R 0-14-0, V 4-5-0; Higher Straie Parke, A 2-3-2, R 0-15-0, V 2-4-0; Little Straie Parke, A 1-2-2, R 1-0-0, V 1-10-0; meadow, A 0-2-30, R 1-6-0, V 0-16-0; Mill meaddows, A 2-2-30, R 1-10-0, V 3-15-0.

Sum A 28-2-2, V 24-14-0.

H24. Richard Hawkins holds Taviton Broome Parkes, date 21 Jan. 1701[*/2*], R £1 4s, heriot £2 13s 4d, lives said Richard (40), Patience (35), his wife.

Hall and parlour, an under roome, four chambers over, and a stable, a barne, a bakehouse and 3 other outhouses and hogs houses.

Orchard, A 0-1-9, V[*?with house*] 4-0-0; Barne field, A 1-1-6, R 1-5-0, V 1-11-0; Burrow Parke, A 2-3-1, R 1-0-0, V 2-15-0; Drye meaddow, A 1-2-19, R 1-10-0, V 2-5-0; Rack

Parke, A 1-1-31, R 1-5-0, V 2-0-0; Furze Parke, A 2-0-6, R 1-0-0, V 2-0-0; Tangeer meaddow, A 0-3-30, R 1-3-4, V 1-0-0; the Splatt.

Sum A 10-1-22, V 15-11-0.

H25. James Leer holds Taviton Barton, rent £6 13s 4d and a capon, heriot best beast or £3, lives said James (56), Elizabeth (54), his wife, Dorothy (22), his daughter.

A dwelling or farme house: a kitching, two parlours, a dayry, a butterry, two cellers, a maulthouse, a kiln, a brewhouse, eight chambers, foure clossets, a corne chamber, an aple chamber and wool chamber, a cyder celler, a barne, stable, sheppin, calves house, 3 hogs houses, a poultry house, a pound house, two linneys, etc.

Orchard, A 0-2-28, V[?*with house*] 3-10-0; Lower meaddow, A 1-1-8, R 2-0-0, V 2-10-0; Mowhay or Long Park mead, A 1-3-0, R 1-10-0, V 3-0-0; Moorey meaddow, A 1-3-0, R 1-0-0, V 1-15-0; Little Hill meaddow, A 1-1-20, R 1-2-6, V 1-10-0; Dry meaddow, A 2-1-8, R 1-4-0, V 2-10-0; Shullake meaddow, A 3-1-8, R 1-5-0, V 3-14-0; Furze Parke, A 4-3-24, R 0-8-0, V 1-15-0; Inner Hill, A 5-13-4, R 0-8-0, V 2-5-0; three Outer Hills, A 9-0-0, R 0-10-0, V 4-10-0; Outer Gratner, A 9-0-0, R 0-10-0, V 4-10-0; Inner Grattner, A 7-1-4, R 0-6-8, V 2-10-0; Outer Taviton, A 4-0-11, R 0-5-0, V 1-0-0; Inner Taviton, A 12-2-21, R 0-6-8, V 4-0-0; Crift, A 8-0-0, R 0-4-0, V 1-12-0; Lower and Midle Long Parkes, A 8-2-24, R 0-10-0, V 4-5-0; Higher Long Parkes, A 7-0-8, R 0-8-0, V 2-16-0; Bate Parke, A 9-2-10, R 0-10-0, V 4-15-0; Bate meaddow, A 2-2-35, R 1-10-0, V 4-0-0; Whitechurch Parke, A 10-1-15, R 0-10-0, V 5-0-0; Whitechurch Parke Grove, A 2-2-29, R 0-16-0, V 2-0-0; Great Dunscomb, A 8-2-26, R 0-6-8, V 2-16-0; Little Dunscomb, A 3-3-30, R 0-8-0, V 1-10-0; Fursey Dunscomb, A 5-0-0, R 0-6-8, V 1-13-4; Dunscomb Marsh, A 3-0-6, R 0-6-0, V 1-0-0; Pitt Parke, A 9-0-26, R 0-5-0, V 2-10-0; Torr Parkes, A 22-1-1, R 0-3-0, V 3-6-0; Taviton Downe, A 33-1-35, R 0-1-0, V 1-13-0.

Sum A 199-3-11, V 77-15-4.

H26. Catherine Glanvill holds Taviton Barn Parks, date 20 Nov. 1650, rent £2 16s 8d, heriot 13s 4d, life said Catherine (70). A barn; Lower meddow, A 3-0-4, R 1-16-8, V 5-10-0; Barne Parke, A 4-0-12, R 1-0-0, V 4-0-0; Higher field, A 5-1-1, R 0-18-0, V 4-10-0; Quarry Parke, A 3-2-28, R 0-13-4, V 2-0-0; Higher and Little meadows, A 5-1-32, R 1-8-0, V 7-0-0.

Sum A 21-1-37, V 23-0-0.

H27. Stephen Maddaford holds Sprig Bagator, date 24 June 1684, rent £1 6s 8d and a capon, heriot best beast or £3, lives said Stephen (20), Arthur (28), his brother.

A hall, two under roomes, 3 chambers, a barne, a shepping, a bakehouse and linney, old V 30-0-0. [A 245-2-28][3]

H28. Henry Vosper holds in right of his wife Sellars and Sweethams Close, date 20 June 1678, rent £1 6s 8d, heriot £2 10s, lately held by David Serjant, lives Walter Serjant (50), Mary (46), his wife. A barn; Northermost field, A 6-3-32; Souther field, A 2-0-28; Higher meddow, A 3-0-32; Lower meddow, A 2-0-20; Cellars close, A 6-0-20.

Sum A 20-2-10.

[p.34] Hurdwick Mannor: The Northeast Quarter of Tavistock Parrish

H29. Walter Shellabeer holds Brayes Hill in ye Burrough, date 4 June 1684, rent 13s 4d, heriot £1 13s 4d, lives Elizeus Bray (56), Elizabeth (50), his wife, Walter Shellabeer junior (30).

Two under roomes, a shopp, three chambers, herb garden, V 3-0-0; a little meaddow, A 0-2-4, R 2-10-0, V 1-5-0; the field, A 2-3-28, R 1-10-0, V 3-15-0.

Sum A 3-1-32, V 8-0-0.

H30. Elizabeth Maynard holds Sandy Close, date 9 Aug. 1686, rent £1 13s 4d, heriot best beast or £3, life said Elizabeth (40).

A barn and linney; Eastern field, A 6-1-32, R 0-16-0, V 5-0-0; North field, A 4-1-26, R 0-16-0, V 3-10-0; Western field, A 4-3-20, R 0-17-0, V 4-0-0; Barne field, A 4-0-2, R 0-17-0, V 3-10-0; meadow, A 3-1-32, R 1-4-0, V 4-0-0.

Sum A 23-0-32, V 20-0-0.

H31. Catherine Glanvill holds Parke Wood, date 20 Nov. 1650, rent £2, heriot £1, life said Catherine (70).

(Glanville 9)[4] Field next the lane, A 1-2-1, R 1-10-0, V 2-0-0; (Glanville 8) next field to that, A 7-0-4, R 0-13-4, V 4-10-0; (Shellabear 7) Little Furze field under, A 1-2-14, R 0-13-4, V 1-0-0; the Hames or meadows under, A 4-3-11, R 1-1-0, V 5-0-0; (Trout 6) field called Teixes close, A 6-3-7, R 0-10-0, V 3-10-0; Little Hill meaddow under, A 1-0-0, R 1-10-0, V 1-10-0; the Hamms under that, A 6-3-14, R 0-15-0, V 5-0-0; (Payne 3) next field called Goodbyes, A 8-1-0, R 0-15-0, V 6-0-0; Little field to the higher end, A 1-1-10, R 0-16-0, V 1-0-0; meadow under called Peakes, A 2-3-0, R 2-0-0, V 5-10-0; (Richards 2) Lower meaddow next Tavy, A 1-3-7, R 2-10-0, V 4-0-0; meadow next above it, A 1-3-10, R 2-10-0, V 4-0-0; (Richards 1) Lower Hamm next Tavey, A 3-0-9, R 1-3-4, V 3-10-0; 3 Corners meaddowes inside it, A 1-3-12, R 1-0-0, V 2-10-0[*sic*]; Higher Ham, A 4-3-32, R 0-10-6, V 2-10-0; (Shellabear 7) Deakes Poole Ham or Marsh, A 2-2-8, R 1-0-0, V 2-10-0; 2 meaddowes next above it, A 2-2-19, R 1-14-0, V 3-0-0; (Cudlip 5) field and barne called Tollers, A 3-3-24, R 0-18-0, V 3-0-0; Hams or marsh under it, A 2-3-24, R 0-18-0, V 2-0-0; (Cudlip 4) meaddow next above the barn, A 1-2-0, R 1-13-0, V 2-10-0; meaddow next above that, A 1-3-18, R 1-13-0, V 2-17-0; Hill field or meaddow, A 1-3-0, R 1-0-0, V 1-15-0; Rack field, A 1-0-0, R 0-16-0, V 0-16-0.

Sum A 73-1-24, V 65-8-0.

[3] No fields given, but in 1726 the area was 245-2-28 (L1258, surveys, Tavistock 5, No. 28).

[4] This holding was later split up, and the new tenants' names were added in the margin, each with a number. These are given here in brackets, each referring to the fields before the next entry.

H32. In Hand: a waste plot by Two Bridges.

H33. Nicholas Gill rents a little garden from the waste, rent 4s (let to Richard Cudlip with part of Park Wood).

H34. Richard Cudlipp holds Kembles Meddow, A 5-3-18, R 1-4-0, V 6-18-0, old V 7-0-0, date 3 Nov. 1701, rent 12s, heriot best beast or £2 10s, lives said Richard (40), Eliza Masters (60), Susanna (30), his wife.

H35. Richard Cudlipp holds Crosse Parkes and house in Towne (Burrough), date 3 Nov. 1701, rent £2 10s, heriot £2, lives said Richard (40), John (20), his son, Richard (14), his son.

Three under roomes, five chambers, a fore shopp and backe shopp and stable and court in the Back Street.

Two fields between the wayes leading to Two Bridges and Indescemb [*sic*], A 5-1-29, R 1-2-0, V 6-10-0, old V 10-0-0.

H36. Richard Cudlipp holds Indescomb Mills, [*lease as H34*], rent £1 10s 8d, heriot best beast or £2.

Two under rooms, two chambers, two mills, V 7-0-0. Stroule field, A 1-3-8, R 0-8-0, V 0-14-0; Wood field, A 2-3-32, R 0-4-0, V 0-10-0; meaddow, A 0-3-3, R 2-0-0, V 1-16-0; Barne and close, A 4-0-0, R 1-0-0, V 4-0-0.

Sum A 9-2-3, V 14-0-0, old V 11-0-0.

H37. Phillip Williams holds Lumhole, date 15 Feb. 1693 [*/4*], rent 10s, heriot 10s, lives John Elford (30), Ralph Elford (28).

Two under rooms, shop, two chambers over, pound house, out house. Hearb garden and orchard, A 1-1-0, R 2-0-0, V 5-0-0; Lower field, A 1-0-2, R 1-0-0, V 1-1-0; Higher field, A 1-2-26, R 1-0-0, V 1-10-0.

Sum A 3-3-28, V 7-11-0, old V 6-0-0.

H38. William Spry holds Indescomb, date 3 Mary 1696, rent £1 13s 4d and a capon, heriot best beast or £3, lives William Spry (21), his son, John Spry (19), Hannah Carpenter (17).

Hall, parlour, two under roomes, four chambers over, a stable, a barn and shipping with a fulling mill, orchard and herb garden, A 0-2-20, V 8-10-0.

Northermost field, A 2-3-24, R 0-17-0, V 2-4-0; Two Hills, A 4-3-1, R 0-7-0, V 1-10-0; Long meaddow, A 2-0-9, R 1-5-0, V 2-10-0; Lower Meaddow, A 3-1-38, R 1-14-0, V 5-10-0; Middle Parke, A 4-1-29, R 0-16-0, V 3-10-0; Rack Parke, A 4-1-0, R 0-16-0, V 3-10-0.

Sum A 22-2-1, V 27-4-0, old V 24-0-0.

H39. Edward Greenwood holds [*at*] Willminston, date 6 Aug. 1675, rent £1 6s 8d and a capon, heriot £3 or best beast, life Catherine Couch (60).

A hall, a parlour, two other ground roomes, four chambers over, a shipping, stable and barne.

Herb garden and orchard, A 1-1-38, R 1-2-0, V 1-10-0; Middle Parke, A 3-2-14, R 0-12-0, V 2-0-0; Bates parke, A 2-0-27, R 0-12-0, V 1-4-0; Threata Parke or field, A 2-3-30, R 0-12-0, V 1-16-0; Willands, A 4-2-39, R 0-12-0, V 2-16-0; North Ground, A 5-3-17, R 0-12-0, V 3-10-0; Under Hill, A 2-3-21, R 0-7-0, V 1-0-0; Two Longlands, A 9-0-38, R 0-11-0, V 5-0-0; meaddowes, A 5-0-25, R 1-2-0, V 6-0-0; field above, A 3-3-0, R 0-11-0, V 2-0-0; Commons on Heath field Downes, V 0-10-0.

Sum A 42-1-9, V 27-6-0, old V 27-0-0.

H40. William Cole holds [*at*] Willminston, date 20 Aug. 1663, rent 13s 4d and a capon, heriot 13s 4d, life said William (60).

A hall and one other under room, a shopp, three chambers over, a poundhouse, a barne and stable.

Herb garden and orchard, A 0-3-37, R 2-0-0, V 1-10-0; Mannas, A 13-3-31, R 0-12-0, V 7-10-0; Two West Parkes, A 2-2-39, R 0-12-0, V 1-10-0; Parke above the towne, A 1-0-19, R 1-4-0, V 1-4-0; Homer meaddow, A 0-3-21, R 1-6-0, V 1-2-0; the Ham, A 0-3-30, R 1-10-0, V 1-6-0; the Common mead and comon on Heathfield, V 0-9-0.

Sum A 20-2-17, V 14-11-0, old V 24-0-0.

H41. John Martin, late Peake holds [*at*] Willminston and Terrell, date 24 April 1681, rent 15s and a capon, heriot best beast or £3 13s 4d, life Mary (40), his now wife.

A hall, two other under rooms, three chambers over, a barne, stable and shipping, a linney house and hogs houses. Herb garden and orchard, A 0-2-26, R 3-0-0, V 1-10-0; Hang parke, A 2-3-27, R 0-15-0, V 2-0-0; Cley parke, A 2-1-16, R 0-13-4, V 1-10-0; Hilley parke, A 6-0-12, R 0-5-0, V 1-10-0; Comforts, A 2-3-33, R 0-13-4, V 1-10-0; Rack Parke, A 0-2-25, R 0-13-4, V 0-7-0; two new parkes, A 5-1-38, R 0-10-0, V 2-18-0; Higher meaddow, A 3-0-10, R 1-3-4, V 3-10-0; Little meaddow, A 0-2-5, R 1-12-0, V 0-16-0; Comfort meaddow, A 0-0-24, R 1-0-0, V 0-5-0; Homer meaddow, A 1-3-12, R 2-0-0, V 2-18-0; Hamm, A 1-2-15, R 1-4-0, V 1-16-0; Iveter meaddow, A 1-0-9, R 1-3-0, V 1-4-0; common meaddow, his parte, A 0-3-0, R 0-18-0, V 0-14-0.

Sum A 30-0-12, V 22-8-0, old V 31-0-0.

H42. Joan King, late Lake holds [*at*] Willminston, date 20 Oct. 1670, rent £1 and a capon, heriot best beast or £3, life Eliza Davey (56). A hall, two under roomes, a shopp, a barne, shipping, stable and linney.

Orchard and gardens, A 1-0-20, R 2-0-0, V 2-0-0; the Ley, A 5-2-26, R 0-11-0, V 3-0-0; New Parke, A 2-3-22, R 1-0-0, V 2-11-0; the Gratten, A 2-0-29, R 0-12-0 V 1-5-0; Great meaddow, A 2-2-8, R 1-4-0, V 3-0-0; Little meaddow, A 0-1-26, R 2-10-0, V 0-16-0; East Hill Corner and Strould, A 11-1-13, R 0-6-8, V 3-10-0; Six Acre, A 5-3-12, R 0-12-0, V 3-5-0; Horna Parkes, A 1-3-22, R 0-15-0, V 1-4-0; Derley, A 2-0-28, R 0-12-6, V 1-5-0; Two Hamms, A 2-2-19, R 1-6-8, V 3-10-0; Rounda Mead, A 0-3-27, R 1-6-0, V 1-0-0; Acre Peice, A 1-0-0, R 0-5-0, V 0-5-0; field above the orchard, A 4-2-4, R 0-14-0, V 3-0-0; Coppice Wood and Common meaddow, A 0-3-0.

Sum A 45-3-10, V 29-11-0, old V 24-0-0.

H43. Daniell Cudlipp holds [*at*] Willminston, date 1 June 1691, rent £1 4s and a capon, heriot best beast or £3 6s 8d, life said Daniell (30).

A hall, a parlor, two other under roomes, foure chambers, a barne, stable, shipping and linney.

Herb garden and orchard, A 0-2-37, R 4-0-0, V 2-10-0; Wheat Parke, A 0-3-0, R 1-4-0, V 0-18-0; Two Leyes, A 8-2-16, R 0-12-0, V 5-0-0; Two Manna's, A 11-2-18, R 0-9-0, V 5-0-0; Berry Parke, A 4-0-4, R 0-12-6, V 2-10-0; Little New Parke, A 2-2-1, R 0-12-0, V 1-16-0; Sandy Land, A 4-1-18, R 0-11-0, V 2-10-0; Lanna Parke, A 2-3-1, R 0-12-0, V 1-10-0; Bakes Parkes, A 3-0-28, R 0-13-4, V 2-0-0; Great Moorey Meaddow, A 3-1-22, R 1-5-0, V 4-0-0; Ivetor meaddow, A 0-3-28, R 1-12-0, V 1-4-0; Gratton meaddow, A 0-2-22, R 2-0-0, V 1-0-0; Holland meaddow, A 0-3-6, R 1-6-8, V 1-0-0; West Ham, A 0-2-0, R 1-0-0, V 0-10-0; Cleine, A 2-1-35, R 0-5-0, V 0-10-0; Common Meaddow his part and Heath field, A 0-3-0, R 0-18-0, V 0-14-0.

Sum A 47-3-36, V 32-6-0, old V 44-0-0.

H44. Richard Cudlipp holds [*at*] Willminston, date 24 June 1706, rent £1 6s 8d and a capon, heriot best beast or £2 13s 4d, lives said Richard (60), John Cudlipp (23), [*blank*] his wife (22).

A hall, two under roomes more, three chambers over, a barne, shipping, stable and linney.

Herb garden and orchard, A 1-1-8, R 1-12-0, V 2-0-0; Lower and Higher Parkes, A 6-1-18, R 0-13-4, V 4-0-0; Two Grattners, A 5-3-19, R 0-11-0, V 3-0-0; Two Lawnes, A 11-3-7, R 0-9-0, V 5-0-0; Huckna, A 1-3-31, R 0-9-0, V 0-16-0; North Parkes, A 3-2-1, R 0-10-0, V 1-16-0; Two West Parkes, A 8-2-6, R 0-10-0, V 4-5-0; Two Church Hills, A 8-3-3, R 0-10-0, V 4-5-0; Three meaddows, A 5-1-9, R 1-0-0, V 5-5-0.

Sum A 53-1-22, V 30-7-0, old V 37-0-0.

H45. Daniel Reddaclift holds [*at*] Willminston, Arscotts, rent £1 and a capon, heriot best beast or £3, lives Daniell Cudlipp (23), son of Robert Cudlipp deceased, said Daniell Reddaclift (35), Roger Veare (30).

Two under rooms, two chambers, barn, linney.

A little hearbe garden, V 0-10-0; Wester Derley, A 6-2-27, R 0-12-0, V 3-18-0; the next, A 7-3-32, R 0-11-0, V 4-10-0; Lower Derley, A 5-3-17, R 0-14-0, V 3-18-0; Smalla Parke, A 1-1-31, R 0-16-0, V 1-0-0; Moore, A 5-1-3, R 0-10-0, V 2-12-6; Two Hills, A 3-0-15, R 0-5-0, V 0-16-0; Two Bicknells, A 9-2-10, R 0-12-0, V 9-10-0; Two Edymeads, A 2-2-26, R 2-0-0, V 7-0-0; Coppice Wood, A 2-1-0, R 0-3-0, V 0-6-0; Common meaddow and common on Heath Field, V 1-4-0.

Sum A 44-3-4, V 35-4-6, old V 31-10-0.

H46. John Grendall holds Idleshill, alias Idleshelf, rent 6s 8d, heriot best beast or £2 13s 4d, life Walter Batten (55). Two under roomes, two chambers, barn, linney.

Garden and orchard, A 0-1-18, R 1-0-0, V 0-10-0; Little meaddow, A 1-1-17, R 1-0-0, V 1-5-0; Lower field, A 4-0-7, R 0-8-0, V 1-12-0; next field, A 3-3-23, R 0-8-0, V 1-10-0; the next to that, A 2-1-5, R 0-10-0, V 1-3-0; field at head, A 2-1-5, R 0-10-0, V 1-3-0; commons on Heath field, V 0-5-0 .

Sum A 15-0-8, V 7-15-0, old V 10-0-0.

H47. William Cake, gentleman, holds Glanaclieve, rent £3 and a capon, heriot best beast or £3, lives Roger Cake (60), his brother, said William (40).

Three fields next Mana Butts, A 14-1-24, R 0-10-0, V 7-0-0; field below them, A 15-3-28, R 0-10-0, V 7-10-0; Hill under it, A 3-2-28, R 0-8-0, V 1-10-0; Two meaddows, A 3-1-11, R 1-0-0, V 3-5-0; the Grove, A 0-3-20, R 0-1-6, V 0-5-0; North Hill, A 4-1-2, R 0-7-0, V 1-8-0; field above it, A 11-2-24, R 0-10-0, V 5-15-0; field next Idleshill, A 12-1-30, R 0-6-8, V 4-0-0.

Sum A 66-2-7, V 30-13-0, old V 33-0-0.

H48. Jeffery Reddaclift holds Burnford, rent £1 and a capon, heriot best beast or £3, life said Jeffrey (45), old V 28-0-0 [*no more details given*].

[p.43] Southwest Quarter of Tavistock Parish

H49. Hugh Pyne, gentleman, holds Croundwell, date 2 Sept. 1706, rent £4 6s 8d, heriot best beast or £4, lives said Hugh (35), Thomas Pyne (40), his brother, Arthur Pyne (9), his nephew.

A hall, a little and grate parlour, a buttery, a dary, five chambers, a brew house, barne, stable, shipping and pound house; ye lower house, two ground rooms, two chambers; two herb gardens.

Three orchards, A 3-2-0, R 2-0-0, V 7-0-0; West Parke, A 15-1-18, R 0-8-0, V 5-10-0; Two Moores, A 4-2-21, R 0-13-4, V 3-0-0; Two Lower Hams, A 15-3-12, R 0-12-0, V 9-0-0; Above Towne, A 13-0-36, R 0-7-6, V 5-10-0; Two Oxen Parkes, A 18-1-1, R 0-6-0, V 5-18-0; Stoney Parke, A 11-3-30, R 0-6-8, V 4-0-0; Long Meads, A 4-2-2, R 1-6-8, V 6-0-0; Two Inner Hams, A 11-3-30, R 0-10-0, V 6-0-0; Outer or Mill Hams, A 8-2-9, R 0-7-6, V 3-10-0; Great meaddow, A 7-1-14, R 1-1-0, V 7-10-0; Wood Parke, A 12-1-22, R 0-6-8, V 4-0-0; Higher Will Parke, A 8-3-7, R 0-7-0, V 3-10-0; Lower Will Parke, A 4-3-7, R 0-9-0, V 2-0-0; Two Little Parkes, A 11-2-39, R 0-17-0, V 9-0-0; Coppice Wood, A 4-3-24, R 0-5-0, V 1-2-6; Towne Place, V 1-0-0.

Sum A 157-2-32, V 83-10-6.

H50. Joseph Davy junior holds [*at*] Shillamill, rent £1, heriot best beast or £2 13s 4d, lives Thomas Reddall (55), Julian (50), his wife, said Joseph (40).

A hall and two other under roomes, three chambers over, an out house, two under roomes and two chambers over, barn, stable and pound house.

Garden and orchard, A 1-3-31, R 2-0-0, V 3-10-0; Three Hams, A 6-2-29, R 0-18-0, V 6-0-0; the meaddow, A 0-3-31, V 2-10-0; two fields next Crowndell, A 2-3-5, R 0-10-0, V 1-10-0; field above the orchard, A 2-3-2, R 0-12-0, V 1-12-0; Mill Parke, A 1-3-28. R 0-10-0, V 0-18-0; Woody

Parke, A 2-0-26, R 0-10-0, V 1-0-0; the Hills, A 14-2-26, R 0-3-0, V 2-4-0.

Sum A 2-3-27, V 19-4-0, old V 20-0-0.

H51. Henry Vosper holds [*at*] Shillamill, date 28 [*blank*], rent £1, heriot best beast or £2 13s 4d, lives George Tucker (22), son of Ichabod Tucker, Francis Davey (23), son of Francis Davey.

Lower Hilley Ground, A 12-1-0, R 0-10-0, V 6-0-0; Grove, A 3-0-32, V 0-20-0; Higher field, A 8-0-38, R 0-10-0, V 4-0-0; meaddow, A 2-3-16, R 1-4-0, V 3-10-0.

Sum A 26-2-6, V 14-0-0, old V 20-0-0.

H52. Thomas Riddolls holds Woods Shillamill, date 20 Nov. 1659, rent 13s 4d, heriot 13s 4d, lives said Thomas (50), Elizabeth (36), wife of Joseph Davey, Thomas Riddols (46), son of Jesper Riddols.

Two lower rooms, one chamber over, orchard and herb garden. A meaddow, A 1-1-30, V 2-0-0.

(**H53**. John Bealey holds Uppaton, late Mr. Rolls, rent £2 10s.)

H54. James Leere holds Hartshole, rent £1 3s and a capon, heriot best beast or £3, lives John Horseman (60), Dorothy Leere (22), his daughter.

Three under roomes, three chambers over, backhouse, barn, stable, shipping.

Gardens and orchard, A 1-1-30, V 1-10-0; Newton Parke, A 7-1-1, R 0-3-0, V 1-1-0; Three Acre, A 4-1-29, R 0-3-0, V 0-13-0; Little Parke, A 2-1-14, R 0-5-0, V 0-11-0; Hartshole Hill, A 2-2-24, R 0-4-0, V 0-10-0; Moorey Plott, A 1-2-24, R 0-6-0, V 0-9-0; Warns Nest, A 0-1-12, R 0-12-0, V 0-3-0; Horne Parke, A 3-2-27, R 0-4-0, V 0-14-0; two meaddows and grove, A 5-3-30, R 1-0-0, V 5-10-0; Six Acre, A 6-1-25, R 0-3-0, V 0-18-0; West Parke, A 7-1-0, R 0-3-0, V 1-1-0; Spillers Marsh, A 2-2-32, R 0-5-0, V 0-12-6; Long field and Spillers Corner, A 4-2-37, R 0-2-0, V 0-10-0; Souther Grove, A 6-3-26, R 0-4-0, V 1-7-0; Grattner, A 6-1-0, R 0-5-0, V 1-11-0; Rumley Hills, A 2-2-0, R 0-2-0, V 0-5-0.

Sum A 66-1-31, V 17-5-6.

H55. Nicholas Screech holds Higher Blackmoreham, rent 13s 4d, heriot best beast or £2, lives said Nicholas (60), John (26) and Charles (24), his sons.

Two under roomes, barn, stable.

An orchard, A 1-0-28, V 1-0-0; Little meaddow and Lay Moore, A 1-0-29, R 1-4-0, V 1-4-0; Six Hams, A 13-0-37, R 0-8-0, V 5-4-0; Quilletts, A 0-2-35, V 0-6-0; meaddow behind the house, A 1-3-2, R 0-8-0, V 0-14-0; Downe parke, A 5-3-10, R 0-4-0, V 1-3-0; Two Will Parkes, A 4-1-25, R 0-7-0, V 1-10-0.

Sum A 28-1-6, V 11-1-0.

H55a. In Hand: Lower Blackmoreham.

H56. Elizabeth Masters holds [*at*] Buckstor Cross, date 30 Sept. 1654, rent £1 6s 8d, heriot best beast or £4, lives said Elizabeth (64), Samuell Sowton (66).

A barn; Grate and Little meaddow, A 4-0-39, R 1-15-0, V 7-0-0; Barne field, A 6-0-13, R 1-10-0, V 6-10-0; field above it, A 2-1-27, R 1-0-0, V 2-5-0; field next that, A 5-1-24, R 0-19-0, V 5-0-0.

Sum A 18-0-23, V 20-15-0.

H57. John Hoggison holds [*at*] Buckstor Cross and a house in Town, rent £2 1s and a capon, heriot best beast or £3, life Susanna Coringdon (43).

In the Burrough: Two shopps, two other under roomes, four chambers over, stable, and hearb garden, V 6-0-0.

Nethermost field, A 3-1-14, R 1-0-0, V 3-5-0; Easter field, A 2-3-30, R 1-0-0, V 2-10-0; Barne Parke, A 2-3-22, R 1-0-0, V 3-0-0; meaddow, A 2-1-32, R 2-0-0, V 4-0-0.

Sum A 11-2-18, V 18-15-0.

H58. John Payne holds Great Beercause, date 30 May 1696, rent £2 3s 4d, heriot £2, lives Robert Hoggison (60), Humphry Hoggison (44), John Badcock (23).

A barne; Homer field, A 3-3-27, R 1-0-0, V 4-0-0; Northermost field, A 5-2-16, R 1-0-0, V 5-10-0; field adjoyning to the Buttes, A 9-1-4, R 1-0-0, V 9-5-0; meaddow, A 4-3-38, R 1-10-0, V 7-10-0.

Sum A 23-3-5, V 26-5-0.

H59. Arthur Lumley holds Little Beercause, rent £1 1s, heriot best beast or £3

Three Pease Hills, A 5-1-34, R 0-12-0, V 3-5-0; Two Moores, A 2-1-9, R 0-10-0, V 1-2-6; Clewres, A 5-1-6, R 0-13-4, V 3-10-0; Barne Parke, A 3-0-0, R 0-16-0, V 2-8-0; meaddow, A 4-0-32, R 1-4-0. V 5-0-0.

Sum A 20-1-1, V 15-5-6.

H60. Samuell Sowton holds Lumburne Parks, date 4 [*blank*], rent £1 13s 4d, heriot best beast or £3, life Ann (46) his now wife.

A barn; Three Corner meaddows, A 1-3-1; Barne field, A 4-2-35; Two Long meaddows, A 2-0-10; three fields above the barne, A 12-2-7; North Parke, A 6-1-8.

Sum A 27-1-21.

H61. John Cudlipp holds Badcock Parkes, date 1 Feb. 1681 [/2] rent £1 4s, heriot £2 13s 4d, lives Elizabeth Masters (60), said John (22).

A barne; Two meaddows, A 3-2-32, R 1-0-0, V 3-15-0; Barne field, A 2-3-38, R 1-0-0, V 3-10-0; Lower field, A 3-0-38, R 1-0-0, V 3-5-0.

Sum A 9-3-28, V 10-10-0.

H62. Henry Vosper holds Crease, alias Bounds Parks, date 1 July 1690, rent £1 6s 8d and a capon, heriot best beast or £3, lives Esira Sprag (30), Amy Sprag (28), daughter of John [*Sprag*].

A barne; Great field, A 7-1-19; Little field, A 3-3-16, [*both*] R 0-15-0, V 8-5-0; field above the barne, A 6-0-38; field below the barne, A 5-0-0, [*both*] R 0-15-0, V 8-5-0; meaddow, A 1-3-8, R 1-0-0, V 1-15-0.

Sum A 34-1-1, V 18-5-0.

H63. Blanch Reddaclift holds Crease, date 20 June 1686, rent £1, heriot best beast or £2, lives said Blanch (63), Mary (40), her daughter, Daniell (43), her son.

Great field, A 4-2-0, R 1-0-0, V 4-10-0; Lower field, A 2-3-8, R 1-0-0, V 2-15-0; meaddow, A 2-0-12, R 1-0-0, V 2-15-0; meaddow, A 2-0-12, R 1-0-0, V 2-0-0.

Sum A 9-1-20. V 9-5-0.

H64. Elizeus Cruise and John Edgecombe hold Crease Cottage, life said Elizeus (60).

H65. John Edgecombe holds Bowrish, date 21 Aug. 1704, rent £1 13s 4d, heriot best beast or £3, lives Edward Willcocks (40), said John Edgecombe (32), Ann (26), his wife.

Two under roomes, three chambers, shipping, stable, herb garden.

An orchard, A 0-0-24, R 2-0-0, V [*?with house*] 2-0-0; Two fields next the Mills, A 3-3-25, R 0-16-0, V 3-0-0; Home Parke, A 4-2-19, R 1-0-0, V 4-10-0; Hilley field, A 4-3-20, R 0-10-0, V 2-7-6; three meaddows, A 3-3-39, R 1-8-0, V 5-10-0.

Sum A 17-2-7, V 17-7-6.

H66. Stephen Rundle holds Lumburne Meadow, rent 9s, heriot 5s, life said Stephen (60).

H67. Mary Widdicombe holds Lumburne Cottage, life said Mary.

H68. Henry Vosper holds Nutton, date 22 Mar. 1696[*/7*], rent £1 9s 4d and a capon, heriot best beast or £2 13s 4d, lives George Southall (10), Elizabeth Southall (12).

A house; orchards, A 0-2-23, V 1-0-0; Rack Parke, A 2-2-26, R 0-18-0, V 2-6-0; Two Hilley fields, A 3-3-0, R 0-18-0, V 3-5-6; Souther meaddow, A 2-3-10, R 1-10-0, V 4-2-6; Norther meaddow, A 2-0-18, R 1-10-0, V 3-2-6; Above Towne, A 2-0-11, R 0-16-0, V 1-12-0; Goose Hill, A 1-3-2, R 0-16-0, V 1-12-0; the Moorey meaddow, A 0-1-35, R 1-4-0, V 0-12-0.

Sum A 16-1-5, V 17-12-6.

H69. Roger Rundle holds Crebar, alias Newton, date 9 Mar. 1675[*/6*], rent £2, heriot best beast or £2 13s 4d, life said Roger (60).

A house; garden and orchards, A 1-0-15, R 1-10-0, V 1-10-0; Grate Parke, A 8-1-16, R 0-12-0, V 5-0-0; Two Green Parkes, A 6-0-16, R 0-10-0, V 3-0-0; Higher fields, A 7-0-38, R 0-8-0, V 2-17-0; Above Towne, A 4-2-32, R 0-10-0, V 2-6-0; meaddow, A 1-3-12, R 1-10-0, V 2-13-0.

Sum A 29-1-9, V 17-6-0.

H70. John Wood holds Newton Chapple and [two] Meddows, A 1-3-37, V 2-15-0, date 9 Aug. 1675, rent 11s 4d, heriot 5s, life said John (60).

A litle dwelling house; one under roome and two chambers over.

H71. John Wood holds Newton Mills, [*lease as H70*], rent 13s 4d, heriot 13s 4d.

H72. Dorothy Cudlipp holds Newton Cottage, rent 6s 8d, heriot 6s 8d.

H73. John Parsons holds [*at*] Newton, date 21 Jan. 1686[*/7*], rent £2 8s 6d, heriot best beast or £4, lives said John (56), Eliza (58), his wife.

A house; gardens and orchard, A 1-2-37, R 2-0-0, V 3-0-0; Three meaddows, A 7-2-9, R 1-0-0, V 7-10-0; Easter Towne, A 4-2-0, R 0-13-4, V 3-0-0; New Parke, A 9-1-39, R 0-10-0, V 4-10-0; Kennester, A 11-0-15, R 0-9-0, V 1-18-0; Little New Parke, A 5-2-35, R 0-12-0, V 3-12-0; Hill, A 3-0-24, R 0-10-0, V 1-10-0; Homer Easter Towne, A 3-1-30, R 0-15-0, V 2-10-0; Crooked Parke, A 2-2-3, R 0-10-0, V 1-5-0; Canna Parke, A 5-0-16, R 0-10-0, V 2-10-0; Two Canna Parkes, A 15-3-32, R 0-13-0, V 18-10-0; Wheat Parke, A 10-1-10, R 0-10-0, V 5-2-0.

Sum A 80-2-10, V 54-17-0, old V 50-0-0.

H74. Joan Rundell holds [*at*] Newton, date 20 Jan 1676 [*/7*], rent £1 13s 4d, heriot best beast or £3, life said Joan (50).

A hall and parlours, a milkehouse and drinkhouse, and foure chambers over, barn and shiping and wean house and house ye other side the highway.

Orchard and garden, A 0-2-13, R 2-0-0, V 2-0-0; foure Leys by the house, A 9-2-25, R 0-10-0, V 4-15-0; Two Tor Parkes, A 4-0-14, R 0-7-0, V 1-18-0; Five meaddows, A 4-0-8, R 1-10-0, V 6-5-0; Five Ridge Parkes, A 8-0-12, R 0-5-0, V 2-0-0; Foure Furze Parkes, A 12-1-3, R 0-5-0, V 3-0-0; Seven North Parkes, A 19-3-6, R 0-6-8, V 6-10-0.

Sum A 58-2-1, V 26-0-0, old V 30-0-0.

H75. Samuell Hawksworth holds [*at*] Newton, date 10 June 1686, rent £1 and a capon, heriot best beast or £3 6s 8d, lives said Samuell (50), Mary (43), his wife.

A house; Three orchard, A 1-2-33, V 3-0-0; Western garden, A 0-3-28, V 1-10-0; Hill Croft, A 4-3-8, R 0-3-0, V 1-18-0; Three North Downes, A 7-2-28, R 0-3-0, V 3-0-0; Two Acres, A 1-3-26, R 0-12-0, V 1-4-0; New Parke, A 2-0-38, R 0-12-0, V 1-5-0; Two Hills, A 2-2-3, R 0-13-0, v 1-12-6; Three meaddows, A 2-3-33, R 1-10-0, V 4-5-0; garden and mowhay, A 0-0-30.

Sum A 24-3-27, V 17-4-6.

H76. Samuell Hawksworth holds Luscombe Downe, A (about) 182-1-1, R 0-1-6, V 13-10-0, date 16 Aug. 1661, rent 13s, heriot 10s, life said Samuell (50).

H77. Dorothy Cudlipp holds Lana Parks, date 30 Sept. 1654, rent £1 and a capon, heriot best beast or £2 10s, life Richard Cudlipp (64).

A barne; Souther field, A 2-1-27; Wester field, A 3-0-32; meaddow, A 1-0-38; Norther field, A 3-2-3; Eastern field, A 3-3-12.

Sum A 14-0-32, V 9-6-8, old V 16-0-0.

H78. John Wood holds Little Artiscombe, rent 13s 4d, heriot best beast or £2, lives Mary Youle (46), Joan Youle (43).

A barn; Higher Parke, A 1-0-30, R 0-12-0, V 0-13-0; Middle Parke, A 3-3-33, R 0-15-0, V 3-0-0; Lower Parke, A 2-0-25, R 0-15-0, V 1-10-0; meaddow, A 1-2-1, R 1-0-0, V 1-10-0; Coppice Wood, A 1-0-32, R 0-10-0, V 0-12-0.

Sum A 10-0-1, V 7-5-0, old V 7-0-0.

H79. Roger Facy holds Great Artiscombe, date 24 June 1685, rent £1 2s, heriot 10s, lives said Roger (45), George Edgecombe (40).

Souther field, A 7-2-2, R 0-14-0, V 5-5-0; Wester field, A 5-2-16, R 0-14-0, V 3-17-0; Two meaddows, A 4-0-14, R 1-0-0, V 4-0-0; field next the barne, A 3-2-24, R 0-12-0, V 2-2-0; field next the wood, A 2-1-19, R 0-14-0, V 1-10-0; Coppice Wood, A 2-2-26, R 0-10-0, V 1-5-0.

Sum A 25-3-21, V 17-9-0.

H80. Daniell Sleman holds Artiscombe, Tor Parks, rent 8s, heriot best beast or £1 10s.

Long Parks, A 0-3-21, R 0-10-0, V 0-8-0; Coumb Parke, A 2-1-30, R 0-7-0, V 0-16-0; Grate Parke, A 4-1-24, R 0-9-0, V 2-0-0; Home Parke A 2-1-9, R 0-10-0, V 1-2-6; meaddows, A 2-0-30, R 1-0-0, V 2-0-0; the [*blank*], A 0-1-0, V 1-10-0.

Sum A 12-2-4, V 7-16-6.

H81. John Edgecombe holds Honyes Tore, rent £1 17s 8d and a capon, heriot best beast or £3, lives English Mounyaine (60), Ann (26), his wife.

A house; Orchard and gardens, A 1-0-9, V 1-10-0; Three Beat Lands, A 11-2-26, R 0-5-0, V 3-0-0; Rougha Ground and Under Towne, A 7-1-5, R 0-7-0, V 2-10-0; Pumple Curey and Barne Parke, A 2-3-7, R 0-10-0, V 1-7-6; Bakes Parke and Above Towne, A 3-0-21, R 0-10-0, V 1-10-0; Week Parke, A 3-0-2, R 0-8-0, V 1-5-0; Five Corner Parkes, A 10-3-16, R 0-10-0, V 5-8-0; Tow South Parkes, A 6-1-22, R 0-7-0, V 2-5-0; Little South Parke, A 1-0-22, R 0-10-0, V 0-10-0; New Parke, A 6-3-14, R 0-4-0, V 1-5-0.

Sum A 54-0-24, V 20-10-6, old V 20-0-0.

H82. John Hunn holds Hatchmoore, A 8-3-10, R 0-8-0, V 3-10-0, old V 3-6-8.

H83. Richard Cudlipp holds Impham, date 1 July 1689, rent £1 2s 8d, heriot £2 1s 8d or best beast, lives Richard Cudlipp (22), his brother, Richard Gerry (31).

A house; Orchards and gardens, A 0-0-35, V 0-10-0; Hamm, A 6-0-21, R 0-16-0, V 4-16-0; Long A Lee, A 1-2-6, R 0-10-0, V 0-15-0; Ball, A 3-2-32, R 0-2-6, V 0-10-0; Hill, A 1-0-7, R 0-4-0, V 0-5-0; What Lane Head, A 3-1-22, R 0-2-6, V 0-10-0; Bridge meaddow, A 0-2-0, R 0-10-0, V 0-5-0; Downe Parke, A 12-2-0, R 0-2-6, V 1-10-0; Knocking Mill, R 1-0-0, V 1-0-0.

[*margin*] The Hath Wood with it, entered in Morwell Mannor, No. 9.

Sum A 29-0-3, V 10-1-0, old V 20-0-0.

H84. Richard Dabson holds Coxter Lands, date 2 Sept. [*blank*], rent 4s, heriot 4s, life Willmitt (65), wife of Stephen Collier.

A house, Orchards, A 0-0-31, V 0-10-0; Higher field, A 2-3-6, R 0-5-0, V 0-13-0; Midle field, A 2-2-28, R 0-4-0, V 0-8-0; Lower field, A 5-0-32, R 0-4-0, V 1-0-0; Litle Parke, A 1-2-26, R 0-6-0, V 0-9-0.

Sum A 12-2-3, V 3-0-0.

H85. Richard Dabson holds Coxter Lands, alias Great Tor, date 20 Oct. 1688, rent £2 6s 8d, heriot best beast or £4, lives said Richard (37), Mary Ellis (35), his sister, Roger Vere (40), son of Roger Vere.

A house; Orchard and Towne Place, A 2-3-19, R [*?for V*] 2-0-0; Torwall foure fields, A 16-3-9, R 0-5-6, V 4-10-0; the Well Parke, A 2-1-10, R 0-10-0, V 1-2-6; Bladder Parkes, A 14-0-8, R 0-8-0, V 5-12-0; Six Easter Wayes, A 35-0-3, R 0-9-0, V 15-15-0; South Parke, A 6-2-32, R 0-8-0, V 2-10-0; Undertowne, A 2-0-16, R 0-12-0, V 1-5-0; Three meaddows, A 5-1-0, R 1-0-0, V 5-5-0; Two Above Townes, A 9-1-13, R 0-10-0, V 4-12-6.

Sum A 94-1-30, V 40-12-0, old V 40-0-0.

H86. John Pyke holds [*at*] Woodovis, rent 16s;, heriot best beast or £2 13s, 4d, life John Cudlipp (24), son of Roger Cudlipp.

A house; The orchards, A 1-0-8, R 2-10-0, V 2-10-0; the Moore Splatt, A 4-1-4, R 0-6-0, V 1-8-0; Green Lane Head, A 1-1-1, R 0-8-0, V 0-10-0; Two Hollow Grattners, A 5-1-6, R 0-12-0, V 3-12-0; Two West Downes, A 6-0-12, R 0-2-6, V 0-15-0; Two Above Townes, A 4-0-34, R 0-10-0, V 2-2-0; East Downes, A 8-0-8, R 0-2-6, V 1-0-0; Little Parke, A 0-2-9, R 1-0-0, V 0-10-0; Two meaddows, A 1-1-29, R 1-10-0, V 1-18-0.

Sum A 32-0-23, V 14-5-0, old V 16-0-0.

H87. John Rowe holds [*at*] Woodovis, rent £1 6s 8d and a capon, heriot best beast or £3, lives said John (59), Patience (54), his wife, John (28), their son.

Orchards, A 0-2-2, V 3-0-0; Foure meaddows, A 6-3-4, R 1-5-0, V 8-10-0; Beer Parke, A 4-2-9, R 0-12-0, V 2-16-0; Two Rinnoules, A 9-0-12, R 0-3-4, V 1-10-0; Barne Parke, A 3-2-32, R 0-12-0, V 2-2-0; New Parke, A 4-0-19, R 0-12-0, V 2-8-0; Two Wrims in hay, A 12-3-24, R 0-5-0, V 3-5-0; Three Downes, A 11-1-31, R 0-2-6, V 1-10-0; Two Outishes, A 4-1-38, R 0-5-0, V 1-5-0; Two Forgett Parkes, A 5-0-11, R 0-6-0, V 1-10-0.

A 62-2-32, V 27-16-0, old V 30-0-0

H88. John Rowe holds Cole Towne, rent 18s and a capon, heriot best beast or £4, lives William (21), Walter (23) and John Rowe (28).

A house; Orchards, A 2-1-6, R 1-5-0, V 3-0-0; Two Above Townes, A 3-3-27, R 0-10-0, V 1-18-0; Wattkins, Gratten and Little Parke, A 4-3-24. R 0-10-0, V 2-8-0; Two Midle Parkes, A 6-3-29, R 0-9-6, V 3-6-0; Two Cross Parkes, A 8-

2-38, R 0-7-6, V 3-5-0; Moore, A 0-2-25, R 0-16-0, V 0-8-0; Two South Parkes, A 7-2-3, R 0-10-0, V 3-15-0; Two meaddows, A 4-2-20, R 1-8-0, V 6-6-0.

Sum A 39-2-12, V 24-6-0.

H89. Henry Mattacott holds Cassell Parkes, old V 4-12-0, rent 4s, heriot 3s 4d, life Thomas Winzor (56).

H90. Richard Cudlipp holds Heele, date 24 June 1693, rent £1 1s 4d, heriot best beast or £2 13s 4d, life John Cudlipp (26), son of Robert Cudlipp, deceased.

Orchards, A 0-2-0, V 2-12-0; North Parkes, A 2-3-1 R 0-4-0, V 0-10-6; Two Middle Parkes, A 2-2-8, R 0-5-0, V 0-12-6; West and East Parkes, A 3-2-29, R 0-6-0, V 1-2-0; Little Parke, A 0-2-13, R 0-10-0, V 0-5-0; Burrough Parke, A 2-2-26, R 0-4-0, V 0-10-0; Wood Earish, A 0-2-20, R 0-8-0, V 0-5-0; Rid Parke, A 4-3-6, R 0-4-0, V 0-19-0; Three meaddows, A 2-1-20, R 1-6-0, V 3-0-0; Squigder, A 0-3-33, R 0-10-0, V 0-9-6; Splatt, A 2-1-24, R 0-8-0, V 0-19-0; Mare meaddow, A 2-3-24, R 0-12-0, V 1-5-0.

Sum A 26-3-4, V 12-19-6.

H91. Richard Rundle holds Heele, rent £1 2s, heriot best beast or £4, lives said Richard (60), Charles Rundle (30), his son, [*blank*] (28), his wife.

Orchards, A 1-0-13, V 4-0-0; Two Northe Downes, A 8-0-30, R 0-2-6, V 1-0-0; Little Parke A 1-2-20, R 0-6-0, V 0-10-0; Two Blindvills, A 6-3-24, R 0-5-0, V 1-10-0; Long and Burrough Parkes, A 5-0-0, R 0-5-0, V 1-5-0; Above Towne, A 3-1-26, R 0-10-0, V 1-12-6; Heele Downes, A 15-1-20, R 0-2-0, V 1-10-6; Little Downe and Gratten, A 10-1-26, R 0-3-0, V 1-11-0; Bush Parke, A 2-3-2, R 0-6-0, V 0-16-0; Bengies, A 6-2-3, R 0-8-0, V 2-12-0; South Parke, A 4-0-32, R 0-6-0, V 1-5-0; Quarry Parke, A 2-2-32, R 0-15-0, V 1-18-0; Barne Parke, A 2-0-35, R 0-15-0, V 1-12-0; Three meaddows, A 3-0-26, R 1-8-0, V 4-0-6; Little Parke, A 1-1-1, R 1-0-0, V 1-5-0; Canna Parke, A 1-0-32, R 0-16-0, V 1-0-0.

Sum A 76-0-2, V 27-7-6.

H92. John Rowe holds Blanch Downe, date 31 Aug. 1663, rent £13 6s 8d, heriot 10s, life Thomas Rowe(59).

A house; Orchards, A 2-0-10, V 2-0-0; Ham and field above, A 6-1-15, R 0-9-0, V 5-15-0; field next the Ileand, A 5-0-0, R 0-6-8, V 1-13-4; Three Higher Hams, A 22-1-29, R 0-5-0, V 5-10-0; Two meaddows, A 1-2-20, R 1-4-0, V 1-16-0; Horse Parke and Splatt, A 2-12-9, R 0-9-0, V 1-0-0; Water Grate Parke, A 4-2-16, R 0-8-0, V 1-17-0; the Downe, A 98-1-39, R, 0-1-6, V 7-5-0; Twenty Acres, A 28-3-8, R 0-1-6, V 2-2-0; Pasture of the woods, V 2-0-0.

Sum A 171-3-6, V 30-18-4, old V 30-0-0.

H93. Joan Facey holds Midle, alias Cakeshill, old V 10-0-0, date 1 Nov. 1697, rent £1 3s 4d, heriot £1 3s 4d, life Joane (26), her daughter.

H94. Henry Vosper hold Pixon, date 23 June 1683, rent £2 and a capon, heriot best beast or £4, lives Amy Doidge (25), Henry Willcocke (28).

A barn, hoppy and mowhay, A 0-2-16, R 1-0-0, V 0-10-0; Three Way Parkes, A 12-3-28, R 0-18-0, V 11-10-0; Burrough Parkes, A 3-2-24, R 0-18-0, V 3-4-0; Shagg Parke, A 5-1-8, R 0-15-0, V 4-15-0; Goosey Parke, A 3-3-36, R 0-18-0, V 3-12-0; Two Barne Parkes, A 6-2-26, R 0-19-0, V 6-5-0; Two meaddows, A 3-0-27, R 1-6-8, V 4-0-0.

Sum A 36-1-5, V 33-16-0, old V 35-0-0.

H95. Mr. Abraham Trowt holds Downehouse, date 24 June 1698, rent £2 13s 4d, heriot best beast or £2 13s 4d, lives said Abraham (66), John Pearse (26), his nephew.

A house, orchard and Towne Place, A 2-0-17, R 1-5-0, V 2-10-0; Souther field, A 5-3-1, R 0-18-0, V 5-5-0; Easter field, A 12-0-33, R 0-16-0, V 9-12-0; Two North Parkes, A 11-2-25, R 0-18-0, V 10-0-0; West Parkes, A 7-1-27, R 0-18-0, V 6-16-8; meaddows, A 7-0-15, R 1-0-0, V 7-0-0.

Sum A 46-0-38, V 41-3-8.

H96. George Courtenay, esquire, holds Stileswell, date 6 Oct. 1670, rent £4 13s 4d and two capons, heriot best beast or £5, lives said George (50), James (56), his brother.

Orchards and Towne Place, A 2-0-20, R 1-5-0, V 2-10-0; Hams and Coppice, A 3-2-0, R 0-5-0, V 1-5-0; Downe Parke, A 16-1-20, R 0-10-0, V 8-2-6; Eleven Acres, A 11-1-30, R 0-15-0, V 10-5-0; Great meaddow, A 3-1-1, R 1-6-8, V 4-6-8; Hill Parke, A 7-2-4; Poore Parke and Mill Parke, A 20-3-28, R 0-12-0, V 12-10-0; Little Parke, A 2-0-14, R 1-0-0, V 2-0-0; Two Homer meaddows, A 2-0-27, R 1-4-0, V 2-10-0; Cornogs Parke, A 9-3-24, R 0-16-0, V 7-5-0; field under itt, A 10-3-6, R 0-14-0, V 7-10-0; meaddow under itt, A 2-2-0, R 0-16-0, V 2-0-0; Marsh, A 2-2-32, R 0-5-0, V 0-13-0; Eighteen Acres, A 17-2-24, R 0-17-0, V 14-15-0.

Sum A 113-0-0, [*incomplete V 25-12-2*].

H97. Sir Francis Drake, baronet, holds the fishing of Tavy, date 15 Feb. 1697, rent 6s 8d, heriot 6s 8d, lives Francis (14) and Pollexson (13), his sons.

H98. John Couningham holds Culver Meddow. A 1-1-18, R 2-10-0, V 3-2-6, lives said John, Katherin, his wife, Joseph Davis.

[p. 69.] Cottages built on the Waste of Hurdwicke Mannor in Tavistock Parish

H99. Walter Symons holds [*at*] Dovin, rent 2s, heriot 2s, lives said Walter (66), Joan (62), his wife, Walter (30), his son.

A hall, a shopp, two chambers over and a garden, Old V 1-10-0.

H100. Walter Whitchurch holds Dolvin Meddow, one little meadow, A 0-2-0, date 1 Aug. 1703, rent 2s, heriot 2s, lives said Walter (22), Elizabeth (29), his sister, Old V 2-0-0.

H101. John Stephens holds Dolvin Tucking Mill, rent 6s 8d, heriot 6s 8d, lives said John (40), Danniell (20), his son.

One under roome, a milkehouse and one fulling mill, three chambers over, a hogs house and two gardens, Old V 4-0-0.

H102. Richard Spiller, late White, holds [*at*] Dolvin, rent 6s 8d, heriot 6s 8d, lives Thomassin White (66), John White (32), her son, William Spiller (14), son of Richard.

A hall, a cellar, a brewhouse, a little parlour and milkehouse, five chambers over, a stable, two hogshouses, two herb gardens and linney.

H103. John Russell holds Carons Cottage, alias Morwell Downe Lane End, date 1 Aug. 1703, rent 5s, heriot 5s, lives said John (40), Jane (36), his wife.

[*Margin*] Entered in Morwell Manor

Two under roomes, three chambers over, hogshouse and linney, an hearb garden and orchard and one plot of land, Old V 2-0-0.

H104. Symon Leach, clarke, holds Deep Lane, one little meadow, rent 6s 8d, heriot 6s 8d, lives said Symon (24), John Robins of Treelga, Old V 3-0-0.

H105. In Hand: A garden at Two Bridges, old V 0-4-0. (Granted with part of Park Wood to Richard Cudlip.)

[*Intervening sections without house descriptions omitted:*
[p. 76] *Ogbear manor*, 2 holdings

[p. 78] *Morwell manor*, 6 holdings

[p. 85] *Ottery manor* [Lamerton], 11 holdings

[p. 91] *Estate, late Sir James Butler's* 24 holdings

[p. 107] *Plymstock manor*, 46 holdings.]

[p. 133] Oreston Cottages [*Plymstock Parish*]

O1(73)[5] Ellias Lang, late Rouses, holds Gutter, V 3-0-0. Foure chambers, three cellers and a little plat.

O2. Jonathan Herderick and Thomas Hatch hold Herderick and Hatches tenement, lives Thomas Hatch (40), Fran' (50), his wife, John Hatch (20).

Foure under rooms, foure chambers, one outhouse, one hearb garden.

One field, A 1-2-0, V 7-0-0.

O3(33). Roger Phillips holds the Kings Arms, V 6-0-0. Two under roomes, three chambers, a brew house, two cellars, a courtlidge, one field, A 0-3-0.

O4(71,72). Richard Geffery holds, late Skinners, V 3-0-0. Two chambers and a cellar, two ground roomes and a spence, and five chambers new built.

O5(70). Rebecca George, late Curtises, holds, rent 1s, lives Eliza' Lang (60), John Endrick (20), V 1-0-0.

One ground room, one chamber.

O6(74). Mary Anderson holds the Ileand House, rent 1s, lives said Mary (28), her two sisters (20), V 1-0-0.

One under roome, one chamber and a little backside.

O7(69). John Watts holds, late Markeworth's, rent 2s, lives said John (60), Robert, his son,[6] V 2-10-0.

Two ground roomes, two chambers and a backside.

O8(68). Paul Bickford holds Norses Cottage, rent 1s, lives said Paul (30), Barbara (25), his wife, Mary Hoard (30), V 2-10-0.

Fowre ground roomes and foure chambers and a little platt.

O9(67). Grace Loud holds Burts Cottage, rent 1s, lives said Grace (55), Jonathan and William (22), her sons, V 1-0-0. Two ground roomes, two chambers and a little platt.

O10(66). Elias Lang holds Woodwalls Cottage, rent 1s, V 2-0-0.

Foure ground roomes, five chambers and a garett and an hearb garden.

O11(65). Rebecca Lang holds Gutters Cottage, rent 1s, V 1-0-0.

O12(64) Richard Veysey holds Huttsons Cottage, rent 1s, lives said Richard (60), his wife, Elizabeth George (34), V 2-0-0.

Two ground roomes and three chambers.

O13(63). Sarah Norse holds Dedlakes, rent 1s, lives Mary and Sarah her sister (34), V 1-0-0.

One ground roome, one chamber and a plott.

O14(62). Grace Trenawrth[*sic*] holds late Collings Cottage, rent 1s, lives said Grace, her two daughters (22), V 2-0-0. Two ground roomes, three chambers and a platt.

O15(61). Daniell Coleman, alias Courtis, holds Colemans Cottage, rent 1s, lives said Daniel (55), his wife, his son (25), V 1-10-0.

Two ground roomes, two chambers, a garden and [two little ?permars][7]

O16(60). Mary Cumins holds Burrows Cottage, rent 1s, lives said Mary (50), her son (25), V 2-0-0.

Two ground roomes, two chambers and a backside.

O17(59). Mary Cumins holds Dedlakes, rent 1s, [*lives as O16*], V 1-10-0.

One ground roome, one chamber.

O18(58). Richard Harris holds Hunkins Cottage, rent 1s, lives said Richard (70), his wife (60), Patience (20), his daughter, V 1-0-0.

One ground roome, one chamber.

O19(57). Arthur Stone holds Hunkins Cottage, rent 1s, lives said Arthur (40), his wife (40), V 1-0-0.

One ground roome, one chamber.

O20(56). Mary Parrager holds late Sweets Cottage, rent 1s, lives Thomas Sweet (50), two lives (50), V 2-0-0.

O21(55). Thomas Sweet holds Sweets Cottage, rent 1s, V 2-10-0.

Three ground roomes and three chambers.

[5] The numbers in brackets in this and the next section, are those pencilled in, keying this survey to the map of 1754.

[6] Note *query if living*.

[7] From version A, illegible on C.

O22(54). James Pollard holds Cannuch, rent 1s, V 1-10-0. Two little ground roomes and two chambers.

O23(53). Barbara Shilburt holds Toopes Cottage, rent 1s, V 2-0-0.

Two ground roomes and two chambers.

O24(52). John Witheridge holds Burry, rent 1s, V 1-0-0. One ground roome, one chamber and linney.

O25(51). Mary Lawry holds Slips, rent 1s, lives said Mary (40), Grace (14), her grand-daughter, V 3-10-0.

Three ground roomes, three chambers.

O26(50). Christian Edgecomb holds Jenkins, rent 1s, V 3-0-0.

Foure ground roomes, five chambers and a garden.

O27(49). Thomas Hatch holds Crosmans, rent 1s, lives said Thomas and his wife (40), Mary Candish (21), V 1-10-0. Two ground roomes, two chambers and a garden.

O28(48). Thomas Sladden holds Brownes, rent 1s, lives Anne (25), his wife, Elizabeth and Mary (27), his daughters, V 1-10-0.

Two ground roomes, two chambers and a garden.

O29(47). Alexander Vass holds Teegs, rent 1s, lives Henry Teeg (50), Alexander Vass (50), Willmitt (50), his wife, V 2-0-0.

Two ground rooms, two chambers and a backside.

O30(46). Joane Parkes holds Cornishes, rent 1s, life said Joan,[8] V 1-10-0.

Two ground roomes and two chambers.

O31(45). Matthew Thomas holds Broones, rent 1s, lives said Matthew (28), his wife (30), V 2-0-0.

Two ground roomes, two chambers, two gardens.

O32(44). Tamzine Boone holds late Langs, rent 1s, lives said Tamzine (50), her daughter (20), V 2-10-0.

Three ground roomes, three chambers and one backside.

O33(?43). Amy Harris holds Harrises Cottage, rent 1s, lives son and daughter (21), V 2-0-0.

Two ground roomes and three chambers.

O34(42). Mary Toboise holds Toboise's Cottage, rent 1s, life said Mary (50), V 2-0-0.

Two ground roomes, two chambers and a backside.

O35(41). Robert Jenkin holds Langs Cottage, rent 1s, V 1-10-0.

Two ground rooms, two chambers and garden plott.

O36(35). John Payne holds Mathews Cottage, rent 3s 4d, lives said John (60), Christopher Burn (35), Mary (30), his wife, V 4-0-0.

Three ground roomes, two chambers, one cellar and two stables.

[8] Note *query if alive*.

O37(34). Christian Edgcomb holds Cartuses Cottage, rent 1s, lives David Phillips (70), Grace Edgcomb (14), V 2-10-0.

Three ground roomes, three chambers.

O38(14). Thomas Colibete holds Bulls Cottage, rent 1s, V 3-0-0.

Three ground rooms, three chambers.

O39(32). Lawrence Couches holds Ashes Cottage, rent 4s, lives said Lawrence (35), his wife (30), his child (4), V 2-0-0.

Three ground roomes and three chambers.

O40(31). William Spicer holds Lawrys and Smiths Cottage, rent 3s, lives Elizabeth Spicer (50), Elizabeth and Mary Bowger (20), V 4-0-0.

Two ground roomes and five chambers.

O41(15). Sarah Quick holds Eustices Cottage, rent 1s, lives said Sarah (30), Agnes Ustace (30), V 2-0-0.

Three ground roomes, three chambers and a backside.

O42(16). Sarah Lawes holds Phillipes Cottage, rent 1s, lives said Sarah (50), John and James (18), her sons, V 1-10-0.

Two ground roomes, two chambers and one court.

O43(17). Jane Batten holds Brownes Cottage, rent 1s, V 2-10-0.

Three ground roomes, foure chambers and a backside.

O44(29). Adam Lang holds Whites Cottage, rent 1s, lives said Adam (60), his wife (45), V 2-10-0.

Three ground roomes, foure chambers, backside and court.

O45(28). William Sellwood holds Meaders Cottage, rent 1s, lives said William (60), his wife (50), Sarah (22), his daughter, V 4-0-0.

Eight ground roomes, nine chambers and garden.

O46(18). Tamzine Browne holds Brownes Cottage, rent 3s, lives said Tamzine (60), Sarah Avent, Hannah Avent (20), V 2-10-0.

Three ground roomes, five chambers.

O47(19). Tamzine Browne holds Brownes Cottage, rent 1s, lives said Tamzine, Sarah and Elizabeth, her daughters, V 2-10-0.

Five ground roomes, six chambers, one garden and backside.

O48(27). Amy Fa holds Drakes Cottage, rent 1s, lives said Amy (60), Eleanour (25), her daughter, Amy (6), her grand-daughter, V 2-10-0.

Two ground roomes, two chambers and a backside.

O49(21). John Pope holds Pope's Cottage, rent 1s, lives Joane Pope (60), his daughter (25), V 1-10-0.

Two ground roomes, two chambers and little backside.

O50(10). Elizabeth Rowe holds Griffids Cottage, rent 1s, lives said Elizabeth, Mary, her daughter, V 2-0-0.

Three ground roomes, two chambers and a backside.

O51(22). Abraham Boger holds Burts Cottage, rent 1s, lives Mary (55), his wife, Cornelius (22), his son, V 1-10-0 Two ground roomes, two chambers and a little backside.

O52(23). Grace Ellford holds Lawrys Cottage, rent 1s, lives said Grace (32), John and Mary (8), her children, V 3-0-0. Three ground roomes, three chambers, an outhouse, a celler and garden plott.

O53(24). John Sanders holds Bickfords Cottage, rent 1s, V 3-10-0.

Three ground roomes, foure chambers, a celler and a garden.

O54(25). Grace Effoard, late Lawrys, holds Hutchings Cottage, rent 1s, V 1-10-0.

Two ground roomes, two chambers, a little backside and a garden plott.

O55. Mr. Prinn holds Prins Cottage, rent 1s, V 2-0-0. Three ground roomes, three chambers and a celler on the Key.

O56(40). Edward Elliott, late Jenkins, late Skinners, holds Jenkins Cottage, rent 1s, lives James Jenkins (70), Edward Elliott (32), William (2), his son, V 5-0-0.

Three ground roomes, three chambers, two outhouses, lechlofts,[9] and garden plott and stable and pallace.

O57(39). Robert Story holds Shiphards Cottage, rent 1s, V 1-0-0.

One ground room, one chamber and a little herb garden.

O58(37). Nicholas Miller holds Burts, alias Millers, rent 2s, lives Nicholas Miller's wife (55), Judith and Sarah (18), his daughters, V 1-15-0. Two leases; Burt holds one. One ground roome, one chamber, one shipping and a garden plott.

O59(36). Christian Edgcomb holds Davises Cottage, rent 1s, V 2-0-0.

Two ground roomes and three chambers.

[p. 162] The Street going to Plymstock.

O60(11). Humphrey Gilbert, late Barletts, holds Barletts, rent 1s, V 1-10-0.[10]

One ground roome, two chambers, a shipping and little garden.

O61(10). Elizabeth Row holds Giffords Cottage, rent 1s, lives Elizabeth Row (50), Mary (20), her daughter, V 1-10-0.

Two ground roomes, two chambers.

O62(9). Christopher Burne, late Candishes, holds Candishes, rent 1s, lives said Christopher (40), Mary (40), his wife, his childe (14), V 1-10-0.

Two ground roomes, two chambers and a little garden plott.

O63(8). Richard Avent holds Avents Cottage, rent 1s, lives said Richard (60), Jane (60), his wife, Jane (21), his daughter, V 1-10-0.

Two ground roomes, two chambers and a little garden.

O64(6). John Fletcher, late Mewfields, holds Meryfields[11] Cottage, rent 1s, lives said John (60), his wife (50), his daughter (24), V 1-10-0.

One ground room, one chamber and one garden.

O65(7). John Williams, late Mewfields, holds Meryfields,[12] rent 1s, lives said John (32), Hester (30), his wife, V 1-10-0.

One ground roome, one chamber and a garden.

O66(5). Nicholas Effoard, late Lawrys, holds Polehey,[13] rent 1s, life Mary Lawry, V 1-0-0.

Two ground roomes, two little roomes and foure chambers.

O67(4). Grace Trenworth, late Lakes, holds Lakes, alias Wakehams, rent 1s, V 2-0-0.

Three ground roomes, three chambers and a large garden the other side the way.

O68(3). George Wakeham holds Burts Cottage, rent 1s, lives said George (60), Joane (55), his wife, Katherine (22), their daughter, V 1-10-0.

Two ground roomes, two chambers and an hearb garden.

O69(12). Mary Joslin holds Gaudes Cottage, rent 1s, lives said Mary (60), Elizabeth Gaud (48), V 1-0-0.

One ground roome, one chamber and a garden.

O70(13). Jane Batten, late Mathews, holds Mathews, rent 1s, lives said Jane (55), Jane (25) and Joane (17), her daughters, V 3-0-0.

Four ground roomes, four chambers and a little garden.

O71(2). William Candish holds Stutfords, rent 1s, lives John (22), his son, Christian, his daughter, William (12), his son, V 1-10-0.

One ground roome, one chamber and a garden pretty large.

O72(1). Brays house. In decay.

O73.[14] Withams. In decay. A lease of itt to Captain Smith.

[p. 170] Plymstock Cottages: the North End

P1(2). Margrett Binmore holds Binmore, rent 1s, lives Ann (21) and John Binmore (18), V 1-10-0.

Two ground roomes, two chambers, an orchard and hearb garden.

P2(3). James Addams, late Gaudes, holds Gaudes Cottage, rent 1s, life said James (35).

---

[9] Perhaps in error for cocklofts, though this is the reading in all versions.

[10] Note *query if not in hand*

[11] *Mewfields* in A

[12] *Meryfields* in A.

[13] Amended in pencil to *Polehouse*.

[14] Pencil note that map numbers 20, 26, 30, 38 and 43 were absent.

Two ground roomes, one chamber, and a little plott of ground.

P3(4). Lucie Briant, late Gates, holds Gates Cottage, rent 1s, lives said Lucie and one more life, V 1-10-0.

Two ground romes, two chambers and a small orchard.

P4(6). Mary Blake, late Grumeses, holds Brumes's,[15] rent 1s, lives said Mary and John Hawkins, V 1-0-0.

Two ground roomes and a little orchard.

P5(5). Mary Blake, late Burts, holds Burts Cottage, rent 1s, [*lives as P4*], V 1-10-0.

Three ground roomes, three chambers, an orchard and garden.

P6(7). Elinor Miller holds Millers Cottage, rent 1s, lives Mary Miller (50), Elizabeth Miller (38). V 0-15-0.

One ground roome and one chamber.

P7(8). John Barlett holds Barletts Cottage, rent 1s, lives said John, John, his son, V 0-10-0.

One ground roome and one chamber.

P8(9). John Giddey, late Balls, holds Balls Cottage, rent 1s, lives said John, Elizabeth, his sister, V 1-0-0.

Two ground roomes and two chambers.

P9(10). Margery Hendey holds Hendeys Cottage, rent 5s, lives said Margery (55), William and John (34), her sons, V 3-10-0.

Three ground roomes, three chambers, an orchard and a field, A 0-3-0.

P10(11). Jacob Ball, late Passes, holds Passes Cottage, rent 1s, lives said Jacob (40), his wife (40), his daughter (19), V 0-10-0.

Two ground roomes, two chambers and little plott of ground.

P11(12). Margrett Sladdon, late Giles, holds Gileses Cottage, rent 1s, lives said Margrett (50), Thomas and Racher [*sic*] (24), her children, V 1-0-0.

Two ground roomes and two chambers.

P12(13). Richard Hake, late Woodcocks, holds Woodcocks Cottage, rent 1s, V 2-0-0.

Three ground roomes, foure chambers, a cellar and stable.

P13(14). Richard Hake, late Harrises, holds Harrises Cottage, rent 1s, lives his wife and Susanna Ward (40), V 0-15-0.

One ground roome, one chamber and hearb garden.

P14(15). Thomas Millards holds Millards Cottage, rent 1s, life said Thomas, V 1-5-0.

Two ground roomes, one chamber and a little orchard.

P15(16). Richard Philles holds Philles Cottage, rent 1s, lives Jeane Philles (55), Richard, her son, V 1-0-0.

Three ground roomes, three chambers, a garden and courtlidge.

[15] *Grumes* in A.

P16(17). Joan Willkinson holds Batchwells, rent 1s, lives Susanna and Elizabeth (24), her daughters V 1-10-0.

Three ground roomes and three chambers.

P17(18). Thomas Pike holds Blakes Cottage, rent 1s, lives Elizabeth, Joane and John Doidge, V 1-10-0.

Two ground roomes, three chambers and an orchard.

P18(19). John Candish holds Barnacotts, rent 1s, lives said John (40), Elizabeth (21), his sister, Eliazer (21), his cozen, V 1-0-0.

Two ground roomes, two chambers and little hearb garden.

P19(20). Elizabeth Woodward holds Woodwards, rent 1s, lives said Elizabeth (60), Jonathan Rundell and Joane, his wife (25), V 1-10-0.

Three ground roomes, three chambers.

P20(21). Elizabeth Dill, late Bayleys, holds Bayleys, rent 1s, lives said Elizabeth (50), Hannah (28) her daughter, V 1-0-0.

Two ground roomes, two chambers, and a little hearb garden.

P21(22). Francis Trig, late Elliotts, holds Elliotts, rent 1s, lives said Francis (48), his wife (47), Mary (14):, his daughter, V 1-10-0.

Two ground roomes, three chambers and a garden plott.

P22(23). Jonathan Luscombe, late Hoopers, holds Hoopers, rent 1s, lives same Jonathan and his son John (31), V 1-10-0.

Two ground roomes, two chambers and a smiths shopp.

P23(24). Jonathan Credicott, late Guists, holds Guists, rent 1s, lives same Jonathan and his wife (40), V 1-0-0. Two ground roomes, two chambers and a shopp.

P24(25). Sylas Beckfoard, late Jesseps, holds Jesseps, rent 1s, lives Thomas Keswill (60), John Pyke (40), V 1-15-0. Two ground roomes, three chambers and an hearb garden.

P25(26). Margrett Physick, late Keswill, holds Keswill, rent 1s, lives Obediah (70) and Thomas Keswill (60), V 1-10-0. Two ground roomes, two chambers and a little orchard.

P26(27). Margrett Physick, alias Sale, holds Bennetts, rent 1s, [*lives as P25*], V 1-10-0.

One ground roome, one chamber and an herb garden.

P27(28). John Josling, late Trigs, holds Trigs, rent 1s, lives John Josling (50), John (40), his brother, V 1-10-0.

Three ground roomes, three chambers and a garden.

P28(29). Richard Sanders holds Sanders, rent 1s, life same Richard (48), V 1-10-0.

Three ground roomes, three chambers and a little plott.

P29(30). Richard Wood holds Woods, rent 1s, lives William Salmon, Joane (40), his wife, John Pyke (20), V 2-10-0.

Three ground roomes, three chambers, an orchard and an herb garden.

P30(31). Mary Daberell holds Pole house, rent 1s, lives said Mary (22), William (14), her brother, V 0-15-0.

Two ground roomes and two chambers.

[*Intervening sections without house descriptions omitted:* [p. 199] *Week manor [Milton, Abbot]* (7 holdings)

[p. 209] *West Liddaton manor [Brentor]* (5 holdings); its last holding, Mill Parkes, of 5 acres, gives a minimum house description: *two under roomes and three chambers.*]

[p. 221] Milton Manor [Milton Abbot]

M1. Richard Doidge, gentleman, holds Leigh Barton, date 18 Nov. 1670, rent £8 6s 8d, heriot best beast or £3, lives said Richard (60), Maurice Doidge (58), his brother.

A hall, a parlour, a kitching, a dary, a buttery, a cyder house, five chambers adjoyning over, halfe the barne on the west side, the west oxen house and shepping [*in A* the barne yt is in the west side, the wester oxen house and shipping] adjoyning with haylofts over the same, the cowhouse, 3 piggs houses adjoyning the kitching, the poundhouse, the court adjoyning and 3 hoggs houses, the easter youcking house, the chappel, the stable and shepping, and halfe the towne place and waterings, Broadparke garden, Chapple parke orchard neer the first garden, the chaple orchard nigh the youcking house and necessary [*in A* nissery] adioyning. Ley Ball Topp, A 27-1-19, R 0-12-0, V 16-10-0; South Ley Balls, A 15-3-14, R 0-9-0, V 0-7-0; Midle Balls, alias Cross Parks, A 9-3-32, R 0-10-0, V 5-0-0; Ley meadow, A 1-0-0, R 1-10-0, V 1-10-0; Little meadow, A 1-2-0, R 1-12-0, V 2-8-0; Wixen meaddow, A 1-0-0, R 1-0-0, V 1-0-0; Moore meaddow, A 4-0-0, R 1-0-0, V 4-0-0; Oxen Parke meaddow, A 1-2-0, R 1-2-0, V 1-13-0; Six Youlls including Wood, A 80-0-0, R 0-6-8, V 26-13-4; Oxen Parke, A 12-2-22, R 0-17-0, V 10-0-0; Three Lemans, A 17-1-4, R 0-13-4, V 11-10-0; two Chaple Parks, A 8-2-30, R 0-14-0, V 6-0-0; White A Borrough, A 9-3-20, R 0-10-0, V 5-0-0.

Sum A 118-2-21, V 98-4-4.

[*also*] North Ley alias Ley Balls, A 35-0-0, R 0-12-0, V 15-0-0; Blendwills, A 25-1-6, R 0-13-0, V 16-0-0.

M2. Richard Doidge holds Leigh Barton, date 26 March 1671, lives Amos Doidge (56), Henry Doidge (50), John Doidge (46).

A hall, a parlor, a kitching, a dry house, a pooke over, and 5 chambers over, the higher stable and woodhouse adjoyning, one piggshouse at the end of the dry house and 2 other piggs houses at the south end of the stable, the youcking house nigh the poole parke and piggs houses adjoyning, the east oxen house, the little oxenhouse, the maultehouse and granary over the same, and halfe deale of the courts and water-courses. The east oxen house, orchard and hearb garden adjoyning to Poole parke, and a plott of ground lying on the North side of the bee garden [*in A* side garden or bee garden].

Six Broad Parks; Broad Parke meaddow; East Grattner; West Grattner; Poole Parke and Mowhay; Six Homer Leys; halfe of the sheare of Millton Meaddow. [*Areas omitted but total in L1258, Surveys A3 is 94-3-39*].

[*Fifteen more properties in Milton Manor lack house descriptions. The last three had unusual tenures, paying 6s 8d normal rent, and also 1s 8d mill rent, perhaps commuted from suit to the lord's mill. They also owed five days service: one harving (*harrowing*) day, two mowing days, two reaping days and two out-taking days.*]

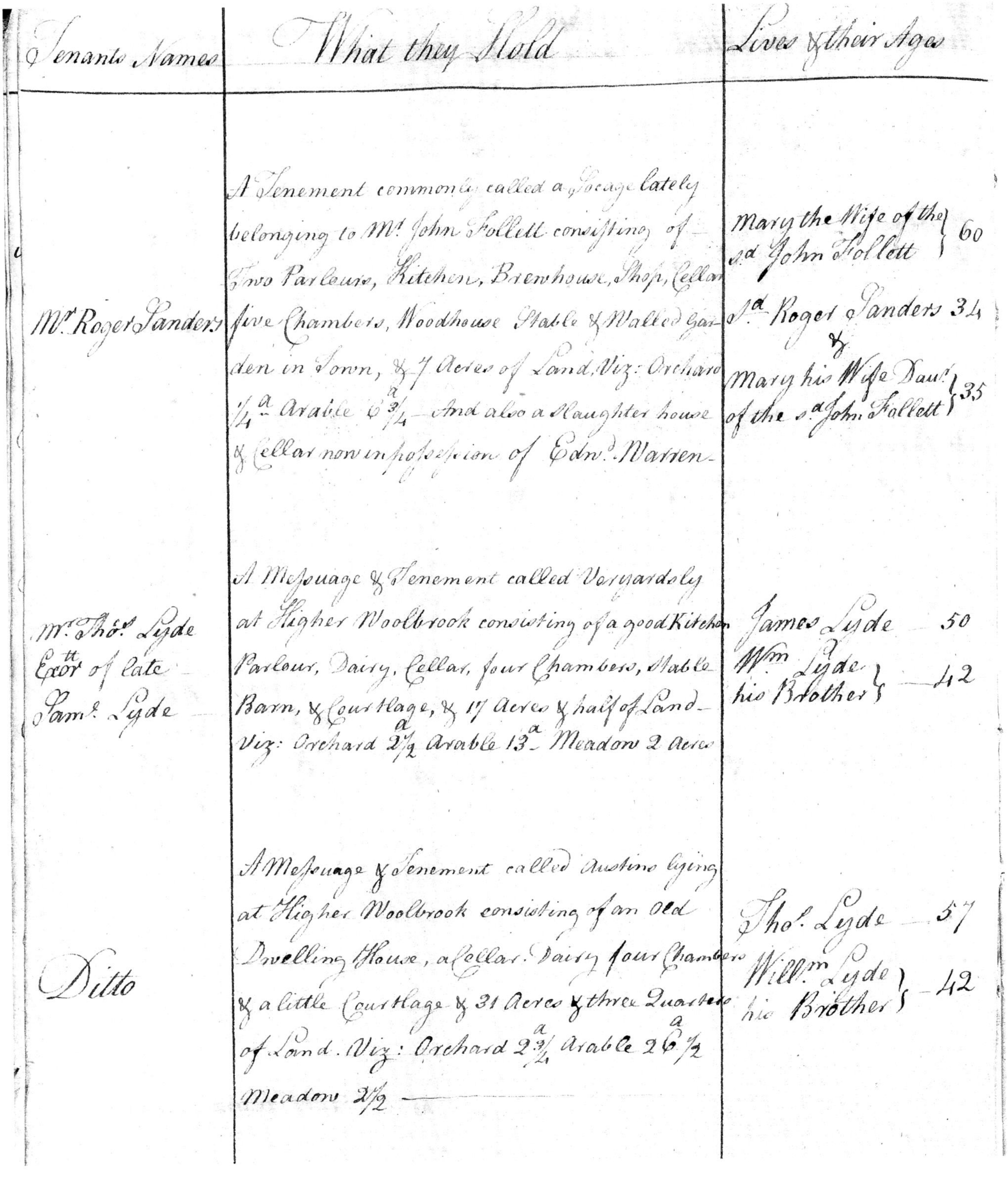

Tenants Names	What they Hold	Lives & their Ages
Mr. Roger Sanders	A Tenement commonly called a Soccage lately belonging to Mr. John Follett consisting of Two Parlours, Kitchen, Brewhouse, Shop, Cellar five Chambers, Woodhouse Stable & Walled Garden in Town, & 7 Acres of Land, Viz: Orchard 1/4 a Arable 6 3/4 a And also a Slaughter house & Cellar now in possession of Edwd. Warren	Mary the Wife of the sd John Follett 60 sd Roger Sanders 34 & Mary his Wife Daur. of the sd John Follett 35
Mr. Thos. Lyde Exor of late Saml. Lyde	A Messuage & Tenement called Veryardsley at Higher Woolbrook consisting of a good Kitchen Parlour, Dairy, Cellar, four Chambers, Stable Barn, & Courtlage, & 17 Acres & half of Land Viz: Orchard 2a 1/2 Arable 13a Meadow 2 Acres	James Lyde 50 Wm Lyde his Brother 42
Ditto	A Messuage & Tenement called Austins lying at Higher Woolbrook consisting of an Old Dwelling House, a Cellar, Dairy four Chambers & a little Courtlage & 31 Acres & three Quarters of Land. Viz: Orchard 2a 3/4 Arable 26a 1/2 Meadow 2 1/2	Thos. Lyde 57 Willm Lyde his Brother 42

Figure 28. A page (left side of opening only) of the survey of Sidmouth, Devon, 1764 (SM32-5) (D.R.O. 1334M/M5, p.7, reproduced with permission)

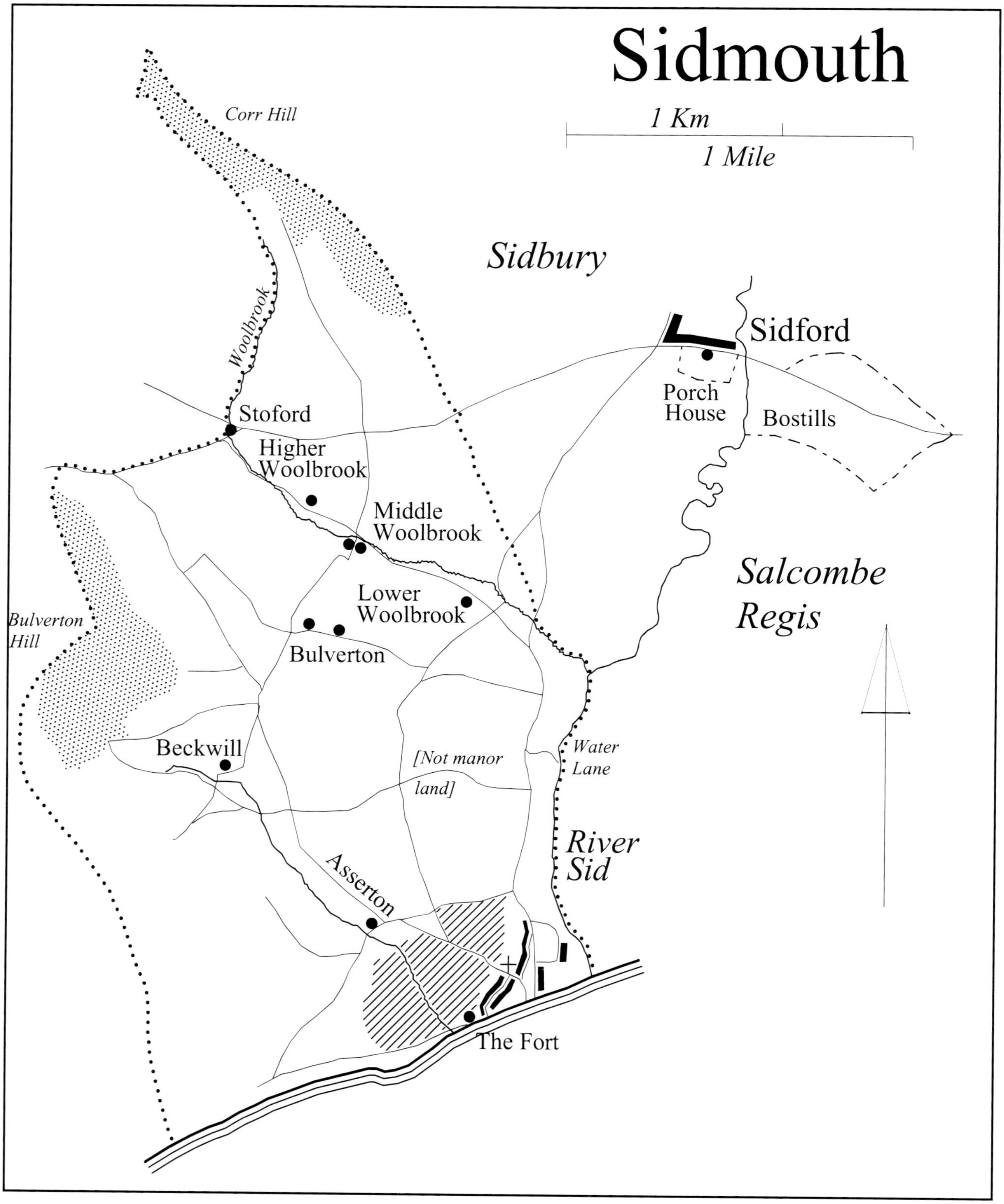

Map 11. Sidmouth parish and manor, Devon

Source: map of 1789 (see p. 209). Commons are stippled, and the small remaining open field area is shaded. The land in Sidbury and Salcombe is excluded from the 1789 map, but Porch House (though not its land), and Bostills can be located from other sources. Most of the land within the parish boundary (dotted) belonged to the manor, apart from an area in the centre (where labelled).

CHAPTER 14

Sidmouth

Sidmouth (SM): 1764 *Map 11*

In its survey, Sidmouth shows many similarities to Seaton, which is partly accounted for by their both being large seashore villages, and partly by a close resemblance in their topography. During the nineteenth century, Sidmouth became popular as a watering-place,[1] and it now has a very different character from its neighbour, but even in the seventeenth century, the occupations recorded[2] suggest that it was much more of a town. There was the expected dominance of seafaring trades—mariners, seamen and sailors. This group probably also included fishermen; though none are included as tenants, there was a fish-driver and a fishmonger. A significant number of people were involved with cloth—mercers, clothiers, tailors and a serge-maker. The urban character is confirmed by an edge-smith (making edged tools) as well as the usual and some less usual trades, baker, blacksmith, butcher, carpenter, cheese-monger, glazier, mason, maltster, thatcher and watchmaker. The wool-washing house (SM105), the dye-house (SM72) and the tucking mill (SM15) had served the woollen industry, but all had been abandoned; the last had also been used at some time as a blade mill, presumably by the edge-smith.

A small part of Sidmouth still lay in common fields (Map 11), and this may partly account for the schematic land descriptions. The larger holdings were described by the number of farthings of land they contained, although the exact acreage was also stated, and it appears that here a farthing was fifteen acres, in contrast to Kenton's thirty-two acres. The survey demonstrates the importance of the common pasture on Bulverton and Corr Hills; it was usually rated by the number of sheep that could be pastured there. The 'marsh' was used by a number of cottagers for gardens. It probably flooded intermittently in the winter, but was fairly dry in summer.

In 1764, Sidmouth Manor was the property of Sir John Prideaux of Netherton Hall, Farway; his holdings were, however, much interspersed with those of the other owners. He also owned four nearby farms in Sidbury and Salcombe parishes (SM115-118). The survey was taken in 1764, probably in the course of normal estate administration, but it exists in a copy of 1780, which was almost certainly made as a preliminary to the sale of the estate by the executors of Sir John Prideaux; he died in 1766, and after considerable difficulty with lawsuits, the sale to Thomas Jenkins was completed in 1789, when the manor was mapped for the new owner.[3] It is not clear what changes were made in preparing the 1780 copy; the 'lives' on which the leases depended had almost certainly been brought up to date by the omission of people who had died, although the ages refer to 1764 not 1780 (*cf.* SM13).

Tenure was mainly by leases for three lives, but hardly any leases had been renewed since 1764 and 29 of the 118 holdings had fallen into hand. They were presumably being let at rack rents, on a year-by-year basis, a policy probably adopted by the executors to make the estate more attractive to prospective purchasers. It does, however, reflect the general drift at this period away from leases for lives.[4] A few holdings were described as 'socages' (SM3, 25, 32, 55, 114), presumably because they had been held by socage tenure;[5] by 1764 they were indistinguishable from the remainder. Many more were termed 'lydworthy' (e.g. SM4, 7, 12, 13), a term that seems to be entirely unrecorded elsewhere. It would also appear to have lost any significance by 1683 (the date of the first surviving lease using it) because no distinction can be seen between these and the other holdings. It possibly described some type of burgage tenure, as the lydworthy holdings seem to be fairly uniform in size, between 1½ and 3½ acres (most commonly 2½ acres).[6] The existence of some of the functions typical of a borough is shown by SM16, leasing the benefit of the market place, shambles and Chezwell.[7]

The survey has one striking implication, that subtenancy was extremely important. This appears from the groups of holdings held by one person (and from the two holdings that contained a pair of houses, SM51, 52). Most notable was Samuel Follett, who leased SM11-31 and had previously held SM36 and 92-93. The Lyde family was also prominent (SM33-45, 51, 96), as were Samuel Cawley, father (SM2-4) and son (SM5-9, 76-78): one of these was described (SM14, 91) as Landlord Cawley. These people were clearly *rentiers*, a new element in society, and one that is surprising because they must have drawn off profit from the estate. It may well be that their appearance was one reason for the change to leases for terms of years, that could be better controlled. The leases describe one Samuel Cawley (elder ?) as a merchant, and another as a net-maker. Samuel Follett was also a merchant, like his father who was a mercer. Several members of the Lyde family were yeomen, but three were also described as mariners.

The Houses

The Sidmouth holdings fall into three clear groups, with areas respectively less than one, less than five, and five to ninety acres (Figure 1Q). The largest appear to be ordinary farms, although with a wide size range, but the distinction between the first two groups is not clear. The middle group correspond very closely to the 'lydworthies'. Of the twenty-three holdings with houses on them, all but five were lydworthies, while only one lydworthy (SM104) had less than one acre, and this was the result of subdivision. In all the survey gives details of seventy-four houses (31, 23 and 20 in the three groups).

A number of the farms have simple descriptions, giving the number of under rooms and chambers;[8] most had three or four rooms on the ground floor, and one had five rooms, with the same range in the number of chambers. It is significant that the surveyor had no need to specify the first floor rooms as such—the chambers were upstairs, the rooms downstairs. Two holdings (SM3, 51) each included a cellar and woodhouse, while SM91 had two cellars.

Five of the remaining farmhouses were fairly similar, typified by SM1 with a kitchen, hall, parlour, together with six chambers, a dairy and a separate cellar with another chamber over it. SM115 (see below) had three cellars and eight chambers, and also a brewhouse, while SM116 (only a seven acre farm) had a brewhouse but no cellars. SM101 and 48 were rather smaller, each lacking the parlour, and the latter had no cellar either.

The last five farms (SM32, 33, 41, 53, 89) differed notably from these in that none had a hall.[9] However, each had a kitchen and a parlour (or in SM32 two parlours), and the smallest (SM51) had in addition only a pantry and three chambers. SM89 included a brewhouse and two cellars, and also a closet with its five chambers; SM33 had a dairy, cellar, and four chambers. SM41 was the largest of this group, with a pantry, dairy, cellar and brewhouse. SM32 included the widest range of ancillary rooms accompanying its kitchen, two parlours and five chambers; it had a brewhouse, shop, cellar and woodhouse, and had previously also included a slaughterhouse with another cellar.

Despite the different terminology, these two groups may have been similar in plan, based on the three-room and cross-passage lay-out, and physical reality can be provided for SM115, Porch House (Figures 10-11, Plate IIIb). In spite of its nineteenth-century conversion to cottages, the original lay-out can still be followed. Like very many of the East Devon farms, it is in origin a medieval house. The principal evidence for this is found in the roof, which is very finely carpentered, with jointed cruck trusses (the central one arch-braced) and with wind-braces; it is heavily smoke-blackened and indicates a date around 1450. In plan, this medieval house probably consisted of the main transverse range only. It was modernised in 1574 by Nicholas and Elizabeth Isaac (the tenants, probably with a three-life lease). They created a splendid first-floor chamber in one end bay with a corbelled chimney, ceiled the hall and added its fireplace. The house probably reached its fullest extent around 1640, with the addition of the rear wings and perhaps the 'porch', though this was later removed, apparently before 1764.

On the smaller holdings, a number of houses were very much larger than would be expected. This might have been due to consolidation of farms, leaving houses without their land. A more likely explanation is that tenants were supported by business activities. Indeed, in some cases they can be identified as the 'Landlords' considered above. Half a dozen houses fall into this class; SM18 is characteristic, the home of 'Mr. Samuel Follett', with a parlour, hall, shop, kitchen, brewhouse, little cellar and eight chambers. SM5 and 7 had both apparently been the homes of

Samuel Cawley, senior, the first with a parlour, a little parlour, a hall (but no kitchen), a pantry and four chambers, the second even more sophisticated, a 'good house' with a kitchen, three parlours, a pantry and a cellar.[10] Could it have been a four-square Georgian house? It even had a walled garden, and another very similar Cawley house, SM91, had a 'little pleasure house in the garden'.[11] SM50, 'a good dwelling house', and the main house of SM68 were almost identical, each with a kitchen, parlour (two in SM68), cellar, buttery[12] and four chambers. No special trade is apparent for the former, but the latter was the Anchor Inn, a sufficient explanation for a large house. SM91 had also been an inn, the Dolphin, before it was taken over by the Cawley family.[13]

As at Seaton, a few cottages had been built in the seventeenth century (SM64, 70, 83) with a number of other constructions. A barn was converted to a house (SM85), a 'stable or cellar' was built on the waste (SM77) and another stable near the beach was converted to a cellar with a chamber over (SM22). Like Oreston, these were presumably cellars for fish; what was more significant than the new houses was the division of existing houses and the addition of extra houses to a holding. Notable is SM49, 'now three dwelling houses', two of which were in one building of five under rooms and six chambers, and SM79 with two houses in one building of two under rooms and two chambers.[14] In contrast to these, a number of houses had been abandoned at an unspecified date (SM31), 'lately' (SM40), '70 or 80 years ago' (SM90), or 'several years ago' (SM102). On holding SM58, an old house had become a stable and woodhouse, perhaps because a new house had been built. Holding SM72, consisting of two stables and two hogsties on the beach, was waste, perhaps destroyed by storms.

Table 29: Sidmouth smallholdings

Number of under rooms	1	2	3	4
Holdings of less than 1 acre	2	10	3	6
Holdings of 1 to 5 acres	1	7	7	2

Most of the houses of the smaller holdings are only described by the number of rooms. Subdividing the holdings into those with 1-5 ac land and those with less than 1 ac reveals a curious difference (Table 29).[15] The houses in both groups ranged from one to four rooms in plan. However, the larger holdings are dominated by the expected two and three room houses, while the second group included far more with four ground rooms. This must surely indicate multiple occupancy, as with the various divided houses noted above.

The houses on the smaller Sidmouth holdings reflect the same changes as the grander ones: the importance of the parlour rather than the hall, and the presence of pantries and closets. SM60 is characteristic, with kitchen, parlour, pantry and three chambers; it was identical to SM61, and almost to SM62 and 84, which had 'little parlours' (and a cellar in SM62), and to SM74 with a cellar and also an upstairs closet. The five other houses described all had shops.[16] SM83 was as simple as possible; a shop and chamber over, and probably not lived in.[17] SM14 and 112 each had a kitchen and a shop with three chambers over,[18] while SM59 also had a parlour and an 'under room'. The oddest was SM9 with a shop, two little kitchens and two little chambers. Was this perhaps used by two households, who were both involved with the shop?

As would be expected, these houses had few ancillary buildings, and apart from a few cellars, the only buildings recorded were woodhouses.

The Farm Buildings (Table 30)

Sidmouth in 1767 had developed much further towards the barn, stable and linhey economy than the Bedford estates on which it is first recorded. The 1709 survey of the latter was taken at a moment when plough horses and stables were just beginning to supersede draught oxen and their traditional stalls. Similarly, linheys for fattening cattle were increasingly preferred to older forms of cattle housing. Sixty years later and in areas of richer land those transformations were almost complete. In Sidmouth, stables outnumbered even barns, and twenty linheys (sometimes two to a farm) had replaced all but two shippons (SM117, 48) and a single cowhouse (SM89). Other changes were evident too. Six larger farmers tended orchards extensive enough to make a pound house convenient for crushing cider apples. Although these relatively fertile coastal farms required scarcely a third as much land as the Bedford estates on the edges of Dartmoor, the buildings used to carry on the blend of arable and

Table 30: Sidmouth: Occurence of farm buildings

Ref. Number	Acres	Barn	Stable	Shippon	Linhey	Pound House	Other Buildings & Notes	Ref. Number	Acres	Barn	Stable	Shippon	Linhey	Pound House	Other Buildings & Notes
SM18	0		•					SM32	7		•				
SM63	0	•						SM3	7½		•				
SM77	0		•				no house	SM116	7½		••				
SM111	0		•					SM118	11	•					no house
SM65	1½	•						SM101	16	•	•		••		
SM49	1¾		•					SM42	16	•					no house
SM52	1¾	•						SM33	18	•	•				
SM93	1¾	•						SM117	18	•		•	•		no house
SM7	2		•					SM100	18	•	•			•	
SM58	2		•					SM47	19	•	•		•		
SM62	2¼				•			SM92	20	•	•		•	•	
SM12	2½	•			••			SM89	29	•	•	*	•		*cowhouse
SM20	2½		•				pigsty	SM41	29		•		•	•	
SM30	2½	•					no house	SM48	31	•	•	•		•	
SM50	2½	•	•				other outhouses	SM36	31	•					
SM84	2½		•					SM10	32	•	•		••		
SM56	2¾		•		•			SM34	32						
SM43	4¼	•						SM11	40	•	•		••		
SM55	5	•	•				no house	SM97–8	41	•	•		•		
SM53	6¼	•	•					SM115	63		•		••	•	
SM51	6¾	•	•					SM1	90	•	•		••	•	

Note: 42 holdings of up to 2¾ acres with a house only are omitted, as are holdings with no buildings at all and those whose buildings are not described.

pasture farming had more in common with each other by the eighteenth century than they had with the old-fashioned structures that had long stood in the very same farmyards. This contrast is immediately clear on looking back from Sidmouth to Seaton and Farway (Figure 22F-G), dominated by shippons or oxstalls, with stables in only a subsidiary role.

In one respect, Sidmouth's buildings had an urban rather than agrarian significance. As in Tavistock, the community found a use for stables, in the back yards of their 'town-houses'.

1 The first 'gentlemen visitor's house' was Peak House, built by Emmanuel Baruch Leusada in 1795 (according to a guide to the town of 1830).

2 These are absent from the survey, but are given in the large series of leases that survive (D.R.O. D1334M. add. 2, L1-270), and have been added as footnotes to the survey text.

3 D.R.O. D1334M. Map 11 is based on this map; it is the property of the Sid Vale Association, and was used with their kind permission. Unfortunately the corresponding survey is lost.

4 See W. G. Hoskins, *Devon* (Newton Abbot, 1972), 92.

5 Cf. p. 75, n. 7.

6 The term occurs regularly in the medieval court and account rolls of Sidmouth Manor (in the British Library and the National Archives), but the contents do not provide further clarification; the earliest spelling is 'Ledwyrth' (list of tenants, temp. Edward I, British Library Add. Ch. 46927). See also R. E. Wilson, 'What is a Lydworthy', *Devon and Cornwall N. & Q.* 22 (1973), 218.

7 The meaning of *Chezwell* is unknown.

8 SM11, 36, 51 (both houses), 92, 98, 100. SM53 also included a small house with one under and one over room. SM10 and 34 have incomplete descriptions, giving only the number of chambers, while that of SM47, with only kitchen, brewhouse and four chambers must be suspect.

9 See p. 40 for further discussion of this characteristic change in late 17th-18th century Devon.

10 No chambers are listed, surely just an omission.

11 The lessee, until his death, was Oliver Cawley, perhaps the brother of Samuel, senior.

[12] The only ones named in Sidmouth. The usual 'pantry' was probably virtually equivalent to a buttery.

[13] SM32 was the George and SM63 the Red Lion, though both had ceased to be inns by 1764. The Ramshorne, of the latter, was not an inn name but a place in the river where nets were set to take fish (perhaps a long narrow channel that could be blocked by the net, named for its shape).

[14] Other examples are SM51, 53, 107, 63, 68 (double), 75, 76, (divided).

[15] The holdings included are: Smallest plots: SM21, 54, 63(a-b), 69-71, 73, 78, 80-1, 85, 95, 104,106, 109-111. Larger plots: SM12, 19-20, 23, 43, 49b, 52, 56-58, 65, 93, 103, 107a-b, 114.

[16] SM63(a) also had a shop, but only the number of rooms is given.

[17] This, and the cellar with chamber over (SM22), make it plausible that by this date 'chamber' meant no more than an upper room.

[18] SM112 also included part of the 'School House'; the other half was in SM104.

Survey of Sidmouth: 1764 (Figure 28, p. 207)

(Devon. Rec. Off. 1334M/M5. Sidmouth Manor Muniments)

This survey occupies a complete thin paper-bound book, copied and updated in 1780 from the original of 1764 (which has not survived). The entry for each holding is written across the full page opening in eight columns, whose headings are given under SM1. The survey is in three sections: Sidmouth holdings still leased in 1780 (SM1-85); holdings fallen into hand since 1764 (SM86-114); holdings at Sidford, etc. (SM115-8). There are no problems with the text, apart from the loss of one page of the MS. This has destroyed minor information for holdings SM26-31, and the main details for the four following holdings (called SM31a-d); these have been reconstructed as far as possible.

The main additional evidence comes from a large series of leases and counterparts, starting in the 1650's (Devon Rec. Off. 1334M.add.2/L1-270, cited here as L1, etc.). There is also a survey of 1750 (1334M/M4). These are useful for background information, particularly on occupations, but they do not provide much direct evidence on the houses, and so have not been quoted extensively. All but half a dozen of the leases can be identified with survey entries (and most of the exceptions are isolated leases of the 17th century), but some fifteen of the survey entries have no associated leases. References to the leases are included in the footnotes, and the status or occupation of the tenant is included in parentheses when it can be obtained from the leases.

TEXT

Copy of a Survey of the Manor of Sidmouth in the County of Devon in 1764.

Note: the tenements which were under lease in 1764, and fallen into hand between that year and the year 1780, are omitted in this copy, which was taken in 1780 from the survey of 1764.

SM1.[1] *Tenants Names*:[2] Mr. George Cooke. *What they hold*: The messuages or tenements called Middle Woodbrook [*for Woolbrooke*] and Bulverton, consisting of a Kitchen, hall and parlour, with six chambers over, a dairy, poundhouse, barn, stable, courtlage, two linhays, a cellar and chamber over, and 89 Acres and half of land, viz: Orchard 3¾ac., Arable 78¾ac., Meadow 7 ac., with common of pasture upon Bulverton and Corr Hills. *Lives and their Ages*: Micheal Cooke 27, Samuel Cooke 24; *Heriots*: £10; *High Rents*: £1 12s; *Capons or Dishes of Fish*: Two capons; *Yearly Value*: £84; *Land Tax, Poor Rates and Church Rates yearly about*: Rated in £60; L.T. [Land Tax] £7 14s; P.R. [Poor Rate] £5 5s; C.R. [Church Rate] £1 4s; [total] £14 3s.

SM2.[3] Mr. Sam. Cawley (gentleman): tenement at Bulverton, 16½ ac., (orchard 3 ac., arable 13½ ac.) com-

[1] L22-5, 149-152, to a yeoman (1658), a gentleman (1686), and a widow (1704).

[2] The headings of the columns are given in italics.

[3] L31-2, to a merchant (1665) and a yeoman (1726). This and the remaining entries are condensed by omitting common form. For the rates, the figures are normally constant for a particular rateable value and are only given once for each value; the abbreviations are as for SM1, with the addition of V = value.

mon for 30 sheep on Bulverton Hill; life: said Samuel Cawley 51; heriot best beast or £4; rent 4s 6d; V £15; rate £10, L.T. £1 5s 8d, P.R. 17s 6d, C.R. 4s, total £2 7s 2d.

SM3.[4] Ditto (gentleman); messuage or dwelling house in town called a socage, late Channons, 5 under rooms, 4 chambers, 1 woodhouse, stable, cellar, courtlage, two gardens, 7½ ac. (orchard 2 ac., arable 5½ ac.); lives: said Samuel Cawley 51, Samuel his son 20; heriot best beast or £2; rent 17s 4d, a capon or 1s; V £13; rate £6, L.T. 14s 8d, P.R. 10s, C.R. 2s 8d, total £1 7s 8d.

SM4.[5] Mr. Samuel Cawley (gentleman): Lydworthy in Western Town, late Channons, now consisting of three small tenements, a garden, 3½ ac. (orchard ½ ac., arable 3 ac.); lives: Samuel Cawley junior 20, Dorothy Cawley 22; heriot 13s 4d; rent 6s 8d; V £8; rate £3, L.T. 7s 4d, P.R. 5s, C.R. 2s, total 14s 4d.

SM5.[6] Mr. Sam. Cawley junior: dwelling house in town, wherin his father lived, a parlour, hall, little parlour, pantry and four chambers, garden near the beach; life: Samuel Cawley senior 51; heriot 7s; rent 3s; V[*with SM6*] £4 10s; not rated.

SM6. Ditto: garden plott called Harrisons, previously held by Robert Parkman; life as last; rent 1s; not rated.

SM7.[7] Mr. Sam. Cawley junior: Lydworthy called Rowes, being a good dwelling house (wherin the said Mr. Cawley's father lived), a kitchen, 3 parlours, pantry, stable, cellar, with a curtlage and walled garden in Town, 2 ac. (Orchard ½ ac. arable 1½ ac.). Note: the whole in the lease is called 2½ ac. Lives: Samuel Cawley senior 51, John Sandford 48; heriot best beast or £3 6s 8d; rent 5s 10d; V £11; rate £3 [*as SM4*].

SM8.[8] Ditto: messuage or dwelling house in town, near Chapple Hill, lately called the Barkhouse; lives: Samuel Cawley senior 51, Samuel Lyde 55; heriot 2s; rent 1s; V £2; not rated.

SM9. Mr. Samuel Cawley junior: house in town called Cole's, now in posession of John Veryard, two little kitchens, shop and two little chambers; lives: said John Veryard 36, John his son 7; heriot 5s; rent 2s; V £1 10s; not rated.

SM10.[9] Richard Doidge, esquire: messuage and tenement in Middle Woolbrook called Griggs, with two farthings of land, dwelling house, cellar, three chambers, barn, stable and 2 linneys, 31¾ac. (orchard 4¾ac., arable 27 ac.), common of pasture; life: Dorothy, his wife, formerly Connant 63; heriot best beast or £4; rent £1 and a dish of fish or 1s; V £30; rate £20, L.T. £2 11s 4d, P.R. £1 15s, C.R. 8s, total £4 14s 4d.

SM11.[10] Mr. Samuel Follett (merchant): messuage and tenement at Bulverton, three under rooms and 3 chambers, stable, barn, 2 linhays, curtilage, 39½ ac. (orchard 7 ac., Arable 32½ ac.), common of pasture for 60 sheep on Bulverton Hill; lives: said Samuel Follett 66, John his son 32; heriot best beast or £4; rent 5s 2½d and a capon or 1s; V £38; rate £20 [*as SM10*].

SM12.[11] Ditto: tenement called a Lydworthy, late Mares, lying near the Town, two under rooms and two chambers, a barn, two linneys, 2½ ac. (orchard 1½ ac., arable 1 ac.); life: John his son 32; heriot best beast or 12s; rent 6s; V £5; rate £3 [*as SM4*].

SM13.[12] Ditto: messuage and tenement comonly called a Lydworthy, 2½ ac. of land, meadow and pasture, previously held by Daniel Slade; lives: said Samuel Follett 66, Florence his sister 62; heriot 8s 2d; rent 4s 1d; V £3 10s; rate £3 [*as SM4*].

SM14.[13] Ditto: a little dwelling house at the South end of the Shambles, a kitchen, shop and three chambers, and a garden in the marsh, now rented by Landlord Cawley; lives: Florence his sister, now Mrs. Scadding 62, Benjamin Follett his brother 55; heriot £1 4s; rent 12s; V £3; not rated.

SM15. Mr. Samuel Follett: a waste plot whereon a Tucking or Blade Mill stood, 3 rods, formerly held by John Westcott, deceased, and now converted into a Nursery; lives: [*as last*]; rent 6d; V 5s; not rated.

SM16. Ditto: the benefit of the Market Place, Shambles and Chezwell, together with a chamber over the said Shambles, heretofore belonging to a Lydworthy at Westown;[14] lives: the said Samuel Follett 66, John his brother 63; heriot 4s; rent 4s; V £10 10s; rate £10 [*as SM2*].

SM17.[15] Ditto: cottage and garden plot, late Crammars, and also the plot of ground on which the Pound now or heretofore stood; lives: said Samuel Follett 66, Benjamin his brother 55; heriot 1s; rent 1s; V £1 1s; not rated.

[4] L169-73, to a husbandman (1680), a widow (1689), a yeoman (1727) and a gentleman (1752).

[5] L217-8, to a yeoman (1719) and a gentleman (1753).

[6] L83-4, to a mercer (1680).

[7] L202-5, to a yeoman (1707), a merchant (1731), and a netmaker (1735).

[8] L130-2, to a mercer (1681), a yeoman (1714) and a merchant (1731). In 1680 it was a stable. The last lease is endorsed *1871 Marlboro' Place*.

[9] L167, to a yeoman (1695).

[10] L26-30, to yeomen (1661, 1682) and a merchant (1741).

[11] L191-3, to a husbandman (1689), a yeoman (1712), and a merchant (1747).

[12] L187-8, to a yeoman (1683) and a mercer (1707). Florence Follet's age is given as 4 in 1707.

[13] L117-21 and 78-9. SM14 and 15 are combined in the last lease (L121). The former was leased to a mercer (1653), yeomen (1682,1703,1728), and a merchant (1747). SM15 was a newly erected fulling mill in 1674 (L78), leased to a fuller, and was probably a blade mill in 1708 when one tenant was an edger.

[14] This is probably SM27 (q.v.)

[15] L111, to a mariner (1731).

SM18.[16] Ditto; messuage and dwelling house in Town, wherein the said Samuel Follett now lives, heretofore in posession of Daniel Gundry, gentleman, and John Carpenter, part of a tenement called a socage formerly in posession of Erasmus Carpenter, a parlour, hall, shop, kitchen, brewhouse, little cellar, eight chambers, a stable, garden and curtilage; life: Florence, wife of Mr. Scadding 62; heriot £1 13s 4d; rent 7s; V £8; rate £1 10s, L.T. 3s 8d, P.R. 2s 6d, C.R. 1s, total 7s 2d.

SM19.[17] Ditto: moiety of a tenement called a Lydworthy, two under rooms, two chambers, garden, 1½ ac. in the common fields, heretofore held by William Carpenter; lives: said Samuel Follett 66, John his son 32; heriot 6s; rent 3s; V £L2 10s; rate £1 10s [*as SM18*].

SM20.[18] Ditto: messuage or tenement called Carpenters Lydworthy, also Princes, two under rooms, two chambers, stable, pigloose, 2½ ac. arable land; lives: [*as last*]; heriot 6s; rent 6s; V £4; rate £3 [*as SM4*].

SM21.[19] Ditto: cottage on the Beach, two under rooms and one chamber; lives: said Samuel Follett 66, Benjamin his brother 55; heriot 2s; rent 1s; V £1; not rated.

SM22. Ditto: stable now converted into a cellar with a chamber over, lying on the Green near the Beach; life: said Samuel Follett 66; heriot 6s; rent 6d; V 12s; not rated.

SM23.[20] Ditto: messuage and tenement in Town called a Lydworthy, late John Leatts, three under rooms and two chambers, a woodhouse, garden, 1¾ac. land (orchard ¾ac., arable lac.); life: Samuel Leatt his son 31; heriot 11s 8d; rent 5s 10d; V £3 10s; rate £2 5s, L.T. 5s 6d, P.R. 3s 9d, C.R. 2s, total 11s 3d.

SM24.[21] Ditto: messuage and tenement called Sandfords Lydworthy, 2½ ac.; lives: Benjamin his brother 55, John Sandford junior 46; heriot best beast or £2; rent 5s 9d; V £3 15s; rate £3 [*as SM4*].

SM25.[22] Ditto: part of Erasmus Carpenters Higher Tenement, called a Socage, containing (as appears by the counterpart of the lease 4½ ac. (orchard 2¼ ac.). N.B. the dwelling house etc., part of this tenement, was granted in another lease to Agnes Hare (now Cloade) for her life, and Moses and Jane, her son and daughter; and Richard Radford hath a cellar etc., also part of this tenement, for the lives of Mrs Scadding and the said Agnes Cloade. Lives: Mrs Florence Scadding 62, said Agnes Cloade 30; heriot £1 5s; rent 3s and a capon or 1s; V £5 10s; rate £2 5s [*as SM23*].

SM26.[23] Mr. Samuel Follett (merchant): tenement heretofore in posession of Grace Mitchell, since of Edmund Carpenter, an old dwelling house, 2½ ac. (orchard 1¼ ac., arable 1¼ ac.); life: John Follett his son 32.

SM27.[24] Ditto: messuage and tenement lying in Westown, called a Lydworthy, 2½ ac.; lives: said Samuel Follett 66, Florence his sister, now Scadding 62.

SM28.[25] Ditto: Pines Lydworthy, 2 ac. (orchard ½ ac., arable 1½ ac.); lives: [*blank*].

SM29.[26] Ditto: garden in the marsh, now in the posession of Joseph Sandford; lives: [*blank*].

SM30.[27] Ditto: Lydworthy called Lardys (late Mr. Follets), 2½ ac. arable land in the fields, with a barn and mowbarton; lives: Fanny Follett, now Saunders 36, Daniel Follett 34, Abraham Follett 33.

SM31.[28] Ditto: garden in the marsh, in posession of John Ellis, and a plot of ground in Town, wheron Bucknoles House stood; lives [*as last*].

SM31a.[29] [*From L61-64*: a house with eight acres of land, tenants Hannah Cornish and Mary Carter, *in 1750*; lives: Mary and Elizabeth Carter;] heriot best beast or £2 13s 4d; rent 3s 4d; V £9; rate £3 [*as SM4*].

SM31b.[30] [*from L259-61*: a messuage and half farthing, late Henry Carpenter, *in 1750* at Asserton, containing 15 ac.; tenant Robert Follett; lives Sarah and Robert Follett;] he-

---

[16] L174-83. The original socage was leased to a blacksmith (1680) and a mariner (1699). It was divided in 1719, and SM18 probably comprised the original house (leased to a yeoman in that year). The second part was leased to a yeoman (1728) and a merchant (1747), but was itself split in 1752 into SM25 (mainly the land), and another house (SM31c). A further part, the cellar referred to under SM25 is not identifiable in the survey (unless it is SM22 or SM31d).

[17] Perhaps L219-20. The other part may be SM93.

[18] L226-7, to a merchant (1741).

[19] L136, to a merchant (1733).

[20] L198-200, to a husbandman (1702), a yeoman (1714), and a mariner (1743).

[21] L225, to a merchant (1741). This followed a copyhold which expired as late as 1731. The lease is endorsed (presumably by the tenant) with a terrier of the lands: *½ ac. in Newclose; ½ ac. in Poyfields; 1 ac. in Gothils Lane; ½ ac. in Blackmore; court behind my house.*

[22] See note to SM18.

[23] L138-40, to spinsters (1686, 1716) and a merchant (1742). The rent, valuation and rate figures have been lost for SM26-31.

[24] Probably L201, to a mercer (1707) of *a Lydworthy in Westowne, 2½ ac., reserving the chamber over the Shambles, rent 6s.* Cf. SM16.

[25] From 1750 survey, rent 6s; heriot: best beast or L3 6s 8d.

[26] Unidentified in the 1750 survey or the leases.

[27] L189-90, to a widow (1684) and a merchant (1766). Although the latter post-dates the ostensible date of the survey, it includes the details of this lease; the rent was 6s.

[28] L99, to a merchant (1766); As for SM30, the survey includes details from this lease. The rent was 2s.

[29] The main details are lost for SM31a-SM31d. L61-64 and L259-61 probably refer to SM31a and b (which have the same rent).

[30] See note to SM31a.

riot best beast or £2 13s 4d; rent 3s 4d; V £11; rate £5 [*as SM32*].

SM31c.[31] [*from L182*: a house, being a socage, late Erasmus Carpenter; tenant Agnes Hare; lives: hers and Moses and Jane, her son and daughter;] heriot 8s 4d; rent 3s; V £3 10s; rate £1 10s [*as SM18*].

SM31d.[32] [*Unidentifiable, as entry blank except*:] V 15s.

SM32.[33] Mr. Roger Sanders: tenement commonly called a Socage, lately belonging to Mr. John Follett, two parlours, kitchen, brewhouse, shop, cellar, five chambers, woodhouse, stable, and walled garden in Town, 7 ac. (orchard ¼ ac., arable 6¾ac.); and also a slaughter house and cellar, now in posession of Edward Warren; lives: Mary, the wife of the said John Follett 60, said Roger Sanders 34, Mary his wife, daughter of the said John Follett 35; heriot 13s 4d; rent 17s; V £16; rate £5, L.T. 12s 10d, P.R. 8s 9d, C.R. 2s, total £1 13s 7d.

SM33.[34] Mr. Thomas Lyde, executor of late Samuel Lyde: messuage and tenement called Veryardsly at Higher Woolbrook, a good kitchen, parlour, dairy, cellar, four chambers, stable, barn and courtlage 17½ ac. (orchard 2½ ac., arable 13 ac., meadow 2 ac.); lives: James Lyde 30, William Lyde, his brother 42; heriot best beast or £3 6s 8d; rent 4s 8d and a capon or 1s; V £16 10s; rate £20 [*as SM10*].

SM34.[35] Ditto: messuage and tenement called Austins, lying at Higher Woolbrook, an old dwelling house, a cellar, dairy, four chambers and a little courtlage, 31¾ac. (orchard 2¾ac., arable 26½ ac., meadow 2½ ac.); lives: Thomas Lyde 57, William Lyde, his brother 42; heriot best beast or £3 6s 8d; rent 6s 8d; V £29; rate £20 [*as SM10*].

SM35.[36] Ditto: tenement called Greenways, an old dwelling house, 14 ac. arable land with common of pasture for 30 sheep on Bulverton Hill; life: James Lyde 30; heriot best beast or £2 13s 4d; rent 2s; V £11 7s; rate £8, L.T. £1 2s, P.R. 15s, C.R. 4s, total £2 1s.

SM36.[37] Ditto: messuage and tenement in Lower Woolbrook, lately belonging to Elizabeth Cawley, widow, deceased, four under rooms and four chambers, barn, courtlage, 31 ac. (orchard 3 ac., arable 28 ac.), with common of pasture upon Corr Hill for 60 sheep. Note: in the counterpart of the lease it appears that this estate is 32 ac. Lives: William Lyde 42, Thomas Lyde, son of James Lyde 8; heriot best beast or £3 6s 8d; rent £1 and 2 capons or 2s; V £29 10s; rate £20 [*as SM10*].

SM37.[38] Ditto: tenement or overland near Cottinton called Crutchmore (heretofore part of an estate belonging to William Warren, now Mr. Follets), 14½ ac. arable land. Note: in the counterpart of the lease, it appears to be 15 ac., and there are three pits planted to orchards. Common of pasture is also granted in the lease. Life: Samuel Cawley junior 20; heriot best beast or £3 6s 8d; rent 5s 7d; V £12 16s; rate £8 15s, L.T. £1 3s 10d, P.R. 16s 3d, C.R. 4s, total £2 4s 1d.

SM38. Ditto: cottage and orchard in Middle Woolbrook, late Pines; life: Thomas Lyde, son of James Lyde 8; heriot 6s; rent 6s 8d; V £1; not rated.

SM39.[39] Mr. William Lyde (gentleman): messuage and tenement containing two farthings of land, called Loverings, an old dwelling house, 26¾ac. (orchard 1 ac., arable 22¼ ac., meadow 3½ ac.), with common of pasture; life: said William Lyde 42; heriot best beast or £3 6s 8d; rent 6s 6d; V £25 10s; rate £16, L.T. £2 4s, P.R. £1 10s, C.R. 8s, total £4 2s.

SM40.[40] Ditto: toft, whereon a dwelling house lately stood with a garden plot and orchard thereto belonging, about ½ ac. land, called Broaddea, lying at Higher Bulverdon; lives: said William Lyde 42, Thomas Lyde, son of James Lyde 8; heriot 4s; rent 4s; V 10s; not rated.

SM41.[41] Ditto: messuage and tenement at Bulverton, containing two farthings of land, late in posession of William Orchard, gentleman, deceased, called Purchases, a kitchen, parlour, milkhouse, pantry, cellar, brewhouse and five chambers, a stable, poundhouse, linneys, courtlage, 29 ac. (orchard 1¾ac., arable 26½ ac., meadow ¾ac.); life: said William Lyde 42; heriot best beast or £3 6s 8d; rent 5s 3d, and a dish of fish; V £29; rate £20 [*as SM10*].

SM42.[42] Ditto: messuage or tenement at Bulverton, called Maynards, a cellar (formerly a dwelling house), a barn, 16 ac. (orchard 1 ac., arable 15 ac.), with common of pasture in and upon the commons belonging to the manor of Sidmouth for such quantity of sheep, beast and cattle, as may be depastured and fed upon the said tenement in the time of winter. Note: tis said to be 18 ac. of land in the counterpart of the lease. Lives: said William Lyde 42, Sam. Cawley junior 20; heriot best beast or £3 6s 8d; rent 9s; V £15; rate £10 [*as SM2*].

SM43.[43] Mr. James Lyde (mariner); cottage or tenement called Courthayes, 2 under rooms and two chambers, a barn, courtlage, 4¼ ac. (orchard ¾ac., arable 1½ ac., meadow 2

31 See note to SM18.

32 See note to SM18.

33 In 1692 (L73) this was *The George*, leased to a widow. The lease was only surrendered 65 years later in 1757 (L184-5; a lease to a merchant).

34 L155-6, to yeomen (1682, 1727).

35 L166, to a yeoman (1687).

36 L163-5, to a yeoman (1714).

37 L153-4, to yeomen (1681, 1765).

38 L65-7, to mariners (1711, 1729) and a gentleman (1756); before 1711, this was combined with SM92 (L141-4).

39 L49A,B, to a widow (1686) and a yeoman (1732).

40 L47-8, to a yeoman (1732) and a gentleman (1762).

41 L44-5, to a gentleman (1714) and a yeoman (1749).

42 L40-3, to a yeoman (1683) and a gentleman (1757).

43 L58-60, to a yeoman (1689), a widow (1702) and a mariner (1745).

ac.), with common of pasture. Note: tis said to be but 4 ac. in lease. Life: said James Lyde 50; heriot best beast or £3 6s 8d; rent 8s 8d; V £5; rate £4 10s, L.T. 11s, P.R. 7s 6d, C.R. 2s, total £1 6d.

SM44.[44] Ditto: tenement in Bulverton, lately belonging to James Board, 14¼ ac. (orchard 4¾ac., arable 9½ ac.), Note: there was formerly a house in Madwestcots Orchard, part of this estate, which has been down for more than 30 years. Tis called in the lease only 14 ac. Life: James Board 35; heriot best beast or £3 6s 8d; rent 6s; V £15; rate £8 [*as SM35*].

SM45.[45] Mr. Thomas Lyde (mariner): messuage and tenement called Forwards, 3 small dwelling houses in Town, 4½ ac. arable; lives: said Thomas Lyde 57, William Lyde his brother 42; heriot £1 3s; rent 11s 6d; V £9; rate £4 10s [*as SM43*].

SM46.[46] John Barrett: messuage or dwelling house, garden and orchard, 20 rods of land lying at Stoford, with common of pasture for 6 sheep upon Corr Hill, formerly Pearses, since Carpenters; life: Richard Carpenter 34; heriot 5s; rent 5s; V £1; not rated.

SM47.[47] Moses Purchase: messuage or tenement, called Lower Tenement or Lower Farthing, a kitchen, brewhouse, four chambers, stable, barn, linney, garden, 19 ac. (orchard and garden 4 ac., arable and meadow 15 ac.); lives: Mary Carter 45, Sarah Carter 44; heriot best beast or £3 6s 8d; rent 12s; V £20; rate £11 10s, L.T. £1 9s 4d, P.R. £1, C.R. 4s, total £2 13s 4d.

SM48.[48] Sarah Wood: messuage and tenement in Higher Woolbrook, a hall, kitchen, milkhouse, four chambers, poundhouse, barn, stable, shipping, courtlage, 30½ ac. (orchard 2½ ac., arable 28 ac.), with common of pasture for 60 sheep on Corr Hill; life: Thomas Wood 36; heriot best beast or £3 6s 8d; rent 6s; V £30; rate £18 10s, L.T. £2 7s 8d, P.R. £1 12s 6d, C.R. 8s, total £4 8s 2d.

SM49.[49] Ditto: messuage, tenement and cottage in Town, now three dwelling houses; two of them, 5 under rooms and 6 chambers, with stable and garden; the other of three under rooms and three chambers; 1¾ac. (orchard ¾ac., arable 1 ac.); life: [*as last*]; heriot 6s; rent 6s; V £8; rate £2 5s [*as SM23*].

SM50. Ditto: messuage or tenement called a Lydworthy, a good dwelling house in Town, a kitchen, parlour, buttery, four chambers, cellar, stable, with other outhouses and garden, also a barn in Blackmore, 2½ ac. (orchard 1¼ ac., arable 1¼ ac.), with right of common; life: [*as last*]; heriot 13s 4d; rent 6s and a capon or 1s; V £8; rate £3 [*as SM4*].

SM51.[50] Mr. Thomas Lyde, executor of late Samuel Lyde: tenement containing two dwelling houses, one of them lying by the church, four under rooms, five chambers, a cellar, barn, stable and courtlage; the other at Longwell in Western Town, three under rooms and three chambers, with a little garden and woodhouse; 6¾ac. (orchard 1 ac., arable 5¾ac.), called Maynards, formerly Perrymans; life: Joseph Baker 28; heriot best beast or £1; rent 9s 6d; V £14; rate £6 15s, L.T. 16s 6d, P.R. 11s 3d, C.R. 3s, total £1 10s 9d.

SM52.[51] Mary Garland (widow): messuage and tenement called a Lydworthy, lying in town, a dwelling house, three under rooms and four chambers, barn, woodhouse and garden, 1¾ac. (orchard ½ ac., arable 1¼ ac.); lives: Sarah Carter 43, Mary Garland 65, Ann Coles, her daughter 33; heriot 5s 9d; rent 5s 9d; V £5; rate £2 5s [*as SM23*].

SM53.[52] William Furze in right of his wife: messuage and tenement in Town, late Thomas Warrens, two dwelling houses; one of them, a kitchen, parlour, pantry, three chambers, barn and stable; the other, one under room and one chamber; 6¼ ac. (orchard 2¼ ac., arable 4 ac.); life: Jane, the daughter of Mr. Samuel Cawley 18; heriot best beast or 14s; rent 14s; V £10 10s; rate £3 [*as SM4*].

SM54.[53] Sarah Lee: a house in Town, 4 under rooms and three chambers, a garden, woodhouse, and orchard, 1 ac. arable ground in Waterfields; life: said Sarah Lee 33; heriot 13s 4d; rent 6s 8d; V £3 10s; rate £2 5s [*as SM23*].

SM55.[54] Florence Drake, widow: socage, late Elias Perrymans, an old barn, little stable, 5 ac. arable; life: said Florence Drake 60; heriot best beast or £3 6s 8d; rent 6s 8d; V £5 5s; rate £3 15s, L.T. 9s 2d, P.R. 6s 3d, C.R. 2s, total 17s 5d.

SM56.[55] Walter Denning: messuage and tenement, called Ladds Lydworthy, a dwelling house in Town, three under rooms and four chambers, with a garden, stable, linney, courtlage, 2¾ac. (orchard ½ ac., arable 2¼ ac.). Note: in the lease tis called only 2½ ac. Life: said Walter Denning 38; heriot best beast or £2; rent 2s 10½d; V £6; rate £3 [*as SM4*].

SM57.[56] Ditto: messuage or tenement, called Pages Lydworthy, a dwelling house in town, two under rooms and

[44] L264-5, to a mariner (1715) and a yeoman (1751).

[45] L250-2, to a yeoman (1704) and a mariner (1746).

[46] L126-8, to a husbandman (1678), a mariner (1715), and a yeoman (1742).

[47] L146-8, to a yeoman (1672) and a gentleman (1719).

[48] L157-62, to yeomen (1687, 1706) and mariners (1714, 1727).

[49] Probably L16-20.

[50] L74-7, to mariners (1671, 1689) and edgers (1709, 1735).

[51] L214-6, to a yeoman (1714), a mariner (1732), and a widow (1755).

[52] L112-4, to a mariner (1736), a gentleman (1754) and a spinster (1757).

[53] L55-6, to a widow (1730) and a mariner (1741).

[54] L209, to a mariner (1711).

[55] L194-6, to a baker (1693) and yeomen (1721, 1756). The last lease is endorsed *Part of Ladds Lydworthy*. See note to SM76.

[56] Possibly L54.

two chambers, 2½ ac. arable; life: [*as last*]; heriot 5s 9d; rent 5s 9d; V £3 10s; rate £3 [*as SM4*].

SM58.[57] Betty Potbury, late Andrews: messuage and tenement called a Lydworthy, a dwelling house in Town, four under rooms and four chambers, also an old house, now supposed to be converted into a stable and woodhouse, 2 ac. arable; life: said Betty Potbury 40; heriot 12s; rent 6s 6d and a dish of fish or 1s; V £4 10s; rate £2 5s [*as SM23*].

SM59.[58] Rebecca Carpenter, spinster: dwelling house in Town, a parlour, shop, kitchen, and another under room, and four chambers, with a large garden; 1 ac. (orchard ¼ ac., arable ¾ac.); lives: said Rebecca Carpenter 40, Elizabeth Godfrey, her sister 42; heriot 4s; rent 4s; V £5 10s; rate £1 10s [*as SM18*].

SM60.[59] Honour Potbury, widow: dwelling house in Town, kitchen, parlour, pantry, and three chambers, with a little garden in the marsh; life: Sam. Cawley junior 20; heriot 2s; rent 4s and 1 capon or 1s; V £3; rate 15s, L.T. 1s 10d, P.R. 1s 3d, C.R. 8d, total 3s 9d.

SM61.[60] Mr. Edward Warren (butcher): messuage and tenement called a Lydworthy, a dwelling house in Town, kitchen, parlour, pantry, and three chambers, 2½ ac. (orchard ½ ac., arable 2 ac.); life: Edward Warren junior 28; heriot best beast or £1 10s; rent 5s 10d and 1 capon; V £6; rate £2 5s [*as SM23*].

SM62.[61] Ditto: messuage and tenement called a Lydworthy, and a dwelling house in Town, a kitchen, little parlour, pantry, cellar, and three chambers, a courtlage and linney, with a garden near the Middle Field, 2¼ ac. (orchard ½ ac., arable 1¾ac.); life: Ann his daughter 23; heriot 13s 4d; rent 6s; V £5; rate £2 5s [*as SM23*].

SM63.[62] James Toby: messuage or dwelling house in the Marsh, late Birds, now divided into two dwellings; one of them, two under rooms and two chambers, a shop, cellar and little garden; the other is of two under rooms, two chambers, and stable. The Ramshorne is included in the above lease. Life: John Bird 60; heriot 6s 8d; rent 6s 8d and two dishes of fish. One is said to be for the Ramshorne. V £3 10s; rate 15s [*cf. SM60*], L.T. 1s 10d, P.R. 1s 3d, C.R. nil, total 3s 1d.

SM64.[63] Richard Wood (glazier): a house called Furze House; life: said Richard Wood 35; heriot 1s; rent 6d; V 10s; not rated.

SM65.[64] Ann Wood, widow: messuage or tenement, a dwelling house in Town, three under rooms, four chambers, and woodhouse, also a barn and garden. 1½ ac. arable land in Middle Fields; life: said Ann Wood 40; heriot 6s; rent 6s; V £4; rate £2 5s [*as SM23*].

SM66.[65] Richard Stone: dwelling house in the Marsh, called Carpenters, late Courtises, two under rooms, and two chambers, with two little gardens, one of them by Godfer Hoopers; lives: Hannah Cox 60, Jane, heretofore Courtice 36; heriot 4s; rent 4s; V £1 6s; not rated.

SM67.[66] Noah Sandford: dwelling house in Town, four under rooms and two chambers, with a little orchard in the Marsh; lives: Sarah Clapp, now Bishop 30, Elizabeth Clapp 19; heriot 1s 6d; rent 3s; V £1 10s; not rated.

SM68.[67] Samuel Sandford (yeoman): messuage or dwelling house in Town, two under rooms, and two chambers, and a little garden; also a dwelling house in Town, formerly the Chapple, now the Anchor, a kitchen, two parlours, cellar, buttery, and 4 chambers, with garden in the Marsh; life: said Samuel Sandford 63; heriot £1; rent 5s; V £8; rate £1 10s [*as SM18*].

SM69.[68] Prudence Southwood, widow: dwelling house in the Marsh, late William Godfrey's, two under rooms and two chambers, with a garden; life: Mary Stone 45; heriot 3s 4d; rent 5s; V £1 5s; not rated.

SM70.[69] Thomas Heifer (thatcher): cottage in the Marsh, four under rooms, two chambers, and a garden; lives: said Thomas Heifer 44, Grace, his wife 44; heriot 5s; rent 5s; V £2; rate 15s [*as SM60*].

SM71.[70] Richard Faber (carpenter): house in the Marsh, four under rooms and three chambers, with a garden; lives: said Richard Faber 42, Elizabeth, daughter of Benjamin Faber 25; heriot 5s; rent 5s and a capon or 1s; V £1 10s; not rated.

---

[57] L107-10, to a carpenter (1699), a fish-driver (1707), and a mariner (1739).

[58] L257-8, to a cheesemonger (1708) and a yeoman (1737).

[59] L95-7, to a spinster (1728).

[60] L228, to a butcher, the same as SM62 (1748).

[61] L103, to a butcher (1748).

[62] L115-6, to a yeoman (1696) and widow (1722). This was *The Red Lion*; the Ramshorne was a place *where nets can be set and fish taken.*

[63] L71-2. Built by Thomas Hellier, white-baker, on a waste plot 50ft by 16ft (1698); leased to a glazier in 1758.

[64] L100-2, to mariners (1671,1758) and a spinster (1738).

[65] L88-90, to the daughter of a yeoman (1700), a husbandman (1711) and a spinster (1733).

[66] L241-2, to mariners (1686,1742).

[67] L51-3, to a widow (1681), a mariner (1722), and a yeoman (1733). The last lease includes a house description: *a hall and chamber over, shop and chamber over, seller and chamber over, two outhouses commonly called linneys on each side of the back door on the north side of the messuage, with a house and smiths shop erected on the Cliffe or Strand.*

[68] L98, to a mariner (1729).

[69] L104-6, to a widow (1684, when it was *newly erected*), a sergemaker (1706), and a thatcher (1748). It was the *Norther Cottage*; cf SM95.

[70] L80-2, to a miller (1680), a husbandman (1727), and a carpenter (1754).

SM72.[71] William Potbury: two stables and two hogstyes on the beach, late Edmund Forwards. Note: the above premises have been down many years, and now become part of the waste on the beach. Life: Samuel Cawley 57; heriot 2s 6d; rent 2s 6d; V 1s; not rated.

SM73.[72] Joan Potbury, widow: dwelling house in Town, four under rooms and three chambers, late Coles's; life: Joan Potbury 64; heriot 2s 4d; rent 2s 4d; V £1 15s; not rated.

SM74.[73] Ann Gregory, widow: dwelling house in Town, a kitchen, parlour, cellar, pantry, three chambers and a closet, with a garden; life: said Ann Gregory 70; heriot 1s; rent 6d; V £4; rate 15s [*cf. SM60*], L.T. 1s 10d, P.R. 1s 3d, C.R. 4d, total 3s 5d.

SM75.[74] Richard Wyatt (mason): messuage or dwelling house in Town, now divided into two tenements, six under rooms and six chambers, with 2 gardens and woodhouse; life: Richard Wyatt 27; heriot 5s 4d; rent 5s 4d; V £4; rate 15s [*as SM74*].

SM76.[75] Samuel Cawley junior: a moiety of a Lydworthy, heretofore in posession of Simon Ladd, two dwelling houses, three under rooms and three chambers, garden, 1¼ ac. (orchard ½ ac., arable ¾ac.); lives: Edward Warren 60, Margaret, the widow of Robert Crammer 48; heriot best beast or 13s 4d; rent 4s 1d and a dish of fish or 1s; V £4; rate £1 10s [*as SM18*].

SM77. Ditto: stable or cellar built on waste; life: Margaret Crammer 48; heriot 3s 4d; rent 1s; V 10s; not rated.

SM78. Ditto: a house, one under room and one chamber; life: Samuel Follett 66; V 15s; [*rest blank*].

SM79.[76] George Cross (husbandman): messuage, 2 dwelling houses, two under rooms and two chambers, with a garden; lives: George Cross 34, Sarah his wife 34, [*blank*] their son; rent 1s 4d; V £1 15s; not rated.

SM80.[77] John Smith: cottage near the Fort, two under rooms and one chamber, with a little garden; life: Mary Gregory 15; heriot 2s; rent 2s; V £1; not rated.

SM81. Elizabeth Pinn, widow: house in Weston Town, three under rooms and three chambers, with little garden; [*life blank*]; heriot 2s; rent 2s; V £1 10s; not rated.

SM82. Ditto: a garden plot adjoining, granted with the above; rent 6d; V [*included with last*].

SM83.[78] Mr. James Scaddon (watchmaker): shop and chamber over, late Overbacks; life: Benjamin Follett 55; heriot 4s; rent 4s; V £1; not rated.

SM84.[79] Mrs. Joan Kingman (widow): messuage and tenement called a Lydworthy, a dwelling house in Town, a kitchen, little parlour, pantry and three chambers, with a garden and stable, 2½ ac. arable; lives: said Joan Kingman 65, Amey Giles 38; Alice Kingman 27; heriot 4s; rent 4s; V £6 10s; rate £3 [*as SM4*].

SM85.[80] Alice Kingman (spinster): dwelling house (formerly a barn), three under rooms and 2 chambers, with a garden plot; lives: said Joan Kingman 65, Alice Kingman 27, said Amy Giles 38; heriot 2s 6d; rent 6d; V £1 10s; not rated.

[f.18v] IN HAND

In the year 1780, when this copy was taken of the survey made in 1764.[81]

SM86.[82] Tobias Hooper: a green in the Marsh, late Tobias Hooper's, now in posession of John Burroughs; heriot 8d, rent 4d, V 3s.

SM87.[83] [*Blank*]: Allingtons garden plot, lying at Yard Lane, in posession of Phillip Pine; rent 2s 8d; V 3s.

SM88. Christian Baker: tenement called a Lydworthy (formerly Hancocks, since Perrys), 3½ ac. (orchard ½ ac., arable 3 ac.), with a garden plot in the Green: last life: said Christian Baker; heriot best beast or £1 10s; rent 11s 6d; V £4 10s; rate £3 [*as SM4*].

SM89.[84] Mr. Samuel Cawley: messuage and tenement called Beckwell, a kitchen, parlour, brewhouse, five chambers, a closet, two cellars, barn, stable, cowhouse, courtlage and linney, 28½ ac. (orchard 1 ac., arable 25 ac., meadow 2½ ac.), with common of pasture for all manner of cattle in and upon the common or waste called Pickhill; last life: Thomas Stocker; heriot £4 4s; rent £1; V £30 [*including next*]; rate [*including next*] £20 [*as SM10*].

SM90.[85] Ditto: a green and orchard called England, ½ ac., on which about 70 or 80 years ago stood a cottage house; last life: [*as last*]; rent 4s.

---

71 L246-7, to a widow (1701) and a baker (1732). As well as being a cottage, this had been a stable and either was or adjoined a dyehouse (L129,133-4 may also relate to SM72).

72 L262-3, to mariners (1714,1741).

73 L77 shows that this was split off from SM51 in 1733.

74 L236-9, to a spinster (1672), a tailor (1698), a mariner (1731), and a mason (1753).

75 L210-3, to a tailor (1712), a yeoman (1726), a mariner (1738), and a widow (1755). The other half may have been SM56.

76 L266-7, to a widow (1719) and a husbandman (1751).

77 L69, to a husbandman (1758).

78 L230-3, to a mercer (1658,60), a widow (1691), and a watchmaker (1732). In 1658, it was *to be erected*, adjoining the house of the tenant.

79 L223-4, to a tailor (1729) and a widow (1758).

80 L248-9, to a widow (1703) and a spinster (1758).

81 In this section, the first column is headed *Names of the last tenants*. The 'last life' comes from the column headed *Names of those on whose death it fell into hand.*

82 L85-6, to a husbandman (1688) and a widow (1765).

83 L240, to a yeoman (1680).

84 L13-15, to yeomen (1668,1713) and a spinster (1723).

85 Formerly part of SM89.

SM91.[86] Mr. Oliver Cawley: dwelling house in Town (formerly called the Dolphin), a kitchen, two parlours, pantry and four chambers, and a garden in the Marsh, now rented by Landlord Cawley. Note: Mr. Cawley lately built a little Pleasure house in the garden. Also, a little plot of ground lying in the Marsh, about ¼ ac.; last life: said Oliver Cawley; heriot 11s; rent 5s; V £8 10s; rate 15s [*as SM60*].

SM92.[87] Mr. Samuel Follett: messuage or tenement in Lower Woolbrook, four under rooms, three chambers, stable, barn, linney, two cellars, poundhouse and courtlage, 19½ ac. (orchard 4¼ ac., arable 11¼ ac., meadow 4 ac.); last life: Nicholas Warren; heriot best beast or £3 6s 8d; rent 5s 7d; V £20; rate £10 [*as SM2*].

SM93.[88] Mr. Samuel Follett: moiety of a tenement called Rowe's Lydworthy, one under room and two chambers, a barn, little garden, 1¾ac. (orchard ¾ac., arable 1 ac.); last life: Julian Carpenter; heriot 3s; rent 3s; V £3; rate £1 10s [*as SM18*].

SM94. Mr. Robert Follett: the Town Mills and Millhouse, etc.; last life: Francis Gwyn esquire; heriot £3; rent £1 10s; V £20; rate £30, L.T. £3 17s, P.R. £2 12s 6d, C.R. 12s, total £7 1s 6d.

SM95.[89] Sarah Davis: cottage, formerly Pines, in the Marsh, one under room and one chamber, with woodhouse and garden; last life: said Sarah Davis; heriot 4s; rent 4s; V £1 5s; not rated.

SM96.[90] Ann Lyde: a Lydworthy, formerly Haymans, a dwelling house in Town now is posession of Robert Cranmer, three under rooms and three chambers, a garden plot in the Marsh, 2½ ac. arable land in the common fields; last life: Mr. Samuel Lyde; heriot 13s 4d; rent 6s 8d; V £5 5s; rate £2 5s [*as SM23*].

SM97.[91] Mr. John Stocker Pearce: tenement or overland, called Slade, lying at Bulverton, a barn, stable, shipping, 18½ ac. (orchard 1½ ac., arable 12 ac., meadow 5 ac.), with common of pasture for 30 sheep on Bulverton Hill; last life: said J. Stocker Pearce; heriot best beast or £3 6s 8d; rent 4s 7d; V £16; rate £10 [*as SM2*].

SM98.[92] Ditto: messuage and tenement called Bulverton, otherwise Channons, three under rooms, four chambers, a courtlage, linney, 22¾ac. (orchard ¾ac., arable 15½ ac., meadow 4½ ac., pasture 2 ac.). The premises in the lease are said to be only 16 ac. Last life: [*as last*]; heriot best beast or £2 13s 4d; rent 4s 7d and a capon or 1s; V £20; rate £10 [*as SM2*].

SM99.[93] Mrs. Mary Pearce: two fields called Furzys and Tinway, 6 ac. arable land lying at Higther Woolbrook; last life: John Stocker Pearce; heriot 10s; rent 1s 4d; V £5; rate £3 15s [*as SM55*].

SM100.[94] Ditto: messuage and tenement at Bulverton, called Farrants, a dwelling house, four under rooms and four chambers, with a courtlage, stable, barn, poundhouse and garden, 17¾ac. (orchard 2 ac., arable 15ac); last life: John Stocker Pearce; heriot best beast or £3 6s 8d; rent 4s 5½d; V £16; rate £10 [*as SM2*].

SM101.[95] Mrs. Elizabeth Goodwin: messuage and tenement containing one farthing of land, lying at Asserton, a kitchen, hall, milkhouse, brewhouse, little cellar, five chambers, barn, stable, two linneys, and courtlage, 15½ ac. (orchard 1 ac., arable 14½ ac.); last life: said Elizabeth Goodwin; heriot best beast or £3 6s 8d; rent 6s 8d; V £16; rate £10 [*as SM2*].

SM102. Joseph Leate: messuage or dwelling, and a little orchard and garden at Bulverton. The house and premises, being in a ruinous state, were seized to the use of the lord several years ago, but Phillip Pine, the last life, is now living; life: Philip Pine 50; heriot 1s 8d; rent 3s 4d; V £1 5s; not rated.

SM103. Sarah Baker, widow: messuage and tenement called a Lydworthy, a dwelling house in Town, four under rooms and three chambers, with a little garden, 2 ac. (orchard ½ ac., arable 1½ ac.); last life: said Sarah Baker; heriot 16s; rent 8s; V £3 15s; rate £2 5s [*as SM23*].

SM104.[96] Sarah Baker, widow: dwelling house, etc. in Town, part of Channons Lydworthy, two under rooms and two chambers, with an orchard, garden and courtlage, heretofore in posession of Phillip Robbins, the orchard and garden about ½ ac.; last life: said Sarah Baker; heriot moiety of best beast or 10s; rent 3s; V £2 10s; rate £1 10s [*as SM18*].

SM105.[97] Mr. John Pearce: a house in the Marsh, called the Wash house, used for washing wool, since called the Coach House; last life: said John Pearce; heriot 2s; rent 2s; V 5s; not rated.

---

86 L68, to a net-maker (1733).

87 L145, to a yeoman (1723). Before 1711, this was combined with SM37 (L141-4, to yeomen (1658,1692) and a spinster (1703)).

88 L197, to a seaman (1694). Cf SM19.

89 L124-5, to a widow (1684) and a spinster (1736). This was the *Souther cottage, lately erected*, probably in 1684, Cf SM70.

90 L91-3, to a widow (1702), a mariner (1739), and a yeoman (1746).

91 L46, to a yeoman (1716).

92 L37-9, to yeomen (1670, 1699, 1716).

93 L70, to a yeoman (1716).

94 L33-6, to a yeoman (1665, 1716) and a gentleman (1728, 1735).

95 Possibly L168.

96 L253-5, to a sailor (1707), a spinster (1712) and a mariner (1734). This is described as the *west of the house, part of Channons Lydworthy, containing the hall, little parlour and two chambers over, the barn and part of the schoolhouse.* The other part is SM112.

97 L87, to a clothier (1699). It is described as *a plot 20 feet by 16 feet to the west side of the mill leat, near the Red Lion, part of the marsh*, to be used for the erection of a wool-washing house.

SM106.[98] William Clapp (mariner): dwelling house and garden in Town, called Pullmans, two under rooms and two chambers, little orchard, ¾ac. arable land; last life: Mary his wife; heriot 5s; rent 4s 4d and a dish of fish; V £3 10s; rate £1 10s [*cf. SM18*] L.T. 3s 8d, P.R. 2s 6d, C.R. 8d, total 6s 10d.

SM107. William Potbury: a Lydworthy, late Roger Potbury's, a dwelling house in Town, three under rooms and three chambers, with little garden. Also, another dwelling house in Town, two under rooms and two chambers, with a little garden, 2½ ac. arable land in the common fields; last life: John Carpenter; heriot £1; rent 7s 8d; V £5 10s; rate £3 [*as SM4*].

SM108. Ditto: garden near the Marsh; last life: [as last]; heriot 1s 4d; rent 1s 4d; V [*included in last*]: not rated.

SM109. Joshua Evans: tenement in Western Town, late Welshes, two under rooms and two chambers, with a garden; last life: said Joshua Evans; heriot 4s; rent 2s; V £1 5s; not rated.

SM110.[99] Peter Wilcocks (husbandman): a cottage house, three under rooms and three chambers, with little garden; last life: said Peter Wilcocks; heriot 5s 4d; rent 5s 4d; V £1 10s; not rated.

SM111.[100] Mr. William Carslake: [*a*] dwelling house, formerly Warrens, late Potbury's, 4 under rooms and four chambers, with a garden in the Marsh; [*b*] by the same lease, a stable or woodhouse cald Sanders's; last life: Ann, wife of William Furze; heriot [*a*] 4s 8d, [*b*] 1s; rent [*a*] 5s 8d, [*b*] 6d; V [*both*] L4; rate [*a*] 15s [*as SM60*], [*b*] not rated.

SM112.[101] John Johnson (tailor): a house in Town, belonging to a tenement called Channons Lydworthy, a kitchen, shop and three chambers over, and part of the School House, as it is or heretofore was divided, together with 2¾ac. of ground to the said Lydworthy belonging (orchard 2¼ ac., arable ½ ac.); last life: said John Johnson; heriot moiety of best beast or 10s; rent 3s; V £7; rate £3 [*as SM4*].

SM113.[102] Ditto: a shop and little plot of ground lying near the Market Place; last life: Sarah Baker, widow; heriot 2s; rent 1s; V [included in last]; not rated.

[98] L243-4, to a husbandman (1693) and a mariner (1727).

[99] L135, to a husbandman (1731).

[100] L123, to a mariner (1740).

[101] L256, to a tailor (1731), the same as in SM113-4. Cf. SM104.

[102] L122, to a tailor (1733).

SM114.[103] Ditto: messuage or tenement called a Socage, heretofore in posession of Robert Veryard, a house, two under rooms and two chambers, with a garden, 3¼ ac. (orchard ½ ac., arable 2¾ac.); last life [*as last*]; heriot best beast or £3 6s 8d; rent 3s 10d; V L6; rate L3 [*as SM4*].

[f.24v] A Copy of a Survey of the Estates in Sidford, etc.[104]

SM115.[105] Mr. William Daniel (yeoman): all that mansion house, farm or tenement called Porch House tenement, lying in the parishes of Sidbury and Salcombe, a good dwelling house, a kitchen, parlour, hall, brewhouse, dairy, three cellars and eight chambers, with a stable, poundhouse, two linneys, two courts, 63 ac. (orchard 4 ac., arable 50 ac., pasture 9 ac.), with common of pasture for 60 sheep on Corr Hill; lives: said William Daniel 43, William his son 12; heriot best beast or £5; rent £3 and two capons or 2s; V £60.

SM116. Mrs. Sarah and Mary Farthing: messuage or tenement called Staves, a dwelling house, a kitchen, hall, parlour, brewhouse, milkhouse and 5 chambers, with two stables and 7½ ac. (orchard 1½ ac., arable 6 ac.), with common of pasture on Salcombe Hill for 61 sheep; lives: Said Sarah Farthing 58, Mary Farthing 54; Julian their niece 23; heriot best beast or £3 6s 8d; rent £1 17s 4d and two harvest days on the Barton of Netherton or 1s; V £13.

SM117.[106] Mr. William Raymond, a tenement, late Warrens, called South Bostills, a barn, shippen, linney and 17½ ac. (orchard ½ ac., arable 14 ac., meadow 2 ac.); life: William Raymond 22; heriot £1 13s 4d; rent £2 6s 8d and two days labour or 1s; V £17.

SM118.[107] William Westcott (miller): tenement called Yard, a barn and 10½ ac. (orchard 2½ ac., arable 8 ac.); lives: Mary, the daughter of said William Westcott 13, Samuel his son 8, Elizabeth his daughter 4; heriot best sheep or 6s 8d; rent £1 3s 4d and 1 capon; V £11.

[103] L186, to a tailor (1733).

[104] These holdings were not in hand, and the arrangement of the entries is as for SM1, except that no tax or rate figures are included. The column for capons is headed *capons or harvest days*.

[105] L9-12, to a merchant (1651), a mariner (1697), a gentleman (1707), and a yeoman (1754). See pp. 38-9, 210.

[106] L1-5, to a wheelwright (1655) and a yeoman (1708). It is described as being in Salcombe parish, south of the highway from Sidford to Colyford.

[107] L6-8, to yeomen (1676, 1708) and a miller (1766).

Bibliography

1. Primary Sources

See the list of surveys on p. xiii. Other primary sources are cited when used.

2. Secondary Sources

Alcock, N .W., 'Vernacular Architecture: Historical Evidence and Historical Problems,' in I. M. Quimby, ed., *Material Culture and the Study of American Life* (Winterthur, 1978).

Alcock, N. W., 'A Provisional Hand-list of Detailed House-by-House Surveys,' *Vernacular Architecture*, 1 (1970), 13.

Alcock, N. W., 'Further House-and-Estate Surveys,' *Vernacular Architecture*, 5 (1974), 27.

Alcock, N. W., 'Devon Farmhouses II,' *Trans. Devonshire Assoc.*, 101 (1969), 83.

Alcock, N. W., 'Houses in an East Devon Parish,' *Trans. Devonshire Assoc.*, 94 (1962), 185-232.

Alcock, N. W., 'Devonshire Linheys: A Vernacular Tradition,' *Trans. Devonshire Assoc.*, 95 (1963), 117.

Alcock, N. W., 'Fields and Farms in East Devon Parish,' *Trans Devonshire Assoc.*, 107 (1975), 109.

Alcock, N. W., 'An East Devon Manor in the Later Middle Ages, Part II,' *Trans Devonshire Assoc.*, 105 (1973), 141.

Alcock, N. W. and Cox, Nancy, *Living and Working in Seventeenth Century England*, (London, 2000), CD-ROM of Randle Holme, *Academy of Armory* (Chester, 1688).

Alcock, N. W., *Stoneleigh Villagers, 1597-1650* (Coventry: University of Warwick Open Studies, 1975).

Anon., *Complete Parochial History of Cornwall* (Truro 1867-72).

Barley, M. W., *English Farmhouse and Cottage* (London, 1961).

Barley, M. W., 'Rural Housing in England' in Ag. Hist. V(ii), p.659.

Barley, M. W., 'Glossary of names for rooms in houses of the sixteenth and seventeenth centuries,' in I. L. Foster and L. Alcock, eds., *Culture and Environment*, 1963, 479-501.

Barley, Maurice [M. W.], *Houses and History* (London, 1986).

Beresford, M. W. and Finberg, H. P. R., *English Medieval Boroughs: a Handlist* (Newton Abbot, 1971).

Brunskill, R. W., *Vernacular Architecture of the Lake Counties*, (London, 1974).

Cash, M., *Devon Inventories of the Sixteenth and Seventeenth Centuries*, Devon and Cornwall Record Soc. NS11 (Torquay, 1966).

Cherry, John, 'Post-medieval Britain in 1976,' *Post-Med. Archaeol.*, 11 (1977), 96-7.

Chesher, V.M. and F.J., *The Cornishman's House* (Truro, 1968).

Collison, John, *History and Antiquities of the County of Somerset* (Bath, 1791).

Dartnell, G. E. & Goddard, E. H., *Glossary of Wiltshire Words* (London: English Dialect Soc., 1893).

Dudley, D. and Minter, E. M., 'The Medieval Village at Garrow Tor,' *Medieval Archaeol.*, 6 (1963), 272-294.

Dyer, C. C., 'English peasant buildings in the later Middle Ages,' *Medieval Archaeol.*, 30 (1986), 19.

Field, R. K., 'Worcestershire Peasant Buildings,' *Medieval Archaeol.*, 9 (1965), p.112.

Flower, N. L., 'The Flower Family of Somerset,' *Somerset and Dorset Notes & Queries*, 29 (1973), 277-288.

Forman, H. C., *Early Nantucket and its Whale Houses* (New York, 1966).

Fox, H. S. A., 'Outfield Cultivation in Devon and Cornwall,' in M. A. Havinden, ed. *Husbandry and Marketing in the Southwest, 1500-1800* (Exeter, 1973).

Fox, H. S. A., 'The Chronology of Enclosure and Economic Development in Medieval Devon,' *Economic Hist. Rev.*, 28 (2nd ser.) (1975), 181-202.

Fox, H. S. A. & Padel, O. J., eds., *The Cornish Lands of the Arundells of Lanherne, Fourteenth to Sixteenth Centuries*, Devon & Cornwall Record Soc. NS41 (Torquay, 1998).

Fox, Harold [H. S. A.], *The Evolution of the Fishing Village: Landscape and Society along the South Devon Coast, 1086-1550* (Leicester, 2001).

Fox, Sir Cyril and Raglan, Lord, *Monmouthshire Houses* (Cardiff, 1951-54).

Gover, J. E. B., Mawer, A. and Stenton, F. M., *Place-Names of Devon* (Cambridge, 1931-2).

Gray, Todd, ed., *Harvest Failure in Cornwall and Devon: The book of orders and the corn surveys of 1623 and 1630*, (Redruth: Institute of Cornish Studies, 1992).

Holme, Randle, *Academy of Armory* (Chester, 1688), see Alcock, N. W. and Cox, Nancy, 2000.

Hoskins, W. G., *Local History in England* (London, 1959).

Hoskins, W. G., *Devon* (Newton Abbot, 1972).

Hoyle, R., 'Vain projects' in J. Chartres and D. Hey, eds., *English Rural Society 1500-1800* (Cambridge 1990), pp. 73-101.

Hurst, J. G. and Beresford, M. W., *Deserted Medieval Villages* (London, 1971).

Kerridge, E., *Surveys of the Manors of Philip, First Earl of Pembroke and Montgomery, 1631-2*, Wiltshire Archaeol. Natural Hist. Soc. Records Branch (Devizes, 1953).

Kussmaul, A., *Servants in Husbandry in Early Modern England*, (Cambridge, 1981).

Laslett, P., *The World we Have Lost* (London, 1971).

Machin, R., *The Houses of Yetminster* (Bristol: University of Bristol, 1979).

Marshall, William, *The Rural Economy of the West of England* (London, 1799).

Martin, D., *Historic buildings in East Sussex*, I (No. 2), 18-20 (Rape of Hastings Architectural Survey, 1977).

Peters, J. E. C., *Discovering Traditional Farm Buildings*, (Princes Risborough, 1981).

Potts, R., *Cornish Glebe Terriers*, Devon and Cornwall Record Soc. NS19, (Torquay, 1974).

Pounds, N. J. G. (ed.), *Parliamentary Survey of the Duchy of Cornwall*, Devon and Cornwall Record Soc., NS25, 27 (Torquay, 1982, 1984).

Powell, Anthony, *John Aubrey and His Friends* (London, 1948).

Royal Commission on Historical Monuments, *West Cambridgeshire* (London, 1968).

Smith, J. T., 'Lancashire and Cheshire Houses; some problems of architectural and social history,' *Archaeol. J.*, 127 (1970), 156-181.

Somerset Vernacular Building Research Group, *Somerset Village: Compton Dundon*, Crewkerne, 2004.

Thirsk, J., ed., *Agrarian History of England and Wales* (Cambridge). vol. IV (1967); vol. V(i) (1984); vol V(ii) (1985).

Vancouver, Charles, *General View of The Agriculture of the County of Devon*, (London, 1808).

Watkins, H.R., *Dartmouth* (Exeter, 1935).

Williams, E. H. D., 'Poltimore Farmhouse, Farway,' *Trans. Devonshire Assoc.*, 106 (1974), 215-229.

Williams, E. H. D. & Penoyre, J. and J., 'The George Inn, Norton St Philip,' *Archaeol. J.*, 144 (1987), 317-327.

Wilson, R. E., 'What is a Lydworthy,' *Devon and Cornwall N. & Q.* 22 (1973) 218.

Wood, M. E., *The English Medieval House* (London, 1965).

Wright, J., *English Dialect Dictionary* (1898-1905).

Wyatt, Peter (ed.), *The Uffculme Wills and Inventories*, Devon and Cornwall Record Soc. NS40 (Torquay, 1997).

Wyatt, Peter & Stanes, Robin, *Uffculme, a Peculiar Parish* (Uffculme, 1997).

Index of Subjects

Index of Persons

Index of Places